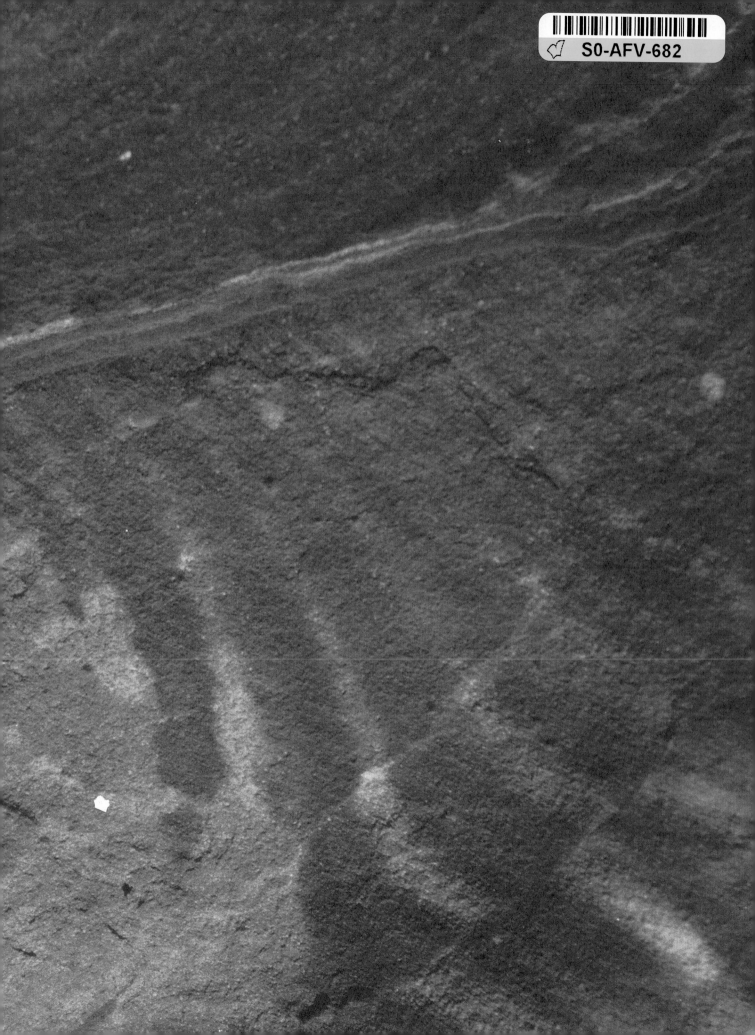

© 1998 Martha Sharp Joukowsky
Providence, Rhode Island

This book was designed and produced
by Simon M. Sullivan and Kirsten K. Hammann.

Printed by E. A. Johnson Company,
East Providence, Rhode Island 02914

Library of Congress Cataloging in Publication Data
Petra Great Temple Volume I: Brown University Excavations 1993-1997 /
by Martha Sharp Joukowsky
Includes bibliographical references and index.

ISBN 0-9668024-0-3

10 9 8 7 6 5 4 3 2 1

Typeset in Bembo
Titles typeset in TRAJAN
Printed in the United States by E. A. Johnson Company

Title page  *1997 site aerial, post excavation, looking south.*
*Photograph by Artemis A. W. Joukowsky.*

Title page inset  *Head of Tyche. Photograph by David L. Brill, 1995.*

Front cover  *Excavation at the Great Temple of the Brian Stairway and Suleiman Column, Petra, Jordan. Photograph by John Forasté, 1997.*

Back cover and Table of Contents (facing page)  *Hypothetical reconstruction of an elephant-headed capital from the Great Temple. Drawing by Jean Blackburn.*

# PETRA GREAT TEMPLE
# VOLUME I:

## BROWN UNIVERSITY EXCAVATIONS
### 1993-1997

# PETRA GREAT TEMPLE
## VOLUME I:

## BROWN UNIVERSITY EXCAVATIONS
## 1993-1997

BY
MARTHA SHARP JOUKOWSKY

Contributions by

Christian Augé, Deirdre G. Barrett, Joseph J. Basile,
Jean Blackburn, Leigh-Ann Bedal, Donna J. D'Agostino,
Sara G. Karz, Elizabeth E. Payne, Thomas R. Paradise,
Erika L. Schluntz, Monica L. Sylvester, Simon M. Sullivan,
Loa P. Traxler, Stephen V. Tracy, Terry E. Tullis, Peter Warnock,
Constance Worthington and Paul C. Zimmerman

# TABLE OF CONTENTS

*Color Plates*

# LIST OF FIGURES

*All photographs in this volume by A. A. W. Joukowsky,*
*unless otherwise noted in the chapters.*

# CHAPTER THREE

*All photographs in Chapter Three by Thomas R. Paradise.*

# CHAPTER FOUR

# COLOR PLATES

# CHAPTER FIVE

## CHAPTER SIX

## CHAPTER SEVEN

## CHAPTER EIGHT

# TRANSLITERATION FOR SITES AND MONUMENTS

The names of sites and monuments in Petra and Jordan as presented in this report are based on the official transliteration system used by the Royal Jordanian Geographic Center (RJGC). They follow the system used by the United Nations, the Board on Geographic Names (a division of the United States Defense Department) and the British Permanent Committee on Geographic Names. The aim is to use a consistent method of writing Arabic names in English based on formal Arabic.

# INDEX OF ABBREVIATIONS

| | |
|---|---|
| *AA* | Archäologische Anzeiger |
| *AAS* | Annales archéologiques de Syrie |
| *AASOR* | Annual of the American Schools of Oriental Research |
| *ACOR* | American Center of Oriental Research, Amman |
| *ADAJ* | Annual of the Department of Antiquities of Jordan |
| *AfO* | Archiv für Orientforschung, Graz |
| *AI* | Art International |
| *AJA* | American Journal of Archaeology |
| *AN* | American Center of Oriental Research Newsletter |
| *ANRW* | Aufstieg und Niedergang der römischen Welt |
| *Antiquity* | A Quarterly Review of Archaeology |
| *Antk* | *Antike Kunst* |
| *Aram* | First International Conference. The Nabataeans. Oxford, 26-29 September 1989. |
| *Archéologia* | Archéologia (Paris) |
| *Archaeology* | Archaeology Magazine, Archaeological Institute of America |
| *'Atiqot* | 'Atiqot, Journal of the Israel Department of Antiquities |
| *BA* | The Biblical Archaeologist |
| *BAM* | Brown Alumni Monthly |
| *BAR* | British Archaeological Reports |
| *BAR-IS* | British Archaeological Reports, International Series |
| *BASOR* | Bulletin of the American Schools of Oriental Research |
| *Berytus* | Berytus Archaeological Studies, Museum of Archaeology, American University of Beirut |

| | |
|---|---|
| *BJ* | Bonner Jahrbücher des Rheinischen Landesmuseums in Bonn im Landschaftsverband Rheinland und des Vereins von Altertumsfreunden im Rheinlandes |
| *BTS* | Bible et Terre Sainte |
| *BUFB* | Brown University Faculty Bulletin |
| *CAH* | Cambridge Ancient History |
| *CIS II* | *Corpus Inscriptionum Semiticarum. Pars II. Tomus II. Fasc. I. Sectio Secunda. Inscriptiones Nabataeae.* Paris. |
| *CQ* | Church Quarterly |
| *CRAI* | Comptes rendus de séances de l'Académie des inscriptions et belles lettres (Paris) |
| *DaM* | Damaszener Mitteilungen |
| *Das Altertum* | *Das Altertum* |
| *DHA* | Les dossiers d'archéologie |
| *Hesperia* | Hesperia, Journal of the American Schools of Classical Studies at Athens |
| *HI* | L'histoire |
| *HTR* | Harvard Theological Review |
| *IEJ* | Israel Exploration Journal, Jerusalem |
| *I.F.A.P.O.* | Institute Français d'archéologie du Proche-Orient |
| *ILN* | Illustrated London News |
| *JA* | Journal Asiatique |
| *JANES* | Journal of Ancient Near Eastern Society, Columbia University |
| *JEOL* | Jaarbericht Vooraziatisch-Egyptisch Gezelschap "Ex Oriente Lux" |
| *JNES* | Journal of Near Eastern Studies, Chicago |
| *JQR* | Jewish Quarterly Review |
| *JRA* | Journal of Roman Archaeology |
| *JRGZM* | Jahrbuch des Römisch-Germanischen Zentralmuseums Mainz |
| *JRS* | The Journal of Roman Studies |

| | |
|---|---|
| *Levant* | Journal of the British School of Archaeology in Jerusalem, London |
| *LIMC* | *Petra and the Caravan Cities.* Proceedings of the Symposium organized at Petra in September 1985 by the Department of Antiquities of Jordan and the Iconographic Lexicon of Classical Mythology with the financial support of UNESCO, Amman, Department of Antiquities. |
| *Man* | A Monthly Record of Anthropological Science |
| *MASCA* | Museum Applied Science Center for Archaeology, University Museum, University of Pennsylvania |
| *NC* | The Numismatic Chronicle |
| *NM* | Jahresmitteilungen der Naturhistorischen Gesellschaft |
| *PAPS* | Proceedings of the American Philosophical Society |
| *PEQ* | Palestine Exploration Quarterly |
| *Qadmoniot* | Quarterly for the Antiquities of Eretz-Israel and Biblical Lands, Jerusalem |
| *QDAP* | Quarterly of the Department of Antiquities in Palestine |
| *Qedem* | Monographs of the Institute of Archaeology of the Hebrew University of Jerusalem |
| *RB* | Revue biblique |
| *RR* | Research Reports |
| *SHAJ* | Studies in the History and Archaeology of Jordan |
| *SIMA* | Studies in Mediterranean Archaeology |
| *Syria* | Revue d'Art Oriental et d'Archéologie, Paris |
| *ZDPV* | Zeitschrift des Deutschen Palästina-Vereins |

## Other Abbreviations

| | |
|---|---|
| A.D. | *anno domini* (year) |
| B.C. | before Christ |
| BCE | before the common (or Christian) era |
| a.s.l. | above sea level |
| b.s.l. | below sea level |
| CE | common (or Christian) era |

| | |
|---|---|
| cm | centimeter(s) |
| E | east |
| ed. | editor(s), edition, edited by |
| e.g. | *exempli gratia* (for example) |
| et al. | *et alii* (and others) |
| etc. | *et cetera* (and so forth) |
| ibid. | *ibidem* (in the same place) |
| km | kilometer(s) |
| m | meter(s) |
| m.s.l. | mean sea level |
| N | north |
| no. | number |
| S | south |
| SP | Special Project-sondage, probe |
| W | west |

Petra Great Temple Elements:

| | |
|---|---|
| P | Propylaeum |
| LT | Lower Temenos |
| UT | Upper Temenos |
| T | Temple |
| LW | Lapidary West |

# PETRA — SELECT BIBLIOGRAPHY

Note: The Great Temple bibliography is listed separately after the general Petra bibliography.

The abbreviations used in this bibliography, for the most part, follow those used by the *American Journal of Archaeology*, 1991, 95:4-16. Works cited are those considered to be most helpful. A comprehensive Petra bibliography can be found in L. Nehmé's *Provisional Bibliography on Petra and the Nabataeans* (1994) ERA 20 du CNRS, 3, rue Michelet 75006, Paris. A comprehensive bibliography can also be found in Judith S. McKenzie's *The Architecture of Petra*, 1990:173-180, and a complete, yet dated bibliography of Nabataean sites is given in A. Negev, 1983, *Tempel, Kirchen und Zisternen, Ausgrabungen in der Wüste Negev.* Stuttgart:250-254, as well as in D. Homes-Fredericq and J.B. Hennessy, *Archaeology of Jordan,* Vol. I, 1986, Akkadica, Peeters, Leuven.

'Amr, K.
1986    "Instrumental Neutron Activation Analysis of Pottery and Clay from the Zurrabah Kiln Complex," *ADAJ* 30:319-328.

————.
1987    *The Pottery from Petra: A Neutron Activation Analysis Study, BAR-IS* 324.

————.
1991    "The Petra National Trust Site Projects: Preliminary Report on the 1991 Season at Zurrabah," *ADAJ* 35:313-323.

Albright, W.F.
1935    "The Excavation of the Conway High Place at Petra," *BASOR* 57:18-26.

Augé, C.

    1990    "Sur la figure de Tyché en Nabatène et dans la Province d'Arabie." In *Petra and the Caravan Cities,* ed. F. Zayadine. 131-146.

————.

    1991    "Les monnaies antiques de Pétra," *DHA* 163:46-47.

Avi-Yonah, M.

    1978    *Hellenism and the East, Contacts and Interrelations from Alexander to the Roman Conquest.* Ann Arbor, MI, Jerusalem: Hebrew University.

Avi-Yonah, M. and A. Negev.

    1960    "A City of the Negeb: Excavations in Nabataean, Roman and Byzantine Eboda," *ILN* 237:944-947.

Bachmann, W., T. Watzinger and T. Wiegand.

    1921    *Petra, Wissenschaftliche Veröffentlichungen des Deutsch-Türkischen Denkmalschutz-Kommandos.* Berlin and Leipzig.

Balty, J.-C.

    1980    "Architecture et société à Pétra et Hégra. Chronologie et classes sociales; sculpteurs et commanditaires." In Collection de l'École Française de Rome 66, *Architecture et société de l'archaisme grec à la fin de la République romaine.* Paris and Rome: Centre National de la Recherche Scientifique and École de Rome. 303-324.

Banning, E.B. and I. Köhler-Rollefson.

    1986    "Ethnoarchaeological Survey in the Beda Area, Southern Jordan," *ZDPV* 102:152-170, pl. 15B-18.

Bartlett, J.R.

    1979    "From Edomites to Nabataeans: A Study of Continuity," *PEQ* 111:53-66.

Bennett, C.M.

    1962    "The Nabataeans in Petra," *Archaeology* 15:233-243.

————.

    1964    "Umm el-Biyara-Pétra," Chronique archéologique *RB* 71:250-253.

————.

    1965    "Tombs of the Roman Period." In *Excavations at Jericho II.* London: The British School of Archaeology. 516-545.

————.

    1966a    "Des fouilles à Umm el-Biyarah: les Edomites à Pétra," *BTS* 84:6-16.

————.

    1966b    "Fouilles d'Umm el-Biyara. Rapport préliminaire," *RB* 73:372-403, pl.14-25.

————.

    1983    "Petra," *AI* 26.3-38.

Bennett, C.M. and P.J. Parr.

    1962    "Soundings from Umm el-Biyara, Petra," *Archaeology* 15: 277-279.

Blagg, T. and M. Lyttelton.
    1990    "Sculpture in Nabataean Petra, and the Question of Roman Influence." In *Architecture and Architectural Sculpture in the Roman Empire*, ed. M. Henig. Oxford University, Committee for Archaeology. 29:91-107.

Boardman, J., et al.
    1967    *The Art and Architecture of Ancient Greece*. London.

Bowersock, G. W.
    1971    "A Report on Arabia Provincia," *JRS* 61:219-242.

———.
    1975    "Old and New in the History of Judaea," *JRS* 65:180-195.

———.
    1982    "Review of A. Spijkerman, *The Coins of the Decapolis and Provincia Arabia*," *JRS* 72:197-198.

———.
    1983    *Roman Arabia*. Cambridge, MA.

———.
    1986    "An Arabian Trinity," *HTR* 79:17-21, 465.

———.
    1990a    "The Cult and Representation of Dusares in Roman Arabia." In *LIMC*, ed. F. Zayadine. 31-36.

———.
    1990b    "Edward Lear in Petra," *PAPS* 4.309-320.

———.
    1991    "The Babatha Papyri, Masada and Rome," *JRA* 4:336-344.

Bowsher, J.
    1986    "The Frontier Post of Medain Saleh." In *The Defence of the Roman and Byzantine East, BAR*, ed. P. Freeman and D. Kennedy. 297:23-29.

Browning, I.
    1982    *Petra*. Chatto and Windus Ltd., London.

Burdon, D. J.
    1959    *Handbook of the Geology of Jordan* (To Accompany and Explain the Three Sheets of the 1:250,000 Geological Map of Jordan East of the Rift by Albert Quennell). Amman: Government of the Hashemite Kingdom of Jordan.

Broshi, M.
    1992    "Agriculture and Economy in Roman Palestine: Seven Notes on the Babatha Archive," *IEJ* 42:230-240.

Brünnow, R. E. and A. von Domaszewski.
    1904    *Die Provincia Arabia*. 3 vols. (A detailed list of pre-1904 publications of visitors to Petra.) Strasburg. 481-510.

Cantineau, J.
    1932a    *Le Nabatéen. I. Notions générales, écriture, grammaire*. Paris.

———.

1932b     *Le Nabatéen. II. Choix de textes, lexique.* Paris.

Casson, L.

1980     "*Periplus Maris Erythraei*: Three Notes on the Text," *CQ* 30:495-497.

Charlesworth, M.P.

1974     *Trade-Routes and Commerce of the Roman Empire.* 2nd ed. Chicago: Ares Publishers.

Clermont-Ganneau, C.

1898a     "La statue du dieu Obodas, roi de Nabatène." In *Recueil d'archéologie orientale* 2. Paris.

———.

1898b     "La statue du roi Rabel I à Pétra." In *Recueil d'archéologie orientale* 2. Paris.

Cohen, S.

1962     "Nabataeans." In *The Interpreter's Dictionary of the Bible. An Illustrated Encyclopedia.* New York.

Comer, D.C.

1997     *Enhancing the Utility of SIR-C Radar Imagery in the Analysis and monitoring of Archaeological Sites by Georeferencing with Larger Scale Imagery: A Test Project at Petra, Jordan.* National Park Service, Denver Service Center, RPG, Applied Archeology Center, Progress Report.

Conway, A.E.

1930     "Exploring a City of Mystery. The First Excavations at Petra: Discoveries in the Remains of the 'Built' City, and a New Explanation of the Rock-Cut 'Sanctuaries'," *ILN* 1 February:160-161.

Conway, A. and G. Horsfield.

1930     "Historical and Topographical Notes on Edom: With an Account of the First Excavations at Petra," *The Geographical Journal* 76:369-390.

Cotton, H.M.

1993     "The Guardianship of Jesus Son of Babatha: Roman and Local Law in the Province of Arabia," *JRS* 83:94-108.

Dalman, G.

1908     *Petra und Seine Felsheiligtümer.* Leipzig.

Dentzer, J.-M.

1979     "À propos du temple dit de 'Dusarès à Sî'," *Syria* 56:325-332.

———.

1984     "Sondages près de l'Arc nabatéen à Bosrà," *Berytus* 32:163-174.

———.

1985     "Six campagnes de fouilles à Sî': Développement et culture indigène en Syrie méridionale," *DM* 2:65-83.

———.

1986     "Les sondages de l'Arc nabatéen et l'urbanisme de Bosrà," *CRAI* 62-87.

Dentzer, J.-M. and J.
    1981    "Les fouilles de Sî' et la phase hellénistique en Syrie du sud," *AAS* 32:177-190.

Dentzer, J.-M., P. Gentelle and M. Gory.
    1989    Contribution française a l'archéologie jordanienne, *I.F.A.P.O.*

Dentzer, J.-M., et al.
    1982    "Fouille de la porte monumentale à 'Iraq al-Amir la campagne de 1978," *ADAJ* 26:301-321.

Dentzer, J.-M., et al.
    1982a    "'Iraq el Amir: Excavations at the Monumental Gateway," *SHAJ* 1:201-207.

Dentzer-Feydy, J.
    1985-1986 "Décor architectural et développement du Hauran du Ier s. av. J.-C. au VIIe s.ap. J.-C." In *Hauran I*, ed. J.-M. Dentzer. Paris. 261-310.

De Vries, B.
    1992    "Archaeology in Jordan," *AJA* 96:503-542.

De Vries, B. and P. Bikai.
    1993    "Archaeology in Jordan," *AJA* 97:457-520.

Dunand, M.
    1934    *Mission archéologique au Djebel Druze. Le Musée de Soueïda: Inscriptions et monuments figurés.* Bibliothèque archéologique et historique 20.

Dussaud, R.
    1904    "Numismatique des rois de Nabatène," *JA* 3:189-238.

Eadie, J.W. and J.P. Oleson.
    1986    "The Water-Supply Systems of Nabataean and Roman Humayma," *BASOR* 262: 49-76.

Farajat, S.
    1991    "The Nabataean Hydraulic System in the area of Humeima," *ADAJ* 35:17-30 (Arabic Section); also *Natural Resources Authority*, 1991. The Geological Map of Petra.

    1994    "The Role of the Nabataean Hydraulic System in the Protection of the Monuments at Petra." In *siti e monumente della Giordania*. 25-32.

Fiema, Z.T.
    1990    "The Nabataean King-List Revised: Further Observations on the Second Nabataean Inscription from Tell Esh-Shuqafiya, Egypt," *ADAJ* 34:239-248.

————.
    1993    "The Petra Project," *AN* 5:1-3.

————.
    1994    "Une èglise byzantine à Pétra," *Archéologia* 302:26-35.

————.
    1998    "The Roman Street in the Petra Project — A Preliminary Report," unpublished manuscript (submitted to *ADAJ*).

Freeman, P.
      1996      *The Annexation of Arabia and imperial Grand Strategy. In The Roman Army in the East, JRA Suppl.*, ed. D.L. Kennedy. 18:91-118.

Gerber, Y. and R. Fellmann Brogli.
      1995      "The Late Roman Pottery from Ez Zantur, Petra," *SHAJ* V:649-655.

Glueck, N.
      1933-1934  "Explorations in Eastern Palestine I," *AASOR* 14:1-113.

————.
      1934-1935  "Explorations in Eastern Palestine II," *AASOR* 15:1-202.

————.
      1937a      "Explorations in Eastern Palestine III," *BASOR* 65:8-29.

————.
      1937b      "The Nabataean Temple of Khirbet et-Tannûr," *BASOR* 67:6-16.

————.
      1937-1939  "Explorations in Eastern Palestine III," *AASOR* 18-19:1-288.

————.
      1939      "The Nabataean Temple of Qasr Rabbah," *AJA* 43:381-387.

————.
      1942      "Nabataean Syria," *BASOR* 85:3-8.

————.
      1956      "A Nabataean Painting," *BASOR* 141:13-23.

————.
      1965      *Deities and Dolphins: The Story of the Nabataeans*, New York.

————.
      1993      "Tannur, Khirbet et-." In *The New Encyclopedia of Archaeological Excavations in the Holy Land*, ed. E. Stern. Oxford. 4:1441-1446.

Goodman, M.
      1991      "Babatha's Story," *JRS* 81:169-175.

Graf, D.F.
      1990      "The Origin of the Nabataeans," *Aram* 2:45-75.

————.
      1992.     "Nabataeans." In *Anchor Bible Dictionary*, ed. D.N. Freedman, et al. 4:970-973.

————.
      1995      "The *Via Nova Traiana* in Arabia Petraea." In *The Roman and Byzantine Near East: Some Recent Archaeological Research, JRA Suppl.*, ed. J.H. Humphrey. Ann Arbor.

Greenfield, J.C.
      1993      "'Because He/She Did Not Know Letters': Remarks on a First Millennium C.E. Legal Expression," *JANES* 22:39-43.

Greene, K.
      1986      *The Archaeology of the Roman Economy.* London.

Gunneweg, J., I. Perlman and F. Asaro.
    1988    "The Origin Classification and Chronology of Nabataean Painted Fine Ware,"
           *JRGZM* 35:315-345.

Hadidi, A.
    1980    "Nabatäische Architektur in Petra," *BJ* 180:231-236.

    See also his 1982, 1985 and 1987 reports in *SHAJ*.

Hammond, N.G.L. and H.H. Scullard.
    1970    *The Oxford Classical Dictionary*. 2. Oxford.

Hammond, P.C.
    1960    "Excavations at Petra in 1959," *BASOR* 159:26-31.

————.
    1965    *The Excavation of the Main Theater at Petra, 1961-1962*. London.

————.
    1973    "The Nabataeans — Their History, Culture and Archaeology," *SIMA* 37.

————.
    1975    "Survey and Excavation at Petra, 1973-1974," *ADAJ* 20:5-30.

————.
    1977    "The Capitals from the 'Temple of the Winged Lions', Petra," *BASOR* 226:47-51.

————.
    1977-1978  "Excavations at Petra 1975-1977," *ADAJ* 22:81-101.

————.
    1980    "New Evidence for the 4th-Century A.D. Destruction at Petra," *BASOR* 238:
           65-67.

————.
    1996    *The Temple of the Winged Lions, Petra, Jordan, 1974-1990*. Arizona: Petra Publishing.

Hanson, J.
    1959    *Roman Theater-Temples*. Princeton.

Hayes, J.W.
    1972    *Late Roman Pottery*. London: British School at Rome.

————.
    1980    *A Supplement to Late Roman Pottery*. London: British School at Rome.

————.
    1985    "Sigillate orientali, Atlante delle forme ceramiche II," *Enciclopedia dell'arte antica*.
           1ff.

————.
    1997    *Handbook of Mediterranean Roman Pottery*. British Museum.

Healey, J.F.
    1989    "Were the Nabataeans Arabs?" *Aram* 1:38-44.

———.
      1993     *The Nabataean Tomb Inscriptions of Mada'in Salih*. Oxford.

Hendrix, R.E., P.R. Drey and J.B. Storfjell.
      1996     *Ancient Pottery of Transjordan: An Introduction Utilizing Published Whole Forms, Late Neolithic through Late Islamic*. Institute of Archaeology, Horn Archaeological Museum.

Horsfield, G. and A. Horsfield.
      1938     "Sela-Petra, The Rock of Edom and Nabatene I & II," *QDAP* 7:1-60.

———.
      1938-1939  "Sela-Petra, The Rock of Edom and Nabatene III: The Excavations," *QDAP* 8:87-116.

———.
      1939-1942  "Sela-Petra, The Rock of Edom and Nabatene IV: The Finds," *QDAP* 9:105-204.

Ilan, T.
      1992     "Julia Crispina, Daughter of Berenicianus, a Herodian Princess in the Babatha Archive: A Case Study in Historical Identification," *JQR* 82.3-4:261-281.

———.
      1993     "Premarital Cohabitation in Ancient Judea: The Evidence of the Babatha Archive and the Mishnah (*Ketubbot* 1.4)," *HTR* 86.3:247-264.

Iliffe, J.H.
      1934     "Nabataean Pottery from the Negev: Its Distribution in Palestine," *QDAP* 3:132-135.

———.
      1938     "Sigillata Wares in the Near East: A List of Potters' Stamps," *QDAP* 5:4-53.

Isaac, B.
      1992     "The Babatha Archive: A Review Article," *IEJ* 42:62-75.

Jaussen, J. and R. Savignac.
      1909-1914 *Mission archéologique en Arabie*. Vols. 1 and 2. Paris.

Johnson, D.J.
      1987     *Nabataean Trade: Intensification and Culture Change*. Ph.D. dissertation, University of Utah.

Josephus.
      1960a    *Jewish Antiquities*, trans. W. Whiston. Grand Rapids, Michigan.

———.
      1960b    *Jewish Wars*, trans. W. Whiston. Grand Rapids, Michigan.

Joukowsky, M.S.
      1980     *A Complete Manual of Field Archaeology*. New Jersey: Prentice Hall.

Kanellopoulos, C.
      1993     *The Great Temple of Amman: The Architecture*. Amman: ACOR. (See also articles by P. Warnock and M. Pendleton in Appendix B.)

Katzoff, R.
>1991    "Papyrus Yadin 18 Again: A Rejoinder," *JQR* LXXXII.1-2:171-176.

Kennedy, Sir A.B.W.
>1925    *Petra, its History and Monuments*. London.

Khairy, N.I.
>1975    *A Typological Study of the Unpainted Pottery from the Petra Excavations*. Dissertation (unpublished), University College, London.

———.
>1982    "Fine Nabataean Ware with Impressed and Rouletted Decorations," *SHAJ* I:275-283.

———.
>1984    "Preliminary Report of the 1981 Petra Excavations," *ADAJ* 28:315-320.

———.
>1987    "The Painted Nabataean Pottery from the 1981 Petra Excavations," *Levant* 19:167-181.

Kirkbride, D.
>1960a   "A Short Account of the Excavations at Petra in 1955-1956," *ADAJ* 4-5:117-122.

———.
>1960b   "Le temple nabatéen de Ramm. Son évolution architecturale," *RB* 67:65-92, pl. 3-9.

———.
>1960c   "The Excavation of a Neolithic Village at Seyl Aqlat, Beidha, near Petra," *PEQ* 92:136-145, pl. 25-30.

———.
>1961    "Ten Thousand Years of Man's Activity Around Petra: Unknown and Little-known Sites Excavated or Explored," *ILN* 239:448-451.

———.
>1964    "Seyl Aqlat, Beidha, près de Pétra," Chronique archéologique *RB* 71:246-250.

———.
>1968    "Beidha: Early Neolithic Village Life South of the Dead Sea," *Antiquity* 42:263-274, pl. 37.

———.
>1984    "Beidha 1983: An Interim Report," *ADAJ* 28:9-12, pl. 1.

———.
>1985    "The Environment of the Petra Region during the Pre-Pottery Neolithic." In *SHAJ*, ed. A. Hadidi. II:117-124.

Knauf, E.A.
>1986    "Die Herkunft der Nabatäer." In *Petra. Neue Ausgrabungen und Entdeckungen*, ed. M. Lindner. Münich. 74-86.

Kolb, B. and R.A. Stucky.
1993    "Preliminary Report of the Swiss-Liechtenstein Excavations at ez-Zantur in Petra 1992. The Fourth Campaign," *ADAJ* 37:417-423, 425, pl. 1.

Kraeling, C.H.
1941    "The Nabataean Sanctuary at Gerasa," *BASOR* 83:7-14.

Laborde, L. de.
1838    *Journey through Arabia Petraea to Mount Sinai and the Excavated City of Petra, the Edom and the Prophecies.* London.

Lapp, N.L.
1979    "The Hellenistic Pottery from the 1961 and 1962 Excavations at 'Iraq el-Emir," *ADAJ* 23:5-15.

Lapp, P.W.
1961    *Palestinian Ceramic Chronology 200 B.C. - A.D. 70.* ASOR Publications of the Jerusalem School, Archaeology. Vol. III.

————.
1976    "'Iraq el-Emir." In *Encyclopedia of Archaeological Excavations in the Holy Land*, ed. E. Stern. Oxford. II:527-531.

Lewis, N. (ed.)
1989    *The Documents From the Bar Kokhba Period in the Cave of Letters: Greek Papyri.* Jerusalem: Judean Desert Studies 2, Israel Exploration Society, Hebrew University, Shrine of the Book.

Libbey, W. and F.E. Hoskins.
1905    *The Jordan Valley and Petra.* 2. New York, London.

Lindner, M.
1980    "Deutsche Ausgrabungen in Petra," *BJ* 180:125-136.

————.
1982a    "Über die Wasserversorgung einer antiken Stadt," *Das Altertum* 28, 1:27-39.

————.
1982b    "An Archaeological Survey of the Theater Mount and Catchwater Regulation System at Sabra, South of Petra, 1980," *ADAJ* 26:231-242.

————.
1982c    "Eine Grabung in Sabra (Jordanien)," *NM* 1982:67-73.

————.
1984    "Archäologische Erkundungen des Der-Plateaus oberhalb von Petra (Jordanien) 1982 und 1983," *AA* 1984:597-625.

————.
1985    *Petra, Der Führer durch die antike Stadt, The Guide Through the Antique City.* Fürth.

————.
1986    Ed. *Petra Neue Ausgrabungen und Entdeckungen.* München.

————.
1989    *Petra und das Königreich der Nabatäer.* 3rd. ed. Nuremberg, 5th ed.

Lyttelton, M.B.
    1974    *Baroque Architecture in Classical Antiquity.* London.

———.

    1990    "Aspects of the Iconography of the Sculptural Decoration of the Khasneh at Petra." In *LIMC*, ed. F. Zayadine. Amman. 19-29.

MacDonald, W.
    1986    *The Architecture of the Roman Empire.* Vol. II. New Haven.

Mattingly, G.L.
    1990    "Settlement on Jordan's Kerak Plateau from Iron IIC through the Early Roman Period," *Aram* 2:309-335.

McKenzie, J.S.
    1985    "The Measurement of Inaccessible Mouldings by a Surveying Method: As Applied at Petra," *Levant* 17:157-170.

———.

    1987a    "Corpus of the Principal Monuments at Petra," *RR* 19:217-218.

———.

    1987b    "The Dating of the Principal Monuments at Petra and Khirbet Tannur," *PEQ* 120:81-107.

———.

    1988    "The Development of Nabataean Sculpture at Petra and Khirbet Tannur," *PEQ* 120:81-107.

———.

    1990    *The Architecture of Petra.* New York.

McKenzie, J. and A. Phippen.
    1983    "Preliminary Report on the Measurement of Architectural Elements on the Façades at Petra," *ADAJ* 27:209-212.

———.

    1987    "The Chronology of the Principal Monuments at Petra," *Levant* XIX:145-165.

Meshorer, Y.
    1975    *Nabataean Coins. Qedem 3.*

Milik, J.T.
    1959    "Inscription nabatéenne de Turkmaniye à Pétra. IIIe partie." In "Notes d'épigraphie et de topographie palestiniennes," *RB* 66:550-575, pl. 13-14.

———.

    1976    "Une inscription bilingue nabatéenne et grecque à Pétra," *ADAJ* 21:143-152.

———.

    1980    "Quatre inscriptions nabatéennes." In "Petra, la cité rose du désert," *Le Monde de la Bible*, ed. J. Starcky. 14:12-15.

———.

    1982    "Origines des Nabatéens," *SHAJ* I:261-265.

Millar, F.
    1993    *The Roman Near East 31 BC-AD337.* Cambridge: Harvard.

Miller, J.I.
    1969    *The Spice Trade of the Roman Empire 29 B.C. to A.D. 641.* Oxford.

Murray, M.A. and J.C. Ellis.
    1940    *A Street in Petra.* London.

Musil, A.
    1907    *Arabia Petraea.* Vol. 2. *Topographischer Reise-bericht.* Vienna.

Negev, A.
    1966    "The Date of the Petra-Gaza Road," *PEQ* 98:98-99.

————.
    1977    "The Nabataeans and Provincia Arabia," *ANRW* II 8:520-684.

————.
    1983    *Tempel, Kirchen und Zisternen, Ausgrabungen in der Wüste Negev.* Stuttgart.

————.
    1986a    "The Late Hellenistic and Early Roman Pottery of Nabataean Oboda," *Qedem 22.*

————.
    1986b    *Nabataean Archaeology Today.* New York.

————.
    1993    "Petra." In *The New Encyclopedia of Archaeological Excavations in the Holy Land,* ed. E. Stern. 4:1181-1193.

Negev, A. and R. Sivan.
    1977    "The Pottery of the Nabataean Necropolis at Mampsis," *ReiCretActa* 17-18:109-131.

Nielsen, I.
    1994    *Hellenistic Palaces: Tradition and Renewal.* Aarhus.

Oleson, J.P.
    1986    "The Humayma Hydraulic Survey: Preliminary Report of the 1986 Season," *ADAJ* 32: 157-169.

Paradise, T.R.
    1993    "Analysis of Weathering-Constrained Erosion of Sandstone in the Roman Theater of Petra, Jordan," National Science Foundation (#SES-9205055) Regional Science Program in Washington D.C. and the United States Information Agency as administrated through the American Center of Oriental Research.

————.
    1994    "Limestone Weathering Rate Analysis." In *Great Temple of Amman, The Architecture,* Chrysanthos Kanellopoulos. 110-114.

Parker, S.T.
    1987    *The Roman Frontier in Central Jordan: Interim Report on the Limes Arabicus Project, 1980-1985.* 2 vols. *BAR-IS* 340. Oxford.

Parlasca, I.

1986a     "Die nabatäischen Kamelterrakotten — Ihre antiquarischen und religionsgeschichtlichen Aspekte." In *Petra. Neue Ausgrabungen und Entdeckungen*, ed. M. Lindner. Münich. 200-213.

———.

1986b     "Priester und Gott. Bemerkungen zu Terrakottafunden aus Petra." In *Petra. Neue Ausgrabungen und Entdeckungen*, ed. M. Lindner. Münich. 192-199.

———.

1990     "Seltene Typen nabatäischer Terrakotten. Östliche Motive in der späteren Provincia Arabia." In *Das antike Rom und der Osten. Festschrift für Klaus Parlasca zum 65. Geburtstag*, ed. C. Börker et M. Donderer. Neustadt/Aish. 1990:157-174, pl. 26-39.

Parr, P.J.

1957     "Recent Discoveries at Petra," *PEQ* 89: 5-16.

———.

1960     "Excavations at Petra 1958-1959," *PEQ* 92:124-135.

———.

1962     "Le 'Conway High Place' à Pétra, une nouvelle interprétation," *RB* 69:64-79.

———.

1963     "The Capital of the Nabataeans," *Scientific American* 209:94-103.

———.

1965a     "The Beginnings of Hellenization at Petra." *8th Congrès International d'Archéologie Classique*. Paris. 527-533.

———.

1965b     "Pétra," *RB* 72:253-257.

———.

1967     "La date du barrage du Sîq à Pétra," *RB* 74:45-49.

———.

1967-1968     "Recent Discoveries in the Sanctuary of the Qasr Bint Far'un at Petra: Account of the Recent Excavations," *ADAJ* 12-13:5-19.

———.

1968a     "Découvertes récentes au sanctuaire du Qasr à Pétra: Compte rendu des dernières fouilles," *Syria* 45:1-24.

———.

1968b     "The Investigation of some 'Inaccessible' Rock-Cut Chambers at Petra," *PEQ* 100:5-15.

———.

1970     "A Sequence of Pottery from Petra." In *Near Eastern Archaeology in the Twentieth Century: Essays in Honour of Nelson Glueck*, ed. J.A. Sanders. New York. 348-381.

———.

1978     "Pottery, People, and Politics." In *Archaeology in the Levant, Essays for Kathleen Kenyon*, ed. P.R.S. Moorey and P.J. Parr. Warminster. 202-209.

———.
    1986a    "Vierzig Jahre Ausgrabungen in Petra (1929 bis 1969)." In *Petra. Neue Ausgrabungen und Endeckungen*, ed. M. Lindner. Münich. 139-149.

———.
    1986b    "The Last Days at Petra." In *Proceedings of the Symposium on Bilad al-Sham During the Byzantine Period*, ed. M.A. Bakhit and M. Asfour. Amman. 192-205.

———.
    1990    "Sixty Years of Excavation in Petra: A Critical Assessment," *Aram* 2:1 and 2:7-23.

———.
    1996    *The Architecture of Petra:* Review Article. (J.S. McKenzie, 1990). *PEQ* 28:63-70.

Parr, P.J., K.B. Atkinson and E. Wickens.
    1975    "Photogrammetric Work at Petra, 1965-1968 An Interim Report," *ADAJ* 20:31-45.

Patrich, J.
    1990    "The Formation of Nabataean Art: Prohibition of a Graven Image Among the Nabataeans: The Evidence and its Significance," *Aram* 2:185-196.

———.
    1993    *Petra und die Weihrauchstraße.* Zürich-Basel: Ausstellungskat.

*Periplus Maris Erythraei.*
    1989    Trans. and ed. L. Casson. Princeton: Princeton University Press.

Polotsky, H.
    1962    "The Greek Papyri from the Cave of Letters," *IEJ* 12:259.

Raschke, M.G.
    1978    "New Studies in Roman Commerce with the East." *Aufstieg und Niedergang der Römischen Welt*, II, ed. M. Temporini and W. Haase. Berlin, New York: De Gruyter. Principat. 9.2:604-1378.

Roche, M.-J.
    1996    "Remarques sur les Nabatéens en Méditerranée," *Semitica* 45: 73-99.

Rostovtzeff, M.
    1957    *The Social and Economic History of the Roman Empire.* Oxford.

Rotroff, S.I.
    1982    "Silver, Glass, and Clay: Evidence for the Dating of Hellenistic Luxury Tableware," *Hesperia* 51:329-337.

Russell, K.W.
    1980    "The Earthquake of May 19, A.D. 363," *BASOR* 238:47-64.

———.
    1993    "Ethnohistory of the Bedul Bedouin," *ADAJ* 37:15-35.

Schmid, S.G.
    1995a    "Nabataean Fine Ware from Petra." Paper presented at the Vth International Conference on the History and Archaeology of Jordan, April 1992, Irbid (Jordan), in *SHAJ* V:637-647.

————.
    1995b    *Die Feinkeramik der Nabatäer. Typologie, Chronologie und kulturhistorische Hintergründe.* Dissertation, University of Basel.

————.
    1996    "Die Feinkeramik der Nabatäer im Spiegel ihrer kulturhistorischen Kontakte." In *Hellenistische und kaiserzeitliche Keramik des östlichen Mittelmeergebietes*, Kolloquium Frankfurt, 24-25, April 1995. 127-145.

Schmidt-Colinet, A.
    1980    "Nabatäische Felsarchitektur. Bemerkungen zum gegenwärtingen Forschungsstand," *BJ* 180:189-230.

————.
    1983a    "A Nabataean Family of Sculptors at Hegra," *Berytus* 31:95-102.

————.
    1983b    "Dorisierende nabatäische Kapitelle," *DaM* 1:307-312, pl. 66-67.

————.
    1987    "The Mason's Workshop of Hegra, its Relations to Petra, and the Tomb of Syllaios," *SHAJ* III:143-150.

Schmitt-Korte, K.
    1968 [1968-1969] "Beitrag zur nabatäischen Keramik," *AA* 83:496-519.

————.
    1971    "A Contribution to the Study of Nabataean Pottery," *ADAJ* 16:47-60.

————.
    1983    "Die bemalte nabatäische Keramik: Verbreitung, Typologie und Chronologie." In *Petra und das Königreich der Nabatäer*, ed. M. Lindner. Lebensraum, Geschichte und Kultur eines arabischen Volkes der Antike. 5:174-197.

Schmitt-Korte, K. and M. Cowell.
    1989    "Nabataean Coinage, Part I. The Silver Content Measured by X-Ray Fluorescence Analysis," *NC* 149:33-58, pl. 11-17.

Seetzen, U.J.
    1854-1859 *Reisen durch Syrien, Palästina, Phönicien, die Transjordan-Länder, Arabia Petraea und unter-Aegypten.* 2 vols. Berlin: Herausgegeben und kommentiert von Pr. Dr. Fr. Kruse.

Segal, A.
    1995    *Theatres in Roman Palestine and Prvincia Arabia.* Leiden.

Siculus, Diodorus.
    1933-1967 Trans. C.H. Oldfather, et al. London: Loeb.

Sidebotham, S.E.
    1986    *Roman Economic Policy in the Erythra Thalassa 30 B.C.-A.D. 217.* Leiden, E.J. Brill.

Sourdel, D.
    1952    *Les cultes du Hauran à l'époque romaine.* Paris.

Speidel, M.
    1984    *Roman Army Studies I*: 229-273. Amsterdam: Gieben.

Starcky, J.
    1955    "The Nabataeans: A Historical Sketch," *BA* 18:84-106.

———.
    1965    "Nouvelles stèles funéraires à Pétra," *ADAJ* 10:43-49, pl. 21-22.

———.
    1966    "Pétra et la nabatène," *Dictionnaire de la Bible*, Supp. 7:886-1017.

———.
    1980    "Pétra, la cité rose du désert," *Le Monde de la Bible,* 14, July, 9-11.

Starcky, J. and C.M. Bennett.
    1967-1968  "Recent Discoveries in the Sanctuary of the Qasr Bint Far'un at Petra. III.
            The Temenos Inscriptions," *ADAJ* 12-13:30-50, pl. 22-26.

Starcky, J. and J. Strugnell.
    1966    "Pétra: deux nouvelles inscriptions nabatéennes," *RB* 73:236-247, pl. 8-9.

Strugnell, J.
    1959    "The Nabataean Goddess Al-Kutba' and her Sanctuaries," *BASOR* 156:26-36.

Stucky, R.A., et al.
    1990    "Preliminary Report 1988 Schweizer Ausgrabungen in Ez-Zantur, Petra.
            Vorbericht der Kampagne 1988," *ADAJ* 34:249-283.

———.
    1991    "Swiss-Liechtenstein Excavations at ez-Zantur in Petra 1989: The Second
            Campaign," *ADAJ* 35:251-273.

———.
    1992a   "Preliminary Report 1991 Swiss-Liechtenstein Excavations at Ez-Zantur in
            Petra: The Third Campaign," *ADAJ* 36:175-192.

———.
    1992b   "Das nabatäische Wohnhaus und das urbanistische System der Wohnquartiere in
            Petra," *Antk* 35:129-140.

———.
    1994    "Swiss-Liechtenstein Excavations at Ez-Zantur in Petra 1993: The Fifth
            Campaign," *ADAJ* 38:271-292.

———.
    1995    "The Nabataean House and the Urbanistic System of Habitation Quarters in
            Petra," *SHAJ* V:193-198.

Tacitus.
            Histories and Annals. (*Ann.*) C.H. Moore and J. Jackson. Loeb Classical Library.

Teixidor, J.
    1973    "The Nabataean presence at Palmyra," *JANES* 5:405-409.

———.

1977     *The Pagan God. Popular Religion in the Greco-Roman Near East.* Princeton.

———.

1991     "Les inscriptions nabatéennes du Musée de Suweida." In *Le djebel al-'arab; Histoire et Patrimone au musée de Suweida,* ed. J.-M. Dentzer et J. Dentzer-Feydy. Paris. 25-28.

Vickers, M.
1994     "Nabataea, India, Gaul and Carthage: Reflections on Hellenistic and Roman Gold Vessels and Red-Gloss Pottery," *AJA* 98:231-248.

Villeneuve, F.
1979     "Pétra et le royaume nabatéen," *HI* 11:50-58.

———.

1984     "Le Qasr al-Bint de Pétra." In *Contribution française à l'archéologie Jordanienne,* ed. F. Villeneuve. Amman.

———.

1986     "Khirbet edh-Dharih (1985)." In Chronique archéologique *RB* 93:247-252, pl. 5-6.

———.

1991     "Tannour et Dharih sanctuaires de la Nabatène," *DHA* 163:58-61.

Ward-Perkins, J.B.
1981     *Roman Imperial Architecture.* Harmondsworth.

Wasserstein, A.
1989     "A Marriage Contract From the Province of Arabia Nova: Notes on Papyrus Yadin 18," *JQR* 80.1-2:93-130.

Weber, T. and R. Wenning. (eds.)
1997     *Antike Felsstadt zwischen arabischer Tradition und griechischer Norm.* Sonderheft/ Antike Welt, Zaberns Bildbände zur Archäologie. Verlag Philipp von Zabern. Mainz.

Weippert, M.
1979     "Nabatäisch-römische Keramik aus Hirbet Dor im südlichen Jordanien," *ZDPV* 95:87-110.

Wenning, R.
1987     *Die Nabatäer — Denkmäler und Geschichte. Eine Bestandesaufnahme des archäologischen Befundes.* Novum Testamentum et Orbis Antiquus 3.

———.

1990     "Das Nabatäerreich: seine archäologischen und historischen Hinterlassenschaften." In *Palästina in Griechisch Römischer Zeit,* ed. H. Weippert and H.P. Kuhren. Münich. 367-415.

———.

1992     "The Nabataeans in the Decapolis/Coele Syria," *Aram* 4.1-2:79-99.

———.

1993     Eine neuerstellte Liste der nabäische Dynastie. *BOREAS.* Munstersche Beiträge zur Archaeologie. Band 16, 25-38.

Wiegand, T., W. Bachmann and C. Watzinger.
    1921    *Petra*. Wissenschaftliche Veröffentlichungen des Deutsch-Türkischen Denkmalschutz-Kommandos, Heft 3. Leipzig.

Wright, G.R.H.
    1961a    "Structure of the Qasr Bint Far'un. A Preliminary Review," *PEQ* 93:8-37.

———.
    1961b    "Petra — the Arched Gate, 1959-60," *PEQ* 93:124-135.

———.
    1962    "The Khazne at Petra: A Review," *ADAJ* 6-7:24-54.

———.
    1966    "Structure et date de l'arc monumental de Pétra," *RB* 73:404-419.

———.
    1967-1968    "Recent Discoveries in the Sanctuary of the Qasr Bint Far'un at Petra: Some Aspects Concerning the Architecture and Sculpture," *ADAJ* 12-13:20-29.

———.
    1970    "Petra — the Arched Gate 1959-1960: Some Additional Drawings," *PEQ* 112:111-115.

———.
    1973    "The Date of the Khazne Fir'aun at Petra in the Light of an Iconographic Detail," *PEQ* 105:83-90.

———.
    1985    "The Qasr Bint Fir'aun at Petra. A Detail Reconsidered," *DaM* 2:321-325.

Yadin, Y. (ed.)
    1963a    "The Nabataean Kingdom, Provincia Arabia, Petra and En-Geddi in the Documents from Nahal Hever," *JEOL* 17:227-241.

———.
    1963b    *The Finds From The Bar Kokhba Period In The Cave of Letters*. Jerusalem: Judaean Desert Studies 1 Israel Exploration Society, Hebrew University, Shrine of the Book.

———.
    1971    *Bar Kokhba*. Jerusalem and London.

Zayadine, F.
    1974    "Excavations at Petra (April 1973)," *ADAJ* 18:81-82.

———.
    1979    "Excavations at Petra (1976-1978)," *ADAJ* 23:185-197, pl.83-94.

———.
    1980    "Art et architecture des Nabatéens," *Le Monde de la Bible* 14:16-26.

———.
    1981    "L'iconographie à'Al 'Uzza-Aphrodite." In *Mythologie gréco-romaine. Mythologies périphériques. Etudes iconographiques.* (Colloques internmationaux du CNRS, 593). Paris.

————.
  1982      "Recent Excavations at Petra, 1979-1981," *ADAJ* 26:365-393.

————.
  1984      "Al-Uzza Aphrodite," *LIMC II,* 1, Zürich, Münich.

————.
  1985a     "Recent Excavation and Restoration at Qasr el Bint of Petra," *ADAJ* 29:239-249.

————.
  1985b     "Caravan Routes Between Egypt and Nabataea and the Voyage of the Sultan Baibars to Petra in 1276 AD," *SHAJ* 2:159-174.

————.
  1986a     "Tempel, Gräber, Töpferöfen." In *Petra. Neue Ausgrabungen und Endeckungen*, ed. M. Lindner. Münich. 214-272.

————.
  1986b     "Recent Excavations at the Qasr al-Bint of Petra," *AfO* 33:177-180.

————.
  1987      "Decorative Stucco at Petra and other Hellenistic Sites," *SHAJ* 3:131-142.

————
  1990      *Petra and the Caravan Cities. Proceedings of the Symposium organized at Petra in September 1985 by the Department of Antiquities of Jordan and the Iconographic Lexicon of Classical Mythology (LIMC) with the financial support of UNESCO.* Amman: Department of Antiquities.

Zayadine, F. and P. Hottier.
  1976      "Relevé photogrammétrique à Pétra," *ADAJ* 21:93-104.

Zayadine, F. and S. Farajat.
  1991      "The Petra National Trust Site Projects: Excavation and Clearance at Petra and Beida," *ADAJ* 35: 275-311.

Zeitler, J.P.
  1990a     "Houses, Sherds and Bones: Aspects of Daily Life in Petra." In *The Near East in Antiquity, German Contributions to the Archaeology of Jordan, Palestine, Syria, Lebanon and Egypt.* I:39-44.

————.
  1990b     "A Private Building from the First Century B.C. in Petra." In "First International Conference, The Nabataeans." Oxford 26-29 September 1989. *Aram* 2:385-420.

————.
  1993a     "Excavations and Surveys in Petra 1989-1990," Chronique Archéologique *Syria* LXX, 257-259.

————.
  1993b     "Petra und die Wiehrauchstrasse," Exhibition Catalog for Zürich and Basel.

# THE PETRA GREAT TEMPLE — SITE BIBLIOGRAPHY
## (BY YEAR SINCE 1993)

### 1993

1) Joukowsky, M.S.
  1993  "The Southern Temple at Petra," *ACOR Newsletter* 5.2:11.

2) Khuri, R.
  1993a "Results of First Year Dig," *Jordan Times*, September 8.

3) ———.
  1993b "Results of First Year Dig," *Al Ra'i Daily Newspaper*, September
  8 (in Arabic).

4) Zeitler, J.P.
  1993  "Excavations and Surveys in Petra 1989-90," Chronique Archéologique *Syria*
  70:205-273.

### 1994

5) Joukowsky, M.S.
  1994a "1993 Archaeological Excavations and Survey of the Southern Temple at Petra,
  Jordan," *ADAJ* XXXVIII:293-322.

6) ———.
  1994b "Archaeological Survey of the Southern Temple at Petra, Jordan," *L'Orient Express*
  2:43-44.

7) ———.
  1994c "Petra Southern Temple." In "Archaeology of Jordan," *AJA*, ed. Glenn L. Peterman
  98:543-544.

8) ———.
  1994d "Petra — The Brown University Excavations," *BUFB* VI.3:15-18.

9) Rodan, S.
  1994  "Bedouin Secrets," *The Jerusalem Post Magazine,* 29 July.

### 1995

10) Joukowsky, M.S.
  1995a "Le "Temple Sud" a` Pétra," *le monde de la bible Archéologie et Histore* 94,
  Septembre–Octobre, 43.

11) ———.
  1995b "Petra the Southern Temple." In "Archaeology of Jordan," *AJA*, ed. Patricia M.
  Bikai and Deborah Koorings. 99:518-520.

12) ———.

    1995c    "Archaeological Survey of the Southern Temple at Petra," *Syria* LXXII.1-2:133-142.

13) ———.

    1995d    "Petra Southern Temple," *ACOR Newsletter* 7.2:7-8.

14) Joukowsky, M.S. and E.L. Schluntz.

    1995     "The Southern Temple at Petra: 1994 Excavations," *ADAJ* XXXIX:241-266.

15) Mamalaki, D.

    1995     "From the Field," *Haffenreffer Museum Newsletter.*

16) Myers, J.W. and E.E. Myers.

    1995     "Low altitude aerial photography," *JRA Suppl.* 14:284-285, fig. 5-7.

17) Negev, A.

    1995     "The Petra Southern Temple," *Qadmoniot* XXVIII.2:110 (in Hebrew).


# 1996


18) Barrett, D.G.

    1996     *How Can the Ceramic Analysis of Lamps Reveal the Impact of Empire on the Southern Temple at Petra?* M.A. thesis, Brown University, Department of Anthropology.

19) Blackburn, J.

    1996     "Ancient City in the Sands," *Views,* Rhode Island School of Design Alumni Magazine, Summer 8.3:20-21.

20) Joukowsky, M.S.

    1996a    "Petra, The Southern Temple." In "Archaeology in Jordan," *AJA* 100.3:525-526.

21) ———.

    1996b    "The Petra Southern Temple: or What I do on my Summer 'Vacations,'" *BUFB* VIII.3:30-35.

22) ———.

    1996c    "The Petra Southern Temple: The Fourth Season, 1996," *Archaeological Institute of America, Abstracts*, 98th Annual Meeting 20:6-7.

23) ———.

    1996d    "Petra, The 'Great' Southern Temple," *ACOR Newsletter* 8.1:6-7.

24) ———.

    1996e    "1995 Archaeological Excavations of the Southern Temple at Petra, Jordan," *ADAJ* XL:177-206.

25) Khouri, R.

    1996a    "Excavations unravel mysteries of Petra's Great Southern Temple," *Jordan Times,* April 23, 1996:6-7.

26) ———.
    1996b    "Fourth Season of Excavation Clarifies Important Architectural Aspects of Petra's Southern Temple," *Jordan Times,* December 14:7.

27) Schluntz, E.L.
    1996    "The Architectural Sculpture of the Southern Temple at Petra, Jordan," *Archaeological Institute of America, Abstracts*, 98th Annual Meeting. 20:7.

28) Zimmerman, P.C.
    1996    "MiniCad 6 — Another View," *CSA Newsletter: A Quarterly Newsletter for Architectural Historians and Archaeologists* 9:3: 9-11.


## 1997

29) Basile, J.J.

    1997    "A Head of the Goddess Tyche from Petra, Jordan," *ADAJ* XLI:255-266.

30) Freyberger, K.S. and M.S. Joukowsky.
    1997    "Blattranken, Greifen und Elefanten: Sakrale Architektur in Petra und ihr Bauschmuck neuausgegrabene Peripteral-tempel." In *Petra: Antike Felsstadt Zwischen Arabischer Tradition Und Griechischer Norm*, ed. T. Weber and R. Wenning. Mainz: Verlag Philipp Von Zabern. 71-86.

31) Joukowsky, M.S.
    1997a    "The Water Canalization System of the Petra Southern Temple," *SHAJ* VI:303-311. Sixth International Conference on the History and Archaeology of Jordan, "Landscape Resources and Human Occupation in Jordan Throughout the Ages." Torino (Italy).

32) ———.
    1997b    "The Southern Temple at Petra." In *Encyclopedia of Near Eastern Archaeology.* Oxford University Press and the American Schools of Oriental Research. 4:306-307.

33) ———.
    1997c    "The Petra Southern Temple: The Fourth Season, 1996," *AJA* 101:339.

34) ———.
    1997d    "Brown University Petra Great Temple Excavations," *BUFB* X.1:29-32."

35) ———.
    1997e    "Brown University Excavations at the 'Great' Temple of Petra. Jordan," *ASOR Newsletter* (Abstracts) 47.2:A-35.

36) ———.
    1997f    "Petra: Great Temple," *ACOR Newsletter* 9.1:7.

37) ———.
    1997g    "The Great Temple at Petra," *AJA*, ed. P.M. Bikai and V. Eagan. 101.3:520-521.

38) ———.
    1997h    "1997 Brown University Excavations at the "Great" Southern Temple of Petra," *Archaeological Institute of America, Abstracts*, 99th Annual Meeting. 21:100.

39) ———.
    1997i    "1996 Brown University Archaeological Excavations of the 'Great' Southern Temple at Petra, Jordan," *ADAJ* XLI:195-218.

40) Schluntz, E.L.
    1997    "The Architectural Sculpture of the Southern Temple at Petra, Jordan," *AJA* 101:339.

41) Twair, P.M.
    1997    "Temple at Petra Challenges Veteran American Archaeologist," *The Washington Report on Middle East Affairs Monthly*, March 1997:55,98.


# 1998


42) Boucher, Norman.
    1998    "Mystery in Stone and Sand," *BAM* 98.3:30-37.

43) Joukowsky, M.S.
    1998    "Re-Discovering Elephants at Petra!" In *Ancient Egyptian and Mediterranean Studies: In Memory of William A. Ward*, ed. Leonard H. Lesko. Brown University, Department of Egyptology. 133-148.

# Media

## Television

1996  *Search, Archaeology 101*, North Carolina State University. Short appearance as Brown University's Director, Petra 'Great' Temple Excavations.

1995  "Ancient Mysteries" Arts and Entertainment (Arts and Entertainment Network Series) documentary. Film produced by Bram Rose, et al. "Petra." 52 minutes, color program, narrated by Kathleen Turner.

1995-1994  *Archaeology* series, "Petra, City in the Sand." *Learning Channel*, New Dominion Films, color, narrated by John Rhys Davies. (Re-aired six times during 1995 and several times during 1996.)

1995  Video Lecture on Petra 'Great' Southern Temple for the St. Louis Society of the Archaeological Institute of America. Martha Sharp Joukowsky, October 17, 1995.

## Web Pages

1995  "Southern Temple Excavations at Petra, Jordan," Brown University.
<petra@stg.brown.edu>

1996  "Petra" on *ASOR Digs 96*, The American Schools of Oriental Research, Committee on Archaeological Policy: Reports of Affiliated Projects.
<http://www.cobb.msstate.edu/asordigs.html>

1997  "The Petra 'Great' Temple."
<http://www.brown.edu/Departments/Anthropology/Petra/>

# Other

1997  Mannis, Avi. "Coins of the 'Great' Southern Temple, Petra," *The Digital Archive Project* (CD-ROM). Honors thesis, Brown University, Center for Old World Archaeology and Art.

May 20, 1998

# PREFACE

This report by a collaborative team of archaeologists, scientists, computer specialists and engineers presents as complete a picture as possible of the archaeological remains discovered over the past five years in the Great Temple at Petra, Jordan. The results of the first five years of excavations supplement the history and archaeological remains of Petra, under investigation starting in 1898 by the Germans R.E. Brünnow and A. von Domaszewski and in 1929 by the British researcher George Horsfield, who led the first archaeological excavations at Petra.

As the center of the peak of prosperity for the Nabataean kingdom from the second century BCE until it was subsumed by the Romans in 106 CE, Petra was given life by its Nabataean founders in the context of its ancient landscape. During the Roman period, the metropolis continued to thrive, since it was linked to the wider history of Arabia Petraea and the eastern Roman Empire. Our excavations reflect the changing fortunes of Petra. The importance of the Great Temple can now take its place in the study of Petra, including the fuller evaluation of the role that the Great Temple played in the chapters of Nabataean and Roman history.

The Great Temple was first brought to my attention in 1992 by Pierre M. Bikai, Director of the American Center of Oriental Research in Amman. The need for the investigation of this extensive, semivisible archaeological site was apparent, although the task was daunting because of the enormous overburden of the collapsed Great Temple. Ironically, these conditions were probably responsible for the survival of one of the most interesting and best-preserved free-standing buildings of the classical Nabataean and Nabataean-Roman periods in Petra.

In 1992, permission was requested and received from the Department of Antiquities of the Ministry of Tourism of the Hashemite Kingdom of Jordan to explore the structure. Annual summer investigations have taken place from 1993 through 1997. It is planned that excavations at the Great Temple will continue for some years to come.

This volume includes a compendium of results over a five-year period; it is meant to form a unified and coherent corpus of what we have identified up to this point in our investigations. This report is aimed at two different constituencies: professional archaeologists researching the magnificent site of Petra or related sites and the interested public who are fascinated with seeing something at this extraordinary site in a new and different light.

## Consultants

In 1993, expertise in several subdisciplines was discussed with Peter J. Parr. It was suggested that Petra coins might be referred to expert numismatist, Christian Augé, of the University of Paris I - Sorbonne. As for the epigraphic record, I depended on the advice of Glen W. Bowersock of the Institute for Advanced Study in Princeton, New Jersey. Upon several occasions I have consulted with Glen W. Bowersock, whose advice has been invaluable. In 1993, Javier Teixidor was willing to undertake the Aramaean and Nabataean epigraphic analyses, should such textual evidence be recovered. Stephen V. Tracy of Ohio State University volunteered to work on the Latin and Greek analysis in 1997. Each of these experts agreed to act as consultant/advisors, and most of them have been active participants in the site recovery as well.

A most profitable dialog was established and maintained over the years with expert Petra architectural historian, Judith S. McKenzie. I am grateful to Judith for her continuing interest in our research and for her many helpful suggestions. Archaeologists Zbigniew T. Fiema and Peter J. Parr have served as consultants to the project. All have generously shared their wealth of knowledge about Petra and archaeology. In 1994, Parr and his wife, Madelaine, worked with us in the field, which brought enormous pleasure to all. Special mention must be given to Nicholas and Katherine Clapp, who have been a constant source of moral support. Nick instigated the investigations of the so-called 'Baths' adjacent to the Great Temple's Lower Temenos in 1995. An additional room was discovered, but unfortunately time has precluded further investigations of this structure.

The University of Pennsylvania Museum, under the auspices of the Museum Applied Science Center for Archaeology (MASCA) and its director, Stuart Fleming, has aided in the electronic surveying coverage of the site, conducted by Douglas Pitney in 1993, Paul C. Zimmerman in 1994, 1996 and 1997, and Loa P. Traxler in 1995 and 1996. We are also grateful to Fleming for his sponsorship of the neutron activation testing conducted by Leigh-Ann Bedal at the University of Missouri at Columbia.

Since 1993, Peter Warnock of the University of Missouri has undertaken the analysis of our botanical remains, and in 1996 he also participated in our excavations and supervised Trench 33. Thomas R. Paradise of the University of Hawaii, an expert in Petra sandstone weathering patterns, spent several weeks with us on site in 1997. In 1993, Ricardo J. Elia of Boston University undertook a study of the site with regard to its drainage problems and conservation. Terry E. Tullis of Brown University has mapped the Subterranean Canalization System. Working with Constance Worthington, Terry spent three weeks on site during the 1995 season, during which he undertook subsurface radar to aid in our understanding of the site configuration as to the lacunae that could not be detected from above-ground observations.

## Sponsors and Acknowledgments

The Jordanian Department of Antiquities has aided us in every way possible, and a great part of the success of our project can be ascribed to Ghazi Bisheh, the Director General of the Department. Our work would not have been possible without the interest, permission and aegis of the Directors of the Department of Antiquities: Safwan Tell in 1993-1994 and Ghazi Bisheh in 1995-1997. They put at our disposal as excavation headquarters the then Nazzal's Camp (which is now the renovated J.L. Burckhardt Archaeological Center) and made annual contributions to our research by allowing us the use of their heavy equipment to lift the enormous ashlar overburden that covered the site and to remove the backfill. Additionally, in 1997, they provided support for workers.

Fortunately, we are under the general supervision of Suleiman Farajat and his assistant, Mohammad Abd-Al-Aziz Al-Marahleh, as our Jordanian Department of Antiquities representatives. I would like to take this opportunity to express my deepest gratitude to Suleiman Farajat, Superintendent of the Department of Antiquities of Petra and now of the Petra Regional Planning Council, and to Mohammad Abd-Al-Aziz Al-Marahleh, who has served as our inspector for the past three years. In 1997, Kamel Mahadin was placed in charge of the Petra Regional Planning Council. He has been most helpful and well-disposed towards our efforts. Furthermore, without the continued support of His Royal Highness, Prince Ra'ad bin Zeid Al-Hussein, this work would not have been as pleasant as it has been — the Royal Family has supported our research from its inception. Additionally, we have been aided for aerial coverage by the Royal Air Force of the Hashemite Kingdom of Jordan. The United States Embassy and the United States of America's Ambassador and his wife, Wesley and Virginia Egan, also have followed our research with keen interest. All of those mentioned above have become part of our extended family.

Throughout this project, I have benefited enormously from the valuable advice and thirty-year friendship of Pierre M. Bikai, Director of the American Center of Oriental Research in Amman. As the excavator of many sites, Pierre has been a constant guide, and he helped me make the initial contacts with the Department of Antiquities and, through his good offices, has helped me maintain those contacts. My longtime friend, colleague and fellow archaeologist Patricia M. Bikai, Director of the Petra Ridge Church Excavations, has always been at my side to offer helpful suggestions. The success of this project is also due in large part to the American Center of Oriental Research (ACOR), which placed at our disposal tools, administrative help and housing before and after the excavations. Kathy Nimri and others at ACOR were always generous in briefing us on various questions of detail.

The Committee on Archaeological Policy (CAP) of the American Schools of Oriental Research (ASOR) has granted us affiliation since 1994. As a peer review committee, their annual visits to the site have provided us with constructive advice. Our excavations were participants in an on-line edition of ASOR-approved excavations, known as "ASOR Digs 1996." This can be accessed from the home page and the URL:

*<http://www.cobb.msstate.edu/asordigs.html >*

This difficult work in Petra could not have been accomplished without the collaboration of Dakhilallah Qublan and the skill, loyalty and hard work of the team of Bedouin workers, so ably supervised by Dakhilallah. In large measure, our success can be attributed to Dakhilallah, our most trusted, competent foreman, who has helped us turn over, inspect and document every ashlar block. It is the heavy mechanical equipment loaned to us by the Department of Antiquities that has also made this possible. In consultation with me, Dakhilallah has been in charge of consolidation and restoration efforts that have been directed to endangered elements of the Great Temple precinct. These efforts were undertaken as the excavation progressed but in major part in the fall of 1996, in consultation with Paul S. Fay, Conservator, and architects Zaki Aslan of the Jordanian Department of Antiquities and May Shaer of Yarmouk University, who is also an expert on Nabataean mortars.

Raising funds for our field campaigns requires an appreciable amount of time — about 30% of my time annually — and we are ever grateful to our many sponsors-supporters who have helped us over this five-year period. We are particularly grateful to the loyalty of several major sponsors during the past few years, including several major foundations, without whom this great monument would never have been recovered. In 1996 and 1997 we were most grateful to The Luther I. Replogle Foundation for their support.

The Brown University research at the Great Temple has been conducted with the enormous assistance and loyal support of Brown University. In 1996, I was the recipient of Brown University's Richard B. Salomon Faculty Research Award. Since 1995, several of the students engaged in the excavation have received Undergraduate Teaching Research Assistantships from Brown University. The recipients of these fellowships have been: Elizabeth E. Payne in 1995, Brian A. Brown and Kimberly A. Butler in 1996 and Elizabeth A. Najjar and Laurel D. Bestock in 1997. Also in 1997, the Brown University Royce Fellowship Committee awarded Benjamin H. Kleine a grant to research at the site, and Brian A. Brown, a graduating senior at Brown, was awarded the American Center of Oriental Research, Jennifer C. Groot Fellowship.

Ongoing research also requires graduate student support. Support from Brown University Graduate School and Anthropology Department was awarded in 1996 and 1997 to Deirdre G. Barrett and in 1997 to Sara G. Karz. Erika L. Schluntz, who is writing her dissertation on the sculptural program of the Great Temple, was awarded a graduate school travel grant in 1996, as well as the Samuel H. Kress Foundation Research Fellowship from the American Center of Oriental Research. During the fall of 1997, at the American Center of Oriental Research in Amman, Erika completed her study researching the architectural decoration of the Great Temple, and it is hoped that her dissertation will soon be completed.

Most particularly I am grateful to Vartan Gregorian, President of Brown University until September 1997, for the intense personal commitment, year after year, with which he approached these excavations. In spite of University budget cuts, he shared in my vision and has encouraged my commitment to this research. I have also received encouragement from my colleagues at the Brown University Center for Old World Archaeology and Art, R.

Ross Holloway, Director, and the Department of Anthropology Chair, Philip Leis. Since the beginning of our work, I am grateful for the patience of Neil Johannessen who has been in charge of procuring our supplies and packing them for shipment. Additionally, I am most indebted to the indefatigable Shirley Gordon, Administrative Assistant, Department of Anthropology, who provided the great assistance in keeping the finances straight — my bookkeeping can hardly be efficient without guidance!

Among the individual benefactors that have provided support for our work, mention should be made of Ronald Margolin and David J. Zucconi of the Brown University Development office, who have helped us find support from donors since the beginning of our work. Additional help has been received from Michael and Betsy Alderman, Richard Ballou, Thomas and Francesca Bennett, Richard Carolan, David A. Detrich, Norbert Donelly, Sarah Dowling, Mr. and Mrs. Martin Granoff, C. Martin Hames, George Hisert, Frederick Lippitt, Gerard T. Lynch, Cynthia Miller, Barbara Mitten, Peter Nalle, John Payne, David S. and Sandra L. Perloff, Charles M. Royce and W. Chesley Worthington.

During these past five years, we have received a number of grants to support our consolidation work. A 1996-1997 and 1997-1998 subvention from the World Monuments Fund partly made possible the consolidation, conservation and preservation of the Temple precinct architecture. This grant (KFEPP/WATCH 96.053) was from the Samuel H. Kress Foundation as an American Express Award through World Monuments Watch, a program of the World Monuments Fund. Describing 1996-1997 site protection and consolidation, a final report entitled "Petra, Brown University Excavations at the Great Temple" was submitted to the World Monuments Watch, a Program of the World Monuments Fund for an American Express Award. A summary of these activities can be found under "Site Protection" in Chapter 2.

In 1995, the original Petra Southern Temple Web page was designed by Erika L. Schluntz and Geoffrey Bilder <*petra2stg.brown.edu*>. In 1997, it was updated by Brown University undergraduate Benjamin H. Kleine and can be referenced at <*http://www.brown.edu/Departments/Anthropology/Petra/*>.

Without the continued support of my wonderful husband, Artemis A. W. Joukowsky, who has been at my side and has sustained me through my many years of research, this work would never have been completed. My immediate family, Nina Joukowsky Köprülü, her husband, Murat Köprülü, and their daughter, Süreya; Artemis 'Timi' A. W. Joukowsky III, his wife, Peggy, their daughters, Lydia Elena and Alexandra Sophia, and Michael 'Misha' W. Joukowsky, his wife, Jane, and their daughter, Elena Maria, have all shared in this great adventure. I sincerely hope they, as well as my Brown University students, colleagues and staff will feel rewarded by this volume.

## About This Volume and the CD-ROM

This five-year Great Temple report has two objectives. The first is to present an overview of the Great Temple excavation together with its major features. The second objective is to provide the researcher with the details, other photographs and plans of our work, as well as the databases created for the sizable collections of many kinds of artifacts recovered. For this data, Simon M. Sullivan and the Scholarly Technology Group at Brown University will be creating a CD-ROM that parallels the course of the book. Thus, Chapter 6 of this volume contains the representative objects from the catalog, and Chapter 6 of the CD-ROM will include the complete catalog entries. In evaluating the results of our analysis that are presented in the book, researchers will have the tools to perform their own analysis with the data. It would be surprising if some details in our databases did not invite reconsideration of our authors' conclusions. And that is precisely why we are creating it.

## Research Credits

In 1992, before our field investigations began, J. Wilson Myers and Eleanor E. Myers conducted an extensive aerial photographic survey of the site with low-altitude aerial photographic and photogrammetric coverage. The aerial photographs at the conclusion of the 1993 and 1994 seasons were taken by Jane Taylor. Pia Ward served as site photographer during the 1993 season. The day-by-day photography of both the site and the small finds has been under the direction of Artemis A.W. Joukowsky, who has been in charge of photographic coverage since 1994. All the photographs in this work are his, unless otherwise credited. Since 1994, Michael F. Slaughter has been in charge of photographic recording and on-site film development and printing. I am extremely grateful to the Royal Jordanian Air Force for providing helicopters so that annual aerial coverage could be attained.

For the most part, the main architectural plans were originally executed by our team of surveyors; they were then revised in the field by the archaeologists and were drafted for publication by Amy E. Grey in 1993 and in successive years (from 1994-1997) by Ala H. Bedewy. The reconstruction drawings of the Great Temple were executed by Chrysanthos Kanellopoulos. Jean Blackburn drew many of the cataloged artifacts presented in this report and supervised the architectural and artifactual presentation as a whole. Additional drawings of finds have been contributed by this author and Simon M. Sullivan.

Chapter 1 is devoted to an introduction to Petra and the Nabataeans so that the uninitiated can best place the site in its setting.

The History of the Brown University Excavations is presented in Chapter 2.

Scientific studies of the Great Temple have gone hand-in-hand with archaeological research; these are presented in Chapter 3. The geology of Petra and the weathering patterns found at the Great Temple are contributed to Chapter 3 by Thomas R. Paradise of the University of Hawaii. This is followed by the work of Peter Warnock, a graduate student at the University of Missouri at Columbia, who has worked on our botanical analysis; his report is presented in Chapter 3 as well.

Elizabeth E. Payne's results from 1993-1995 excavation of the Subterranean Canalization System are presented in Chapter 4. Following up on Payne's excavation, in 1995, Terry E. Tullis, of the Brown University Geology Department, surveyed an extensive series of test-passes over the Great Temple precinct utilizing ground-penetrating radar. It is from these results that he has been able to piece together the path of the Subterranean Canalization System also found in Chapter 4.

Erika L. Schluntz joins with Joseph J. Basile of the Maryland College of Art in a discussion of the Great Temple architectural plan, which is the topic of Chapter 5. Erika's analysis of the Great Temple sculpture is also presented in Chapter 5.

It is impossible to adequately express my thanks to all of those professionals who have so generously and devotedly contributed their knowledge, talents and time. I am deeply indebted to Donna J. D'Agostino for wrestling with FileMaker Pro 3.0 for the architectural fragment database, as well the Petra Great Temple artifact database analysis, familiarly known as 'Grosso Modo.' These results are presented in Chapter 6.

Deirdre G. Barrett has been in charge of the catalog of small finds since 1996, succeeding Katherine Mallak of the Semitic Museum at Harvard University, who was in charge of the catalog in 1994-1995. In Chapter 6 is Deirdre's presentation of the Artifact Catalog. Also presented in this study is the analysis of the lamps, also initiated by Deirdre in 1995 and continued through to 1997. A study of the glass was undertaken in 1997 by Sara G. Karz, graduate student in the Anthropology Department at Brown University. Sara's analysis can also be found in Chapter 6.

Christian Augé of the University of Paris I - Sorbonne has kindly undertaken the analysis of the numismatic evidence also using FileMaker Pro 3.0 for the Great Temple catalog — the results of all seasons are presented in Chapter 6. Augé has been ably assisted by David Smart in working and organizing this evidence — this has been a co-operative effort in every sense for which I am most grateful. Working in 1996-1997 for a Brown University Senior Honor Thesis, undergraduate Avi Mannis created a multimedia archive using CD-ROM to show the find spots of coins set against the stratigraphy, for a three-dimensional analysis. He produced a digital archive project entitled: "Coins of the Great Southern Temple, Petra: A Multimedia Archaeological Site Archive on CD-ROM" by integrating image, text and three-dimensional space to foster intuitive access to the archaeological record. The current archive documents three years (1993-1996) of coin recovery for 158 coins. The support for this research was given by an undergraduate Brown University Research At Brown grant.

In the research of the pottery, Stephan G. Schmid and Yvonne Gerber, of the University of Basel, and the excavations of Az-Zantur, under the direction of Rolf Stucky, have generously shared their expert knowledge. In 1995-1996, Leigh-Ann Bedal, graduate student at the University of Pennsylvania, undertook the neutron activation analysis testing at the MURR Reactor at the University of Missouri at Columbia; the results of this analysis are presented in Chapter 7.

Epigraphic recovery from the Great Temple excavations has been scanty. The Brown University Classics Department and William Wyatt helped me contact Stephen V. Tracy, then Visiting Mellon Professor at the School of Historical Studies at the Institute for Advanced Study in Princeton, who analyzed the Latin inscription recovered in 1996 from the floor of the Temple 'Adyton' room. In Amman, Robert Daniel, epigrapher with the Petra Church Scrolls Project, also offered help with this analysis. Stephen V. Tracy's interpretation of this find is presented in Chapter 8.

In the preparation of the manuscript, I am grateful to Kirsten K. Hammann for the final preparation of the manuscript. I am also grateful to Simon M. Sullivan for the drafting of maps and preparing the design and layout of this volume. This work has been three years in planning and execution; it was completed in December 1998.

As far as editing is concerned, I am indebted to David A. Detrich who has tried to correct the knotty problems of my prose in Chapters 1 and 2. Robert Reichley reread Chapter 1 and helped me reorganize and develop the text. I extend great personal gratitude to the experts on Roman Arabia, Glen W. Bowersock, Stephen V. Tracy, Judith S. McKenzie and Zbigniew T. Fiema for their generosity and assistance in reviewing the manuscript of Chapters 1 and 2. Their suggestions, constructive criticisms and corrections were invaluable and are gratefully acknowledged. I should also like to thank Peter J. Parr for the help he provided. All have been most patient, detail-oriented and, with great effort, have helped my ideas come together.

The material from the Great Temple excavations will be exhibited in the site museum in the Petra Museum. Much of the material has been reburied on site or is stored in the caves at the site under the jurisdiction of the Jordanian Department of Antiquities.

*Martha Sharp Joukowsky*
*Director and Editor, Brown University,*
*Petra Great Temple Excavations*

*December 18, 1998*

# PETRA GREAT TEMPLE

# CHAPTER ONE

# INTRODUCTION

## BY
## MARTHA SHARP JOUKOWSKY

*Djin Block situated in the Bab as-Siq*

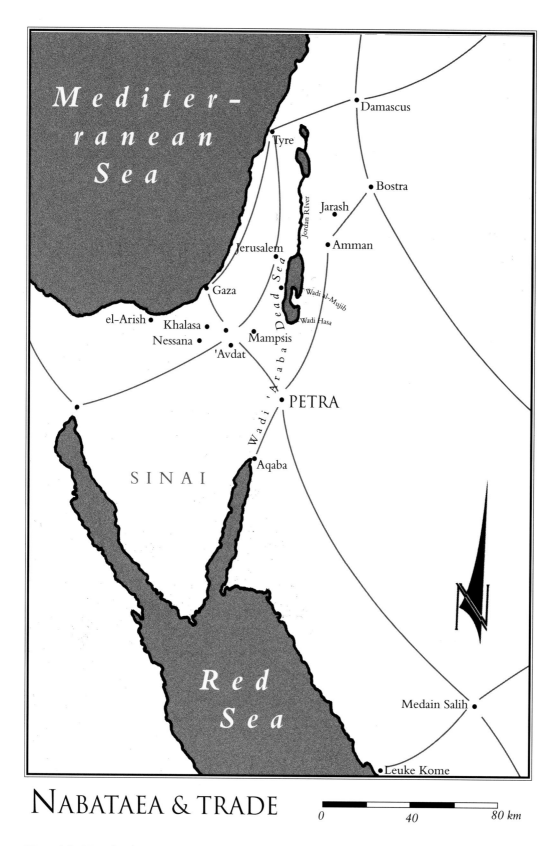

# NABATAEA & TRADE

*Figure 1.1. Map of Nabataea.*

Petra is an international treasure. This awe-inspiring, 2000-year-old site is a vast natural wonder with unique architectural beauty. When it first fell under the jurisdiction of the Nabataeans, a new spirit rose among her untamed, rocky ravines. Employing thousands of masons, the Nabataeans carved out their city with a scale and character that was unmatched in the ancient world. It may be that the Nabataeans regarded their city and its setting as a special gift from their gods, believing that it was shaped by the supernatural in that it held a holy meaning. The haunting beauty of its landscape holds a special mystique. Today this hidden city still inspires the visitor, as it may well have inspired the souls of its original citizens.

Modern civilizations are characterized as much by their affluence as by their control and preservation of the environment. In the first century BCE, Petra awaited the dramas for which it would serve as a setting. We have inherited a scenic and historic wonder; Petra, however, is not a renewable resource. Its architectural structures are endangered by tourism. Now, Petra is waiting to be rescued, so the loveliness of the valley and her monuments will be preserved. Petra is fighting for her survival, and we must help. Indeed, her only hope of survival lies in the hands of the preservationists and the archaeologists who are demanding that her monuments be rescued.

Petra provides a spectacular backdrop within which people over the millennia lived out their lives. With a paucity of written records, it is the mission of the archaeologist to bring life to those who built and lived in the site. This is the intrigue of archaeology, for every shred of information rewards us with excitement. That is exactly why Brown University archaeologists are so committed and challenged by Petra and Nabataea, to which we now turn.

## Geography

The Nabataean Kingdom is strategically located. It is interlaced with east-west routes traversing the desert of the region, now designated as the Israeli Negev (south of Beersheba), to the ports of Gaza, Ascalon and Raphia (Rafa, in the Sinai)[1] on the Mediterranean Coast. It also includes the vast desert of the Sinai. Serving as the nexus for redistribution of goods to caravan traffic,

Petra's most important route to the west crossed the Negev to the Sinai. Here the Nabataeans established settlements in the Negev that served as their intermediary links either to the Mediterranean or to Jerusalem and Phoenicia in the north. The best known of these towns include Nessana (Auja al-Hafir in Arabic, Nitzana in Hebrew) and, in the Negev area, Sbeita or Sobata (Isbeita in Arabic, Shivta in Hebrew ), Elusa (Khalasa in Arabic, Halutza in Hebrew), Oboda (Abda in Arabic, 'Avdat in Hebrew), Rehovot-in-the-Negev (Ruheibeh in Arabic) and Mampsis (Kurnub in Arabic, Mamshit in Hebrew). From Mediterranean ports, ships sailed westward to Egypt and Alexandria[2] on the North African coast and northwards to Palestinian and Phoenician ports, primarily Caesarea and Tyre, and to Anatolian ports, such as Miletus. Goods were then transshipped further afield to Europe.

Petra is most important in the history of the Near East because of the major role she has played in the control of the crossroads for trade and communication — the main north-south desert route as well as the east-west routes from the desert to the Mediterranean coast. The city settlement served as a prized desert stronghold and refuge between the Wadi 'Araba and Arabia for the intrepid travelers and traders who traversed the hostile region.

The geography of Nabataea is complex. In modern terms, this region, which the Romans referred to as *Provincia Arabia*, comprised southern Syria, all of modern Jordan[3] and the northwestern part of Saudi Arabia, known as the Hejaz — from the ancient kingdoms of Edom and Moab in the east to the Wadi[4] al-Arish (ancient Rhinocolura) in the Egyptian Sinai to the west. The Jordan River[5] and its north-south valley bisects the east part of the Nabataean Kingdom from the west (Figure 1.1).

Before the Nabataeans ruled this fertile mountain plateau, there were two kingdoms in the area: Edom and Moab. Ancient Edom includes the land from the Dead Sea[6] in the north to the north shore of the Gulf of Aqaba in the south. Located in present-day southern Jordan, it includes the territory east of the Wadi 'Araba.[7]

Ancient Moab occupies a narrow land strip in central Jordan, above the Dead Sea and between the eastern flank of the Dead Sea and the Arabian Desert. Moab is 90 km (60 miles)

north-south-x-25 km (15 miles) east-west.[8] Dividing Edom are east-west rivers, the Wadi al-Mujib (Arnon)[9] and the Wadi al-Hasa, which flow into the Jordan River. The fertile plateau between these river systems provided Moab with more protection against human and natural threats than the land to the south did for the Edomites.

North-south caravans from Syria to the Gulf of Aqaba followed the main route, The King's Highway (so known to the Israelites of the Exodus), which linked northern cities in the central Syrian Hawran and Damascus to the Red Sea in the south. Following the ancient caravan route, the paved Roman superhighway, *Via Nova Traiana*,[10] was constructed between 107 and 114 CE. It also linked Bostra in the Hawran (modern Syria) with the Red Sea port of Roman Aila (Aqaba).[11] Aqaba is modern Jordan's only outlet to the sea.

Precious merchandise from the Orient would be transported over the Indian Ocean, across the Persian Gulf to the ports of Leuke Kome on the eastern shore of the Red Sea and from there overland to Petra and onto Rhinocolura or to Gaza.[12] Other goods might have been shipped to Berenike on the Red Sea's western shore and from there to Myros Hormos and other Egyptian ports to the Nile Valley. Many goods were carried northwards either by ship or by caravan to Aila (Aqaba) and on to the distribution center, or entrepôt, at Petra, where they would be redistributed for export.

To the south of Nabataea, lay the kingdom of Saba or Sheba[13] (Yemen and probably Aden), which was known as 'Arabia Felix' to the Romans. Trans-Arabian overland routes would carry exotic cargo from the land of incense, myrrh and perfumes, Aden or Qana, northwards over the vast western Saudi Arabian desert to the area of present-day Medina and ancient Dedan. From there, they went on to the strategically located Nabataean caravan marketplace-emporium of Medain Saleh and on to Petra. Nabataea also embraced the large area of northwestern Saudi Arabia, which served as a trading station to the south.

## Petra

Well over 300 million years ago, shifting tectonic plates created the dramatic Great Rift Valley that extends from southern Turkey into Lebanon and Syria to the Dead Sea[14] and from there to Aqaba, the Red Sea and Africa. Located in a deep north-south canyon approximately 80 km south of the Dead Sea, some 260 km south of Amman via the Desert Highway, Petra is enclosed by the towering majesty of the scarp that forms the Dead Sea Rift System. The northern edge of this rift system can be found within the sterile salinity of the Dead Sea — the lowest point on earth. To the south is the Great Rift Valley, which extends through the desert-like Wadi 'Araba to Aqaba, where it descends to sea level. Further south, the Great Rift rises and again plunges into the Red Sea.

Of incredible beauty and wonder, the ancient site of Petra (Πέτρα, meaning "rock" or "stone" in Greek, was also given the Semitic name Rekem/Raqmu) lies in a Great Rift Valley east of Wadi 'Araba in the present-day Hashemite Kingdom of Jordan. To the east of Petra are the Shara (Sharra) Mountains that tower to heights of 1700 m (5000 feet). These mountains share their name with the most venerated of Nabataean deities — Dushara (Dusares), meaning "Lord of the Shara."

Located to the east of the Wadi 'Araba, Petra (30°19'N, 35°25'E) is nestled in a north-south basin bordered by unusually dramatic and precipitous, east and west sandstone, limestone and porphyry hills measuring 100 m (300 feet) in height (Figure 1.2). One of the highest western points of central Petra is the lofty rock massif known as Al-Habis, but it is the sheer, flat-topped outcrop of Umm al-Biyara (meaning "Mother of Cisterns") that dramatically towers over the central city. With its single approach, which was for strategic refuge and defense, Umm al-Biyara was used as an Edomite fortress. Traveling to the southwest of Petra is Mount Hor, or Jabal Harun, where according to legend Moses' brother, Aaron (Harun, in Arabic), died. There, a small shrine, venerated by Moslems, Christians and Jews, commemorates him (Figure 1.3).

Petra lies between the pastoral desert and the agriculturally sown area of the desert. Water has been, and remains today, a precious commodity.[15] In the present time, as in antiquity, water plays a pivotal role in Petra. Fortunately, Petra is bisected by deep river gorges — water from perennial springs is naturally carried down into the valley by gravity. The most important is the 'Ayn Musa ("Moses' Spring"), located some 3 km (2

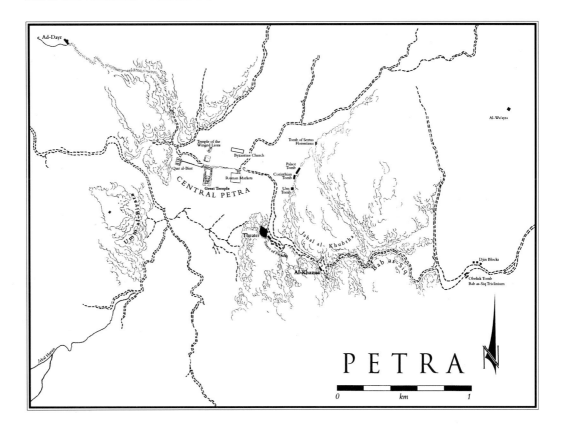

*Figure 1.2. Map of Petra.*

miles) to the northeast of the site in the hills of the Village of Wadi Musa (Al-Ji). Other perennial springs that were connected by pipes and aqueducts to the Petra Valley include the 'Ayn Brak east of Petra and the 'Ayn Debdebeh in Al-Bayda' (Beidha).[16] Additional water is provided by flash floods, which can occur from October to April; these floods also wreak havoc on the area.[17] The water supply cannot be said to be constant, but it is enough to supply the dry, yet fertile, alluvial soil with enough moisture to support the basic herding and agricultural needs of the people. With time, as the city expanded, intensive agricultural systems were developed, and these depended on additional water resources.

Among the most remarkable of Nabataean achievements are the hydraulic engineering systems they developed for water conservation. Utilizing their ingenuity, they constructed dams, terraces and aqueducts to divert and harness the rush of swollen winter waters. In addition to dams and great tunnels, the Nabataeans constructed a brilliant engineering system to divert the flash flood waters around the rugged Jabal al-Khubtha Mountain so they could bring this precious resource of the Wadi

al-Mudhlim into the city, via the Wadi al-Mataha. The Nabataeans also tapped water found in the mountain springs surrounding the city, and they diverted it to Petra by a complex series of channels and pipes. In the interests of water conservation, they harnessed and stored this critical commodity in extensive reservoirs and cisterns.

Although there are entries to Petra from the north and south, the principal and most dramatic entrance to the site is on the east through a serpentine cleft of rock in the Al-Khubtha ridge, known simply as the Siq. The Bab as-Siq (entry or door to the Siq) is at the very beginning of the Siq near the dam. Throughout the millennia, the Siq has been worn away by the swollen waters of winter flash floods rushing through its narrow, winding passage. As would be expected, the Nabataeans constructed a series of intricate, rock-cut water systems (some laid with ceramic pipe) that lace the Siq on both its north and south faces to bring the waters of the 'Ayn Musa into the city. The walls of its passage become so narrow at points (5 m) that it can be easily blocked for defense of the city.

*Figure 1.3. Mount Hor, or Jabal Harun.*

## Nabataean Architecture and the City of Petra

Before the outside entrance to the Bab as-Siq are marvelous freestanding tombs,[18] in particular the Egyptian-inspired Obelisk Tomb with four obelisks cut into the solid rock, which originally stood to a height of 7 m. The Nabataean Bab as-Siq Triclinium[19] was carved below it with its broken pediment, which is typical of the Petra architectural canon. (The pediment is the part that crowns the building and is generally triangular in shape; a broken pediment consists of two half pediments with a space between them.)

Following the path, which takes a right turn, the dam can be seen on the left, and this marks the entrance to the Siq[20] of Petra. The entry to this 1.5 km defile, which is a natural fault in the mountain, gently slopes downhill, and, although there are places where it widens, the further down one travels the narrower are the towering side walls. Carved into the side wall are niches, baetyls[21] (small shrines) and the water channels mentioned previously. The most striking feature, however, is the beauty of the colored sandstone, on which the bright sun dramatically contrasts with the gloom of dark shadows.

At the Siq entrance to the city, there is a spectacular view that partially opens up as the Siq begins to end. The traveler walks through the cleft of rock to an architectural marvel — the Al-Khazna (Figure 1.4). Here is an elaborate monumental classical façade — more properly known as the Al-Khazna Fir'awn ("The Pharaoh's Treasury"). Its name derives from the folklore that treasure filled the 3.3 m-high stone urn that adorns the second story of its broken pediment façade. Scarred by bullets, the urn still stands, as do the remains of figurative reliefs that are visible on the façade.

Deeply carved into the rock face, from the top to the bottom, this structure measures 40 m in height and 28 m in width. On the right side are two squared rows of cuttings that may have been used by the architects for scaffolding or to gain access to the top story. Their presence, as well as other factors, lead architectural historians to conclude that this building may never have been completed. Further, it is not known to whom it was dedicated — king or deity — or when it was carved. The date of the Al-Khazna has been debated by scholars (McKenzie 1990:7, Table 2), who date it from the reign of Aretas IV or to the end of the first century BCE to the first century CE. Some, like the Jordanian archaeologist Fawzi Zayadine, date it earlier, to Aretas III, who reigned from 85 to 62 BCE.

*Figure 1.4. Al-Khazna.*

The Al-Khazna façade looks like two temples, one atop the other. The lower temple has a six-column façade, which appears to be completely independent of the upper temple. On the lower temple are two colossal male riders. Above its delicately carved Corinthian columns is a frieze decorated with vases and winged animals. The upper temple is divided into three sections with a tholos — a small round temple — in the middle, and its sides are crowned by broken pediments. Decorating this order are nine figures carved in relief

one al-Jinn block (Djin Block, a large, rectangular, stone block sacred to the Nabataean god Dushara). Also here is the "Streets of Façades," which has tombs with either classical features or Assyrian crow-steps.[22]

Upon leaving the Outer Siq, the next structure that comes into view is the 7000-seat[23] Theater cut out of the living rock with 33 rows of seats and a stage approximately 40 m in width (Figure 1.5). Its excavator, Philip C. Hammond,

*Figure 1.5. The Roman Theater.*

possibly representing Amazons and Nikes. The central figure is draped; she holds a cornucopia with ears of corn and a pair of horns framing the solar disk. These are sacred items emblem-atic of the goddesses Fortuna or Isis. Inside the columnar portico on either side are two small rooms, possibly for priests. Steps lead into a 12-x-12 m room with two small rooms on either side and one behind it. All were adorned with decorative plaster.

Leaving the Al-Khazna, along the Nabataean road, is an area known inappropriately as the 'Outer Siq,' inappropriate because it is inner to the site, not outer. This area is adorned with rock-cut tombs and monuments, including

dates its construction to the Nabataean period or to the first century BCE. The auditorium was cut into the pre-existing tombs. The orchestra is 38 m in width. On both sides of the stage are vaulted entrances leading to the orchestra. Today the Theater can be seen from the street, but in antiquity a wall completely blocked it from the sight of passersby.

Beyond the Theater, central Petra opens to view (Figures 1.2 and 1.6).

The main city area is bordered by the Jabal al-Khubtha (the Al-Khubtha Mountain). Carved into the western flank of the mountain are the Royal Tombs. The Urn Tomb, with its lower vaults, served as a church in the Byzantine period. The Corinthian Tomb is terribly weathered. One of Petra's largest monuments, the three-story Palace Tomb looks like a Nabataean imitation of a Roman palace.

The central city grew up around its 6 m-wide Colonnaded Street in the first century CE, and by the mid-first century had witnessed rapid urbanization. Covering approximately 3 km² and following the flow of the Wadi Musa, the city-center was laid out on both sides of the

of the straight course of the Colonnaded Street where the Wadi Musa and the Wadi Mataha merge together.

After passing the Nymphaeum, the visitor walks on the paved Roman Colonnaded Street with its recently excavated shops and monumental stairway leading up the southern slope to the as yet unexcavated Upper Market (Figure 1.7). Directly opposite, across the Wadi Musa on the north slope of the cityscape (now under a protective shelter), lies the Byzantine

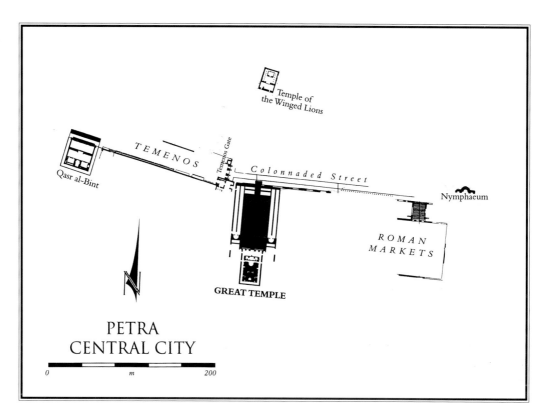

*Figure 1. 6. Map of the Central City of Petra.*

main artery, the Colonnaded Street, which today has several restored columns and shops on its southern side. The city was designed on an elongated plan between the Theater in the east and the Qasr al-Bint in the west with markets, residences and temples on the sloping hillsides. This main city thoroughfare was also entered through side arteries served by a series of now-collapsed bridges that forded the Wadi Musa.

With an estimated population of 20,000-30,000 at its peak, Petra was a thriving city. In addition to public buildings, there were houses, city walls and a plethora of water works, including a Nymphaeum located at the beginning

Church where papyrus scrolls as well as important mosaics have been recently excavated. Beyond is the Nabataean Temple of the Winged Lions. This temple, named for the lions adorning its capitals, is dedicated to the goddess Al-'Uzza, the consort of the patron deity of Petra, Dushara. Returning to the Colonnaded Street, the remains of bridges again can be seen to mark the crossing of the Wadi Musa, and to the south of the street are the steps that lead to the monumental entrance or Propylaeum of the Great Temple.

The Great Temple Complex is one of the major archaeological and architectural components of central Petra, and since 1993,

*Figure 1.7. The Colonnaded Street, 1997.*

*Figure 1.8. The Petra Great Temple, looking west, 1997. Photograph by John Forasté.*

American archaeologists from Brown University have been excavating this site (Figure 1.8). The Great Temple precinct measures an estimated 7560 m² and is comprised, north to south, of a propylaeum (monumental entryway), a lower temenos (sacred area), twin exedrae (semicircular structures) flanked by broad stairways and an upper temenos — the sacred enclosure for the Temple itself. In the Lower Temenos are triple colonnades on the east and west. Here, large, white hexagonal pavers are positioned above an extensive water canalization system.

With its red and white, stuccoed exterior, the Great Temple must have had a dramatic impact when set against its rose-red environment. The Temple is tetrastyle in antis — four columns on the porch with solid outer walls, typical of Nabataean architecture. Approximately 15 m (45 ft.) in height, the Porch columns plus the entablature, with its pediment they carried, would place the Temple's height at a minimum of 18 m (57 ft.).

The Great Temple measures 28 m (84 ft.) in east-west width, and it is some 42.5 m (127.50 ft.) in north-south length. A stairway leads into a broad, deep pronaos (porch), which, in turn, opens into a 550-630-seat *theatron,* or theater-like area, which may have served as the seat for the most important religious activities.[24] The style and quality of the Temple's elaborate floral friezes and acanthus-laden, limestone capitals suggest that the sanctuary was constructed late in the first century BCE by the Nabataeans, who combined their native traditions with the classical spirit. The Great Temple precinct, but not necessarily the Temple itself, was in use until some point in the late Byzantine period.

The Great Temple steps are adjacent to the so-called 'Baths' with a finely frescoed, columnar, octagonal hall. This, in turn, is adjacent to the tripartite Temenos Gate — a triple-arched gate that formed the entry for the large sacred courtyard of the largest free-standing structure in the city, the Qasr al-Bint Fir'awn ("the Palace of the Pharaoh's Daughter").

With the active trade relations with Seleucid Syria, Persia and India, Nabataea enjoyed increased prosperity enabling her to import master stonemasons and sculptors. The capitals, some crowned by animals (lions from the Temple of the Winged Lions and elephant heads from the Great Temple precinct), are carved with consummate naturalistic skill and originality. Beautifully carved masks decorate the entablature of the Great Temple. The Great Temple capitals too are deeply chiseled with rhythmic, foliated acanthus leaves and delicate canopies of flowering vines with the richest imaginable profusion of flowers and fruits. These capitals define the character of the architecture and are truly one of Petra's sculptural delights.

Although the influences of the Hellenistic — Seleucid, Ptolemaic and, to a lesser extent, Parthian — sculptural decoration are clear, a strong native style asserts itself.

Decoration of the elaborate capitals of the Great Temple or the Al-Khazna ("The Treasury") must be perceived as part of the Nabataean architecture. We can see in the monuments a gradual process of change that was brought about by the assimilation of influences principally from Rome. By the Roman period, most of the recovered sculpture is more bold and crude in character. It has less warmth, and a metamorphosis has taken place resulting in a style that has all but lost its individuality. This post-106 CE sculptural style is characterized by the bold rosettes carved on the Temenos Gate (Figure 1.11).

Returning now to the Colonnaded Street, the Temenos Gate is but a few steps away. Passing through the Temenos Gate, visitors find themselves in a sacred area 150 m in length — the sacred area or temenos for the Temple, the so-called 'Qasr al-Bint' (Figures 1.9 and 1.10). This sacred area was probably the site of religious festivities, feasts and sacrificial offerings. A row of well-preserved benches, where there is an inscription of Aretas IV, borders the south side of the precinct, and on the west is a well-constructed exedra.

Built in the beginning of the first century CE and dedicated to 'Zeus Hypsistos' or Dushara, the Qasr al-Bint is an enormous square temple (32 m in width and length), which one approaches by a monumental staircase. Oriented north-south on a high podium, like the Great Temple, it too is tetrastyle in antis but with a broad cella (the main room of the Temple) and a tripartite adyton (the inner sanctuary). Its second story is reached by interior staircases in the side walls.

*Figure 1.9. Qasr al-Bint, 1997.*

The Qasr al-Bint itself, the Temple of the Winged Lions and now the Great Temple mark the most sacred precinct of the ancient city.

In the ancient world, the implementation of a great building program became a status symbol, and if a city were ambitious and wealthy it could seize the opportunity of self-

aggrandizement by not only constructing monumental public edifices, but its people also took the opportunity to demonstrate their wealth by constructing monumental tombs. Into the vertical walls of the hills surrounding the site and well into the hills beyond, the Nabataeans chiseled out their tombs. There are two types of tombs found at Petra, shaft

*Figure 1.10. Ornamental detail, Qasr al-Bint.*

*Figure 1.11. Rosette relief panels, Temenos Gate.*

*Figure 1.12. Ad-Dayr.*

tombs and those that were sculpted into the cliff walls of sandstone. The tomb façades were divided into seven different stylistic groups by A. von Domaszewski in 1904.[25] These include: 1) the Pylon — with one or two rows of crow-steps; 2) the Step — with two sets of five steps facing each other; 3) the proto-Hegr — the same as the Step Tomb with pilasters supporting a cavetto cornice; 4) the Hegr — the same as the Step with the addition of an Attic and classical entablature; 5) the Arch — decorated with an arch supported by pillars; 6) the Gable — with a pediment supported by pilasters, and 7) the Roman Temple — having pediments or broken pediments. The most important tombs include Ad-Dayr ("The Monastery"), the Palace Tomb, the Corinthian Tomb and the Al-Khazna ("The Treasury"). These structures are characterized by façades of two-story buildings with two or more superimposed orders of architecture.

High in the hills above the city, and not visible from the central city, is The Monastery, or Ad-Dayr — the largest monument of all in Petra (Figure 1.12). Ad-Dayr is entered by crossing the Wadi Musa, walking past the Museum and through a sandy area filled with oleanders. Just beyond this is a flight of steps through a spectacular mountain gorge bordered with caves and carved niches. After climbing to the top, visitors find themselves in the sacred temenos court that Nabataean architects had carved out of the parent rock. Pausing in the court, one feels like an ancient worshipper, for the area in front of this great monument was sacred space where the ancients took part in festivals. Also in this court are cisterns, caves, steps carved into the rock face, niches and an open air altar.

Ad-Dayr in the afternoon light is breathtaking. Here is the largest two-story façade in Petra — 40 m in height-x-46 m in width. Sometime between 40-70 CE, Ad-Dayr was chiseled out of the mountain. Its tripartite upper story is crowned by a gigantic urn (Figure 1.13), and its doorway measures 8 m in height. Illuminated by light coming through the doorway is a single large chamber 11.5-x-10 m in width. It has a niche that probably served as an altar platform and biclinia, which were used in funerary rites.

Petra is surrounded by hundreds of monuments, cultic high places and cisterns. Other major monuments[26] include the tomb of Sextius Florentinus, which was constructed for

*13*

*Figure 1.13. The urn crowning Ad-Dayr. Photograph by Simon M. Sullivan.*

the Roman governor of Petra by his son. It can be dated to ca. 127/130 CE. One cannot help but be amazed by the architectural fabric of Petra.

How could the Nabataeans, who were originally nomads, have had the imagination to construct the massive free-standing buildings as well as the 800 or more monumental tomb façades and other structures found at Petra?[27] They clearly worked to make Petra a reflection of the enormous wealth and power that came to them from their control of the desert trade routes.

These monuments were constructed within a 200-year period. The artisans who designed and executed them were probably imported, perhaps from Alexandria — a city that boasts decorative architectural elements similar to those we find in Petra. However, hundreds of local masons, stucco workers and painters took part in these projects. With time, the stylistic development of the sculptural decoration became simplified, and it has been assumed that this was perhaps due to trained local masons taking over the sculptural tradition.

What characterizes the architecture of Petra? It exhibits an eclecticism achieved by a combination of styles, with Nabataean and Greek, Seleucid, Ptolemaic and Egyptian influences. Nabataean architects borrowed Hellenistic concepts, which they combined with their own sense of Orientalism. They constructed architectural façades hewn into the living rock — the Al-Khazna ("The Treasury") and Ad-Dayr ("The Monastery"), as well as free-standing structures like the Qasr al-Bint, the Temple of the Winged Lions, the Temenos Gate and the Great Temple. The quarries were in full use by the first century BCE, if not before, and there followed the virtually continuous chiseling out of buildings through the first and second centuries CE. Many structures are built on rock terraces or on terraces that have been cut away for them or, in the case of the free-standing Great Temple, on fill imported to create height.

Nabataean construction primarily employs ashlar blocks of sandstone — either bonded together with mortar or dry laid. The free-standing buildings like the Great Temple have walls faced with ashlar blocks and a rubble and mortar core. Their walls are set with timber string courses that provide tensile reinforcement against earthquakes. The diagonally chiseled surfaces are designed to hold the stucco commonly used for decoration. Stucco decoration, consisting of mixed limestone and sand with plastic modeling of cornices and the use of rich colors — reds, blues, greens and yellows — covered the walls and columns of the buildings. Ornamented plaster, and sometimes marble imported for use as revetments, also decorated many of the buildings.

Petra exerts a strong appeal on the imagination. What are the qualities that make it so spellbinding? Is it its isolation and its spectacular beauty? Is it its imposing native culture with the admixture of traditions representing both the orient and the occident? To be sure, Petra embodies the national pride and power of the Nabataeans as the seat of a stable government for some 300 years. But for many who work in Petra, and others know it well, its qualities are ultimately intangible. The monuments carved almost magically out of solid rock, the panoramic vistas and the tremendous sense of the past almost mesmerize us.

## A Brief History of Petra

Intimate acquaintance with the terrain was a prerequisite for understanding Roman contact with the Arabs of the province. Antiquity left no narrative history for western scholars to rely upon as a substitute for discovery and autopsy. There was no Arab Polybius, no Arab Josephus. It was essential, therefore, to build the history from scattered references in ancient authors, in conjunction with the surviving monuments and inscriptions, viewed within the context of the land itself.

Glen W. Bowersock (1994.4)

The Nabataeans (Gk. *Nabataioi*) are identified as people from the Arab kingdom of Nabataea. They referred to themselves as *Nabatu* on their Aramaic inscriptions. Among other scholars, David Graf (1992:IV.970) states that their origins are controversial but that "the Nabataeans arose within the Aramaic-speaking world of the so-called 'Fertile Crescent.'" (Graf cites Hieronymus of Cardia *apud* Diodorus Siculus 19.95). Graf also suggests that they may have been a subtribe from Qedar or the Persian Gulf. Philip C. Hammond (1973:11) places their origins in the Arabian Hejaz. The fact is that we don't know where they came from, and the evidence available is not sufficient to allow us to identify their origins.

Ya'akov Meshorer writes (1975:1):

> No regular account of the history of the Nabataeans is to be found in any of the ancient sources. There are only chance, sparse descriptions occasioned mainly by the meeting of various rulers of the ancient world with the Nabataeans, for the most part against a military background. Yet these few descriptions combine to present a clear, though superficial, picture of the emergence of the Nabataean kingdom.

What little is known of Nabataean history is through Greek, Latin, Hebrew and Nabataean sources that have been extensively researched by the Abbé J. Starcky (1966), Philip C. Hammond (1973), R. Wenning (1987, 1993) and Glen W. Bowersock (1983). These references suggest that Petra had a rich history through several different periods. Although it was never on the same level as contemporary cities such as Jerusalem or Jarash (Gerasa/ Jerash), Petra nevertheless appears, albeit

infrequently, in written tradition. Petra came into prominence in the late first century BCE through the lucrative success of her trade, particularly in spices as well as other luxury items, such as precious gems, silks and medicinal products. The Nabataeans also became prosperous as the purveyors of asphalt or bitumen, which they harvested from the Dead Sea and sold. The city was the capital of ancient Nabataea and was famous, above all, for its extraordinary architecture, its pottery and its hydraulic systems. It was autonomous until the reign of Trajan, and it flourished under Roman rule.

### Early History

For millennia before the Nabataeans, Upper Palaeolithic Stone Age peoples lived in Petra. Camp sites and chipping stations can be found at undisturbed sites behind the main city. The site of Al-Bayda' (Beidha), located just to the north of Petra, is the earliest settled culture in the area. Its lowest deposits are Natufian,[28] and Diana Kirkbride, the excavator, suggests that the site was first settled by a Mesolithic community followed by an early wave of Neolithic[29] settlers in ca. 7000 BCE (Figures 1.14 and 1.15). The latest levels have been dated to the Pre-Pottery Neolithic B culture,[30] or ca. 6500 BCE, when the site became a center for exchange systems.

There then appear to have been small settlements at sites in the area later known as Edom from the Chalcolithic, Early Bronze Age, ca. 3000-1900 BCE, through the Middle Bronze Age, ca. 1900-1600 BCE, and Late Bronze Age, ca. 1600-1200 BCE. Chalcolithic pastoralists' remains have been located in the region, and copper smelting was also being practiced in the Aqaba area. There have been settlements charted on the plateau in the Early Bronze period.

Although no Middle or Late Bronze Age sites have been excavated at Petra itself, that doesn't mean they don't exist. Unfortunately, little is known about the region, including the details of its development during the Middle Bronze (1900-1600 BCE) and the Late Bronze (1600-1200 BCE) periods. It is probable that Edom was occupied to some degree during these periods. As for the Middle and Late Bronze Ages, the archaeological record is mute.

**Figure 1.14. Al-Bayda'.**

It is in the thirteenth and twelfth centuries BCE that there is an increase in villages, and Edom begins to gain its identity. What is known of the Iron Age of Palestine, which roughly extends from about 1200 BCE to the coming of Alexander the Great in 331 BCE, has been grouped on historical and cultural evidence into three phases: Early (Iron I), Middle (Iron II) and Late Iron (Iron III).

The Early Iron Age covers the first three centuries from 1200-900 BCE. It embraces the Israelite Exodus to the emergence of the United Kingdom of Israel. This is a very complicated political time, for there are various tribes, including the Israelites, who in spite of their frequent revolts did not gain independence until the reign of David.

According to biblical tradition, in ca. 1200 BCE, the Petra area (but not necessarily the site itself) was populated by itinerant pastoralists, the Edomites, and the area was known as Edom ("red"). It was the capital of Arabia, known as *Raqmu* — the town's Semitic name. When Moses reached Edom, he asked permission to travel through the territory. The Edomite King refused and the Israelites were forced to take another route before they reached their Promised Land.

**Figure 1.15. Interior wall construction, Al-Bayda'.**

Flavius Josephus, a leader of the Jewish rebellion of 66-70 CE and later a Roman citizen, served as a historian for the Jews writing two important works: *The Jewish War* and *Jewish Antiquities*. In *Antiquities* 4.161, he associates Petra with Rekem when he refers to the Israelite trek under Moses to Canaan. It is reported in Numbers 31:8, "And they slew the kings of Midian...namely Evi, and Rekem..." This reference also recounts the Israelite defeat of five Midianite kings, and Rekem is a town named for its founder and is referred to as the capital of Arabia. A Nabataean inscription found at Petra dated to the first century CE refers to *Raqmu*, the Semitic name for Petra. Although this biblical reference is very early, it is clear that both the Nabataeans and the city of Petra had a life and history well before the time of this writing.

Biblical accounts also mention the nearby kingdom of Moab, through which the Israelites were also refused permission to travel during the Exodus.[31] The Israelites eventually conquered this "land of milk and honey" and settled in the areas of the Ammonites (the region of modern Amman). This period is chronicled by the inscription on the Moabite Stone, now in the Louvre.[32] Many of our previous notions concerning the Nabataeans and the Edomites have been heavily influenced by the biased biblical accounts of the Israelites, who described them as their uncultured, ruthless enemies.[33]

In the Early Iron Age there are more small villages and farms scattered throughout Edom, and mining centers again have been found and excavated in the Aqaba area. From the archaeological record, however, there is little continuity of settlement.

Dating to ca. 1000 BCE, one of King David's first military victories was against Edom and Moab. As security he left his general, Joab, to slaughter the males. He reported having killed two-thirds of the Moabite population and all the males of Edom. He enslaved the remaining natives, who eventually regained their freedom. Rabbath Ammon (modern Amman) was under Israelite rule for some time, but with the death of David in 960 BCE, it regained its independence.

Before the Israelite incursions, the Edomites controlled the trade routes from Arabia in the south to Damascus in the north. Little is known about the Edomites at Petra itself, but as a people they are remembered for their wisdom, their writing, their textile industry, the excellence and fineness of their ceramics and their skilled metal working. The Edomite King list from the time of Moses to ca. 688 BCE can be found in Iain Browning's *Petra* (1986:60). Browning (1986:32) points out that the Edomites were a settled folk, whereas the Nabataeans were nomadic. In folklore, both tribes are said to have descended from Ishmael, each from a different daughter.[34]

King David had established the United Kingdom (Judah and Israel), which King Solomon (970/960-930/920 BCE) inherited. While maintaining a strong military, Solomon developed Israel into a larger entity by establishing diplomatic ties with neighboring countries. Peace, prosperity and trade flourished as a result, and enormous wealth was brought to Israel, especially to Jerusalem. King Solomon's trade interests included Arabia, and he controlled the port at Ezion Geber (the modern city of Elat in Israel) on the Gulf of Aqaba.

The Middle Iron Age (Iron II) extends roughly from 900 to 550 BCE, and it covers the era of the divided kingdoms of Israel and Judah and their subjugation to the status of tributary states. The northern kingdom of Israel first succumbed to the Assyrians and then to the Babylonians, while the southern kingdom of Judah survived as a tribute-paying state; Judah later was conquered by the Neo-Babylonians. From ca. 796 to 781 BCE, the ruler of Judah was King Amaziah who conquered Sela and renamed it Joktheel (2 Kings 14, 2 Chronicles 25). Although the biblical Sela is equated with Petra, there is no evidence to substantiate that reference.

It is during this time that we have archaeological evidence for Petra. Situated on a terrace just outside Wadi Musa and Petra is the site of Tawilan where C.M. Bennett excavated a large, unfortified, agricultural Edomite settlement dating to this period. Bennett concluded there was no occupation earlier than the eighth century BCE and suggested that the remains should be dated to the seventh through sixth centuries BCE.

In Petra, Nelson Glueck made soundings on the top of Umm al-Biyara (Figure 1.16), and Bennett undertook excavations here from 1963-1965. Umm al-Biyara means "Mother of Cisterns," and true to that meaning, some 50 large cisterns were found, along with a domestic settlement with houses constructed along a north-south wall. These houses had bedrock floors, and the finds included many loom weights and undecorated pottery. The site was dated by a royal seal impression of an Edomite king who ruled around 670 BCE. It was concluded that the Umm al-Biyara settlement lasted only for 50 years.

There is, therefore, no stratified continuity between the settlements of either Tawilan or Umm al-Biyara with the Nabataean settlement of Petra and its surroundings.

*Figure 1.16. Umm al-Biyara, with the Temenos Gate in foreground.*

## The Persian Period

The next chapter of history belongs to the Late Iron Age or the Persian period, which extends from 550-330 BCE. During this time it is believed the Nabataeans, one of many nomadic Arab tribes, gradually migrated into Edom, probably forcing many of the Edomites to relocate in southern Palestine. Looking for safety and protection, the Nabataeans may have settled in Petra and begun to charge taxes on those who passed through this crucial passage between the Red Sea and Syria. Evidence at Petra from the Persian and Hellenistic period, however, is scanty. If there was life at the site in the Persian period, we have no archaeological evidence for it.

## The Nabataeans and the Hellenistic Period in the Near East

Alexander the Great captured the Persian Empire and ruled the largest empire ever known before him. After the area passed into his hands, there was building or rebuilding and beautification of the major cities in the Near East. With the death of Alexander the Great in 323 BCE, the Greek Empire was divided up among his generals. Ptolemy seized Egypt, became the first king of the Hellenistic dynasty in Egypt and built the city of Alexandria, an

architectural masterpiece. At the outset, Palestine and Transjordan belonged to the Ptolemies.

Little is known about Petra proper until about 312 BCE, by which time, according to some historians, it is thought that the enterprising Nabataeans occupied the stronghold and later made it the capital of their kingdom. Also in 312, these historians suggest that the Nabataeans were attacked by one of Alexander's generals.[35] There are no written sources to support this claim, so we have to rely on the archaeological evidence. The archaeological evidence provides no record that Petra was occupied in the late fourth century BCE. Thus, the early development of Petra is unknown to us.

Writing in the Augustan period, two scholars are particularly important for our understanding of the Nabataeans. One is the first-century-BCE, Sicilian-born, Greek historian, Diodorus Siculus. In his *Bibliotheca historica* (19.94-100) he took his information largely from Hieronymus of Cardia. The second historian is Strabo, who wrote about the Nabataeans in his *Geography*.

Petra is first mentioned by Diodorus Siculus (II:48-49) not as a specific place, but as a "rock" or site where the nomadic Nabataeans (who were involved in the merchandising of exotics from Arabia, Africa and India) took refuge when they were attacked by 4000 infantry and 600 calvary of the King Antigonus I in 312 BCE. The "rock" to which he referred may have been Petra, for it was a specific place — a unique location — where the Nabataean people protected their elders, women and children during their annual meetings. In this passage is a description of how a surprise midnight attack was mounted, and, in the absence of the Nabataean men who were away at a "fair," besieged and plundered the Rock, which may have been Umm al-Biyara. As booty, the Greeks stole frankincense, myrrh, and 500 silver talents. Once the Nabataean men realized what had befallen their families (and their spies made them aware of the possibility that they would again be attacked), they counterattacked, killed many of the invading force and recovered their booty. They did not trust the Greeks, as can be seen from the quote from I. Browning (1986.33), who rephrases the passage from Diodorus Siculus (19:96-98):

> Once back at the Rock, they sent a slightly apologetic letter to Antigonus explaining the whole incident. Antigonus pretended to accept the explanation and sent back the most felicitous reply, blaming the whole affair on the dead Athanaeus [the commander of the forces who had been killed], who he said had acted without orders. After a discreet lapse of time, during which he hoped that the Nabataeans would drop their guard, he sent another army under the command of his son, Demetrius, to storm the Nabataeans. They, however, still having much of the bedouin in them, were suspicious, and when Demetrius arrived he found the stronghold — the Rock— stoutly defended by a small force. The remainder of the Nabataeans had, on hearing of the advancing army, packed up all their belongings and departed into the secrecy and safety of the mountainous desert. Demetrius's attempts to storm the Rock were futile and in the end he allowed himself to be bought off with 'such gifts as are most precious among them.'[36]

Wherever their origins, by 312 BCE, we do know that the Nabataeans may have been living in Petra, where "they defended themselves successfully from an attack by Antigonus the One-Eyed, a veteran commander from Alexander the Great's eastern campaigns" (Graf ibid.).

A view of the Nabataean nomadic nature, Diodorus Siculus (19.94.3) remarks:

> It is their custom neither to plant grain, set out any fruit-bearing tree, use wine, nor construct any house; and if any one is found acting contrary to this, death is his penalty.

In this description, the Nabataeans are a nomadic people who live under the open sky in a country without springs or rivers — some of them have camels, while others have cattle.

Writing a generation or so later than Diodorus is the Greek geographer, Strabo. His secondhand account about Nabataean customs provides an interesting insight on life at Petra. Strabo (16.4.21-26) is worthwhile quoting in full:

> The metropolis of the Nabataeans is Petra, as it is called; for it lies on a site which is otherwise smooth and level, but it is fortified all round by a rock, the outside parts having springs in abundance, both for domestic purposes and for watering gardens...Petra is always ruled by some king from the royal family; and the king has as Administrator one of his companions, who is called "brother." It is exceedingly well governed; at any rate, Athenodorus, a philosopher and companion of mine, who had been in the city of the Petraeans, used to describe their government with admiration, for he said that he found both many Romans and many other foreigners sojourning there, and that he saw that the foreigners often engaged in lawsuits, both with one another and with the natives, but that none of the natives prosecuted one another, and that they in every way kept peace with one another.
>
> The Nabataeans are a sensible people, and are so much inclined to acquire possessions that they publicly fine anyone who has diminished his possessions and also confer honours on anyone who has increased them. Since they have but few slaves, they are served by their kinsfolk for the most part, or by one another, or by themselves; so that the custom also extends even to their kings. They prepare common meals together in groups of thirteen persons; and they have two girl-singers for each banquet. The king holds drinking bouts in magnificent style, but no one drinks more than eleven cupfuls, each time using a different golden cup. The king is so democratic that, in addition to serving himself, he sometimes even serves the rest himself in his turn. He often renders an account of his kingship in the popular

assembly; and sometimes his mode of life is examined. Their homes through the use of stone, are costly, but on account of peace, the cities are not walled. Most of the country is well supplied with fruits except olive; they use sesame oil instead. The sheep are white-fleeced and the oxen are large, but the country produces no horses. Camels afford the service they require instead of horses. They go out without tunics, with girdles about their loins, and with slippers on their feet — even the kings, though in their case the colour is purple. Some things are imported wholly from other countries, but others not altogether so, especially in the case of those that are native products, as, for example, gold and silver and most of the aromatics whereas brass and iron, as also purple garb, styrax, crocus, costaria, embossed works, paintings and moulded works are not produced in their country. They have the same regard for the dead as for dung, as Heracleitus says: "Dead bodies more fit to be cast out than dung;" and therefore they bury even their kings beside dungheaps. They worship the sun, building an altar on the top of the house, and pouring libations on it daily and burning frankincense.

In contrast to the earlier passage from Diodorus, Strabo portrays an entirely different picture of the Nabataeans who now live in luxurious stone houses, who practice viti-culture and who are traders. We can assume that by this time they are a cosmopolitan, settled people who are acquisitive, ruled by a monarch and boast a fleet in the Red Sea. They are said to number 10,000 men, and they are known for their wealth from their merchandising of spices, incense and myrrh.

Returning to the history of the time, it is known that the Macedonian, Seleucus I, who was also a general of Alexander the Great, took Syria, and, not to be outdone by Ptolemy, constructed the great cities of Antioch on the Orontes and Seleucus on the Tigris. From 305-64 BCE, the Seleucids controlled the largest kingdom (from Thrace in Europe to Syria and Babylonia to India) in the Near East during the Hellenistic period. Seleucus I was quickly advanced from being the governor of Babylon to becoming the king of the Seleucid Empire. From 305-281 BCE, he administered the empire from both Syria and Iran.

The Zenon Papyri (*Papyri greci e latini,* 406) of 259 BCE identify the Nabataeans with the Hawran and northern Transjordan, which they may have controlled as they expanded their territory and influence to the north. Nabataean settlements are found on the Edomite plateau that may predate their fortress in Petra where the earliest Nabataean building takes place in the mid-third century BCE. Finds of this period include black-glazed wares and Phoenician, Ptolemaic and Seleucid coins. The now wealthy Nabataeans borrowed art and architectural ideas from those who surrounded them; Hellenistic culture was pervasive, and they co-opted Egyptian, Assyrian, Arabian and Greek ideas both for their buildings and their artifacts.

By 198 BCE, Antiochus III the Great, crushed the Ptolemaic army near modern Baniyas, and Petra, Jerusalem and all Asia Minor passed into Seleucid hands. Under these successors of Alexander the area flourished. In 190 BCE, Antiochus was defeated by the Roman armies when he attempted to take Greece, and he had to surrender most of Asia Minor and pay the Romans a heavy tribute.

The son of Antiochus the Great was Seleucus IV *Philopater* ('father loving'), who initially ruled with his father and then alone. During an unsuccessful *coup d'état* in 175 BCE, Seleucus IV was assassinated, and the throne passed to his brother, Antiochus IV Epiphanes, who had to contend with the rise of the Maccabees who seized most of Palestine and a greater part of Jordan. The anti-Jewish decrees of the Seleucid king led Judas Maccabaeus to lead a revolt against Antiochus IV. The Maccabees were under the command of John Hyrcanus I, son of Simon Maccabee — Simon had taken Jerusalem from the Seleucids. John Hyrcanus then set about to enlarge Simon's holdings. Thereafter, as Seleucid power declined, the Hasmonaeans, successors of the Maccabees, ruled an independent Judaea from 142-63 BCE. (They were a family of Jewish high priests descended from Mattathias, the father of Judas Maccabaeus, who died in 165 BCE.)[37] Thus, from 135-104 BCE, the high priest-civil governor-king, John Hyrcanus I, essentially controlled the area, conquering the Negev and taking land as far north as Galilee. His son and successor, Aristobulus, took all of the Galilee.

Aristobulus' brother, Alexander Jannaeus, gained the throne in 103 and held it until he died in 76 BCE. He ruled from Dan to Beersheba, calling himself king as well as high priest. Alexander Jannaeus was opposed to religious freedom and Hellenism; his mission was to Judaize the area. In this effort he became a warring, ruthless, military monarch who was successful in his goal of subjugating all of Palestine. Alexander Jannaeus provoked a conflict with the Nabataeans, who were in control of the trade routes and cities that he coveted. The Nabataeans were greatly concerned when their trading interests were interrupted as Alexander Jannaeus' forces reduced to shambles the coastal cities of Gaza and Raphia. Threatened, the Nabataeans joined forces with the Seleucid King Demetrius III, and although together they temporarily defeated the Hasmonaeans, Alexander Jannaeus regained control. He then constructed fortresses along the Jordanian front to protect his line of defense. He died leaving his capable queen and widow, Salome Alexandra, as his successor who ruled from 76-67 BCE.

The two sons of Salome Alexandra and Alexander Jannaeus, John Hyrcanus II and Aristobulus, began their own civil war and fought, initially, with Aristobulus as the victor. But with the critical aid of the brilliant strategist, John's advisor, the Idumean Antipater,[38] and the military support of the Nabataean King Aretas III, John Hyrcanus II took his brother captive.

Paradoxically, it is during the time of the Ptolemies and the Seleucids that Petra and her caravan cities flourished with increased trade and the establishment of new, independent, non-Nabataean trading towns, such as Philadelphia (Rabbath Ammon, modern Amman) and Jarash (modern Jerash/Gerasa). Infighting between the Seleucids and Ptolemies allowed the Nabataeans to maintain their control over the caravan routes between Arabia and Syria. Although there were struggles between the Jewish Maccabeans and their Seleucid overlords, Nabataean trade continued, and Greater Petra became a metropolis with an estimated population of 20,000 to 30,000.

The Roman conqueror Pompey the Great arrived in Damascus in 63 BCE, and although they did not know it at the time, this sounded the death knell for the Hasmonaeans. Pompey forced Aretas III's troops to withdraw from Jerusalem, and Pompey selected John Hyrcanus II to rule but only as high priest. Pompey stripped him of both his title as king and most of his territory, which he annexed into the Roman province of Syria. Aristobulus and his sons were exiled to Rome, where they attempted to start a rebellion against John. This insurrection was soon halted by Mark Antony, and after a second rebellion in 55 BCE, the Romans appointed Antipater governor. Technically, the Seleucids ruled Syria until Pompey annexed it as a Roman province. The Parthians invaded Palestine in 40 BCE and put the Hasmonaean Antigonus on the throne in Jerusalem, taking John Hyrcanus II prisoner. The Nabataeans made a tactical blunder by siding with the Parthians. Rome, backing Herod the Great, defeated the Parthians and captured Jerusalem. After the defeat of the Parthians, Petra was forced to pay a heavy fine to Rome.

In 37 BCE, Jerusalem fell to Herod the Great, the Roman vassal king, who invaded Nabataean territory when the Nabataeans neglected to pay tribute to Rome. Of Nabataean descent, Herod the Great was the son of Herod Antipater, the advisor of John Hyrcanus; his mother, Cypros/Kypros, was a noblewoman from Petra. In 38, the Roman Senate appointed him King of Judaea, and with the help of the Roman legions, he captured Jerusalem in 37 BCE and Nabataea in 31 BCE, thereby gaining control over a large area of Nabataean territory and ending its independent status. Although geopolitically the Nabataeans lost their "national identity," their culture continued to flourish. They contributed and left their imprint on Roman culture — in particular, architectural and ceramic designs — until finally their cultural individuality was lost, sometime in the third or fourth century CE.

The forces of Malichus I were defeated at Philadelphia (modern Amman). That same year also marked the defeat of Antony and Cleopatra at Actium by Octavian. Plutarch (*Ant.* 69.3) reported that the Nabataeans played a part in the destruction of Cleopatra's fleet near Suez, when she fled from Actium to return to Egypt. It was hoped this would place the Nabataeans in a favorable light as far as the new Roman order was concerned; however, the Nabataean effort was hardly noticed by Rome. There was little necessity for any recognition, for by this time the Roman Empire effectively controlled the Near East. Octavian received the title Augustus Caesar, and he became the first Roman Emperor.

But we are getting ahead of the sequence of events. Let us now turn to Nabataea and those who ruled her during these events.

## The Rule of the Nabataean Kingdom[39]

Little is known about Nabataean rulers. There has been scholarly controversy over their names, the dates of their rule and their accomplishments. Since inscriptions are extremely rare, we can only interpret the archaeological evidence in general terms. It would seem that the system was patrilineal, but it is difficult to know the rules of succession. Although the known rulers are male, there is clear evidence of the high status accorded queens, for the coinage demonstrates that both the king and the queen occupied prominent positions. And, in some cases, they may have served as joint rulers.

Trade routes covered a broad swath of territory, and the prosperity of the kingdom depended on controlling them. In essence, these kings were in the business of controlling trade routes, and the king must have served as the supreme commander of the army. The Nabataean military protected the kingdom and its caravan traffic. This placed on their rulers a constant burden of leadership. It will be noted that Obodas I outsmarted Alexander Jannaeus, and Aretas III expanded the kingdom to the north to include Damascus. Additionally, they undertook to cement international contacts through diplomacy and intermarriage with other royal houses.

The men and women who ruled Nabataea were no doubt proud of their kingdom and must have been brilliant administrators. They had access to vast resources of wealth, which allowed them to indulge in the massive building projects found throughout Petra. However, we know little about when specific structures were built or who built them. Aretas IV brought to his rule extraordinary abilities; he is credited as the builder of the city on a grand scale. The Nabataeans rose to great power, but the span of their civilization — their brilliance — lasted only some 300 years.

The chronologies of Nabataean monarchs for these periods (Figure 1.17) are provided by Abbé J. Starcky in his "Petra et la Nabatene," in *Supplément au Dictionnaire de la Bible*, Vol. VII,

1966. Although the early rulers are shrouded in mystery, the list begins with a reference to the Nabataeans in the war with the Seleucid King Antigonus of Syria. The Nabataean King **Aretas**[40] **I** (ca. 168 BCE) is referred to as the 'tyrant of the Arabs' and the 'King of the Nabatu,' or King of the Nabataeans. It is also Aretas I who is cited as the protector of the High Priest Jason, who asked for asylum in Petra and ruled when cordial hospitality was offered to the Maccabean leaders Judas and Jonathan.

Thus, if we look at the extant biblical record of the Roman period, we find that the Nabataean King Aretas I appears in 2 Maccabees 5:8 as the first known Nabataean king-ruler. There he is asked by Jason, the deposed Maccabean High Priest, for asylum:

> Even so, he [Jason assuming that Antiochus, the Seleucid king was dead] did not succeed in seizing power; in the end his conspiracy brought him nothing but disgrace, and once again he took refuge in Ammonite territory. His career of wickedness was thus brought to a halt. Kept under restraint by Aretas the Arab despot, fleeing from town to town, the quarry of all men, hated as a rebel against the laws, abhorred as the butcher of his country and his countrymen, he drifted to Egypt.

Although this reference is thought by some scholars to be problematic, there are others who believe in its veracity.

In 1 Maccabees 5:24–28, the Nabataeans are shown giving support to the Maccabeans Judas and Jonathan.

> Meanwhile Judas Maccabaeus and his brother Jonathan crossed the Jordan and made a three days march through the desert, where they encountered the Nabataeans, who came to an understanding with them and gave them an account of all that had happened to their brothers in Gilead. Many of them, they said, were shut up in Bozrah [Bostra] and Bosor, Alemo, Chaspho, Maked and Carnaim, all large fortified towns. Others were blockaded in the other towns of Gilead, and the enemy planned to attack and capture these strongholds the very next day, and wipe out all the people inside them in a single day. Judas and his army at once turned off by the desert road to Bozrah; having captured the town, he put the entire male population to the sword, plundered the town and set it on fire.

| The Chronology of Nabataean Kings | |
|---|---|
| Aretas I | ca. 168 BCE |
| Rabbel I | Uncertain |
| Aretas II | 120/90-96 BCE |
| Obodas I | 96-85 BCE |
| Aretas III Philhellenos | 85-62 BCE |
| Obodas II | 62/61-59 BCE |
| Malichus I | 59/58-30 BCE |
| Obodas III | 30-9/8 BCE |
| Aretas IV Lover of His People | 9/8 BCE-40 CE |
| Malichus II | 40-70 CE |
| Rabbel II | 70-106 CE |

*Figure 1.17. The Chronology of Nabataean Kings.*

And 1 Maccabees 9:35:

> Jonathan sent his brother, who was in charge of the convoy, to request his friends the Nabataeans to store their considerable baggage for them.

There is scholarly debate (Bowersock 1983:71-73) as to whether Aretas I was or was not succeeded by a king known as **Rabbel I**.

We can assume, however, that by ca. 110 BCE **Aretas II** ruled, and he is mentioned as the victor in the siege of Gaza, opposing the Hasmonaean King Alexander Jannaeus who attempted to capture the port city from the Nabataeans.

In ca. 96 BCE, the son of Aretas II, **Obodas I,** ascended the Nabataean throne and ruled until 85 BCE, inheriting the struggle against Alexander Jannaeus. In ca. 90 BCE, Josephus writes in his *Antiquities* (13.375ff), "after subduing the Arabs of Moab and Gilaadites, whom he forced to pay tribute...[Alexander] engaged in battle with Obedas [Obodas], king of the Arabs. Falling into an ambush in a rough and difficult region, Alexander Jannaeus was pushed by a multitude of camels into a deep ravine near Garada...and barely escaped with his own life, and fleeing from there came to Jerusalem." Thus, Obodas I thereafter took land in Moab and Galaaditis from the Hasmonaean.

In a crucial battle that took place at Cana in southern Syria in 87 BCE, King Obodas I and his forces defeated the army of the Seleucid ruler, Antiochus XII, who was killed. As a result, Obodas was so revered that after his death the city of Oboda in the Negev was named for him and is said to have served as the seat of his royal cult.

From 85-62 BCE, Petra was ruled by **Aretas III** (also known on his coins as 'Philhellene,' Philhellenos or Philhellen, meaning "lover of 'Hellenism'"). Aretas III expanded Nabataean territory up to and including Damascus in southern Syria. It was during his reign that the earliest Roman governor of Syria, Marcus Aemilius Scaurus, unsuccessfully carried out a military campaign against Petra.

It will be remembered from the foregoing discussion that Aretas III also contested Alexander Jannaeus for the control of Moab and Gilead. (He was the friend and supporter of the Idumean, Antipater, the father of Herod the Great.) In 76 BCE, Alexander Jannaeus died, and as was mentioned above, his sons waged civil war over the power to rule Judaea. Together the two rulers, Aretas III and Antipater, joined forces in support of the Hasmonaean John Hyrcanus II, the son of Alexander Jannaeus, for the throne. In 63 BCE, the Roman general Pompey captured Jerusalem and ended the Judaean civil war — Jerusalem was then placed under the tribute of Rome, and Judaea became a Roman dependency. Thereafter, Nabataea became a client state of Rome. It appears that Nabataean control over Damascus was not secure, and the troops of Åretas III had to evacuate the city when the Armenian King Tigranes attacked central Syria.

In the absence of written sources, we have to rely on the archaeological data. One of the most significant indicators is the evidence of coinage. A great honor in celebration of Nabataean royalty was their minting of their own coins. The earliest Nabataean coins were struck during the period of 60-62 BCE. Nabataean coinage was minted for 170 years, and these coins are important sources of information about Nabataean political standing. Ya'akov Meshorer (1975.3) states:

> The expansion of the Nabataeans into territory formerly under the rule of the Seleucid dynasty, and under their 'protection' by the Romans after Pompey's domination of the East in 63 BCE, enabled the Nabataeans to strike their own coins. This was initially done in the first century BCE (62-59 BCE) by Obodas II and then by Malichus I and Obodas III. It was to meet their specific military needs that these kings minted coins, for their appearance coincided mainly with years of strenuous warfare.

King **Obodas II** (62/61-59 BCE) ruled during this interval.[41] Obodas II was succeeded by **Malichus I** (59/58-30 BCE).[42] This was a time of political upheaval in Rome when fortunes changed. In 55 BCE, Malichus I was attacked by Gabinius, the governor of Syria, who forced him to pay tribute.

Meanwhile, Caesar had defeated Pompey at Pharsalus, and Pompey was murdered in Egypt in 48 BCE. Malichus I supplied military aid to Caesar at Alexandria in 47 BCE, but he shifted his alliance to support the Parthians in their invasion of Judaea. In 40 BCE, the Parthians invaded Syria and captured Jerusalem. (King Herod fled to Masada with his family.) The Parthian invasion incurred the bitter enmity of Mark Antony as well as Herod the Great, who in 41 BCE became allies. With the assassination of Antipater, Herod became the governor of Judaea. After the Roman victory, Malichus I was forced to pay an indemnity to Rome.

By this time, Mark Antony was amorously involved with Queen Cleopatra of Egypt. The queen sought for herself the great city of Petra. When Antony took control of the eastern area of the Roman Empire, Cleopatra demanded Petra as well as Judaea. Some lands were sacrificed, but Petra was one of the few requests that Antony turned down.

With King **Obodas III** (30-9/8 BCE) Nabataean relations with Rome and Judaea were peaceful, and in 26 BCE Obodas III sent his minister-general, Syllaeus, with 1000 Nabataean troops to support the Roman march of Aelius Gallus into southern Arabia, *Arabia Felix*. Obodas also had cordial exchanges with the paranoid Herod the Great — Syllaeus wanted to marry Herod's sister Salome, but Josephus in *Antiquities* (16.7.6) tells us that since the match would have been contingent on Syllaeus' conversion to Judaism, the attempt was aborted. With the death of Obodas III, the ambitious Syllaeus tried to take control of Nabataea. On his way to Rome to defend his claim and his reputation, his ship stopped in Miletus on the western shore of Anatolia, where he dedicated a bilingual Nabataean-Greek inscription to Dushara. Syllaeus' attempt to exonerate himself was unsuccessful, and Strabo (16.4.24) states that by an order from Augustus Syllaeus was decapitated in Rome in 6 BCE.

The rule of **Aretas IV** (9 BCE-40 CE) marks a 48-year golden age for the Nabataeans. To his people he was known as *hrtt mlk rhm amh*, "Haretat [Aretas] the King who loves His People." On his coinage his queens, Huldu (until 16 CE) and Shuqailat (from 18 CE), are shown in profile. They are identified as "Huldu, the Queen of the Nabataeans" or *sqylt mlkt nbtw*, "Shuqailat, the Queen of the Nabataeans" (Glueck 1965:10). The representation of the queen on the Nabataean coin issue implies that royal women at least enjoyed a high status and perhaps even a position of some power in the Nabataean court, such as regent.

An expert of Nabataean numismatics, Ya'akov Meshorer (1975), states that, additionally, Aretas was responsible for the most prolific minting of Nabataean coins.[43] Aretas' two queens, Huldu and later Shuqailat (or Shaqilat I), appear with him on his coinage. He proudly mentions his sons and daughters on an inscription from Petra.[44]

Once again, Damascus came under Nabataean control.[45] The monuments at Petra reflect a flourishing economy and unsurpassed wealth from international trade. Aretas IV reigned over a cosmopolitan Petra, which Strabo states in his *Geography* 16.4.21 was where Romans and other foreigners frequently could be seen. He built splendid temples and tombs not only in the capital of Petra, but at Hegra (Egra) in the Hejaz (Medain Saleh, in present-day northwestern Saudi Arabia) and along the route to Gaza in the Israeli Negev. In 1964, Peter J. Parr found an inscription of Aretas IV on a bench in the Forecourt of the Temenos area of the Qasr al-Bint, in which Aretas IV credits himself with the Temenos' construction.

By 4 BCE, Herod the Great's kingdom had been divided between his three sons.[46] Relations between Nabataea and the Herodians were generally peaceful, but sometimes they could be at each others' throats. For example, one of the daughters of Aretas IV was the wife of the ambitious and greedy Herod Antipas (a son of Herod the Great). He divorced Aretas' daughter[47] to marry Herodias, who was his niece and the wife of his half-brother as well as the mother of the luscious and well-endowed temptress, Salome. This lack of morality deeply upset John the Baptist, whose life, as a result, was sacrificed for Salome. We read in Matthew 14:3-12:

> For Herod had laid hold on John, and bound him, and put *him* in prison for Herodias' sake, his brother Philip's wife.
>
> For John said unto him, It is not lawful for thee to have her.
>
> And when he [Herod Antipas] would have put him to death, he feared the multitude, because they counted him as a prophet.
>
> But when Herod's birthday was kept, the daughter [of] Herodias danced before them, and pleased Herod.
>
> Whereupon he promised with an oath to give her whatsoever should ask.
>
> And she, being before instructed of her mother, said, Give me here John Baptist's head in a charger.
>
> And the king was sorry: nevertheless for the oath's sake, and them which sat with him at meat, he commanded *it* to be given *her.*
>
> And he sent, and beheaded John in the prison.
>
> And his head was brought in a charger, and given to the damsel: and she brought *it* to her mother.

> And his disciples came, and took up the body, and buried it, and went and told Jesus.
>
> When Jesus heard *of it,* he departed thence by ship into a desert place apart: and when the people had heard thereof, they followed him on foot out of the cities.
>
> And Jesus went forth, and saw a great multitude, and was moved with compassion toward them, and he healed their sick.

The aftermath was a conflict between the armies of Aretas IV and the Herodians under Herod Antipas. A sound, well-deserved thrashing was given to the Herodians.

We know that the Nabataeans fluctuated between symbiotic and actively hostile relations with the Jews. In 2 Corinthians 11:32-33, the Apostle Paul mentions the Nabataean King Aretas IV.

> In Damascus the governor under Aretas the king kept the city of the Damascenes with a garrison, desirous to apprehend me:
>
> And through a window in a basket was I let down by the wall, and escaped his hands.

**Malichus II** (40-70 CE) was referred to by the Nabataeans as *mlkw mlk, mlk nbtw,* "Malichus the King, King of the Nabataeans." His queen, Shuqailat II[48], was called *sqylt 'hth, mlkt nbtw,* "Shuqailat, his Sister, queen of the Nabataeans" (Meshorer 1975.107). With the rule of Malichus II (40-70 CE), Nabataea is thought by some scholars to have witnessed a decline in its fortunes. This may not, however, have been the case, for it has now been confirmed by scholars that Malichus II was the king referred to in the *Periplus Maris Erythraei* 19.[49] This citation describes a great commercial success resulting from a linking of the Red Sea port city of Leuke Kome to Petra. The Nabataeans also seem to have been commercially and militarily successful at Hegra, and they occupied the north Arabian oasis in Wadi Sirhan of Dumah (Jauf). In 67 CE, Josephus (*Jewish Wars* III.IV.2.68) states that Malichus II sent 5000 infantrymen, including archers and 1000 cavalry, to suppress the First Jewish Revolt.

**Rabbel II** (70-106 CE) ascended the throne with his queen-mother, Shuqailat II, serving as regent until he came of age in 75 CE. Rabbel II married two of Malichus II's daughters, who are also referred to as his "sisters" — Queen Gamilat (76-102 CE) and Queen Hagru (102-106).

This was a time of trouble for Nabataea and particularly for the royal house ruling from Petra, its capital. The royals at Hegra revolted, led by one known as Damasi, who was supported by northern Nabataean tribes as well as his fellow Hejaz people. David Graf (1992.IV.971) suggests that the phrase ascribed to Rabbel II as one "who brought life and deliverance to his people" is a reference to the king's successful outcome in stamping out this rebellion.

At this time, the city of Bostra in the Hawran (modern Syria) may have become a prominent city of Nabataea. The ruling family now resided here instead of Petra. Bostra served as the nexus of the important inner trading route through the Wadi Sirhan. The move was probably a military precaution, to have the seat of Nabataean power be further removed from the Hejazi troublemakers.

It is thought that Rabbel II came to an agreement with Rome that, if they did not attack during his lifetime, the Romans could take control after his death. Rabbel II's reign ended in 106 CE, and in the same year Rome absorbed Nabataea. Nabataea completely succumbed to Roman hegemony when the Roman legate of Syria, A. Cornelius Palma, on behalf of Trajan took control. Whether or not this action was a peaceful or hostile takeover is not known, but it probably was an administrative formality carrying out the agreement between Rabbel II and Rome. Trajanic coinage carries the legend *Arabia adquista* instead of *Arabia capta,* which would seem to confirm the routine nature of the annexation. As would be expected, Roman coinage came with the creation of the province, and Nabataean coinage was being overstruck by the Romans. The Roman Province of *Provincia Arabia* was created out of the annexed territory of Nabataea.

In 64-63 BCE, before Roman domination, the Nabataeans were conquered by the Roman general Pompey. Nabataea was regarded as a client state of Rome; the area was taxed by the Romans and served as a buffer territory against the desert tribes. In 25-24 BCE, Aelius Gallus started an unsuccessful expedition from Nabataea to conquer *Arabia Felix,* the kingdom that lay to the south, Saba, present-day Yemen — the land of frankincense and myrrh. The Roman propaganda of the day made this expedition out to be a success.

The Nabataeans had their political ups and downs — they supported the Syrian Seleucids against the Ptolemies, the Hasmonaeans against the Seleucids and the Parthians against the Romans. Clearly Petra's position made her vulnerable to the fortunes of conflicts in the region.

## The Roman Period Post 106 CE

After 106 CE, the world of the Nabataeans was politically Roman. Therefore, we can assume that Petra and Nabataea were completely and formally subsumed by the Romans under the Emperor Trajan in 106 CE and then became part of the Roman province known as *Provincia Arabia,* with major centers at Bostra and perhaps at Petra as well. Did the *Pax Romana* ("the Roman Peace") allow the Nabataeans to worship as they had before? Did the Nabataean pantheon of gods continue to be worshipped, albeit with Hellenistic and Roman overtones?

It is ironic that Nabataean success was directly related to Roman imperialism. After Nabataea was taken over by Roman imperial interests, the Nabataeans were certainly assimilated to some degree,[50] but the Nabataean script is found on inscriptions dating to the second half of the fourth century, and Nabataean deities continued to be worshipped. With the Roman development of a seafaring trade around Arabia, which was directly related to the discovery of the monsoons and the increased influence of Palmyra as an entrepôt, Petra began its decline as the leading trade center.

Although the Nabataean geopolitical fortunes had changed, at least in the beginning of the Roman takeover, the Roman control of the area seems to have had little effect on the flourishing Nabataean economy. With Roman domination, the Roman *Legatus*[51] maintained order, which clearly manifested the dependence of the now allied city.[52] The Nabataean language continued in use for administrative and legal purposes, although Greek and to a lesser extent Latin were in use as well. The potters of Nabataean fine wares maintained their production, although the yield from this time demonstrates a decline in the painting, and the wares become coarser and more sandy to the touch.

By 114 CE, Trajan had granted Petra the title of *metropolis,* and it served the Romans as the principal center for their southern holdings in the area, which extended from the south shore of the Dead Sea to the Gulf of Aqaba. Nabataean kings were no more, having been replaced by Roman legates or deputies — members of the senatorial rank serving as governors.

Discovered at Nahal Hever near En-Gedi was the Babatha archive, which dates from 93 to 132 CE. (A portion of the archive dates to the time of T. Aninius Sextius Florentinus, a Roman governor appointed by the Emperor Hadrian.) This archive is ascribed to the Judaean Jewess Babatha, and it gives us some insight about this period of time. The archive spans the time when the area was under the control of the Nabataean kingdom and the beginning of the Roman province, and it shows settlement patterns south of the Dead Sea.[53] (It refers to a crown prince named Obodas in 98 CE but provides no mention of a Nabataean ruler after the annexation.) In particular, this document is important, because it also refers to the Judaean Babatha's ownership of property in Nabataea and her desire for legal retribution from the Nabataean-Roman judicial system for herself and her son. Repeatedly, Babatha was ordered to appear before Roman authorities at the court in Petra. It is obvious that there were continued close relationships between the Judaeans and Nabataeans (Glueck 1965.8-9),[54] although the fortunes of both peoples were now decided by Rome.

The Nabataeans and Judaeans enjoyed shared interests. They had strong commercial ties, and intermarriage took place between those of high social and economic status. Glueck (1965:39) points out the Nabataeans had political ties with the Hasmonaeans and the Herodians as well, for they had common interests that brought them into conflict with the Seleucids and the Ptolemies.

In 131 CE, Hadrian (117-138 CE), the Roman emperor, visited the site and named it after himself, *Hadriane Petra* (Ηαδριανη Πετρα).[55] The city continued to flourish, at least up to this time in the Roman period, with a monumental Arch in the Bab as-Siq (which possibly carried an aqueduct) and tomb structures either carved out of the living rock or built free-standing. Under Roman rule, Roman classical monuments abounded; however, many continued to be embellished with Nabataean motifs.[56] With time, in the third and fourth centuries CE, the once flourishing caravan towns in the Negev lost their luster and began to wither away as their populations migrated to more important commercial centers. The Romans carried more of their goods by ship from Arabia to Egypt. They no longer had to be dependent on Nabataean routes, and the Nabataeans suffered from economic decline, Bedouin raids and piracy.[57]

Petra's apogee was from the first century BCE to the second century CE. Its material culture reached its zenith in the second half of the first century BCE, before the Romans established control.

## The Byzantine Period

By 313 CE, Christianity had become a state-recognized religion. In 330 CE, the Emperor Constantine established the eastern Roman Empire with its capital at Constantinople. In the fourth century, the Byzantines divided the area into two parts; the southern region was known as *Palestina Salutaris/Tertia,* and Petra became its capital. (No longer was the area considered to be the Roman Province of Arabia.)

On the 19th of May 363 CE an earthquake destroyed half of the city. This earthquake did not affect Petra's rock-carved monuments (e.g., the Al-Khazna), but it probably brought ruin to many of its free-standing structures, such as the Temple of the Winged Lions and perhaps the Great Temple, which may have been partially demolished at this time. This earthquake also may have had a devastating effect on the social and economic institutions. This may have marked the beginning of Petra's decline.

It is said that Petra became a place of exile for heretical priests who found unacceptable either the imperial decisions or those of the early church councils. Perhaps that is the reason Eusebius, the Christian chronicler, accused Petra of being "filled with superstitious men, who have sunk in diabolical error," yet Christian martyrs from Petra are known from the persecutions of Diocletian. In 451, the bishopric of Petra was placed under the patriarchate of Jerusalem. Petra became the seat of a bishopric and many Nabataean descendants now became Christianized. However, pagan worship remained. The city may have been the center of a local ecclesiastical culture. One of the bishops of Petra (Theodore) wrote the *enkomion* of Saint Theodosios Koinobiarches, who died in 529.

The newly excavated Petra Church, with its extraordinary mosaics and papyrus scrolls, documents this period, especially in the sixth century, a phenomenon less well attested in other sites so far south in Jordan. As a trading center, Petra was obscured by Palmyra in the Roman period, and this trend continued as the main trade routes slowly moved east to the Euphrates and the Persian Gulf, leaving Petra and her caravan cities "out of the loop." With this change in trade routes, Petra's commercial decline was inevitable. Just as Petra seems to have held on to some of its former glory, some of its former caravan towns in the Negev, once again, became independent centers of commerce. Pagan temples in the Negev were replaced with richly decorated Christian churches.

Thereafter, one can read the archaeology of a fragmented Byzantine community living among and reusing the abandoned limestone and sandstone elements of Petra's classical past. The inhabitants during the Byzantine period recycled many standing structures and rock-cut monuments, while they also constructed their own buildings, including churches: the now restored Petra Church and the Ridge Church, lying on the ridge above the Petra Church, excavated by Patricia M. Bikai. And the shops along the Colonnaded Street were reconstructed. Among the rock-cut monuments the Byzantines reused is the Urn Tomb, which was modified into a church.

An even more devastating earthquake occurred on the 9th of July in 551 CE, which some scholars believe brought the city, once again, to ruin. But, because the Petra Church Papyri document land holdings for another decade or so, we now know that Byzantine Petra may have been a community more important and affluent than these historians have assumed. Petra, serving as the seat of a Byzantine bishopric, retained its urban vitality into late antiquity. It appears that city life continued, although Petra was absorbed by the Byzantine Empire.

## The Islamic Period 636-1097 CE

The Islamic period begins with the foundation of this world religion by the Arabian apostle or prophet, Mohammad, in the seventh century. In 636 CE, the "Sword of Islam" — the Muslim Conquest — destroyed the Byzantine forces at the Battle of the Yarmuk River, and Petra, like most of Palestine, came under Muslim rule. All of the area comprising present-day Jordan fell to Muslim rule between 630-640 CE. The Muslim invasion probably left Petra as it was. We find little evidence of Islamic occupation.

The Umayyads ruled from 660-750 CE, establishing their dynasty in Damascus in 661 CE. During this time (in 747/8 CE), Petra suffered yet another great earthquake, which was as devastating as its predecessor. The Abbasid Dynasty transferred its capital to Baghdad, and the center of power was focused farther to the east than ever before. At Petra, the Bedouin way of life returned. Thus, with the rise of Islam, Petra became a backwater community.

## The Crusader Period 1099-1268 CE

The Crusaders, who captured Jerusalem in 1099, built an outpost in Petra in the twelfth century. Transjordan was known as *Oultre-Jourdain* by the Crusaders. Ruled by King Baldwin I, there is little known until the Kingdom of Jerusalem claimed *Oultre-Jourdain* as part of its fiefdom. Coveting the north-south trade route, King Baldwin I built a fortress at Ash-Shawbak (Shobak) in about 1114-1115. Kennedy (1925:36) quotes A. Musil:

> Baldwin established a new garrison post in the course of eighteen days, so that he might the more effectively subdue the land of the Arabitae and that merchants might no longer be allowed to pass hither and thither across it without his permission, and that no ambuscades or forces of the enemy might suddenly make their appearance without showing themselves to the King's loyal subjects posted in the citadel.

When the Crusaders arrived in Petra, they probably also found a small community of Christian monks still living in the Monastery of St. Aaron on Jabal Harun. (These monks had asked King Baldwin for help against the Saracens who were raiding them.) In 1127,

*Figure 1.18. Al-Wu'ayra Crusader fortress, tower.*

Baldwin occupied Petra and constructed fortresses in the area the Crusaders called *Li Vaux Moise* ("the Valley of Moses"). The Al-Wu'ayra fortress (Figures 1.18 and 1.19), as it is known today, was constructed just outside the central city where the king garrisoned his troops. It was lost in several battles but was later recaptured by Baldwin III. To quote from William of Tyre:[58]

> The Turks with the support and on the invitation of certain inhabitants of these regions, had occupied a certain strong place of ours, called the Vallis Moysi in Syria-Sobal...On learning, therefore, that the

*Figure 1.19. Al-Wu'ayra Crusader fortress, entryway.*

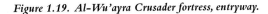

enemy were holding the aforesaid place, our lord the King sets out, and crossing with his expeditionary troops the famous valley where now the Dead Sea lies...they arrive at the point they aimed at. Now the inhabitants of that district had taken themselves into the fort, taking for granted the strength of the place for the reason that it seemed impregnable. When our men, seeing the difficulty and insuperable strength of the place, after having spent some days in casting great stones, in many a discharge of arrows and other methods of offence, had found their labour useless, they had recourse to other tactics. The whole of that region was thickly planted with fertile olive trees — so thickly that they overshadowed the whole surface of the land, like very thick woods. It was resolved, therefore, to grub up these trees and burn them all.

It is known that then the fort capitulated, but it was captured by Salah-ed-Din (Saladin) in 1188-1189.

In Petra, the Crusaders also built a fort on the top of Al-Habis and converted the Qasr al-Bint into a stable. After the Crusaders abandoned the city to Salah-ed-Din in 1189 CE, they were forced to retreat to the Mediterranean. Petra's rock-cut tombs and caves were again inhabited by the Bedouin, and the city was left, once again, to its own way of life.

## The Ottoman Period 1517-1831 CE

In the sixteenth century, the area submitted to Ottoman rule and became part of the vilayet of Damascus. In the nineteenth century, the Turks, in order to protect and further their communications with Arabia, constructed the Hejaz railway system from Damascus to Medina and settled Circassian and Caucasian refugees in the area. In the Petra area, they cut down many trees causing irreparable environmental damage.[59] Petra disappears from the record for five centuries until its rediscovery.

## The Modern Period 1831 CE-Present

Petra was revealed to the western world in 1812, for the first time since the Crusades, when it was rediscovered and identified on August 22 by the Swiss explorer Johann Ludwig Burckhardt (Figure 1.20). Its stunning and incredible beauty and its extraordinary array of architectural monuments made it attractive to visitors; however, in the early nineteenth century tourists entered the site essentially at their own risk.

In the early days after the rediscovery of Petra, there was no protection for travelers for the region was independent — there was neither centralized authority, nor any administration. Many travelers were frightened away by the ignorance and superstition of the wild Bedouin. The natives resented outsiders, for they thought they were visiting for financial gain. There were the risks of being cheated or robbed and even the risk of violent death. Another hazard was disease, for cholera was common. There was also the unattractive possibility of being stalked by wild cats, foxes and hyenas roaming the all-but-abandoned hills.

Petra's image since has been recorded by artists (Figure 1.21), including the Englishman William John Bankes, who went to Petra and drew the earliest known drawings in 1818.[60] There were also engravers like the British Royal Academician David Roberts, who after his visit to the site in 1839, said that he "grew more and more astonished and bewildered with this extraordinary city...I have often thrown my pencil away in despair of ever being able to convey any idea of this extraordinary place."

The landscape painter, Edward Lear painted scenes of Petra in 1858.[61] Overwhelmed by the site, he said:

> [It is a]...magical condensation of beauty and wonder...I felt 'I have found a new world — but my art is helpless to recall it to others, or to represent it to those who have never seen it.' Yet, as the enthusiastic foreigner said to the angry huntsman who asked if he meant to catch the fox — 'I will try.'

And there were photographers like Francis Frith in the 1860s who captured the uniqueness associated with Petra that give it its reputation today as one of the most extraordinarily beautiful and haunting sites in the world. The first American painter to visit Petra was Frederick Edwin Church,[62] who spent five months in the Near East in 1867-1868; his most remarkable painting of this period is of the Al-Khazna.

In the late 1890s, orientalists like R.E. Brünnow and the classicist, A. von Domaszewski began their investigations of the city. (These researchers will be discussed *infra*.)

The Arab revolt against the Turks, in part under the leadership of T.E. Lawrence (Lawrence of Arabia), followed in 1916. In 1920, Abdullah of the Hashemites was persuaded to lead the government that was created as Transjordan in 1921. This was recognized as an independent constitutional state in 1927, although it was still under British control. In 1946, Abdullah became the first king of the Hashemite Kingdom of Transjordan (which later became Jordan). Abdullah's grandson, the present King Hussein, came to the throne in 1952.

*Figure 1.20. Johann Ludwig Burckhardt.*

***Figure 1.21. Lithograph of Al-Khazna by David Roberts, 1839.***

## The Bedouins
(Arabic, sing. *Badawi* — pl. *Badawiyin*)

For centuries Petra has been the home of the Bedouin tribes. Traditionally, the Bedouins of the Arabian desert were camel breeders who patrolled the desert. Traders and desert cities had to pay them for the protection of their caravans. Even the Ottomans reported that they had to buy security from these nomadic people.

The Bedouins (Figure 1.22) are divided into clans, which are ruled by a sheik (generally the eldest). Each clan is sovereign, and there is constant fighting between them for the possession of good grazing lands. Modern political boundaries are irritating to them for their nomadic ways are not limited by a specific territory. The vast majority do not think about the Middle East peace process for it matters little to them. They are devoted to King Hussein, but on the whole, they spend their time fighting to survive, keeping mind, body and soul together. They coax the soil to provide them with enough food to live and follow their goats and sheep through the hills of Petra. In the summer, they take their flocks to graze on higher ground, and they move into the lower areas around central Petra for their winter pasture grounds.

Many Bedouin customs like vendetta, polygamy and blood-money are in practice today. But once trust is established, the Bedouin are honorable, generous to a fault, hospitable beyond belief, loyal and kind, and their friendship knows no bounds. These are the best of people with whom one could ever collaborate.

The Bedouin living in and around Petra are composed of five major families, and the population presently numbers approximately 2000. East of Petra is the village of Al-Ji, or in modern terms, Wadi Musa (Figure 1.23), where the Al-Layathina (Liyathna) tribe settled. This is the local Jordanian government administrative center where civil authority has been established. Just to the north of Petra is Wadi al-Bayda' (Beidha, the Neolithic site mentioned earlier) where the 'Amarin (Amareen) tribe live — a tribe with whom the Al-Budul of Petra maintain close contact, although there have been bitter hostilities between them. Each of these tribes will not tolerate subservience either to one another or to any outside authority.

The Bedouins who have been born in and have lived in Petra are known as the Al-Budul tribe. Most likely the word "Budul" derives from the Arabic word *badala*, meaning "to change," although the Hebrew root *badel*, meaning "dissent," is also a possible derivation. Although there is no proven link between them, Al-Budul claim their tribe descends from *Badl*, one of the sons of the mythical Nabataean King *Nabt*. Their tribal name means "clan of Badl." Speculations about the Al-Buduls' origins link them with the traditional ancient inhabitants of Petra, and they are also associated with Moses' Exodus; there is an early Al-Budul religious association with Judaism. The present-day Al-Budul, however, think of themselves as descendants of the Nabataeans.

The growth of the tourist industry exacerbates the problems caused by modernization of the culture and lifestyles of these indigenous peoples. The pastoral Al-Budul are vulnerable to tourism. They have been forced to leave their caves in Petra to live in brick or cinder

block, crowded, government-sponsored housing in the newly created village of Umm Sayhun, outside the Petra Basin. Before the move, the Al-Budul traditionally lived in Petra, herded goats, bred camels, seasonally cultivated barley, tobacco and wheat and hunted and gathered plants. Although the Al-Budul continue to use donkeys and camels as beasts of burden, Toyota small trucks have become the norm. Their decreased mobility has resulted in increased population (3000 vs. 150).

There has always been rivalry between the tribes. Today these tribes are in conflict and rivalry over tourism, a major component of Jordan's economy. In just 10 years, most of the young Al-Budul have adjusted to their housing, but there is a wistful reverence for the old life that stirs in the hearts of the older generation. Few Al-Budul tend flocks or are involved in agriculture anymore. Instead they operate tea shops and jewelry stands or lead tourists through the ruins of Petra on camels and donkeys. The benefits of their new lifestyle include a larger school, a school for girls, a local clinic and protection of the government authorities. Because of their native acumen, they are advancing from being under-appreciated into a dynamic force of modern Jordan. To be sure, within the context of modern Jordan, tribal territory no longer holds the value it once did, and the Al-Budul know and resent it.

Anthropological researchers posit that the Al-Budul have created a folklore about their origins to fit in with contemporary political circumstances. Somehow the Arab-Israeli conflict, the Al-Budul belief in their Nabataean ancestry and their opposition to relocation have all become part of the Al-Budul ethos.

## A Word About Nabataean Language and Writing

The most meticulous and important study of Nabataean Tomb Inscriptions was written by John F. Healey and published in 1993.[63]

The earliest Nabataean inscription found at Petra is dated to Obodas I or to the first year of his reign in 93 BCE. It is engraved on the triclinium at the entrance to the Siq and is a dedication to Dushara and Obodas:

> for the life of Obodas, king of the Nabataeans, the son of Aretas, king of the Nabataeans. Year 1.

*Figure 1.22. Bedouin workers on the Petra Great Temple site. Photograph by John Forasté.*

David Graf (1992:IV.972) states that the Nabataeans were multilingual. Their native language was Arabic; many of their personal names were in Arabic, and they spoke Arabic, but they adopted the *lingua franca,* Aramaic, which they wrote in their own script for formal inscriptions. David Graf remarks (ibid.)

> Instead, the fact that the Nabataeans preserved the indigenous cults of the

*Figure 1.23. Wadi Musa, 1997.*

Edomites, Moabites and Syrians, wrote in diverse scripts and spoke several languages suggests a heterogeneous society in which the indigenous populations of Transjordan, N. Arabia, and elsewhere were assimilated under the Nabataean hegemony. The term "Nabataeans" should then be understood as a vast political alliance of various peoples.

After the Romans occupied the area and established a strong military presence, Petra continued to retain its native language but used Greek for business. They also started to incorporate Roman institutions and began to use Latin for government and business.

The most comprehensive study of Nabataean inscriptions has been undertaken by J. Cantineau, who published two volumes entitled *Le nabatéen* in 1930-1932. As for their own writing, there are some 4000 inscriptions that have been recovered. These have helped in establishing their chronology.

## Nabataean Religion[64]

In researching the Nabataeans, one is struck by the mixed information about the spiritual nature of their deities. Who was their creator god or goddess? Who among their deities represented weather? Who among the deities worshipped were the spirits that can be defined? Although a few Nabataean deities can be identified, the question remains how were they worshipped? We have some idea of their mixed environment, that of Moabites, Edomites, Judaeans and Syrians and how they became "Nabataeanized," yet their environment was ever changing according to the various stages of their social, religious and economic development. The paucity of information from written sources is serious; the Nabataean world and their gods remain a mystery to us.

The main deities of the Nabataeans are Dushara and Al-'Uzza. They may have also worshipped Illaalge, Manawat and Sai' Al-Qaum, who will be briefly described as well.

As we mentioned previously, **Dushara** — Dusares in Greek, Dus-sara (or "Lord of the Shara," pronounced Dushara) — is the tutelary deity of Petra, the supreme deity of the Nabataeans and of Petra. He is associated with vegetation and fertility. He is also the everlasting, deathless god.

At Petra, Dushara has been recognized by a black obelisk and huge rectangular blocks of stone, known as the Saharij al-Jinn (Djin Blocks), that carried his spirit (Glueck 1965:Pl. 215a). The tradition handed down by Arab folklore is that the al-Jinn blocks and tower tombs are representations of Dushara and embody his spirit. The al-Jinn are considered to be evil, malevolent spirits that inhabit some 26 of these blocks of stone found at Petra. Dushara is also thought to be worshipped in carved, quadrangular niches with baetyls in them. The pair of obelisks carved out of bedrock, standing like sentinels on the High Place of Sacrifice at Jabal Madhbah, may also have been representative of Dushara and the Egyptian goddess Isis. They are thought to have been sacred to his worship and that of Al-'Uzza (*infra*), who scholars believe was associated with Isis. Sacred to Dushara are the eagle and the panther, and his attributes include the vine stem.

In the Hellenistic period Dushara became equated with Dionysos, and he has also been syncretized with the Egyptian gods Serapis and Osiris. Later he may have been identified with the Hellenistic Zeus and Ares.

At Petra he may also have been represented as the handsome bearded god (perhaps the Egyptian deity Serapis) that is associated with the Temenos Gate sculpture (Figure 1.24). This attribution is doubted by many, because unlike other gods in the Nabataean period, Dushara seems to have escaped any sort of anthropomorphic representation either on coins or in sculpture. It is only in the Roman period that not only is his representation aniconic, but he is given the human form of a young man with long, flowing hair. This, however, is found on the coinage of Bostra, not Petra.

The At-Turkmaniyya Tomb boasts the longest Nabataean inscription yet found at Petra. It threatens the despoilers of the tomb, but the inscription begins with a description of the tomb itself — two rock chambers with graves, a courtyard, benches and triclinium, water cisterns, rock walls and retaining walls. It then states:

> These are sacred to Dushara, God of our
> Lord, his throne Harisa and all the gods, by
> acts of consecration as commanded therein.
> Dushara and his throne and all the gods
> watch over the acts of consecration so they

will be observed and there will be no change..., and no one will be buried in this tomb except him who is authorized...according to the acts of consecration which are eternal.

**Al-'Uzza** (sometimes associated with the Syrian Atargatis, meaning "the mighty One," and also with the Egyptian goddess Isis) is the Nabataean mother goddess, the Arabian Aphrodite sometimes referred to as Al-'Uzza-Aphrodite. She symbolizes fertility and is a vegetation goddess. She is also the paramount queen, the sky-mother and the patroness of travelers. Most important of all, she is the creator and sustainer of life. There are several dedications to her at Petra (Zayadine 1979:197), including two at Wadi Musa. The famous schematic figurative representation, the "eye idol" found by Philip C. Hammond in the Temple of the Winged Lions, is also thought by some scholars to be a schematic representation of her (Figure 1.25).[65] In Wadi as-Siyyagh, she is mentioned, and on the passage to Al-Khubtha she is referred to "with the 'lord of the house.'" At various times she can be thought to embody Isis, Hera, Demeter and Fortuna (Tyche). Sacred to her is the dolphin, and she is represented as the fish-goddess, the lion and the leaf.

Al-'Uzza was also worshipped at Khirbat Tannur and Wadi Ramm, Nabataean sites not far from Petra. At Khirbat Tannur, a site to the north of Petra, she is represented as a vegetation goddess in different ways such as grain, cornucopiae, leaves, fish and felines. She has celestial characteristics including the zodiac, and she wears the Tyche mural crown as Fortuna, the guardian of the city. At Khirbat Brak,[67] Nelson Glueck associated her with dolphins, and she is depicted as a mermaid. Dolphins have also been associated with her at Petra's Temple of the Winged Lions. She may be shown carrying a cornucopia or holding a bird in her hand. Often she is shown flanked by lions.

Al-'Uzza can be linked with the goddess Tyche, who represents fortune and wears a mural crown as the guardian of the city. She is the consort of Dushara, and in the Hellenistic period, she is described as a radiate goddess, which may suggest that she also symbolized the sun. Al-'Uzza also enjoys strong links with the Egyptian goddess Isis, who was worshipped in Petra. Representations of Isis-Al-'Uzza-Isis

*Figure 1.24. A possible representation of Dushara.*

have been found carved in relief on the Al-Khazna, and there are numerous votive figurines that have been found as well.

**Allat** is also a tutelary goddess; she was not worshipped in Petra but in Wadi Ramm. At some point, however, her characteristics may have been syncretized with Al-'Uzza. Like Al-'Uzza, the lion is sacred to her, as is the camel. In some cases, she borrows attributes from Al-'Uzza and Atargatis. She is the domestic guardian who is associated with Astarte. During the Hellenistic period, she becomes syncretized with Athena, the goddess of war. Herodotus called her Alilat-Aphrodite. She also may be associated with Alarsamain, the morning star, or Venus.

**Illaalge** (Illa al-ge, i.e., Allah al-Ji, "the god of Al-Ji") is a local god about whom little is known except that he was worshipped in Wadi Musa.

**Manawat** is the goddess of destiny — chance and luck— who is mentioned in a large number of inscriptions.

**Sai' Al-Qaum** (the good and the beautiful god who does not drink wine) was another local guardian deity who is known from two inscriptions at Palmyra. This god was the protector of caravans, and his attributes include the helmet. It is not known if he was worshipped at Petra; the archaeological evidence is lacking.

The prime role of the gods is to protect us and help us in governing our lives. With so little to go on, it is difficult to know the time in which a deity became identifiable, the effect on beliefs when cultures were merged and how syncretizations took place. The original meaning of a god or goddess may have become corrupted over time. It must be noted that Nabataean gods undergo changes during time and from place to place. Nabataea is a composite population, and one deity may borrow attributes from another.

*Figure 1.25. Stele found in the Temple of the Winged Lions of a goddess/deity. Photograph courtesy of the Jordanian Department of Antiquities and Philip C. Hammond.*

## Nabataean Pottery

Nabataean pottery is unique. It is what archaeologists refer to as an "horizon-marker" or an "index fossil," because it is different from any other wares produced at this time. Not only has it been found in prodigious numbers at Petra and known Nabataean sites in Jordan, but it is also found in large quantities in Saudi Arabia, the Negev and the Sinai. The origins of Nabataean pottery are obscure, but it makes its earliest appearance at Petra during the reign of Aretas II, or between 100-92 BCE.

Nabataean pottery is a well-levigated ware, meaning that there are few inclusions in the clay, which has been well purified in water. It is wheel-thrown, thin, crisp and a so-called ringing ware. Characteristically, its colors are salmon to red, which in part are created from its even firing temperatures. The most common shape is the open bowl, which is decorated on the interior with red, dark brown or black designs of feathers, dots, branches, pomegranates and other fruits (Color Plate 5). Rouletted decoration is commonly found to embellish the rounded, slightly pointed base or the ring base, and rouletted patterns are often found around the rim as well.

Numerous pottery studies of Nabataean wares have been undertaken by Khairieh 'Amr (1986, 1987), M. Avi-Yonah and A. Negev (1960), Philip C. Hammond (1973), J.H. Iliffe (1943),

N.I. Khairy (1975), Peter J. Parr (1970), Stephan G. Schmid (1995a, 1995b, 1996) and Yvonne Gerber (1995). Figurines have also undergone study by I. Parlasca (1986a, 1986b, 1990). Nabataean pottery kilns have been found just outside Petra at the Zurrabah kilns and have been excavated by Fawzi Zayadine. Khairieh 'Amr (1986, 1987) has published the neutron activation results.

## A Brief History of Research and Excavations at Petra

As one of the most spectacular sites in the Middle East, Petra has long attracted travelers and explorers. Ulrich J. Seetzen visited Petra in 1806 but did not understand its significance. As was mentioned earlier, in 1812 the Swiss explorer, Johann Ludwig Burckhardt visited the site, and it is to Burckhardt that the credit for its rediscovery is given. The site was visited and documented by several Europeans, including Charles Irby, James Mangles and the artist William John Bankes, in 1818, and the Frenchman Léon de Laborde, in 1828. In 1839, the great British artist David Roberts produced his extraordinary lithographs of the site. British archaeologist Sir Austin Henry Layard, the excavator of Nimrud in Mesopotamia, visited Petra in 1840 and remarked on his disappointment with the ruins. In 1858, the renowned Edward Lear drew the ruins. Another intrepid British

*Figure 1.26. Temple of the Winged Lions.*

*Figure 1.27. Aerial view of the Petra Church showing mosaics in side aisles. Photograph by J. Wilson Myers and Eleanor E. Myers. Courtesy of the American Center of Oriental Research.*

traveler, Charles Doughty, who visited Petra in the 1870s, published *Travels in Arabia Deserta,* in which he referred to Petra as "an eyesore," with the exception of the Al-Khazna ("The Treasury") of which he said:

> That most perfect of all monuments whose sculpted columns and cornices are pure lines of crystalline beauty without blemish, whereupon the golden sun looks from above, and Nature has painted that sand-rock ruddy with iron-rust.

In 1896, the Dominican fathers from the École Biblique at the Archéologique Française in Jerusalem published their explorations of Petra. In 1905, W. Libbey and F.E. Hoskins published a synthesis of Petra, presenting one of the earliest overviews in print.

Further explorations began in earnest at the turn of the century, with the first scientific expedition being published in *Arabia Petraea* in 1907 by Alois Musil. The orientalist, R.E. Brünnow, and the classicist, A. von Domaszewski, who had surveyed the site in 1897-1898, published an ambitious three-volume mapping project in their *Die Provincia Arabia* (1904-1909). Sponsored by the German Evangelic Institute for Exploration of the Antiquities of the Holy Land in Jerusalem, G. Dalman explored the high places of worship and the necropolis before World War I. Orientalists, including R. Dussaud, A. Jaussen, R. Savingac and M. Dunand, explored evidence that related to Nabataean culture by researching crosscultural links with other sites. German interest in Petra continued with the German Society for Oriental Research sponsoring H. Kohl's exploration of the Qasr al-Bint. During World War I, W. Bachmann, C. Watzinger and T. Wiegand investigated the city structures under the Committee for the Preservation of Monuments of the German-Turkish Army.[67]

In 1929, when Palestine was under the British Mandate, the Department of Antiquities of Palestine undertook the first archaeological excavations at Petra. They investigated the tombs, town dumps (on the Al-Katute[68] ridge), some of the rock-cut houses and the city wall, under the direction of British researchers George Horsfield and Agnes C. Horsfield. Under the auspices of the American School of Oriental Research in Jerusalem, American scholars including William Foxwell Albright researched Petra in 1934.

Meanwhile, beginning in 1933, Nelson Glueck surveyed Transjordan. The British School of Archaeology in Egypt sponsored excavations by Margaret Murray and J.C. Ellis, who continued the excavation of more rock-cut houses and tombs. This work was subsequently published by the British School of Archaeology in Egypt.

In the 1950s, modern scientific archaeological research brought British archaeologist Diana Kirkbride to Petra. From 1955-1956, she excavated the Colonnaded Street and a few of the shops bordering it. Peter J. Parr, under the auspices of the British School of Archaeology in Jerusalem, excavated the Temenos Gate and the Colonnaded Street, where he discovered walls of buildings dating from the third century BCE, and he found the first stratified Nabataean pottery sequence. Parr also excavated a domestic structure at Al-Katute, surveyed the town walls, drafted plans of the Baths and instituted damage control of the swollen waters of the Wadi Musa by the construction of revetment walls. Additionally, he instituted a photogrammetric plan of the city and studied the elevations of the tomb façades. In 1958, along with C.M. Bennett of the British School of Archaeology, Parr began an excavation of the city center, which remains the most informative and scientific to date. He later excavated the great Temenos of the Qasr al-Bint; he also excavated the podium and demonstrated that its placement was important evidence in its relationship to the Bench Inscription of Aretas IV found in the Temenos area.

The Al-Khazna ("The Treasury"), which had suffered from earthquakes and erosion over the years, was excavated, studied, consolidated and partially restored in 1960 by G.R.H. Wright. In collaboration with Fawzi Zayadine of the Jordanian Department of Antiquities, he undertook the detailed architectural study of the Qasr al-Bint, and Wright also consolidated the Temenos Gate. Mohammad Murshed for the Jordanian Department of Antiquities excavated the entrance to the Baths. Also among these pioneers was the American Philip C. Hammond, Director of the American Expedition to Petra, who, under the sponsorship of the Princeton Theological Seminary and the Jordanian Department of Antiquities, excavated the Main Theater from 1962-1963, publishing his findings in 1965. Later in 1971, Hammond began the excavation of the Temple of the Winged Lions

(Figure 1.26) and adjoining buildings; his latest excavation report was published in 1996. These excavations continue today.

The University of Basel's Rolf Stucky has been actively engaged in the Swiss exploration of Petra for some time. Stucky has excavated the Az-Zantur residential structures located to the south overlooking the Great Temple. He has published his findings annually in the *Annual of the Department of Antiquities of Jordan* (*ADAJ*), and his final report, *Petra-Ez Zantur I*, covering 1988-1992 campaigns appeared in 1996. The Jordanian archaeologist Fawzi Zayadine has excavated and written about several tombs of the Al-Khubtha triclinia in the Siq al-Barid in Al-Bayda' and pottery kilns in Wadi Musa. From 1973, Manfred Lindner of Nuremberg, with the Jordanian Department of Antiquities, has studied various aspects of the ancient city as well as the graves, roads, flora and geology of the nearby Nabataean Petra suburb of Wadi Sabra (as-Sabra), where he discovered extensive copper smelting activities and surveyed the small theater there.[69] Lindner has also surveyed the Ad-Dayr ("The Monastery"). These surveys have since undergone many necessary revisions, the most recent of which was published by Judith S. McKenzie in 1990. McKenzie undertook extensive field work by recording the rock-cut façades and their moldings, and she made a comprehensive survey of tomb plans.

In 1991, the American Center of Oriental Research (ACOR) in Amman undertook the excavations of the Petra Church, under the direction of Kenneth Russell. These excavations have continued under the direction of Pierre M. Bikai and Zbigniew T. Fiema, and a shelter was constructed in 1997 over the area to protect its precious mosaics (Figure 1.27). In 1992, ACOR began the excavations of the Petra Ridge Church, under the direction of Patricia M. Bikai, and these excavations continue to the present time. In 1996, the preliminary investigation of the Colonnaded Street was conducted by Chrysanthos Kanellopoulos, architectural historian, and Zbigniew T. Fiema, archaeologist on behalf of ACOR. In 1997, ACOR conducted the actual fieldwork of the Roman Street in the Petra project. The project, directed in the field by Zbigniew T. Fiema, concentrated on exposing several shops, the

Monumental Stairway to the Upper Market and the sidewalk along the street. Following was the partial restoration of the uncovered structures, under the direction of Chrysanthos Kanellopoulos. Now joining these projects are the extensive Brown University, American excavations of the Petra Great Temple, which were initiated in 1993 and continue to the present time. Annual publications of these excavations have appeared in various locations (see the Site Bibliography in the introductory material).

Architectural remains now visible at Petra indicate a thriving city. However, despite almost 100 years of excavation, only one percent of the city has been investigated. Modern excavations, like those of Brown University, continue to increase our understanding of Petra and correct the work of earlier scholars. Future excavators will further interpret and evaluate what we have accomplished.

The Nabataeans were well known as merchants in the trade of oils, aromatics and spices and frankincense and myrrh from southern Arabia. By the second century BCE, they were in control of Red Sea coastal cities and were considered unwelcome competition by Ptolemaic shipping interests (Diodorus 3.43.5). Soon thereafter the expansionist Nabataeans established settlements on the lucrative trade route, dominating the passage from the Hejaz through Petra to Damascus and from Petra through the Negev to the Mediterranean port city of Gaza. Nabataean remains have been found in over 1000 sites in this area. In modern terms, at their height they controlled and colonized part of Syria, Jordan, the Israeli Negev, Sinai, parts of eastern Egypt and a northwestern section of Saudi Arabia.

Petra is most important as a testament to the dynamism of the human spirit. During the period the Great Temple was constructed, Nabataea enjoyed a prosperity never to be seen again in Petra. The Nabataean kings commissioned temples of worship, and master artists helped them embellish their city. They created a highly organized city that was a tangible expression of their fabled wealth and success. And in this they succeeded in creating a masterpiece!

It seems fitting to close this chapter with the Victorian traveler Dean J.W. Burgon's Newdigate Prize Poem, entitled "Petra."

It seems no work of Man's creative hand,
By labor wrought as wavering fancy planned;
But from the rock as if by magic grown,
Eternal, silent, beautiful, alone!
Not virgin-white like that old Doric shrine,
Where erst Athens held her rites divine;
Not saintly-grey, like many a minster fane,
That crowns the hill and consecrates the plain;
But rose-red as if the blush of dawn
That first beheld them were not yet withdrawn;
The hues of youth upon a brow of woe,
Which Man deemed old two thousand years ago,
Match me such a marvel save in Eastern clime,
A rose-red city half as old as Time.

---

# Endnotes

[1] This is a border town between Gaza and Egypt; it is now located in Israel.

[2] Founded by Alexander the Great in 332 BCE after he captured Egypt, Alexandria was the center of Ptolemaic-Hellenistic culture from 323 BCE until the time it was taken over by Rome in 30 BCE. It was the center of Arab, Greek and Jewish ideas. Ptolemy I (323-285) founded here the greatest library of all times, fabled to have 700,000 papyrus rolls. The library was lost in the fire when Caesar attacked the city in 48 BCE.

[3] Modern Jordan lies between the Levant and the Arabian Desert, Israel and the occupied West Bank to the west, Syria to the north, Iraq to the east and Saudi Arabia on the east and south. In area it is 96,188 km², and there are three main environmental climatic zones: the Jordan Valley, the mountainous Plateau where Petra lies and the eastern desert known as the Badia — about 75% of Jordan.

[4] A wadi is a river bed or valley created by river flow.

[5] The sources for the Jordan River are in the Syrian Anti-Lebanon Mountains, from which it flows south to 212 m below sea level to Lake Tiberias or the Sea of Galilee, and from there to its termination point in the Dead Sea. The Jordan Valley, however, continues on to the Wadi 'Araba.

[6] The Dead Sea is 75 km in length and varies from 6-16 km in width.

[7] Between 1934-1938, the American scholar, Nelson Glueck conducted surveys in the area. He excavated Khirbat Tannur, south of the Wadi al-Hasa, in 1937 and 1938 and Tall (Tel) al-Kheleifih, north of Aqaba, from 1938-1940. Both of these sites he dated between 25 BCE-125 CE, but Tall al-Kheleifih also has earlier deposits.

[8] This area is known as Ghor and is more fertile by far than the south, because it has a higher rainfall, fertile soil and a mild climate.

[9] With its deep, 1000 m valley, the Wadi al-Mujib forms a natural dividing point between Amorite Ammon in the north and the Moabite territory in the south.

[10] See the *Michigan Papyri* VIII, Papyri and ostraca from Karanis. Glen W. Bowersock reminded me that work was already underway in 107. This route largely follows the King's Highway, but in the south between Ash-Shawbak (Shobak) and Aineh, its course is further east.

[11] For Nabataean and Roman trade routes, see D.J. Johnson 1987, M.G. Raschke 1978, S. Sidebotham 1986 and J.I. Miller 1969.

[12] Strabo 16.4.24 states: "Now the loads of aromatics are conveyed from Leuce Come to Petra, and thence to Rhinocolura, which is in Phoenicia near Aegypt, and thence to the other peoples; but at the present time they are for the most part transported by the Nile to Alexandria; and they are landed from Arabia and India at Myus Harbour; and then they are conveyed by camels over to Coptus in Thebaïs, which is situated on a canal of the Nile, and then to Alexandria."

[13] Saba or Sheba was commercially strong, cf. I Kings 10, for the story of the Queen of Sheba's visit to Solomon. Its principal cities are San'a and Marib.

[14] The Dead Sea is approximately 407 m below sea level, and no plant or animal life can survive in it because of its high salt and mineral content.

[15] Much of Jordan has less than 200 mm annual rainfall.

[16] I am grateful to Zbigniew T. Fiema for this information.

[17] In 1963, 28 tourists were killed in a flash flood.

[18] All of these tombs were robbed out in antiquity.

[19] At Petra, the triclinium is a room with benches cut out of the living rock along three sides. These were used for relaxation, sitting or reclining on while dining. There are also biclinia, rooms with benches along two sides of the room. Both triclinia and biclinia were presumably used for banquets related to funerary rites.

[20] The original Nabataean paving of the Bab as-Siq has now been revealed by excavation, and the 2 m depth of debris covering the ancient road will be completely removed so that the original surface of the Nabataean roadway can be seen.

[21] A baetyl is a roughly shaped stone, which was held sacred and worshipped in a small shrine, because its origin was thought to be divine. Often meteorites were worshipped, for they were thought to come from a divine origin.

[22] These are either free-standing crenellations or, in Petra, more commonly in relief. They are characterized by having stepped sides like battlements, and they are often used to decorate Nabataean tombs. Because they are found in Assyria, they are often referred to as Assyrian crow-steps.

[23] The capacity of the Theater as reported by Browning (1995:138) is 4000. A. Segal (1995:101) places its capacity at 7000.

[24] The excavations have shown that this theater installation was created after a major Temple rebuilding in the early second century CE. It was not an original component of the Temple.

[25] These are not necessarily in chronological order.

[26] The accepted periods for these structures that have been agreed upon by scholars date the Qasr al-Bint, the Theater and the Al-Khazna to the reign of Aretas IV. The Triumphal Arch in front of the Agora is Trajanic in date (see Bowersock 1983.61, Starcky and Strugnell 1966 and Wright 1961a and b).

[27] Judith S. McKenzie's (1990) rigorous approach to the study of the architecture of Petra covers the most comprehensive analysis of the subject. Not only does McKenzie examine the façades at Petra, but she draws on comparative materials from Medain Saleh in Saudi Arabia and Alexandria in Egypt, and in her analysis of the wall paintings she uses Pompeiian comparative material as well. Nabataean architecture at Petra has also been researched by R.E. Brünnow and A. von Domaszewski (1904), W. Bachmann, C. Watzinger and T. Wiegand (1921), Peter J. Parr (1957-1996), G.R.H. Wright (1961-1985), Philip C. Hammond (1960-1996), Schmidt-Colinet (1980), Fawzi Zayadine (1974-1990), Rolf Stucky (1990-1995) and now by our Brown University team (see the Site Bibliography).

[28] This is a late Mesolithic culture named for its type site at Wadi an-Natuf in Palestine. The site's subsistence was hunting and gathering, although some communities had permanent villages.

[29] As used here, this term implies food production as well as the domestication of animals.

[30] This culture was Neolithic but had not yet produced pottery.

[31] As a historical source, the biblical story of Moses was probably written approximately in the seventh century BCE. The Exodus is dated ca. 1270 BCE, some 600 years before Edom can be thought of as a Kingdom!

[32] King Mesha ruled the small kingdom of Moab in the ninth century, from Madaba (Medaba), which King David had captured. King Mesha is credited with taking the region north of the Wadi al-Mujib, part of the Moab, from the Israelites. This is recorded on the Mesha Stele, also known as the Moabite Stone — a basalt slab 1 m (3 ft.) high, which is inscribed in Canaanite and dated to 850 BCE. The Ammonites took Madaba in ca. 165 BCE, but it was captured by John Hyrcanus I in ca. 110 BCE. John Hyrcanus II gave the city to the Nabataeans for their help in the recovery of Jerusalem. Madaba is known for its spectacular Byzantine mosaics, the most famous of which is the Madaba Map of Palestine dated to ca. 560 CE.

[33] It is identified with the biblical Selah (Sela) in the Old Testament and is positively referred to, in most cases, by numerous ancient authors including Eusebius, Josephus and Strabo — all of whom wrote many centuries after this period.

[34] The biblical 'Nabayot' (Genesis 25:13, 28:9, 36:3), or the people who are associated with Edom or Esau — the Nabaitaeans of Arabia — who battled against Ashurbanipal from 668-633 BCE, are not to be confused with the later Nabataeans.

[35] The Diadochs were the successors to Alexander the Great. It is still a matter of debate as to whether or not this report of Antigonus' raid was against people who were Nabataeans.

[36] It is not secure that this quote actually refers to Petra. Scholars have not agreed if the "Rock" referred to in this passage actually refers to Umm al-Biyara at Petra or to another site with a rock. Nonetheless, it is informative.

[37] For Mattathias' instructions to his sons see 1 Maccabees Chapter II.

[38] Antipater was forcibly converted to Judaism under John Hyrcanus' rule. His son was Herod the Great.

[39] This list of Nabataean kings is based on Zbigniew T. Fiema and R.N. Jones, *ADAJ* 1990.34:245.

[40] Aretas is the dynastic name of four known kings of Petra.

[41] See Meshorer 1975.16 ff. Meshorer describes this coinage of this monarch; he dates Obodas III from 62-60 BCE.

[42] I am grateful to Zbigniew T. Fiema for this correction; see his and R.N. Jones' contribution, *ADAJ* 34.

[43] The coinage of Aretas IV had widespread distribution. They have been found at Curium in Cyprus, at Dura-Europos in Syria and at Susa in Iran.

[44] (Meshorer 1975.48): (...for the life of Aretas, king of the Nabataeans, the lover of [his] people [and Shuqailat] / his sister, queen of the Nabataeans, and Malichus and Obodas and Rabbel and Phasael and Se'udat and Hagru, his children, and Aretas the son of Hagru, his grandson]...)

[45] In his correction of an earlier statement I had made, Glen W. Bowersock wrote in a personal communication: "This is too vague for a highly complex problem. All we know is that it probably was under Nabataean control near the end of Aretas' reign when Paul was there. We don't know when Damascus came back to the kingdom, nor what territories linked it to Nabataean possessions in the Hawran. I had thought that the return to Damascus came after the death of Philip the tetrarch in 34, but this need not be so. In 18, Germanicus and Piso had a grand dinner with Aretas, according to Tacitus, *Ann.* 2.57.4. Since Piso was governor of Syria, and Germanicus is attested in Cyrrhus and Palmyra around this time, I have begun to wonder whether the meeting with the Nabataean king was in Damascus. It is certain that the king would not have left his kingdom to receive these Romans. Cf. the Parthian monarch, Artabanus, who graciously consented at the same time to advance as far as the banks of the Euphrates to honor Germanicus. But he did not enter the Roman province."

[46] Herod Antipas (4 BCE-39 CE) was tetrarch of Galilee and the east Jordanian plateau. Herod Philip (4 BCE-34 CE) was the tetrarch of Batanaea, Trachontis, Aurantis and Iturea. Archeleus (4 BCE-6 CE) was the ethnarch of Samaria, Judaea and Idumaea.

[47] Glueck (1965:41) states that the Nabataean princess escaped to Machaerus and thereafter to Nabataea.

[48] Shuqailat is the favored name among Nabataean queens. Aretas IV married Shuqailat I (there is a misprint in Glueck 1965:10, which has Aretas I married to her), and Malichus II married Shuqailat II.

[49] See Lionel Casson's 1980 commentary in *CQ* 495-497.

[50] The Roman Empire was ruled by Tiberius from 14-37 CE, Gaius (Caligula) from 37-41 CE, Claudius from 41-54 CE, Nero from 54-68, Galba, Otho, Vitellius from 68-69 CE, Vespasian from 69-79 CE, Titus from 79-81 CE, Domitian from 81-96 CE, Nerva from 96-98 CE, Trajan from 98-117 CE and Hadrian from 117-138 CE.

[51] Zbigniew T. Fiema corrected my earlier statement by writing: "The governor of Arabia was...legatus *Augusti pro pretore* and the commander of Arabia's single legion."

[52] For Nabataean presence in the Decapolis cities, see Wenning's excellent article, 1992:79-99.

[53] As stated here, the significance of this archive has been suggested by Glen W. Bowersock (personal communication).

[54] Petra is identified in the Septuagint with the biblical Selah (in Hebrew) in Edom. This attribution is accepted by Eusebius (*Onomasticon* 36.13;142.7; 144.7) who identifies Petra with Selah Jokteel.

[55] In 132 CE, there is the Jewish revolt against Rome led by Bar Kokhba. Jerusalem is in Jewish hands. In 133, Hadrian built a Roman city on the ruins of Jerusalem and named it Aelia Capitolina.

[56] The Roman governor, T. Aninius Sextius Florentinus was buried in Petra ca. 127/130 CE, his tomb offers one good example.

[57] Glen W. Bowersock (1983.21) discusses Nabataean piracy.

[58] *Historia Rerum* XVII, 6. This is dated to 1144.

[59] Deforestation, leading to desertification and reduced productive land, continues to be an environmental threat — productive land has been reduced to desertification over the years.

[60] I am grateful to Glen W. Bowersock for bringing these extraordinary drawings to my attention.

[61] See Glen W. Bowersock, 1990b:309-320.

[62] See F. Kelly 1989, *National Gallery of Art,* p. 67. "For some modern observers Church's major Near Eastern paintings are less original and more conventional than his earlier masterpieces...But others, including 'El Khasne [Al-Khazna], Petra' (cat 46), are notable for their portrayal of scenes that were little if at all known in the Western world."

[63] I thank Glen W. Bowersock for this reference.

[64] Those interested in the various deities should refer to Sourdel 1952.

[65] But the excavator, Philip C. Hammond 1996:101-111, vehemently disagrees with this identification.

[66] Nelson Glueck 1965:60, Pl. 4, mistook the identity of at least one of the dolphins he found at Khirbat Brak; it is not a dolphin but an elephant! Could Al-'Uzza also have had the elephant sacred to her? If so, the Great Temple was probably dedicated to her worship.

[67] The Deutsch-Türkische Denkmalschutz-Kommandos.

[68] Al-Katute is the ridge on the south side of the city that rises behind the structures, including the Great Temple and the Colonnaded Street.

[69] In Robert Wenning's book, published in 1987, there are summaries of the excavations up to that time.

## CHAPTER TWO

# HISTORY
## OF THE
# BROWN UNIVERSITY
## EXCAVATIONS

BY
MARTHA SHARP JOUKOWSKY

*Figure 2.1. Bedouin workers excavating in situ column drum, 1997. Photograph by John Forasté.*

*Figure 2.2. Bedouin workers removing soil from Brian Stairway and Suleiman Column, 1997. Photograph by John Forasté.*

The Great Temple was first explored by R.E. Brünnow and A. von Domaszewski, but it was W. von Bachmann, in his revision of the Petra city plan, who postulated the existence of a 'Great Temple' aligned with the Colonnaded Street, lying on the hillside to the south. They speculated that the Temple was approached through a monumental propylaeum with a grand staircase leading into a colonnaded, terraced lower temenos, or sacred precinct. Another broad monumental stairway led to the Upper Temenos. At its center was the Temple, with a flight of stairs leading into it. While no standing structures were revealed before our excavations, the site was littered with architectural fragments, including column drums that were probably toppled by one of the earthquakes that rocked the site. Given the promise of the Great Temple precinct and its importance in understanding Petra's architectural and intercultural history, it is remarkable that its precinct remained essentially unexcavated[1] until 1993, when our Brown University investigations began.

## The Brown University Excavations

Long fascinated with the region — having visited Petra numerous times over a stretch of 30 years since the 1960s — and long interested in the Nabataeans and the Nabataean-Roman contact period, the criteria I used in selecting the site for excavation were largely due to the exceptional challenges it offered. I chose to excavate the Great Temple for the following interdependent research interests:

• There was the opportunity to define the Nabataean time period — a Nabataean model might be determined and explained.

• The site should provide an explanation of how and why the Nabataeans made the decision to build a monumental edifice at this site.

• This structure and its location should provide an important architectural component of the central metropolis of Petra.

• The definition of the Temple's function and its relationship to other significant structures within the city fabric might be determined.

• We would be able to determine the architectural styles employed.

• This was a spatially defined area — an isolated structure within the city fabric.

• The Temple and its precinct should reflect the socio-religious and economic interests of the Nabataean, Nabataean-Roman and perhaps Byzantine populations.

• It might be possible to excavate the site giving it as total a coverage as possible.

• The investigations could be undertaken with sample units providing data that could be defined.

• The size of the samples would be reliable representatives of the population. Sample sizes would be large enough to give a reliable measure of the smallest independent subclass of Nabataean cultural systems.

• And on a personal level, it might be excavated within my lifetime!

The Great Temple excavations have been under the sponsorship of Brown University and the auspices of the Jordanian Department of Antiquities, and they have been active from 1992-1997 (please refer to the Site Bibliography).

The Great Temple is sited on the north edge of the Al-Katute slope, rising to an elevation of 895 m above sea level. Its northern border parallels the Colonnaded Street, its south, the ridge of Al-Katute, and walls extend along its east perimeter delimiting it from the so-called 'Lower Market' and on the northwest from the 'Baths.' Its two great terraces overlook the Colonnaded Street and the Wadi Musa to its north, the Qasr al-Bint to its west and the Lower Market to its east. The site topography can be divided into three sectors: the Propylaeum, the Lower Temenos (which is approximately 8 m higher than the Colonnaded Street) and the Upper Temenos and the Temple (which rise some 6 m above the Lower Temenos).

## Identification

When we began our work in 1992, because of its location, I identified the project as the 'Petra Southern Temple;' it seemed logical, for the precinct was constructed to the south of the Colonnaded Street. In 1996, the structure was officially renamed the 'Great Temple' at the suggestion of many, including Ghazi Bisheh, Director of the Jordanian Department of Antiquities. The adjective 'Great' was originally used in 1921 by W. von Bachmann, who designated the area as the 'Great Temple.' In the intervening years from 1993-1996, the publications of these Brown University excavations have referred to either the 'Southern Temple' or the 'South Temple.'[2] The precinct, however, is now to be designated as the *Great Temple* of Petra. I beg the tolerance of the scholarly community, and hopefully no further confusion between names will take place.

## Background, Research Design and Documentation

In 1992, a five-year feasibility plan was submitted to the Jordanian Department of Antiquities. The plan was accepted; however, following established procedure, it was understood that each year the excavation permit had to be reapplied for and would be granted on an annual basis.

The Brown University surveys of the Great Temple have consisted of historical research, archaeological testing, laboratory analysis and report preparation. The first stage of the project involved documentary research, whose principal goal was to identify all recorded ancient and modern structures, features and activity areas located within the Great Temple precinct. This led to the development of a comprehensive field strategy, incorporating a broad coverage of the area in a physical sense, which also allowed the investigation of a range of potential research topics.

When we began our research we wanted to know answers to the "what," "where" and "when" of the Temple precinct and to understand the "how" and "why" of the processes that took place. Unfortunately, there have been few in-depth, detailed and systematic studies of the Nabataeans and the region they were known to control. Current archaeological research undertaken by a number of archaeological teams, however, is slowly beginning to give us some clues. The isolation of Petra and the definition of the Nabataean cultural systems in Petra, and most specifically those of the Great Temple alone, were viewed as a research objective. It was reasoned that the accomplishment of such an intensive study could begin to augment what was already known of the content and structure of Nabataean culture; this would offer additional clues and provide another benchmark for an understanding of Nabataean socio-religious and political ideas.

Several methods were used for charting the changes of culture systems within the site itself. Quantitatively, spatial-formal relationships could be structured around the architectural, artifactual and ecofactual records. We assumed that different sectors of the precinct would have served different tasks, and these, we also assumed, could be gleaned from the depositional, architectural, artifactual and ecological records. We reasoned that the spatial clustering of the artifact record set against the architecture and stratigraphy would reveal the archaeological structure and changes that took place within the cultural processes.

## Background

In preparation for the Petra excavations, the spring and early summer of 1993 were occupied with several interdependent tasks, including research design, formulation of field forms, tool acquisition and budget preparation. Finding additional consultants to serve on the team to help in monitoring our progress was also a top priority. Visits were made to review the plans for the excavation with Peter J. Parr[3] of the Department of Archaeology, University of London, on July 7-8, 1993. Although Peter J. Parr at that time was excavating at Tell Nebi Mend, Syria, he continued his interests in Petra and assured me of his advice. On July 11-12, discussions were also held with Jean-Louis Huot of the University of Paris I - Sorbonne. A number of helpful suggestions, beneficial to our projected plans, also resulted from these discussions.

In the beginning of our work in 1993-1994, surveys and excavations were divided among five complementary strategies: I. Survey, II. Excavation, III. Artifact and Ecofact Analysis — Data Collection and Sampling, IV. Conservation and Consolidation and

V. Site Deposition Analysis — Phasing. With the exception of V. Site Deposition Analysis, which concludes this chapter, each of these strategies will be briefly presented, after which summaries of the annual campaigns will be given.

Those systems we put in place in 1993 continue today to be an integral part of our research objectives. It will become clear that those site-specific excavation strategies created in 1993 were further developed in each of our five field campaigns.

## I. Surveying Strategy

Based on what was known before we undertook our survey in 1993, several plans were reviewed prior to the archaeological field season. The Bachmann map afforded what was presumed to be a fairly accurate depiction of the layout of structures along the Colonnaded Street, although in relation to the Great Temple itself, it was proven to be based on conjecture. A revised plan, originally drawn by Peter J. Parr and University College, London, published by Judith S. McKenzie (1990:Map 7),[4] indicated that the extant building elements of the city (a total of nine or 10 major structures) were located north and south of the Colonnaded Street and along the Temenos area of the Qasr al-Bint. The building plan clearly indicated that the Great Temple, lying to the south of the Colonnaded Street and to the southeast of the Temenos Gate, was very fragmentary. We quickly discovered that this plan was a pastiche of various periods and teams. We questioned which plans were based on the ground survey of the actual remains and which included hypothetical information. What was clear at that time was that all these plans indicated that the Great Temple precinct was in a position of paramount importance, but each plan suggested different sets of information. We could only assume that accurate survey data were lacking and that one of our missions would be to survey and accurately draw a new plan for the Great Temple site (Figure 2.4).

Petra site plans were supplemented by aerial photographs. In 1992 and 1993, before our excavations began, J. Wilson Myers and Eleanor E. Myers[5] conducted an aerial photographic balloon survey of the site.[6] With each successive season, we have continued to

extensively document the area with low altitude aerial photographic and photogrammetric coverage. In 1997, the National Park Service ran a Test Project at Petra. Led by Douglas C. Comer, this project established coordinates for the site with a global positioning system (GPS). Because the Great Temple was visible, these studies began the processing of radar-generated and related imagery. Additionally, geo-referencing was begun. The net result of such map research, as well as our own aerial photography, laser EDM (electronic distance measurement) surveys and the use of CADD (computer-aided design) programming, has produced one of the most detailed and accurate site-specific Petra maps for the archaeological record.

Our general approach to survey (and its primary objectives)[7] is to automate and integrate the collection of field data. We use a series of programs to chart and document the site, and the systems we deploy have proven so successful that they have been used as the model for other archaeological field operations. We utilize software packages that include a CADD program (MiniCad 6) and the COMPASS/ForeSight program, a survey data acquisition and plotting package developed at the University of Pennsylvania Museum. These software packages combined with our use of a Topcon laser transit, ensure the continuity of all our data files. Our system, therefore, is a combination of computer hardware (Macintosh laptop computers) and software that allows input, editing, storage, retrieval and display of spatially referenced data.

In 1993, once preliminary research and general site assessments were completed, one of the first and most critical tasks to be performed before excavation was the charting of master site plans and establishing Control Points. Utilizing the Topcon laser transit to establish elevations and distances, a topographic survey was initiated. Control Points had to be selected and tied into the known benchmarks on the Al-Katute ridge. On top of the east wall of the precinct, we established the Site Datum Point known as CP 103 with an elevation of 895.48 m; a second point was located to the south of the West Exedra wall, CP 104, which had an elevation of 884.34 m, and a third point, CP 10, was located at the top of the Stairs of the Propylaeum at an elevation of 878.73 m. Each of these points was clearly marked with cemented stakes and

*Figure 2.3. Loa P. Traxler, surveyor, 1995. Photograph by David L. Brill.*

have served our surveying needs since the inception of the excavations. Thus, all elevations listed in this report are referenced to these datum points.

A comprehensive grid system of nominally 10 m squares aligned north-south also served as a control for the excavations. Illustrated in Figure 2.5, this grid allowed us the flexibility to record architectural surface finds.

These data also appear in tabular database files to which other digital data, such as scanned images, may be added. These files can be viewed as displays or printouts according to the field researcher's needs. Thus, these programs provide a means for accessing data sets from a variety of sources. Additionally, their capability renders them an excellent tool for the storage, retrieval and interpretation of archaeological information. These surveys are the backbone of this excavation, for they have produced cumulative multidisciplinary data necessary for our research and long-term management of the site.

Data currently combined in this project include architectural plans, datum and sub-datum points, topographic features and trench maps with loci. The location of each trench and locus allows us the flexibility to determine

if the architecture is associated or not. For example, daily field data processing produces maps of each trench's characteristics, which then are documented the following day in the field, and significant features are recorded, measured, drawn and photographed. Copies of all of these maps have been turned over to the Department of Antiquities in Petra for their use as a reference tool.

In 1996, our voluminous multiple-year survey data files were converted to a new system — a most time-consuming undertaking, which involved the conversion of the COMPASS data files and the updating of the data collection program. The new program, known as ForeSight, developed by our surveyor, Paul C. Zimmerman (1994, 1996, 1997), is more versatile, speeds up results and is easier to manipulate.[8]

## II. Excavation

In 1993 and 1994, we partitioned the site and established the grid. The results of the topographic survey (Figure 2.4), provided the spatial control for the location of sampled units. Because we judged the same soil types were common to the surface of the precinct, we elected to sample its different parts to understand the potential variations for depositional distinctions between them. Logistically, each trench represented the major topographic and cultural areas — the Stairs of the Propylaeum, the Lower Temenos, the Upper Temenos and the Great Temple itself. Thus, a set of four excavation units in 1993 and nine in 1994 were originally selected from different areas of the Temple precinct.

In the first two seasons of excavation, units were thus selected from each part of the site ensuring an even coverage of a portion of each area. The sampling of artifactual and ecofactual materials was as complete as possible. The objective evaluation of the site density provided clues as to the intensity of activities in the precinct as a whole, as comparative deposition patterns became clearly differentiated. As activity loci and architectural components became functionally identified, our research plan was modified according to the locational context and our methodological frame of reference shifted. At that time, we thought we were able to define spatially the architectural characteristics of each area sampled, and as the work progressed,

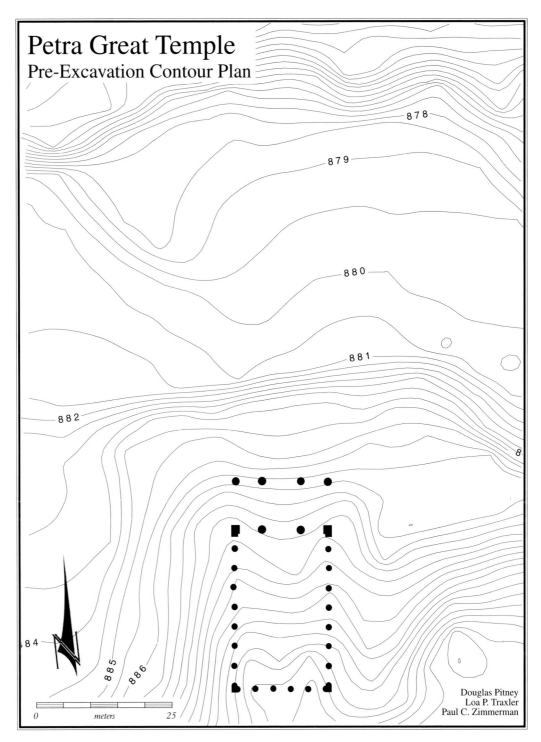

*Figure 2.4. Pre-excavation Contour Plan.*

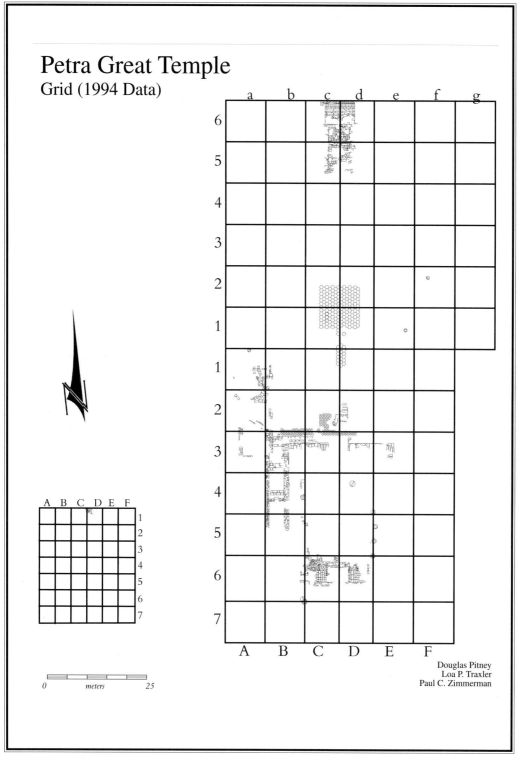

# Petra Great Temple
## Grid (1994 Data)

Douglas Pitney
Loa P. Traxler
Paul C. Zimmerman

*Figure 2.5. Grid (1994 Data).*

cultural features were mapped. But looking back on those days, some of our assumptions were faulty. The site held many surprises for us; it became abundantly clear that we had not excavated enough.

Trenches as well as 'Special Projects' (SP), localized test trench excavation areas, were also used to investigate architectural features. These were both numbered with Arabic numerals. In the beginning, the 10-x-10 m trench was utilized as our standard-sized trench, with a 0.25-0.30 m balk on all sides; thus, the actual area excavated was 9.40-x-9.40 m.[9] Each Control Point and trench had sub-datum points registered by EDM, and their elevations were marked on the nearest permanent feature.[10] In 1993, four trenches (Trenches 1-4) were excavated along the Temple Stylobate and Forecourt. In 1994, one trench was excavated in the West Exedra (Trench 5); the sixth was in the Lower Temenos (Trench 6), and Trench 7 was excavated in the Lapidary West (where architectural fragments were stored) to the west and beyond the formal confines of the Temple precinct. These were selected for the comparison of their stratigraphy, for we wanted to understand if a stratified, aligned systematic probability existed between them.[11] As architecture became revealed, trenches were positioned where more elucidation was warranted.

Excavations in all areas were highly systematic following many of the procedures outlined by Martha S. Joukowsky (1980), but as excavations progressed, systems were refined and updated.[12] All measurements were taken along the north-south, east-west axes of the trench sub-datum Control Points. When the depth of a trench became a deterrent to excavation, ramps or sand bags were used for access.

1993 was an investigative season. We attempted probability sampling of areas along the Great Temple Stylobate, so that we might develop a site typology in structural and functional forms that would be relevant for the entire range of the site's occupational history. We found, though, that our assumptions were based on incorrect information. Although we had been told by the Department of Antiquities that there had been no excavations at the site, we found the soils to the Temple North in what is now the Temple Forecourt to have been disturbed. Additionally, many blocks were marked with green, painted numbers. We later found that a German team had investi-

gated and surveyed the site, and J.P. Zeitler had published their results in *Syria* (1993). Thus, our initial season's survey and limited excavations to determine the density and distribution of activity loci awaited the 1994 season for confirmation of the results.

During the subsequent seasons of excavation from 1994-1997, 50 irregularly configured trenches have been excavated in different precinct sectors (see each respective trench plan, infra). Additionally, some 53 small-scale architectural soundings (special projects) have been made to locate columns and precinct walls and to confirm the results of the stratigraphic analyses.

Thus in successive seasons, we opened up large areas with excavation units that were contiguous to others researched in previous seasons. Once the annual excavations were completed, or at the end of each season, the architectural and stratigraphic units were placed into temporal phases, and an annual Great Temple Phasing Chart was created.

## Recording

In preparation, before work started at the site, weekly meetings were held by the staff at Brown University with Geoffrey Bilder, who was initially in charge of the computer systems and the conversion of the field forms into database programs. The formulation of field forms and reporting procedures were those that I had found successful in previous field campaigns. But if these were going to be converted to the computer, certain features had to be refined.[13] We worked with the field forms to find overlaps in the recording process, and I began the design of new forms in consultation with Erika L. Schluntz and Geoffrey Bilder. For ease in recording, we transferred the forms to a hand-held computer. When the machine crashed, we realized that we had to use traditional paper methods for field recording that could then be backed up by computer systems. The documentation systems on the CD-ROM of the Trench Reports should provide an overview of our field recording systems.

Petra Great Temple Site Codes were developed in 1993, using the Bachmann reconstruction of the precinct as a guide. The standard codes are as follows:

**Site:** [Petra Southern Temple] = **P/ST**.

We encode the Area as well as the grid alphanumeric designations. There are **five** main building **Areas** for the site, identified as follows:

> **P** — Propylaeum
> **LT** — Lower Temenos
> **UT** — Upper Temenos
> **T** — Temple
> **LW** — Lapidary West (added in 1994)

These are subdivided as follows:

**Propylaeum** (sing.) = **LT (Prop)** Stairs of the Propylaeum (*Area 1*) Elevation of the Colonnaded Street and lowest steps: 871 m; top of steps 878.73 m.

**Lower Temenos = LT** (*Area 2*) Elevation: 878.50 m.

> • Colonnade W = **LT (W)**; Hexagonal Court = **LT**, and Colonnade E = **LT (E)**.

> • There are two lateral **exedrae** (exedra, sing.) located in the Lower Temenos to the east and west of the stairways that lead from the Lower Temenos to the Upper Temenos. These have been assigned their own designations, or **LT (EE)** = East Exedra and **LT (WE)** = West Exedra.

> • Stairways = **LT**. As this is a large area, it has been excavated in several trenches/special projects. Thus, West Stairway = **(SW)**; East Stairway = **(SE)**.

**Upper Temenos = UT** (*Area 3*) Elevation: 884.41 m.

> Upper Temenos East = **UT (E)**;
> Upper Temenos North = **UT (N)**;
> Upper Temenos South = **UT (S)**;
> Upper Temenos West = **UT (W)**.

**Temple = T** (*Area 4*) Elevation: 885.91 m.

> The Temple, **T**, is subdivided into Temple North = **T (N)** (From the Stylobate to the Cella wall is the Pronaos.);
> Temple South = **T (S)** (Referred to as the 'Adyton.');
> Temple East = **T (E)**;
> Temple West = **T (W)**.

## A Note About the Naming of Great Temple Components

During the excavations conducted over the years, the Great Temple columns, antae and several stairways have been brought to light. Each column, anta and stairway has been assigned a locus number, by its trench or by its special project (SP) designation. Because there was no standard nomenclature that could easily be remembered by workers, staff and visitors, confusion about their positions resulted not only in field descriptions, but also in the field notebooks. One of us might be describing a column's position as "the fourth column on the Temple East from the East Anta from the north" or the same column as "the eastern fourth column from the south." Consequently, in 1994, I decided to identify these elements by assigning them names of staff and supporters of our work. Figure 2.6 identifies the columns, antae and stairways by their "names," and in the following text when describing an area, the "name" of the column, anta wall and stairway will also be used.

## Field Forms — Reporting Procedures

We have a total of eleven field forms for the Petra Great Temple excavations. These essential customized forms were developed, each with an address that inter-related one to the other so that a centralized network of information was created. Thus, each of these color-coded forms was designed to provide the field excavator and the entire team with information and insights allowing them to sequentially follow the work progress.

> • **Daily Field Form** to be filled out every day (white);
> • **Locus Form** to be filled out for every locus (yellow);
> • **Burial Form** (blue);
> • **Number Log** to be updated daily (pink) — this provides the documentation for each of the applications that had taken place in the field;
> • **Artifact Field Form** a special field form to be used when a special find is

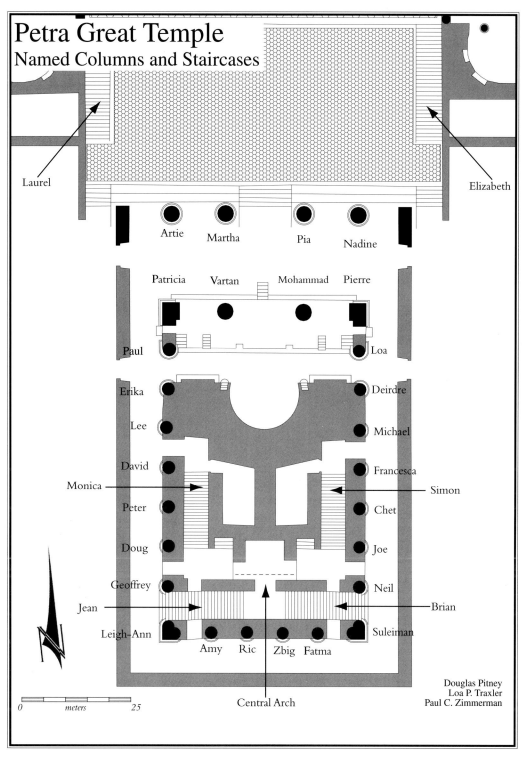

**Figure 2.6.  Named columns and staircases.**

excavated (green), and
• **Architectural Fragment Form** (white).

There are also **Special Finds** 'tickets' (orange), which accompany every small find to the catalog. In addition, there are six computerized artifact forms that are converted for computer input: for the general Catalog and for the Lamps, Glass and Coin Catalogs.

*Figure 2.7. Josh Bell and Lawrence Sisson excavating the Lower Temenos Colonnade, 1995. Photograph by David L. Brill.*

For artifact groups there is the Grosso Modo Form. There is a also a computer-generated Bag List Form. (More will be said about the find forms in Chapter 6.)

Although these systems have been in place since 1993, they have been refined over the years and have helped our researchers be more productive. Our field recording led to unprecedented levels of efficiency as we expanded our scope of excavation. I manage a team that maintains these recording systems as they evaluate changes and problems in the archaeological record. The greatest asset of the systems in use is the consistency of reporting.

A word should be said about the **sequence number** (seq. no.), for it is allocated as a distinct serial number to each form used,

thereby tracing the sequence of the excavation and recording as data is recovered. Every record carries its own sequence number that is also a discrete (i.e., not to be repeated) field number given to every Daily Field Form, locus, artifact or collection container. The Number Log, which has its own sequence number, is the log for these sequence numbers that follows the work as it progresses.

Once processing records are compiled in the field, they are edited, saved in the Macintosh hard drive memory and backed up with floppy disks and Zip drives.[14] Several printers are used; we also utilize an optical scanning device, which works with our printers for adding photographs[15] and drawings to our reports and catalogs.

The field methods and recording systems employed were those the field director has used successfully over the years. Sections, plans, copious field notes, phasing charts and computer systems allowed for the control over each unit of excavation, as well as horizontal and stratigraphic position of individual artifacts. The result of utilizing this methodology has been the ability to coherently discuss the nature of these sites both in terms of loci (generally the smallest unit) or in terms of larger features and architectural components and their largest horizontal units.

## III. Artifact and Ecofact Analysis — Data Collection and Sampling

Artifacts represent different sets of populations. Not only did we want to know where and when artifacts were made, used and disposed of, but we also wanted to know their inter-relationships and the changes they underwent in relation to formal, temporal and spatial dimensions. Beyond this we wanted to identify their physio-chemical properties.

Portable artifacts were photographed *in situ*, and they then were taken to the field laboratory at the J.L. Burckhardt Archaeological Center for processing — washing, sorting, counting, analyzing, detailed recording and temporary storing. After these artifacts had been fully documented, the artifacts for the catalog were cleaned, processed and, at the close of the season, deposited with the Department of Antiquities in Petra. The remaining artifacts and smaller architectural

*Figure 2.8. Deirdre G. Barrett, cataloger, and Christian Augé, numismatist, examining coins, 1997.*

fragments were replaced on the site and reburied.

*Artifact Recording.* In the field, the trench supervisor presorted bulk finds by material (i.e., stone, bone, glass, metal and pottery) into color-coded containers. These buckets were also used for construction materials such as tiles, which were resorted, classified and counted in a special area.[16]

Given the range of variability of the collected artifacts and ecofacts, interdependently, in 1993-1994, a provisional typology was drawn up reflecting the taxonomic variations found through survey and preliminary excavation. I identified this as 'Grosso Modo,' implying that it was to be an unbiased, across-the-site recording procedure to chart the full range of materials, including ecofacts. If there were to be formal distinctions between phases or loci, within trenches or between them, this system would capture the quantitative populations of items and might give us clues as to the depositional history of the site. We assumed that this data would help us understand the historicity of the areas excavated as well as provide a key to the functional and cultural progression of the areas under scrutiny. From the stratigraphy, it seemed likely that there were internal variations particularly in the use and reuse of each area. If we could correlate the distribution of the cultural materials, we could gain a better understanding of the various activities conducted in each area. Additionally, the dependent relationships between parts of the artifact repertoire could be better understood.

*The Catalog: Special Finds.* Special finds were not placed into field containers, but were measured *in situ*, recorded on the Grosso Modo Form and then bagged separately and taken directly to the cataloger, who annotated each special find with a detailed description,[17] sketch and photograph. Objects selected for cataloging were numbered according to season and material and then assigned a serial number. Thus, 93-P-103 indicates that the artifact was unearthed in 1993, that its material was pottery and that it was the 103rd pottery artifact registered. In a few cases, joins between fragments were found, so one of the two assigned artifact numbers was deleted, and the fragments were listed together as one number. (This change of number was noted in the catalog.[18]) Coins were differentiated from metals and were labeled with a "C" (i.e., 94-C-1), whereas other metal objects were labeled with an "M" (i.e., 94-M-33). The catalog numbers were also recorded on the appropriate sequence sheet within the field notebook as well as in the catalog log in each trench field notebook.

For the field collection of pottery, bone, stone, shell, stucco, glass,[19] wood and metal, Grosso Modo evolved. From its initial predefined template, it has been upgraded over the years.

Thus, Grosso Modo was used to capture the distribution, form, function (when known) and structure of the population of all portable artifacts, with the exception of the catalog, architectural fragments and glass: each of which had its own database. Almost all aspects of fieldwork were affected by computer technology at the most basic level. The computer promises to allow the archaeologist to effectively sift and organize the mountains of data that is accumulated during a typical excavation. At the Great Temple Excavations we record the particulars of hundreds of thousands of architectural fragments, ceramic remains and small finds. Our interpretation of the site can only be accomplished through the careful analysis and comparison of this data.

A database computer program was used for their inventory, listing the artifact's material, function, shape and, whenever possible, its date of manufacture. The database allowed study of the artifact assemblage by the production of summary tables, study and graphs.

For software we have used FileMaker Pro to create the relational database. In our five years

of excavation, this database has grown to include a total of 115,742 objects, of which 90,793 (or 78%) are ceramics. We have been able to analyze the distribution of fields by setting them against the stratigraphy and phasing of the excavations. This database, about which more will be discussed in Chapter 6, has served as an indispensable tool.

*Pottery.* Although earlier excavations had published their ceramic analysis, we elected to compare our ceramics with those recovered from the contexts closest to the Great Temple. The Az–Zantur excavations, undertaken since the late eighties by Rolf Stucky of the University of Basel, Switzerland, are located on the hilly rise just to the southeast of the Great Temple. These excavations have yielded a stratified, stylistic ceramic sequence that has been captured by Stephan G. Schmid (1995a, 1995b, 1996) for the fine wares and by Yvonne Gerber (1995) for the plain wares. It is these two researchers who have developed a regional chronology for ceramic stylistic characteristics. We asked them to serve as consultants and to study the ceramics we identified as coming from important loci, which they have done since the beginning of our work. Clearly, the pottery characteristics that have been collected over the years in the Grosso Modo database have been analyzed by multiple factors, but

***Figure 2.9.** Artemis A. W. Joukowsky, photographer. Photograph by John Forasté.*

these factors are not as refined in their analysis as those given to the special loci of pottery by Schmid and Gerber.[20]

*Architectural Fragments.* It was assumed that we would be overwhelmed by our architectural fragment recovery — so characteristic of Petra sites. However, we did not find this to be the case, with the exception of decorative architectural fragments used for the embellishments of capitals and entablatures. Elements of carefully carved, floral capitals abounded with a rich and lively ornamentation of acanthus leaves interspersed with vegetal elements, including detailed renditions of pomegranates or poppies, pine cones, hibiscus petals and vines. Not only were these elements found carved in limestone, but many were recovered in plaster. Often they were found to be painted, and in a few cases, gold leaf had been applied to their surfaces. The deeply incised ornamentation clearly demonstrated the Nabataean aesthetic sense for light and shadow. The painted elements were striking for their coloration, which in many cases was what we would call "gaudy." What was clear was that each of these architectural details had to be documented, and an architectural fragment database evolved, which included the description and dimensions of each architectural fragment — those of particular interest were surveyed, photographed and drawn.[21] This Architectural Fragment Database was converted to FileMaker Pro in 1997. The results of this study are presented in Chapter 6.

Analysis was made of the preserved architectural elements, including the sandstone column drums lying on the site (which in more than a few instances obstructed our analysis of the area). In the main these were elements of Nabataean construction — isodomic, ashlar sandstone blocks with the characteristic oblique, 45°, sometimes coarse surface dressing. The *in situ* positions of thousands of architectural components were recorded, numbered, cataloged, photographed and drawn, and those that had collapsed onto other architectural components were re-erected and consolidated, if we knew where they belonged. If we had no indication of where they originated, they were removed to prepared lapidaries.[22] The east Temple Porch column collapse was left on the site by design, although this fall prevented our investigation of the east Temple Forecourt. (The measurements

of the Temple Porch columns can be found on the CD-ROM under Upper Temenos.)

*Ecofactual data and analysis.* The study of soils, pollen and animal remains was also used to understand the ways the Nabataeans and their successors participated in the ecosystem. (Peter Warnock undertook this study and he reports on its findings in Chapter 3.)

Thomas R. Paradise of the University of Hawaii has long been interested in the geology of Petra. We asked Tom to help us understand the geologic formation of the area as well as the weathering patterns of the region and the quarrying of nearby sites that might have been used by the Temple architects. (The results of his analyses have been included in Chapter 3.)

Putting theoretical interests aside, I selected flexible field procedures that I thought would provide data relevant to a number of problems. I knew that research interests would be broadened as our work continued, and to identify the cultural processes involved, I would have to make additional efforts to work on the development of other, new processes. From the beginning of our work, I have been concerned that the methodologies I have instituted are not adequate to supply facts pertinent to the data — but that is the underlying fear of archaeology as a discipline.

## IV. Conservation and Consolidation

Conservation involves the analysis, treatment and preservation of the Great Temple. It is hoped that we have helped to preserve this monument and its precinct, for we have routinely maintained records of both the condition and treatment of the various sectors of this site that we have participated in recovering.

These Brown University excavations uphold the principles put forth by the International Council on Monuments and Sites (ICOMOS) and the International Committee on Archaeological Heritage Management (ICAHM) Charter,[23] the 1966 Venice Charter, the Hague Convention and the tenets of the 1956, 1970 and 1985 UNESCO Conventions.[24] We adhere to field treatment that is *safe* and *reversible* — that is, anything that is done must be capable of being undone (Joukowsky 1980.246).

*Figures 2.10 and 2.11. West Stairway (Laurel Stairway) before consolidation, 1996, and after consolidation, 1997.*

Our archaeological investigations of the Great Temple are important in increasing our knowledge of the past. However, they also have produced serious side effects by exposing the friable, sandstone and limestone structural elements to the environment and vastly increasing the rate of their deterioration. Salts play a key role in the deterioration of elements. They set in motion a chain of events. The stone reacts and expresses its reaction in a number of ways, the least of which is exfoliation.

From the beginning, the fundamental philosophy of the Petra Great Temple excavations has been that the site is a fragile and nonrenewable resource that would require protection. One of our concerns before excavation was undertaken was that we would do everything possible for the consolidation of the site while the excavations were in progress. It should be made clear that we have not undertaken architectural restoration, in its true sense — restoration awaits further excavation and the expertise of an architectural historian. The measures we have taken are geared only to the reversible preservation of the structural integrity of the precinct. Exposure of the architectural features has been of serious concern, for the site is susceptible to the havoc created by heavy rains and earth tremors. This has been acknowledged and instituted by the incorporation of several additional consolidation procedures that have become part of our research design.

Approval to carry out conservation was vigorously supported by the Department of Antiquities of the Hashemite Kingdom of Jordan. Aware of the threats caused by winter rains and earthquakes, Ghazi Bisheh, Director of the Department of Antiquities, was anxious to have consolidation carried out during the excavation or as soon as possible after the close of the excavation season. During our annual excavations, consolidation plans were undertaken, and those measures that interfered with the excavation process were postponed until the excavations had concluded. Annual measures were put forward to the Jordanian Department of Antiquities, and all procedures were discussed; all problems were addressed, and most of the time, solutions were found.

Whenever possible, an experienced architect, May Shaer, and an experienced conservator, Zaki Aslan, also supervised the consolidation of the Temple architecture. (The involvement of all of these parties was fully endorsed by the Jordanian Department of Antiquities.) In 1996, Paul S. Fay envisioned a more extensive, organized plan for the consolidation of the Great Temple architecture, which has been ongoing under the expert guidance of Dakhilallah Qublan and some 20 local workmen. Their work has been fully supported by the Jordanian Department of Antiquities.

We have also made several studies of consolidants[25] for the conservation and restoration of standing structures. We have diagnosed a wide variety of sensitivities, for example, to slow this process of sandstone and limestone deterioration. We have employed certain conservation measures either simultaneously with the excavation or during the post-excavation season. With this in mind, yearly conservation surveys of the excavated portions of the Temple have been carried out with a view to preserving and restoring various architectural features.

Now that all the Temple columns have been located, their reversible re-erection (no mortar is used between the drums) has to be undertaken. However, the columns in the opening of the West Exedra have been restored with mortar, because they were *in situ* or collapsed in an order that could be restored. Using a tested mortar, which in composition is similar to the original Nabataean mortar, we have consolidated architectural elements — the aforementioned columns and walls that have been imperiled both from 2000 years of erosion and by recent excavations.

Applications have been made to the World Monuments Fund, which has granted us two awards expressly for site preservation, conservation and consolidation. The Great Temple Consolidation Project was made possible in part by a grant from the Samuel H. Kress Foundation and the American Express Company through World Monuments Watch, a program of the World Monuments Fund. These funds were matched several times over by special subventions through Brown University. Briefly stated, budget constraints forced us to be selective in what we could undertake.

The protective fencing that was placed around the Temple in 1995 had to be increased in length in 1996 for the site's protection and extended even more in 1997. In addition,

63

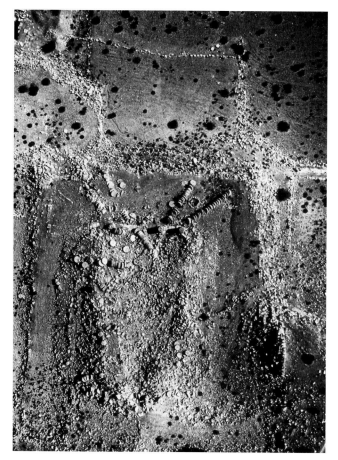

*Figures 2.12 and 2.13. Aerial views of the Petra Temple site pre-excavation, 1992. Top, drawing by Amy E. Grey. Bottom, photograph by J. Wilson Myers and Eleanor E. Myers.*

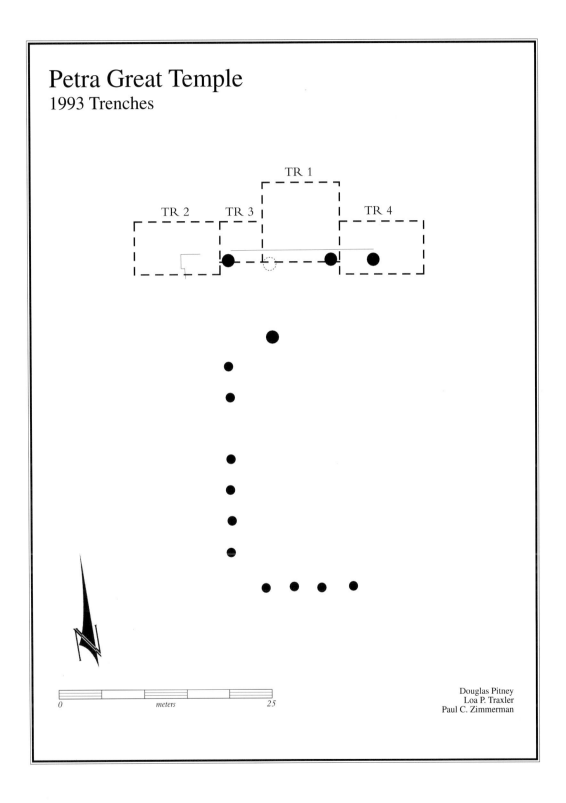

**Petra Great Temple**
1993 Trenches

*Figure 2.14. 1993 Trenches.*

continuous excavation requiring that certain trenches be left open from season to season, creates safety hazards for the numerous visitors to a site such as Petra. In order to insure tourist safety, we thought it essential to partition off opened trenches and stairways.

Keeping our strategy in mind, we now turn to an appraisal of our annual field campaigns.

The following discussion summarizes the annual investigations of the past five years. Each year lists the staff, the goals of the season, the results, a summary of the catalog and the consolidation measures that were put in place. A list of publications concludes each annual summary. Projects undertaken between excavation seasons are also given. Specific trench reports can be referenced on the CD-ROM.

## 1993 — First Year

The long hours of research, including map study and extensive library research, planning and consultation described in the previous section, took place before the 1993 excavation.

1993 Excavation

The first year of Brown University archaeological survey and excavation of the Great Temple at Petra, Jordan, was conducted under the auspices of the Jordanian Department of Antiquities from July 23 to August 25, 1993 (please refer to Figure 2.14 for the position of trenches during this first season).

The Great Temple was opened to explorations in 1993, consisting of historic research, archaeological testing by the excavation of the Temple Stylobate (Trenches 1-4) and the examination of other architectural components, such as the Stairs of the Propylaeum and *in situ* features in the Lower Temenos. Fieldwork also consisted of field reconnaissance, site survey and mapping the ancient landscape and its drainage. Additionally, Ricardo J. Elia, a consultant for the Great Temple expedition, spent two weeks examining the questions of site preservation and management.

## 1993 Staff

The staff was comprised of Martha S. Joukowsky, Director; Amy Grey, Assistant Director and Draftsperson; Artemis A.W. Joukowsky, Administrator; Douglas Pitney, Engineer- Architect-Surveyor; Geoffrey Bilder, Computer Analyst; Pia Ward, Photographer; Senior Archaeologists, Erika L. Schluntz, David Thorpe, Meredith Chesson, Nadine Shubailat, Elizabeth A. Smolenski, and Archaeological Assistants, Elizabeth E. Payne and Peter G. Lund.

Great appreciation must be extended to Safwan Tell, Director of the Jordanian Department of Antiquities, for his enthusiastic reception of our project. Suleiman Farajat conscientiously served as the resident representative of the Jordanian Department of Antiquities. With us daily on site, he contributed faithful and effective support and was a pleasure to work with in every sense.

## 1993 Goals

The goals of the 1993 season were to:

• Investigate and assess the nature, extent and depth of deposit;

• Identify specific areas of the Great Temple precinct;

• Provide recommendations for the management of cultural resources;

• Assess the potential of the site for further research and to recommend, if warranted, an additional multiyear excavation and research project, and

• Interpret the Petra Great Temple through publication.

## 1993 Results

Once site datum and sub-datum points were established, the topographic survey (Figure 2.4) and the *in situ* positions of architectural components were acquired in relation to set points with absolute elevations. (These architectural components along with the positions of 1993 trenches can be seen in Figure 2.14.) A grid system was established across the site, and excavations were conducted in accordance with this grid, with maps generated on various scales of 1:100 and 1:50 m.

A detailed archaeological site plan was compiled to include standing features, such as

# GREAT TEMPLE
# 1993 TRENCHES EXCAVATED

| Trench | Location | Position | N–S by E–W Dimensions (m) | Excavator(s) |
|--------|----------|----------|---------------------------|--------------|
| 1 | Upper Temenos | Temple Forecourt | 9-x-9 | Schluntz |
| *SP 4* | Upper Temenos | Canalization System | 1-x-1.5 | Schluntz |
| 2 | Upper Temenos Temple | Stylobate West | 6-x-10 | Smolenski Thorpe |
| 3 | Upper Temenos | Stylobate Center West | 4.5-x-5 | Joukowsky, M. |
| 4 | Upper Temenos | Stylobate East | 4-x-10 | Shubailat |
| — | Upper Temenos Temple | Porch Columns | — | Payne |

fallen columns and walls. It was ascertained at that time that the Great Temple and its precinct approximately covered some 7000 m² — a north-south length of 113 m-x-an east-west width of 55.5 m. In 1993, the four main areas were identified, from north-to-south: 1) the Propylaeum, 2) the Lower Temenos, 3) Upper Temenos with 4) the Great Temple.

## 1993 Propylaeum

The Stairs of the Propylaeum, leading up to

*Figure 2.15. Canalization, Upper Temenos, 1993.*

the Great Temple precinct from the Colonnaded Street, were cleaned and the lowest courses were consolidated. In total, these stairs measure 17.66 m in length. They appear to have been constructed at least three times. The lowest portion of steps abutting the Colonnaded Street measure 7.24 m in length and 5.6 m in width. The middle stair portion measures 6.67 m in length, and the upper portion, which is in a very poor state of preservation, measures approximately 5.4 m in length. From the initial analysis it was ascertained that these stairs were constructed at a later phase than the Great Temple. They were positioned at an oblique angle to the street; the lowest stairs also appeared to have been modified when the Colonnaded Street was constructed later than 76 CE.[26]

## 1993 Lower Temenos

We posited that the original large ashlar wall (the retaining wall for the Lower Temenos), positioned to the west of the Stairs of the Propylaeum, was synchronous with the building of the Temple but that it was abutted and modified by the insertion of this later stairway and was not bonded to it. We further speculated that the original access into the

*Figure 2.16. 1993 Brown University Excavation Team.*

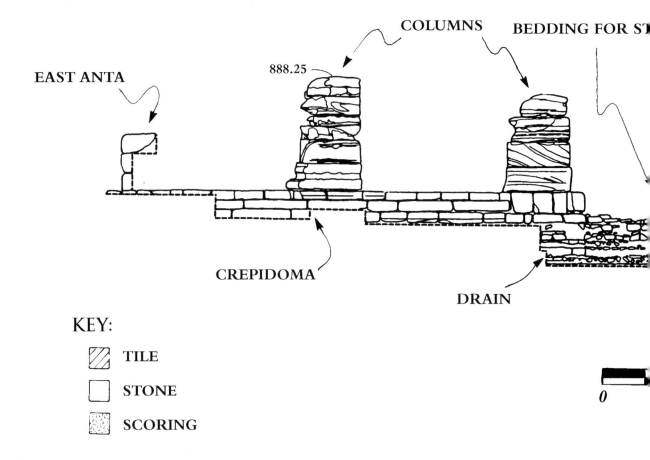

COLUMNS     BEDDING FOR ST

EAST ANTA

888.25

CREPIDOMA

DRAIN

KEY:

▧ TILE

☐ STONE

▨ SCORING

0

*Figure 2.17. Temple Stylobate and Porch columns. Drawing by Amy E. Grey.*

Temple precinct from the main artery of the city would be found when the Propylaeum entrance underwent extensive excavation.

## 1993 Upper Temenos

Of great interest under the Upper Temenos of the Temple itself was what was initially thought to be a four-branched Subterranean Canalization System (Figure 2.15). This was positioned under the floor of a disturbed portion of the Temple Forecourt Hexagonal Pavement in Trench 1. One branch was located to the north, another to the west and the others to the southeast and southwest. Constructed with five to six courses of ashlar blocks, they could be seen to extend to a distance of more than 5 m in each direction, and the southwest branch took a dramatic curve and sloped downward to what appeared to have been a stepped area. At these distances, collapse obstructed further investigation of this feature. Unfortunately, time restrictions during the 1993 season precluded our further study of

this area. (This feature is reported by Elizabeth E. Payne in Chapter 4.)

## 1993 Great Temple

Also in the Upper Temenos and on the Temple Porch, modest excavations were conducted along the north Great Temple Stylobate and Podium. These consisted of four irregularly sized trenches (Trenches 1-4), positioned between fallen column drums so that the character of the Temple Stylobate and its founding courses might be ascertained. Figure 2.17 shows the position of these trenches and what was then known about the position of the Temple Porch columns. With the excavation of these trenches, we were able to obtain more precise information regarding the plan of the Temple and gain a better understanding of its architectural components. From our excavation of the east-west Porch Stylobate and crepidoma or Podium, the Temple Stylobate was found to measure approximately 28 m (east-west), and the *in situ*

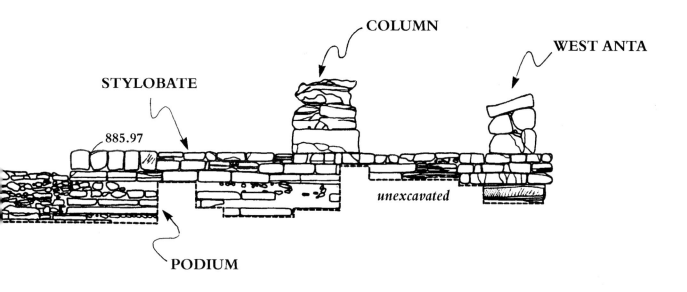

width of the limestone blocks was found to be 2.13 m. We posited that the length (north-south) of the Temple itself was 42 m, if not more. The bottom of the crepidoma and Podium was reached at approximately 1.5 m below the Stylobate edge at the northwest Temple corner. There we discovered the Great Temple Forecourt Hexagonal Pavement, consisting of small hexagonal pavers (Figure 2.18).

Our preliminary analysis was that the Great Temple was tetrastyle in antis, with widely spaced (7.1 m) central columns at the entrance, with the two end columns located 5 m to the east and west, respectively, and with anta walls at an approximate distance of 4.4 m enclosing them. The original stairway constructed up to the Stylobate from the Upper Temenos measured 4.5 m in width (its original length could not be determined), and it accessed the level of a broad Pronaos, measuring some 6.6 m in depth.

The interior Temple measurements were approximate: from the Pronaos columns to the columns in the rear, its north-south length was measured to be 28 m-x-18 m in width. To the south at the end of the building were six columns, and eight were located along each of its east and west flanks. These columns were smaller in diameter (1.20 m) than those of the Temple Porch or Pronaos. (Of the 22 columns

that hypothetically decorated the Cella, only 12 were known by the end of the 1993 season from their original *in situ* positions.)

From our measurements of the Temple Porch columns (the shaft plus the base and the capitals recovered), they originally stood 15-16 m in height. Added to this would have been the superstructure, including the entablature (i.e., the architrave, frieze and cornice) and the pediment. Given this information, we hypothetically placed the height of this colossal edifice to approximately 19-20 m. Unfortunately, there was no evidence to reconstruct the pediment and the entablature of the Temple Porch.[27]

## 1993 Catalog

There were only five artifacts that were considered to be of quality that were cataloged in 1993: a partial Latin marble inscription, a blue-green faience bead, a polished limestone pendant, an iron clamp and a bronze palette. These can be referenced in the Catalog in Chapter 6 or on the CD-ROM.

As for the processing of artifacts, once the Grosso Modo system was established, 7023 items were classified, of which 6211 (88%) were pottery fragments. The number of architectural fragments processed was 697.

*Figure 2.18. Temple Forecourt showing placement of Canalization System (center), 1993.*

## 1993 Field Conservation

The analysis, treatment and hoped-for preservation of the Temple Stylobate was undertaken in the field to ensure the survival of parts of its ashlars. Special thanks were due to the Jordanian Department of Antiquities, for they supplied us with a trained restorer for this undertaking.

## 1993 Publication

I published the results of the 1993 excavations in several periodicals. Jordanian journalist Rami Khouri published "Results of First Year Dig," in the *Jordan Times*, and J.P. Zeitler published the results of the German survey in *Syria*. (Please refer to the Site Bibliography.)

## At Home 1993-1994

Planning for the 1994 season consumed the fall of 1993 and the winter of 1994. Articles were submitted for publication; a number of papers were presented at scholarly conferences, and there was revision of special reporting systems, such as field forms and Grosso Modo input forms. Special instructions were drawn up for field supervisors to achieve standardized completion of all field forms. A great deal of energy was also put towards the listing of architectural fragments by trench (a system we later discarded in favor of a comprehensive database).

## 1994 — Second Year

The second year of archaeological survey and excavation continued to be conducted under the auspices of the Jordanian Department of Antiquities, Safwan Tell, Director, as part of an ongoing Brown University research project. These archaeological investigations were undertaken from June 15 to August 15, 1994. Additional time was spent both on site and in Amman at the American Center of Oriental Research, where we presented the season's results at a public lecture.

Please refer to Figure 2.20 for the 1994 trench plan, and the excavation plan is found in Figure 2.19.

## 1994 Staff

The staff was comprised of Martha S. Joukowsky, Director; Artemis A.W. Joukowsky, Administrator and Photographer; Erika L. Schluntz, Assistant Director; Douglas Pitney, Engineer, Chief Architect-Surveyor; Loa P. Traxler and Paul C. Zimmerman, Architect-Surveyors; Geoffrey Bilder, Computer Analyst; Michael F. Slaughter, Photographic Recorder and Photo Developer; Leigh-Ann Bedal, Ceramic Analyst and Archaeologist; Kathleen Mallak assisted by Madelaine Parr, Finds Recorder; Karen Jacobsen, Draftsperson; Peter Nalle, Mining Engineer; Senior Archaeologist, Peter J. Parr, with Elizabeth E. Payne, Gyles J. Austin, Heather Beckman and Alexandra R. Retzleff, and volunteers, Margaret Nalle, Kate Patrecci, Francesca Bennett, Marilyn C. Greenleaf, Mary-Kay Hunt and Betsy and Michael Alderman. Besides Peter J. Parr, Great Temple Consultants in 1994 included Christian Augé, numismatics, and Peter Warnock, botanical materials analysis. Again, we were fortunate to have Suleiman Farajat serve as the Jordanian Department of Antiquities Representative.

## 1994 Goals

The Great Temple had been opened to exploratory research in 1993, and these investigations continued in 1994 with historic research and archaeological testing by the survey and excavation of several Temple areas, such as the Propylaeum and other *in situ* features in the Lower Temenos. Field research also consisted of reconnaissance and analysis of the ancient landscape and ancient and contemporary drainage problems.

The goals of the 1994 season were to:

• Clear the Great Temple precinct of more earthquake debris and excavate and clarify its architectural plan;

• Investigate and assess the nature, extent and depth of the stratigraphy within the Canalization System, the Lower Temenos, the West Exedra and the Lapidary West;

• Provide a working plan of the Great Temple design by survey;

• Prepare the site for further research and excavation, and

Petra Great Temple
1994 Overall Excavations

0      *meters*      25

Douglas Pitney
Loa P. Traxler
Paul C. Zimmerman

*Figure 2.19. 1994 Overall Excavations.*

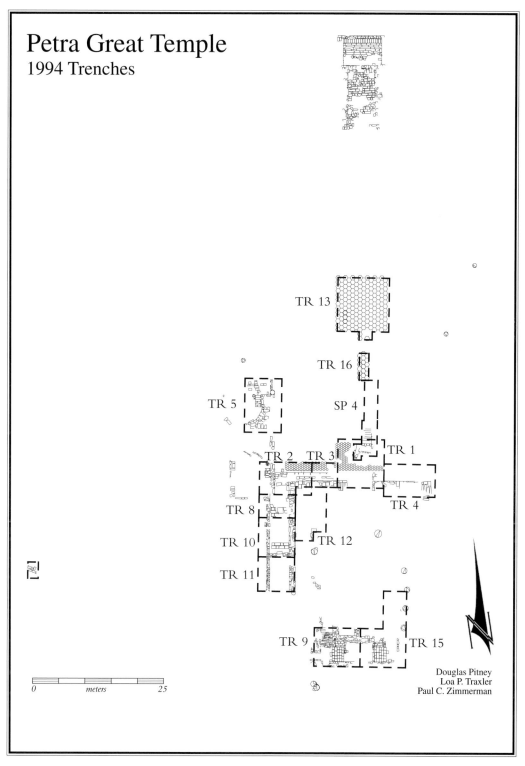

# Petra Great Temple
## 1994 Trenches

TR 13

TR 16

TR 5

SP 4

TR 2    TR 3    TR 1

TR 8    TR 4

TR 10    TR 12

TR 11

TR 9    TR 15

0    meters    25

Douglas Pitney
Loa P. Traxler
Paul C. Zimmerman

*Figure 2.20. 1994 Trenches.*

## GREAT TEMPLE
## 1994 TRENCHES EXCAVATED

| Trench | Location | Position | N–S by E–W Dimensions (m) | Excavator(s) |
|---|---|---|---|---|
| — | Propylaeum | Steps | 20-x-6 | Joukowsky, M. |
| 7 | Lapidary West | West of Temple | 2-x-3 | Retzleff |
| 5 | Lower Temenos | West Exedra | 7-x-10 | Beckman Retzleff Schluntz |
| 6 | Lower Temenos | Center | 9-x-4 | Payne |
| 13 | Lower Temenos | Center | 10-x-10 | Joukowsky, M. |
| 2 | Upper Temenos | Stylobate West | 6-x-10 | Schluntz |
| SP 4 | Upper Temenos | Canalization System | 4-x-2 | Payne |
| 8, 10, 11 | Temple West | West Walkway | 18.5-x-7 | Slaughter Joukowsky, A. |
| 12 | Temple | Interior Anta (Patricia) West | 10-x-10 | Parr |
| 9 | Temple | 'Adyton' Southeast | 7.5-x-10 | Bedal |
| 15 | Temple | 'Adyton' Southeast | 6-x-5 | Austin |

• Interpret the Petra Great Temple's phases of use and function(s).

## 1994 Results

A detailed topographic map begun in 1993 was completed so that the relationship between the Great Temple and its immediate surroundings could be ascertained. The Site Grid system had been established across the Upper Temenos in 1993, but this year we were able to extend it to the Lower Temenos, the Lapidary West and the Propylaeum. Excavations were conducted in accordance with the grid, using maps generated on scales of 1:100 and 1:50. Archaeological site plans were compiled to include all visible features, such as fallen columns and walls. By the end of the 1994 season, this plan (Figure 2.20) encompassed the Great Temple and its entire precinct. A fifth area was added to the four main areas established in 1993 — 1) the Propylaeum, 2) the Lower Temenos, 3) the Upper Temenos with 4) the Great Temple, and 5) the Lapidary West (prepared field for the temporary storage of architectural fragments). All of these areas were documented by excavation in 1994.

Beginning north to south, the 1994 survey and excavations will be briefly described.

*Figure 2.21. 1994 Brown University Excavation Team.*

### 1994 Propylaeum

The Stairs of the Propylaeum had been partially documented in 1993. In 1994, however, the side walls and each block were surveyed (block by block — over 350 individual blocks), and further consolidation of the steps was undertaken. It was clearly established that this later entrance, as seen today from the Colonnaded Street, was in direct alignment with the Temple but not with the street and, therefore, was used at some later point in its development as an integral part of the precinct.

### 1994 Lower Temenos

In the Lower Temenos, column drums had been moved by the local farmers to divide the area for their fields; these can be clearly seen in the pre-excavation aerial photograph (Figure 2.12). Positioned across the width of the Lower Temenos, these column drums were recorded and moved to the west of the area. A sondage (Trench 6) was excavated to determine the Lower Temenos' depth of deposit, as well as to investigate the northern route of the Subterranean Canalization System. The limestone Hexagonal Pavement, with pavers measuring an average of 0.77–0.78 m (the largest pavers presently known in Jordan), was found under an approximately 1.50 m

deposit of fill. This pavement was found again in the 10-x-10 m excavation of Trench 13, which was located 4 m to the north of Trench 6. This indicates that the Hexagonal Pavement did in fact continue and, in all likelihood, covered the entire Lower Temenos (Figure 2.22). However, Trench 13's south balk was found disturbed, and it had been impacted by the collapse of the Subterranean Canalization System, which also coursed underground north from the Temple Forecourt (Trench 1, 1993) under the Central Stairs to the Lower Temenos.

Another investigatory probe in the Lower Temenos was the excavation of one half of the West Exedra (Trench 5) to what we then believed was one of its original floor levels (Figure 2.23). Just above the Hexagonal Pavement, resting at the base of an eastern engaged column of the West Exedra, was found a capital with an unusual embellishment; the usual corner volutes were replaced with Asian elephant heads (Figure 2.25)! We posited these decorative elements originally adorned either this West Exedra structure or some other structure in the Lower Temenos.[28] Several other carved limestone fragments, including elephant ears, cheek pieces and trunks, were identified and registered as having come from this area, which suggested that the Lower Temenos was the origin of this decorative capital.

## 1994 Upper Temenos

Within the Upper Temenos, to the immediate north of the Great Temple itself, the northern branch of the four-branched Subterranean Canalization System uncovered in 1993 was mapped underground for 11 m, and soil samples were taken to analyze its botanical content (Figure 2.24).[29] The Upper Temenos was further examined by the completion of Trench 2 initiated in 1993 and with a block-by-block survey of the Temple Stylobate. In the excavation of Trenches 8, 10 and 11, which border the Great Temple West, a paved walkway was partially uncovered.[30] An excavated 20.1 m length of this 'West Walkway' was excavated to its 3.84 m in width (Figure 2.26). Delicately sculpted facial mask fragments, many finely decorated architectural elements and coins were recovered from this area.

## 1994 Temple

In the Great Temple, excavations were also conducted along the north interior, consisting of one irregularly sized trench (Trench 12) positioned behind and to the south of the Temple Stylobate. It was hoped that the character of the Great Temple proper might be further ascertained, and it was. Found here was a massive West Anta wall (Patricia Anta) resting on a finely carved Attic base, which we associated with the original Temple construction (Figure 2.27).

Additionally, in the Temple South, two trenches (Trenches 9 and 15) were excavated in the rear of the Temple structure, which we tentatively identified as the 'Adyton.' We found this area to be dominated on a lower level by a large, now partially consolidated vaulted Central Arch. Its northern face had collapsed, so extra measures had to be used to consolidate it. To the far west of this Central Arch was found a north-south, 11 m, stepped, vaulted stairway passage (Monica Stairway). Set into this West Stairway's west wall were arched windows and a doorway located at the lower landing on the north (Figure 2.28). At the time, it was thought that these steps led either down into the Temple Cella or to an interior corridor. At the top and to the east side of the West Stairway and on the east as well, were paved platforms or landings, which

*Figure 2.22. Lower Temenos Hexagonal Pavement, 1994.*

*Figure 2.23. West Exedra pre-excavation, 1994.*

with a 90° turn accessed twin, incompletely preserved, four-step flights of stairs positioned towards a feature to the north. Whatever this feature was, it no longer existed on this level. At that time, it was premature to speculate whether the Great Temple was a two- or three-level structure, but we suspected that the rear was three-storied. (The 1997 excavations have provided us with a better understanding of this sector's architectural plan.)

A number of special projects were undertaken to locate the columns on the Temple East as well as on the Temple South. These were very productive investigations that resulted in the revised Temple plan. To the south, at the rear of the Great Temple, were six columns, five of which had now been located; eight had been located along each of the structure's east and west flanks.

At that time, the easternmost Pronaos column (Mohammad Column) and the northeast side column had yet to be found. (In sum, of the 22 columns that hypothetically decorated the Temple, 20 were known to be *in situ* by the end of the 1994 season.) The interaxial intercolumniation (from the center of one column to the center of another) between the side and rear columns measured between 3.47-3.50 m, and from one column edge to the other measured approximately 2.23 m. Thus,

we were able to obtain more precise information regarding the plan of the Temple and gain a better understanding of its architectural components.

## 1994 Lapidary West

The Lapidary West was investigated by a sondage (Trench 7) to determine if it held cultural deposits.[31] Under a 2 m deposit of topsoil, several Nabataean levels were located with a wealth of Nabataean pottery. Over 150 of the pottery fragments from this area were drawn, photographed and described. Samples underwent petrographic and neutron

*Figure 2.24. Temple Forecourt, Canalization cleared, 1994.*

*Figure 2.25. Elephant-headed capital, Lower Temenos, West Exedra, 1994.*

activation (NAA) testing at the University of Missouri at Columbia, under the sponsorship of the Applied Science Center of the University of Pennsylvania Museum (MASCA). (See Leigh-Ann Bedal's report in Chapter 7.)

The building and use phases of each area were arranged in chronological sequence, and the inter-relationships between architectural

components were tentatively established. Based on the 1994 excavations, the general sequence or phases of the Great Temple precinct were determined.

## 1994 Catalog

The 1994 catalog of more than 150 items was prepared for the Jordanian Department of

*Figure 2.26. West Walkway, 1994.*

*Figure 2.27. West Anta (Patricia Anta), 1994.*

*Figure 2.28. Discovery of the West Stairway (Monica Stairway) wall, 1994.*

Antiquities at the Petra Museum, and all registered artifacts were placed in storage there. Recovered were some 36 coins, six limestone facial mask elements, 47 lamps (most of which were fragmented), a delicate Roman glass head vase and some 49 ceramics, which included a figurine fragment with sandals, two Nabataean bowls and several complete small cups, juglets and bowls.

Grosso Modo had 18,416 items registered, of which 15,330 (83%) were ceramic fragments. Glass fragments numbered 525, and the architectural fragment database had some 1409 fragments analyzed.

## 1994 Publication

Martha S. Joukowsky published the 1993 report in the *Annual of the Department of Antiquities of Jordan,* and reports appeared both in *L'Orient Express* and the *American Journal of Archaeology.* Additionally, nine public lectures were delivered about our results.

## 1994 Field Conservation

The proper protection and conservation of each of the Temple sectors was a major responsibility of the 1994 project. One of the site's most important consolidation efforts was the anastylosis (reconstruction stone by stone)

of the lower curbing of the Stairs of the Propylaeum. Other such projects prioritized the consolidation and conservation of the Stylobate and crepidoma of the Temple façade.

Other completed 1994 projects included:

• The removal and reinstallation of the east buttress in the West Exedra;

• The construction of steps at the Temple entry;

• The replacement of column drums with better-preserved elements in the Temple façade and in the East Colonnade of the eastern Lower Temenos;

• The retirement of heavily eroded drums;

• The construction of a fence around the Temple to protect it from animals and pot hunters;

• The construction of a massive flood control channel to divert water away from the structure;

• The backfilling of trenches so they were not exposed to air and water seepage during the rainy periods, and

• The protection of delicate areas by roofing them over with zinc sheeting held in place by sandbags.

*Figure 2.29.  Aerial view of the site post-excavation, 1994.  Photograph by Jane Taylor.*

## At Home 1994-1995

This was an opportune time to catch up on the drafting and scanning of site sections and plan drawings. Interdependently, Deirdre G. Barrett worked on the computer catalog database and Jean Blackburn drafted the architectural fragments. Besides grant writing and applications to foundations, the Petra Excavation Fund was formally established at Brown University. Public lectures were delivered at home as well as at the Jordanian conference in Torino, Italy; there, the preliminary results of the Subterranean Canalization System were presented along with a comparative discussion of other known Nabataean water conservation systems.

## 1995 — Third Year

### 1995 Excavation

Brown University archaeologists conducted excavations at the Great Temple from June 17 to August 10, 1995. An additional four days (August 11-14) were spent in Petra phasing and writing final reports, and two days (August 15-16) were spent in Amman, where we reported the 1995 excavation results at a public lecture at the American Center of Oriental Research on August 16.

### 1995 Staff

The 1995 staff was comprised of Martha S. Joukowsky, Director; Artemis A.W. Joukowsky, Administrator and Photographer; Erika L. Schluntz, Assistant Director; Loa P. Traxler, Chief Architect-Surveyor; Geoffrey Bilder, Computer Analyst; Michael F. Slaughter, Photographic Recorder and Photo Developer; Leigh-Ann Bedal, Ceramic Analyst and Archaeologist; Kathleen Mallak, Finds Recorder; Jean Blackburn, Draftsperson; Terry E. Tullis, Geologist; David Brill, Professional Photographer; Senior Archaeologists, Deirdre G. Barrett, Joseph J. Basile, Josh Bell, Elizabeth E. Payne, Lawrence Sisson, John Rucker, Laurent Tholbecq; additional Field Researchers, Faisal Ra'ad, Lamya Khalidi, Ann Harris, Zain Habboo, and volunteers, Richard Ballou, David Barrett, Francesca Bennett, Christina Bennett, Nina Köprülü, Patricia Boczkowski, Daniel Quigley, James Nicholas, Constance Worthington, W. Chesley

Worthington, Whitney Azoy, Stephanie Scott, Fr. Anthony Scott and Monica L. Sylvester. Ghalib Abbadi was assigned to us by the Department of Antiquities for help in moving architectural components and soil removal. His service to us was indispensable. Besides Terry E. Tullis, 1995 Great Temple Consultants included Christian Augé, numismatics; Stephan G. Schmid, Nabataean fine ware analysis; Yvonne Gerber, plain ware analysis, and Peter Warnock, botanical materials analysis.

We are grateful to the Jordanian Department of Antiquities and to newly appointed Ghazi Bisheh, Director, for this season's assistance. The Jordanian Department of Antiquities has been unceasingly generous with their time and support. Under the general supervision of Suleiman Farajat, the Department of Antiquities assigned Mohammad Abd-Al-Aziz Al-Marahleh as our Jordanian Government Department of Antiquities Representative. Dakhilallah Qublan and some 25 Bedouin workmen helped in our site recovery.

### 1995 Goals

The goals of the 1995 season were to:

• Trace the Subterranean Canalization System by ground-penetrating radar (GPR) to determine if this could be accomplished with above-ground methods;

• Expose enough of the east Lower Temenos to understand its character in relation to the Hexagonal Pavement and, if possible, find the east perimeter wall of the precinct;

• Locate the positions of the Temple columns, in particular the Pronaos columns, and determine what effects might have been caused by earthquake damage so excavation strategies could be modified to meet these needs;

• Locate the architectural elements on the Temple East, despite the Porch column fall here, better define this area and determine if in fact there was correspondence on the Temple West, and

• Continue our investigations of the Temple Rear stairway systems to find if their arrangements were symmetrical and gain an understanding of how and why these stair systems accessed the Great Temple.

# Petra Great Temple
## 1995 Overall Excavations

Douglas Pitney
Loa P. Traxler
Paul C. Zimmerman

0    *meters*    25

*Figure 2.30. 1995 Overall Excavations.*

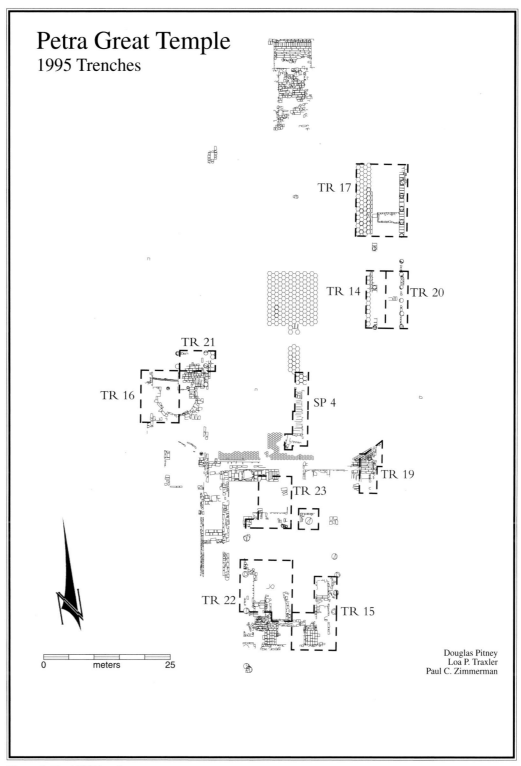

# Petra Great Temple
## 1995 Trenches

TR 17

TR 14

TR 20

TR 21

TR 16

SP 4

TR 19

TR 23

TR 22

TR 15

0    meters    25

Douglas Pitney
Loa P. Traxler
Paul C. Zimmerman

*Figure 2.31. 1995 Trenches.*

# GREAT TEMPLE
# 1995 TRENCHES EXCAVATED

| Trench | Location | Position | N-S by E-W Dimensions (m) | Excavator(s) |
|---|---|---|---|---|
| 5 | Lower Temenos | West Exedra | 9-x-4 <br> 2 m probe | Basile Rucker |
| 16 | Lower Temenos | West Exedra | 7-x-10 | Basile Rucker |
| 21 <br> *SP 26/SP 31* | Lower Temenos | West Exedra | 4-x-7 | Rucker Basile Khalidi |
| *SP 20* | Lower Temenos | Center | 1.5-x-2.5 | Payne Barrett |
| 14 | Lower Temenos | East Colonnade | *SP 22, 24, 29 combined* <br> 8.2-x-11 | Sisson Bell |
| 20 | Lower Temenos | East Colonnade | 9-x-4.3 | Sisson Bell |
| *SP 22* | Lower Temenos | East Colonnade | 4-x-2 | Sisson Bell |
| *SP 24* | Lower Temenos | East Colonnade | 7-x-2.2 | Sisson Bell |
| *SP 29* | Lower Temenos | East Colonnade | 2-x-2 | Sisson Bell |
| 17 <br> *SP 25* | Lower Temenos | East Colonnade | 10-x-14 <br> *1.6-x-2.5* | Payne |
| *SP 4* | Upper Temenos | Central Staircase | 9.75-x-2.8 | Payne Slaughter Barrett |
| *SP 30* | Upper Temenos | East | 4.6-x-7.2-x-8.2 | Tholbecq |
| 19 | Temple East | East Walkway | 5.2-x-3.4 | Tholbecq |
| 23 <br> *SP 23* <br> *SP 10* | Temple | Pronaos West | 10-x-6.5 <br> 3-x-3.6 | Schluntz Harris |
| 15 | Temple | 'Adyton' Southeast Staircase | 7.35-x-2.23 | Harris Khalidi |
| 22 | Temple | 'Adyton' Southwest Staircase | 7.5-x-10 | Bedal |

*Figure 2.32. 1995 Brown University Excavation Team in the West Exedra.*

## 1995 Results

The Great Temple architectural plan was clarified with excavation backed up by EDM equipment, and there was a partial re-erection of the columns in the Lower Temenos sacred area as well as in the Temple itself. The recovery of the principal columns of the Temple, as well as its gigantic decorative capitals carved with complex floral designs, again confirmed that the Temple structure originally stood to about 19-20 m in height. Ground-penetrating radar (GPR) was used to trace the Subterranean Canalization System, which extended under the principal buildings of the site (see this report in Chapter 4).

## 1995 Lower Temenos

In 1995, the archaeological investigation of the Lower Temenos Hexagonal Pavement area was undertaken in Trenches 14 and 17 and a number of special projects. There was reconstruction of elements of the East Colonnade, then thought to be a double colonnade. Here, the limestone stylobate of the Colonnade was exposed and found to extend over 50 m — the north-south extent of the Lower Temenos (Figure 2.33). From the 1994 evidence, we assumed the Hexagonal Pavement covering this open plaza was constructed on fill. We were correct, but we

did not suspect that originally the pavement and the fill below it overlay a massive construction of arches and well-constructed Nabataean walls. These were found to extend more than 6 m below the East Colonnade Hexagonal Pavement!

*Figure 2.33. Excavation of the East Colonnade in the Lower Temenos, 1995.*

*Figure 2.34. West Exedra during excavations, 1995.*

*Figure 2.35. East–West Retaining Wall during excavations, 1995.*

The limited exposure of the investigation of this buildup was undertaken in Trench 17, SP 25, and in Trenches 14 and 20, SP 29. These as yet enigmatic deposits indicated that the Lower Temenos had an earlier monumental construction phase. We conjectured that access into the then Temenos was on the same level as the Colonnaded Street. If this was the case, the Stairs of the Propylaeum (which serve as the present-day access from the street to the Lower Temenos) were not in use at this time.

The Lower Temenos now appeared to have been constructed as a massive, monumental, artificial platform. At least in the east, it was not found to be solid but was constructed on a system of arches and walls that were founded on approximately the same elevation as the Colonnaded Street. We were not sure if this structure had a functional purpose, perhaps as a cistern, or if it served as a substructure for architectural support in creating a platform for the Lower Temenos.[32]

The construction of the Subterranean Canalization System was confusing, for in its later phase it had construction deposits that were superimposed on the massive arches and walls. SP 4 saw continued excavation to understand the construction of the Subterranean Canalization System. What was recovered was the bedding for a central stairway, 8 m in length, that led from the Lower Temenos to the Upper Temenos Temple Forecourt. The dressed limestone ashlars on the east stair wall indicated that this was an earlier staircase. Cutting across this staircase was a massive, east-west wall with the lower courses of large, sandstone orthostats, some measuring more than 2 m in width and 1 m in height. Clearly, these 'Central Stairs' had been decommissioned when the East-West Retaining Wall and the Hexagonal Pavement of the Lower Temenos were constructed, for the wall cut off stair access to the Lower Temenos (Figure 2.35). This indicated that this stair bedding had served as an earlier access to the Temple. The evidence also suggested that part of the original stepping had been incorporated into the Canalization System when the system underwent repair (Figure 2.36). This difference in plan also reflected that the original staircase did not seem to have been built as a monumental structure to cover the complete east-west slope of the area but was contained in an approximate 3 m width.[33] Zbigniew T. Fiema has suggested the possibility that in the earlier Temple phase these Central Stairs may have continued through the Lower Temenos down all the way to the level of the Colonnaded Street.

*Figure 2.36. Trench 13, Lower Temenos, Subterranean Canalization System, 1995.*

### 1995 Upper Temenos

The Great Temple Upper Temenos was further examined by the completion of a special project (SP 30) located under the column fall of the easternmost exterior column (Nadine Column). Below the column fall, a 1 m fill was found; this led us to speculate that the Great Temple did not collapse at one time but that the eastern columns fell after this fill had accumulated and after the Porch and Pronaos columns had tumbled to the north and west. Within the Upper Temenos to the immediate east of the Temple itself and under the small Hexagonal Pavement of the Temple Forecourt, an upper eastern branch of the Subterranean Canalization System was uncovered and mapped, and, again, soil samples were taken to analyze its botanical content.

The excavation of Trench 19 uncovered a well-preserved series of seven steps from the Temple Forecourt leading up to an east walkway. We then knew that the 'East Walkway' had been added to flank the Temple on its east, and it paralleled the West Walkway recovered in 1994. (The unexcavated portion of the West Walkway, partially recovered in 1994, was left until there was disposal of backfill from more southerly trenches.)

### 1995 Temple

A number of special projects were undertaken in the Great Temple to excavate more columns on the Temple North, in particular the eastern Pronaos column (the Mohammad Column, SP 23). Additionally, a second block-by-block survey of the eastern Temple Stylobate was undertaken. These were very productive investigations that resulted in a redefined, more accurate Temple plan.

In 1994, excavations had been conducted along the north Temple interior, consisting of one irregularly sized trench (Trench 12) positioned behind and to the south of the Temple Stylobate and east of the West Walkway area, so that the character of the Temple proper might be further ascertained. Excavated in 1995 was Trench 23, from the West Anta wall (Patricia Anta) to the Temple Center. Resting on finely carved Attic bases, the massive Pronaos columns (Mohammad and Vartan Columns) were recovered still bearing traces of red plaster decorating their drums Figure 2.37). We have identified these

columns with the original Phase I Temple Construction.

In antiquity, the inner western Porch column (Martha Column) had completely fallen from the Temple Stylobate. Even its base was absent. It probably toppled from its position when it was struck by the falling collapse of the Pronaos west column (Mohammad Column). This inner western Porch column (Martha Column) was reconstituted from five fallen drums. There were some reasonably well-preserved drums that littered the Temple Forecourt. It was reasoned that their service might be best employed in re-erecting the column elements, rather than moving them to the lapidary. Thus, we were able to give the public a more coherent idea of the Temple façade and provide a better understanding of the structure's architectural statement.

In the Pronaos east, we recovered the top course of the massive eastern Anta wall (Pierre Anta). It was left unexcavated in 1995, but it served to define the symmetrical plan of the Temple.

In the Temple South, the 1994 trench (Trench 9) underwent continued excavation in the so-called Temple 'Adyton,' and Trench 15 was reopened on the west where we had found an indication that there was an East Stairway (Simon Stairway) that was aligned parallel to the 1994 West Stairway (Monica Stairway) recovered in Trench 9. In 1995, Trench 15, the East Stairway (Simon Stairway), was completely excavated. It was in a reasonable state of preservation and measured 10 m in length-x-2.26 m in width. Although we were disappointed by the partial collapse of its eastern Inter-Columnar wall (which had slumped to the east), there also was a vaulted stairway with arched windows and a door that mirrored those in the Inter-Columnar wall of the West Stairway (Monica Stairway). Thus, west and east of the Central Arch (also recovered in 1994) were twin, stepped, arched passages (Simon and Monica Stairways) leading to west and east paved platforms (Figure 2.40). We reasoned that these twin stairways may have led either into the Temple main room from the rear of the structure or to East and West Walkway exits. Decorated and finely sculpted capital fragments in excellent condition, lamp fragments and several coins were recovered from the West Stairway (Monica Stairway) in Trench 9. Because the architecture continued into another adjacent

*Figure 2.37. Pronaos column (Mohammad Column) during excavation, 1995.*

*Figure 2.38. West column (Joe Column) collapse, 1995.*

*Figure 2.39. East Walkway with Canalization System disturbance in foreground, 1995.*

room to the east of the stairway, beyond the confines of the original trench, Trench 9 was enlarged and was reassigned as Trench 22.

The building and use phases of each area were arranged in chronological sequence, and the inter-relationships between architectural components were tentatively established. Based on the 1995 excavations, the general sequence of construction phases of the Great Temple precinct were assessed.

## 1995 Catalog

The catalog of more than 300 objects was prepared for the Department of Antiquities, and all registered artifacts except the lamps, coins and architectural fragments were placed in storage at the Petra Museum.[34] Of especial interest were the 37 elephant-head fragments, 29 of which were elephant trunks. Recovered and registered were some 57 coins, 172 lamps (most of which were fragmented), four figurine fragments, 12 bone artifacts (including two complete bone pins and two spoon fragments) and five metal objects (including a finger ring and a probable bracelet). The most spectacular find of this year was the over life-sized head of the city goddess, Tyche, wearing a diadem with the crown of the city gates (see Figures 6.79 and 6.80). Tyche has been analyzed and published by Joseph J. Basile (1997); see the Site Bibliography.[35]

Thousands of architectural fragments and pottery elements were registered in the Grosso Modo database and subsequently stored on site. A record 35,914 objects were classified, of which 30,478 (85%) were ceramic fragments. Additionally, glass fragments numbered 826,

*Figure 2.40. West Stairway (Monica Stairway) during excavation, showing collapse, 1995.*

*Figure 2.41. 1995 Overview of Porch columns looking north.*

## 1995 Consolidation and Preservation

and 1235 architectural fragments were registered. Animal bones were transported to Amman where they have yet to undergo analysis.

The stabilization, reconstitution and re-erection of *in situ* column drums was undertaken. Also attended to was the consolidation of the west Porch columns (Artie and Martha Columns) (Figure 2.42) — previously mentioned was the complete re-erection of the central west Porch column (Martha Column). Consolidation of the central east and west Pronaos columns (Vartan

*Figure 2.42. Workers removing architectural elements, 1995.*

*Figure 2.43. Aerial view of the site post-excavation, looking south, 1995.*

and Mohammad Columns) was accomplished (Figure 2.43).

Due to the increased area excavated, additional fencing was placed around the site to protect it from animals and to serve as protection for tourists. The 1994 ditch that served successfully to divert water from the site was rebuilt. Consolidation measures were undertaken as the excavation progressed to treat ashlars that were in jeopardy of collapse.

## At Home 1995-1996

As in previous seasons, all drawings of the stratigraphy and site plans were inked by Ala H. Bedewi, our Assistant Draftsperson. They were scanned by Elizabeth E. Payne into computers at Brown University's Scholarly Technology Group headquarters and were prepared for site use in the following year. These total some 250 images of the site stratigraphy.

Thousands of ceramic data files were also under scrutiny using the FileMaker Pro database, which was updated. We also developed a new database to assist us in publishing our catalog data. At this point we had four on-line site databases — Grosso Modo, the Architectural Fragments Catalog, the Coin Catalog and the general Site Catalog, which were all backed up with Zip disks.

To better understand the chemical "finger-print" for the different wares represented at the site, the results of the neutron activation analysis (NAA), undertaken by Leigh-Ann Bedal, were completed. Of the 149 samples that were tested on the pottery recovered in 1994 from Trench 7 in the Lapidary West, five different compositions were represented. These results are presented in Chapter 7.

## 1995 Publication

In the fall of 1995, Geoffrey Bilder and Erika L. Schluntz created a Home Page for the Internet. Martha S. Joukowsky published reports in *le monde de la bible Archéologie et Histoire, American Journal of Archaeology, Syria* and *American Center of Oriental Research Newsletter.* Joukowsky and Erika L. Schluntz published the 1994 report in the *Annual of the Department of Antiquities of Jordan.* Additionally, Avraham Negev published a report on the Great Temple

in *Qadmoniot, A Journal for the Antiquities of Eretz-Israel and Bible Lands.* Educational films were also produced during this year, which fostered a public awareness of our excavations. Copies of these films were widely distributed in America. (Full citations can be found in the Site Bibliography.)

## 1996 — Fourth Year

## 1996 Excavations

1996 was the fourth year of two-month excavations by Brown University at the Great Temple. Our investigations took place from June 16 to August 12, 1996. As in previous seasons, at the end of the excavation the staff remained on site for a few days for phasing, and during their stay in Amman, they delivered a public lecture at the American Center of Oriental Research.

One of the most time-consuming surveying undertakings was the updating of the COMPASS program by its conversion into a new database. The new program, known as the ForeSight Program, was developed in part by Paul C. Zimmerman. The new system was more versatile, sped up results and was easier to manipulate. All of our voluminous data files were converted to the new system.

## 1996 Staff

The staff was comprised of Martha S. Joukowsky, Director; Artemis A. W. Joukowsky, Administrator and Photographer; Joseph J. Basile, Associate Director; Elizabeth E. Payne, Assistant Director; Paul C. Zimmerman, Chief Architect-Surveyor; Michael F. Slaughter, Assistant Director, Photographic Recorder and Photo Developer; Leigh-Ann Bedal, Ceramic Analyst and Field Supervisor; Deirdre G. Barrett, Finds Recorder; Monica L. Sylvester, Computer Database Manager; Jean Blackburn, Draftsperson; Erika L. Schluntz, Senior Archaeologist (who was with us until illness precluded her work on site); Archaeologists, Laurel D. Bestock, Brian A. Brown, Kimberly A. Butler, Juliette Gimon, David Goldstein; Field Excavators, Zain Habboo, Randy Takian, Evan Wolf, and volunteers, Francesca Bennett, Candace Hisert, Katherine Hisert, George A. Hisert and Faith Erickson-Gini. Again, besides Terry E. Tullis, Geologist, 1996 Southern

94

**Petra Great Temple**
1996 Overall Excavations

Douglas Pitney
Loa P. Traxler
Paul C. Zimmerman

0          *meters*          25

*Figure 2.44. 1996 Overall Excavations.*

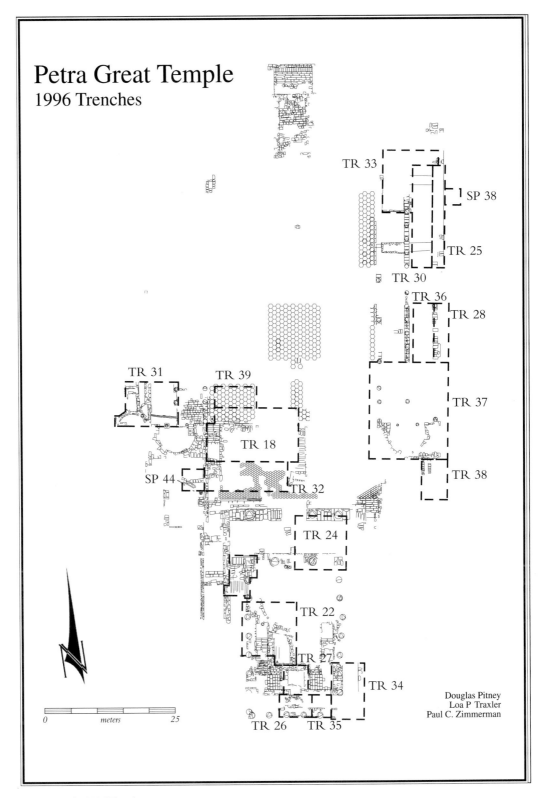

# Petra Great Temple
## 1996 Trenches

TR 33

SP 38

TR 25

TR 30

TR 36

TR 28

TR 31

TR 39

TR 37

TR 18

SP 44

TR 32

TR 38

TR 24

TR 22

TR 27

TR 34

Douglas Pitney
Loa P Traxler
Paul C. Zimmerman

N

0      *meters*    25

TR 26    TR 35

*Figure 2.45. 1996 Trenches.*

## GREAT TEMPLE
## 1996 TRENCHES EXCAVATED

| Trench | Location | Position | N-S by E-W Dimensions (m) | Excavator(s) |
|---|---|---|---|---|
| 31<br>*SP 41* | Lower Temenos | West Exedra West | 7.5-x-9.72<br>1.65-x-1.65 | Butler<br>Goldstein |
| 18 | Lower Temenos | West Stairway and E-W Retaining Wall | 17.5 (S)-x-16 (N)<br>14.5 (E)-x-10 (W) | Basile |
| 17<br>*SP 25* | Lower Temenos | East Colonnade | 10-x-14<br>*1.6-x-2.5* | Payne |
| 28 | Lower Temenos | East Colonnade | 13-x-2.8 | Bestock<br>Gimon |
| *SP 38* | Lower Temenos | East Colonnade | 3-x-3 | Goldstein<br>Butler |
| *SP 39* | Lower Temenos | East Colonnade | 19-x-4.1-x-1.9 | Joukowsky, M. |
| 25 | Lower Temenos | East Colonnade | 26.67-x-2.37 | Slaughter<br>Butler<br>Goldstein |
| 30 | Lower Temenos | East Colonnade | 19-x-4 | Joukowsky, M. |
| 36 | Lower Temenos | East Colonnade | 11-x-4 | Bestock<br>Gimon |
| 33 | Lower Temenos | Northeast Colonnade | 4.7-x-6 | Warnock |
| 37 | Lower Temenos | East Exedra | 19-x-15 | Joukowsky, M. |
| 32 | Upper Temenos | Stylobate and Pavement | 17.65 (N)-x-3.6 (E)<br>15.36 (S)-x-16.45 (W) | Brown |
| 39<br>*SP 44* | Upper Temenos | Forecourt West | 4-x-4 | Brown |
| 38 | Upper Temenos | East Archway | 7.5-x-4 | Joukowsky, M. |
| 24 | Temple | Pronaos East | 9.8-x-9.95 | Bestock |

| GREAT TEMPLE 1996 TRENCHES EXCAVATED | | | | |
|---|---|---|---|---|
| Trench | Location | Position | N–S by E-W Dimensions (m) | Excavator(s) |
| 29 | Temple | Northwest Corridor | 8.25-x-3.36 | Slaughter |
| 22 | Temple | 'Adyton' West Staircase and Vaulted Room | 7.5-x-10 | Bedal |
| 26 | Temple | 'Adyton' South | 5.5-x-4.5 | Payne |
| 27 | Temple | 'Adyton' South | 4.75-x-3.5 | Payne |
| 35 | Temple | Rear East–West East Staircase | 3.75-x-3.5 | Payne |
| 34 | Temple | Southeast Corridor | 14-x-5 | Joukowsky, A. |
| SP 40 | Temple | Suleiman Corner Column | 5-x-2.6 | Joukowsky, M. |
| SP 42 | Temple | Neil Column | 2-x-1.5 | Hiserts |

*Figure 2.46. 1996 Brown University Excavation Team.*

*Figure 2.47. Brown University Team posing as Lower Temenos East Colonnade, 1996.*

Temple Consultants included May Shaer, Zaki Aslan and Paul S. Fay, consolidation and preservation; Christian Augé, numismatics; Stephan G. Schmid, Nabataean fine wares analysis; Yvonne Gerber, plain wares analysis,

*Figure 2.48. SP 25, Trench 17, showing depth of deposit, 1996.*

and Peter Warnock, botanical materials analysis.

As in former years, the support and efforts of Ghazi Bisheh, Director of the Department of Antiquities, was very much appreciated. Ghalib Abbadi served as our back hoe operator, which was essential to the continued removal of backfill and the transport of large architectural elements. Under the general supervision of Suleiman Farajat, the Department of Antiquities assigned Mohammad Abd-Al-Aziz Al-Marahleh as our Jordanian Government Department of Antiquities Representative. Dakhilallah Qublan, Foreman, oversaw the 24 Bedouin workmen who assisted us in the site recovery.

## 1996 Goals

The goals of the 1996 season were to:

• Understand the architectural program of the Lower Temenos;

• Find the access to the Great Temple from the Lower and Upper Temenoi;

• Locate the East Exedra and excavate it, time permitting;

*Figure 2.49. East Exedra after excavation, 1996.*

• Carry out the search for the location of a floor under the arch springer wall in the Trench 17 sondage, SP 25;

• Clear the Temple East Pronaos;

• Explore the West Corridor and the West Anta (Patricia Anta);

• Complete the excavation of the West Stairway (Monica Stairway) in the Temple Rear and its adjacent vaulted room;

• Make preliminary explorations of the Temple Cella, and

• Excavate the Temple West rear to better understand its layout.

## 1996 Results

### 1996 Propylaeum

No work was undertaken in this area during the 1996 season.

### 1996 Lower Temenos

There were confirmed revelations about Nabataean Temple architecture. The most

significant 1996 architectural features indicated a penchant for formal symmetry with the discovery in the Lower Temenos of east and west triple colonnades adorned with a

*Figure 2.50. West Stairway (Laurel Stairway) during excavation, 1996.*

*Figure 2.51.  Porch column (Pia Column), 1996.*

minimum of 96 columns to a hypothetical maximum of 120 columns — 48 or 60 flanking each side of the Lower Temenos Hexagonal Pavement (Figure 2.47). These columns were approximately 0.80 m in diameter, and their interaxial intercolumniation measured approximately 2.50 m. The east of the Lower Temenos was

*Figure 2.52.  West Anta (Patricia Anta), 1996.*

*Figure 2.53. West Corridor with Paul Column, 1996.*

*Figure 2.54. West Stairway (Monica Stairway), 1996.*

cleared in Trenches 25, 28, 30 and 36, with an additional sondage (SP 39) to investigate the perimeter wall between the Lower Temenos and the Lower Market.

Additionally, one of the season's most significant discoveries was the excavation of a monumental West Stairway (Laurel Stairway) leading from the west Lower Temenos to the

*Figure 2.55. West vaulted room ('Adyton'), 1996.*

*Figure 2.56. Reconstruction of the Neil Column, 1996.*

Upper Temenos (Figure 2.50). Measuring 10 m (north-south) in length-x-2.23 m (east-west) in width, the West Stairway was also defined in Trench 18, where it was found to bond with the West Exedra. Extending from the east wall of the West Stairway, the continuation of the massive East-West Retaining Wall, which had been discovered in 1995 in the center of the Lower Temenos, was recovered. (SP 4, 1995 found that this East-West Retaining Wall cut off and blocked the Central Stairs from the large Hexagonal Pavement of the Lower Temenos.)

Six courses of the elegantly apsed East Exedra were excavated in Trench 37 (Figure 2.49). The East Exedra's interior depth (north-south) was 6 m; its interior width measured 7.2 m, and its exterior width was 12 m. Like its counterpart to the west, the East Exedra was embellished with interior buttresses, with twin columns at the entrance. Additionally, lying to the east of the East Exedra, the eastern peripheral wall of the precinct was defined in SP 38.

The 1995, Trench 17, SP 25 sondage excavated in the East Colonnade of the Lower Temenos was re-entered, and once the floor was cleared, it was finally closed at a 6 m depth below the stylobate wall of the East Colonnade (Figure 2.48).

In Trench 38 in the Upper Temenos, just above and behind the East Exedra, the tops of twin arch passages leading to the Lower Market to the east were exposed.

## 1996 Temple

In the Great Temple proper, the interior Pronaos east was completely excavated in Trench 24. Thus, the complete expanse of its width (24.5 m) was finally exposed. In Trench 29, there was the completed recovery of the northwest interior Anta wall (Patricia Anta) (Figure 2.52) and the founding levels of three of the eight western columns (Paul, Erika and Lee Columns). The Attic base of the northwest engaged column (Paul Column) was found to be built into the wall extending to the south of the interior Anta wall (Patricia Anta) (Figure 2.53). An opening in this wall, located between the Patricia Anta and the Paul Column, led to a small interior staircase, whose function was difficult to understand unless it was used as a viewing platform. A portion of the West Corridor was also exposed during these excavations, and it was found to measure some 2.79 m in interior width, and 8.25 m was its excavated length.

The massive overburden was cleared, allowing the exploration in Trench 26 of the central

*Figure 2.57. Suleiman Column in situ, 1996.*

*Figure 2.58. West Stairway (Monica Stairway) and vaulted room, 1996.*

'Adyton' on both the north and south sides of the rear Central Arch. Other 'Adyton' features included the completed excavations in Trench 22 of the vaulted West Stairway (Monica Stairway), which was found to measure 10 m in length-x-2.26 m in width (Figure 2.54). Adjacent to the West Stairway (Monica Stairway) was a vaulted chamber measuring 5.29 m (north-south)-x-2.96 m (east-west), with a depth of approximately 4 m (Figures 2.55 and 2.58). On its floor, five fragments of a Trajanic inscription were unearthed. (For a discussion of this inscription, see Chapter 8). All of these factors combined to confirm that the Temple South rear was a three-storied structure.

Of particular interest was the discovery of the upper courses of a major east-west semicircular wall opening north into the central room of the Temple. Projected 1997 excavation plans made us reason that this structure would clearly define the 'Adyton.' It promised to be a major architectural component of the Great Temple architectural plan.

On the Temple Southeast in Trench 34, the outer east wall, the southeastern heart-shaped Temple corner column (Suleiman Column) and the Inter-Columnar wall were defined. Since the east part of the Temple had fallen to

the east, the excavation of the Interior Corridor was difficult due to the collapse of large architectural elements (Figure 2.57). Two capital elements — a one half acanthus lower order and a one-fourth (of the four-part) upper order were re-erected on the Neil Column to give the public greater understanding of the architectural decoration (Figure 2.56).

As in previous years, before leaving the field, the phasing of each of the Temple area trenches was set forth in chart form, so that the inter-relationship between areas could be demonstrated, and a public lecture was presented at the American Center of Oriental Research in Amman.

## 1996 Catalog

Not only was there a wealth of finds (including 60 coins, the fragmentary Trajanic Latin inscription, some 72 Nabataean, Roman and Byzantine lamp fragments and large amounts of ceramic assemblages that included unguentaria and bowls), but there were also an additional 31 fragments of elephant sculpture, including eyes, trunks and faces. Of interest was the recovery of a large brain coral, presumably brought in antiquity from the Gulf of Aqaba. It was unearthed in association with many coins and the fragmented Trajanic inscription in Trench 22, the Temple 'Adyton' area. There was continued study of the Great Temple sculptural program, including the richly adorned capitals embellished with hibiscus petals, pine cones, pomegranates or poppies, acanthus leaves and vines. The corpus of small finds inventoried included broken glass bowls and several bone items (including bone needles and a spatula). Bronze decorative pieces were found, including a decorative leaf, a petal and a bronze buckle — all of which can be found in the Catalog, Chapter 6.

Our Grosso Modo database for artifact collections (bone, stone, ceramics, stucco, shell and metal) was consolidated into the FileMaker Pro program. The total number of artifacts in this database now numbered 84,561 artifacts, with 69,493 pottery sherds registered. In 1996, 23,208 pieces were registered, of which 17,474 (75%) were ceramics. These artifacts were then distributed over the phases we assigned to the Great Temple stratigraphy. The glass database had 316 pieces, and architectural fragments registered numbered 905.

## 1996 Conservation

The following abbreviated listing includes the diagnosis and measures we undertook for preservation, consolidation and safety considerations, beginning with the Stairs of the Propylaeum in the north.

### Propylaeum

• The step foundations were partially consolidated with mud mortar and small field stones prior to the restoration of the steps, using newly cut ashlar blocks.

• Vegetation located on the steps (and along the Colonnaded Street) was removed in order to prevent damage by roots to surrounding structures.

### Lower Temenos

#### 1. West Exedra

• Gaps along the eastern portion of the walls were filled with mud mortar and small stone wedges.

• The faces of the walls were treated by pointing with mud mortar and stone wedges.

• Gaps occurring between the column drums in the West Exedra entry were treated either by removing and re-placing the drums and injecting mud mortar (grouting) between them (Figure 2.61).

• The drainage channel in front of the West Exedra was covered with sand and backfilled.

#### 2. West Stairway (Laurel Stairway) between the Lower Temenos and the Temple Forecourt (Figures 2.59 and 2.60)

• East and west staircase walls were treated with pointing, and missing ashlars were replaced with new blocks.

• The staircase foundation was treated by filling missing sections with mud mortar and small field stones prior to the stair restoration. The original ashlars uncovered in the excavation were re-placed in their *in situ* positions, whereas new ashlars had to be quarried and cut for the upper steps.

#### 3. Lower Temenos South — Hexagonal Pavement

• Hexagonal Pavement tiles were to be re-placed after refilling and leveling the interstices between the capstones and the pavement level. However, further investigation of the Lower Temenos substructure was thought to be required; the type and weight of the fill had to be determined before restoration could begin.

### Upper Temenos

#### 1. Temple Forecourt

• Exposed ceramic drainage pipes were covered with clean sand and backfilled.

• The damaged Hexagonal Pavement in the Forecourt was covered with a thin layer of sand until such time as the pavement could be consolidated and restored. Further excavation would be required in order to determine how to proceed with the consolidation of the pavement and its subsurface. (Unfortunately, the use of geo-technic cloth to cover this area was precluded by our budget.)

• The Central Stairs foundation was consolidated by using mud mortar and large pebbles. A safety barrier was erected at the top the staircase.

• Exposed sections of the Canalization System underlying the Forecourt and the extreme eastern side of the Forecourt underwent consolidation. Their crumbling edges were reinforced by the use of mud and lime mortars. These exposed sections also required safety barriers, which were installed.

*2. West Exterior Walkway*

• Gaps in the eastern walls were replaced with worked field stones, bonded with mud mortar and reinforced by pointing.

The Great Temple

*1. West Corridor*

• There was the replacement of the fallen ashlars recovered in the excavation to their original positions in the northwest wall.

• The northwest section of the corridor was treated by pointing both to reinforce the wall and to close large gaps between the ashlars.

• Safety barriers were erected around the exposed section.

*2. West 'Adyton' Stairway (Monica Stairway)*

• In order to insure safe access to the West 'Adyton' room, a partial restoration of

*Figures 2.59 and 2.60. Consolidation of the West Stairway (Laurel Stairway), 1996.*

*Figure 2.61. West Exedra after consolidation, 1996.*

the stairs was undertaken by completing the foundation level using mud mortar and small field stones. There was the replacement of stair treads found in the lapidary from previous excavation seasons. Additional limestone blocks also had to be quarried and cut to size. As time precluded the completion of this project, it awaited 1997 consolidation efforts.

### 3. West 'Adyton' Room

• Gaps between the wall stones were filled with a combination of mud mortar, stone wedges and small field stones, and the blocks were pointed. The niche found in the south wall was reinforced by placing flat core fill stones and mortar to shore up the surrounding wall.

• Reinforcement of the remaining vault stones on the east side of the room was undertaken (anastylosis) by removing and replacing them. They were then bonded with a local mud mortar.

### 4. Southeast Cella Corridor

• There was the rebuilding of the northern wall-support niche of the heart-shaped column (Suleiman Column). The ashlars were numbered, removed and have been rebuilt in their original positions.

• The gaps above the designated ashlars have been cleared of debris, and new ashlars have been inserted.

• A drainage trench was constructed parallel to the southern wall of the Temple, north of the column niche, to divert water.

### 5. 'Adyton' Central Arch

• The preservation of the Central Arch required simultaneous work by both excavators and conservators in order to clear out debris and repair damage prior to further excavation of adjoining areas. Further study of the construction of the arch is still required by conservators along with architectural historians before excavation can proceed.

### 6. East 'Adyton' Stairway (Simon Stairway)

• Preliminary restoration of the first two rows of the vaulted ceiling was required before the consolidation of the lower section of the surrounding walls could be undertaken.

• A safety barrier was put in place to limit public access to the stairway.

### 7. Pronaos

• Remnants of plaster stucco decoration on the exterior southwest Pronaos column (Vartan Column) were treated professionally with sealants. Injections of sealants to their interior surfaces were undertaken in order to forestall further deterioration and to bond the red stucco to the column.

• Deteriorated column drums were removed, and drums from the fall of the Porch columns were re-erected in their place. (No bonding agent was used between these drums.)

### 8. The Pronaos and the Temple Forecourt

• The foundations were consolidated by using mud mortar and small field stones. This preceded the restoration of the stairs using existing worked stones.

## At Home 1996–1997

Several interdependent researches were undertaken after leaving the field in August 1996, although the consolidation and restoration work at the Great Temple, just described, continued.

All drawings of the stratigraphy, site plans and artifacts were drafted. Special artifact drawings and reconstructions were undertaken by our Chief Draftsperson, Jean Blackburn, of the Rhode Island School of Design. The 150 drawings of plans and stratigraphy were inked by Ala H. Bedawi, our Assistant Draftsperson. Once the final plans were found to be acceptable, they were scanned by Laurel D. Bestock into the computer and labeled. All the plans that we had stored in other computer files at Brown University had to be brought together and occasionally had to be rescanned so that the site file was up-to-date.

Stephen V. Tracy, Visiting Mellon Professor at the Institute for Advanced Study, Princeton, translated, dated and interpreted the partial inscription found in 1996 in the west room of the 'Adyton.' He publicly reported on these

*Figure 2.62. 1996 site aerial, post-excavation, looking west.*

results at a lecture sponsored by the Brown University Classics Department. (The results of his analysis can be found in Chapter 8.)

The fine wares were given intensive study by Stephan G. Schmid of the Ecole Suisse d'archeologie en Grece, and once again Yvonne Gerber of the University of Basel, Switzerland, analyzed our plain wares and dated them. Deirdre G. Barrett of Brown University continued her analysis of the Great Temple lamps.

Since 1993, the Great Temple coins have undergone continued study by Christian Augé of the University of Paris I - Sorbonne. David Smart has coordinated the effort. All of the coins were mechanically cleaned. When necessary, chemical cleaning was undertaken. They were cleaned first by Martha S. Joukowsky and Pierre M. Bikai in the ACOR Laboratory in Amman. A follow-up cleaning and stabilization was undertaken by professional conservator, Clifford Crane, assisted by Avi Mannis. The coins were then measured, weighed and given preliminary identification by David Smart. The collection was then photographed in color by Asher Keshet and in black-and-white by Artemis A.W. Joukowsky. The collection was then re-examined, and final identifications were made by Christian Augé, whose notes were translated from French into English by David Smart and Deirdre G. Barrett for the Coin Catalog (presented in Chapter 6). All the coins have been stored in acid-free paper envelopes with a desiccant, and they have been turned over to the Petra Museum.

For his Senior Honor Thesis at Brown University, Avi Mannis instituted a digital archive project entitled: "Coins of the Great Southern Temple, Petra: A Multimedia Archaeological Site Archive on CD-ROM." The archive documented three years (1994-1996) of coin recovery for 158 coins. Avi Mannis integrated image, text and three-dimensional space to foster intuitive access to the archaeological record. He created a Digital Archive Project taking the three-dimensional representation of the excavations, in which the *in situ* positions of the excavated coins had been marked. The selection of a marker brought up a record of the coin with a color photograph, an analysis of its composition, cultural origins, inscriptions, mint marks and conservation history. The user was also able to search the archive for specific characteristics,

e.g., all the Nabataean coins from the reign of Aretas IV. This effort has produced a working CD-ROM archive of the Great Temple coins. (This archive can be referenced on our five-year report on the CD-ROM.) While this archive was limited in scope, we hope in the future to expand it to encompass the whole range of materials excavated from the site. The support for this research was given by an Undergraduate Research at Brown (RAB) Grant.

The 1996 site plan was refined by Paul C. Zimmerman of the University of Pennsylvania. This "cleaned up" the 1996 plan for publication. This was an important task, for our data files were so extensive that we had to constantly be aware that they may have been confusing to the first-time viewer.

Signs were designed for visitors to the Great Temple by Artemis A.W. Joukowsky and Erika L. Schluntz in English and Arabic (translated by Kemal Abdul Malek and Pierre M. Bikai).

Graduate student, Sara G. Karz began an analytic study of the 2054 fragments of glass found during the excavations. She prepared a report entitled: "Succession of Glass in Form and Function at the Great Temple, Petra, Jordan," which is a section of Chapter 6 in this report.

Regarding 1996-1997 site protection and consolidation, a final report entitled "Petra, Brown University Excavations at the Great Temple" was submitted to the Samuel H. Kress Foundation, World Monuments Watch, A Program of the World Monuments Fund. A summary of these activities can be found under "1996 Conservation" (*supra*).

The Great Temple excavations have engendered a great deal of interest. To make our investigations available to the public, we created a web page in 1995. In 1996, a new web page was designed by Benjamin H. Kleine, Brown University '98. It can be accessed at <http://www.brown.edu/ Departments/Anthropology/Petra/>. This updated home page reflects the work that had been carried out in the last years. The funding for this project was donated by a Brown alumnus who has shown a keen interest in our computer systems. Additionally, I submitted a general statement for the web page of the American Schools of Oriental Research, which can be accessed at <http:// www.cobb.msstate.edu/asordigs/petra.html>.

The program and assignments for the five-year publication of the site were outlined. All the contributors were given standard guidelines for reporting both the 1997 results and their contributions for the five-year report. All the trench reports were edited for consistency in format and were readied for publication in this five-year report. The corrections and their insertion into PageMaker were undertaken by Kirsten K. Hammann. Thus, we went into the field prepared to correct our earlier assumptions and to continue the excavations of the Great Temple precinct.

## 1996 Publication

Several scholarly articles (see the Site Bibliography for full citations) were submitted for publication, and some 20 lectures were presented on the excavation. In addition, for the *Brown University Faculty Bulletin,* I wrote an informal article on the excavations, and I submitted final reports to the *Annual of the Department of Antiquities of Jordan* and the *American Journal of Archaeology.*

The excavation staff wrote a number of articles. Jean Blackburn wrote a description for the Rhode Island School of Design Alumni Magazine. Erika L. Schluntz reported on the architectural sculpture at the 98th Annual Meeting of the Archaeological Institute of America. Paul C. Zimmerman wrote an article on MiniCad 6. Deirdre G. Barrett submitted her M.A. Thesis on the ceramic lamps.

Jordanian author and columnist, Rami Khouri, continued his coverage of the excavations with two articles in the *Jordan Times.*

## 1997 — Fifth Year

### 1997 Excavations

With the continuing support of the Department of Antiquities of the Hashemite Kingdom of Jordan and Ghazi Bisheh, Director, excavations were carried out at the Petra Great Temple from June 14 to August 11, 1997.

### 1997 Staff

The staff was comprised of Martha S. Joukowsky, Director; Artemis A. W. Joukowsky, Administrator and Photographer; Joseph J. Basile, Associate Director; Elizabeth E. Payne, Assistant Director; Paul C. Zimmerman, Chief Architect-Surveyor; Michael F. Slaughter, Assistant Director, Photographic Recorder and Photo Developer; Deirdre G. Barrett, Finds Recorder; Monica L. Sylvester, Computer Database; Simon M. Sullivan, Draftsperson, and Sara G. Karz, Glass Analyst and Archaeologist. Senior Archaeologists included Leigh-Ann Bedal, Laurel D. Bestock, Brian A. Brown, Katrina M. Haile, Elizabeth A. Najjar, Margaret G. Parker, and the Field Excavators were Hilary Mattison, Constantinos Sistovaris, Thomas Smolenski and Benjamin H. Kleine, who also served as our 1997 Web Page Designer. John Forasté, Brown University Photographer, and his wife, Diane, spent one week recording our work. Volunteers included Betsy F. Alderman, David Barrett, Francesca and Thomas Bennett, Fr. David Clark, Patricia and John Payne and Joyce and Frank Coffey.

Besides Terry E. Tullis, Geologist, 1997 Great Temple Consultants included Architectural Historians, Judith S. McKenzie and Jacqueline Dentzer-Feydy; Thomas R. Paradise, Geologist; Zbigniew T. Fiema, Archaeologist; May Shaer, consolidation and preservation; Christian Augé, numismatics; Stephan G. Schmid, Nabataean fine wares analysis, and Yvonne Gerber, plain wares analysis. Our intrepid Foreman, again, was Dakhilallah Qublan, who was also responsible for carrying out the consolidation and conservation of the Great Temple.

Ghalib Abbadi was again assigned to us by the Department of Antiquities for help in moving architectural components and soil removal. His service to us was indispensable. Once again, the Jordanian Department of Antiquities appointed Mohammad Abd-Al-Aziz Al-Marahleh as our Jordanian Government, Department of Antiquities Representative.

### 1997 Goals

1997 marked the fifth year of two-month excavations by Brown University at the Great Temple. Not only did this season of excavation research, consolidation and publication planning promise to be productive, but also it was intended to serve as a time of

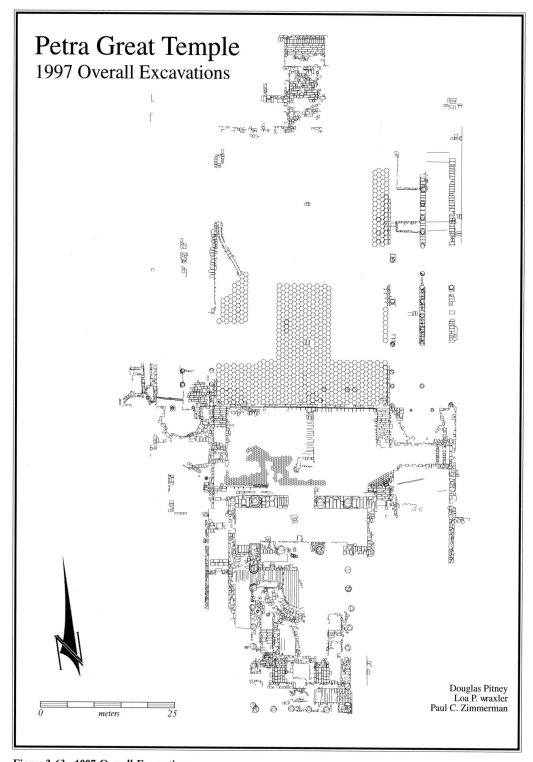

**Petra Great Temple**
1997 Overall Excavations

Douglas Pitney
Loa P. wraxler
Paul C. Zimmerman

0                meters                25

*Figure 2.63. 1997 Overall Excavations.*

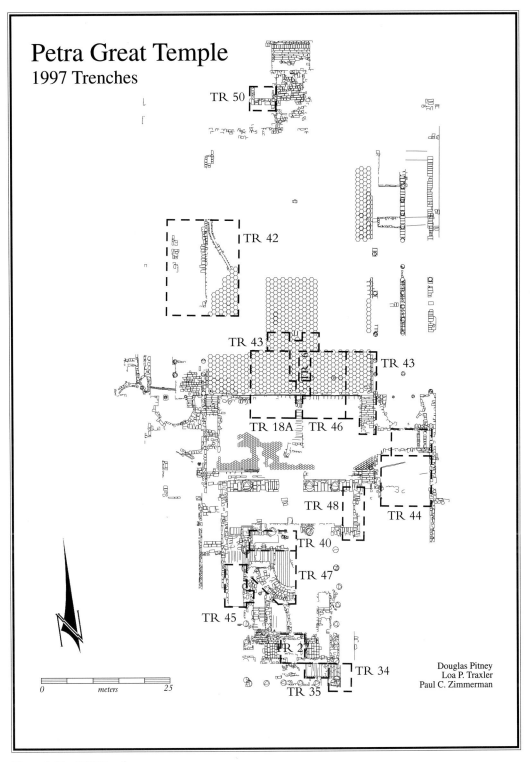

**Petra Great Temple**
1997 Trenches

TR 50

TR 42

TR 43

TR 43

TR 18A TR 46

TR 48

TR 44

TR 40

TR 47

TR 45

TR 2

TR 34

TR 35

Douglas Pitney
Loa P. Traxler
Paul C. Zimmerman

0    meters    25

*Figure 2.64. 1997 Trenches.*

| | | | N-S by E-W | |
|---|---|---|---|---|
| Trench | Location | Position | Dimensions (m) | Excavator(s) |
| | | **GREAT TEMPLE** | | |
| | | **1997 TRENCHES EXCAVATED** | | |
| 50 | Propylaeum | West of Stairs | 4.55-x-4.75 | Haile Parker |
| 42 | Lower Temenos | Center West | 18-x-14 | Haile Parker |
| 18A | Lower Temenos | Retaining Wall between West Stairway and Central Stairs | 7.35 (N)-x-7.5 (S) 14.5 (E-W) | Basile Najjar Sylvester |
| 6 | Lower Temenos | Center | 8-x-3 | Basile Najjar Sylvester |
| 43 cut | Lower Temenos | Center | 4-x-9.7 1.45-x-2.3 | Basile Najjar Sylvester |
| 46 | Lower Temenos | Center East Retaining Wall | 7 (N)-x-8 (S) 14.5 (E-W) | Basile Najjar Sylvester |
| 49 | Lower Temenos | East Stairway | 6-x-17.7 (E) 14.5 (W) | Basile Najjar Sylvester |
| 41 | Upper Temenos | East Archway | 4.5-x-9.5 | Bestock Mattison Sistovaris |
| 44 | Upper Temenos | Temenos East | 10.1-x-8.85 (W) 9.75 (E) | Bestock Mattison Sistovaris |
| 48 | Temple | East Pronaos | | Slaughter |
| 45 | Temple | West Corridor | 7.5-x-3 | Payne Joukowsky, M. |
| 47 | Temple Center West | Theatron | 9.8-x-6 | Bedal |
| 40 | Temple Center West | Theatron | 6-x-9.8 | Slaughter |
| 27 | Temple South | 'Adyton' South | 4.75-x-3.5 | Payne |
| 34 | Temple Southeast Corridor | Suleiman Column | 5-x-4 | Brown Joukowsky, M. |
| 35 | Temple 'Adyton' | Rear E-W East Stairway | 2.47-x-4.38 | Brown Parker |

*Figure 2.65. 1997 Brown University Excavation Team.*

reflection of our work during the past four years. Additionally, it was to be a field season designed to carry out priorities established in 1996. Our research design was in place, and our focus was on the multidisciplinary nature of the documentation of the excavations. We looked forward to our 1997 excavation-documentation plans with confidence, however ambitious we thought they might be.

Excavations were planned to continue in several areas.

• In the Lower Temenos, the area east of the West Stairway and the East-West Retaining Wall (Trench 18, 1996) would undergo excavation until the area west of the Central Stairs was cleared.

• Excavation also would be undertaken in the west Lower Temenos to better understand its shared connection with the Hexagonal Pavement and the East Colonnade as well as to confirm their architectural plans. The East Stairway (Elizabeth Stairway) from the Lower Temenos to the Upper Temenos would be located and excavated.

• Once excavation had been completed in the above two areas, the East Exedra, which had been partially excavated in 1996, was to undergo continued investigation.

• In the Upper Temenos, excavation would continue in the 'Arched Passage' from the Upper Temenos to the presumed Lower Market (Trench 38, 1996).

• In the Great Temple, a new trench would be located behind the West Anta wall (Patricia Anta) in the Temple Cella to define the architecture of this area. Of particular interest was our 1996 discovery of the upper courses of a major east-west semicircular wall. We speculated that this wall might clearly define the area and that it held the promise of being a major architectural component of the Great Temple. This curvilinear wall would be cleared on the west in a new trench to expose its upper courses and to understand how it inter-related with the West 'Adyton' Stairway (Monica Stairway) and the West 'Adyton' room.

• Research also would continue in the rear of the Temple (Trenches 34, 35 and 26, 1996) to better understand the inter-relationship between the 'Adyton' arch and the Temple Rear.

• Continued excavation would also take place on the east side of the Temple Rear, near the Suleiman Column in the East Corridor (Trench 34), to locate its founding level.

To aid visitors, signs with the site plan and explanation of the major features of the site, in

Arabic and English, were placed on site. The major objective of 1997 was to further clarify the ground plan of the Great Temple and to publish the results of our five years of research.

## 1997 Projected Publication Program The Five-Year Report of 1993-1997 Excavations

A working copy of the record of the past four years of our Brown University investigations was in a preliminary stage. Much work had yet to be done to finalize this report, and the 1997 season was also intended to be a work-study season. Therefore, the four years of field reports, as well as specialist studies on surveying, architecture, inscriptions, coins, sculpture and lamps and the neutron activation analysis of the pottery, were taken into the field. Some of these reports already had been readied for publication but required additional documentation, and there were the 1993-1996 artifact and field reports to update and edit. Some of the artifacts, like the coins, required additional documentation, thus much of our time was given over to the myriad of the details for this publication.

## 1997 Results

### 1997 Propylaeum

In order to better understand the Propylaeum, work was initiated in Trench 50 to the west of the Stairs of the Propylaeum. Defined here was a columned terrace structure with limestone stylobate blocks, many of which bore mason's marks (Figure 2.66). This structure extended 5 m (east-west)-x-3.28 m (north-south). Once a series of wall structures were cleared, the column drums found lying nearby were re-erected. The small, exquisite limestone sculpture of a lion's head was re-covered in this excavation. More excavation must take place in this area if we are to define the Propylaeum and its relationship to the stairs.

### 1997 Lower Temenos

Lying to the west of the Temple precinct near the Temenos Gate was the backfill from the so-called 'Baths' excavations, left there from the 1950s and 1980s. This fill, conspicuous in our 1994-1996 aerial photographs, was covering an area of possible excavation that might delineate the architecture of the Lower Temenos and locate what interconnections, if any, existed between the Temple and the Baths. After days of work, this backfill was finally removed. Excavations in this area will take place in the future. We designed a drainage abutment, with the soil reinforced by stone, so that the winter rains would be drawn away from collecting in the excavated 6 m depth of the Bath structure excavations.

Excavation was undertaken in the west Lower Temenos to better understand its shared connection with the central sector of the Hexagonal Pavement and the East Colonnade and to confirm their architectural plans. In Trench 42, a large portion of the Hexagonal Pavement was cleared. To the trench west, under the Hexagonal Pavement, a portion of the Nabataean rebuilt-reconstructed Canalization System was excavated. Extending southeast to northwest, this shallow canal presumably connected to the system discovered in the center of the Lower Temenos (Figure 2.67). This part of the system was found in 1994, when the disturbed pavers had lost their support and had tumbled into the early Nabataean Subterranean Canalization System drainage. Recovered from a segment of this shallow canalization, at a point where the water system took an abrupt turn to the west, was an extraordinary cache of first-century CE Nabataean wares, which in antiquity had clogged the canal. These are presented in Chapter 6, along with other ceramics.

Excavations continued in several areas along the East-West Retaining Wall of the Lower Temenos (Figure 2.68). The area east of the West Stairway and the East-West Retaining Wall (Trench 18, 1996) underwent excavation until the areas east and west of the Central Stairs were cleared. This major project was undertaken in Trenches 18A, 43 and 46 to recover the full expanse of the massive East-West Retaining Wall, which when fully exposed measured some 27 m in east-west length.

From the east corner of the East Exedra to the west corner of the West Exedra, the width of structural elements in this southern terminus of the Lower Temenos was now found to measure approximately 55.7 m in total length. Time, however, precluded the continued excavation of the East Exedra.

*Figure 2.66. Propylaeum, looking northwest, 1997.*

*Figure 2.67. Canalization System, west Lower Temenos, 1997.*

*Figure 2.68. East-West Retaining Wall, looking east, 1997.*

*Figure 2.69. East Stairway (Elizabeth Stairway), looking south, 1997.*

*Figure 2.70. Arches of 'Cistern' during excavation, east Upper Temenos, 1997.*

Time permitted the East Stairway (Elizabeth Stairway) from the Lower Temenos to the Temple Forecourt to be located and excavated in Trench 49 (Figure 2.69). Two-thirds of the East Stairway, or 7.20 m in north-south length-x-2.61 m in east-west width, was excavated. Many of the stair treads of this stairway were found cracked, broken and slumped at downward angles into a branch of the Nabataean Subterranean Canalization System, which lay below the stairs.

For better public understanding of the precinct, we continued to re-erect columns in the east triple colonnade (SP 48).

## 1997 Upper Temenos

In the Upper Temenos, excavation continued in the Arched Passage from the Upper Temenos to the presumed Lower Market (Trench 38, 1996; Trench 41, 1997) (Figure 2.70). Found in Trench 41 (Trench 38, 1996) and bonding with the rear wall of the East Exedra were an elegant series of seven arches; however, all but the two recognized and consolidated in 1996 had collapsed in antiquity and could not be reconstructed. Excavated to a 5 m depth (Figure 2.71), a portion of this probable cistern contained numerous Nabataean wares as well as stacks of imported marble pavers. It is estimated that the original

measurements of this structure were 10 m in east-west length-x-3.23 m in north-south width. More work has to be undertaken in this area before the full extent of this structure is fully understood. (The excavation of this area is planned for 1998.)

*Figure 2.71. Looking down into the 'Cistern,' 1997. Photograph by Sara G. Karz.*

Undertaken as SP 50 in the Temple Forecourt, the massive, precariously fallen, one-ton sandstone drums that had tumbled from the Temple Porch were stabilized in 1997 to prevent their further collapse onto the Lower Temenos. This involved repositioning the drums and providing them with additional support to arrest slippage that might be caused by earthquake action or winter rains.

### 1997 Great Temple

The earth choking the east exterior wall by the excavation of the interior East Anta (Pierre Anta) was removed in Trench 48 so that the full sweep, measuring approximately 6.40 m in width-x-24.5 m in length, of the Temple Pronaos could be viewed. Here it was found that the East Corridor wall, extending between the Temple Stylobate, the Anta wall and the beginning of the East Colonnade, was in a better state of preservation than its twin counterpart (Patricia Anta) excavated in 1994 on the west.

### The *Theatron*-shaped Structure and Related Features

In the Great Temple several new initiatives were undertaken. One of the major excavations was that of the east-west semicircular wall (the upper courses of this wall had been discovered in 1996). We posited that this excavation would define the Cella — it held the promise of being a major architectural component of the Great Temple. In exposing the upper courses of this wall, we also wanted to understand how it inter-related with the West 'Adyton' Stairway (Monica Stairway), the West 'Adyton' room, the Central Arch and, of course, the Great Temple architecture as a whole. Our expectations were more than met!

Here was found a theater structure; a summary of our findings are presented below under the subdivisions: Cavea, Orchestra, Pulpitum or Platform, Walkway between the Orchestra and the Cavea, West Corridor and Temple Rear. This is followed by a discussion of the structure's tentative flow pattern.

**Cavea.** Trench 40, measuring 9.8-x-6 m, was located to the west of the Lee Column, and it extended to the center of the Cella. Before excavation we thought this would define the front wall of the curvilinear Cella. In an irregularly shaped Trench 47, excavation was undertaken to define the rear wall of the Cella. One half of an apsidal structure with tiers of seating was discovered, which we tentatively identified as a Nabataean structure in the form of a theater (from the Greek *theatron*, meaning "a place of seeing"). Facing north were five

*Figure 2.72. Theatron, 1997.*

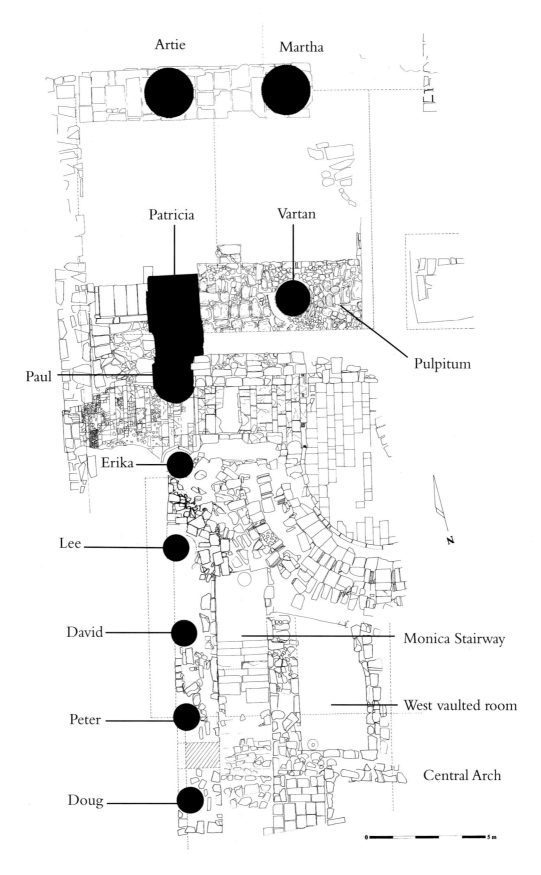

Artie
Martha

Patricia
Vartan

Pulpitum

Paul

Erika

Lee

David — Monica Stairway

West vaulted room

Peter

Central Arch

Doug

0 ▬▬▬▬▬▬▬▬▬▬▬ 5 m

N

*Figure 2.73. Plan of Theatron and surroundings. Drawing by Martha S. Joukowsky, 1997.*

extant courses of carefully hewn, limestone seats, with two six-step stairways (scalaria) in the cavea (Figure 2.72). This cavea was above a 1.5 m-high plastered apsidal wall. Below the lowest tier was a paved diazoma (horizontal passageway or aisle) on the lower cavea wall, measuring 1.5 m in width and set with alternating white and dark red sandstone pavers. The extant, lower, five-course cavea wall was constructed with carefully dressed blocks, 0.20-0.30 m in height with curved faces. Unquestionably, the auditorium was central to the structure, and it dominated the monument's interior.

The cavea seats averaged 0.35-0.40 m in height and 0.55-0.70 m in depth. The second to fifth tiers were of white sandstone ashlars, which were divided into four wedge-shaped sections (cunei). Based on the excavated evidence, we can predict that the cavea was divided by three staircases — with one in the center and two on either side. Although the collapse of the West Colonnade scarred the structure, further evidence for the seating was found to continue up to the east and west platforms to where the rear of the cavea must have stood in antiquity. The complex is built up to the casemate Inter-Columnar walls, over the vaulted substructures of the East and West Stairways (Simon and Monica Stairways), over the 3-x-5.5 m vaulted west chamber, over the as yet unexcavated east chamber (which is presumed to exist), and over the center area of the Central Arch.

Of note was that some of the blocks in the seating area were channeled ashlars — their tops and facing surfaces had been chiseled out to produce narrow, 0.02-0.05 m-deep, rectilinear, channel-like slots, which may have served as the socles for wooden arm rests or dividers. We hypothesized they may have delineated single and double seats.[36] In the massive collapse that fell into the West 'Adyton' Stairway (Monica Stairway), the West 'Adyton' room and the Central Arch area, many channeled ashlars were found in the debris — we reason these slotted blocks were used throughout the cavea. To reiterate, the cavea extended over the Monica and Simon Stairways, the vaulted rooms and the Central Arch to the rear of the Temple.

Unfortunately, the upper portions of the structure were either in poor condition or were completely missing. In spite of this, we project that there may have been as many as 20

original courses of seats, with a diazoma bisecting the cavea between the tenth and the eleventh row of seats.[37] A conservative estimate of the seating capacity would be a minimum of 550 and a maximum of 630 persons. This is based on the probability that the excavated preserved portion held at least 52 people, and if there were originally a total of 20 tiers of seats extending to the South Stairways, this would account for substantial additional seating. These calculations must remain tentative, however, until we can confirm the extent of the cavea to the south.

On the north is a small, narrow, 0.7 m, stepped, sandstone stairway that leads up to the cavea. Although there are post holes for a railing, it does not appear as if this stairway provided a major access to the auditorium; it is so poorly constructed that it may well have been a later addition for access into the cavea.

**Orchestra.** The projected preserved diameter of the orchestra is approximately 6.5 m (Figure 2.73). The floor of the orchestra is paved with rectilinear sandstones placed longitudinally, north-south, and perpendicular to the center of the cavea. These were set in place after the cavea was constructed. A line of red pavers led us to speculate that originally this floor may have had a variegated, patterned design. Unfortunately, the damage to it is appreciable — perhaps in our future excavations of the remaining part of the structure, the floor design may become better delineated.

The orchestra area is too restricted and small for any large function but may have been used for speeches, dramatic presentations, simple religious rituals and ceremonies. In the east balk of Trench 47, the orchestra, is a collapsed stone feature of four ashlars that has yet to be excavated. This may have served as a platform, as the base for a statue or even as an altar. Future excavation will clarify the function of this feature.

**Pulpitum or Platform.** The east-west excavations in Trench 40, between the Paul Column (to the rear of the East Pronaos) and the Mohammad Column, were very productive, for there is an architectural component that we tentatively identified as a pulpitum or the front of a raised platform, which at this time has been incompletely excavated. Constructed of sandstone ashlars four courses in height, the excavated portion of this feature is 1.3 m in height-x-5.66 m in length-x-approximately 1 m in width. It is curbed by sandstone ashlars, 0.4 m in width, which lie 0.3 m above the orchestra floor. In the south wall facing the cavea, interrupting the wall of diagonally dressed sandstone blocks, are two small staircases, and in the center there is a niche 0.5 m in width-x-0.4 m in depth. It is assumed that this feature, if a *scaenae frons* (stage building), cut off the visibility to the Temple Pronaos and the entrance of anyone seated in the cavea, but if it was a raised platform, visibility to the Temple Forecourt would still have been possible.

**Walkway-entry.** A paved walkway of some 3m in width lies between this stage-like structure or platform — either the pulpitum or the *scaenae frons* (stage building) — and the orchestra. At the east end of the excavated portion of this walkway and positioned perpendicular to the pulpitum or platform is a threshold, 3 m in length-x-0.30 m in width, with deeply cut, squared, hollow cavities in its upper surface. Because quantities of metal were found in this area, it is probable that these cavities supported a gate or door with metal fittings.

**West Corridor.** As in past years, the interior of the Great Temple was found to have been highly decorated. The 1.9 m casemate walls of the West Corridor (Trenches 45 and 47), constructed up to and behind the West Anta pier (Patricia Anta, Trench 48), were frescoed with red, yellow, green and blue stucco. More columns were found covered with vestiges of red and white stucco serving as decorative idioms.

Excavations also took place in the West Corridor to define the architecture of this area. These investigations took place behind the West Anta wall (Patricia Anta) and from the engaged Paul Column to the Erika Column, extending to the Temple Center west. Recovered were many well-preserved, worked, decorative stucco fragments, some with egg and tongue and egg and dart motifs, some vegetal elements and some painted cornice fragments. One limestone, acanthus capital fragment still had traces of gold leaf adhering to its surface!

In the southeast of Trench 45 (between the Lee and David Columns), we also excavated the arched doorway in the casemate Inter-Columnar wall at the bottom of the West 'Adyton' Stairway (Monica Stairway), between the West Stairway and the West Corridor (Figure 2.74). Presumably this arched doorway provided access to the steps that led up to the platforms in the rear of the cavea. Erosion damage to the arched doorway had been appreciable from annual winter rains that had been trapped at the bottom of the exposed stairs. Therefore, the main purpose of this work was to open this area for the passage of water from winter rains. During excavation, the structural integrity of the arch, its Inter-Columnar wall and the Lee Column showed a serious need for stabilization. The ashlars had not fallen but had been jostled out of their original positions and were listing to the west. This stabilization was completed during the fall of 1997 before the advent of the winter rains.

**Temple Rear.** Continued research was devoted to the rear of the Temple (Trenches 34, 35 and 26, 1996) to better understand the inter-relationship between the 'Adyton' Central Arch and the Temple Rear. Excavation resumed under the now consolidated Central Arch in Trench 26, but when the arch ashlars were found to be further compromised by earthquake, the project was abandoned until additional consolidation measures could be put into effect.

To our great surprise in the center south of the Temple, leading up to the platform that was supported by the Central Arch, was the recovery of an east-west flight of stairs (Brian Stairway) extending from the upper 'Adyton' to the interior East Corridor, approximately 7m in length-x-2.2 m in width. At the foot of these stairs (elevation 885.93 m), we discovered that they were built around, and therefore constructed after, the Attic heart-shaped, column base of the Suleiman Column in Trench 34 (Figures 2.75 and 2.76). A large window and an arched doorway were found in the south wall of the stairway. At their top, they accessed the small paved platform and the north-south East Stairway (Simon Stairway) excavated in Trench 15 in 1995. (The elevation of the East Corridor floor lies at a 7 m depth below present-day ground level.)

In the Temple Rear, continued excavation also took place on the east side of the Temple in the East Corridor (Trench 34) to locate its founding level. (This operation continued the Trench 34 excavations initiated in 1996.) Eight courses of the massive heart-shaped, southeast column (Suleiman Column) were

*Figure 2.74. View through west arched doorway, looking east, 1997.*

*Figure 2.75. Excavation of Brian Stairway and Suleiman Column, 1997.*

*Figure 2.76. Brian Stairway with lower courses of heart-shaped column (Suleiman Column), 1997.*

removed, section by section, for re-erection. Here too, large amounts of multicolored — green, red, blue and yellow — decorative stucco were recovered.

## Design — Flow Pattern

Now, given a new plan for this building, how did it work? We found the flow pattern at the time it was used as a theatron to be extraordinarily well planned and efficient (Figure 2.77).

On the ground level, access was from the Lower Temenos, up the East or West Stairways, (Laurel and Elizabeth Stairways) to the East or West Walkways and from the Walkways into the East or West Corridors. Alternatively, access might also have been gained though the Temple Entrance, if it too was not blocked,[38] to the front of the now blocked Temple Pronaos. (As the pulpitum wall had been constructed between the two center columns, the participant was obliged either to turn to the right and then to the left into the West Corridor or to turn to the left to gain entry into the as yet unexcavated East Corridor.)

Once in the corridors, the major route that would have been taken by most participants who wished to access the cavea would have

been from the now excavated West Corridor. The major access would have been through the arched doorway between the Lee and David Columns. (We anticipate a similar entrance to the East Stairway (Simon Stairway) from the East Corridor, between the Michael and Francesca Columns.) Returning to the structure west, once the West Stairway (Monica Stairway) had been mounted, access to the cavea was via the paved platforms at the top of these stairs, which with a 90° turn accessed the twin small flights of steps that may have led to an arched passage that exited at the middle diazoma. Once in the cavea, the participant would have had the option either to descend to the lower rows of seats or mount the scalaria that led to the upper seating and up to the diazoma, if one existed, at the upper reaches of the cavea.

Entry or egress from the rear of the Temple Theatron could also have been from the East or West Corridors. These participants would have elected to walk up the recently excavated Trench 35 Southeast Stairway (Brian Stairway) or the as yet unexcavated Southwest Stairway (Jean Stairway), which led from the East and West Corridors to the twin platforms that accessed the rear of the cavea. Also from the corridors, entry or exit could have been gained through the exterior East and West Walkways.

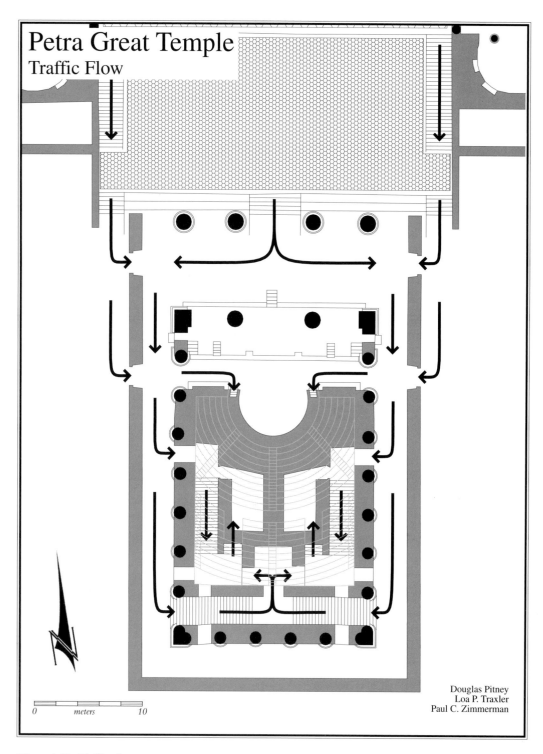

**Petra Great Temple**
Traffic Flow

Douglas Pitney
Loa P. Traxler
Paul C. Zimmerman

0    meters    10

**Figure 2.77.** *Traffic Flow.*

As for the narrow series of steps found leading up the side of the cavea to the lower west cavea walkway, it would appear that this was a minor access, perhaps for special purposes, and that these served as "emergency" steps to the front of the cavea walkway (and from there to one of the three major scalaria).

For the performers, from the west, we do know that between the Paul and Erika Columns there must have been a secondary entrance along the paved walkway that led to the orchestra on the west. (We assume the same plan existed on the east between the Loa and Deirdre Columns.) This access would also have served the performers, the speakers, in short — any person who was to perform on the orchestra floor. An additional entry onto the top of the platform is the narrow 0.8 m passageway from the West Corridor that is cut into the wall between the Patricia Anta and the Paul Column. (It will be interesting to excavate the corresponding East Anta (Pierre Anta) and the Loa Column wall to find if an opening existed here as well.)

Before turning to the discussion of this structure, charts are presented on pages 126 and 127 with the major elevations and distances of the Great Temple components.

## Discussion

The Great Temple stands alone above a large colonnaded Lower Temenos among thousands of architectural fragments, including elephant-headed capitals. The Temple itself is embellished with floral Nabataean capitals, and it cannot be forgotten that this well-preserved building is also decorated with masks, recovered from the West Walkway in 1995. The whole precinct is built with an emphasis on axiality and frontality.

Interpreting this large public edifice is at the heart of the archaeological process — there has been a great deal of debate regarding the identity of this building. If our structure is, in fact, a Great Temple, the hypaethral (open-air) Theater is certainly its dominant architectural element.[39] On one hand, this structure is built like a temple, and on the other, it has a theater-like structure in place of the cella. It cannot have served as a sacred space, a religious building that was decommissioned and desacralized. In other words, it could not have been built as a temple and then have become

transformed into a civic structure; I have to assume that a shift in function would go against Nabataean religious tradition. Therefore, it must have served either as a religious or as a secular structure. And if it is a religious structure, why could it not have served as an instrument of religio-political propaganda? The kings of Nabataea certainly utilized religion to further their political ambitions.

For some time I have been puzzled about this monumental structure. Although the conventions of classical architecture proscribe this building to be the Great Temple, it is clear that Nabataean creativity, their lack of preconceived ideas and their unusual architectural borrowings from the classical world could have led them to utilize the Great Temple either for ritual or administrative purposes. The purpose of this structure has yet to be determined — it remains a riddle. We know that this theater-like structure must have served as the central focus for the Great Temple after it was rebuilt. Since the interpretation of this building is somewhat enigmatic, future excavation will hopefully clarify its function.

In future seasons we will test several hypotheses to explain and understand this building.

1) It was a temple or a theater-temple, or

2) It served as the civic center for Petra in the Nabataean and Nabataean-Roman periods as,

> a) a bouleuterion where the boule (city council) met or as a *comitium* or *curia*, a Roman political meeting place;
>
> b) an odeum or small concert hall, or
>
> c) a law court, council chamber, meeting hall.

Now it is possible that this is a civic structure — perhaps it is where the Nabataean "popular assembly" held their meetings. It is worth requoting Strabo (16.4) who states:

> Petra is always ruled by some king from the royal family; and the king has as Administrator one of his companions, who is called "brother." It is exceedingly well governed; at any rate, Athenodorus, a philosopher and companion of mine, who had been in the city of the Petraeans, used to describe their government with

| ELEVATIONS OF MAJOR TEMPLE PRECINCT COMPONENTS I (in m a.s.l.) | |
|---|---|
| **Site Datum Points** | |
| Al-Katute | 911.23 |
| CP 103 | 895.48 |
| CP 104 | 884.34 |
| CP 10 | 878.73 |
| **Colonnaded Street** | |
| Crown, directly north of Propylaeum | 870.77 |
| South gutter, directly north of Propylaeum | 870.59 |
| **Stairs of the Propylaeum** | |
| Curbing | 871.10 |
| Lowest step | 871.19 |
| Upper step | 877.69 |
| **Lower Temenos** | |
| Hexagonal Pavement | 879.12 ± 0.12 |
| Easternmost Colonnade, pavers and stylobate slope downward slightly | 879.07 ± 0.16 |
| Sondage, SP 25, depth | 872.41 |
| West Exedra | |
|    Height (maximum) | 883.96 |
|    Porch column Stylobate | 879.79 |
|    Byzantine platform | 880.69 |
| West Stairway (Laurel Stairway) | |
|    Lowest step-curb | 879.58 |
|    Restored upper step | 884.38 |
| East Exedra | |
|    Height (maximum) | 885.60 |
|    Porch column Stylobate | 879.59 |
| East Stairway (Elizabeth Stairway) | |
|    Lowest step-curb | 879.58 |
|    Last excavated upper step | 883.02 |
| **Upper Temenos** | |
| West Corridor | 885.91 ± 0.06 |
|    Height (maximum) | 889.46 |
| East Corridor | 885.87 ± 0.03 |
|    Height (maximum) | 890.51 |
| Temple Forecourt | 884.46 ± 0.04 |
| East Archway 'Cistern' | |
|    Arch upper elevation | 885.67 |
|    Lowest excavated elevation (quarry) | 879.20 |
|    Lowest plaster floor | 881.06 |
| **Subterranean Canalization System** | |
| Temple Forecourt, capstone upper elevation | 884.29 |
| Floor elevation | 882.04 |
| Trench 13, lowest elevation below Hexagonal Pavement | ~ 878.68 |
| **Temple** | |
| Stylobate | 886.07 ± 0.05 |
| Pronaos | 885.79 ± 0.04 |
| West Anta (Patricia Anta), preserved height | 2.6 |
| Fatma Column, preserved height in south | 8.5 |
| Restored Porch columns, average | 888.40 ± 0.10 |
| West Anta (Patricia Anta), elevation | 889.59 |
| East Anta (Pierre Anta), elevation | 888.19 |
| West Walkway | 885.98 ± 0.01 |
| Theatron | |
|    Orchestra | 885.97 ± 0.02 |
|    Lowest diazoma | 887.55 ± 0.02 |
|    Lowest seating | 887.94 ± 0.01 |
|    Uppermost excavated seating | 889.03 |
|    Projected last seat | ~ 895.11 |
|    Lowest step | 886.42 |
|    Restored uppermost step | 890.93 |
|    Upper platform | 890.93 |

| ELEVATIONS OF MAJOR TEMPLE PRECINCT COMPONENTS II (in m a.s.l.) | |
|---|---|
| East Stairway (Simon Stairway) | |
| Floor at the bottom of stairs | 886.05 |
| Lowest step | 886.42 |
| Restored uppermost step | 890.96 |
| Upper platform | 890.97 |
| West Stairway (Monica Stairway) | |
| Floor at the bottom of stairs | 886.07 |
| Lowest step | 886.42 |
| Restored uppermost step | 890.93 |
| Upper platform | 890.93 |
| Central Arch | |
| Top of keystone | 890.95 |
| East rear column (Suleiman Column), restored height | 892.93 |

| DIMENSIONS OF GREAT TEMPLE PRECINCT COMPONENTS (in m) | |
|---|---|
| **Precinct, from portico wall in the Propylaeum to the preserved south precinct wall** | |
| North-south | 135 |
| East-west | 56 |
| Total area | 7560 m² (3/4 hectare) |
| **Stairs of the Propylaeum** | |
| Width | 7.4 |
| Length | 17 |
| **Lower Temenos, from the Propylaeum retaining wall to the East-West Retaining Wall** | |
| North-south | 49 |
| East-west | 56 |
| Retaining wall west | 28 |
| Expanse of Lower Temenos from the East Exedra to the West Exedra | 32.7 |
| East Colonnade | |
| Width | 11.8 |
| Length from the exedrae to Propylaeum terrace wall | 54 |
| East Exedra | |
| North-south depth | 5.4 |
| East-west | 6.8 |
| West Exedra | |
| North-south depth | 5.3 |
| East-west | 6.5 |
| **Temple** | |
| Porch Stylobate, east-west | 28 |
| Temple, north-south | 42.5 |
| East Anta and the East Porch column (Nadine Column), interaxial distance | ~ 4.4 |
| East Porch columns (Nadine and Pia Columns), interaxial distance | 5.03 |
| Central Porch columns (Pia and Martha Columns), interaxial distance | ~ 7.06 |
| West Porch columns (Martha and Artie Columns), interaxial distance | 5.03 |
| Pronaos | |
| Width from the Stylobate south edge to the front of the Pierre and Patricia Antae | 6.5 |
| Length | 24.7 |
| Side columns, interaxial distance east and west | 3.51 |
| Rear columns, interaxial distance | 3.27 |
| Theatron | |
| Orchestra floor diameter | 6.43 |
| Proposed diameter of outermost seats in Zimmerman reconstruction | 33.2 |
| Estimated seating capacity | |
| 0.5  m per person | 565 |
| 0.45 m per person | 620 |
| West Corridor | |
| Length from front of the West Anta (Patricia Anta) to the rear | 12 |
| Width | 3 |
| West Walkway | |
| Excavated length from the front of the West Anta (Patricia Anta) | 33.3 |
| Width | 3.7 |

admiration, for he said that he found both many Romans and many other foreigners sojourning there, and that he saw that the foreigners often engaged in lawsuits, both with one another and with the natives, but that none of the natives prosecuted one another, and that they in every way kept peace with one another...

The king is so democratic that, in addition to serving himself, he sometimes even serves the rest himself in his turn. He often renders an account of his kingship in the popular assembly;[40] and sometimes his mode of life is examined.

We must be mindful of the Latin Imperial inscription studied by Stephen V. Tracy and dated between (?)112 and 114 CE, found in the rear west vaulted room on the floor.[41] Further investigations of the parallel room to the east (the east chamber has yet to be excavated) may determine the actual purpose of these interior chambers in the rear of the Temple. There is but a single entry into this west chamber, measuring 3.5 m in width-x-5.5 m in depth with walls 4 m in height. It did serve for storage in the late Nabataean-Roman period (for stacks of roof tiles were found here lying in an earth deposit above the Latin inscription), but originally it may have served as a secure space for keeping records, a room for the storage of arms, a holding pen for prisoners or, although dark, a changing room for actors. Or its purpose may have been solely for the support of the cavea extending above it.

But perhaps the Great Temple was rebuilt as a bouleuterion? We should not forget the multiple references to the boule at Petra in the Babatha Archives discovered by Yigael Yadin from the *Cave of the Letters.*[42]

The Great Temple precinct's location adjacent to the Temenos Gate and the most sacred Qasr al-Bint is not accidental. A Great Temple or a bouleuterion-odeum should be accessible to the citizens of Petra and provide a gathering place where the decisions of the day could be announced and discussed by the populace. So, was the Great Temple a center of worship where performances of a ritual nature were performed, or was it the location of the highest court? Or did this structure serve other or perhaps even multiple civic functions? We seek scholarly discussion of this issue.

Even if we restrict the interpretation of the function of the building, we are still left in the dark with a number of compelling questions. If it is a temple, what deity is worshipped here? And if it served as a civic center, what was its intended use — bouleuterion, odeum, bouleuterion and odeum; it is conceivable that it could have been used for both purposes.[43] How does this precinct relate to the urban fabric of the city itself? It must be considered in relation to the city plan of central Petra. While the function of this structure remains obscure, it surely presents a significant architectural component of Petra.

Although we have shed new light on urban Petra, the implications of these finds have certainly opened new questions about the site and the city. The reappraisal of the Great Temple architecture, chronologically and stratigraphically, will greatly enhance our understanding of the socio-political and religious culture of Petra. More discussion will be given to the interpretation of these interesting architectural and functional questions by Joseph J. Basile and Erika L. Schluntz.[44] Although we, as archaeologists, have the same general frame of reference, there may be differences in our interpretations. As this is an interim report, many questions may be answered by further excavation, but additionally, we are hopeful that our readers will reassess the evidence and provide us with the answers.

## 1997 Catalog

The 1997 catalog contains an additional 33 coins, 68 lamps and 46 other items, including Nabataean wares, a partial Greek inscription, a Rhodian-style stamped amphora handle dated from ca. 146 to 108 BCE (see Chapter 8), two bronze finials and the extraordinary sculpture of a lion's head found in Trench 50 of the Propylaeum. Portions of elephant-headed capitals continued to be recovered in the Lower Temenos; although they fit the diameters of the Lower Temenos column drums, the mystery remains as to what part of the Lower Temenos these capitals adorned. Architectural decorative elements continue to be prolific, but of particular interest is a pilaster found in the Lower Temenos fill above the Hexagonal Pavement. This is a limestone block with the relief of a life-sized, headless torso, whose identity has yet to be discovered.

*Figure 2.78. 1997 site aerial, post-excavation, looking south.*

*Figure 2.79. Arched doorway, West Corridor, looking southeast, 1997.*

*Figure 2.80. Arched doorway, West Corridor, requiring consolidation, 1997.*

Sara G. Karz has been studying the glass fragments, which had not been given close attention up to now, and has prepared her research for Chapter 6. Additional drawings and photographs were made of our architectural fragments and the pottery. Our database now stores some 115,742 items; in 1997 the Grosso Modo database had 31,181 objects recorded, with approximately 21,300 (68%) representing pottery sherds. Our architectural fragment database, totaling 5078 fragments, saw an additional 832 pieces recorded in 1997, many of which were again capital elements. Thus, our corpus of objects was updated not only with the new finds but also with a fuller documentation of those we have identified as having been unearthed in important loci.

## 1997 Consolidation and Preservation

1997 consolidation projects continued the work of previous years. An additional 75 m of fencing was installed to protect the areas excavated as well as the large architectural fragments that were recovered. Before excavation can resume, we are devoted to the time-consuming quarrying and cutting of new blocks for step areas that have been robbed and to the pointing and consolidation of the architectural elements of the precinct.

In the **Lower Temenos**, there are three projects. The East Exedra, excavated in 1996, suffered structurally during the 1996 winter rains. Because it was in danger of collapse, this structure underwent extensive consolidation. Now that it has been reinforced, it is planned for excavation in 1998.

The curbing in front of the East-West Retaining Wall has been consolidated, for its blocks over time have shifted from their original positions.

The 1997 excavations found the East Stairway (Elizabeth Stairway) from the Lower to the Upper Temenos in varying states of collapse into the Subterranean Canalization System that extended below them. It is planned to create extra support for these steps before they are consolidated and reinstalled.

In the **Upper Temenos** and the **Great Temple**, columns that had collapsed from earthquake tremors continued to be re-erected. In addition, there was the consolidation of deteriorated blocks found in all areas of the site.

Both the East and West 'Adyton' Stairways (Simon and Monica Stairways) suffered erosion from the heavy rains of 1996. An enormous effort has been made for their consolidation and restoration. The re-erection of seven courses of the five- to six-part engaged drums of the heart-shaped Suleiman Column in the rear east of the Great Temple now has been completed. Before this process could be undertaken, the Nabataean support wall behind the Suleiman Column had to be dismantled and reconstructed, for it had all but collapsed to the west and was intruding on the area occupied by the column.

The Central Arch, once again, required support before further excavation. Partially conserved in 1995 and 1996, this area was partially excavated again in 1997, because we wanted to see it in its entirety. To our disappointment, further consolidation has to be undertaken before further excavation can take place. This will be completed before the onset of the 1998 season.

The West Corridor and the Inter-Columnar wall arch required complete dismantlement for anastylosis to take place. The west flank of this wall, its arch and the Lee Column were excavated in 1997. It was discovered that these architectural elements had undergone significant earthquake damage — both the wall and the arch had slumped out of position at awkward angles to the west (Figures 2.79 and 2.80 — see also Plates 14-16). The Lee Column had to be completely dismantled and re-erected during the 1997 field operations Figure 2.81). This time-consuming re-erection during the 1997 field season placed an enormous strain on the progress of the 1997 field schedule. But, because of logistics, it had to be completed before work in the theater-like structure could be initiated.

The theater-like structure requires consolidation. We thought it better to postpone this effort until some point in the future when this structure will be fully excavated.

We continue to be committed to the consolidation of this great edifice, which in part has been made possible by the World Monuments Fund. Although our major subventions are through Brown University, we have received significant support not only from the Department of Antiquities, but also from the newly formed Petra Regional Council.

## 1997 Publication

Again, 1997 was an active year, for some 20 scholarly lectures were delivered, and several publications appeared (see the Site Bibliography).

## At Home 1997-1998

Awarded a Kress Fellowship for her dissertation research on the Temple architecture, Erika L. Schluntz spent the fall in Amman and on site in Petra.

In Petra, major-scale consolidation was carried out under the direction of Dakhilallah Qublan. Knowing that the site was susceptible to deterioration from the winter rains, the main areas of focus were the repair of the East 'Adyton' Stairway (Simon Stairway), the

*Figure 2.81. Lee Column showing re-erection, 1997.*

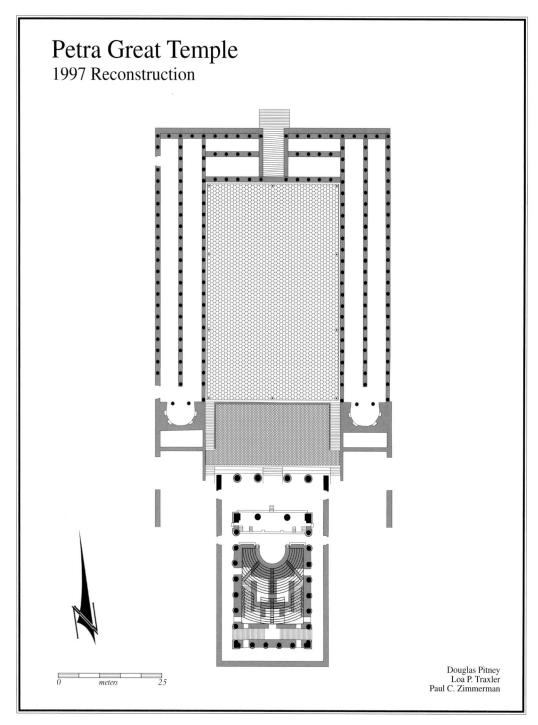

*Figure 2.82. 1997 Reconstruction.*

Trench 45 arch and wall at the bottom of these stairs and the Inter-Columnar wall between the Lee and David Columns, which required complete removal and re-erection. In the Temple Rear, the Suleiman Column was also re-erected with the elements that had been removed during the 1997 excavation season. Once this project had been completed, a dam was constructed at the east rear of the Great Temple to divert rainfall.

Donna J. D'Agostino created an upgrade of the architectural fragment database, and I spent an appreciable amount of time (two months) entering the data. Sara G. Karz kept working on the glass database and photographed the glass catalog. At the American Center of Oriental Research, the elegant bronze finials were restored by Fatma Marii. The 1997 coins, which had been given a preliminary reading during the field campaign by Christian Augé, were cleaned in Amman also by Fatma Marii. After Yvonne Gerber had studied the pottery, the Trench 42 fragments were sent to Providence, where I drafted and described them. Simon M. Sullivan undertook the drawing of cataloged items and several of the architectural features, but in the main, the trench drawings were drafted in Amman by Ala H. Bedawi. The site catalog was organized for publication by Deirdre G. Barrett.

The plans for a full digital reconstruction and virtual reality tour of the Great Temple were prepared by Eileen L. Vote, Brown University graduate student in the Department of the History of Art and Architecture. The complete model of the whole edifice, generated in Auto CAD, was exported to a modeling program (3D Studio MAX©). Because a large part of the Great Temple is no longer standing, producing such a simulation will enable our archaeology colleagues, architectural historians and anthropologists to work on a visual reconstruction of the site as a whole and to experience how the Temple may have looked during the various stages of its use. A digital simulation will also provide us with the ability to show in a realistic way what the architecture of the central part of Petra looked like in antiquity. The completed project will allow the viewer to experience the whole building in its setting by creating a full virtual environment. It is projected that this study will be completed in 1999.

The compilation and final editing of this report was the focus of our home schedule during this time. Editing was completed by David A. Detrich, and I corrected and annotated the text as Kirsten K. Hammann put it into PageMaker and Simon M. Sullivan oversaw the layout. Interdependently, Simon M. Sullivan consulted experts for the CD-ROM, for there was far too much data to be presented in book form. What we attempted to do was to plan ahead for problems, i.e., the illustrations that had to be selected and given size considerations as the publication was put together.

Now that the summaries of our five years of excavation have been discussed, we turn to our phasing of the site and place its progressive stages of architectural development into a chronological scheme.

## V. Site Deposition Analysis

If possible, we wanted to find the primary building phases of the site, as it became abundantly clear that the Great Temple precinct had a complex deposition history. Moreover, there were multidepositional contexts whereby soils and features had been spatially altered. There were multiple occupations as well as long-term occupations that had also altered the site over an extended period of time. Additionally, there had been geophysical changes and erosion that had to be dealt with and analyzed. We realized the complexities of the situation and implemented our recovery methods to provide us with data on the phasing of structures. Our understanding and constant restudy of the stratigraphy of the Temple site itself has been hampered by the lack of sealed archaeological contexts. Thus, our conclusions must remain tentative.

Based on site deposition, our annual excavations have determined the general sequence or phases of the Great Temple construction, collapse and abandonment. Seven phases have been tentatively identified. These may be modified by subsequent excavations, but at present they are used as the backbone of the archaeological evidence. The ideas espoused below are tentative and hypothetical. Please refer to the in-depth contributions by Joseph J. Basile and Erika L. Schluntz in Chapter 5 for a contrast of

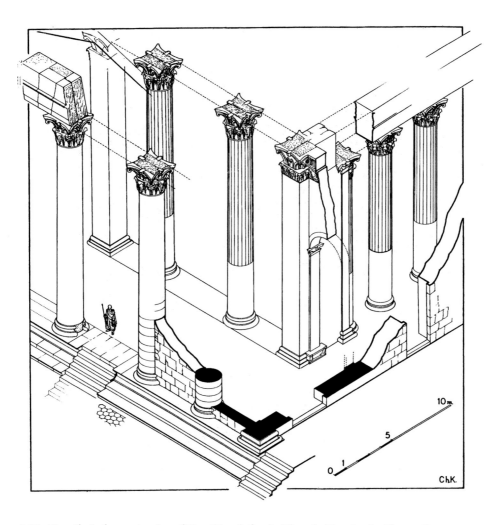

*Figure 2.83. Hypothetical reconstruction of Great Temple façade, Phase I. Drawing by Chrysanthos Kanellopoulos.*

Ch.K.

*Figure 2.84. Hypothetical reconstruction of Great Temple façade, Phase II. Drawing by Chrysanthos Kanellopoulos.*

opinion. Each set of ideas was written independently; the reader is left to judge the evidence for themselves. A summary of the evidence is as follows:

**Phase I** is labeled **Nabataean I**.[45] This represents a major construction of the Temple precinct. The major goal of the project was to construct a building of importance in Central Petra and to orient it toward the main thoroughfare of the city. The dramatic backdrop of the Al-Katute provided a perfect siting for the building. Built into the rocky site, an enormous amount of fill was brought in to create the setting for an imposing structure set on a high terrace platform. As the upper terrace sloped away, a flat terrace had to be leveled out in the planning for the Great Temple. An early Canalization System was also constructed, perhaps even before the Temple was laid out. This had to be functional, for it was feared that the terrace fill might otherwise erode. A central stairway was built to lead up to this structure. It probably originated from what then was the central artery of the city (the later, paved Colonnaded Street), through the then nonexistent Lower Temenos, up to the Upper Temenos.[46] (These are the Central Stairs that were later blocked off in Phase II.) The Lower Temenos may not have been developed in this phase, or it may have seen the building of the arched system excavated in the east. At some point in Phase I, we assume that this Lower Temenos Arch System was put in place.

The massive **Great Temple** was then constructed. The building façade became what we see today as tetrastyle in antis — four columns in the front of the building with wall ends or pilasters at the extremities of the Antae walls of the Temple Cella. A roof probably existed between the Porch columns and the Pronaos columns, but its architectural design is unclear. The Porch columns could have been surmounted by either a "regular" pediment or a broken pediment, but as for this structural detail, we have no archaeological evidence. What we do see today are the Great Temple Stylobate (the upper step or platform on which the columns rested) and the Pronaos (the Porch in front of the Temple Cella), and we assume they were built at roughly the same time.

As far as the building's interior was concerned, Phase I also included the erection of the eight interior, bichrome, plastered, sandstone columns on the building's flanks and six

columns at the rear. At least in late Phase I, these columns were decorated with flat, red plaster on the bottom and white, ridged plaster above, for there is still evidence for this decor. These columns were decorated with deeply carved, limestone capitals with fine sculptural decoration. The side corridors were also constructed and decorated with multicolored plaster. To protect both the wall and column plaster, roofing probably extended around the structure from the side columns to the tops of the corridor walls.

What the central part of the structure looked like in the Phase I architectural plan is not clear. If this structure is a temple, it must have held a cella and an adyton, but no traces of these components remain. On the basis of the few roof tiles found, the center of the structure may have been open to the sky, or hypaethral.

From the style of the floral decoration, especially the limestone capitals, the Petra Great Temple iconographic evidence appears to be similar to that of the Al-Khazna.[47] Tentatively, the evidence suggests this structure was constructed sometime in the last quarter of the first century BCE[48] by the Nabataeans who combined their native traditions with the classical spirit. By this reckoning, therefore, this structure was built during the reign of either King Malichus I (59/58-30 BCE) or Obodas III (30-9 BCE), or perhaps both.

**Phase II** is what we refer to as **Nabataean II**. There is a new, complete monumental rebuilding program — an architectural metamorphosis was launched in this phase. The architects wanted to make a strong statement, and they might have drawn their inspiration for the precinct perhaps from Alexandria, which at that time epitomized the architecture of a great city. It is obvious that the rulers of Petra took pride in the embellishment of their precinct while providing for its functional demands with a sense of spatial logic. The precinct had to emanate a sense of power befitting Nabataean wealth. This construction period is placed in the later Nabataean period based on the Trench 18, Locus 10 pottery identified as belonging to the last quarter of the first century BCE.[49]

So, what did these Phase II architects have in mind? To begin with, there had to be a building of an elegant, columned **Propylaeum** for access to the precinct, and a

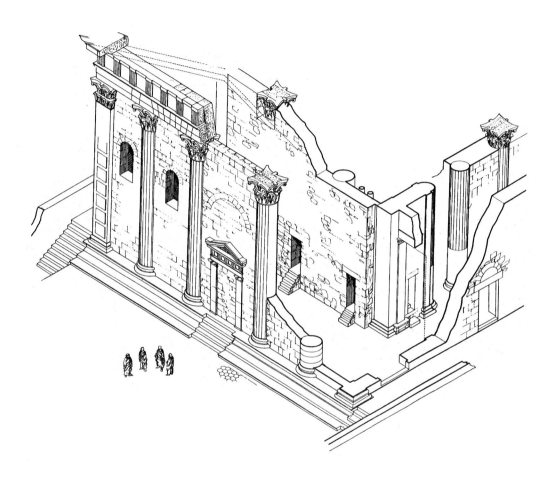

*Figure 2.85. Hypothetical reconstruction of the Great Temple, later Phase II. Drawing by Chrysanthos Kanellopoulos.*

series of new steps had to be laid to be built up to the level of the Lower Temenos.

At the same time, the architects ably conceptualized the **Lower Temenos** as a symmetrical, formal presence that purposefully emphasized the Great Temple. The Central Stairs may have remained in use for part of this time, but there was a challenging and exasperating problem confronting the planning of the area. It was the Canalization System. It must have been either inadequate or nonfunctional, or both. The answer, as with so many architectural questions, was clear: the Canalization System had to be reconfigured, and the most expedient way to do this was to completely rebuild its interior for drainage and enlarge its exterior, reusing a portion of the Central Stairs for water flow. With this rebuilding, the Phase I Central Stairs had to be blocked off. This set in motion a completely new series of changes that made the design of the Lower Temenos radically different from what it had been before. Although a new standard was about to be set, this created a difficult situation, for the architects had to decide how to lead people from the Lower Temenos to the Upper Temenos. This may have provided the impetus for a scheme that would involve precise planning for the complete remodeling of the Lower Temenos. The architects approached all aspects of the Lower Temenos design simultaneously, from laying out the stairways and the exedrae to enhancing the area with triple colonnades. In short, they converted the area, creating a vast architectural foreground for the Great Temple.

For the bold new plan to work, the Phase II Lower Temenos had to serve as a functional space on its own. The wall with arch springers had to be filled in with earth; this was key for this area had to be level and had to have proper drainage. Because the Central Stairs were dysfunctional, there had to be lateral staircases, and these had to have accompanying luxurious exedrae and other appurtenances to complete the finished look of the ensemble.

In closing off the Central Stairs, a massive east-west retaining wall had to be built on the same line as the twin lateral stairways and the exedrae, which delimited the Lower Temenos on its south. This east-west wall would also serve to support the Upper Temenos fill. New lateral stairways on the east and west (Elizabeth and Laurel Stairways) also had to be built to lead people from the Lower Temenos to the Upper Temenos and the Temple Forecourt. Other monumental structural changes in the Lower Temenos included the construction of the roofed triple colonnades with elegantly carved, elephant-headed capitals that flanked the area on its east and west sides. This Lower Temenos court-plaza was then embellished with a sweeping, white, limestone Hexagonal Pavement, which tied all the elements together and gave them, and the area as a whole, the feeling of association.[50] These architectural components were all interconnected features that boldly defined the area's spacious importance.

The **Phase II Temple** continued to crown the composition of space, and the edifice we know today as the Great Temple emerged. The exterior was enlarged with exterior walkways on its flanks that connected with the twin east and west lateral stairs leading from the Lower Temenos. These walkways may have been roofed, but this is not at this point clear from the archaeological record. This is also when the limestone pavement of small hexagonal pavers was put in place to embellish and finish off the Great Temple Forecourt, and if it had not been there in Phase I, a nine-step stairway was installed to lead into the Temple from the Temple Forecourt.

In the Great Temple interior, there was the careful construction of the Inter-Columnar walls (walls with arched doorways and windows between the columns). The building of these Inter-Columnar walls disturbed and all but destroyed the plaster decoration of the columns. How high these casemate walls were is still a matter of conjecture, but we do know they fell short of covering the capitals. As some of the Phase I capitals had been damaged, restoration had to be undertaken, and we have evidence for their repair. Figure 2.84 shows the reconstruction of the structure in this phase.

Also at this time, there was the major reconfiguration of the Temple interior. The Phase I core of the Great Temple, the Cella, was reconstructed as an approximate 600-seat *theatron*-like structure, open to the sky and descending to the orchestra or pulpitum. The building of the pulpitum between the two Antae (Pierre and Patricia Antae) and the Pronaos columns (Vartan and Mohammad Columns) postdates the building of the cavea and orchestra. Its bottom courses, still *in situ*, are definitely superimposed on the Theater flooring that extends under it. The heart of the Great Temple was now the Theater, and the architects blended the proportions of the Theater to blend in with the Phase I architecture. Its transformation must have reflected the changed circumstances of Petra royalty. Figure 2.82 represents the Temple reconstruction in this phase.

Additionally, multiple sets of new stairs were installed in the Temple Rear — East and West (east-west) Stairways (the Brian Stairway and the probable Jean Stairway). These accessed the lateral Inner Corridors and the East and West (north-south) Stairways (Monica and Simon Stairways) with adjacent east and west vaulted rooms. These four stairways accessed the Inner Corridor, which led to the Temple exits — the walkways.

This renovation we have placed sometime near the end of the reign of Aretas IV (ca. 40/44 CE) or to the rule of Malichus II (40/44-70 CE) and possibly to the reign of Rabbel II (70-106 CE). It is therefore suggested that these modifications took place sometime in the first or early second centuries CE. But questions persist: What was the transition between the earlier Nabataean structure and what we know as the Great Temple? Why was the transition from one type of installation to another so swift, less than 100 or so years?

The next phase, **Phase III**, we call **Nabataean-Roman**. Serving as a buffer state against the desert tribes, Nabataea retained its independence but paid taxes to Rome. Completely subsumed by the Romans under the Emperor Trajan in 106 CE, Petra and Nabataea then became part of the Roman province known as *Arabia Petraea*. Under Roman rule, Roman classical monuments abounded, many with Nabataean overtones; thus, it is appropriate to identify this time (post-106 CE) as the Nabataean-Roman phase.

When Petra entered into the "Roman" world in the second century CE, we assume that the Great Temple was recycled by Nabataean-Roman architects, and this is our Phase III or Nabataean-Roman period. The precinct continued to serve the Romans as one of the principal monuments of the city. And if there were post-106 CE changes made to the Temple and its precinct, these changes are not altogether clear from the stratigraphy.

We posit, however, that at some point during the Nabataean-Roman period — in the last half of the second century CE — the lower Stairs of the Propylaeum were modified to conform with the paving of the Colonnaded Street and were added to for ease of entry into the precinct.

As we know, Petra continued to flourish during the Roman period, with a Monumental Arch spanning the Siq and tomb structures either carved out of the living rock or built free-standing. There is no reason why the Great Temple should not have continued to serve as a principal monument of the city, and the fragmented Latin Imperial inscription, if we assume it is in some way associated with this building, attests to its importance and one of its last uses.

The evidence suggests that the Great Temple continued to serve the people of Petra until some point in the late third or early fourth centuries CE. This is our **Phase IV**, in which the evidence suggests that there was a minor **collapse and abandonment** of the structure. In the archaeological record, this period was represented on the Temple West by the accumulation of fill, 1 m in depth. The areas in use were worn with neglect, but the precinct as a whole was remarkably well preserved.

By 313 CE, Christianity had become the state-recognized religion of the Roman Empire. In 330 CE, the Emperor Constantine established the eastern Roman Empire, with its capital at Constantinople. Although the 363 CE earthquake destroyed half of the city, it appears that Petra retained its urban vitality into late antiquity, when it was the seat of a Byzantine bishopric.

Our **Phase V** begins with a **major destruction**, probably related to the fourth century CE earthquake. At least part of the structure collapsed onto the fill accumulated in Phase IV. Up to this point, we have no evidence to suggest the Great Temple continued to function. What is clear, however, is that the Temple structure was devastated by the earthquake presumed to have taken place in the fourth century. This earthquake is said by some to have brought the city of Petra to the brink of ruin and total abandonment, but we have reason to believe that this was not the case.

In **Phase VI**, dated to the **Byzantine period**, there was reuse of the Temple precinct, but this reuse was probably domestic in nature. At this point in our investigations, the Byzantine reuse does not provide us with a clear picture of how the various architectural components of the precinct were used and were inter-related, if they were at all. Therefore, this phase is problematic, with a series of differing activities that take place in different sectors of the Temple precinct, each having varied time spans; these are difficult to correlate. In the Great Temple, the floor pavers and the upper stair treads were robbed. Numerous surface drains were constructed over the extant remains, and some doorways were narrowed, indicating that only parts of the structure were in use at this time. In the Lower Temenos, a platform and stairs were constructed the West Exedra, and later this area was used either to house a kiln or to serve as a dump for burned debris.[51] In the east Lower Temenos, lime slaking was a major activity, which probably consumed many of the limestone elements of the Great Temple's decorative program — architrave blocks and capitals would have been perfect fodder for such activity. Slowly fill accumulated and the precinct was worn by time and neglect.

**Phase VII** represents the **modern reuse** of the site. Although, thankfully, the major portion of the Great Temple lies under its massive collapse, farming activities had taken place in the Lower Temenos, which had been subdivided by the Bedouin farmers into two plots of ground using fallen column drums to separate the areas. Here too it is a miracle that any of the Hexagonal Pavement remains, for in the north, the farmer's fill lies centimeters below the modern ground level surface, whereas to the south near the East-West Retaining Wall, the soil buildup is greater (1-2 m in depth).

At the turn of the century, European scholars began to explore the area, but notice of a Great Temple received scant reference in the record. In the 1930s, Petra began to capture scholarly and tourist interest. Accommodation was at first provided with tents, and then Nazzal's Camp was constructed behind the Qasr al-Bint as a hotel for tourists and visitors, with the hotel dump positioned in the Great Temple Forecourt between the east Porch column fall of the Nadine and Pia Columns.[52] Now renovated, this complex is known as the J.L. Burckhardt Archaeological Center, which serves as the headquarters for our archaeological campaigns.

As excavations continue, it must be borne in mind that this phasing is tentative and may be revised in light of future excavation. Our understanding of the site has been difficult, not because of the lack of dateable materials, but because the mixture within archaeological contexts of artifact stylistics ranges from the first century BCE to the early fifth century CE in date — the Great Temple precinct was in use for approximately 500 years. There are few sealed deposits, and much more has yet to be explored before we can understand the archaeological deposition of these remains.

The existence of the Great Temple is now an established fact. Our discoveries over the past five years will enable scholars and the public at large to study and visit this great edifice. Before the excavation is closed, I hope to not only reveal more of the architectural layout of the building and its sacred precinct, but also to better understand its function, its phasing and how it was woven into the fabric of its Nabataean, Nabataean-Roman and Byzantine urban environment.

The wealth and importance of Petra as the Nabataean capital had to be made clear to both her subjects and those powers with whom she interacted. In the heart of the city, the Great Temple must have been impressive. The visitor entering the complex from the Propylaeum and crossing the great open expanse of the Lower Temenos became involved in a great architectural experience. The drama of the Nabataean planning is evident — there are exciting vistas of the exedrae, the double great staircases, the seemingly limitless rows of columns and the remarkable façade of the Great Temple itself. The fabulous architectural decoration of the elephant-headed capitals set against the monumental architecture of the Lower Temenos and the height and breadth of the impact of the Temple structure with its deeply sculpted, elaborate, floral capitals demonstrated power and wealth. The overall construct of the precinct must have been directed by royal patronage, and it clearly is a response to the needs of the Nabataean court and its administration.

## In Conclusion...

Some of the questions about this structure that still abound we hope will be answered as our work progresses. We now know why this Temple seems to be so different in architectural plan from the traditionally established canon of the classical temple. What is the relationship of the theater-like emplacement to the Temple? Could this be a theater-temple?[53] Or could it be a civic bouleuterion? Could it have served dual or several functions, be they either religious or secular, or does it have yet other functions? What is the relationship of this structure to the fabric of the city? What are the earliest structures constructed on this site, and what modifications took place to the Temple Complex and when?

## Postscript

To be celebrated is our Brown crew and superb Bedouin work force. Needless to say, without the support of Brown University, the Jordanian Department of Antiquities, the American Center of Oriental Research in Amman and the devotion of Pierre M. and Patricia M. Bikai, the loyalty of the American Embassy, the help of H.R.H. Prince Ra'ad bin Zeid Al-Hussein and, most important of all, the friendship and affection of all of our participants these excavations would not have been realized.

## Endnotes

[1] At the time we started our excavations, we did not know there had been a previous survey at the site.

[2] Because the Great Temple is on the southern side of the street, the normal expectations of directions are reversed. As one moves into the structure from the street, one is moving from the north to the south. This means that as one is moving into the Temple and turns left, one is moving east.

[3] Peter J. Parr's observations from his extensive research and excavation at Petra have been both valuable and insightful.

[4] Peter J. Parr reminded me that this plan was produced from air photographs by the Department of Photogrammetry, University College, London. It was first published in 1976 (P.J. Parr, K.B. Atkinson and E.H. Wickens in *ADAJ* 20.31-45, figure 1).

[5] We mourn the untimely death of Eleanor E. Myers. "Ellie" was a supportive friend and guide, and we miss her.

[6] Interdependently during the spring of 1993, our team set to work with various project goals, including electronic distance measurement systems, computer systems and architectural nomenclature, and library research was devoted to the archaeological and cultural history of the site.

[7] This section was contributed by Paul C. Zimmerman.

[8] During the 1998 season of excavations at the Petra Great Temple, we had the opportunity to collaborate with the surveyors of the Petra Mapping Project (a joint project of ACOR and the Hashemite University). In the course of their survey, our control points CP103 and CP104 were shot in along with the Al-Katute datum. Since the PMP survey is keyed in to sub-centimeter GPS coordinates, these data will allow us to correlate our site plans with UTM coordinates (WGS84 datum) — and, therefore, the entire site of Petra and indeed the world. The transformations are as yet uncompleted, but cursory inspection of the data suggests a correction of approximately 0.6 m in elevation and 2° rotation about CP103.

[9] To prevent balk cave-ins, sandbags were placed alongside the trench on top of the balk between the inner and outer trench perimeters.

[10] Elevations were resurveyed at the beginning of each field season.

[11] Charles L. Redman 1974:15-16. *Archaeological Sampling Strategies,* Reading MA.

[12] In regards to digging technique, picks, shovels, hoes, trowels and, when needed, mechanical equipment were used for the removal of dirt. Care was used to identify and separate different layers as well as maintain vertical balks.

For each layer or locus identified, separate marked containers served to collect artifacts. Artifacts were presorted in the field by material, i.e., stone, ceramics, bone, shell, metal and glass. At the onset of a new locus and at the end of the day, all artifacts were physically removed from the trench to the processing areas.

When a feature such as a wall, pit or floor was encountered, a special series of excavation techniques were employed. For instance, pits or hearths were generally bisected in order to have a clear picture of their stratigraphy. Walls were excavated by placing a temporary balk line perpendicular to each face. Either side of the wall was then excavated and documented separately as a locus so that interiors and exteriors could be separately identified, and possible builders trenches were noted. In the plotting of features, loci and architectural components, a 0.20 cm:1 m scale was used. All of these drawings were maintained in the field notebooks along with their descriptions.

Last but not least, no systematic sifting or faunal analysis of the excavated earth occurred. The mixed nature of most deposits and the time constraints imposed upon our efforts, unfortunately, made these techniques unfeasible.

[13] John Smolenski donated three days to start the field recording process on its way.

[14] The Macintosh was chosen for field use for several reasons. First, it has a simple, icon-based interface that is easy to learn and use, even for non-English speakers. In addition, the Macintosh's graphic capabilities are excellent. Pictures can be stored as data, and maps and stratigraphic records can be entered directly into the computer. The Macintosh is small, relatively inexpensive and easily transportable. We used four laptops in the field. Upgrades to mainframes for batch-type data analyses have been easily accomplished.

Several different computer programs were utilized to organize and analyze this data. Briefly, the FileMaker Pro database program was used to store and systematize the information drawn from the objects excavated at these three sites. Microsoft Word (a word processing program) was used to produce all documents, including the daily site diary and final trench reports.

[15] The photographer's record, emphasizing the shape and surface features, has been vital for the understanding of these sites. Both Kodachrome color slides and two sets of either Kodak-Plus-X or Kodak TMX black-and-white photographs are taken simultaneously as a standard procedure during the course of excavation, and these are processed during the course of excavation. Two sets of contact sheets are made — one for the field notebook and the other for the notebook containing general site information. Black-and-white and color photographs are taken daily of the trenches and special features. Standard tools used in all photographs include the one-meter scale, the north

arrow and a sign board that identifies the date and the subject. A separate film log is maintained by the photographers. Five Nikon 35 mm camera backs and seven lenses (1:14 50 mm, 1:2 50 mm, 1:3.5 28 mm, 1.2 50 mm, 1:2.8 135 mm, 1:3.5 2.8 mm) have been used for this coverage. In addition, Polaroid 600 Sun, LMS cameras provided photographs for an immediate visual record to supplement the information in the site notebooks. When necessary, a Kodak Gray Card and/or Kodak Color Correction Panels are used in photographs.

To maximize artifact coverage, photographs of significant or important assemblages were taken in their *in situ* positions, often with a gray card. Again using the 35 mm camera, cataloged artifacts were photographed both in black-and-white and in color with scale and often with a color chart. In most cases, artifacts were lit from the left or photographed with standardized natural light against either a white or black background. The scale and the color correction panel could be cropped if necessary, and emphasis was given to filling the frame. A tripod was always used, as well as two light meters — incident and reflected types. Coins were taken vertically (i.e., from above) with reference to scale with a lens extension tube so that focal length could be reduced. Most objects were also taken vertically with a macro lens.

Aerial photographs were taken before we began our work and after the completion of each year of excavations. In the first instance, these photographs were photographed from a balloon mounted with a remote-controlled camera by J. Wilson Myers and Eleanor E. Myers, while in the later instances, helicopters were employed. Not unexpectedly, these different techniques produced varying results. Whatever the technique, all of these photos have enabled us to better understand the site and its surround.

The use of a digital camera might have greatly enhanced some aspects of our recording process. It could have been used to create instant color photographs in situations where we would normally use a Polaroid. The advantage would have been that the photographs would be in digital form and could have been included in our databases and site reports. Because digital cameras do not use film, the number of photographs that we take would only be limited by the amount of storage space. We did experiment with digital cameras but returned to traditional photographic coverage, because the photographs were unclear.

[16] Due to our procedures, it was understood that large amounts of pottery and other artifacts would be recovered. The trench supervisor labeled each bucket, and its contents were washed on a daily basis, then sorted, read, counted and recorded, and finally entered into the computer. In order to understand the material culture and to chart changes in the artifact record, a simple system of attribute classification based on mutually exclusive color and ware types was selected for the understanding of change in pottery manufacture and culture. All artifacts (ceramic, glass, metal, stone, shell, stucco/plaster, vegetable matter and bone) considered distinctive were documented and retained for study. At this time, the vast majority of the artifactual remains have yet to be analyzed either for cultural type, date or minimum vessel count. After processing was complete, nondescript body sherds were discarded (except for those loci that might provide either a *terminus post quem* or information regarding particular activities within a given area — then everything was retained for study). Study artifacts were then transferred to numbered plastic bags, placed in plastic crates. A master bag list was filled out weekly in triplicate. The three copies were distributed among the trench supervisor, the field director and the excavation files. Bag numbers include the initials of the site (P/ST = Petra Southern Temple), followed by the trench number, followed by the bag number. Thus, P/ST101 stands for the Great Temple (formerly the Southern Temple), Trench 1, Bag No. 1. The year excavated appears on the top of the form, and the bag contents are described on the master list. Thus, each collection of distinctive material bore a field container number and a storage disposal bag number.

After processing, all distinctive artifacts were removed to the Petra Museum. Distinctive pottery was transferred to Yvonne Gerber or Stephan G. Schmid, who were directing the artifact research of plain and painted wares, respectively.

[17] This description contained information concerning the artifact's provenience, dimensions and any special features. Such data was entered into the artifact catalog, which was maintained independently in the field notebook and computer.

[18] Care was taken not to reuse the number, so there would be no confusion between past designations.

[19] After the 1997 field season, the glass recorded in Grosso Modo was removed for specialist study by Sara G. Karz.

[20] Joseph J. Basile worked on the reorganization of the painted pottery typology from earlier Petra material, published before 1993.

[21] In 1996, Erika L. Schluntz drew up an outlined sequence for capturing the recording of stucco architectural fragments.

[22] There were two prepared fields for the temporary storage of architectural fragments (where they await possible reconstruction). The larger is located beyond the western flank of the Temple, and the second is to the east of the site itself. The fallen column drums in front of the Temple were left *in situ* by choice.

[23] See Ricardo J. Elia, in the 1993 *Journal of Field Archaeology,* Vol. 20 97-104, for "ICOMOS Adopts Archaeological Heritage Charter: Text and Commentary." This article presents the background for the Charter, the text of the Charter and some explanatory comments.

[24] Published in 1956 is the UNESCO *Recommendations on International Principles Applicable to Archaeological Excavations.* These guidelines establish professional standards for excavations, preservation of sites, public access to excavations, finds documentation and disposal and the publication of the excavation report. Also see UNESCO 1970, *Convention on the Means of Prohibiting and Preventing the Implicit Import, Export and Transfer of Ownership of Cultural Property.* Paris: United Nations Educational, Scientific, and Cultural Organization, and 1985, *Conventions and Recommendations of UNESCO Concerning the Protection of Cultural Heritage.* Paris, United Nations Educational, Scientific and Cultural Organization.

[25] Whether or not these mortar consolidants have limitations is a complex question. Stone, particularly sandstone deterioration is appreciable in the Temple's erosion. The long-term effects of the mortar on the sandstone are difficult to predict. It is a matter of judgment of the conservator. For each stone there are differing porosities, differing salt, water and acid absorption rates and a difference in how they react to sunlight. Here is a very complex question, for each individual stone has its own problems.

[26] Peter J. Parr. "A Sequence of Pottery from Petra," in Sandars, J.A., ed., *Near Eastern Archaeology in the Twentieth Century: Essays in Honour of Nelson Glueck,* 1970: New York 348-81. See pp. 366-370 for the dating of the Colonnaded Street. But Judith S. McKenzie (1990:35-36) argues for an earlier date. She suggests it was constructed as early as 9 CE.

[27] I suppose there is a possibility that the building did not have a pediment, but that would make it a most unusual structure.

[28] I am grateful to Peter J. Parr for his identification of this feature. See Thomas F.C. Blagg's "Column Capitals with Elephant-Head Volutes at Petra," in *Levant* Vol. XXII, 1990:131-137.

[29] For safety, this investigation was undertaken with the on-site advice of an experienced mining engineer, Peter Nalle.

[30] This is similar in design to the walkway of the Qasr al-Bint.

[31] We wanted to know the character of its stratigraphy before using it as a lapidary and covering it with Temple blocks for reconstruction.

[32] It could be similar to Herod's Temple Platform.

[33] See the Bachmann reconstruction in Browning (1995) Fig. 75, p. 150.

[34] Nabataean fine wares typological analysis has been undertaken by Stephan G. Schmid, and drafting of architectural details and small finds has been undertaken by Jean Blackburn and Simon M. Sullivan, assisted by Ala H. Bedewy. The continued study of the numismatic evidence has been documented by Christian Augé, assisted by David Smart, and the lamp analysis was submitted as a 1996 M.A. Thesis by Deirdre G. Barrett, a Ph.D. candidate at Brown University's Anthropology Department.

[35] This head was rediscovered by us in 1995 lying in a Lower Temenos spoil heap. After this published article had gone to press, we were bearded by the fact that this head was originally published by Bachmann (1921.45. Abb.37), and we had not noticed its publication until Leigh-Ann Bedal brought it to our attention. Presumably, in 1921 there was no authority to take care of her, and she remained on site for some 76 years! She is now safely stored in the Petra Museum.

[36] That these served as water channels or as roof supports has also been suggested, but these ideas have been rejected.

[37] This estimate has been arrived at by our architect-surveyor, Paul C. Zimmerman.

[38] Erika L. Schluntz believes that it may have been blocked by a screen wall that extended between the Porch columns and that the former Pronaos area should now be considered "backstage."

[39] Few roof tiles were excavated in the center of the structure; for that reason, we believe the side colonnades may have been roofed. Because few roof tiles were found in the Temple Center, I believe the area over the auditorium was unroofed.

[40] In Greek, in the strict sense of the word, this building would have been for the meeting of the *deme* (the popular assembly) not the boule (city council).

[41] Can we state that this find adds the appropriate force to the argument that this should be identified as a civic structure? Glen W. Bowersock states: " The monumental Latin inscription is perfectly compatible with a temple, particularly one in which the emperor might have been a *sunnaos theos*. There is nothing about this find to suggest identification of the building as civic. Of course, it does not weigh against this possibility either."

[42] Babatha was a wealthy Jewess from the village of Maoza in the provincial administrative center of Zoara, located on the shores of the Dead Sea. Her father, Simon, son of Manahem, held a considerable amount of land, consisting of houses and palm groves in the then kingdom of Nabataea, where he was comfortably established. After the annexation of the Nabataean kingdom by the Romans in 106 CE, Babatha's family retained their land in the newly created Roman province of Arabia. (We have to remember that the Romans seized Judaea in 68 CE, some 38 years before Nabataea was annexed.) Dating from 93/94–132 CE, the double documents (two copies of the text on the same papyrus) of the Babatha archive contain deeds, money settlements and lawsuits in which Babatha was involved.

The 35 papyrus archives were found in a leather purse in 1961 by Yigael Yadin at the cave of Nahal Hever on the west shore of the Dead Sea. The languages of the documents were: six in Nabataean, three in Aramaic and 26 in Greek. The latest document was written in the year the Bar Kokhba Revolt began (132 CE), and it is possible that Babatha hid these documents at that time in the cave, where she too sought refuge to escape from the Romans. (It is not known if Babatha was one of the approximately 20 corpses found by the excavator, but Yigael Yadin assumed that she was.)

From the Nahal Hever cave, these priceless finds are known as documents from "the Cave of the Letters." Published in 1989 by the Israel Exploration Society, The Hebrew University of Jerusalem and the Shrine of the Book, as *The Documents from the Bar Kokhba Period in the Cave of the Letters,* Naphtali Lewis, ed., the letters and transactions tell us that Babatha was married twice, once to a Maozene Jew named Jesus, son of Jesus, and then to a Jew from En-Gedi in Judaea named Judah, son of one Eleazar Khthousion.

Babatha and Jesus have a son, who is given the patronymic, Jesus, and is referred to as "Jesus, a Jew, son of Jesus." Sometime before 124 CE, Babatha's husband, Jesus, dies, and her son

Jesus is considered to be an orphan. Because Babatha is not a Roman citizen, she has to find guardians for her son, and between the end of February and June 28, 124 CE, she petitions the provincial governor and has her case heard by the town council (boule) of Petra. Two guardians are appointed by the town council of the metropolis Petra — a Jew, John, the son of Joseph Eglas, and a Nabataean, 'Abdoöbdas, son of Ellouthas. It is stated in Document 12 that these minutes have been displayed in the Temple of Aphrodite in Petra. Four months later, in October 125 CE, Babatha again petitions the governor of Provincia Arabia, one Julius Julianus; the two guardians have been giving her an insufficient sum (two denarii a month) for her son's living expenses. (She complains bitterly that her brother-in-law, Joseph, also did not contribute to Jesus' upkeep.)

Although illiterate, Babatha knows that the guardians have not been contributing the fair and just amount, for they have been paying only one-half denarius per 100 denarii, or one half of one percent, which is not what was prescribed by law. Because she summons the guardian, John, to appear in the court (boule) at Petra, it may mean either that the Nabataean guardian had by this time paid his fair share or that the procedure could only be brought against one person at a time. In yet another document, it is revealed that the guardians had invested Jesus' assets in loans yielding one percent a month, and she states that they have paid only one half of that amount. She accuses them of embezzlement and wants them to be accountable for Jesus' real assets. With her security of a mortgage on her own property, she says that she can increase the interest for the upkeep of her son to three times the amount they are contributing! This document, written in October 125 CE, asserts that Judah, Babatha's second husband, is Babatha's transactional guardian; therefore, it can be assumed that by this time they were married.

At the time of Babatha's second marriage, it appears that Judah was a bigamist, for he was already married to a woman named Miriam, with whom he had a daughter, Shelamzion.

In a letter dated February 17, 128 CE, Judah acknowledges that he has borrowed 300 silver denarii from Babatha. A little later Judah's daughter, Shelamzion, marries with a comfortable dowry of 500 denarii. Not long thereafter, in ca. 130 CE, Babatha's husband, Judah, dies. In Documents 20-26, Babatha takes over Judah's properties of date palms and three orchards, which she declares he owes her for past debts. She and her step-daughter, Shelamzion, in turn are sued by the guardians representing her brother-in-law's children (her brother-in-law, another Jesus, had also died at about the same time as her husband). The case is dropped against Shelamzion, but the case against Babatha carries on for more than a year. Because she had received nothing from Judah's estate, on September 11, 130 CE, Babatha, in frustration, sells off the dates harvested from Judah's three orchards.

By November 17, Besas, along with a Roman citizen, one Julia Crispina, are appointed as the co-guardians of Jesus' (Judah's brother's) children. Besas again summons Babatha to the court in Petra to give up the date orchards that he says belong to the orphans. There are summons and counter summons, and this time it is Julia Crispina (because Besas is ill) who summons Babatha to Rabbath-Moab to appear before the governor there. (It appears as if the governor spent July in Rabbath and October-November in Petra. It was customary for the governor to make an annual trip around the province to hold assizes.) In addition to this already complex affair, Judah's first wife, Miriam, tries to gain possession of that part of Babatha's wealth that Miriam had jointly held with Judah; she also summons Babatha to appear in court. Summonses and litigious petitions continue to be served.

For reasons still not fully understood, sometime around the beginning of the Bar Kokhba Revolt, Babatha and her family left the region of Mazoa for En-Gedi, where they hid in the cave at Nahal Hever until their untimely demise around 132 CE. When Babatha fled to the cave near her second husband's home in Judaea, she took with her this extraordinary collection of legal documents that were obviously vital to her and her family. Nearly 2000 years later, these priceless documents, which were once merely family archives, have become our single most important source of information on the legal affairs of the inhabitants of the province of Roman Arabia.

[43] Fawzi Zayadine further suggested that the structure may have served as the seat of the Principia. Zbigniew T. Fiema dismisses this suggestion by commenting that the archaeological evidence suggests that the Headquarters of the Arabian Legion were in Bostra and that the Principia would have had to be there as well.

[44] Please refer to Chapter 5.

[45] I suggest that there may have been an earlier small temple that was distyle in antis (two massive columns on the façade set between wall ends or pilasters — the Vartan and Mohammad Columns). This is an almost square structure, measuring approximately 18 m (east-west)-x-22 m (north-south). If there was a roof, there is no evidence for it. This structure then underwent a transformation and with remodeling had its side and rear walls dismantled when the building scheme was enlarged to construct a grander edifice by later Nabataean architects — our now Phase I structure. This modified Phase I structure saw the extension of the building to the north by approximately 9 m, with the construction of the Pronaos, plus two new antae with four new columns between them.

A paucity of masonry indicates this phase, and I have little stratigraphic evidence to support it, but it appears to me that the construction of the Pronaos and the Stylobate as seen today is considerably different than the Patricia and Pierre Antae walls and the Pronaos columns that served the original structure. Future excavations will clarify if this earliest building existed, but I suspect it did. This then was a small structure, probably a temple that crowned the hill and could be viewed from all parts of Central Petra. With the construction of the Phase II Lower Temenos and Propylaeum, the Temple was not visible from the Colonnaded Street.

[46] This good suggestion, offered by Zbigniew T. Fiema, may be confirmed by the GPR results, which seem to indicate a subterranean stepped structure in the Lower Temenos. This structure may also be part of the Canalization System; at this point the evidence is not clear.

[47] As we mentioned in Chapter 1, the most detailed study of Petra monuments has been undertaken by Judith S. McKenzie in her magnificent tome, *The Architecture of Petra,* Oxford 1990. And also see the discussion regarding the site of Medain Saleh in Saudi Arabia. Judith S. McKenzie and Angela Phippen in "The Chronology of the Principal Monuments at Petra," *Levant* Vol.19, 1990:152 summarize their views of Nabataean sculpture by stating, "Simplification of the classical elements of architectural decoration is related to chronological development. This change was seen in the moldings, Doric frieze, capitals, florals and sculpture."

[48] This idea was put forward in a public lecture on August 24, 1993, in Amman, and in the discussion period, the archaeologist Nabil Khairy stated that an early first-century date was accurate. And McKenzie's typology assigns the structures including the Qasr al-Bint, Al-Khazna, the Temple of the Winged Lions and the Baths to this time period.

[49] This is a pocket of pottery that was left *in situ* near the east wall of the lateral West Stairway.

[50] The date of this pavement is also open to question. It can be paralleled to other such pavements at the site, which, at this point, have been imprecisely dated. In a personal communication, Rolf Stucky stated that the pavement he recovered from the Petra site of Az-Zantur and the pavement from the site of Al-Katute, excavated by Nabil Khairy in the 1980s, were Nabataean Classical. At that time, I believed this pavement to be later in our phasing of the Great Temple site. Now, it is agreed to assign its construction to the later of two Nabataean construction phases.

[51] The area may have served as the dump of a praefurnium for the adjacent Baths. But of this we cannot be sure.

[52] This dump can be viewed in pre-1997 aerial photographs. Positioned between the Nadine and Pia Porch column fall in the Upper Temenos, it is a rounded structure bordered by stones, and it is almost 1.5 m in diameter. The fact that it is a dump is hearsay; it has not been excavated.

[53] A most useful source is John A. Hanson's 1959 publication entitled, *Roman Theater-Temples,* Princeton. Hanson looks at the plans of these structures. But those at Dura Europos associated

with the temples of Atargatis, Artemis Nannaia and Artemis Azzanathkona are not in the same design as our structure. The closest Dura parallel in architectural design is "H" associated with the Sanctuary of Artemis Nannaia, but the theater lies outside the sanctuary proper. The lack of models for our structure leaves us without definite answers.

The temple at Seleucia-on-the-Tigris is also hypaethral, but again it is not inside the temple structure. The Nabataean temple of Baal Shamin at Si' has three steps facing the central court; the theater is the courtyard for the temple. This is true also of the theaters at Sur and Sahr.

Hanson explores the concept of the theater-temple, and on pg. 98 he states: "In addition to what may properly be called sanctuary theaters, we find numerous cases in which temples are located near theaters and easily accessible to them, cases which seem to represent more than meaningless accident." And on pg. 77, "What is common to all [theater-temples] is a location on the central axis of the theater overlooking the orchestra with the front facing the stage building, with provision for a statue of the divinity. Most have a colonnaded façade and many are approachable by special steps or entrances through the back wall of the *cavea*."

CHAPTER THREE

# GEOLOGICAL AND BOTANICAL EVIDENCE

## ENVIRONMENTAL SETTING AND STONE WEATHERING
Thomas R. Paradise

## PALYNOLOGICAL ANALYSIS FROM THE PETRA GREAT TEMPLE
Peter Warnock

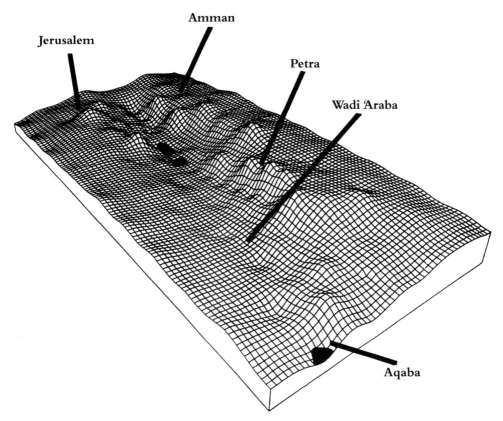

*Figure 3.1. Jordan, Israel, Wadi 'Araba and Petra*
*This digital elevation model depicts a northeast perspective. Note Petra's proximity to the Dead Sea graben, Israel and the*
*Mediterranean Sea. The mountain of Aaron's sarcophagus, Jabal Harun, is situated directly south of the Valley of Petra, along*
*the plateau edge of Jordan's Uplands.*

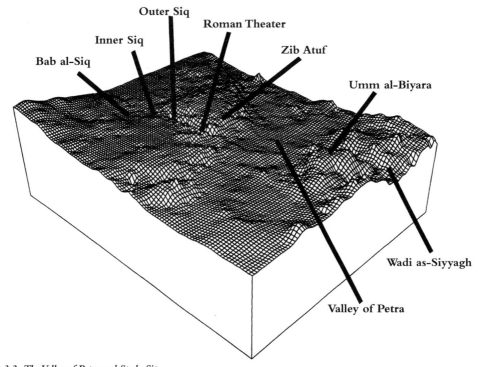

*Figure 3.2. The Valley of Petra and Study Site*
*This digital elevation model depicts a southeast perspective and explains Petra's recently concealed location from its encircling*
*cliffs (50-100 m) and single and obscured entrance through the Siq. A second and more difficult entrance into Petra may be*
*taken through the Wadi as-Siyyagh from the Wadi 'Araba near the Israeli border. The Roman Theater is located at the*
*intersection of the Outer Siq and the Main Valley of Petra.*

# ENVIRONMENTAL SETTING AND STONE WEATHERING

Thomas R. Paradise

---

## The Natural Environment of Petra

The landscape of southwestern Jordan is a stunning mix of bold cliffs, broad plateaus and deep gorges, in a desert environment of xeric vegetation, extreme weather and indigenous cultures. These towering salmon-colored, sandstone cliffs and domes rise atop dark, granitic basements and between broad, buff-colored, desert plains producing a land of visual and geographic contrasts.

An understanding of the physical setting of southern Jordan must begin with its relationship to the great Dead Sea Rift Valley. Separating Israel from Jordan, the Dead Sea Rift Valley has been evolving over 125 million years and measures 375 km in length, although it represents only a small portion of the Great Rift System, which extends over 65° of latitude. From the Mozambique Channel that separates Madagascar from the African mainland, north to the Aegean Sea, this organization of rifting plates is one of the most extensive tectonic plate/fault systems on Earth. The Jordan River Valley, which connects Lake Tiberias (Galilee) with the Dead Sea, and the Wadi 'Araba, which links the Dead Sea to the Gulf of Aqaba, represents a branch of the Rift Complex. Petra is seated atop the edge of an eastern plateau halfway between the southern end of the Dead Sea and the head of the Gulf of Aqaba. From the Dead Sea (-392 m), the Wadi 'Araba rises to the south at Ghorel 'Ajram (240 m) to descend toward the Gulf (Burdon 1982).

This barren corridor of salt playas and desert flora lies at the foot of the Wadi as-Siyyagh, Petra's only primary approach other than the famous Siq to the east. The weathering and erosion that has produced steep-walled wadis (arroyos) and residual sandstone towers and buttes has been linked to the genesis and seismic activity of the adjacent Dead Sea Rift. As the rift valley dropped (grabens) and the highlands rose (horsts), numerous en-echelon transform faults were created that increased erosion along these faults and gouged the land, producing Petra's unique valley (Bender 1968, Osborn 1985).

At an elevation of 900 m and a location of 30°19'N 35°20'E, the ruined city of Petra lies in a roughly crescent-shaped valley. Petra is walled by steep cliffs rising to 100 m above the valley floor and is extensively faced with hewn tombs. The surrounding plateaus and hammadas have minimal plant growth, due to the soil-free landscape atop the weathering limestone and sandstone. In the valleys and wadis, however, sand and clay accumulate, and water availability and retention are greatest. The local loamy, sand soils (*Arenic Haplargids*) display the distinctive attributes of aridisols: little humic accumulation, varied degrees of salt (*Bs*) and carbonate (*Bk*) buildup, few or no soil horizons and minor argillic lensing (*Bt*) in the B horizon (SCS 1990).

Though this weak soil provides a poor substrate for plant growth, xeric plant life exists. Petra is uniquely located at the interface between the vegetation regions of the Saharo-Arabian (western/southern), Mediterranean (northwestern), Sudanian (southern) and Irano-Turanian (eastern) (Fall 1990). Immediately noticeable is the prevalence of summer-blooming *Nerium oleander* in the wadis. The relative abundance

*Figure 3.3. The Landscape of Southern Jordan*
*The landscape of southern Jordan is controlled by its great seismic history. Destructive earthquakes have been recorded every 100-200 years and have produced a land of steep, uplifted cliffs and peaks (horsts) and sheer-walled valleys (grabens). Many of these valley floors are scattered with roving sands burying ancient ruins.*

*Figure 3.4. The Valley of Petra*
*The valley of Petra is dominated by steep, reddish sandstone cliffs and the broad valley of the ancient ruined city. The valley walls contain many carved tomb façades and are a product of the various faults and joints that divide the local sandstone and limestone, uplifting and dropping massive blocks across southern Jordan during its recurrent earthquakes. Pink oleander bushes (Oleander nerium) are found throughout the valley only because its poisonous flowers are not tasty to the abundant goats.*

of pink oleander may be attributed to their poisonous nature, which dissuades the local goat herds from eating their foliage. On the limestone hills above Petra and within the valley itself, the thin desert soils support scant juniper (*Juniperus phoenicea*), oak (*Quercus caliprinos*), pistachio (*Pistacia atlantica, P. palaestrina*), olive (*Olea europaea*), fig (*Ficus carica*) and exotic gum (*Eucalyptus globulus*) trees. Desert scrub vegetation, though sparse, dominates the plant landscape. *Artemisia herba-alba*, *Ephedra alte* and *E. campylopoda*, *Retama raetam*, *Noaea mucronata*, *Suaeda asphaltica* and *S. aegyptiaca* represent the typical shrub taxa (Zohary 1940, Fall 1990).

The arid climate of southern Jordan is typified by mild, relatively rainy winters and hot, dry summers. Only periodically affected by the Mediterranean cyclonic cells, local rainfall occurs in winter as peripheral precipitation from low barometric cells passing through northern Israel and Jordan (JMD 1971). Occasionally, however, low-pressure fronts move across northern Africa or up through the Red Sea bringing torrential downpours and flooding from a combination of cyclonic flow, orographic lifting and convectional propagation (JMD 1971). These rare but recurrent floods played a significant role in the development of progressive irrigation techniques by the ancient Nabataeans. Many of these methods were unknown to the Romans until occupation in the first century CE. (Glueck 1965). The infrequent floods may be the primary agent responsible for the removal of the weathering-produced sands, since observed winds (1-5 m/s) blowing in the Inner and Outer Siqs have little effect on the entrainment and transport of the loose sand.

Climate and weather data are not available from the valley of Petra but are available from nearby Wadi Musa. Mean annual precipitation totals approximately 130 mm (5") in Wadi Musa and occurs primarily from November through March (Water Resources Division 1981). Though trace snowfall is nearly an annual occurrence, most precipitation is recorded as rain. Temperatures may drop below 0°C during the nighttime hours in January; however, these subzero temperatures are infrequent and quickly rise during daylight hours. In Wadi Musa, the January mean temperatures range from 6°C to 12°C and rise toward an August mean temperature range of 15°C to 32°C (JMD 1971). The effect of freezing and thawing upon weathering, rock disaggregation and landscape change has gained recent insight through field analysis and laboratory experimentation (McGreevy 1981, Thorn 1982, Fahey & Dagresse 1984, Hall 1986). However, with few days below freezing in Petra, the potential for frost-induced weathering is minimal. In Wadi Musa, relative humidity exhibits a predictable relationship to precipitation, ranging from 70% in January to less than 25% in August. Mean daily periods of insolation range from seven hours in December to 13 hours in July (JMD 1971). Though convectional clouds in the summer months are common, little rain is ever produced during the hottest season.

Local prevailing wind directions are from the west/northwest for 60% (7 a.m.), 50% (1 p.m.) and 90% (7 p.m.) of the time (JMD 1971) and are attributed to a mixture of cyclonic flow off the Mediterranean Sea and adiabatic winds rising from the Wadi 'Araba. Low-pressure cells originating in the Mediterranean can produce storms with wind velocities reaching 35 mph, though their passage directly through Petra is infrequent. Only katabatic or drainage winds were observed during the late evening and early nighttime hours, with some strong gusts due to the convergence of the winds through the Siq and main valley. The drainage winds that develop in the Petra uplands descend to converge in the Siq. These locally produced katabatic winds can create rare, small dust storms throughout the valley during the nighttime hours. Unusual easterly winds (called ᶜhamsin) may gust from the highlands of southern Jordan, draining into the Wadi 'Araba. Though rare, these strong föhn-like winds have been recorded in nearby Wadi Musa, quickly raising the temperature 5-10°C and often causing great amounts of sand to drift up and over the Transjordan mountain ranges, causing considerable damage to the structures in its path (JMD 1971).

Although high winds may be responsible for the transport of large sand masses across the Petra uplands, winds of this magnitude are relatively infrequent in the Siq or valley. Though Owen's work (1964) established the required entrainment velocity for sand grains to be ~ 11 mph, wind velocities exceeding ~ 9 mph were rarely encountered in the Siq during the summer months, while breezes of 2-3 mph blew constantly throughout the day. Wind gusts in the main valley, however, have been sometimes recorded exceeding 25 mph (JMD 1971).

Overall, although the valley of Petra and its surrounds are classified as a desert climate with xeric biota, its protected setting has enabled a number of relative environmental anomalies — the climate is milder, the vegetation more abundant and the weathering less extreme than in the surrounding areas. However, as its popularity increases as a tourist destination, the rate of general landscape degradation in Petra will increase dramatically.

## The Geology of Petra

Petra's multicolored sandstone with spalling cliffs and fault-bound escarpments has attracted visitors to the area since its earliest days. The ruined city of Petra contains numerous tombs, monuments and structures, all built or carved directly from local sandstone or limestone. The secluded site, steep valley walls and towering crags are related to its geological history and processes. Periodic seismic activity has produced a sandstone landscape wrought with fault-defined valleys and deeply jointed strata. However, it is the character of sandstone's weatherability that has accentuated these valley walls and spires into unique, aesthetic shapes.

The Petra sandstones (Ram, Umm Ishrin, Disi formations) are underlain by an extensive pre-Cambrian (>ca. 550 my) complex comprised of the Aqaba Granite, with gneisses and schists, and the Ahaymir Rhyolite and Diabases. These dark-colored rocks outcrop along the eastern slopes of the Wadi 'Araba, in the eroded walls of the Wadi as-Siyyagh — Petra's western drainage into the Rift Valley. This igneous rock base exhibits a well-defined contact upon which the Cambrian Ram and Umm Ishrin sandstones sit. These are the reddish to buff-colored arenite sandstones that gave Petra its early description as "A rose red city, half as old as time" and into which most of the celebrated tombs, the façades, the Theater, the stairways and the couloirs have been hewn. The famous arenite-type sandstone displays few rosy hues, but was more aptly interpreted by a visiting Italian chef as a "world where everything is made of chocolate, ham, curry-powder and chicken" (Browning 1989). This formation dates from the Middle to Upper Cambrian (~ 530-550 my) and measures up to 300 m in thickness. It has been subdivided into three categories: a) multicolored, medium to coarse quartz grains with some rounded quartz pebbles found at Cambrian/pre-Cambrian contact; b) dark brown-black, often banded, fine quartz grains with a dense, ferruginous and manganiferous composition, and c) buff-colored, fine quartz grains of micaceous, interbedded, shaley/silty lenses. The original environment for the sandstone deposition is believed to have been a continental braided stream complex (Jaser & Bargous 1992).

The younger, blanketing formation is the conforming Upper Cambrian-Lower Ordovician (470-550 my) Disi sandstone. Measuring up to 100 m in thickness, this stratum displays a whitish-beige color and is seen throughout the valley as the capstone bed of Jabal al-Khubtha (the rocks at the Siq's entrance), Zib Atuf, the High Place of Sacrifice and the caprock of Umm al-Biyara (the site of Nabataean cisterns and couloirs). The Disi formation sandstone weathers and erodes into characteristic domed features that can be recognized miles away. Unlike the Umm Ishrin sandstone, which exhibits extensive moment jointing and faulting, the Disi sandstone displays less frequent jointing, though its jointing patterns and orientation conform to those of the underlying formation. Finally, of great additional importance to Petra's early builders is the locally available Cretaceous Shahar limestone (~ 125 my). This is the light gray, banded caprock that is visible atop Jabal ash-Shahar, the prominent mountain rising behind Wadi Musa. This was one of the stronger building materials found in the valley of Petra and nearby Sabra. It may have been the primary material for much of Petra's constructed architecture, including the Temple.

The surrounding hills of Petra, near Wadi Musa, Jabal Harun, Al-Bayda' and Sabra are covered by Quaternary remnants of poorly sorted, fluvial gravels and loess blankets — the fine dust that possibly originated during the lowered sea level of past periods of global cooling and glaciation. Holocene deposition is marked by active scree cones, eolian silt and sand deposition, poorly sorted cobbles, gravel, boulders and sand atop and amongst the Paleolithic, Edomite, Nabataean, Roman and Byzantine ruins (Bargous 1989).

Faulting, jointing and gentle stratigraphic dipping dominates the structural geology of the Petra area. The Al-Mataha and the Abu Ulayqa faults, developed during the Oligocene Epoch (ca. 40 my), respectively, define the eastern and western walls of the valley (Bender 1968). Both trending approximately northeast-southwest, these faults delimit a graben valley, while the adjacent Rift Valley System's rising horsts are slowly forcing the Mediterranean Sea westward as the valley widens. To the west of the Abu Ulayqa fault through Petra's Wadi as-Siyyagh, a series of sympathetic faults have generated a descending horst staircase to the Wadi 'Araba Rift System. These faults have caused great destruction in the Petra area, with recorded earthquakes in 113, 363, 419, 551, 748 and 757 CE (Russell 1985).

On a large scale, the steep valleys and Siq of Petra can be attributed to the extensive faults and joints that run throughout the sandstone and limestone. However, it is the overall smaller-scale weatherability of Petra's cliffs and peaks that produces its unique appearance and character. The unique rounded forms of the whitish Disi formation and the characteristic spalled cliffs of the reddish Umm Ishrin formation add to Petra's mythical air. The early builders of Petra were fortunate to have constructed and hewn such great and numerous architectural wonders in an arid climate, which acts to decrease weathering and erosion. This is why many of the tomb façades

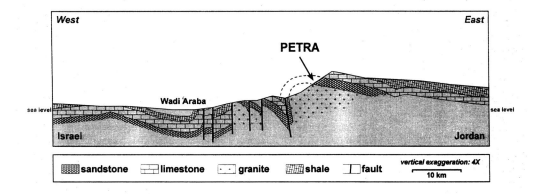

*Figure 3.5. Geological Cross-section of Petra*
*This map illustrates the pre-Cambrian extrusive/intrusive plinth that supports the Cambrian/Ordivician Arenite Sandstones of Petra and the Cretaceous Limestones of nearby Wadi Musa and the Jordanian Uplands. Note the complicated recumbent nature (overturned) of the Petra Sandstones. Map adapted from Quennel 1982.*

and structures have withstood two millennia of nature's influences.

## Previous Weathering Research

### General Weathering Studies

Weathering studies for sandstone and limestone in arid climates are rare. Early observations on sandstone and limestone weathering and their often unusual features in the Middle East were made by Herodotus (ca. 450 BCE), Strabo (ca. 10 CE), Pliny (ca. 50 CE), J.L. Stephens (ca. 1830) and R.F. Burton (ca. 1850); however, it isn't until the twentieth century that we begin to see the conceptual development of weathering studies (Paradise 1995). Bryan (1922, 1928) and Blackwelder (1929) documented previous investigations of the processes responsible for weathering. These were the first works to address the processes responsible for sandstone and limestone weathering and not just weathering feature descriptions.

Later research in arid region weathering mechanisms established the importance of the relationship of weathering to mass wasting (i.e., Schumm and Chorley 1966), lichen overgrowth (i.e., Jackson and Keller 1970, Jones et al. 1980, Paradise 1997), case hardening (Conca and Rossman 1982), permeability (Pflüger 1995), tafoni develop-ment (i.e., Mustoe 1983), salt (i.e., Smith and McGreevy 1988, Young 1987) and insolation

and moisture availability (i.e., Blackwelder 1933, Sancho and Benito 1990, Robinson and Williams 1992, Paradise 1995). Schmidt (1985, 1989) examined cliff face retreat and mass wasting to quantify weathering rates, while Meierding (1993) investigated sandstone inscription legibility in the American Southwest as a function of differing weathering influences. These works either addressed the extrinsic (i.e., climatic, human use) or intrinsic (i.e., lithology) influences of weathering to understand process type and rate and process effect and control. For instance, these studies indicate that sandstone weathers two ways. Since sandstone is made of sandy clasts in a binding matrix, either the clast fractures or dissolves and falls out, or the matrix fractures or dissolves and releases the clast. Both weathering types represent disaggregation, producing loose sand as the weathering product. This is the source of many of the dunes and sand veneers throughout the Middle East.

Since weathering studies investigate the influences of rock decay, its understanding is vital to the varied fields investigating landscape change (i.e., geography, geology, pedology, biology) and material conservation, integrity and protection (i.e., art conservation, material science, architecture, engineering). However, weathering studies require an increasingly multidisciplinary focus, and although holistic weathering studies are increasing, the need to bridge these various studies is becoming increasingly rare since the fields (i.e., art history, climatology and petrology) are often perceived as unrelated, or the crossover training is unavailable.

## The Roman Theater

One of the most extensive sandstone weathering studies completed in an arid region was conducted on the Roman Theater of Petra (Paradise 1995). Nabataean culture was sophisticated and capitalized on the fusion of various exotic attributes into their crossroads society (Glueck 1965) — those of morés, business, technology, art and architecture. This is evidenced in the composite and unique style of their tomb façades, site designs and architecture, including the Roman Theater.

The Roman Theater displays perfectly melded qualities: the exacting acoustical standards, orientation recommendations, stone-dressing techniques and stage design of the Romans,

*Figure 3.6 . Weathering of the Tomb Façades*
*Weathering and erosion threatens the architecture and small-scale landscape of Petra. Running water and wind have been found to be significant influences on stone weathering in arid regions, as is seen in this photograph of water-induced tafoni (patterned cavities) on a tomb façade in the Outer Siq. Nabataean water diversion techniques were successful in redirecting torrential storm waters; however, as these channels fill, water overflows and threatens to accelerate weathering in Petra.*

and the modified drainage and site-specific engineering capabilities of the Nabataeans (McKenzie 1990). Though the Theater was hewn and constructed under Roman specifications for the highest acoustical rectitude, as prescribed by Vitruvius, it was done so before formal occupation of the Romans under the Emperor Trajan in 106 CE, during the reign of Aretas IV (9 BCE-40 CE) (Hammond 1965). The engineering criteria recommended by Vitruvius were so specific that it has permitted historians and architects to locate the structures of his design, of his building authority or those contemporary to his. The acoustical rectitude produced from the designs of Vitruvius was only surpassed by the rigid adherence to the angles, proportions and design used by the architects and workers implementing the Vitruvian canon.

These standards allow a high level of precision in archaeometric field measurements. The difference between the original dressed surface and the current weathered surfaces represents surface recession from weathering after the Theater's construction 2000 years ago. Across the Theater, a two-meter sampling scheme was used to measure these receded surfaces. Over 500 measurements were made on vertical and horizontal surfaces and correlated to the intrinsic variables of sandstone matrix-to-clast ratios, overall densities, matrix chemistry (Si, Ca, Fe, Al concentrations) and to the extrinsic effects of climate and the annual amount of insolation (megajoules/m$^2$). This data set has become the largest sandstone weathering data network of its kind.

It was found that iron in the rock matrix slowed weathering. As iron amounts increase, there is an abrupt decrease in weatherability, until it decreases below measurable limits at 4%. Iron in the matrix may be a sandstone clast-binding agent, which reduces disaggregation. This is easily observed throughout Petra, where the whitish Disi sandstone (containing little iron in the sandstone matrix) is weathering faster and is more friable than the reddish Umm Ishrin sandstone (containing more matrix iron). Since iron concentrations affect the overall color of sandstone, the color of the sandstones can then be used as a rough indicator of its relative weatherability — lighter colors weather faster than darker tones.

This study also found that calcium concentrations affected weathering rates. In sandstone with matrix calcium concentrations exceeding 10%, weathering accelerates when insolation exceeds 5000 megajoules/m$^2$ (the more exposed south-facing rock). Increased heating from insolation may be responsible for clast expansion and contraction, causing micro-fractures to develop between the clast and matrix and leading to disaggregation and subsequent weathering (Somerton 1992).

Moreover, of greatest importance in this study was the estimation of mean weathering rates for sandstone in arid regions, ranging from 15-70 mm/millennium on horizontal surfaces to 5-20 mm/millennium on vertical surfaces. Gross differences in recession rates are attributed to the extrinsic influences of moisture availability (slope) and insolation (aspect), while minor differences are attributed to intrinsic characteristics of matrix chemistry (Fe, Ca), sandstone density and clast-to-matrix ratios. Weathering-rate studies are not only important for rock decay and landscape change but also for an estimation of the quantity of particles produced — a vital aspect of erosion, hydrology and/or water resources.

Overall, this research on the Roman Theater established an essential hierarchy of sandstone weathering influences in an arid region — of primary importance in influencing stone weatherability is the amount of iron and calcium in the sandstone matrix, and of lesser influence is the rocks' exposure to sunlight and the availability of moisture on the rock surface.

## The Djin Blocks and Obelisks

Many of the pre-Roman Nabataean structures in Petra were not constructed but hewn directly from local Paleozoic sandstones. Before the stonework was undertaken, the Nabataeans dressed these rock surfaces with methods similar to the Romans but in a uniquely Nabataean, herringbone pattern dating from 100 BCE to 100 CE (Browning 1989). These dressed surfaces are found throughout Petra and represent excellent surfaces for sandstone weathering studies, since their exposure span is known and they have not been moved or relatively altered.

The Djin Blocks and obelisks were used in this research because of (i) their dressed surfaces of varying aspects, (ii) their weathering features and surface recession as well as their unobscured surfaces of consistent Nabataean stone-dressing and (iii) their relatively vertical surfaces of easy access. Of the four primary Djin Blocks at Bab as-Siq, the fourth block near the diversion tunnel was the most important block for study, since the nearest cliff face is 7 m away — the other blocks have northern faces obscured by nearly adjacent cliffs. The two obelisks on the Atuf Ridge display similar weathering characteristics and surface recession, with the exception of the narrow, white sandstone bed within each obelisk of the Disi formation that shows accelerated weathering due to its lower iron matrix constituents (Paradise 1995).

Using the original Nabataean dressed surface as the measurement standard, weathering features (i.e., tafoni, rillen, alveoli) were measured on vertical wall surfaces of varying aspects. Surface recession since construction was estimated and the weathering features were identified and measured.

These hewn Nabataean-dressed faces (block, obelisks) exhibit weathering features, dimensions and recession influenced by their aspect. Northern aspects ($\pm$ 000°N) show minimal weathering with 90 $\pm$ 5% of the original stone-dressing apparent with no recesses exceeding 0.02 m in any dimension. Original stone-dressing indicates a weathering rate of less than 15 mm since construction. The relatively minor weathering occurring on northern faces can be attributed to (i) decreased surface erosion and increased surface weathering from lichen attachment (Paradise 1995, 1997), since lichens were rarely found on other aspects, and (ii) decreased solar flux and, consequently, less-frequent wetting and drying cycles (Ollier 1984). Southern aspects ($\pm$ 180°N) display 40 $\pm$ 10% of the original dressing remaining with scarce large cavities (tafoni) rarely exceeding 0.015 m in dimension. The increased surface recession on south-facing surfaces (as compared to northern surfaces) can be attributed to increased solar flux, increasing daily heating and cooling cycles (McGreevy 1985). Western ($\pm$ 270°N) and eastern ($\pm$ 090°N) aspects, however, display the greatest surface recession — with little original Nabataean stone-dressing remaining (<10%) and numerous tafoni often exceeding 0.20 m. This increased weathering can be attributed to the ideal daily and yearly balance of moisture and heating cycles that occur on these faces. Moisture availability (as compared to southern faces) and insolation exposure (as compared to northern faces) is high because of a half-day exposure to sunlight and heating. This permits eastern, southern and western faces to exceed summer surface temperatures of 50°C, while still enabling surface moisture from morning dew (when relative humidities are high enough) or from rainfall. Previous research (Young 1992) has shown the efficacy of wetting/drying and heating/cooling in the weathering of sandstone in arid regions. However, this ongoing research in Petra is clarifying the unique balance between moisture and insolation-induced weathering through the comparison of differing aspects on similar sandstones under the same microclimatic influences — a previously obscure relationship. The influence of aspect causing western and eastern surfaces to weather faster than other aspects has been confirmed with additional observations of similar surfaces throughout Petra.

## Observations from the Great Temple

The excavation of Petra's Temple has exposed a number of carved, arenite sandstone and limestone architectural fragments that are ideally suited for a discussion of local weathering. The Temple Complex is located along a hill (886-872 m) sloping toward the Colonnaded Street, and its architectural elements were probably carved from the local sandstones (Disi/Umm Ishrin) and limestone (Shahar) and display both remarkably

weathered and unweathered characteristics. This section will address the variable weathering of the Temple sandstone and limestone: the influences on stone deterioration and the present and future integrity of the Temple's stone architecture.

Sandstone deteriorates from variable microclimatic conditions and/or lithologic constituency, and the sandstone of the Temple displays weathering features from these influences. Conventional sandstone weathering studies have examined stone decay from two different scales: broad-scale studies indicating prevailing influences of rock jointing and lithologic homogeneity (i.e., cliffs and arches) and smaller-scale studies indicating weathering dominated by microclimate and petrographic inconsistency (i.e., tafoni). Large-scale research is used to understand landscape change, while small-scale studies have focused on architectural deterioration and conservation and theoretical foundations. These studies examine both intrinsic and extrinsic agents of weathering. Although the architecture of the Temple displays cracking and spalling from broad structural joints or faults, small-scale weathering will be discussed that is most affected by microclimatic and lithologic variation.

The fallen columns of the Temple are an excellent *in situ* representation of sandstone weathering. Designated 'Pia' and 'Nadine,' these two columns collapsed from a historic earthquake and are visible trailing down the

*Figure 3.7. The Weathering of a Djin Block*
*This diagram illustrates the four sides of the fourth carved sandstone Djin Block near the diversion tunnel at Bab as-Siq. The differences in surface recession and weathering features (i.e., tafoni) are related to the aspects of each block face. Northern aspects display the least amount of surface recession and weathering of the original Nabataean stone-dressing and cross-step motifs, because of its decreased exposure to sunlight and warming. Southern aspects also exhibit decreased weathering from its relative absence of moisture availability. Eastern and western exposures show the greatest amount of weathering from increased moisture and decreased warming, indicating the ideal combination for accelerated weathering in Petra lies in the balance between daily and seasonal wetting/drying and heating/cooling cycles.*

**Surface Recession (Weathering) on the Bab as-Siq Djin Block (#4)**

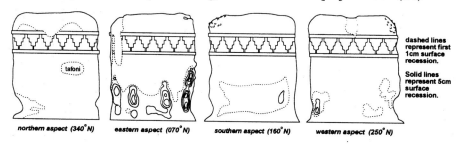

Fallen Columns of the Great Temple

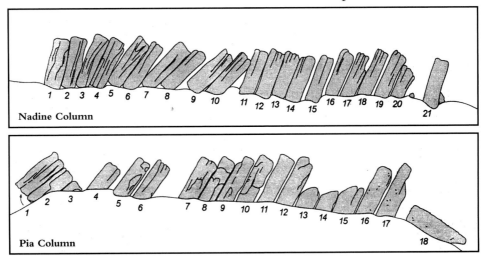

**Figure 3.8.** *The Fallen Columns of the Great Temple*
*This diagram represents the twin columns that toppled during a historic earthquake. The two columns are comprised of both the Umm Ishrin (darker in color and more resistant) and the Disi Sandstones (lighter in color and less resistant). The large, thin drums collapsed and have remained relatively exposed to natural influences since their construction, and they display weathered surfaces and features such as tafoni and spalling.*

slope. The columns trend 031°N and 044°N, respectively, and their upper portions have remained relatively well exposed, since their location is comparatively stable above the wadi flood plain where alluvial sediments can collect. They are facing northeast where daily and seasonal winds hinder sand accumulation common in the recessed areas in the valley. The lower half of each column drum grouping has been cleared and exposed further by the Brown University excavation team, so the drums are now completely cleared of vegetation and accumulated sediments. Only the very bottom of each drum has remained unexposed.

The column drums display weathering features consistent with prior observations and research in Petra. Most of the drums exhibit deterioration influenced by solar flux (sunlight) and lithology, although some of the column drums exhibit decreased weathering because of lichen blankets. Drum portions facing north are often covered with lichen thalli *(Lecanora sp.)* from decreased sunlight and increased moisture. These lichen-covered drums exhibit decreased weathering and original stone-dressing grooves (only visible on Umm Ishrin sandstone), indicating a surface recession rate less than 10-15 mm over two millennia (Pia Column Drums 7 and 8 and

Nadine Column Drums 11, 12 and 21). The lichens may be accelerating weathering beneath the thalli, but they are decreasing the removal of the weathered by-product (erosion), which contains the detached sandstone particles, by attachment (Paradise 1995, 1997). Not only are the lichens decreasing surface recession, but the north-facing portions of the drums are also weathering at a slower rate because of less frequent wetting and drying cycles and cooler surfaces. Drum areas that have remained obscured from sunlight and away from running water display smaller weathering features and less surface recession.

The sandstone used for the column drums varies from the relatively iron-rich Umm Ishrin formation to those from the iron-poor Disi formation. Previous research (Paradise 1995) indicates that iron composition in the sandstone matrix has a dramatic effect on weathering, with a noticeable weathering threshold at 4%, above which weathering decreases below measurable rates. Since the Disi sandstones contain less matrix iron, they weather faster, as evidenced by five of the drums (Nadine Column Drums 9, 10, 13, 14 and 15). These drums exhibit no original stone-dressing or noticeable cracks, and significant wear and surface recession exceeds 500 mm in some areas (~ 25 mm/century).

*Figure 3.9. The Fallen Columns of the Great Temple*
*The fallen columns of the Great Temple may be seen from across the valley. Toppled from a historic earthquake, these thin column drums display diverse weathering and erosion features due to differences in microclimatic influences and lithologic composition. The view is to the west.*

*Figure 3.10. Close-up of the Fallen Sandstone Columns*
*A close-up view of two column drums (Pia Column Drums 5-6) from the dark reddish-brown sandstone of the Umm Ishrin Formation. The grooves across the drums are original stonemason dressing marks, which indicates a weathering rate so slow that 2000 years has not drastically weathered or eroded the surface to remove these grooves.*

Tafoni or honeycomb weathering are also visible on one of the Disi sandstone drums (Pia Column Drum 10). Located on drum portions facing southwest, these features represent an accelerating influence from more frequent wetting and drying cycles and greater heating. Iron-rich nodules (>8%) are visible in many of the column drums protruding from the low-iron weathering mass, remaining relatively unweathered (Pia Column Drums 16, 17 and 18).

On the iron-rich Umm Ishrin sandstone weathering is more affected by variations in rock composition than microclimatic influences. Since sandstone is composed of sandy clasts and matrix, matrix iron increases the binding strength of the sandstone. The lighter-colored sandstones are iron-poor and weather faster than the darker-colored, iron-rich rock. Also, since sandstones originally deposit as sandy accumulations in streams or at coasts, they accumulate in planar, bedded forms. So even if the lithologic composition is consistent, the rock often weathers along these original bedding planes. These weathering characteristics are observed in most of the

Temple sandstones as parallel cracks, flaking or spalling. All of the fallen drums display bedding planes perpendicular to the column axes, which would have eased stone quarrying and drum construction. However, since sandstone develops and hardens under great pressure, once that pressure has diminished (i.e., quarrying) the sandstone expands and develops fine fractures and cracks parallel to original bedding planes (Nadine Column Drums 1-5). This inherent weakness may have been an early influence on column instability, intensifying topple during ground shaking.

Architectural elements constructed of limestone were found throughout the Temple as well. Probably quarried from Jabal ash-Shahar, this sandy limestone is an ideal building material because of its lithologic consistency, relative hardness and abundance. The Shahar limestone is an indurated and siliceous aggregate of quartz sand clasts in carbonaceous matrix, much like the local sandstones with fewer clasts and more matrix (Pflüger 1995). The limestone portions that have been exposed since construction displayed features and surface recession

**Figure 3.11. The Excavated Limestone Attic Base of the Great Temple**
*The excavated limestone Attic base from the Great Temple displays masonry so finely constructed that little weathering has occurred while originally exposed and since buried. This was probably quarried from the local limestone of Jabal ash-Shahar, the towering peak above Wadi Musa. Limestone weathers relatively slowly in arid environments like Petra. Ancient Classical period inscriptions in the Shahar Limestone exhibit similarly slow weathering and erosion since their production 2000 years ago.*

consistent with similar limestone studies in arid regions, such as studies of the Temple of Amman (Paradise 1998). Stone-dressing grooves are not apparent on exposed portions, indicating a recession rate exceeding 15 mm since construction. However, on excavated limestone fragments like the Attic bases of the Temple, original stone-dressing is faintly visible, revealing a minimal weathering rate due to its removal from exposure to natural influences. Local limestones weather through the disaggregation of the clasts (sand or shell) from the matrix or, more commonly, through the dissolution of the matrix. Acidic waters from pollution or decaying biota can accelerate this dissolution. Prior research on the Temple of Amman (Paradise 1994, 1998) indicates that slow weathering (<5 mm/millennia) is not unusual in regions with low precipitation and minimal industry, which increases local acidification of precipitation, which thereby increases limestone dissolution. As vegetation decays and combines with water, it forms humic acid. So in Petra, where vegetation is sparse, ground waters remain neutral or slightly alkaline and are ideal subterranean environments for the preservation of limestone architecture. This can be observed on the excavated portions of the Temple, where limestone weathering has been remarkably slow. It is covered with stone-dressing grooves and chisel marks left by stonemasons nearly 2000 years ago. The relatively unweathered nature also indicates that the groundwater mobility and permeability on the slope of the Temple has been swift. Standing subsurface water would have accelerated limestone dissolution.

## Stone Conservation and Weathering

Globally, stone weathering has been accelerating. In industrialized regions like the United States, Australia and Europe, weathering rates in the past century have doubled and tripled (Meierding 1981, Dragovich 1986, Vavlaikis et al. 1990, Cooke et al. 1995). This has been attributed to increased hydrocarbon combustion and the subsequent combination with moisture, producing acid rain. Moreover, when pollution is combined with an increase in human use like tourism, the association can have disastrous results. As tourism increases, so will the impact from

visitors on architectural structures and archaeological sites. Furthermore, as an increase in human modification and deterioration of these sites compounds, it will become imperative to restrict access to ensure the integrity of these sites. Hopefully, this is not the future of Petra; however, as local and regional industry and automobile use increase in southern Jordan, combustion emissions will increase and consequently accelerate the weathering of sandy limestones or limey sandstones through the slight acidification of precipitation. Even distant upwind locations in Israel, Cairo and Gaza can add to the acidic dew and rainfall. Because of the known human effects on stone weathering, tourist access to these sites may need to be restricted or prohibited, but censored access will not stop the effects of airborne acids. This represents a great dilemma; as populations increase so does industry and its pollution, with an increase in acid rains and the consequent acceleration of stone weathering. As global tourism increases, the need to conserve these susceptible sites becomes increasingly difficult and crucial. There is good news, however, with new research in stone conservation. Currently, a number of surface applicants (i.e., silicic esters) that can decrease permeability and particle disaggregation have been developed. At this time, however, once applied they are not removable — an unacceptable conservation practice. As the research continues, though, we may find removable solutions that will slow stone weathering and save important architecture.

Overall, the sandstones and limestones of the Great Temple exhibit conditions and features typical of weathering in arid regions. Weathered features are visible across the structures and elements; however, the rate of deterioration is relatively slow compared to less arid sites in northern Jordan and Syria. Original stone-dressing is apparent on some of the fallen sandstone columns and the exhumed limestone Attic bases, indicating a surface recession rate of less than 15 mm since construction. However, the whitish sandstones (matrix containing little or no iron, <2%) have weathered at rates exceeding 25 mm/century, or one inch every 100 years, a rapid rate for arid regions. Some sandstones containing high amounts of iron in the matrix (>4%) appear nearly unweathered in 2000 years. This is evidenced by the brownish-blackish portions in sandstones that still exhibit stonemason chisel marks adjacent to low-iron, whitish areas that have receded more than two to four inches.

Weathering studies are essential and are contributing notably to a number of fields.

Broad-scale investigations are adding to an understanding of landscape change, while smaller-scale studies are valuable in materials conservation — one cultivates our appreciation of nature, the other enriches an understanding of our heritage.

---

# Bibliography

Barjous, M.O.

    1989    *The Geology of the Rose-Red City of 'Petra,'* Natural Resources Authority of Jordan, Amman.

Bender, F.

    1968    *Geologie von Jordanien (Geology of Jordan)*, Gebrüder Borntraeger, Berlin, Stuttgart.

Blackwelder, E.

    1929    "Cavernous Rock Surfaces of the Desert," *American Journal of Science* 217:393-399.

    ———.

    1933    "The Insolation Hypothesis of Rock Weathering," *American Journal of Science* 26:97-113.

Browning, I.

    1989    *Petra*, Chatto and Windus Ltd., London.

Bryan, K.

    1922    "Erosion and Sedimentation in Papago Country, Arizona," *U.S. Geological Survey Bulletin* 730-B:19-90.

    ———.

    1928    "Niches and Other Cavities in Sandstone at Chaco Canyon, New Mexico," *Zeitschrift für Geomorphologie* 3:125-140.

Conca, J.L. and G.R. Rossman.

    1982    "Case Hardening of Sandstone," *Geology* 10:520-523.

Cooke, R.U., R.J. Inkpen and G.F.S. Wiggs.

    1995    "Using Gravestones to Assess Changing Rates of Weathering in the UK," *Earth Surface Processes and Landforms* 20:531-546.

Dragovich, D.

    1986    "Weathering Rates of Marble in Urban Environments, Eastern Australia," *Zeitschrift fur Geomorphologie* 30:203-214.

Fahey, B.D. and D.F. Dagresse.

    1984    "An Experimental Study of the Effect of Humidity and Temperature Variations on the Granular Disintegration of Argillaceous Carbonate Rocks in Cold Climates," *Arctic and Alpine Research* 16:291-298.

Fall, P.L.

    1990    "Deforestation in Southern Jordan: Evidence from Fossil Hyrax Middens," in *Man's Role in the Shaping of the Eastern Mediterranean Landscape*, ed., S. Bottema, G. Enjes-Niebord, W. Van Zeist, Rotterdam, A.A. Balkema 271-81.

Glueck, N.

    1965    *Deities and Dolphins: The Story of the Nabataeans*, Farrar, Straus and Giroux, New York.

Jackson, T.A. and W.D. Keller.

    1970    "A Comparative Study of the Role of Lichens and Inorganic Processes in the Chemical Weathering of Recent Hawaiian Lava Flows," *American Journal of Science* 269:446-466.

Jordan Meteorological Division.

    1971    *Climate Atlas of Jordan*, Ministry of the Environment, Royal Hashemite Kingdom of Jordan, Amman.

Hall, K.

    1986    "Rock Moisture Content in the Field and Laboratory and its Relationship to Mechanical Weathering Studies," *Earth Surface Processes and Landforms* 11:131-142.

Hammond, P.C.

    1965    *The Excavation of the Main Theater at Petra: 1961-1962*, Bernard Quaritch, Inc., London.

Jaser, D. and M.O. Bargous.

    1992    *Geotechnical Studies and Geological Mapping of Ancient Petra City*, Natural Resources Authority of Jordan, Amman.

Jones, D., M.J. Wilson and J.M. Tait.

    1980    "The Weathering of Basalt by *Petrusaria corallina*," *Lichenologist* 12:277-289.

McGreevy, J.P.

    1981    "Some Perspectives on Frost Shattering," *Progress in Physical Geography* 5:56-75.

———.

    1985    "Thermal Properties as Controls on Rock Surface Temperature Maxima and Possible Implications for Rock Weathering," *Earth Surface Processes and Landforms* 10:125-136.

Mustoe, G.E.

    1983    "Cavernous Weathering in the Capitol Reef Desert, Utah," *Earth Surface Processes and Landforms* 8:517-526.

Meierding, T.C.

1981      "Marble Tombstone Weathering Rates: A Transect of the United States," *Physical Geography* 2:1-18.

———.

1993      "Inscription Legibility Method for Estimating Rock Weathering Rates," *Geomorphology* 6:273-286.

McKenzie, J.S.

1990      *The Architecture of Petra*, Oxford University Press, Oxford.

Ollier, C.

1984      *Weathering*, Longman Press, London, New York.

Osborn, G.

1985      "Evolution of the Late Cenozoic Inselberg Landscape of Southwestern Jordan," *Paleogeography, Paleoclimatology, Paleoecology* 49:1-23.

Paradise, T.R.

1994      "Limestone Weathering Analysis of Temple of Amman," in *The Great Temple of Amman: The Architecture*, ed., P.M. Bikai, ACOR, Amman, Jordan 110-15.

———.

1995      "Sandstone Weathering Thresholds in Petra, Jordan," *Physical Geography* 16:205-222.

———.

1997      "Disparate Weathering from Lichen Overgrowth, Red Mountain, Arizona." *Geografiska Annaler* in press.

———.

1998      "Limestone Variability and Weathering, Great Temple of Amman, Jordan," *Physical Geography*.

Pfluger, F.

1995      "Archaeo-Geology in Petra, Jordan," *ADAJ* 39:281-295.

Russell, K.W.

1985      "The Earthquake Chronology of Palestine and Northwest Arabia from the Second through the mid-Eighth Century A.D.," *BASOR* 260(Fall):37-60.

Robinson, D.A. and R.B. Williams.

1992      "Sandstone Weathering in the High Atlas, Morocco," *Zeitschrift fur Geomorphologie* 36:413-429.

Sancho, C. and G. Benito.

1990      "Factors Controlling Tafoni Weathering in the Ebro Basin, Spain," *Zeitschrift fur Geomorphologie* 34:165-177.

Schmidt, K.H.

1985      "Regional Variation of Mechanical and Chemical Denudation, Upper Colorado River Basin, USA," *Earth Surface Processes and Landforms* 10:497-508.

_____.

  1989    "The Significance of Scarp Retreat for Cenozoic Landform Evolution on the Colorado Plateau, USA," *Earth Surface Processes and Landforms* 14:93-104.

Schumm, S.A. and R.J. Chorley.

  1966    "Talus Weathering and Scarp Recession in the Colorado Plateau," *Zeitschrift fur Geomorphologie* 10:11-35.

Smith, B.J. and J.P McGreevy.

  1988    "Contour Scaling of a Sandstone by Salt Weathering Under Simulated Hot Desert Conditions," *Earth Surface Processes and Landforms* 13:697-705.

Somerton, W.H.

  1992    *Thermal Properties and Temperature-related Behavior of Rocks*, Elsevier, Amsterdam.

Thorn, C.E.

  1982    "Bedrock Micro-climate and the Freeze/Thaw Cycle," *Earth Surface Processes and Landforms* 72:131-137.

Vavlaikis, E.G., D.A. Haristos and C. Balafoutis.

  1990    "Indirect Influence of Man-made Factors on the Dissolution Rate of Dolomitic Marble in the Thessalonika Area (Northern Greece)," *Zeitschrift fur Geomorphologie* 34:475-480.

Young, A.R.

  1987    "Salt as an Agent in the Development of Cavernous Weathering," *Geology* 15:962-966.

Young, A.R. and R. Young.

  1992    *Sandstone Landforms*, Springer-Verlag, New York.

Water Resources Department.

  1981.    *Rainfall in Jordan*, Royal Hashemite Kingdom of Jordan, Technical Paper #50, Amman.

Zohary, M.

  1940    "Geobotanical Analysis of the Syrian Desert," *Palestine Journal of Botany* 2:46-96.

# PALYNOLOGICAL ANALYSIS
# FROM THE PETRA GREAT TEMPLE

## Peter Warnock

## Introduction

During the 1994 field season of the Petra Great Temple excavations, pollen samples were taken to investigate environmental conditions and cultural activities at the site. Palynological analyses can supply information on the local environment in Petra during the occupation of the Temple as well as cultural activities, including vessel and feature use.

A number of select plaster, whole-vessel soils and washes and soil samples were taken for palynological analysis during the 1994 season. The samples include: plaster from column drums, the soil contents from inside whole vessels, washes from inside whole vessels (to collect the pollen adhering to the vessel walls) and soil samples from particular features. Plaster samples from the Temple at the Amman Citadel contain pollen, used to determine the local environment and investigate cultural practices (Warnock and Pendleton 1994). Soil and pollen washes from inside vessels have been used to determine vessel use and contents, while soil samples are used to investigate cultural practices and environmental reconstruction (Bryant and Holloway 1983, Holloway and Bryant 1986).

## Methodology

The samples were sent to Michael Pendleton at Texas A & M University, where they have been processed using standard palynological procedures (Faegri and Iversen 1989, Moore and Webb 1978, Traverse 1988). Unfortunately, because of time and lab constraints, only seven samples have been processed at this time. Of the samples processed, most do not have the required 200 grain pollen counts per slide to be considered viable samples (Barkley 1934). One sample (Drain location 20, Area UT, Trench 2, Locus 20, Sequence number 55) does have the required 200 grain count, while

a second sample (west channel of Canalization System, tan/brown soil above plaster layer) contained a 154 grain count. All other samples have less than 10 grains per slide.

## Discussion

Both samples contain high counts of pollen and reflect localized environmental conditions. They are both very high in non-arboreal pollen types, suggesting a general lack of forests in the vicinity. Pinaceae, Fagaceae (specifically *Quercus*, oak) and other arboreals make up less than 5.0% of the pollen spectra for both samples. If there were forests nearby, the expected amount of arboreal pollen would be much higher. The samples are composed primarily of non-arboreal field plants, such as grasses (Poaceae), cheno-ams (Chenopodiaceae and Amaranthaceae) and various composites (Asteraceae, Compositiaea, Liguliflorae). This pollen spectra suggests an environment not unlike the current Petra environment — wide open areas with few trees and large numbers of annual flowering plants.

The sample from the drain (Drain location 20, Area UT, Trench 2, Locus 20, Sequence number 55) also contains a large number of spores and fungal bodies. Many pollen grains in the sample are being attacked by fungi. The sample from the Canalization System (west channel of Canalization System, tan/brown soil above plaster layer) also has spores and fungi attacking pollen grains. Fungal destruction of pollen is differential; various fungi prefer particular types of pollen over others. The large numbers of fungi observed may have influenced the numbers and types of pollen that have been preserved in the samples. The high amounts of fungi and spores are consistent with the cool damp conditions found in the Canalization System.

## Conclusions

The pollen samples that did contain pollen offer a view of the local environment. The environment associated with the samples is similar to the present Petra environment — open areas with large numbers of scattered, annual plants and few trees. Unfortunately, it is not possible to determine when the soils were deposited and, thus, what time period the samples and their data represent. While the preservation in the majority of samples is not good, several samples contain adequate amounts of pollen. Future studies may provide more information, which can be combined with studies such as wood and other botanical analyses to provide a broader picture of the environment and cultural activities at the Petra Great Temple.

## Bibliography

Barkley, F.A.

   1934    "The Statistical Theory of Pollen Analysis," *Ecology* 15:283-289.

Bryant, V.M. and Holloway, R.

   1983    "The Role of Palynology in Archaeology," in *Advances in Archaeological Method and Theory, Vol. 6*, ed., M. Shiffer, Academic Press, New York 191-224.

Faegri, K. and J. Iversen.

   1989    *Textbook of Pollen Analysis*, 4th ed., Hafner, New York.

Holloway, R. and V.M. Bryant.

   1986    "New Directions of Palynology in Ethnobiology," *Journal of Ethnobiology* 6(1):47-65.

Moore, P.D. and J.A. Webb.

   1978    *An Illustrated Guide to Pollen Analysis*, Hodder and Stoughton, London.

Traverse, A.

   1988    *Paleopalynology*, Unwin Hyman, London.

Warnock, P. and M. Pendleton.

   1994    Appendix B: Amurca, in *The Great Temple of Amman: The Architecture*, C. Kanellopoulos, ACOR, Amman 104-105.

CHAPTER FOUR

# CANALIZATION
## AND
# GROUND-PENETRATING
# RADAR

## EVIDENCE FOR THE NABATAEAN
## SUBTERRANEAN CANALIZATION SYSTEM

Elizabeth E. Payne

## GROUND-PENETRATING RADAR
## STUDY OF THE PETRA GREAT TEMPLE

Terry E. Tullis and Constance Worthington

*Figure 4.1. Site aerial showing Canalization of the Temple Forecourt and disturbance in the Lower Temenos, 1997.*

# EVIDENCE FOR THE NABATAEAN SUBTERRANEAN CANALIZATION SYSTEM

Elizabeth E. Payne

The Nabataeans were renowned, even in antiquity, for their control and collection of the minimal rainfall received annually. Diodorus Siculus (II.48.2-3; XIX.94.6-8) describes the Nabataean cisterns that dotted the desert and their effect on the Nabataeans' control of the trade routes. Archaeological investigation has greatly expanded our knowledge of Nabataean canalization systems. Excavations at Humeima (Oleson 1990, 1991, 1992a, 1992b), Mampsis (Negev 1988) and Sabra (Lindner 1982a, 1982b), as well as the survey work conducted by the Natur-historichen Gesellschaft Nürnberg of the Al-Habta system within Petra (Gunsam 1980), provide interesting comparisons of construction method and scale.

The discussion that follows will focus only on the evidence for the Canalization System uncovered thus far at the Great Temple of Petra. Here, evidence for the collection of water has been excavated, and suggestions for the water's conservation can be made based on five years of study by the Brown University team.

## Subterranean Canalization System

Perhaps the most spectacular feature of water conservation found at the Great Temple is the Subterranean Canalization System. Evidence for the system appears across the site and will be described in full.

On the final day of the 1993 field season, the first evidence of the Subterranean Canalization System came to light. After excavating an irregularity in the Temple Forecourt (Trench 1, 1993) and removing an ashlar block with a mason's mark (Architectural fragment 776) that had been used as a plug stone, an opening into the system was revealed at the intersection of three channels: the main channel running south-north and two channels joining this main channel — one from the east and one from the west. Because of their well-constructed, bonded corners, these channels are believed to have been built during a single building phase (Joukowsky and Schluntz 1995:246). The upper courses of these walls, however, are less finely constructed and employ abundant chinking stones. This may represent either an enlargement or a repair of the original channel (Joukowsky 1997:305). The following description is based on observations made at the time of discovery (Joukowsky 1994:312-314) and on the 1994 excavation within the system at the point of intersection, designated Special Project 4 (SP 4) (Joukowsky and Schluntz 1995:246-249).

Excavation of a 2.67 m section of the main conduit has revealed walls consisting of five to seven courses of roughly hewn ashlar blocks, averaging 0.65-x-0.30 m in size. These walls show no signs of mortar or plaster coating, but they are covered by a thick gypsum deposit.[1] This portion of the Canalization System ranges from 0.6-0.7 m in width and from 1.7-1.9 m in height (Joukowsky and Schluntz 1995:247).

The roof of the channel is made of large ashlars, averaging 0.75-x-0.57-x-0.16 m in size. These blocks span the distance between the channel walls. Many of these capstones are severely cracked, due most likely to earthquake damage, and were removed prior to excavation within the system. The floor of the channel and the base of its walls are covered with a layer of mortar (Locus 6; 10YR 3/1, very dark gray). The main channel slopes south-north at a 26° angle until both the floor and the ceiling of the channel step downward at the northern extent of excavation (Figures 4.1 and 4.2). These steps would have slowed the speed of

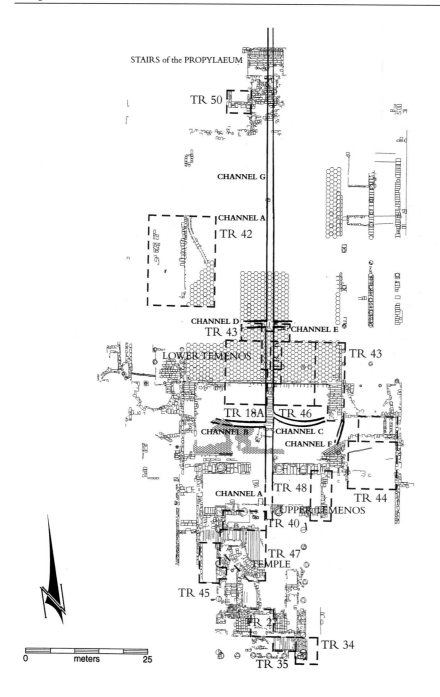

STAIRS of the PROPYLAEUM

TR 50

CHANNEL G

CHANNEL A

TR 42

CHANNEL D

TR 43

CHANNEL E

LOWER TEMENOS

TR 43

TR 18A    TR 46

CHANNEL B    CHANNEL C

CHANNEL F

TR 48

CHANNEL A

TR 44

UPPER TEMENOS

TR 40

TR 47

TEMPLE

TR 45

TR 27

TR 34

TR 35

0    meters    25

*Figure 4.2. Probable route of Canalization channels superimposed upon the 1997 Site Plan.*

the flowing water (Nalle, personal communication)[2] and would have allowed the channel to continue beneath the Central Stairs.

While the techniques used in constructing the east and west channels mirror those of the main conduit, the size of these channels is smaller, with the east channel measuring 0.5 m in width and 1.1 m in height and the west channel measuring 0.5 m in width but only 0.6 m in height. The intersection of these channels is slightly offset with the east tunnel,

0.75 m further north (Figures 4.2 and 4.3). This offset was probably necessary because a single capstone could not have spanned the distance between two adjacent channels (Joukowsky and Schluntz 1995:249).

These channels are believed to represent one of the earliest construction phases in the Temple precinct (Phase Vc). They were built either into the existing natural slope or, more likely, within or prior to the deposit of the artificial fill upon which the Temple was then constructed (Joukowsky 1997:309). After the

*Figure 4.3. Canalization System in the Temple Forecourt looking south, showing channel offset, 1997.*

construction of the channels was complete, the capstones were covered with roughly 0.15 m of a densely packed layer of sand and wadi pebbles (10YR 6/4, light yellowish brown). This technique seems to have been standard in the construction of this system (see SP 4, 1994, Locus 12; SP 20, Locus 6), and it appears to have served as a mortar, preventing the loose, sandy layers of floor bedding from falling through the gaps between the capstones into the channels.

Two strata have been excavated within the channel itself. The upper stratum, SP 4, Locus 4, is a loose, sandy fill that resembles the topsoil excavated across the site (7.5YR 4/6, strong brown). This layer contains few pottery sherds, but of these, there is a slightly higher proportion of Nabataean and Roman sherds than is typical of topsoil. This layer averages 0.35 m in depth and is believed to have been deposited after the system ceased to be in use. The lower stratum, SP 4, Locus 5, covers the mortar floor. This locus averages 0.25 m in depth and differs in both color and texture from the succeeding layer, being darker (2.5YR 4/4, reddish brown) and much finer. The inclusions within this level are also markedly different, consisting entirely of Nabataean and Roman pottery and lamp fragments. One lamp fragment can be securely dated to the first century CE, as 'Amr Type 2

(Figure 4.4) (Joukowsky and Schluntz 1995:247, 'Amr 1987:30). This level was probably deposited while the channels were in use.

While excavation at the intersection of these channels only has been conducted within the main conduit, the route of the other channels can be determined for quite some distance. The main channel can be traced roughly 8 m south, under the Temple Pronaos, before it is completely blocked by collapse and fill. This

*Figure 4.4. Nabataean lamp fragment, first century CE. Drawing by Elizabeth E. Payne.*

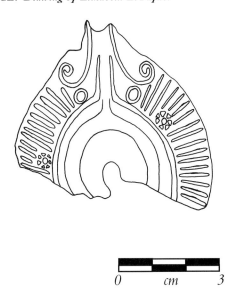

0          cm          3

*Figure 4.5. East Walkway Canalization disturbance, 1997.*

channel is believed to extend to the rear of the Temple Complex. Both the east and west channels extend perpendicularly to the main conduit for roughly 1.5 m before curving to the north (see Figure 4.2). Neither channel can be traced with certainty beyond 5 m from the point of intersection (Joukowsky and Schluntz 1995:249). The water in these channels flowed into the main conduit.

Also in the Upper Temenos, the excavation of Trench 19 reveals an opening into yet another branch of the Canalization System. While this section of the channel has not been excavated, much can be determined. The width of the channel is 0.58 m, and it has an unexcavated height of 1.11 m. This section flows southeast-northwest, but if this channel joins the main conduit, the location is not yet known. The construction of this channel is identical to that discussed above, except that the portion of channel exposed thus far appears to have been plastered, suggesting that all of the channel walls may also have been plastered originally. Repairs done to the small Hexagonal Pavement of the Temple Forecourt directly above this system imply that at some time repair or maintenance work was necessary within the channel (Figure 4.5).

Evidence of the system's course through the Lower Temenos is available from several

locations. The first is in SP 20, an excavation conducted to investigate an anomaly in the southern balk of Trench 13 (Figure 4.6). This anomaly consists of a large mound of rubble in an area otherwise covered with virtually clean fill. In addition, the large Hexagonal Pavement at this point suffers from extensive damage. Excavation has revealed that one of the tunnel's capstones broke and collapsed into the channel, causing both the layers of bedding and the Hexagonal Pavement above the channel to sink into the system. The rubble fill was used to cover the collapse of the Hexagonal Pavement. At this point, the channel runs below the pavers at a depth of 1.3 m. The damaged capstone is still in the channel, and the difficulty of its removal prevents further excavation. Here, another channel also branches off to the east, and the severe damage to the Hexagonal Pavement

*Figure 4.6. Trench 13, Lower Temenos Canalization disturbance, 1997.*

directly northwest of this opening could be explained by a west channel offset further north — the same technique found in the Upper Temenos.

The excavation of Trench 49 exposes portions of a subterranean branch running underneath the East Stairway. While the channel itself (Locus 20) has not been excavated, its walls and capstones are visible underneath the damaged hexagonal drain (Locus 24, see below) and other damaged areas of the Stairway. At 0.57 m, the width of the channel is identical to that found in Trench 19 and may represent a continuation of that branch to the north.

The excavation of Trench 42 reveals another smaller branch of the Canalization System that runs directly under the Hexagonal Pavement on this, its western perimeter (Figure 4.7). The channel in this area flows away from the

*Figure 4.7. Trench 42, Canalization System in the Lower Temenos West, 1997.*

Temple precinct from southeast to northwest. The channel uncovered here has been plastered, which lends support to the hypothesis that the main conduit may also have been originally plastered.

The northern extent of the Subterranean Canalization System is not yet known. A sink hole into the central channel (Figure 4.6) indicates that the system indeed continues to the north. Since there is not yet conclusive evidence of a cistern in the Lower Temenos into which the channels could empty,[3] it is not impossible to conclude that the channels empty directly into the Wadi Musa. Disturbances in the paving stones of the Roman Road are in line with the projected course of our channel and may support this hypothesis (Joukowsky 1997b).

## Above-ground Drains in the Lower Temenos

Perhaps the primary use of the Temple's Subterranean Canalization System was the removal of water collected on the floor surfaces of the Temple precinct. In support of this conclusion are the multiple drains that have been found in the Hexagonal Pavement covering the Lower Temenos, which lead to the subterranean channels (Figures 4.8 and 4.9).

The best preserved of these drains has been excavated in Trench 5, 1995. The drain (Locus 66) is carved into a hexagonal paving stone in the southeast corner of the trench and still retains its bronze fitting (Figure 4.8). This

*Figure 4.8. Bronze drain fitting in the Lower Temenos West, 1997.*

*Figure 4.9. Drain without fitting, Lower Temenos East, 1997.*

hexagonal fitting measures 0.30 m across, with a hole in the center (diameter 0.14 m). From this hole, a bronze pipe extends down vertically for 0.27 m. Shallow channels are also carved into the paver to facilitate the collection of water.

Three other examples of this type of drain have been found in the Lower Temenos (Figure 4.9). These drains are all constructed in the same manner, although in no other case yet uncovered has the bronze fitting been preserved. The measurements of the drains vary in nearly all the examples found: the example in Trench 17 measures 0.28 m across with a diameter of 0.12 m; the drains found in Trench 18A, Locus 16 and the damaged drain found in Trench 49, Locus 24 both measure 0.34 m across and 0.16 m in diameter.

These drains were used to remove the rain water that collected on the unroofed expanse of the Lower Temenos. Drains have been found in all areas excavated on the perimeter of the Lower Temenos Hexagonal Pavement, and it is assumed that subterranean channels run underneath these drains even in the areas where the channels themselves have not yet been seen.

## Conclusions

Evidence for this massive Canalization System has been found across the Great Temple. The tunnels form an extensive network for the removal of water from the Lower Temenos, and further excavation may yield a similar substructure beneath the Upper Temenos. This system is so far unique among Nabataean sites in its construction techniques. Far more common are above-ground channels, carved either into the living rock or into series of ashlar blocks placed for this purpose (Payne, n.d.). What is not unusual, however, is the emphasis its Nabataean builders placed on water collection.

The largest outstanding question concerning this system is its final destination. As stated above, no evidence has been found of a cistern into which this large quantity of water could have been deposited, and there is evidence that the channels may have extended to the wadi. Nevertheless, it seems unlikely that the Nabataeans, a people known for their efficient use of water, would have allowed the water collected from the surfaces of the Great Temple to have been wasted. A conclusive statement on this issue must, however, await further excavation.

## Endnotes

[1] A sample of this coating was analyzed by Bruno Giletti of the Department of Geological Sciences at Brown University. He suggests that the evaporation of moisture from the channel walls could leave gypsum ($CaSO_4(H_2O)_2$) as a residue. Further evaporation would result in the anhydrite crystals ($CaSO_4$) also present in the sample. Continued analysis may provide environmental information from within the Subterranean Canalization System.

[2] Excavation during the 1994 field season was greatly assisted by Peter Nalle, a retired mining specialist, who not only insured that all necessary safety precautions were taken, but was also invaluable in the measurements and interpretation of the Canalization System as a whole.

[3] This is based on the evidence revealed by the Ground-Penetrating Radar; see Terry E. Tullis in this chapter. It should also be borne in mind that the area directly south of the East Exedra is identical in structure to Nabataean cisterns found elsewhere. Further excavation will determine if this was indeed a cistern.

# Bibliography

'Amr, K.

1987    *The Pottery of Petra: A Neutron Activation Analysis Study,* BAR International Service.

Diodorus of Sicily.

1967    *Library of History,* Vol. 2, ed., E.H. Warmington, trans., C.H. Oldfather (from Greek), Harvard University Press, Cambridge, MA.

_____.

1983    *Library of History,* Vol. 10, ed., G.P. Gould, trans., Russel M. Geer (from Greek), Harvard University Press, Cambridge, MA.

Gunsam, E.

1980    "Die nördliche Hubta-Wasserleitung in Petra," in *Petra und das Königreich der Nabatäer,* ed., M. Lindner, Nürnberg:Delp 302-312.

Khairy, N.I.

1984    "Preliminary Report of the 1981 Petra Excavations," *ADAJ* 28:315-320.

_____.

1986    "Nabatäischer Kultplatz und byzantinische Kirche," in *Petra Neue Ausgrabungen und Entdeckungen,* ed., M. Lindner, München:Delp Verlag 58-73.

Joukowsky, M.S.

1994    "1993 Archaeological Excavations and Survey of the Southern Temple at Petra, Jordan," *ADAJ* 38:293-332.

_____.

1997    "The Water Canalization System of the Petra Southern Temple," in *SHAJ* IV, Amman 303-311.

_____.

1997b   "1996 Brown University Archaeological Excavations of the 'Great' Southern Temple at Petra, Jordan," Submitted to *ADAJ* Vol. XL:195-218.

Joukowsky, M.S. and E.L. Schluntz.

1995    "1994 Archaeological Excavations and Survey of the Southern Temple at Petra, Jordan," *ADAJ* 39:241-266.

Lindner, M.

1982a   "Über die Wasserversorgung einer antiken Stadt," *Das Altertum* 28/1:27-39.

_____.

1982b   "An Archaeological Survey of the Theater Mount and Catchwater Regulation System at Sabra, South of Petra, 1980," *ADAJ* 26:231-242.

McKenzie, J.

1990    *The Architecture of Petra,* Oxford University Press, Oxford.

Negev, A.

    1988    *The Architecture of Mampsis: Final Report Vol. I: The Middle and Late Nabataean Periods,* QEDEM 26. The Hebrew University, Jerusalem.

Oleson, J.P.

    1990    "Humeima Hydraulic Survey, 1989: Preliminary Field Report," *Echos du Monde Classique / Classical Views* XXXIV, 9:145-63.

    ———.

    1991    "Aqueducts, Cisterns, and the Strategy of Water Supply at Nabataean and Roman Auara (Jordan)," in *Future Currents in Aqueduct Studies,* ed., A.T. Hodge, Leeds: Francis Cairns 45-62.

    ———.

    1992a    "The Water-Supply System of Ancient Auara: Preliminary Results of the Humeima Hydraulic Survey," in *SHAJ IV, Actes du Congrès de Lyon, 30 May-4 June, 1989,* Amman 269-275.

    ———.

    1992b    "Hellenistic and Roman Elements in Nabataean Hydraulic Technology," in *L'Eau et les Hommes en Méditerranée et en Mer Noire dans l'Antiquité. Actes du Congrès International, Athènes, 20-24 mai 1988,* ed., G. Argoud, et al., Athens: Centre National de Recherches Sociales 473-497.

Payne, E.E.

    n.d.    *Nabataean Water Systems: An Evaluation of the System at the Southern Temple in Petra, Jordan and a Comparison of the Primary Examples Present throughout the Nabataean World.* B.A. Thesis, Brown University, Center for Old World Archaeology and Art, May, 1995.

# GROUND-PENETRATING RADAR STUDY OF THE PETRA GREAT TEMPLE

Terry E. Tullis and Constance Worthington

## Introduction

During excavation of the Petra Great Temple an underground system of tunnels, termed the 'Subterranean Canalization System,' was found to underlay various parts of the site. The Nabataeans who constructed this Temple are well known as experts in management of scarce water supplies in their region. Whether the purpose of the Canalization System was to collect water, to prevent damage to the Temple during flash-flood runoff or a combination of these is not known, although logic suggests it was a combination. In order to better determine the underground geometry of the Canalization System, a ground-penetrating radar (GPR) study was conducted during the summer of 1995. The primary purpose of this study was to trace the Canalization System under as much of the Temple as possible. An auxiliary purpose was to determine if other unexcavated features could be seen.

The suspected locations of several parts of the Canalization System were confirmed by the GPR. Other interesting features were also located during the survey, but as of this writing it is not exactly clear what these represent. Although it seems possible the Canalization System might lead into a cistern, no cistern has been detected. It is possible that further, more sophisticated processing of the radar data might reveal other features in addition to those that we have been able to identify by looking at individual profiles.

*Figure 4.10. Ground-Penetrating Radar. Terry E. Tullis and Constance Worthington in the Temple Forecourt, 1995.*

## Method

### Background on Ground-Penetrating Radar Method

In the GPR method, a radar wave travels downward from a source antenna that is dragged along the ground surface. The radar wave reflects off features in the subsurface and returns upward to a receiving antenna that is also moved along the ground surface. Frequently, as in this study, the sending and receiving antennas are connected to each other and dragged along together, so they have virtually the same location. In order for a radar wave to be reflected in the subsurface, it must encounter material with different electrical conductivity and dielectric constant. Even when two materials differ in other ways, if these electrical properties are nearly the same, no reflection occurs, and the boundary between these two materials is invisible to the radar.

If a radar wave is reflected from a point feature, like a boulder, or from a horizontal linear feature, like a pipe, running at right angles to the direction in which the radar antenna is dragged, the image seen in the raw radar data is not a simple point. It is instead a down-ward-oriented hyperbola, i.e., the shape of a frown. This is because radar waves are reflected back from the object not only when the antenna is directly above the object, but also before it gets to the object and after it passes the object. The time it takes for the waves to go and return will be longer because the object is further from the antenna, hence the object looks deeper when the antenna is not directly over it. The actual location and depth of the object is given by the shallowest point of the hyperbola, because the antenna is closest to the object when it is directly above the object. This characteristic hyperbola pattern of reflection from a point or linear source helps to identify such sources in the raw radar data.

A typical hyperbola reflection from the tunnel is seen in Profile 1 of Color Plate 9, where the location of the tunnel is given by the black rectangle in the center of the image. Ideally, the red center of the uppermost hyperbola should be located at the same depth as the top of the tunnel rectangle. The slight discrepancy in depth is because the radar velocity used in constructing this figure was the average of values taken at several locations, and the velocity varies slightly from place to place. The reason there are several hyperbolae, one above the other, is that ringing occurs after the first reflection. This ringing makes it nearly impossible to see other features for some depth below a good reflection. Thus, even in such textbook examples of hyperbolae as in Profile 1, it is not possible to image the floor of the tunnel.

It is also apparent from this example that the image of the subsurface obtained is rather fuzzy and distorted. The degree of resolution possible with GPR depends on the wavelength, or frequency, of the radar waves. Higher frequency/shorter wavelength waves are able to resolve finer detail, but they become attenuated more easily and so cannot see as deeply. The frequency chosen in a given study, therefore, depends on the size of the features one wants to detect and their expected depth.

To learn more about the GPR method, papers by Davis and Annan (1989:531-551) and Fisher et al. (1992:577-586) offer a place to begin. Some discussions of its use in archaeology are those by Vaughan (1986:595-604) and Imai et al. (1987:137-150).

### Our Methods

During two weeks in late July of 1995, we collected 190 GPR profiles of various lengths. The GPR system used is a GSSI SIR-2 with a 300 MHz antenna. Because we did not have a measuring wheel to record positions along each profile, locations of features along each profile have been determined by assuming that the antenna was being dragged at a constant rate and interpolating from the known end locations. The locations of most profiles have been determined by surveying using a total station EDM. During reconnaissance investigations, some other profiles were located only approximately. In the Lower Temenos area of the Temple, a systematic pattern of mutually perpendicular profiles was used, with a spacing between profiles of 1 m. Due to the surface topography of active trenches and the temporary positions of earth-moving equipment and their piles of dirt, it was not possible to make measurements along all of the possible profiles in the orthogonal grid system.

In other parts of the site, more isolated profiles were taken in order to discover if underground tunnels or other features could be located for later, more detailed measurements.

In order to identify tunnels better in the GPR data, we initially measured profiles across locations where the depth to a tunnel was known (Plate 9, Profile 1). This allows us to identify the character of tunnels in the radar profiles. It also allows us to determine an average radar velocity, so we are able to better determine the depths of unknown tunnels on subsequent profiles. The radar velocity is determined by the dielectric constant of the subsurface material, according to the equation $V = (0.3 \text{ m/ns})/(2 \text{ er})$, where V is the velocity of the radar that relates the two-way travel time to the depth and er is the relative dielectric constant. The two-way travel time is the time that it takes the radar to travel down to the feature and return. It is also the time that appears on the depth axis of the raw radar data. (Because of the very high speeds of the radar waves, times are given in nanoseconds (ns), which are billionths of a second.)

Measuring the two-way travel time to a good reflection in cases where the depths were known allowed us to determine the best value for the relative dielectric constant and hence the radar velocity. A relative dielectric constant of 5.85 was found to be the best average for the several locations with known depths to identifiable features. This is a reasonable value for the sandy soil of the area. With this value, 1 m of depth corresponds to 16.1 ns two-way travel time. Equivalently, the depth reached in a 50 ns-deep profile is 3.1 m and is 6.2 m in a 100 ns-deep profile. The depth is, however, slightly less, because about 5.7 ns (corresponding to 0.35 m) is required for the radar to travel from the antenna center to the ground surface. The maximum "depth" of recording used in our profiles is 50, 80 or 100 ns, and along many profiles we collected both 50 and 100 ns data.

Preliminary analysis of the data was made in the field by looking at the colored CRT display on the SIR-2 system and looking at black-and-white versions of the GPR profiles made on a thermal printer. The data was also stored on a magnetic tape shuttle, so it could be transferred to computers upon return to the United States for more detailed analysis. This analysis is done primarily by visual examination of colored versions of GPR reflections, using the line scan mode provided by GSSI's WinRad software. Most profiles have been examined using color table 11 and color transform 2, and these have been used to create the images in Plate 9. Color table 11 results in the same progression of colors corresponding to increasing amplitude away from zero, with positive reflections as brighter versions of these colors and negative reflections as darker ones. In some cases, the average of the amplitude at any given depth for many positions along the profile has been subtracted from the value at each position (horizontal background subtraction). This is done in order to enhance inclined features obscured by high amplitude ringing at times greater than 50 ns, which is due to reflections from the end of a coaxial cable that connects the sending and receiving antennae. Such horizontal background subtraction has been done, for example, on the lower half (53-100 ns) of profile 76hb on Plate 9. It permits seeing the inclined layer well into the time/depth contaminated by the antenna ringing.

In order to determine the locations of radar features, the profiles were plotted on a map using the MiniCAD software, which was employed in surveying the rest of the Great Temple. The locations of interesting features on each profile were determined by identifying the scan number (proportional to distance along the profile) and sample number (proportional to two-way travel time or depth in any scan) corresponding to the uppermost reflection in the hyperbolae. Scan and sample numbers were converted into distance and depth in meters. Once the locations and depths of the features on all profiles were so identified, their locations were transferred onto the map using MiniCAD.

Because the reflections and hyperbolae corresponding to the features identified are of variable quality, they are graded on a scale from A to D, corresponding to what is considered excellent, good, fair or poor. Examples of A-quality profiles are illustrated for Profiles 1, 16, 34 and the middle of 133 (the feature just below the letter A) in Plate 9. A reflection of D-quality means that some feature in the profile could be a hyperbola, but the shape and often the depth are also unclear. The feature about 30% of the way from the north end of Profile 133 (just below the letter C) in Plate 9 is a C-quality reflection.

## Results and Discussion

### General

A number of profiles showing well-defined hyperbolae or other interesting features are illustrated in Plate 9. The location of these figures is indicated in Figure 4.11. Hyperbolae identified as the tops of tunnels range in depth from 0.6-2.1 m, with 1 m being typical.

The principal results of this GPR survey are shown on the map of Figure 4.11. The light gray background shows the archaeological features described elsewhere in this volume, together with contour lines showing site elevations. Also shown in thin, straight, light gray lines are many of the GPR profiles. Five of these profiles are shown in wider gray lines. These are labeled with their profile number and correspond to the five profiles illustrated in Plate 9.

### Canalization System

The locations of hyperbolae identified along each profile are shown in Figure 4.11 as short, double-headed arrows, aligned along the profile in which they were observed. They have four degrees of darkness corresponding to the quality of the hyperbolae (see legend in Figure 4.11). Our interpretation of the location of tunnels of the Canalization System is given as heavier, darker lines, either solid, dashed or dotted depending on our degree of confidence in its existence/location. The solid lines show tunnel locations of which we are confident. These tunnels are observed in many of the GPR profiles crossing them and/or corresponding to known tunnel locations at one or more places along their length, based on actual excavation. The dashed lines are possible tunnel locations inferred only from connecting GPR hyperbola locations. Question marks at the end of some dashed lines indicate that a logical connection to the rest of the Canalization System is not apparent. These dashed lines could be connecting hyperbolae corresponding to reflections from subsurface features other than tunnels. The dotted lines are drawn where tunnels could exist, based on connecting tunnel locations that are known from drain holes, excavated tunnels or GPR-inferred tunnels.

While many tunnels are identified in the data of Figure 4.11, it is much more difficult than we anticipated simply connecting the locations of hyperbolae to define the locations of tunnels for several reasons. Several complexities of the data set make it difficult to be sure what was imaged. First, the problem of ground irregularities made it difficult to drag the antenna sled at a constant velocity as required to locate features accurately by interpolation. Consequently, a tunnel crossed on several adjacent profiles does not always line up exactly. For example, the region in the Lower Temenos between Profiles 34 and 16 clearly shows a tunnel nearly perpendicular to the east-west profiles. This tunnel is accessed directly at "a man hole" about 2 m south of Profile 16 and also at the intersection point of this and an east-west tunnel about 7 m south of Profile 34. Although the tunnel may not run in a precisely straight line between these two points, the radar images show that the tunnel does span this entire distance. Note that on three of the east-west profiles just north of the trench where Profile 34 was taken, the identified hyperbolae plot is as much as 1.5 m west of the plotted and probable tunnel location. We attribute this to erratic velocity of the sled. In the field, we could mark the location of the sled when hyperbolae for the tunnel appeared on the system's visual display screen, and they always aligned above the plotted tunnel location. Between Profiles 34 and 16 several hyperbolae plot east of the tunnel location by up to 3 m. These are part of a reconnaissance study made using approximately located profiles, prior to establishing the one-meter grid-spacing profiles with the EDM. Hyperbola misplacement on surveyed locations in the orthogonal grid are smaller.

The second complexity encountered is the lack of clear reflection where tunnels are known to exist, examples being the two profiles that run parallel to Profile 16 approximately 3 m to the north. We speculate that the tunnel has collapsed or filled with soil. Thus some tunnel locations are not seen in the GPR.

The third difficulty is in hyperbola reflections that do not correspond to tunnels. Other subsurface features, perhaps walls and large blocks, are difficult or impossible to discriminate from tunnels.

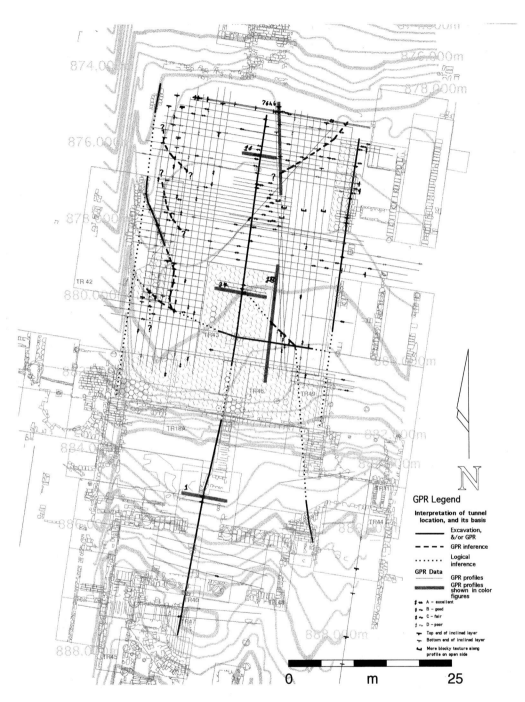

*Figure 4.11. Map showing GPR data and interpretation superimposed upon architectural features and topographic contours (surveying by Loa P. Traxler and Paul C. Zimmerman). The straight gray lines represent GPR profiles. Profiles in the orthogonal grid on the Lower Temenos have been precisely located by survey. The locations of some other profiles have also been determined by survey, but for others the location is only approximate. The five wider gray lines represent the correspondingly numbered profiles in Color Plate 9. Double-headed arrows with varying degrees of darkness, as shown in the legend, indicate four qualities of hyperbola reflections. Symbols indicating differences in general subsurface radar characteristics as well as symbols indicating inclined layers are also plotted (see text for more detail). Tunnels of the Canalization System are indicated in dark lines, solid, dashed or dotted depending upon our confidence in the feature and the method in which we inferred their locations. Those wishing further use of this GPR map and user-navigation may find a full-color digital copy on the CD-ROM archive.*

Because of these problems, determining features to connect and features to ignore is quite arbitrary without additional data from actual excavation. Consequently, our interpretation on Figure 4.11 should be accepted with caution. Careful study of the hyperbola locations, if one can imagine our interpretation lines being removed, will demonstrate the difficulty of a unique interpretation.

Exposure of the Canalization System in the western portion of the Lower Temenos in 1997 validated some of the intermittent 1995 GPR reflections in that area.

We made several profiles on the Colonnaded Street near the bottom of the Stairs of the Propylaeum, both parallel and perpendicular to the Colonnaded Street. We found no evidence for any tunnels of the Canalization System in this location. A few profiles taken immediately adjacent to the Great Temple to its south, east and west also showed no evidence for tunnels.

## Spatial Variability in GPR Character

An interesting observation is that the reflection character of certain regions below the surface differed from others: in some places subsurface features caused irregular reflections, whereas in others little reflection occurred. Some boundaries separating differing regions appear on Figure 4.11 as heavy bracket symbols described in the legend as a "blocky" boundary. On these GPR profiles, the "texture" of the radar reflections differs on opposite sides of the bracket. More complex, scattered reflections occur on the side of the bracket toward which the barbs point than on the other side. On the eastern half of the Lower Temenos, the location of these brackets suggests an east-west boundary with more complex radar reflections to the north and less structure to the south. This suggests that more than one type of fill has been used to elevate and level the Lower Temenos to the surface where the Hexagonal Pavement lies. Our investigation of such textural differences is incomplete.

## Inclined Planar Features

Some of the most interesting and unexpected features seen in the GPR data are inclined planes, the most dramatic example of which is indicated in Profile 76hb, Plate 9 by the arrows on the left and bottom. The reflecting layer extends from 1.2 m below the surface at its north end to 4.9 m below the surface at its south end, over a horizontal distance of 6.5 m and with an incline of 30°. This feature also appears on the parallel profile immediately to the west, but it does not appear on the north-south profiles nearby. However, less well-defined, inclined features do occur on north-south profiles of the grid near the northwest corner of the grid and on one north-south grid profile about 7 m to the east of Profile 76hb.

Inclined features seen on profiles are indicated on the map by a pair of dip-and-strike symbols as used by geologists to indicate sloping layers. The symbol is shaped like a T with a long top bar and a short stem. The stem points in the downward direction of the inclined layer. The pairs of symbols are arranged such that the heavy one corresponds to the location of the shallowest identified end and the light symbol to the location of the deepest identified end of the inclined layer. Compare these inclined features, as represented on the map 76hb (Figure 4.11) with the cross-section view of Profile 76hb. The southernmost dip-and-strike symbol, about 60% of the way from the north end of the map's highlighted profile, indicates the bottom end of the inclined layer seen in the 100 ns-deep cross-section view in Plate 9. In the map view, two light, dip-and-strike symbols appear along this profile. The more northerly one comes from another profile along the same line that sampled only to 50 ns depth, so the inclined layer cannot be seen to extend as far south as on the 100 ns profile.

What is the inclined surface? It could be some artifact of the GPR method and not represent a true architectural feature, but we believe it is real and deserves future excavation.

The inclined features to a depth of nearly 5 m and the different subsurface character in portions of the Lower Temenos suggest that the entire area of the Lower Temenos consists of artificial fill. The inclined reflecting feature could be a stone embankment to hold fill material and bring the level of the Lower Temenos up to the level of the top stair of the Propylaeum. The inclined feature might also be a set of stairs that exists only in the center of the Lower Temenos, in line with the Stairs of the Propylaeum, and it was therefore not seen in profiles to the east. These southward-inclined stairs would be steeper than the northward-inclined Stairs of the Propylaeum, which have a slope of 20°.

## Conclusions

This initial ground-penetrating radar study of the Great Temple in Petra confirms the existence and location of several unexcavated tunnels of the Canalization System. Although it seems logical that the Canalization System would be used both to remove surface rainfall runoff from the site and to collect the water for future use, no cistern can be identified from this GPR study. The GPR also identifies regions with different subsurface character within the Lower Temenos. An inclined surface is found about 1 m below the ground just south of the top of the Stairs of the Propylaeum leading up from the Colonnaded Street. The feature inclines downward to the south at an angle of about 30° to a depth of nearly 5 m. Possible interpretations of the inclined surface include a set of stairs in line with the Stairs of the Propylaeum or a stone embankment to support a thick layer of fill used to bring the ground level up to the Hexagonal Pavement.

Although interpretation of GPR data will always be somewhat speculative, we suggest two improvements in field equipment for future studies. First is the use of a measuring wheel to index distances along the profiles frequently to allow more accurate location of features. Second, the serious ringing that occurred after 50 ns, preventing imaging deeper than 3 m, could be eliminated by an optical fiber connection between the sending and receiving antennae rather than the coaxial cable available to us.

## Acknowledgement

We thank Martha S. Joukowsky for introducing us to field archaeology and the Nabataeans for inviting us to join the excavation team and conduct this survey at Petra. Martha Joukowsky's infectious enthusiasm and talent as a Field General are an inspiration to everyone connected with the project. We also wish to thank Loa P. Traxler for her surveying, professionalism and valuable cooperation in the field and Paul C. Zimmerman for his frequent and patient long-distance help in using MiniCAD. Geophysical Survey Systems, Inc. (GSSI) generously loaned us software for processing the GPR data. We also acknowledge with great affection the hospitality of our Bedouin hosts and the friendship, camaraderie and team spirit of all those who participated in the 1995 summer season. Finally, we lovingly thank the venerable traveler/field archaeologist Chet Worthington for his sense of humor, his love of adventure and for making our trip possible.

# Bibliography

Davis, J.L. and A.P. Annan.

    1989    "Ground-Penetrating Radar for High-Resolution Mapping of Soil and Rock Stratigraphy," *Geophysical Prospecting* 37:531-551.

Fisher, E., et al.

    1992    "Examples of Reverse-Time Migration of Single-Channel, Ground-Penetrating Radar Profiles," *Geophysics* 57:577-586.

Imai, T., T. Sakayama and T. Kanemori.

    1987    "Use of Ground-Probing Radar and Resistivity Surveys for Archaeological Investigations," *Geophysics* 52:137-150.

Vaughan, C.J.

    1986    "Ground-Penetrating Radar Surveys Used in Archaeological Investigations," *Geophysics* 51:595-604.

To our good friend Dr. Martha Joukowsky with my warm wishes
Hussein P. 13.4. 1998

**Plate 1.** *His Majesty King Hussein of the Hashemite Kingdom of Jordan.*

**Plate 2.** *Aerial of Petra surround.* *Photograph by Jane Taylor.*

**Plate 3.** *Jabal Harun.* *Photograph by Artemis A. W. Joukowsky.*

**Plate 4.** *Al-Khazna.* *Photograph by Artemis A.W. Joukowsky.*

**Plate 5.** *Ad-Dayr.* *Photograph by Artemis A.W. Joukowsky.*

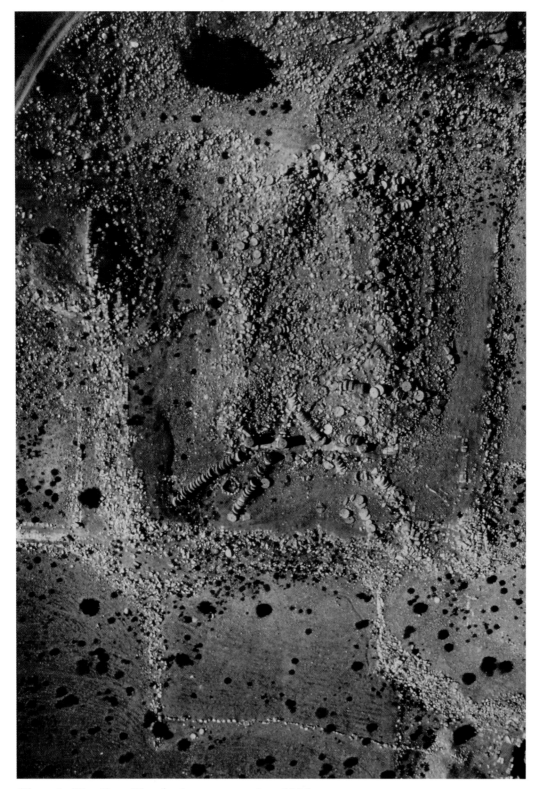

***Plate 6.*** *The Great Temple site pre-excavation, 1993.* Photograph by J. Wilson Myers and Eleanor E. Myers.

**Plate 7.** *The Great Temple site post-excavation, 1997.* Photograph by John Forasté.

**Plate 8.** *The Canalization System exposed, Temple Forecourt, looking north, 1995.*
Photograph by David L. Brill.

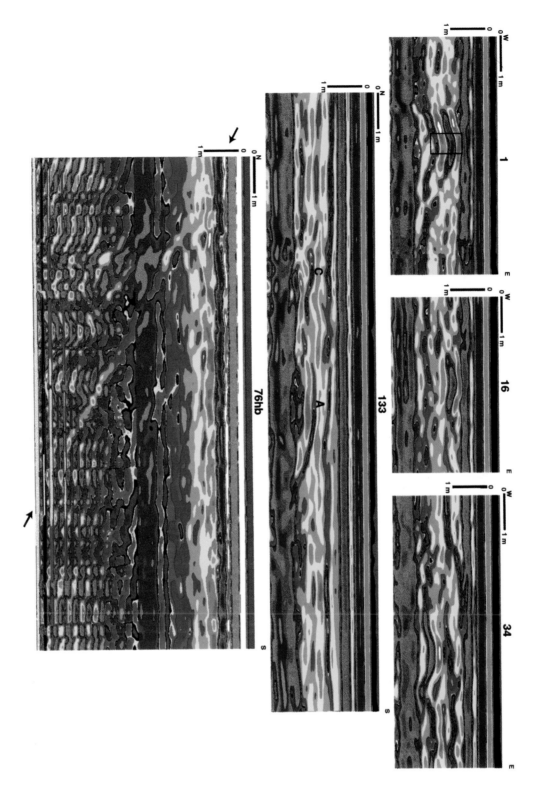

**Plate 9.** *Ground-Penetrating Radar profiles created by Terry E. Tullis.*

**Plate 10.** *The 'Cistern' arch system.* Photograph by John Forasté.

**Plate 11.** *Dakhillallah Qublan.*
Photograph by John Forasté.

**Plate 12.** *Paul C. Zimmerman surveying.*
Photograph by David L. Brill.

**Plates 13, 14 and 15.** *Anastylosis (reconstruction) of the Inter-columnar Wall of the West Corridor, 1997-1998.*

***Plate 16.*** *Drum Removal from the Temple Porch, 1993.* Photograph by Artemis A.W. Joukowsky.

***Plate 17.*** *Painted plaster wall fragment, 'Cistern,' 1997.* Photograph by John Forasté.

**Plates 18, 19 and 20.** *Architectural fragments, details.* Photographs by Artemis A. W. Joukowsky.

**Plate 21.** *Heart-shaped Suleiman Column undergoing restoration.*

**Plate 23.** *Architectural fragments awaiting storage.*

**Plate 22.** *Base detail of the engaged Paul Column, West Corridor.*

**Plate 24.** *94-S-8 and 94-S-3. Mask of a woman, West Walkway, 1994.*
*Photograph by Artemis A. W. Joukowsky.*

**Plate 25** *97-P-9, partial Nabataean plate.* *Photograph by Artemis A. W. Joukowsky.*

26

27

28

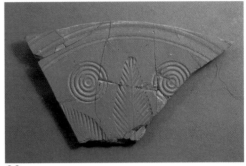

29

32

30          31

**Plate 26.** *97-M-1, bronze chain.*
**Plate 27.** *96-M-16, bronze buckle.*
**Plate 28.** *97-S-36, plaster decoration.*
**Plate 29.** *97-P-8, terra sigillata, fragment.*
**Plate 30.** *94-C-3, Nabataean coin.*
**Plate 31.** *97-C-25, Roman coin.*
**Plate 32.** *97-P-14, Nabataean bottle.*

*All photographs by Artemis A.W. Joukowsky,*
*except Plate 31 by Paul C. Zimmerman.*

*Plates 33a and 33b.* *97-M-3, bronze finial before cleaning.* *Photographs by Artemis A. W. Joukowsky.*

*Plates 34a and 34b.* *97-M-3, bronze finial after cleaning.* *Photographs by Paul C. Zimmerman.*

**Plate 35.** *Elephant-headed capital fragment.* Photograph by David L. Brill.

**Plate 36.** *The Great Temple at the close of the 1997 season, looking west.*

**Plate 37.** *The Great Temple in the snow, 1997, looking west.*

# CHAPTER FIVE

# ARCHITECTURAL SCULPTURE AND RECONSTRUCTION

## THE LOWER TEMENOS
Joseph J. Basile

## THE UPPER TEMENOS AND THE GREAT TEMPLE
Erika L. Schluntz

## THE ARCHITECTURAL SCULPTURE OF THE GREAT TEMPLE
Erika L. Schluntz

*Figure 5.1. Site aerial looking south, showing excavation of Lower Temenos, 1997.*

# THE LOWER TEMENOS

## Joseph J. Basile

The Great Temple at Petra, Jordan (also known as the Southern Temple, the Corinthian Temple, the Podium Temple or the Peripteral Temple), has been excavated by a team from Brown University, under the auspices of the Jordanian Department of Antiquities, since 1993. The Temple dominates the central part of the Petra Valley, south of the Colonnaded Street and the Wadi Musa, east of the Baths complex and the temenos of the Qasr al–Bint, west of the so-called 'Lower Market' and north of the rise of the Zib Fir'awn. It was immediately clear to the excavators, and indeed to earlier explorers,

that the Great Temple and the platform on which it stands are only part of an even larger complex, a complex which includes a lower courtyard, a flight of monumental steps articulating with the famed Colonnaded Street and other ancillary structures like rows of columns and apsidal exedrae. The Stairs of the Propylaeum and the courtyard identified as the Lower Temenos by the excavators (Figure 5.2) are discussed below, in an attempt to arrive at an understanding and interpretation of these important structures.

***Figure 5.2. Plan of the Lower Temenos, 1997.***

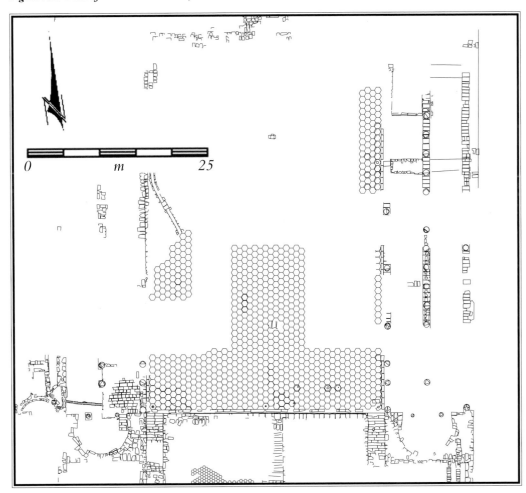

***Figure 5.3. View of the Stairs of the Propylaeum, looking south from the Colonnaded Street.***

## The Stairs of the Propylaeum

The point of entry to the Great Temple Complex is the Stairs of the Propylaeum, which rise just east of the famed Temenos Gate from the level of the Colonnaded Street to the Lower Temenos area of the Temple (Figure 5.3). These steps have always been visible to travelers and archaeologists and were associated with the unexplored Great Temple as early as Bachmann (Bachmann, et al. 41-45), but their exact relationship to the Temple Complex, the Colonnaded Street and its south boundary wall (the retaining wall of the lower Great Temple area and the three 'Market' complexes), and the Temenos Gate was not well understood.

## Description

The Stairs of the Propylaeum were examined by Brown University excavators as early as 1993; it wasn't until the subsequent year, however, that large-scale surveying, documentation and consolidation took place (Joukowsky 1995:133-142). Soon it was established that the steps were directly aligned with the Great Temple but did not meet the Colonnaded Street at a right angle (Joukowsky 1995:133-

142). Indeed, the two-step curb of the street, which is constructed of sandstone ashlar blocks, some 0.4 m wide, clearly overlies the stone pavement of the street. This curb is aligned properly with a landing of well-cut, limestone ashlars each 0.3 m wide, set perpendicular to the curb and creating a platform some 0.8 m across. The landing articulates with the first riser of the Stairs of the Propylaeum (Joukowsky 1994:309). The blocks of the platform, however, *do not* meet the first step riser at a right angle but rather at an awkward angle that is not aligned with the street. In addition, they are not level: the platform of limestone ashlars slopes downward from east to west some 0.15 m. This evidence, as well as an examination of the position and relationships of curb, landing and riser stones during consolidation of the steps in 1993 and 1994 (Figure 5.4), suggests that the Stairs of the Propylaeum were in fact constructed *prior* to the Colonnaded Street and that the sidewalk and curbing of the street were designed to tie into the already-existing steps (Joukowsky 1994:309). Peter J. Parr has already suggested that the extant Colonnaded Street was built over the foundations of a Nabataean predecessor sometime between 9 BCE and 76 CE; this may represent a later Nabataean or

Roman redesign of the street, perhaps to widen it to accommodate an increase in traffic in the central Petra area (Joukowsky 1994:309; Parr 1960:124-135, 1970:348-381).[1] This increased traffic may be, at least in part, a result of the building and subsequent use of the Great Temple.

The steps are built of sandstone, and the full flight would have been approximately 12.8 m long. The best-preserved treads are in the lower nine or 10 courses, which are 7.4 m across. The upper steps are narrower, extending between poorly preserved retaining walls spaced 5.05 m apart. It is estimated that there would have been approximately 38 steps in all, rising from the platform of the limestone landing to the Lower Temenos some 5.8 m above (Joukowsky 1994:309). Like most of the staircases at the Great Temple Complex, the steps here are each about 0.15 m high and 0.35 m deep. The overall effect must have been impressive. Additionally, the height of the south retaining wall of the Colonnaded Street and the Lower Temenos behind it would have served to block the Great Temple from view at street level. The only way to see the imposing edifice, then, would be to ascend the steps to the courtyard above.

Until recently, not much exploration has been done in the areas adjacent to the steps. However, a small excavation by the Brown University team in 1997 just west of the staircase — about 5.6 m south of the point where it narrows to form the upper treads — revealed some interesting structures that may form part of the monumental Propylaeum complex posited by earlier scholars. Specifically, two large piers (or small stylobate platforms) were discovered, measuring 1.90 m east-west and 1.20 m north-south. A wall of coarser stone some 0.65 m long connects the two piers, creating a kind of niche on the south face of the structure. A wall also extends north from the westernmost of the piers, and several column drums were found in the vicinity. More work needs to be done in this area, however, if we are to get a more accurate and complete picture of the Propylaeum complex.

Another puzzle of the Stairs of the Propylaeum regards their relationship to the retaining wall of the Colonnaded Street and the complex of rooms and colonnades included in the famous reconstruction of the Great Temple area, based on Bachmann (Browning 1973:140-141).

*Figure 5.4. Partial consolidation of the Stairs of the Propylaeum.*

First, the east-west retaining wall of the street seemed to cut *across* the steps just above the well-preserved group of nine or 10 risers at the bottom of the steps and below the point where the staircase narrowed. Additionally, some of the ashlars here were dressed less expertly than those of the steps, and some appeared to be reused blocks (Joukowsky 1994:311). Thus, this part of the retaining wall must have been *later* than the steps and represented a period when the steps, and perhaps the whole Temple Complex, went out of use. West of the steps, however, the retaining wall, which was built of well-dressed and fitted blocks (and formed the east wall of the well-known Baths complex),[2] seems to have been cut through and was evidently partially dismantled when the stairway was constructed, making this section of the retaining wall *earlier* than the Stairs of the Propylaeum (Joukowsky 1994:311). The phasing of these structures remains to be clarified.

Also, an altar may have marked the middle of the stairs: fine-grained ash was discovered by the platform at the middle of the Stairs of the Propylaeum. This was originally interpreted as evidence suggesting the existence of such an installation (Joukowsky 1994:311).[3] There have been no further discoveries, however, in this area to support such a hypothesis.

## Interpretation

As we have seen, interpreting the Stairs of the Propylaeum involves defining the relationship of the steps to the architectural elements that they bring together: the Colonnaded Street, the retaining wall of the Lower Temenos, the Baths complex and the Hexagonal Pavement of the Lower Temenos (discussed in more depth below). Excavation has shown that the Colonnaded Street, the Hexagonal Pavement and the western part of the retaining wall (shared with the Baths) seem to have been remodeled to accommodate the Stairs of the Propylaeum, while the Hexagonal Pavement seems to overlap the top of the steps, and a later rebuilding phase of the retaining wall cuts across the middle of the steps, nine or 10 treads up from the limestone landing, rendering the steps useless after that point. To summarize, it would appear that the Stairs of the Propylaeum

were originally built, or rebuilt, earlier than the Colonnaded Street but later than the western part of the retaining wall, the Baths and the Great Temple itself. However, much about this part of the Colonnaded Street and how it appeared in antiquity is poorly understood, and more exploration in this area is necessary.

## The Lower Temenos

The Lower Temenos is the monumental "courtyard" of the Great Temple, measuring 55 m$^2$ and stretching between the Colonnaded Street to the north and the platform of the Temple to the south (Joukowsky in press:10). Reached from the level of the street by the grand flight of the Stairs of the Propylaeum, the Lower Temenos creates a dynamic space where visitors could observe the bustle of the central valley and the great monuments to the north, such as the Temple of the Winged Lions, or gaze upon the massive Great Temple itself (as it was obscured from street level). The complexity of the architecture here suggests that this area was more than just a transitional space between the Upper Temenos of the Temple proper and the busy urban setting of the Colonnaded Street. Rather, it was a multifunctional space with both roofed and open-air elements. It certainly fulfilled an important role in the "life" of the Temple compound.

The Lower Temenos is divided and described by its various architectural features: flanking rows of colonnades that run the whole length of the courtyard on the east and west sides, paired exedrae (one at the south end of each colonnade), a monumental central staircase leading to the Upper Temenos (eventually abandoned), later lateral staircases flanking the exedrae, the massive sandstone retaining wall supporting the Temple Forecourt and the vast and impressive expanse of hexagonal pavers used to embellish the broad Lower Temenos courtyard. Indeed, the Lower Temenos shows the same architectural genius, the same concern for combining modified classical designs and traditional and native design elements that characterizes so many of the great monuments at Petra.

*Figure 5.5. Collapse of the Hexagonal Pavement into the central Subterranean Canalization System.*

## Description

It is easiest to describe the Lower Temenos as we have above — in terms of the architectural elements of which it is comprised. The first feature of the courtyard that one encounters after ascending the Stairs of the Propylaeum is the expansive pavement made of hexagon-shaped flagstones of white limestone, which must have stretched over 50 m, from the northern edge of the Lower Temenos to the southern retaining wall of the Temple platform and approximately 30 m east-west between the two colonnades. Each paving stone measures approximately 0.95 m across, from point to opposite point (0.82 m from flat side to flat side) and is about 0.11 m thick. A number of features make the pavement distinctive, the most important of which is the elaborate drainage system discovered underneath. In the south central area of the courtyard, a large and well-built drainage channel was unearthed when a number of the hexagonal pavers were removed (they had collapsed into the system) (Figure 5.5). In the corners of the pavement, and at the edges equidistant from each of the

*Figure 5.6. Bronze drain cover, southwest corner of the Hexagonal Pavement.*

*Figure 5.7. Drain, east edge of the Hexagonal Pavement.*

corners, the hexagonal stones were cut to receive a total of ten bronze drain fittings. Hexagonal bronze plates, measuring some 0.36 m from point to point, and drain openings led to a bronze cylinder 0.17 m in diameter — all except the example on the southwest are missing, but here the fitting is almost perfectly preserved (Figures 5.6 and 5.7).[4] Large portions of the pavement remain unexcavated. The courtyard is, nevertheless, still an impressive sight today and must have been quite remarkable in antiquity.

Equally impressive would have been the long colonnades on the east and west sides, providing a monumental boundary for the Lower Temenos. These rows of columns created "...ordered private retreats — enclosed spaces for rest and introspection..." and bordered the courtyard with a "...rhythm of light and shadow" (Joukowsky in press:10). Currently, excavation of the East Colonnade suggests that each row of columns stretched the whole length of the Lower Temenos, although on the west only the southern and central parts have been excavated. Each colonnade consisted of rows of sandstone columns standing on substantially built stylobates of squared limestone or white sandstone blocks, measuring 0.52-x-0.96 m, alternating with square limestone slabs, measuring 0.96 m². Between the colonnades were walkways some 4.4 m wide; these are not well-preserved, however, and are missing their foundation blocks, flags and flooring stones (Joukowsky 1997:9). The columns themselves are made up of drums measuring approximately 0.85 m in diameter with varying thicknesses — drums 0.40, 0.60 and 0.80 m thick have been recovered. Each column was spaced some 2.5 m apart, with 16 or 18 or perhaps as many as 21 columns in each row (Joukowsky 1997:9).[5] No bases have been found.

Evidence from the southwest corner of the West Colonnade suggests that each column was plastered in typical Nabataean fashion, with alternating "reverse" (convex) flutes bordered by flattened ridges or arrises. The plaster was white in antiquity; a few fragments of red plaster have been found. A curb of red and yellow stones, 0.37 m wide and extending north-south for the whole length of the Lower Temenos courtyard, marked the articulation point of each colonnade with the Hexagonal Pavement, and archaeological evidence (i.e., the presence of clay tiles) suggests that each colonnade was roofed. The east and west terrace walls that form the limits of the temenos — assuming these existed — are difficult to discern and need to be explored further.

*Figures 5.8 and 5.9. Sondages, East Colonnade, Trenches 17 and 14.*

*Figure 5.10. West Exedra platform, looking west.*

The shoring up of the eastern stylobates with chinking stones and other materials, as well as the remains of roughly built support walls erected between some of the columns in the southern part of the East Colonnade (Figures 5.8 and 5.9), points to a repair and reuse of this area at a later date, perhaps subsequent to one of Late Antique Petra's infamous earthquakes. In the southern portion of the West Colonnade, there is also substantial evidence of reuse: a platform some 5 m wide was constructed here by stringing walls of reused sandstone blocks and column drums between the remains of the last three columns of the inner and central colonnade (Figures 5.10 and 5.11). The rough square formed by these retaining walls was filled with debris and covered by limestone slabs, thus forming the platform. A well-built limestone staircase with six treads leads south and down into the West Exedra (see below). The function of these structures, assumed to be late Roman or Byzantine, remains unknown.

Exploration of the colonnades in the 1994 and 1995 seasons pointed to a double row of columns on each side, and these were duly noted on the site plans of those years. However, exploration of the eastern edge of the East Colonnade in 1996 uncovered yet another stylobate, identical to the other two in dimension and construction, preserved to a length of 42 m with a single *in situ* column drum (Joukowsky 1997:9).[6] This discovery demonstrated that, in fact, the East Colonnade had a *triple* row of columns, creating a broad arcade about 12.5 m wide[7] and prompted a re-examination of the western edge of the West Colonnade. Assuming that the plan of the Lower Temenos was symmetrical, there should have been a third colonnade there as well. What was discovered, however, was the eastern wall of a room or complex of rooms with recognizably late Roman or Byzantine elements but perhaps founded on structures predating these late periods. The size and shape of the rooms (including curved walls and apsidal rooms, drainage elements and hypocaust tiles) and the presence of tremendous deposits of ash have prompted the excavators to tentatively identify the complex as a bath. The aforementioned eastern wall may in fact be the stylobate of the third (outer) column row of the West Colonnade, but any earlier features were obscured by the late remodeling. Could the West Colonnade have had only two rows of columns or perhaps a western boundary wall instead of a row of columns? More exploration in this area will be required before this problem can be put to rest.

*Figure 5.11. West Exedra, detail of west platform face.*

It had been assumed all along that the Lower Temenos was built upon a leveled or terraced hillside lying under the rise of the Upper Temenos. In 1995, however, it was discovered that at least part of the East Colonnade was not built on a natural rise at all but on a complex and extensive artificial terrace,

*Figure 5.12. Subterranean Canalization System, west Lower Temenos, looking south.*

supported by massively built walls, mortared and plastered and extending north-south below the stylobates (Joukowsky 1997:9-10). Much more fragmentary remains of a similar complex were discovered in the area of the West Colonnade in 1997. Arches seem to have tied the walls together: arch springers, extending east-west between the walls and forming a north-south arcade, were discovered protruding from the upper courses of the support walls on the eastern arcade roughly 0.94 m below the level of the stylobates. These arches were approximately 0.56 m in width and must have spanned some 4.3 m (Joukowsky 1997:10). What appeared to be the lowest courses of the walls (signaled by a beaten earth floor and rough-cut string and foundation courses) were not recovered in the eastern sector until 1996, some 6 m below the Stylobate (and just 1.77 m above the Colonnaded Street) (Figures 5.8 and 5.9), at an elevation of 873.22 m (Joukowsky 1997:10). The level of this beaten earth floor, along with the evidence of the artificial terrace,[8] may support the idea that at least parts of the Lower Temenos represent a later phase of remodeling and that originally the Great Temple may somehow have been reached from the level of the Colonnaded Street. At some point, however, the arch system of the eastern arcade was remodeled; it was buttressed with huge, 19- or 20-course cross-walls that extended

*Figure 5.13. Detail of elephant-headed capital recovered in the southwest corner of Hexagonal Pavement, 1994.*

east-west and abutted the north-south walls. This would seem to negate the function of the arches and eliminate the arcade extending between the original north-south walls. Indeed, the whole complex was buried in a massive fill deposit at this point, poured into the compartment-like spaces formed by the original north-south walls and the later east-west cross-walls. The fill included deposits of pottery and other artifactual material; it has been tentatively dated, by its latest material, to the middle of the second century CE (Joukowsky 1997:10). Was it after this remodeling, then, that the elements of the East Colonnade that are visible today were constructed? Or did the colonnades stand directly on top of a functioning arched arcade, the whole complex being filled in and shored up after one of Petra's earthquakes?

Another remarkable aspect of the flanking colonnades was their decorative scheme; the

*Figure 5.14. Drawing of elephant-headed capital, 1994, by Karen Jacobson.*

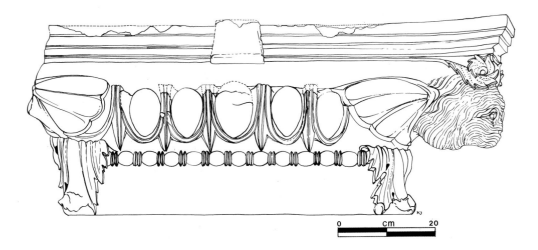

*Figure 5.15. Elephant-head fragment.*

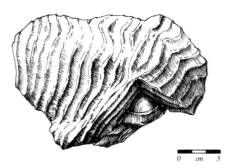

*Figure 5.16. Drawing of elephant-head fragment by Jean Blackburn.*

columns seem to have been decorated with elephant-headed capitals of beautifully carved, white limestone (Figures 5.13 and 5.14). An almost complete example of the capital was discovered resting near the southwest corner of the Hexagonal Pavement, measuring some 1 m across. In addition, 106 fragments of elephant heads, faces and trunks have been recovered to date, almost all from the Lower Temenos area and concentrated around the flanking colonnades (Figures 5.15, 5.16 and 5.17). Such capitals were not unknown prior to the Brown University excavations; three famous examples rest near the Temenos Gate. Fragments, however, have never been discovered in such numbers, and the Temenos Gate examples may really belong to the Great Temple (Browning 1973:141-147, Blagg 1990:131-137). The

elephants decorated the corners of the capital, replacing the volutes; this scheme is very similar to the eponymous capitals of the Temple of the Winged Lions. Exquisitely and naturally carved, their expressive eyes, gaping mouths and wrinkled skin exhibit the skill of the Nabataean carver. The twin dome of the head suggests that the Lower Temenos elephants may be of the Indian variety (*Elephas maximus*) — the preferred military elephant of the Hellenistic and Roman Near East. Though the ears are somewhat large and fanlike, they do not have the folded dorsal edge of the African elephant (*Loxodonta africana*) (Joukowsky 1997:11, Blagg 1990:133). Egg and dart, and bead and reel moldings decorate the capital as well; the whole is a superb example of Nabataean art. Taken together, the rows of tapering, plastered columns, capped with finely carved elephant-headed capitals must have produced a stunning effect as it greeted the visitor to the Lower Temenos.

Each colonnade terminates in a semicircular exedra, borrowed almost wholesale from the Hellenistic-Roman architectural vernacular. The West Exedra is better-preserved and more fully explored than the East (Figures 5.18 and 5.19), but both are fine examples of the skill exhibited by Nabataean builders when adopting classical forms. Almost fully excavated, the West Exedra is about 6 m high; the East Exedra has been excavated to a depth of 4 m (Joukowsky in press:10). Each exedra complex is about 10 m wide and 6 m deep; the apsidal interior space of the exedra is just slightly greater than a semicircle in plan, so it measures 7.5 m wide across the center but only 6.8 m wide at the mouth. Separating each exedra from the colonnade to the north is a pair of sandstone columns made up of segmented drums between 0.30-0.60 m thick and 0.60 m in diameter, standing at the mouth of the apse.

*Figure 5.17. Elephant-trunk fragment recovered in 1995. Photograph by David L. Brill.*

*Figure 5.18. East Exedra during excavation, looking south, 1996.*

They are 4.7 m apart, each 1.2 m from the front corners of the exedrae, and rest on finely carved bases of the Attic type, measuring 0.80 m in diameter. Engaged columns flank the mouth of the East Exedra and are aligned with the outside rows of the colonnade; the center row bisects the pair of exedra columns. On the West Exedra, the easternmost engaged column is extant; this is where the elephant-headed capital was discovered. Where the

*Figure 5.19. Aerial photograph of the West Exedra, looking southwest, 1995.*

western engaged column should be, however, we find instead the enigmatic wall, discussed above in relation to the posited third (outer) row of columns of the West Colonnade. The southernmost part of this wall is as early as the exedra and, in fact, bonds with it, although there are later phases of this wall that include roughly cut and reused blocks. Another interesting feature of the exedrae is a row of seven north-south arches that have been discovered behind the East Exedra. No such arrangement has yet been found behind the West Exedra. These arches bond fully with the south wall of the exedra and seem to have formed an arched arcade over a chamber or passageway 3.5 m wide-x-9.5 m long. The passage was blocked on its east side at some point and plastered, perhaps to be used as a cistern (a clay pipe was discovered leading away from the Temple platform to this passage). Slabs of marble were also discovered here; when the postulated cistern went out of use, the structure may have functioned as a storage room for stone being stripped from the Temple or other nearby buildings. Interestingly, these arches are constructed in the same way as the arches of the colonnade substructures — the blocks are even of the same width. Does this suggest that the arches behind the East Exedra and the arches of the East Colonnade substructure are of the same date?

Both exedrae are finely constructed from well-cut sandstone ashlars, diagonally dressed in typical Nabataean fashion. These blocks — the largest of them measuring 1.5 m in length — are curved where they form the interior of the apse; otherwise, they are square-cut. The interior surfaces of the exedrae are decorated with niches, five in each (1.15 m wide and 0.55 m deep), creating a dynamic, relief-like surface; the niches may have been filled with statuary, although no evidence relating to their decoration or function has been found. Plaster, preserved on some walls but mostly recovered in small fragments in excavation, shows that the interiors of the exedrae were decorated with painted surfaces in dark reds, blue-greens, yellows, blacks and rust-oranges. (The passage behind the East Exedra preserves similarly painted plaster, along with the coarser plaster of the postulated cistern.) Also recovered from the West Exedra were architectural elements in sandstone, limestone and plaster, a corner of a beautifully carved Corinthian capital, which must have capped one of the

paired columns at the mouth of the structure, and many examples of cut and polished slabs of marble, porphyry and other colored stones — at some point the floor of the exedrae may have been decorated with attractive *opus sectile* patterns. Under the floor of the West Exedra a narrow ceramic drain pipe, of typical Nabataean cylindrical type, was discovered extending southeast-northwest for approximately 5 m and leading ultimately to the well preserved, bronze drain cover set in the very southwestern corner of the Hexagonal Pavement (see above). A few blocks with complex, curving faces have been excavated from the West Exedra, and roof tiles were found in both exedrae. It is, therefore, postulated that the exedrae were partially covered with semi-domes and roofed with clay tiles where they met the colonnades.

While there is no direct archaeological evidence regarding the function of the exedrae, it can be assumed from their form and location that they were used in the same way as Roman exedrae: as "additional" and multifunctional space where merchants could set up shop, government officials might have temporary offices or travelers and tourists might rest away from the sun — and the hustle and bustle — of the main courtyard. They could also have been subsidiary shrines or, if provided with fountains or basins, nymphaea where pilgrims could drink or wash before proceeding to the Temple. Indeed, the whole arrangement of the courtyard, with colonnades on both sides that terminate in exedrae, reminds one of a Roman forum. The Lower Temenos probably served as more than just an intermediate point between the Colonnaded Street and Upper Temenos; it may have functioned like a market or civic center, spread out before the magnificent form of the Great Temple.

The southern boundary of the Lower Temenos terminates in a dramatic and fairly regular slope that extends between the two exedrae for some 38 m and rises about 6 m to meet the northern margin of the Upper Temenos and the Temple Forecourt (Joukowsky 1994:312, 1997:11). It has usually been assumed that this slope represents the transition point and staircase by which the Upper Temenos was accessed; the famous reconstruction based on Bachmann, for instance, shows a broad and continuous flight of steps extending all the way across, from one exedra to the

*Figure 5.20. View of the Central Stairs with East-West Retaining Wall, looking south, 1995.*

other (Browning 1973:137, 140-142). Beginning in 1995, the Brown University team began looking for this postulated 'Grand Staircase,' with some interesting results.

Excavation in the very center of the slope did indeed produce immediate and important evidence; the remains of a staircase were uncovered. It was poorly preserved except for the plaster bedding layer that would have been under the treads (now removed) but a staircase nonetheless. The steps clearly did not extend all the way across the slope, however, as posited in the reconstruction based on Bachmann but were bounded on the east by a well-built wall of close-fitting, sandstone ashlars, dressed in Nabataean fashion (Figure 5.20). It is assumed that a similar retaining wall will be found on the west.[9] Thus, the stairs were only some 4.7 m wide and were centrally aligned with the Stairs of the Propylaeum and the staircase of the Temple itself, which ran between the two massive central columns of the façade. Located underneath the stairs was a well-built canalization tunnel, showing evidence of several phases of construction and remodeling. The treads of the Central Stairs functioned as the capstones of the tunnel as it extended down the slope from the Temple platform to the Lower Temenos and underneath the Hexagonal Pavement to the wadi below.[10] Even more puzzling was the massive sandstone wall constructed across the lower courses of these Central Stairs. Its discovery suggests that at some point in the history of the Temple a Retaining Wall extending east-west along the bottom of the slope was created, cutting off the Central Stairs, which were then filled in with a homogenous rubble layer. Above this was constructed the Forecourt of the Great Temple, with its small hexagonal flagstones. Indeed, the whole northern part of the Upper Temenos seems to be supported by this fill layer and its sandstone retaining wall.[11] Thus,

*Figure 5.21. West Stairway (Laurel Stairway) after reconstruction, looking south, 1997.*

*Figure 5.22. East Stairway (Elizabeth Stairway) during excavation, looking south, 1997.*

the question arises: to where did Temple access shift after this event closed off the Central Stairs?

Surveys at the end of the 1995 season suggested an answer: there was a lateral staircase built up against the east side of the West Exedra complex.[12] Excavation in 1996 proved this to be the case. A well-constructed staircase of limestone treads between sandstone retaining walls was revealed, which we called the West, or Laurel, Stairway (Figure 5.21). The complex is fairly well-preserved. The treads in the best condition are the lowest 12, made up of limestone slabs some 0.15 m thick and 0.35 m deep and extending 2.60 m east-west between the north-south, sandstone retaining walls. Where the stairs meet the Upper Temenos, only the bedding is preserved, but we can estimate that there were perhaps 27 steps in all. They terminate properly in what has been called the Temple Forecourt and are aligned with a broad walkway that winds around the Temple itself. In total, the West Stairway (Laurel Stairway) was about 9 m long and rose 6 m from the Hexag-onal Pavement of the Lower Temenos to the Temple Forecourt.

In addition, branching canalization walls were revealed under a layer of fill that was homo-genous with the rubble layer excavated from the Central Stairs in 1995.[13] Pottery deposited against these canals has been tentatively dated by Stephan G. Schmid to the last quarter of the first century BCE, suggesting that at least this part of the Upper Temenos platform fill dates to the first phases of Temple construction (see below). Above these canals was laid a bedding of yellow sand and flint and chert pebbles from the Wadi Musa; the floor of small Hexagonal Pavement in the Temple Forecourt was set over this, completing the upper plaza. Also, a continuation of the East-West Retaining Wall was discovered, constructed of beautifully cut sandstone blocks. The wall is currently preserved to four courses at a height of approximately 1 m; the blocks are mortar-cemented in the three lower courses, which are set on a rough-cut string course (Joukowsky 1997:13). The stones of the wall are set as headers and stretchers; some of the latter are massive and measure over 2 m in length (Joukowsky 1997:13). Above the rows of headers and stretchers is a decorative molding, like a reverse cornice, which was also preserved at the Central Stairs. At the West Stairway, however, the east-west wall turns a

corner to become the eastern retaining wall of the stairway and is, in fact, the same wall. The west retaining wall of this staircase is con-structed separately and may actually be part of the West Exedra complex, since it terminates on the north in the aforementioned engaged column.

Finally, a curb and drain were recovered in front of the East-West Retaining Wall (this was also in evidence at the Central Stairs) (Figure 5.23), which may at one time have carried a narrow lead pipe — a length of such pipe was discovered protruding from the west wall of the staircase just before the engaged column. It would have been set in plaster in the gap between the back of the curbstones and the front of the sandstone wall. The curbstones themselves are finely carved of sandstone and limestone and are similar to the stair treads found throughout the complex in makeup and dimension. Indeed, from the evidence recovered at the foot of the West Stairway, it would seem that the curb also functioned as the bottom stair tread.

After the discovery of the West Stairway in 1996, it was theorized by the excavators that an East Stairway should also exist between the East Exedra and the other corner of the east-west sandstone wall (assuming, of course, that the plan and arrangement of features of the Lower Temenos were symmetrical). Explora-tion in 1997 proved this theory to be true. A stairway was discovered that was an exact counterpart to the West Stairway, except that more treads were discovered *in situ* (Figure 5.22). The top of this staircase could not be fully explored because of the massive fallen drums of the Temple's Porch columns still in place in the Upper Temenos courtyard. It would seem that the East Stairway (Elizabeth Stairway) was buried earlier than the West; the sandstone blocks of the north-south retaining walls are less weathered, and there is evidence of large stones falling into the staircase area. Massive wall blocks were removed during excavation; moreover, many of the stair treads were cracked down the middle and partially caved in, as if struck by heavy objects tumbling down the incline. These cracks exposed another important feature of the East Stairway: a canalization tunnel extending down the slope from the Temple platform to the Lower Temenos underneath the stair treads (which were used as the capstones as in the Central Stairs; see above) and connecting to the small drain at the southeast corner of the Hexagonal

Pavement. This canal then extended north and west, perhaps to the central tunnel that was built under the Central Stairs or to the small drain on the east-center edge of the Hexagonal Pavement. If a similar tunnel existed under the West Stairway, it has yet to be discovered.

Finally, excavation in 1997 provided a clearer picture of the construction techniques and phases of the massive sandstone wall, extending east-west to the lateral staircases and cutting off the Central Stairs. In fact, it was discovered that the wall is not so much a retaining wall as a facing wall. The complex was constructed by putting in place a fairly homogenous layer of rough-cut, square blocks leveled with dirt and chinking stones, which was then faced on the north, east and west with the finely carved sandstone blocks. But based on the irregular arrangement of facing stones across the foot of the Central Stairs — the wall was constructed with a fairly regular header-stretcher pattern elsewhere — it would seem that at least the lower courses of this wall were contemporary with the Central Stairs and "turned the corner" to create East and West Retaining walls, just as in the lateral staircases. Indeed, the corners flanking the Central Stairs appear to be constructed in an manner identical to the corner arrangement discovered in the excava-tion of the East Stairway (the corner at the West Stairway is badly damaged), further suggesting that these structures are contempo-rary. Thus, at least some parts of the facing wall were constructed at the same time as the Central Stairs, namely, the 11.7 m lengths that flank that staircase. The height of the wall during this era is unknown. Later, however, the Central Stairs were replaced by the lateral ones; the facing wall was extended across the bottom of the stairs (connecting the flanking facing walls so that they assumed their full extant length of 28 m) and filled in with debris. The platform was then perhaps extended upward, with layer after layer of roughly squared stones and chinking, faced with well-carved, sandstone slabs that mirrored the style of the previously existing courses. The lateral staircases were then built against the east and west corners of the rising platform. It is possible, in fact, that this redesign resulted in the expansion of the Upper Temenos courtyard, which saw a high platform created and extended to the north, the Central Stairs filled, and the whole area covered with small hexagonal paving stones

that mirrored the larger examples in the Lower Temenos. The phasing certainly suggests it; the layers of rough-cut blocks extend to the level of the Temple Forecourt, almost as far north as the facing wall (it is assumed that parts of the fill here have been eroded), and cross over the Central Stairs in unbroken courses, suggesting a single period of construction after the initial modifications.

Thus, we see that the Lower Temenos was an intricate and complex structure or, more accurately, series of structures, which changed over the "life" of the Great Temple.

## Interpretation

It is clear from the archaeological evidence that interpretation of the Lower Temenos ruins will be a difficult task. The complexity of the remains suggests a number of building phases that may reflect changing attitudes towards the role of the Lower Temenos area and its relationship to the Temple itself. A few things can be said, however, based on the current state of the evidence, especially in regard to relative chronology and the form the Lower Temenos takes in comparison to other examples of monumental courtyards.

As stated above, the relationships of some of the Lower Temenos elements suggest a relative

*Figure 5.23. View of curb, looking west.*

chronology of building phases. It would seem that the Lower Temenos went through a major remodeling at least once in its history. Specifically, the complex substructure of north-south walls and east-west arches discovered under the East Colonnade — which was later shored up with east-west cross-walls and filled in with debris — seems to imply that at least parts of the Lower Temenos that we see today were in fact a later phase of construction. For instance, it is possible that at some point during the history of the Temple at least the eastern part of the Lower Temenos was closer to street level — 871 m as opposed to 878.5 m. In addition, the beaten earth floor that was discovered at an elevation of 873.22 m near the foundation levels of the north-south support walls might suggest that access to the Lower Temenos was originally from just off the Colonnaded Street, perhaps by means of an arched arcade and not by climbing a set of steps (i.e., the Stairs of the Propylaeum) as was necessary later. Then, at some point, a redesign was needed: the arcade was filled in, an artificial terrace was created (which was reached by a monumental staircase) and the whole arrangement was elaborately decorated with rows of columns on the east and west and a plaza of hexagonal, limestone flags between. Alternately, the colonnades may have been built on top of a functioning arcade structure in the same design phase, creating usable space at the level of the Colonnaded Street *and* the graded Lower Temenos. The pavement would have also belonged to this phase, and the cross-walls and fill discovered in the east arcade represent a shoring-up operation — not a complex redesign. The similarity of the arches in the Lower Temenos and behind the West Exedra certainly suggests that they are contemporary, and the location and design of the exedrae complement and refer to the flanking colonnades. Many questions remain unanswered, however, and it is difficult to be sure which model is correct. More excavation is needed before the phasing of the Lower Temenos can be reconstructed definitively.

Additionally, access to the Temple itself changed, from the Central Stairs — aligned as it was with the Stairs of the Propylaeum and the stairs to the Temple — to the lateral East and West Stairways, discovered in 1996 and 1997, respectively. These stairs were part of a remodeling phase that saw the redesign of the massive, sandstone facing wall (to cut off the Central Stairs and create a huge new platform on top of the old one), the filling in of the terrace that stretched in front of the Temple proper and the creation of a courtyard of small Hexagonal Pavement, which could now be constructed in the expanded Temple Forecourt. It is unclear whether this redesign phase is part of the program that sees the Lower Temenos take on its extant form or whether it represents a modification at a different time. The pottery evidence from the Lower Temenos fill has been tentatively dated to the middle of the second century CE, while the fill from behind the sandstone retaining wall and later staircases seems to come from as early as the last quarter of the first century BCE (see above). This could indicate that an early Lower Temenos complex, consisting of the Central Stairs, its early sandstone facing walls and the canals underneath, existed from the end of the first century BCE and that an extensive redesign or repair of the Lower Temenos — as evidenced by the cross-walls and fill of the eastern arcade — took place not earlier than the second century CE. The Stairs of the Propylaeum, the Hexagonal Pavement, the flanking colonnades, the exedrae and the lateral staircases (replacing the Central Stairs, which were walled off) come somewhere in between. It should be stressed, however, that this pottery analysis is preliminary, and more work is needed before an accurate absolute chronology can be constructed for the Great Temple.

As for the relationship of the Lower Temenos with other architectural remains at Petra and the possibility of establishing a chronology based on those relationships, the only part of the Lower Temenos complex that articulates with neighboring monuments and that has also been explored in any detail is the Stairs of the Propylaeum. The phasing of this monument has been discussed above. To summarize, the evidence suggests that the steps predate the current street but postdate the original phases of the Lower Temenos; they would seem to be an integral part of the Lower Temenos redesign and contemporary to this reorganization phase. Indeed, the Nabataean precursor of the Colonnaded Street may have been altered to the form we see today, perhaps to accommodate the increased traffic related to the redesigned Great Temple. If the *terminus post quem* of the street alteration really is between 9 BCE and 76 CE (see above), then the Lower Temenos redesign would predate the end of the first century BCE or the third quarter of the first century CE. This chronology would seem to be supported by the pottery evidence from the fill, which was used to bury the Central Stairs, but not the fill under the East Colonnade. Is it possible that the Lower Temenos redesign was in two stages, or does the evidence suggest a more complex scheme of building?

A comparison between the Lower Temenos and similar monuments may also bear on the chronological questions as well as questions concerning influence and function. The arrangement of the Lower Temenos with apsidal exedrae and a broad pavement is not unique; indeed, there is even another example at Petra. Just to the west of the Great Temple Complex, the Qasr al-Bint is possessed of a broad paved court, more irregular in plan than the symmetrical Lower Temenos of the Great Temple but still with may points of comparison. Perhaps most striking is a preserved exedra, which is at the west edge of the Qasr al-Bint temenos and which flanks the so-called 'altar.' It can be clearly seen on any of the plans based on Bachmann as well as the foundations and few courses of this exedra that are extant today, though they were formerly obscured by one of the tents used to serve beverages and snacks to tourists. These are not the only similarities; excavation in the Upper Temenos of the Great Temple has produced evidence of a ground plan with a divided cella and stairs to a mezzanine level (like the Qasr al-Bint, though with a significant difference in function; see below) and walkways, which wrap around the Great Temple (as at the Qasr al-Bint and the Temple of the Winged Lions). While the temenos of the Qasr al-Bint did not, seemingly, possess a colonnade, the whole arrangement still bears a striking resemblance to the Great Temple Complex, and one should remember that, canonically, the Qasr al-Bint is dated with a *terminus ante quem* of the beginning of the first century CE, roughly contemporary to at least some of the remains at the Great Temple.

The most important similarities, however, occur between the Lower Temenos plan and the plans of contemporary (and preceding) Roman ruins. Temple enclosures throughout the Roman East, for instance, contain broad, square courts, often with colonnades. The sanctuaries of Zeus and of Artemis at Jarash are just two of many examples of this arrangement. Even closer to the arrangement of the Lower Temenos are the plans of fora and temple enclosures from the imperial capital itself, dating from the first century BCE and the first century CE. Although arched arcades and apsidal exedrae appear as early as the famed Republican sanctuaries of Fortuna Primigenia at Palestrina and of Jupiter Anxur at Terracina, better parallels can be found at the great imperial fora of Augustus and Trajan. These well-known complexes possess all of the elements of the Lower Temenos: a symmetrical arrangement based on a square or rectangular plan, flanking colonnades with multiple rows of columns, paired exedrae articulating in some way to the colonnades (in the imperial fora they are aligned with the long sides of the colonnades; at the Great Temple they are at the ends) and a broad paved court between the colonnades. Also, all of these complexes served as the courtyards or "temenoi" for temples — Mars Ultor at the Forum of Augustus and Deified Trajan at the Forum of Trajan. The Roman forum was not just an economic center (i.e., a marketplace) but also a civic and religious center. The Lower Temenos of the Great Temple at Petra seems to have been conceived in the same way.

Indeed, it is quite clear that the whole of the Great Temple Complex is based on a combination of Roman architectural forms (principally from the late Republican and Principate periods) and native Nabataean elements, which results in the expert reconciliation of classical and Near Eastern traditions we see at the site today. It seems likely that the Lower Temenos of the Great Temple formed an important part of the monumental core of the central city; it was a vibrant meeting place for all Petra's citizens.

## Endnotes

1 See Judith S. McKenzie, *The Architecture of Petra,* British Academy Monographs in Archaeology Series, No. 1 (1990:35-6, 131-2).

2 For a complete discussion and bibliography of the Baths, see Judith S. McKenzie (1990:138).

3 Nabataean painted pottery discovered near these ash deposits has been dated to between 20 BCE-50 CE by Stephan G. Schmid.

4 See the discussion by Elizabeth E. Payne in this volume, Chapter 4.

5 The full length of both colonnades is conjectural, as the northern limit of the Lower Temenos has been subject to weathering and collapse, plunging 7.5 m to the Colonnaded Street below. Thus, the whole north margin of the Temenos has been damaged.

6 If there were 21 columns in each colonnade row, there would be an astonishing 63 columns in the East Colonnade.

7 In addition to the surprising third colonnade, a feature was discovered north of the East Exedra in 1996 that resembles a step or the foundation of a step, which seems to lead from the eastern edge of the East Colonnade to the so-called 'Lower Market.' This step may have provided access to the Lower Temenos from the Lower Market area, but its phasing is uncertain, and more exploration needs to be done in this area.

8 For instance, there are the Temple of Jupiter Anxur at Terracina and the Sanctuary of Fortuna Primigenia at Palestrina; both are dated as early as the second century BCE.

9 A fragment of an elephant's head, smaller than the Lower Temenos examples, was found within the Temple in 1996. We have yet to determine whether such embellishments decorated the interior of the Temple or if this Upper Temenos example was brought in from somewhere else.

10 The staircase was not fully excavated but rather bisected; only the east half was uncovered. It is assumed that the west half mirrors the east, and the stairs will be completely uncovered in subsequent seasons.

11 The canals discovered underneath the collapsed center section of the Hexagonal Pavement connect to the Central Stairs canal (see above).

12 See the following section by Erika L. Schluntz.

13 As first observed by surveyors Loa P. Traxler and Michael F. Slaughter.

## Bibliography

Bachmann, W., et al.

    n.d.    "Wissenschaftliches Veroffentlichungen des Deutsch-turkischen Denkmalschutz-Kommandos." In *Petra.* Lepzig. 41-45.

Blagg, T.F.C.

    1990    "Column Capitals with Elephant-Headed Volutes at Petra," *Levant* 22:131-137.

Browning, I.

    1973    *Petra.* London: Chatto and Windus.

Joukowsky, M.S.

1994 "1993 Archaeological Excavations and Survey of the Southern Temple at Petra, Jordan," *ADAJ* 38:293-322.

———.

1995 "Archaeological Survey of the Southern Temple at Petra," *Syria* 72.1-2:133-142.

———.

1997 "The 1996 Brown University Archaeological Excavations at the 'Great' Southern Temple at Petra," *ADAJ* 41:195-218.

———.

n.d. "Exploring the 'Great' Temple at Petra: Brown University Excavations 1993-1996." In *A Volume Honoring James A. Sauer*, ed. L. Stager and J. Greene. Harvard Semitic Museum.

Parr, P.J.

1960 "Excavations at Petra 1958-59," *PEQ* 124-35.

———.

1970 "A Sequence of Pottery from Petra." In *Essays in Honor of Nelson Glueck*. 348-381.

# THE UPPER TEMENOS AND THE GREAT TEMPLE

Erika L. Schluntz

## Introduction

In this discussion of the architecture of the Upper Temenos of the Great Temple Complex, two phases of construction are described. The first, which coincided with the first phase of construction in the Lower Temenos, seems to date to the last quarter of the first century BCE, based on stylistic evidence. This construction phase includes the main structure of the Upper Temenos — the Great Temple itself.[1] The second phase of construction, also coinciding with most of the major renovations undertaken within the Lower Temenos, transformed the Temple building completely, both in appearance and function. The dating of this second phase is also somewhat tenuous, but it probably took place before the middle of the second century CE.

## The Upper Temenos Platform

The Upper Temenos area, measuring 56 m (east-west)-x-60 m (north-south), rose some 6 m above the Lower Temenos courtyard. The Temple itself stands in the center of the Upper Temenos, its tetrastyle-in-antis façade facing north, across a limestone, paved forecourt, towards the broad expanse of the Lower Temenos below.

Approximately 10 m of open space flanked the Temple on either side. Remains of the retaining walls for the Upper Temenos platform, measuring approximately 1.2 m thick, are visible on both the east and west sides. To the west, beyond the limit of the platform, the ground drops off approximately 3.5 m to a large terraced area below. Excavations at the northeast corner of the Upper Temenos have begun to uncover the eastern retaining wall and platform substructure. Future excavation may reveal whether access to the so-called 'Lower Market,' east of the Great Temple precinct, was possible from Upper Temenos platform. The southern limit of the Upper

Temenos area seems to have been the rock face of the Al-Katute slope itself; indeed, the north face of Al-Katute may have been partially cut away to accommodate the Great Temple Complex, as was the case with the vast Lower Market and Upper Market areas to the east.

## The Forecourt

The Upper Temenos area was originally accessed from the courtyard below by a single stairway, measuring 4.7 m wide, centrally positioned at the southern limit of the Lower Temenos. A later large-scale reconstruction, however, covered this axial stairway in favor of two lateral stairways, measuring 2.6 m in width.[2] These stairways opened onto the broad Forecourt area, measuring 28 m in width (east-west) and 13 m (north-south). The Forecourt is overlaid with hexagonal, white, limestone pavers (Figure 5.24); these pavers are similar in design to those covering the Lower Temenos courtyard but are smaller in size and thickness, measuring 0.20 m per side and 0.36 m in diameter (flat side to flat side, 0.40 m point to point), with an average thickness of 0.12 m. The Hexagonal Pave-

*Figure 5.24. Temple Forecourt, looking south, 1993.*

ment, which at one time covered the entire Forecourt area, is in poor condition due to damage caused by the collapse of the superstructure from the Temple building. In a few areas the damaged pavement shows signs of repair — ceramic construction tiles and roof tiles have been positioned directly on top of, and at times actually replace, the crushed pavers. This makeshift repair seems to belong to a very late period of the area's use.

Underlying the Hexagonal Pavement, in the center of the Forecourt, is a main junction area of the Subterranean Canalization System, which runs throughout the entire Great Temple precinct.[3] At some late point in the precinct's history, a supplemental drainage system was installed in the Forecourt, placed directly on top of the Hexagonal Pavement. This system, composed of reused limestone blocks and ceramic piping, extends east-west, abutting the north face of the Temple crepidoma, and is then laid underground, where it eventually empties into a catchment drain situated toward the northwest corner of the Upper Temenos.

## The Great Temple

The Great Temple is fronted with a tetrastyle-in-antis façade and is walled on its three remaining sides. Behind the façade is an enclosed porch, 6.3 m deep, extending the width of the building. At the rear of the Porch are two columns, positioned directly behind the two axial Stylobate columns, and two elongated piers, positioned directly behind the two lateral Stylobate columns. Passing southward beyond these, the interior of the original structure contained a free-standing peristyle, which extended around the south, east and west exterior walls of the building.

The overall Temple structure measures 28 m east-west and is approximately 42.5 m in length. The original height of the building could have been as high as 22 m, if the entablature supported a low pediment. This means that the Great Temple was slightly larger, in overall size, than its more boxy neighbor to the west, the Qasr al-Bint, whose dimensions are 32 m², with an estimated height of about 30 m.[4] Whether or not the Temple building (or for that matter, the Qasr al-Bint) actually had a pediment, however, is a matter for speculation; no remains of such a feature have been recovered within the Great

Temple precinct. Indeed, it is also assumed that the Stylobate column capitals supported some sort of entablature, presumably a frieze running the length of the façade, composed of weight-bearing voussoir blocks. These too, however, have not been found.

Access to the building was gained either through the broad, seven-step Central Stairs or through the two doorways found in both the east and west walls of the building. The Central Stairs, now completely robbed out, were originally 4.8 m in width and ascended 1.5 m from the Hexagonal Pavement of the Forecourt up to the Stylobate level (Figure 5.25). Other than this stairway, no other access was feasible via the front of the building; a two-step, low crepidoma sets the Podium off from the Hexagonal Pavement, but its function is aesthetic — the molded stylobate that rises above it is too high to climb without considerable effort. This is somewhat unusual in monumental sacred architecture of the time; the entire frontage of the Qasr al-Bint, for instance, was stepped.

The side doorways into the building were reached via the West or East Walkways (Figure 5.26); these 3.7 m-wide ambulatories flanking the east and west exterior walls of the Temple building were, like the Temple Stylobate, reached via 1 m-high stairways from the Forecourt level.[5] The walkways are paved with large, rectangular, well-laid flagstones composed of variously colored sandstone and were situated in direct alignment with the long stairways leading up from the Lower Temenos. The first of the side doorways opened onto the Porch; the second, 7 m farther south, opened onto the building's inner corridor (Figure 5.27). Presumably, these walkways extended the entire length of the building; future excavation in the very south of the Upper Temenos area may uncover additional doorways toward the rear of the building.[6]

Although the existence of the Temple building's entablature and pediment remain a matter of conjecture, what has been uncovered, concerning the decoration of the Temple building, is an abundance of carved, limestone capital pieces that originally decorated the building's Porch columns and colonnade. These expertly rendered floral capitals, loosely based on the Corinthian order, sat atop sandstone columns composed of characteristically Nabataean, disk-like drums (Figure 5.27). That these column drums are relatively squat is

*Figure 5.25. Reconstructed Temple steps, looking south.*

*Figure 5.26. View from the West Walkway, looking east.*

*Figure 5.27. Temple Southeast, looking west.*

due to the fact that they are cut from sandstone — the weight and friability of the stone and perhaps the seismic instability of the region presumably forced the Nabataean engineers to build with these smaller but sturdier elements. Such conservative construction methods are also in evidence in the Qasr al-Bint.

The columns of the building façade and the two at the rear of the Porch measure 1.5 m in diameter; the interior, peristyle columns are a narrower 1.1 m in diameter, except for the corner supports at the rear of the building, which are heart-shaped piers composed of engaged half-columns. Some entasis appears to have originally been visible on the contour of the columns; unfortunately, heavy weathering has made this difficult to ascertain at this writing. The estimated heights of the columns are approximately 15.5 m for the larger Porch columns and 12 m for those comprising slimmer inner colonnades. The approximate 3.5 m difference in height between the two sets of supports may have been equalized by a frieze carried atop the peristyle — the top surfaces of these column capitals are grooved and scored, indicating the presence of some type of entablature.

All of the building's columns were covered with a thick plaster, which then held a thin wash of stucco. Some interior columns still

carry plaster with thicknesses of more than 0.1 m, and there is some evidence of later reapplication and redecoration. The lower portions of the columns of the internal colonnades are decorated with red stucco on unfluted plaster; above approximately 2 m, the plaster becomes fluted and is painted white (Figure 5.28). The Stylobate columns are too weathered to determine precisely their decorative scheme, although the columns at the rear of the Porch appear to have carried the same two-color embellishment as the internal colonnade. The lathe-carved Attic bases of the columns are composed of the same white limestone as the capitals. The antae of the building's walls were also decorated with carved, limestone pilaster capitals and bases to duplicate the Porch columns, though all that remains are small fragments of the bases and perhaps a few fragments of pilaster capitals.

The two elongated piers at the sides of the rear of the Porch also mirrored their neighboring columns, constructed with pilasters on their north and inner faces and an engaged column on their south face. These pilasters are decorated with the same Attic limestone bases as the building's columns, and fragments of pilaster capitals with the same decorative motif as the capitals have been recovered. An anomalous feature occurs, however, on the sides of the piers facing the outer walls of the building: on this surface, each pier is decorated with a low,

*Figure 5.28. Upper colonnade column, decorated with white fluted plaster.*

chiseled pilaster base. These 0.9 m-wide bases are carved from the same limestone block as the Attic bases of the north- and inward-facing pilasters but in a different style, looking almost like short pedestals rather than molded bases. The bases are roughly chiseled and heavily scored, clearly for the application of plaster decoration. Rising vertically from these bases are narrow pilaster shafts, cut from the fabric of the sandstone piers themselves. Opposite these slim pilasters, on the interior surfaces of the walls of the building, are identical shafts, again, designed as part of the original wall construction. Neither the piers nor the building walls are preserved high enough in this area to ascertain how high these narrow pilasters extended; the bases and shafts are of a smaller scale than the architecture that loomed up around them. Therefore, they could not have risen much more than half the height of the Porch piers.[7]

The purpose of these small pilasters is a mystery. It may be that they held an arching cross-wall, sprung between the piers and the side walls of the building.[8] These cross-walls, extending from the level of these pilasters up to the height of the piers, would have provided more stability to the outer walls of the structure and helped to screen the transition between the different heights of the Porch and peristyle columns.

The exterior walls of the building are constructed of sandstone, ashlar masonry, 1.4 m thick. The blocks, especially on the exterior faces of the building, are closely fit and horizontally dressed; the interior surfaces of the walls are not as finely finished, no doubt due to the fact that they were plastered and stuccoed. Fragments of plaster and painted stucco still adhere to excavated portions of the west wall. A series of four narrow peg holes in this wall, approximately 1.7 m from the floor, is a probable indication that the wall decoration was partially supported by iron pegs, as was not uncommon. Over the long history of the building's use, these walls must have been decorated and redecorated many times, as changing tastes as well as the building's changing functions dictated. The extant plaster, preserved to a thickness of 0.15 m, shows a rich palette of greens, deep golds, blue, Pompeiian red and black.

The question as to whether the original building structure was roofed or hypaethral must, at this point, remain unanswered. Some roofing was evidently in place after the building was thoroughly remodeled (see below); however, there is as yet no physical evidence for any roofing early on — stone or timber — other than the observation that the limestone of the peristyle capitals, as well as the preserved plastering of these interior columns, shows little evidence of weathering.

It seems probable that at least the peristyle was roofed, forming covered porticos extending around the inside of the building.

As was clear in the discussion of the Lower Temenos, the Great Temple Complex underwent drastic renovations at one point in its history. Within the Upper Temenos, the original Temple building was completely remodeled and transformed into a small theater or odeum structure. Almost no feature of the original structure was left untouched.

What would have been the most striking change to the viewer approaching the building was the screen wall installed along the Stylobate of the building's façade. This wall, erected between the antae and the lateral Porch columns and between the lateral columns and the central columns, would have completely altered the building's façade. No remnant of this screen wall survives; its sometime existence is shown by the presence of deep cuttings into the limestone bases of the Porch columns and shallow cuttings into the Stylo-bate between the central columns. The cuttings into the column bases are .70 m wide and 0.42 m deep; that is, a meter-wide "notch" has been cut out of each base on its east and west sides, with the depth of each notch corresponding to the vertical axis of the column drums above (Figure 5.29). The screen walls were then fitted into these notches and constructed to an undetermined height. Erosion of the Porch column drums has made it difficult to ascertain the height of the screen wall — any sort of surface alteration that the construction of the later wall might have made has been worn away from the extant *in situ* drums. Most likely, however, the wall would have "screened" the entire height of the façade.

It may be that the screen wall was also continued within the central inter-columnation of the Porch, i.e., right across the (former) main entryway into Temple building; a cutting identical to those described above is also present in the west side of the base of the east axial column (the west base is not *in situ*). However, it is more likely that a doorway was installed between these two central columns, limiting but not completely restricting access into the building from the north. The Stylobate surface within the central inter-columnation exhibits shallow indentations, aligned with the cuttings in the bases, which probably signify the placement of door jambs. Such cuttings into the surface of the Stylobate

are not present between the other inter-columnations, indicating that a different form of construction was built here. Given that this was the central and most visible part of the building, this new doorway was probably decorated with a low entablature and pediment. A screen wall would have surmounted the doorway. To the ancient viewer, this new façade to the building would have looked quite familiar — Ad-Dayr, the Corinthian Tomb, the Urn Tomb and countless other later façades within Petra displayed monumental solid façades with engaged columns and a central pedimented doorway.

The purpose of the screen wall was to further limit access to the building from the north; this action coincides with the covering over of the large Central Stairs, which once led from the Lower Temenos courtyard up to the Upper Temenos Forecourt. It was also during this large-scale renovation phase, most likely, that the lateral Porch doorways, which once gave access to the Porch area from the East and West Walkways, were blocked. This allowed the entire Porch area to become a separate room, presumably serving as backstage for the new odeum structure. The main public entrances to the building now seem to be the second set of doorways leading from the East and West Walkways, as well as any entrances

*Figure 5.29. Porch columns showing "notches."*

that may be uncovered in the future toward the rear of the building.

The interior of the building was completely altered as well. A stage was constructed, stretching between the two elongated piers and incorporating the two large columns at the rear of the Porch, which may have served as part of the *scanae frons* structure. The central space of the structure, within the area of the peristyle, was transformed into the orchestra and cavea, with an elaborate substructure of long passageways and broad staircases; the seating capacity of the cavea may have been over 600 people.

To begin, the two elongated piers at the rear of the Porch served as the east and west bounds of the stage structure; thus, its width spanned 15.4 m pier to pier. To date, only the west half of the structure has been excavated (Figure 5.30). The overall depth of the structure was 5.1 m, although approximately 1.2 m of this depth was devoted to the *scanae frons*. As is often the case with stages, this stage platform is not solidly constructed. Rather, two separate, parallel walls extend from pier to pier, with the space between them filled with loose rubble and construction debris and then paved over to provide the stage surface.[9] The "back" (north) wall of the stage structure, which is constructed of hewn and unhewn stones, is

preserved to a height of just over 1 m, approximately 0.3 m below stage level. At three points along its length, narrow makeshift steps are built up to the north face of the wall; these are either steps providing rear access onto the stage or ancillary supports for the *scanae frons*, which would have surmounted this wall and part of the stage flooring. Nothing remains of the *scanae frons*, except for the two large columns original to the Porch. These must have been incorporated as both decorative and structural elements of the *scanae frons*.

Providing the *itinera versurarum*, the principal entryways onto the stage for the actors which are traditionally situated at the side limits of the stage, may have been a conundrum for the engineers who planned this elaborate remodeling phase of the building, since the stage abutted the elongated piers. Excavation of the west pier revealed that their solution was to actually cut a narrow, stepped passageway through the sandstone fabric of the piers themselves. This passageway, 0.8 m in width, is cut approximately 0.9 m from floor level; sandstone blocks provided a step up and into the passageway (Figure 5.31).

The *proscaenium*, the front wall of the stage, was built with considerably more care with finished, white and yellowish, sandstone blocks (Figure 5.32). Its preserved height is 1.3 m,

*Figure 5.30. Theater stage, looking north.*

*Figure 5.31. Entryway to stage from the West Corridor.*

the height of the stage; it is up to 1 m thick. Two narrow stairways from the orchestral level are preserved in its south face. The first, situated at the extreme west of the stage, is 1 m wide, and it abuts the west face of the engaged column that forms the south portion of the elongated pier. The second stairway, 1.5 m to the east of the first, is 0.7 m wide; both rise to the height of the stage. The excavated portion of the *proscaenium* also contains one inset niche, measuring 0.6 m in width and 0.4 m deep. The center of the *proscaenium* appears to have also carried a niche, although at present this area is only partially excavated. The entire stage front rests on a low border of red, purple and white sandstone. This decorative curbing, measuring approximately 0.4 m in depth, rises 0.3 m from the orchestra floor.

The construction of the orchestra and cavea was limited to the space demarcated by the peristyle, just as the width of the stage building was dictated by the distance between the twin elongated piers. The peristyle columns provided a "skeleton" to the 1.9 m-thick, casemate wall that served as a retaining wall to the entire cavea structure (Figure 5.33). While the exterior of this wall appears quite regular, with the dressed, sandstone ashlars laid in regular, well-fitted joins, the interior of these walls is more poorly assembled, with loose-

hewn stones filling its matrix. The columns themselves protrude slightly — not enough to convincingly look like engaged columns but enough to provide decorative embellishment for the wall. The construction of this casemate wall transformed the 2.6 m-wide porticos of the original structure into corridors, starting in the north with the northernmost column, which was left exposed. These corridors provided access to the passageways and staircases within the cavea structure (Figure 5.33).

During this odeum phase of the building's use, a patron's most direct access to the cavea was through the side doorways that led from the external East and West Walkways into the inside corridors. The cavea was constructed so that the *aditus maximus*, the main entryways into the orchestra and cavea, are directly aligned with these side doorways. That is to say, the visitor would proceed from the outside walkway into the building, cross the portico and pass straight through the *aditus maximus*, which was flanked by the elongated pier on the north and the beginning of the casemate wall on the south. This passageway opens onto the orchestra, where steps then lead up to the cavea. Like the stage structure, only the west half of the orchestra and cavea have been excavated to date.

The entire "public" surface of the porticoes, the *aditus maximus* and the orchestra is paved with well-fitted, rectangular, sandstone flagging (Figure 5.36). This is in contrast to the area of the Porch and the area surrounding the elongated piers, now considered "backstage," where the flooring of the original building has been removed and only the sandstone subflooring remains. Set into the flooring at the beginning of the semicircular orchestra are a series of narrow limestone blocks, 0.3 m wide, which span the 3 m distance from the front of the stage to the edge of the cavea. These stones contain four cuttings, presumably post holes, and they must have held a gate or low screen preventing public entry to the central orchestra area.

From this area, access to the cavea seating was gained via 0.7 m-wide stairways, which led up 1.3 m from the orchestra floor to the semicircular aisle that formed the lowest level of the cavea (Figure 5.34). Dovetail post holes within the West Stairway indicate that a banister once aided spectators up this narrow rise. From the semicircular aisle at the center

*Figure 5.32. Stage showing staircases, looking north.*

*Figure 5.33. Inter-Columnar casemate wall interior.*

*Figure 5.34. Aerial view of Temple Rear, showing Simon and Monica Stairways and west vaulted room, looking south.*

*Figure 5.35. Engaged column, West Corridor.*

of the cavea, a 0.7 m-wide stairway rose upward through the seating. Again, post holes indicate the presence of a banister. Positioned between the Central Stairs and the north edge of the cavea is another poorly preserved stairway. Other access to seating was probably provided by similar stairways, rising up the height of the cavea along its north retaining walls. The north retaining wall on the west side of the cavea unfortunately has collapsed, leaving nothing but its foundation course. Perhaps future excavation of the east side of the cavea will reveal a more intact structure.

Given the poor state of preservation of the excavated portion of the cavea, it is difficult to ascertain the number of rows of seats that this odeum structure may have held. Each row of seats is approximately 0.7 m in depth and 0.35 m in height. If the seating did extend back to the southern casemate wall at the rear of the building, a conservative estimate would be a total of approximately 22 rows leading back to the rear of cavea, leaving space for one diazoma, or horizontal aisle, which would have bisected the seating area. This would provide seating for approximately 600 people.

Access to the cavea was also available through a series of stairways constructed within the cavea substructure. Halfway down the West

Corridor toward the rear of the building, an arched doorway leads through the casemate wall, below the seating of the cavea, to a 2.2 m-wide vaulted stairway (Figure 5.37). These broad, dressed, sandstone stairs abut the interior face of the west casemate wall, ascending southward about 9 m, passing a well-constructed, arched window and ending on a wide landing (Figure 5.38). The angle of ascent for this stairway corresponds directly to the angle of ascent of the seating within the cavea.

The landing was embellished with a flooring of large, rectangular, white, sandstone pavers. Another large window, 1.2 m wide, opened in the casemate wall at the level of the landing; small holes drilled into the sides of the window opening presumably secured ropes or some sort of barrier to prevent accidents. It should also be noted, however, that because there was still an exterior wall outside of this casemate wall, these light wells would have emitted only minimal amounts of light. An identical stairway, along with windows and a landing, were also uncovered on the east side of the cavea. Passage between the two landings may have been possible, although the collapse of the vaulted south central area of the cavea has made this difficult to ascertain at this time. From both platforms, a short stairway, measuring 1.7 m wide, led northward to the interior of the cavea, presumably at the level of the diazoma.

*Figure 5.36. Theater, looking south.*

Excavations at the southeast corner of the cavea revealed a sharply ascending, 8.5 m-long stairway, rising westward from the east corridor (Figure 5.39). This vaulted stairway, measuring 2.3 m wide, is constructed between the south casemate wall and a 1 m-wide, interior support wall that spans the width of the cavea, paralleling the casemate wall. A 1.3 m-wide window in the south casemate wall would have provided some light into the stairway; a corresponding window in the support wall is also present. Further excavation should reveal an identical stairway starting from the southwest corner of the cavea structure, which would have met its twin at a landing. The collapse of the vaulted substructure under this

*Figure 5.37. West Stairway (Monica Stairway) door, looking northwest.*

*Figure 5.38. West landing, Temple Rear, looking northeast.*

area of the cavea, again, has made reconstruction tenuous; presumably, another small stairway leading upward to the north would have provided access to the uppermost seats of the cavea. These seats would have been built above the vaulting of the long stairways.

The extensive substructure of vaulted rooms below the seating of the cavea has only been partially excavated. Directly beyond the arched doorway in the west casemate wall, past the foot of the lateral staircase, a narrow doorway opens into a large, vaulted "room" (Figures 5.36 and 5.40). The function of this room, measuring approximately 3 m wide-x-5.5 m long, is primarily structural; the walls that surround this room are unusually thick (1.3-1.8 m), as their vaults must have provided the principal support for the cavea seating above. All of these walls are composed of massive, sandstone ashlars and more roughly hewn stones. Less well-excavated, due to safety concerns, is the room below the collapsed rear portion of the cavea. This centrally located space, again defined by thick walls, also carried a vaulted ceiling. Clearly, the weight of the cavea required such a large, vaulted support system.

## Interpretation

That the Great Temple structure, in its later, remodeled phase, served a civic function as a small theater or odeum seems most probable. Contemporary theaters of a similar size,

*Figure 5.39. Southeast Stairway (Brian Stairway), looking west.*

*Figure 5.40. Temple Rear, looking south from the Theater, showing the west vaulted room.*

employing similar construction techniques, are in evidence throughout Palestine and Arabia.[10] In antiquity, odeum buildings often served as city council halls (bouleuteria); it would seem likely that this building served both of these functions. It is known from papyrological records[11] that Petra had a boule at least by the early second century CE. As no other building has to date been uncovered within Petra that could have properly served as its meeting hall, this newly refurbished structure probably housed such functions.

There is very little evidence that the second-phase structure was a temple with a theater and not a civic odeum. In the late Hellenistic and Roman periods, a few localized theater-temples were in use in northern Arabia and southern Syria. These religious structures, however, were not architecturally similar to the Great Temple structure; their theater seating was quite limited and occupied only a small portion of the temple.[12] Likewise, the building is not suitable for imperial cultic activities. Structures of this size associated with the imperial cult, even ones that may have previously housed a different "god," almost always were embellished with an abundance of imperial religious imagery. Given that so much care was taken and resources expended on the remodeling of the building, some evidence pointing toward this activity would surely have surfaced.

The remodeling of the building into a civic odeum/bouleuterion must bring the 'Temple' interpretation of the original, first-phase structure into question. Due to very strong religious sensitivities, desacralization of religious sites was virtually unheard of in antiquity. Also, in five years of excavation on site, no evidence of religious activity has been uncovered — no confirmed altar, artifacts, iconography or other structures that would indicate that this site was a sacred precinct. It is useful, therefore, to consider another possibility for the use of this rather enigmatic building and its complex.

The closest architectural parallels to the original building structure can be found in the design of late-Hellenistic palace buildings. By this period, palace architectural design had progressed from the compact, inward-looking structures in the early Hellenistic period to more spread out complexes, with separate buildings serving separate functions.[13] By the first century BCE, the triclinia (the banquet halls of these palaces), especially those of the Ptolemies of Egypt, became especially grandiose. Very often, these halls served a double function; not only were they used for large-scale meals and celebrations, but they were also utilized as audience halls, no doubt because they were among the most elegantly decorated structures within the palace complex.

In the Levant, the late first century BCE palaces of Herod the Great were particularly impressive, according to both the literary and archaeological record. The historian Josephus, for one, gives enthusiastic descriptions of the magnificence of the Herodian palaces at Jerusalem, Jericho and Herodium. It is the triclinia of Herod's palaces at Herodium and Jericho, in particular, that bear a striking resemblance, architecturally, to our monumental edifice.[14] The triclinium at the Third Winter Palace at Jericho, for instance, was a solid-walled building with a broad doorway and a peristyle, complete with elongated piers and heart-shaped piers at the rear corners. It also took advantage of its setting upon a hill overlooking a wadi; in Josephus' accounts of the Herodian palaces, he often mentions the "picture window" views that these triclinia afforded. The design of the Great Temple building, with its broad open Porch, certainly takes into consideration its surroundings as well.

Despite his reputation as a rather odious character, Herod's reputation as a builder was first-rate — this monarch built some of the most architecturally significant structures of the late first century BCE. The Nabataean kings of Petra, Herod's rivals and near neighbors, are also known to have spent considerable amounts of their vast wealth on the architectural embellishment of their capital city — an aspect that is still immediately evident to even the most casual visitor to Petra today. That these kings might have tried to "out-Herod Herod" would come as no surprise. The possible late-first-century-BCE

dating of the first phase of construction of the Great Temple Complex would coincide nicely with this scheme.

Clearly, banqueting was an important event in the lives of the Nabataean royal family, and it was imbued with civic and perhaps even religious meaning. Strabo, in his *Geography*, devotes a great deal of effort to describing such activity, "The king calls together banquets (*symposia*) with great magnificence, but nobody drinks more than eleven drinks…The king is so democratic that besides serving himself, he occasionally serves the others himself." In addition, some of the most well-known structures at Petra, including Ad-Dayr and the High Place, are laid out as triclinia, another indication of the centrality of this activity not only to the kings of Petra but to other citizens as well.

If the Great Temple building had in fact been part of the palace complex of the kings of Nabataea, serving as a banqueting or reception hall, then its remodeling into an odeum-bouleuterion after Roman annexation at the beginning of the second century CE would be understandable. No longer needed by the now defunct royalty of Petra,[15] the building could now fill a wholly civic function, yet still retain its nature as a major place of entertainment and assembly.

Of course, only future excavation will provide the information necessary to gain a conclusive understanding of the rich and enigmatic history of the Great Temple Complex.

---

# Endnotes

[1] This author is not entirely convinced that the Great Temple was, in fact, a temple at all. However, for the sake of continuity within this publication, the structure will be referred to in this chapter as a temple. An alternate possibility for the building's identity and function is given in the concluding interpretation.

[2] Of course, there is no evidence to say that such lateral access to the Upper Temenos did not also exist, along with the axial stairway, early in the Great Temple Complex's history; the extant stairway structures are, however, not original to the Complex but were built during the secondary reconstruction phase.

[3] This impressive example of Nabataean hydraulic engineering is discussed in Chapter 4.

[4] A good short description of the Qasr al-Bint can be found in Judith S. McKenzie, 1990:135-138.

[5] Excavations at the northwest corner of the building indicate that these stairways are part of the same construction phase as the Temple building itself — the substructure of the Stylobate and the walkway stairs bond. These ambulatories themselves were, however, remodeled at some point — the low, outer wall of the West Walkway is clearly secondary; it is not particularly well-constructed, and it cuts into the flagstone paving of the walkway, indicating that it was initially wider. It is unknown whether these walkways were roofed — there is no evidence on the exterior surface of the building's walls for support-holes, although such features may have been above the walls' preserved height.

[6] The Qasr al-Bint was also flanked by a broad ambulatory in its east side. This walkway, however, featured no doorways into the building.

[7] There is also no way of determining with what sort of capital these odd pilasters were topped; pilaster bases of this sort most often carried Nabataean capitals, and the mixing of orders was not uncommon in Nabataean architecture. In fact, the main order of the Al-Khazna is the floral order found here at the Great Temple, but Nabataean capitals adorn its doorways.

[8] This suggestion was offered by architect Chrysanthos Kanellopoulos, in discussions at Petra during the fall of 1997.

[9] Partial excavation of this ca. 2.6 m gap in 1995 revealed a thick layer of whitish, sandstone chips among the rubble fill, which confused this excavator. It now seems likely that these chips were the debris from the cutting and fitting of either the stones used to face the front of the stage or the slabs used for the seats within the cavea.

[10] A. Segal (1995) has an up-to-date, analytical survey.

[11] For the intricate legal tribulations at Petra of one woman in early second century CE Palestine see Glen W. Bowersock (1983:76-90). See also the full explanation in Chapter 1.

[12] The most comprehensive discussion of theater-temples in antiquity is still J. Hanson (1959).

[13] An indispensable source for this study has been I. Nielsen (1994).

[14] The large triclinium at Herod's palace at Jerusalem also seems to have been quite similar in structure and in size to the Great Temple building, although all that remains of that palace are the descriptions found in Josephus' *The Jewish War* and his *Antiquities of the Jews*. One of his most thorough descriptions of the Jerusalem banquet hall can be found in *The Jewish War*, 5.4.3-4.

[15] See Glen W. Bowersock (1983:85f) for a discussion on the dismantling of the royal apparatus at Petra.

# Bibliography

Bowersock, G.W.

     1983     *Roman Arabia.* Cambridge, MA: Harvard University Press.

Hanson, J.

     1959     *Roman Theater Temples.* Princeton, NJ: Princeton University Press.

McKenzie, J.S.

      1990     *The Architecture of Petra*. Oxford: Oxford University Press.

Nielsen, I.

      1994     *Hellenistic Palaces: Tradition and Renewal*. Aarhus: Aarhus University Press.

Segal, A.

      1995     *Theatres in Roman Palestine and Provincia Arabia*. New York: Leiden.

# THE ARCHITECTURAL SCULPTURE
## OF THE GREAT TEMPLE

### Erika L. Schluntz

### Introduction

This is a discussion of the architectural sculpture unearthed to date during the excavations
of the Great Temple in Petra, Jordan.[1] After five
seasons of field excavation, an extraordinary
amount of this material has been found; well
over 5000 pieces of sculpted stone have been
recorded. Primarily, these are fragments of
column capitals, elaborately carved with floral
and vegetal elements, but we have also
uncovered a series of very fine mask-like
heads, a fragmentary relief panel and some
rather unique zoomorphic capital embellishments. All of these elements are carved out of
local, rather good-quality, white limestone.

The study of these fragments from the Temple
is significant for two reasons. First, we are now
reasonably certain of the overall decorative
program of the Great Temple itself during the
building's period of use. The exterior order

and the interior order of the original Temple
structure can all now be described and
reconstructed accurately, as can some of the
embellishments that were added later during
the building's secondary use as a small theater
or odeum.

The information gained from this sculptural
material can also be useful in dealing with
other, more far-reaching questions concerning
the Temple. The well-developed style and
excellent quality of these artifacts, when
viewed against the background of existing
Nabataean architectural art, provide important
clues for determining the initial period of
construction and use of the Temple. Because
sealed, original construction phase deposits
within the Temple building itself have yet to be
found and analyzed, this sculptural decoration
has provided us with some of our only information dating the first phase of this structure.

*Figure 5.41. Pronaos column with remnants of red plaster. Photograph by David L. Brill.*

## The Column Bases

The bases of the columns of the Great Temple are expertly crafted Attic bases, made from the same limestone as the column capitals (Figure 5.41). The Porch bases have a maximum diameter of 2.36 m; their height is 0.6 m, and the bases of the colonnade columns are slightly smaller, with a maximum diameter of 1.7 m and a height of 0.42 m. Close examination of the bases reveals very fine, perfectly horizontal lines and grooves running across the surface of the stone, indicating that they were carved on a lathe (Figure 5.42). This fact is rather striking, given their size and weight, and it attests to the exceptional artistic conception and skill with which the entire decorative program of the building was carried out.

*Figure 5.42. Attic base, Pronaos column.*

## The Column Capitals

The capitals that adorned both the Great Temple's Pronaos columns and the internal colonnade are based on the Hellenistic Corinthian order (Figure 5.43). Their upper elements, however, exhibit an elaboration of floral designs not seen in standard Corinthian capitals of the time. These "floral" capitals appear to be a particularly Nabataean interpretation of the order, and they are

present on many of the principal monuments of Petra (Figure 5.44).[2] While some very fragmentary capital pieces have been recovered from the Pronaos area, the best preserved examples are from the internal colonnade capitals.

Squared, pilaster, capital fragments have been recovered in front of the Temple Stylobate and in the Porch area (Figure 5.45). These pieces belong to the antae, the projecting ends of the Temple walls and the internal 'antae' or piers that flank the Pronaos columns; these antae were, in a sense, "dressed up" to look just like their neighbor columns.

The lowest element of the capital is a double row of bushy, curling acanthus leaves, which surmount an astragal. Each acanthus "basket" was constructed in vertical halves (the upper section of the capital, the florals and the volutes with the abacus was constructed in quarters). The bottom diameter of the internal order capital was 1.1 m; the Porch capitals are actually a bit larger, measuring 1.5 m in diameter. The heights of the internal and external capitals are, respectively, 1.46 m and 2 m. In general, the internal and external models are virtually identical, although the Porch capitals do seem to have been executed with slightly more care, due, no doubt, to their prominence.

A close-up of a fragment from one of the Porch columns (Figure 5.46) reveals the "ripple technique" of carving on the leaves, a channeling of the surface that enhances the vegetal or organic aspect of the element and allows for greater play of light and shadow across the enlivened surface. Most of the elements on the capital exhibit this sort of exaggerated texture, no doubt so that these sculptural details, once *in situ*, could be seen by people on the ground.

The upper portion of the capitals exhibits a rich variety of fruits and florals, all set within lively tangles of vines and tendrils, which spring from the acanthus fronds below. The impression the sculpture gives is of lush, energetic growth and abundance (Figure 5.47). Stout, winding vines and stems blossom with hibiscus and wild rose petals, which in turn open to reveal a variety of finely carved pomegranates, poppies and pine cones (Figure 5.48). Framing these floral compositions were robust, deeply channeled, leaf-covered vines, which, sprouting from the acanthus basket

*Figure 5.43. Floral capital — Type I. Courtesy of Judith S. McKenzie, 1990 p. 190: f.*

*Figure 5.44. Typical Temple limestone capital elements (in meters). Lower acanthus order, 34/192, Trench 34, Locus 12, 3-VIII-96. Diameter 117, Width 0.77, Thickness 0.52. Upper order, 58086, Trench 58, Locus 5, 4-VIII-98. Height 0.57, Width 0.82, Thickness 0.78. Pine cone boss, 58103, Trench 58, Locus 5, 5-VIII-98. Length 0.45, Width 0.20, Thickness 0.23. Drawing by Susan B. Tillack.*

*Figure 5.45. Pilaster capital fragment.*

*Figure 5.46. Detail of lower order acanthus decoration.*

below, curve up and outward to form the corner volutes of the capital. Within the arid, often bare landscape of Petra, such luxurious, exuberant images must have been particularly striking and can probably be construed as symbolic of the Nabataeans' well-established prosperity and their dominance over this harsh landscape.

An astragal crowns the floral elements of the capital, which is in turn surmounted by the abacus. Projecting up and out from the center of the abacus is the boss, which consisted of a

broad, rippled acanthus leaf with a large pine cone in the center (Figure 5.49). These bosses were carved as separate elements and were fitted, like a plug, into corresponding deep niches carved into the abacus.

It is interesting to note that among the many hundreds of recovered individual elements — including leaves, vines and pine cones — a number of these are plaster repairs or "copies" of these elements (Figure 5.50). Surely, in the end-stage production of these capitals, a chisel can slip or the carving can somehow become

*Figure 5.47. Capital volute and vegetal decoration.*

*Figure 5.48. Capital vine and blossom decoration.*

damaged, either during installation or over time. Rather than discarding the whole section or trying to secure a heavy stone element back in place, it was much more efficient to just repair it with a bit of light, moldable plaster. The heavier examples of these reproductions were held in place with pegs of wood or stone, as is demonstrated by peg holes on the reverse sides of the plaster fragments. Virtually every element from the capital design has turned up in plaster, occasionally still *in situ* on the stone. And a few large capital fragments, excavated towards the rear of the Temple, have their vegetal decoration molded completely in plaster. Most likely because these out-of-the-way capitals were not as easily viewed, this faster and less expensive means of achieving the same visual effect was employed.

When comparing the Temple building's capitals to other examples of floral capitals in Petra, for instance from the Temple of the Winged Lions or the Temenos Gate, it is readily observable that most of these other examples do not seem to be of the same artistic quality as those that adorned the Great Temple. The execution of these other capitals, usually belonging to the first century CE or later, is more schematic; there is less depth to their relief, and the elements seem less organic or "alive." The monument whose architectural

sculpture does exhibit the same lively quality is Al-Khazna, probably the most well-known edifice in Petra. Its primary order capitals bear a striking resemblance to those of the Great Temple, especially in terms of their deep relief, their curling, serrated acanthus leaves and the complexity and variety exhibited in their floral

*Figure 5.49. Pine cone boss.*

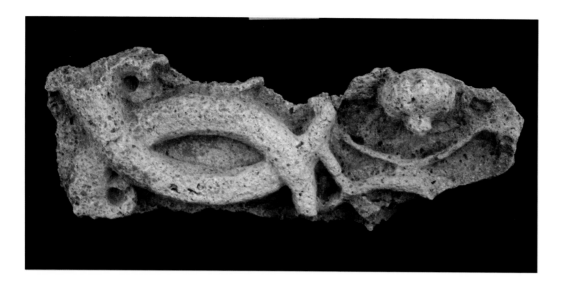

*Figure 5.50. Example of plaster repair fragments.*

arrangements. In addition to the capitals, the profile of Al-Khazna's column bases is identical to that found on the bases of the Great Temple.

Judith S. McKenzie has examined the stylistic development of the floral capitals at Petra and has concluded that over time the lively complexity of these capitals diminished, and their decoration became more "simplified" (McKenzie 1990:39ff). In other words, the more elaborate the capital, the earlier the

building. In her work, conducted before Brown University began excavating the Great Temple, McKenzie pointed to the capitals of Al-Khazna as among the earliest and best examples of the Nabataean floral capital. Thus, it appears reasonable that the Great Temple, whose quality of sculpture is so similar to that of Al-Khazna, must have been constructed not long after that famous mausoleum, some time fairly early in the course of monumental architecture at Petra. This is a departure from what had originally been assumed about the

*Figure 5.51. Capital, upper order.*

Great Temple; before excavation, casual observers had often placed its construction later in the history of Petra, after the Roman domination.

However, as to determining an actual, and not just a relative date for the Temple, that is more problematic. Al-Khazna is currently dated to somewhere in the first century BCE. If that is so, it would be reasonable to speculate that the Great Temple was also constructed some time before the end of the first century BCE.

breast; a bunched chlamys rests on the left shoulder, exposing the anatomical details of the softly delineated chest.

This panel was retrieved from destruction debris close to the West Stairway leading from the Lower Temenos to the Upper Temenos. The original placement of this panel is unknown, although one possible position could be the north faces of the antae of the Temple building itself. Panel devices are not an uncommon decoration for projecting antae, e.g., the nearby Qasr al-Bint displayed a series of stucco geometric panels on its antae, and the Temenos Gate is thought to have carried a series of figural relief panels in both its

*Figure 5.52. Limestone torso panel, Lower Temenos, 1997.*

## The Relief Sculpture

Aside from the finely sculpted capitals, other examples of architectural sculpture have been unearthed in and around the Temple Complex. In 1997, a fragmentary limestone panel depicting a torso was found in the Lower Temenos, although in all probability, it comes from the decoration of the Temple itself (Figure 5.52). The preserved width and height of the panel was 0.82-x-0.24 m; originally the panel would have measured about 0.9 m². The figure is carved in middle relief and is framed by a cyma reversa and a fillet. Because the stone was cut down, presumably for reuse, only a narrow section of the figure is preserved, from just below the top of the shoulders to just below the pectorals. The figure is nude, except for a baldric worn diagonally across the torso, from the right shoulder to below the left

Nabataean classical and Roman phases. On the Great Temple building, 0.9 m-wide figural panels would have fit quite suitably into the 1.5 m-wide antae walls, leaving 0.3 m on each side; that is, an even 1:3:1 ratio would have existed in the wall-panel-wall decorative scheme. In theory, the height of these antae walls would have carried five of these panels.

This panel from the Great Temple bears a striking resemblance, both in composition and artistic quality, to the series of relief panels among the '1967 Group of Sculptures,' which are said to have been found in the general vicinity of the Temenos Gate. The original position of these reliefs, depicting various members of the Greek pantheon, is unknown; it has been theorized that they were part of the decorative program of the original phase of the Temenos Gate.[3] McKenzie dates these panels,

*Figure 5.53. Face mask. Photograph by David L. Brill.*

based on stylistic similarities to the reliefs on Al-Khazna, to the first century BCE.

Compositionally, these sculptural panels use the same framing device of cyma reversa and fillet as does the panel from the Great Temple. Further, the Ares figure from the '1967' sculptures displays a baldric and chlamys in identical positions to those worn by this figure from the Great Temple. Stylistically, the folds of the chlamys on each figure are carved with the same deep, bunched creases. Given these artistic similarities, it could be speculated that these panels are products of the same school or group of sculptors and, presumably, of contemporary date in the first century BCE. It should be noted that the size difference between the '1967' sculptures, whose widths are approximately 0.6 m — 0.3 m smaller than the Great Temple sculpture — precludes their having originally decorated the same structure.

## The Masks

In 1994, seven carved limestone 'head' fragments were recovered in the vicinity of the second, smaller doorway into the west wall of the Temple (Figures 5.53-5.57). These fragments compose six separate 'heads,' five female and one male. These startling heads appear to have adorned a frieze, possibly one

that was situated either across the lintel or on the door jambs within this doorway. The fragments were not carved in the round, but rather appear to have been broken off from a relief. The four female examples are rendered slightly under life-size, while the sole, fragmentary male example is slightly over life-size.

The heads are presumably theater masks, modeled in the standard format of masks: the mouths of each are open, and the eyes are slightly wider than expected. The male mask wears an elegant laurel wreath; one of the female masks sports a thick fillet, and two of the other females do not don a headdress. The other mask is too fragmentary to reconstruct its headgear. The hair on the female masks is heavily carved, giving each thick, voluminous curls; the male mask also displays thick hair and a long mustache. On the male mask and one of the female masks, the pupils of the eyes are raised. This peculiar technique is also seen in most of the reliefs from the '1967 Group of Sculptures,' perhaps representing a Nabataean stylistic preference. The masks also bear a resemblance to these reliefs in their full jaw lines and chin and slightly angular brows, although the masks are generally not as finely executed. There is also an "orphaned" female mask, identical in size and style to the masks from the Temple building, which has resided for many years unprovenienced in a case in the Petra Museum. She is labeled simply as a stray find from "around" the area of the Colonnaded Street; it seems likely that the Great Temple was probably her original home. Given their theatrical nature, the masks of the Temple building were presumably added as embellishments after the building underwent its transformation into a theater/odeum sometime in the second century CE.

## The Zoomorphic Capitals

Other sculptural elements found within the Great Temple Complex are the numerous fragments of elephant-headed, ionic capitals found in the Lower Temenos. These expertly worked capitals, which must have played a significant role in the decorative program of that area, are discussed earlier in this chapter by Joseph J. Basile.

*Figure 5.54*

*Figure 5.56*

*Figure 5.55*

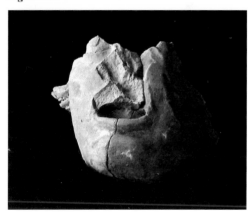

*Figure 5.57*

*Figures 5.54–5.57. Face masks.*
*5.54–5.56. Photographs by David L. Brill.*

## Conclusion

In conclusion, the first phase of sculptural decoration from the Great Temple Complex, dating most probably to the later first century BCE, seeks to symbolically represent the well-established wealth of the Nabataeans. In particular, in the ornamentation of the finely sculpted capitals, the Nabataeans transformed their indigenous vegetation of poppies, pomegranates and pine cones — which grew only sparsely and periodically in the arid climate of Petra — into permanent, lush abundance; literally, they set their prosperity into stone.[4] Stylistically, it has been noted that these capitals bear striking resemblance to Al-Khazna's capitals, with deep carvings, original patterning and lively execution. Given the political prominence and status of Al-Khazna itself, it can be deduced that it would have served as the architectural and sculptural standard upon which all other buildings would have been modeled; in addition, the artistic school that created it would have continued to be vigorously employed.[5]

*Figure 5.58. Fragment of a limestone lion's head, 1997.*

# Endnotes

[1] For the sake of consistency within this publication, this building complex will be called the Great Temple, and its main building referred to as the Temple building throughout this article. Due to the results of the 1997 excavation season, this assumption has been brought into doubt. For the possibility that this Complex was originally a portion of the palace precinct and later transformed into a theater/odeum facility, see my section earlier in this chapter on the architecture of the Upper Temenos.

[2] Judith S. McKenzie's (1990:39ff) is the most comprehensive study to date on the architecture of Petra.

[3] First published by G.R.H. Wright (20-29); see also the discussion in McKenzie (1990:41, 134–135) plates 60-62.

[4] The Nabataeans were certainly not alone in promulgating this sort of iconographical propaganda. One only need glance at the Ara Pacis Augustae in Rome to see a similar scheme at work.

[5] Whether or not the Great Temple Complex is determined to be a temple precinct or the triclinium part of the palace complex of the Nabataean kings, this iconographic program of wealth and abundance is completely suitable. In addition, if this complex is part of the palace, then the figural relief panels would be serving an appropriate propagandistic function as divine patrons of the Nabataean kings, adorning the main building's façade; their presence would have been less appropriate for a temple façade.

# Bibliography

McKenzie, J.S.

    1990    *The Architecture of Petra.* Oxford: Oxford University Press.

Wright, G.R.H.

    1967-1968  "Recent Discoveries in the Sanctuary of the Qasr Bint Far'un at Petra: Some Aspects Concerning the Architecture and Sculpture," *ADAJ* 12-13:20-29.

CHAPTER SIX

# ARTIFACTS
## AND
# ARTIFACT DATABASES

*Plaque depicting Harpocrates.*

## ARTIFACT STUDIES AND DATABASES
Martha Sharp Joukowsky and Donna J. D'Agostino

## THE LAMPS
## OTHER SMALL FINDS
## THE COINS
Deirdre G. Barrett

## THE ROMAN AND BYZANTINE GLASS
Sara G. Karz

*Figure 6.1. Architectural fragments ready to be reburied at the end of the 1997 season.*

# ARTIFACT STUDIES AND DATABASES[1]

Martha Sharp Joukowsky and Donna J. D'Agostino[2]

The basic goal of an excavation is to collect and analyze as much data as accurately as possible. The process of excavation destroys so much of the evidence that it is therefore of paramount importance for the archaeologist to record as much as possible as accurately as possible. Unfortunately, archaeologists have two constraints that often render these two desiderata, "much" and "accurate," to be mutually exclusive.

Traditionally, archaeologists have excavated whilst armed with an elaborate arsenal of arcane manual measuring equipment and complicated forms, and in this we are no exception to the rule. The process of conducting measurements manually and recording the details in the excavators' unwieldy field notebooks is time consuming, tedious and subject to inaccuracies.

## Introduction

In this chapter we shall try to achieve three simple objectives:

1) To examine several of the more important artifact classification systems of the Great Temple;

2) To set these concepts against the phases of time they were in use;

3) To derive a concept of the Great Temple corpus of artifact traits as a frame of reference for the industries, most importantly, for the site itself, and, whenever possible, for the Great Temple's interrelationships with other sites.

One of our major responsibilities was to develop a process to capture our incoming artifact repertoire and, in particular, to lay out how we would be selecting priorities, matching them with available time constraints and ultimately implementing them. The broad goal of these efforts was to enhance all facets of the excavated artifact record. The strategic planning process evolved from a set of recommendations made by a six-person excavation committee over brown-bag lunches in the fall of 1992 and spring of 1993. These recommendations were determined after broad-based discussions had taken place involving all constituents of the excavation — field supervisors and artifact specialists. A series of items were then identified from these discussions and assigned to the appropriate staff members for further consideration. Priorities as well as analyses were completed and have been summarized in our databases.

We determined that it was essential to have a comprehensive control and study of all the artifacts found in every part of the Temple precinct, both those recovered from the surface and others through excavation. These mini-plans focusing on the artifact record incorporated the following artifact analysis: pottery, stone, bone, metal, numismatics, shell, stucco and vegetable matter. The study was governed by several interdependent factors: the staff had to undertake the analysis during excavation, a timesaving approach had to be conceived, and a system had to be devised that would capture the basic provenance data as well as vast amounts of information about the different materials collected. If possible, selected primary physical and functional characteristics would be recorded. Once the stratigraphy had been composed, a reassessment would be made by setting the artifact repertoire against the phasing.

## Computer Use

From its inception, computer application has been essential to every aspect of our field work. The excavation's computing equipment includes four laptop computers, plus a surveying computer for CAD mapping and Zip drives and Zip 100MB cartridges for storage. These computers are used for activities like word processing and data input. Although some sophisticated applications like database analysis have been done in the field, these applications generally have been completed at home on more powerful and dependable machines such as the Power Macintosh 7600/132.

Since the very start of the excavation, we have made extensive use of electronic surveying equipment that interfaces directly to computers. Using this system, we can survey thousands of points a day — an order of magnitude far greater and more accurate than we could have done using manual surveying tools. The ability to collect this amount of information has meant that we can record artifact and feature find spots more accurately.

Thus, almost all aspects of our fieldwork have been affected by computer technology. At the most basic level, the computer has allowed us to more effectively sift and organize the amounts of data that were accumulated during the typical excavation. For the three basic data functions — collection, analysis and dissemination of information — the computer has been of unprecedented help. At the Great Temple Excavations, we recorded the particulars of hundreds of thousands of architectural fragments, ceramic remains and small finds. Our interpretation of the site can only be accomplished through the careful analysis and comparison of this data.

## Database Development

In the following pages the processes and mechanics that governed these studies are presented. These are followed by a complete file of the results that can be accessed on the CD-ROM. Included here are the methodologies and computer use for 'Grosso Modo' and Architectural Fragments. We will, however, begin with a review of our computing hardware and the methodology involved with the field recording systems.

Besides the surveying data, we currently have six major site databases on line: 'Grosso Modo,' Architectural Fragments, Glass, Lamps and the Catalog, with a separate catalog for coins. Each of these files can be accessed on the CD-ROM in Chapter 6. The Grosso Modo and Architectural Fragments Databases were developed in 1993 and 1997, respectively. Before we started the 1995 season, we had already migrated the Grosso Modo input system to FileMaker Pro, thus most of our input for the 1994 season had been undertaken using this new system. In 1995 we developed the database for handling our growing catalog, with a separate catalog for coins. 1997 saw the inception of the Glass Database and the development of the Architectural Fragment Database. We will begin by briefly describing the Grosso Modo and Architectural Fragment Databases.

## Field Recording Systems

Our field input forms perform in two capacities; they serve as an outline for the range of information to be recorded by the excavator, and they serve as the first data input stage for the computer. These two roles have been visually distinguished from each other. The former role allows for a certain latitude in recording practices, while the latter demands a more systematic and consistent recording practice.

Well-understood conventions for the site field forms were employed for standard user interface elements. However, our early forms were cluttered with fields that were never filled in or were filled in rarely. These fields were distracting and made it easy to neglect fields that needed to be annotated. They also took up room that otherwise would have served for the expansion of those fields that were used more often. Thus, over time, we modified our input forms to better reflect the needs of the data. We needed to simplify and refine the forms and did so without sacrificing any of the functionality that we had in use. In fact, by simplifying the forms we were able to relate the disparate data collected in more sophisticated ways. There were three major kinds of revisions that were put into effect:

1) A common "header" allowed the various components of the excavation research, excavation, cataloging, surveying and data input to be more easily integrated;

2) Fields that required absolute consistency in their use were clearly identified and separated from fields that allowed free-form entry;

3) Fields that were to be commonly filled out were clearly distinguished from fields that were rarely filled out.

## Procedures — Sequence numbers

The plethora of different kinds of identifying factors (including the bucket number, bag number, field number, catalog number, trench or special project number and locus number) have one distinct identification scheme — the sequence number. Such a system was used for all elements of the excavation. Every field process and artifact record was uniquely identified by the sequence number.

The typical scenario was that once a trench was established, sequence numbers began with the first digits of the trench number; a Field Form and a Locus Form were filled out, each with their own distinct sequence number. The artifact collection container also was given its own sequence number. When an object was found, an Artifact Field Form was filled out with its sequence number. If the artifact was cataloged, it was assigned a catalog number dependent upon its material, but it still carried the sequence number, for this number was that object's field identification number. All architectural fragments were also assigned discrete sequence numbers. This provided a method for the excavators to safely assign unique identification numbers to all field procedures, i.e., loci as well as artifacts and architectural fragments.

This procedure also allowed us an understanding of the chronology of excavation events, and it was therefore easy to reconstruct the sequence of events in a specific locus or trench. One of the benefits of the sequence number system was that it was also easy to detect a missing sequence number, which among other things indicated missing paperwork, either during the excavation or when the field supervisor was writing a final report. Thus, during the excavation process the sequence number log was kept of these entries to avoid duplication of sequence numbers. This sequence number log provided the history for all the sequence numbers assigned, and any discrepancies between the sequence number log and the existing paperwork was easy to detect. Had

we been ambitious, the sequential reconstruction of the sequence of events for the entire excavation would have been possible!

## Methodology

An initial identification and definition of the artifact corpus was completed before the specific processing of individual materials began in 1993. Interdependently flexible project databases were designed along with inventorying procedures. As the excavations have progressed, new parameters have been established making data entry more efficient. Early studies of the artifacts from the site have revealed that, with the exception of a very few cases, most of the deposits were contaminated — the stratigraphic sequence was mixed.

## The Model

Therefore, the design of a new database consisted of two tables, linked by the unique sequence number. Out in the field, the materials were first recorded on paper. Each page (with its own unique sequence number) was then entered into the Petra Identification (ID) file by Monica L. Sylvester, aided by Elizabeth E. Payne and Martha S. Joukowsky. Behind the scenes, each piece of material that was entered in the ID record created a separate record in the Petra Materials file. (The ID file is menu driven, making it easy for anyone, even with little or no FileMaker experience, to enter data.) Manipulation of the data takes place on the Materials table, always driven from the ID file.

## The Grosso Modo Database

**Pottery:** The system for the recording of the bulk of finds is known as Grosso Modo, because we decided not to record detailed traits, such as ceramic ware colors and ware types. We did not plan to create formalized typologies for the various materials, for there would have been a duplication of effort. These typologies had already been put in place by Yvonne Gerber and Stephan G. Schmid for the pottery of Az-Zantur, the site located behind the Great Temple. At the close of each season, Great Temple trench supervisors selected the pottery deposits from loci they considered to be important or pottery they thought to be most significant for study by Yvonne Gerber for plain ceramics and Stephan G. Schmid for painted or decorated wares.

As far as the pottery was concerned, these analyses were limited to vessel type, shape, function and decoration. All the pottery was assumed to have been wheel-made, with the exception of the lamps and figurines, which were molded and in a few cases hand-modeled. Emphasis was also placed on decorative elements, such as slip and paint colors. No attempt was made to interpret wares in regard to their period of manufacture, with the exception of wares with known traits, e.g., Nabataean and terra sigillata wares.

## 1993-1995 — Development

The earliest database used to record Grosso Modo was created in Fourth Dimension by Geoffrey Bilder of the Scholarly Technology Group at Brown University. Data from material excavated in 1993 and 1994 were entered. In 1995, a new database was developed using FileMaker Pro v2.1. At that time FileMaker was only a flat-file database, meaning that, while the materials could be recorded in the computer, performing quantitative analysis on different groupings of the data was difficult and inefficient. Geoffrey Bilder planned to convert the flat-file database into a relational database he was developing in FoxPro. In the meantime, all 1995 and 1996 materials were entered into the FileMaker database.

By the fall of 1996, Geoffrey Bilder had left academic computing and Donna J. D'Agostino, currently of Northeastern University, Boston, MA, who had considerable FileMaker experience, assisted in analyzing the data we had gathered so far. After discussing the reports we had in mind, we concluded that the data needed to be converted to a relational format. We decided to continue using FileMaker, since its latest version at that time (3.0) was relational. This made the conversion relatively simple and allowed us to continue using an application that was fully supported by Brown University.

The first step consisted of two parts: the cleaning up of the current data and the creation of a new database. Throughout January and February 1997, we checked the 1994 and 1995 data for accuracy. Required fields were filled in; inconsistent labels were fixed; phasing was applied; records with duplicate sequence numbers were combined, and empty records were eliminated. The data from 1993 and 1994 was then imported into FileMaker, and all these records were checked in the same fashion. Data from each year was then merged into one file. Simultaneously, the new relational application was conceived and developed.

At the outset, many of the problems that we experienced with data collection were due to inadequate training of the excavators in the use of our systems. As we sought to improve the design of our field processing systems, we realized there were a number of things that we could do to make the input of site data faster, more accurate and more useful. The simplest procedure we instituted was to make sure that all the excavators met with the excavation director or assistant director for a tutorial on forms and the specifics of artifact analysis before each excavation season began. Thus, a demonstration session was held on site before the beginning of each season. An explanatory text key with codes was developed to make the system easier to "translate" for users. We, therefore, created a standard set of site abbreviations and developed the method for registering them. We also created a manual of site field recording guidelines, wherein field supervisors were given explicit instructions as to how to record.

In addition, in the case of Grosso Modo, we established a threshold for abbreviations. (In other words, now we allow only abbreviations for artifact types that number 100 or more. In a data set of over 115,000 categorized items, it did not make sense to include an abbreviation for an object type that numbered only 50.)

The explanatory text key with codes was developed to make the system easier to "translate" for the users. The following are the codes for Grosso Modo.

**ALL**

| | |
|---|---|
| Indeterminable | IND |
| Other | O |
| Unknown | UN |

**Material**

| | |
|---|---|
| Bone | B |
| Faience | F |
| Glass/Glass Slag | G |
| Stone | S |
| Metal | M |
| Pottery | P |
| Shell | SH |
| Vegetable Matter | Veg |
| Stucco/Plaster | ST |

**Part**

| | |
|---|---|
| Architectural Frag. | AF |
| Base | B |
| Bead | BD |
| Body Sherd | BS |
| Handle/Base | CHB |
| Handle/Neck | CHN |
| Hand./Neck/Rim | CHNR |
| Handle/Rim | CHR |
| Rim/Base | CRB |
| Rim/Neck | CRN |
| Spout/Base | CSB |
| Other composite | CD |
| Construction Mat. | CM |
| Discus | D |
| Handle | H |
| Lid | L |
| Neck | N |
| Rim | R |
| Spout | S |

**Function**

| | |
|---|---|
| Amphora | A |
| Amphoriskos | AS |
| Bowl | B |
| Canalization Tile | CT |
| Cooking Pot | CP |
| Decorative | D |
| Figurine | F |
| Floor Tile | FT |
| Glass Slag | GS |
| Hypocaust Tile | HT |

| | |
|---|---|
| Jar | JR |
| Jar/Jug | JJ |
| Jug | JG |
| Kiln Waster | KW |
| Lacrymatory | LY |
| Lamp | L |
| Lid | LD |
| Large Store Ves. | LSV |
| Loom Weight | LW |
| Mosaic | M |
| Nail | N |
| Opus Incertum | OI |
| Pipe | PP |
| Pithos | P |
| Plate | PLT |
| Roof Tile | RT |
| Small Form | SF |
| Spindle Whorl | SW |
| Stopper | SR |
| Tesserae | T |
| Unguentarium | U |
| Wall Tile | WT |

**Shape**

| | |
|---|---|
| Acanthus Leaf | AL |
| Button | B |
| Disc | D |
| Double-Stranded | DS |
| Everted | E |
| Flaring | FG |
| Flat | F |
| Floral | FL |
| Fluted | FD |
| Horizontal | H |
| Incurving | IG |
| Inverted | ID |
| Lug | LG |
| Ogee/pedestal | OP |
| Ovoid | OV |
| Pendant | PT |
| Plain Vertical | PV |
| Pointed | PD |
| Raised Banded | RB |
| Ring | RG |
| Rounded | RD |
| Squared-Off | SQ |
| String-cut | SC |
| T-Shaped | TS |
| Trefoil | T |
| Triangle | TE |

| | |
|---|---|
| Tubular | TR |
| Twisted | TW |
| Umbilical | U |

**Liquid & Paint Color**

| | |
|---|---|
| Black | BK |
| Blue | BE |
| Brown | BN |
| Glazed | GL |
| Gray | GY |
| Green | GN |
| Multi-colored | MC |
| Purple | P |
| Red | R |
| Salmon | S |
| Self-Same | SS |
| Tan | TN |
| Terra Sig. Black | TSB |
| Terra Sig. Red | TSR |
| Turquoise | T |
| White | W |
| Yellow | Y |

**Motif**

Write-in description

**Plastic Decoration**

| | |
|---|---|
| Appliqué | A |
| Excision | E |
| Impression | IM |
| Incision | IN |
| Molded | MD |
| Perforation | P |
| Ribbing | RG |
| Rouletting | R |

**Culture**

| | |
|---|---|
| Byzantine | B |
| Byzantine/Islamic | B/I |
| Classical | CL |
| Contemporary | CY |
| Crusader | CR |
| Edomite | E |
| Hellenistic | H |
| Islamic | I |
| Nabataean | N |
| Roman | R |
| Roman/Byzantine | R/B |
| Roman/Nabataean | R/N |

*Figure 6.2. Grosso Modo Codes.*

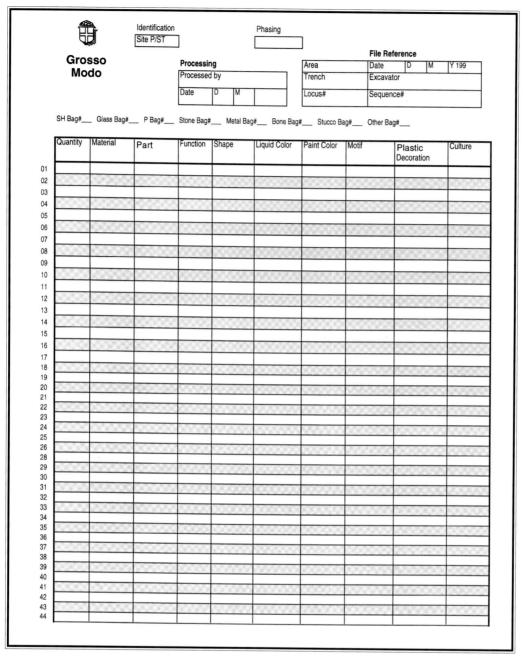

*Figure 6.3. Grosso Modo Form.*

In general, anything that we could do to simplify the forms aided the excavators in recording their finds. In short, with a few changes made in our procedures and the normalization of a few aspects of the recording process, we attempted to make a significant change in the speed, accuracy and quality of the data that we collected. There is as much consistency in reporting as possible.

**Processing:** After artifacts were cleaned and sorted, each artifact (or artifact group) was registered on the Grosso Modo Field Input Form (Figure 6.3) with the information

provided on the container (area, trench, locus, sequence number, date and excavator's initials). At the end of the day, these documents were transferred to an "in box" for computer encoding. The computer encoding form is shown in Figure 6.4. (It currently takes an average of 10 minutes to transcribe a Grosso Modo Form to the computer.)[3]

The encoding, therefore, was handled on a daily basis, and once the data from the original input form was entered, the form was then returned to the trench supervisor for insertion in the field notebook. Thus, in the on-site

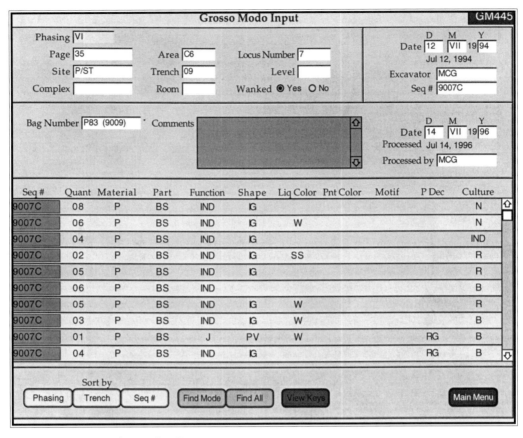

*Figure 6.4. Grosso Modo Encoding Form.*

*Figure 6.5. Grosso Modo Reports Generated.*

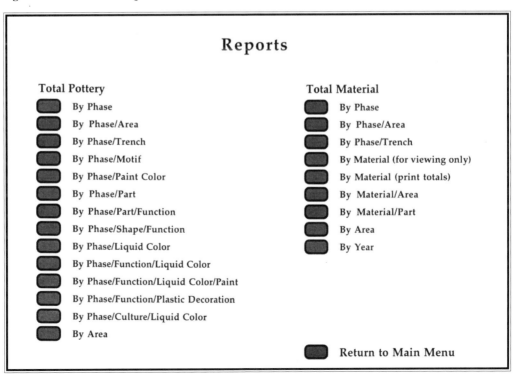

| Material | Total | Percent |
|---|---|---|
| Bone | 7,347 | 6.30% |
| Eggshell | 135 | 0.10% |
| Metal | 1,151 | 1.00% |
| Pottery | 90,788 | 78.40% |
| Stone | 7,682 | 6.60% |
| Shell | 501 | 0.40% |
| Stucco/Plaster | 8,091 | 7.00% |
| Wood | 47 | 0.00% |
| | 115,742 | 100.00% |

**Total Material**

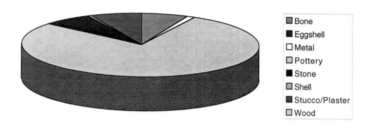

*Figure 6.6. Total Material.*

*Figure 6.7. Material by Phase.*

| Phase | Bone | Eggshell | Metal | Pottery | Shell | Stone | Stucco | Wood | Grand Total |
|---|---|---|---|---|---|---|---|---|---|
| I | 135 | 0 | 7 | 3,924 | 3 | 1 | 220 | 0 | 4,290 |
| | 0.10% | 0.00% | 0.00% | 3.40% | 0.00% | 0.00% | 0.20% | 0.00% | 3.70% |
| II | 374 | 0 | 21 | 4,276 | 5 | 51 | 955 | 0 | 5,682 |
| | 0.30% | 0.00% | 0.00% | 3.70% | 0.00% | 0.00% | 0.80% | 0.00% | 4.80% |
| III | 712 | 0 | 58 | 5,342 | 9 | 108 | 1,424 | 0 | 7,653 |
| | 0.60% | 0.00% | 0.10% | 4.60% | 0.00% | 0.10% | 1.20% | 0.00% | 6.60% |
| IV | 1,007 | 18 | 393 | 7,777 | 20 | 1,167 | 451 | 44 | 10,877 |
| | 0.90% | 0.00% | 0.30% | 6.70% | 0.00% | 1.00% | 0.40% | 0.00% | 9.30% |
| V | 557 | 0 | 130 | 3,059 | 13 | 261 | 558 | 0 | 4,578 |
| | 0.50% | 0.00% | 0.10% | 2.60% | 0.00% | 0.20% | 0.50% | 0.00% | 3.90% |
| VI | 4,562 | 117 | 542 | 66,410 | 451 | 6,094 | 4,483 | 3 | 82,662 |
| | 3.90% | 0.10% | 0.50% | 57.40% | 0.40% | 5.30% | 3.90% | 0.00% | 71.50% |

excavation headquarters, the person in charge of computer entry checked for inconsistencies in the records and entered the data directly into the computer. This system provided the field supervisor with the ability to generate timely statistics and reports to determine if there were any changes taking place in the artifact record.

The Grosso Modo Database has evolved extensively over the past few years[4] and has been used to account for approximately 115,742 entries. This database is the most structurally complicated of the databases that we have. Each Grosso Modo Form must be split into two tables, in order for the data to be analyzed adequately. The first table contains the "header" information of a form (sequence number, dates, excavators, trench/locus), while the second entry table contains records representing each "entry line" on the Grosso Modo Form. These two tables are linked by the sequence number field.

Additionally, we created templates for generating trench/locus reports on function, part and materials found. These reports have been imported into Microsoft Excel for the charting and graphing of results.

Finally, the Grosso Modo key database is kept in FileMaker Pro, and Grosso Modo attribute codes can be produced from within FileMaker itself.

## Reporting

A number of reports were produced to show the quantitative analysis of all materials grouped and sorted in various ways. All the Grosso Modo reports can be found on the CD-ROM; however, the types of reports generated can be found in Figure 6.5. The goal was to determine if there was any significance in the numbers when grouped one way versus another. Scripts were developed to search, group, sort and summarize each combination of groupings, and they were then added to a report menu on the ID file. Each report could be run at the press of a button and would generate up-to-date figures within seconds.

By March 1996, we were ready to import the data into the new database. Once this was completed, we generated the reports and were finally able to see the quantitative results of the last four years of excavations.

| Area | Material | Total | % |
|------|----------|-------|---|
| **LAP** | | | |
| | Bone | 423 | 7.7% |
| | Pottery | 4,851 | 88.2% |
| | Shell | 3 | 0.1% |
| | Stone | 2 | 0.0% |
| | Stucco/Plaster | 222 | 4.0% |
| | | 5,501 | 4.8% |
| **LT** | | | |
| | Bone | 3,054 | 5.6% |
| | Eggshell | 117 | 0.2% |
| | Metal | 192 | 0.4% |
| | Pottery | 46,547 | 85.5% |
| | Shell | 206 | 0.4% |
| | Stone | 1,920 | 3.5% |
| | Stucco/Plaster | 2,388 | 4.4% |
| | | 54,424 | 47.0% |
| **P** | | | |
| | Bone | 21 | 2.2% |
| | Metal | 8 | 0.8% |
| | Pottery | 382 | 39.4% |
| | Shell | 2 | 0.2% |
| | Stone | 490 | 50.6% |
| | Stucco/Plaster | 66 | 6.8% |
| | | 969 | 0.8% |
| **T** | | | |
| | Bone | 2,277 | 8.9% |
| | Eggshell | 18 | 0.1% |
| | Metal | 851 | 3.3% |
| | Pottery | 15,223 | 59.2% |
| | Shell | 21 | 0.1% |
| | Stone | 3,297 | 12.8% |
| | Stucco/Plaster | 3,995 | 15.5% |
| | Wood | 45 | 0.2% |
| | | 25,727 | 22.2% |
| **UT** | | | |
| | Bone | 1,572 | 5.4% |
| | Metal | 100 | 0.3% |
| | Pottery | 23,785 | 81.7% |
| | Shell | 269 | 0.9% |
| | Stone | 1,973 | 6.8% |
| | Stucco/Plaster | 1,420 | 4.9% |
| | Wood | 2 | 0.0% |
| | | 29,121 | 25.2% |
| **Total:** | | **115,742** | |

*Figure 6.8. Material by Area.*

| Phase | Area | Material | Total | % | Phase | Area | Material | Total | % |
|---|---|---|---|---|---|---|---|---|---|
| I | | | | | III | LAP | | | |
| I | LAP | | | | | | Bone | 74 | 13.2% |
| | | Bone | 100 | 14.7% | | | Pottery | 487 | 86.8% |
| | | Pottery | 468 | 68.6% | | | | 561 | 7.3% |
| | | Shell | 1 | 0.1% | III | LT | | | |
| | | Stucco/Plaster | 113 | 16.6% | | | Bone | 335 | 9.4% |
| | | | 682 | 15.9% | | | Metal | 4 | 0.1% |
| I | LT | | | | | | Pottery | 2,982 | 83.4% |
| | | Bone | 35 | 3.5% | | | Stone | 71 | 2.0% |
| | | Metal | 2 | 0.2% | | | Shell | 7 | 0.2% |
| | | Pottery | 956 | 95.8% | | | Stucco/Plaster | 177 | 4.9% |
| | | Shell | 2 | 0.2% | | | | 3,576 | 46.7% |
| | | Stucco/Plaster | 3 | 0.3% | III | T | | | |
| | | | 998 | 23.3% | | | Bone | 303 | 9.5% |
| I | T | | | | | | Metal | 50 | 1.6% |
| | | Metal | 5 | 0.3% | | | Pottery | 1,569 | 49.0% |
| | | Pottery | 1,478 | 95.5% | | | Stone | 36 | 1.1% |
| | | Stone | 1 | 0.1% | | | Shell | 1 | 0.0% |
| | | Stucco/Plaster | 64 | 4.1% | | | Stucco/Plaster | 1,246 | 38.9% |
| | | | 1,548 | 36.1% | | | | 3,205 | 41.9% |
| I | UT | | | | III | UT | | | |
| | | Pottery | 1,022 | 96.2% | | | Metal | 4 | 1.3% |
| | | Stucco/Plaster | 40 | 3.8% | | | Pottery | 304 | 97.7% |
| | | | 1,062 | 24.8% | | | Stone | 1 | 0.3% |
| | | *Phase I Total:* | *4,290* | *3.7%* | | | Shell | 1 | 0.3% |
| II | | | | | | | Stucco/Plaster | 1 | 0.3% |
| II | LT | | | | | | | 311 | 4.1% |
| | | Bone | 316 | 7.6% | | | *Phase III Total:* | *7,653* | *6.6%* |
| | | Metal | 20 | 0.5% | IV | | | | |
| | | Pottery | 3,257 | 77.9% | IV | LAP | | | |
| | | Stone | 47 | 1.1% | | | Bone | 230 | 7.2% |
| | | Shell | 4 | 0.1% | | | Pottery | 2,962 | 92.4% |
| | | Stucco/Plaster | 538 | 12.9% | | | Stone | 1 | 0.0% |
| | | | 4,182 | 73.6% | | | Stucco/Plaster | 11 | 0.3% |
| II | T | | | | | | | 3,204 | 29.5% |
| | | Bone | 58 | 5.7% | IV | LT | | | |
| | | Pottery | 530 | 52.5% | | | Bone | 1 | 0.3% |
| | | Stone | 4 | 0.4% | | | Metal | 3 | 0.9% |
| | | Shell | 1 | 0.1% | | | Pottery | 318 | 96.1% |
| | | Stucco/Plaster | 417 | 41.3% | | | Stone | 5 | 1.5% |
| | | | 1,010 | 17.8% | | | Shell | 1 | 0.3% |
| II | UT | | | | | | Stucco/Plaster | 3 | 0.9% |
| | | Metal | 1 | 0.2% | | | | 331 | 3.0% |
| | | Pottery | 489 | 99.8% | IV | T | | | |
| | | | 490 | 8.6% | | | Bone | 363 | 6.6% |
| | | *Phase II Total:* | *5,682* | *4.9%* | | | Eggshell | 18 | 0.3% |
| III | | | | | | | Metal | 364 | 6.6% |

*Figure 6.9. Material by Phase and Area.*

| Phase | Area | Material | Total | % | Phase | Area | Material | Total | % |
|---|---|---|---|---|---|---|---|---|---|
| | | Pottery | 3,490 | 63.6% | VI | LT | | | |
| | | Stone | 923 | 16.8% | | | Bone | 2,313 | 5.2% |
| | | Shell | 5 | 0.1% | | | Eggshell | 117 | 0.3% |
| • | | Stucco/Plaster | 278 | 5.1% | | | Metal | 161 | 0.4% |
| | | Wood | 44 | 0.8% | | | Pottery | 38,705 | 86.2% |
| | | | 5,485 | 50.4% | | | Stone | 1,763 | 3.9% |
| IV | UT | | | | | | Shell | 186 | 0.4% |
| | | Bone | 413 | 22.2% | | | Stucco/Plaster | 1,665 | 3.7% |
| | | Metal | 26 | 1.4% | | | | 44,910 | 54.3% |
| | | Pottery | 1,007 | 54.2% | VI | P | | | |
| | | Stone | 238 | 12.8% | | | Bone | 21 | 2.2% |
| | | Shell | 14 | 0.8% | | | Metal | 8 | 0.8% |
| | | Stucco/Plaster | 159 | 8.6% | | | Pottery | 382 | 39.4% |
| | | | 1,857 | 17.1% | | | Stone | 490 | 50.6% |
| | | Phase IV Total: | 10,877 | 9.4% | | | Shell | 2 | 0.2% |
| V | | | | | | | Stucco/Plaster | 66 | 6.8% |
| V | LT | | | | | | | 969 | 1.2% |
| | | Bone | 54 | 12.6% | VI | T | | | |
| | | Metal | 2 | 0.5% | | | Bone | 1,135 | 10.3% |
| | | Pottery | 329 | 77.0% | | | Metal | 306 | 2.8% |
| | | Stone | 34 | 8.0% | | | Pottery | 5,978 | 54.1% |
| | | Shell | 6 | 1.4% | | | Stone | 2,169 | 19.6% |
| | | Stucco/Plaster | 2 | 0.5% | | | Shell | 10 | 0.1% |
| | | | 427 | 9.3% | | | Stucco/Plaster | 1,448 | 13.1% |
| V | T | | | | | | Wood | 1 | 0.0% |
| | | Bone | 418 | 12.2% | | | | 11,047 | 13.4% |
| | | Metal | 126 | 3.7% | VI | UT | | | |
| | | Pottery | 2,178 | 63.5% | | | Bone | 1,074 | 4.4% |
| | | Stone | 164 | 4.8% | | | Metal | 67 | 0.3% |
| | | Shell | 4 | 0.1% | | | Pottery | 20,411 | 82.7% |
| | | Stucco/Plaster | 542 | 15.8% | | | Stone | 1,671 | 6.8% |
| | | | 3,432 | 75.0% | | | Shell | 251 | 1.0% |
| V | UT | | | | | | Stucco/Plaster | 1,206 | 4.9% |
| | | Bone | 85 | 11.8% | | | Wood | 2 | 0.0% |
| | | Metal | 2 | 0.3% | | | | 24,682 | 29.9% |
| | | Pottery | 552 | 76.8% | | | Phase VI Total: | 82,662 | 71.4% |
| | | Stone | 63 | 8.8% | | | | | |
| | | Shell | 3 | 0.4% | | | Total : | 115,742 | |
| | | Stucco/Plaster | 14 | 1.9% | | | | | |
| | | | 719 | 15.7% | | | | | |
| | | Phase V Total: | 4,578 | 4.0% | | | | | |
| VI | | | | | | | | | |
| VI | LAP | | | | | | | | |
| | | Bone | 19 | 1.8% | | | | | |
| | | Pottery | 934 | 88.6% | | | | | |
| | | Stone | 1 | 0.1% | | | | | |
| | | Shell | 2 | 0.2% | | | | | |
| | | Stucco/Plaster | 98 | 9.3% | | | | | |
| | | | 1,054 | 1.3% | | | | | |

| Phase | Total | Percent |
|---|---|---|
| I | 3,924 | 4.30% |
| II | 4,276 | 4.70% |
| III | 5,342 | 5.90% |
| IV | 7,777 | 8.60% |
| V | 3,059 | 3.40% |
| VI | 66,410 | 73.10% |
| | 90,788 | 100.00% |

### Pottery by Phase

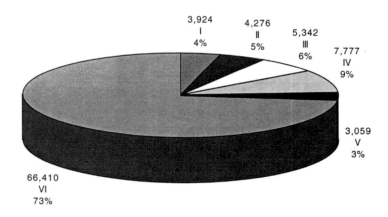

*Figure 6.10. Pottery by Phase.*

*Figure 6.11. Pottery by Area.*

| Area | Total | Percent |
|---|---|---|
| Lapidary | 4,851 | 5.30% |
| Lower Temenos | 46,547 | 51.30% |
| Propylaeum | 382 | 0.40% |
| Temple | 15,223 | 16.80% |
| Upper Temenos | 23,785 | 26.20% |
| | 90,788 | 100.00% |

### Pottery by Area

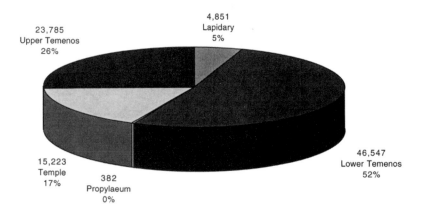

## Grosso Modo Results

As far as the materials by year, 1995 represents 31% of the materials and 1997 27% of all the materials registered.

Figure 6.6 presents the frequency of results of the 115,742 artifact materials entered in the Grosso Modo Database. Pottery accounts for the bulk of the artifacts, representing 78%; stucco/plaster represents 7%, and stone artifacts account for 6.6%. Figure 6.7 presents the materials by phase, and as would be expected, Phase VI accounts for 71%, followed by Phase IV, which has 9.3% or 10,877 artifacts registered. Pottery represents 71% of this Phase IV assemblage; bone accounts for 9% and stone for 10%.

In Figure 6.8 is a frequency of occurrence of all artifact materials by area, and Figure 6.9 gives the frequency of occurrence by phase and area.

**Pottery:** Figure 6.10 gives the frequency of occurrence of the pottery by phase, and again, Phase VI is represented by 73% of the pottery collected, with Phase IV representing 8.5%.

In Figure 6.11 is a frequency of occurrence of all the pottery by area, and Figure 6.12 gives the frequency of occurrence by area and phase.

For the frequency of pottery by trench, for Phase I, Temple, Trench 40 represents 38% of the pottery, with the Lower Temenos, Trench 18 accounting for 23%. SP 4 of the Lower Temenos also represents 25%.

In Phase II, Trench 42 of the Lower Temenos represents 37% of the phase. Also in the Lower Temenos, Trench 18 represents 14%, Trench 21 10%, SP 4 11% and SP 20 8%. Thus, in combining the trenches for the Lower Temenos, the ceramics from here represent 80% of this phase.

Phase III is represented with its greatest counts of ceramics excavated from the Lower Temenos, Trenches 17 and 20, each representing 27% or a combined 54% of the phase. SP 25, the sondage in Trench 17, represents 18% of this phase's pottery, accounting for 72% of the registry.

The majority of Phase IV sherds come from Trench 7 of the Lapidary West. These account for 38% of the phase total. In Trench 22 of the Temple West, there is a 32% representation, and Trench 41 of the Upper Temenos has 13%.

In Phase V, Temple trenches had the highest frequency of pottery (Trench 26 20%, Trench 22 18%, Trench 47 16% and Trench 27 5.6%). Combined, these represent 60% of the ceramics for this phase.

As would be expected, Phase VI is a highly polluted sample, because it contains the uppermost strata of all the site trenches excavated. The highest percentage, or 10%, of the pottery in this phase is found in Trench 5 of the Lower Temenos, but the combined percentages of the Lower Temenos, Trenches 16, 17, 18 and 18A is 23%. When combined

| Phase | Area | Total | % |
|---|---|---:|---:|
| **I** | | | |
| | LAP | 468 | 11.9% |
| | LT | 956 | 24.4% |
| | T | 1,478 | 37.7% |
| | UT | 1,022 | 26.0% |
| | | *3,924* | *4.3%* |
| **II** | | | |
| | LT | 3,257 | 76.2% |
| | T | 530 | 12.4% |
| | UT | 489 | 11.4% |
| | | *4,276* | *4.7%* |
| **III** | | | |
| | LAP | 487 | 9.1% |
| | LT | 2,982 | 55.8% |
| | T | 1,569 | 29.4% |
| | UT | 304 | 5.7% |
| | | *5,342* | *5.9%* |
| **IV** | | | |
| | LAP | 2,962 | 38.1% |
| | LT | 318 | 4.1% |
| | T | 3,490 | 44.9% |
| | UT | 1,007 | 12.9% |
| | | *7,777* | *8.6%* |
| **V** | | | |
| | LT | 329 | 10.8% |
| | T | 2,178 | 71.2% |
| | UT | 552 | 18.0% |
| | | *3,059* | *3.4%* |
| **VI** | | | |
| | LAP | 934 | 1.4% |
| | LT | 38,705 | 58.3% |
| | P | 382 | 0.6% |
| | T | 5,978 | 9.0% |
| | UT | 20,411 | 30.7% |
| | | *66,410* | *73.1%* |
| *Total :* | | **90,788** | |

*Figure 6.12. Pottery by Phase and Area.*

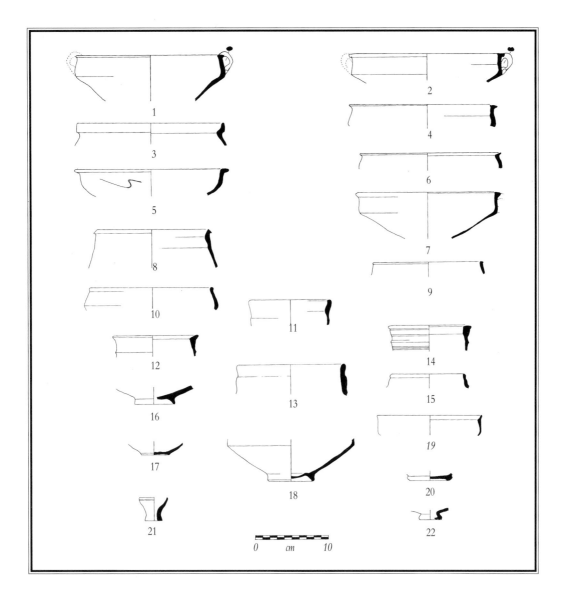

**Figure 6.13**

*Figure 6.13.*
*Lower Temenos, Trench 20, Locus 25, Sequence numbers 210, 215, July 19-20, 1995.*

1. Bowl. Light red 2.5YR 6/8 ware, exterior upper body flaky, pink white 7.5YR 8/2 slip, core light gray, slightly uneven.

2. Bowl. Light red 2.5YR 6/8 ware, white 10YR 8/2 slip over top of body, gray core.

3. Bowl. Light red 2.5YR 6/8 ware, exterior pinkish white 7.5YR slip, even core.

4. Bowl. Light reddish brown 2.5YR 6/6 ware, exterior pink 5YR 7/4 slip, core slightly gray on the interior.

5. Bowl. Red 2.5YR 5/8 ware, exterior white 10YR 8/2 slip, exterior shoulder excised with wave design, core even.

6. Bowl. Reddish yellow 5YR 7/8 ware, exterior-interior pink 5YR 8/4 slip, even core.

7. Bowl. Light red 2.5YR 6/8 ware, exterior upper body white 10YR 8/2 slip, even core.

8. Jar/Jug. Light red 2.5YR 6/8 ware, exterior pink 5YR 8/3 slip, few large limestone inclusions, even core.

9. Bowl. Red 10R 5/8 ware, pinkish white 5YR 8/2 slip over exterior, even core.

10. Bowl. Brown 7.5YR 5/2 ware, interior-exterior self-same slip, even core.

11. Jar/Jug. Light red 2.5YR 6/8 ware, reddish brown slip over exterior and interior rim, even core.

12. Jar/Jug. Reddish yellow 5YR 6/8 ware, pink 5YR 8/3 slip interior-exterior, even core.

13. Jar/Jug. Light red 2.5YR 6/8 ware, reddish yellow 5YR 7/8 wash over exterior and partial interior, even core.

14. Jar/jug. Brown 7.5YR 5/4 ware, self-same slip, even core.

15. Bowl. Reddish yellow 5YR 6/8 ware, interior-exterior pinkish white 5YR 8/2 slip wash, even core.

16. Bowl base. Light red 2.5YR 6/8 ware, exterior self-same slip, discolored to a brown 7.5YR 5/4, core even.

17. Bowl base. Light red 2.5YR 6/8 ware, gray core.

18. Bowl base. Light red 2.5YR 6/6 ware, exterior body pink 7.5YR 8/4 slip, core slightly gray.

19. Bowl. Light red 10R 6/6 ware, pink 7.5YR 8/4 slip exterior, even core.

20. Base. Light red 2.5YR 6/8 ware, self-same slip, even core.

21. String-cut base. Light red 2.5YR 6/8 ware, exterior pinkish white 5YR 8/2 slip wash, even core.

22. Base. Light red 2.5YR 6/8 ware, self-same slip, gray core.

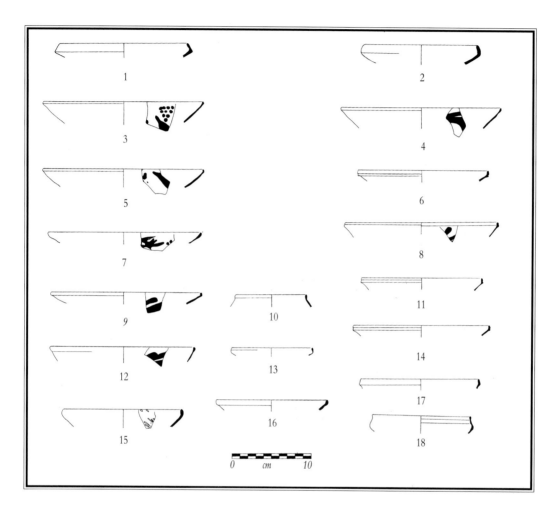

*Figure 6.14*

*Figure 6.14.*
*Lower Temenos, Trench 20, Locus 25, Sequence numbers 210, 215, July 19–20, 1995.*

1. Bowl. Reddish yellow 5YR 8/4 ware, self-same slip, streaked pinkish gray paint on exterior rim, even core.

2. Bowl. Light red 2.5YR 6/8 ware, streaked weak red 2.5YR paint around rim, even core.

3. Bowl. Light red 2.5YR 6/8 ware, interior weak red 10R 5/2 paint, even core.

4. Bowl. Light red 2.5YR 6/8 ware, interior weak red 10R 5/2 paint, even core.

5. Bowl. Light red 10R 6/8 ware, white 10YR 8/2 slip over top of exterior rim flaked-off, interior weak red 10R 5/3 paint, even core.

6. Bowl. Light red 2.5YR 6/8 ware, self-same slip, even core.

7. Bowl. Reddish yellow 5YR 6/8 ware, exterior-interior pink 5YR 8/4 slip-wash, interior painted with pinkish gray 5YR 6/2 design, even core.

8. Bowl. Light red 10R 6/8 ware, exterior rim painted in pink 5YR 8/3, interior dark reddish gray 5YR 4/2 paint, even core.

9. Bowl. Red 10R 5/8 ware, light red slip wash 10R 6/6 over top of exterior rim, interior weak red 10R 5/2.

10. Bowl. Brown 7.5YR 5/4 ware, interior-exterior pinkish white 7.5YR 8/2 slip, even core.

11. Bowl. Light red 10R 6/8 ware, traces of light red 10R 6/6 paint on exterior rim, even core.

12. Bowl. Light red 2.5YR 6/8 ware, white 10YR 8/2 slip over top of exterior rim, interior weak red 10R 5/2 paint, even core.

13. Bowl. Red 2.5YR 5/8 ware, pink 7.5YR 8/4 slip exterior rim, even core.

14. Bowl. Light red 2.5YR 6/8 ware, red 10R 5/8 slip over top of exterior rim, even core.

15. Bowl. Light red 10R 6/8 ware, interior and over top of interior rim light red 10R 6/6 paint feather design, even core.

16. Bowl. Light red 2.5YR 6/8, white 10YR 8/2 slip over top of exterior rim, interior weak red 10R 5/2 paint, even core.

17. Bowl. Light red 2.5YR 6/8, white 10YR 8/2 slip over top of exterior rim, even core.

18. Bowl. Light red 2.5YR 6/8 ware, vestiges of pinkish white 7.5YR 8/2 slip, even core.

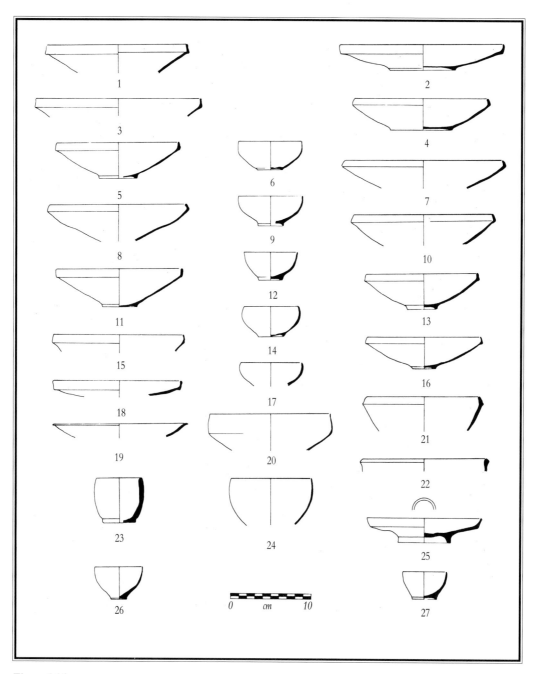

*Figure 6.15*

*Figure 6.15.*
*Trench 42, Locus 24, 6-VII-97.*

1. Bowl. Light red 2.5YR 6/8 ware, pinkish white 5YR 8/2 slip-wash around exterior rim, even core.

2. Bowl. Reddish brown 5YR 5/3 ware, pinkish gray interior-exterior 5YR 6/2 slip, even reddish brown core.

3. Bowl or lid. Red 2.5YR 5/8 ware, self-same slip, pale red 2.5YR 6/2 painted band on exterior rim, even core.

4. Bowl. Red 2.5YR 5/8 ware, interior-exterior pink 5YR 7/3 slip, even core.

5. Bowl. Reddish yellow 5YR 6/8 ware, self-same slip, pink 5YR 8/3 band exterior rim, even core.

6. Cup. Light red 2.5YR 6/8 ware, interior-exterior self-same slip, uneven core.

7. Bowl. Light red 2.5YR 6/8 ware, self-same slip, weak red 2.5YR 5/2 painted band rim exterior, uneven core.

8. Bowl. Light red 2.5YR 6/8 ware, pink 5YR 8/3 paint exterior rim, uneven core.

9. Cup. Reddish yellow 5YR 7/8 ware, self-same slip, even core.

10. Bowl. Light red 2.5YR 6/8 ware, pink 5YR 8/3 paint exterior rim, even core.

11. Bowl. Red 2.5YR 5/8 ware, interior-exterior pink 5YR 7/3 slip, pale red paint 2.5YR 6/2 around exterior rim, even core.

12. Cup. Light red 2.5YR 6/8 ware, self-same slip, even core.

13. Bowl. Brown 7.5YR 5/2 ware, interior-exterior light brownish gray 10YR 6/2 slip, painted very pale brown 10YR 8/3 band exterior rim and top of exterior body, even brown core.

14. Cup. Reddish brown 2.5YR 5/4 ware, even core.

15. Bowl. Light red 2.5YR 6/8 ware, interior-exterior self-same slip, even core.

16. Bowl. Reddish gray 5YR 5/2 ware, interior-exterior gray 5YR 6/1 slip, pinkish white 5YR 8/2 paint on exterior rim, even core.

17. Cup. Reddish yellow 5YR 7/8 ware, pinkish white 5YR 8/2 slip-wash around exterior rim, even core.

18. Bowl. Red 2.5YR 5/8 ware, pale red 2.5YR 6/2 painted band on exterior rim, even core.

19. Bowl or lid. Red 2.5YR 5/8 ware, self-same slip, pale red 2.5YR 6/2 painted band on exterior rim, even core.

20. Bowl. Light red 2.5YR 6/8 ware, self-same slip, even core.

21. Bowl. Light red 2.5YR 6/8 ware, even core.

22. Bowl. Light red 2.5YR 6/8 ware, very pale brown 10YR 8/3 wash slip interior-exterior, even core.

23. Molded cup. Light red 2.5YR 6/8 ware, discolored light red 10R 6/6 slip, even core.

24. Cup. Red 2.5YR 5/8 ware, very pale brown 10YR 8/3 wash slip interior and partial exterior, even core.

25. Green plate. Pinkish gray 7.5YR 7/2 ware, interior exterior pale olive 5Y 6/3 worn-off glaze with green bubbles, even core. Incised double circles on interior base, raised plastic band at base of exterior rim, which in part has broken away.

26. Cup. Pinkish gray 5YR 7/2, self-same slip interior-exterior, even core.

27. Cup. Pink 5YR 7/3 ware, self-same slip, discolored core.

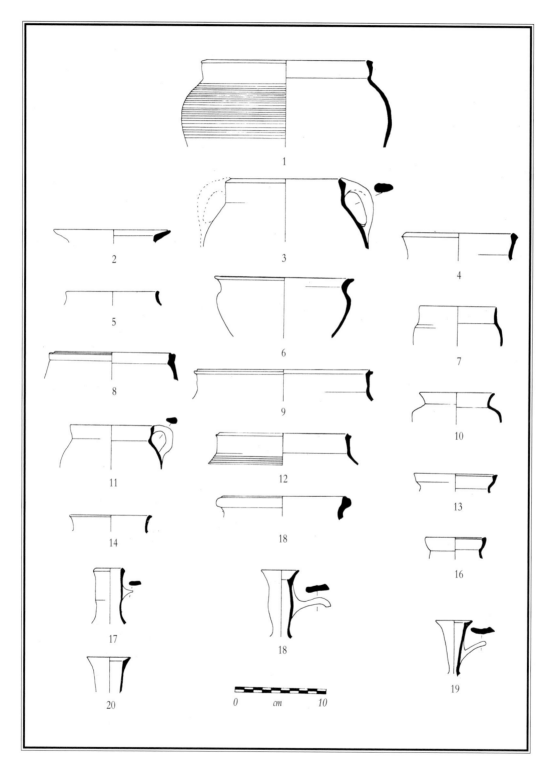

*Figure 6.16*

*Figure 6.16.*
*Trench 42, Locus 24, 6-VII-97.*

1. Cooking pot. Red 2.5YR 5/8 ware, exterior 5YR 7/3 pink slip, even core.

2. Bowl. Light red 2.5YR 6/8 ware, very pale brown 10YR 8/3 slip on exterior, even core.

3. Cooking pot. Red 2.5YR 5/8 ware, very pale brown 10YR 8/3 wash-slip exterior, ribbed body, even core.

4. Jar. Red 2.5YR 5/8 ware, exterior 10YR 8/3 very pale brown slip, even core.

5. Bowl. Reddish yellow 5YR 6/8 ware, white 10YR 8/2 slip on exterior and over top of rim, even core.

6. Bowl. Red 2.5YR 5/8 ware, exterior 10YR 8/3 very pale brown wash-slip, even core.

7. Bowl. Red 2.5YR 5/8 ware, self-same slip, even core.

8. Bowl. Reddish yellow 5YR 7/8 ware, white 10YR 8/2 slip on exterior, even core.

9. Bowl. Reddish yellow 5YR 7/8 ware, even core.

10. Bowl or jug. Light red 2.5YR 6/8 ware, pale red 2.5YR 6/2 wash on exterior, self-same slip interior, even core.

11. Cooking pot/work pot. Red 2.5YR 5/8 ware, exterior-interior 7.5YR 5/2 brown slip, even core.

12. Cooking pot. Light red 2.5YR 6/8 ware, very pale brown 10YR 8/3 wash-slip interior-exterior, even core.

13. Jug. Red 2.5YR 5/8 ware, very pale brown 10YR 8/3 wash-slip interior-exterior, even core.

14. Jug or Bowl. Light red 2.5YR 6/8 ware, interior-exterior 7.5YR 8/4 pink slip, even core.

15. Bowl. Light red 2.5YR 6/8 ware, pale red 2.5YR 6/2 wash on interior and partial exterior, even core.

16. Jug. Red 2.5YR 5/6 ware, very pale brown 10YR 8/3 slip on exterior, even core.

17. Jug. Dark reddish gray 10R 4/1 ware, interior-exterior very pale brown 10YR 8/3 slip, even black core.

18. Jug. Light red 2.5YR 6/8 ware, very pale brown 10YR 8/3 slip exterior and interior rim, even core.

19. Jug. Light red 2.5YR 6/8 ware, interior-exterior self-same slip, even core.

20. Jug. Reddish yellow 5YR 7/8 ware, even core.

with other Lower Temenos trenches, the results are that 46.7% of the pottery is represented as coming from this area.

## Grosso Modo Problems

We face two problems with the Grosso Modo system as it works now.

1) Currently, any reports and/or statistics that we derived from the early Grosso Modo data varied a great deal in their usefulness, for at that time individual excavators varied a great deal in their expertise and in the quality of their Grosso Modo observations. In 1993, we assigned one or two people to be exclusively responsible for recording all Grosso Modo finds, but thereafter site supervisors and their assistant excavators recorded Grosso Modo. Having two people responsible for all Grosso Modo categorization would have allowed us to expect greater consistency in our Grosso Modo data, but it was impractical.

2) Initially we had undermined our ability to generate useful statistics and reports, because we over refined our categorization schemes. As an example, even in the best of circumstances it was difficult to tell if a sherd was "white," "off-white," "gray," "tan" or "cream," and we could hardly trust the various excavator's interpretations of these colors. What this means is that it was unlikely that we might generate any meaningful reports based on the "liquid color" or "paint color" fields. Therefore, in order to generate useful and accurate information from the above fields, we faced a case where "less was more." It saved time (categorizing) and was more useful, for instead of endlessly subdividing and refining the categorization schemes in these fields, we designated a handful of broad ranges to choose from. Adopting the policy of consolidating (rather than refining) the codes that applied for each field sped up input, provided us with more reliable and useful statistics and was more in keeping with the theory behind the Grosso Modo system.

## Current Work

Over the 1997 field season, new materials were entered into an empty file that had been prepared for the field. These 1997 field results were imported into the master file in October 1997. Additionally, since the site had been assigned new phases, this information was recalculated. We then exported cumulative summaries into Excel spreadsheets for the graphic representation of our assemblages.

All the pottery from these sealed contexts has been bagged and saved; however, for the corpus as a whole, undecorated body sherds have been discarded. At present, the Petra Great Temple pottery fragments and the stucco and stone fragments are stored in crates in a sondage on the site. The bone has been moved to Amman, where it is in dry storage, and metal objects have been stored at Petra with the Jordanian Department of Antiquities.

The drawing of a small, selected representative sample of pottery was dependent on those deposits that were sealed and closed. The building and its complex underwent a series of restorations and rebuildings, which we were not able to define both from the stratigraphy and the pottery groups. Since there are so few of these, only the drawing and description of a few deposits have been undertaken by Martha S. Joukowsky; a representative sample of these are presented in Figures 6.13-6.16.

## Conclusion

Other sites share in the potting traditions of the Great Temple. Intersite relationships are a vital component for a site report. In Petra, we are just beginning to target this kind of information to link up excavated sequences securely. (In our Great Temple *Final Report*, we will hope to draw heavily on analogies of excavated material from Petra at large and from other sites.)

**ARCHITECTURAL FRAGMENT FORM** Page_____

**P/ST**_________ Seq.#________ Grid_______Area: P/LT/UT/T Trench______ Locus___

D M

Surface___ Date: 199 Excavator(s)_________

**Material:** limestone __ sandstone__ marble__ porphyry__ stucco__ mortar__ other_________

**Dimensions:** Ht.________Diam._______ Length________ Width_______ Thickness_______

**Composition:** carved__carved & incised__ dressed__ dressed diagonally__ incised__ molded_ bossed__ bossed & drafted__ painted__mason's mark__ unknown__ other__

**Feature:** ashlar__ boss__ capital__ column drum__ column base__ cornice___ floor/pavement___ pediment/entablature__ sculpture__ unknown__ other__

**Function:** abacus__ arch__ column decoration__ door jamb__ stylobate__ wall__ wall decoration__ unknown __ other__

**Paint Color:** red__ black__ green__ blue__ yellow__ gold leaf__ white__ other___

**Motif #1**: acanthus leaf__ beed and reel __ cauliculus__ corner volute___ crow steps__ dart__ dentils__ egg__ egg & dart__ egg & tongue__ elephant__ human__ mask__ helix__ flower petal__ hibiscus petal__ pine cone__ pomegranate/poppy__ ribbed/fluted__ torus__ vine__ volute__ unknown__ other______________________________

**Motif #2:** arm__ body__ eye__ ear__ face__ foot__ hand__ head__ head & ear__ head w/ ear & eye__ head w/out eye__ head w/2 eyes__ head w/ trunk__ leg__ skin__ trunk__unknown__ other_____________________________________________

**Motif #3:** (explain)_____________________________________________

**Comments:**_____________________________________________

*Figure 6.17. Architectural Fragment Form.*

## The Architectural Fragments Database

In 1993, we initiated an architectural fragment recording system, which was modified in 1994. We began recording the Porch column fall so that we might be able to estimate the height of the Temple as well as the earthquake action that had brought the structure down. Columns Nadine, Pia and the Pronaos column, Mohammad, were the first to be recorded. The Great Temple abounded with architectural fragments, and they had also to be recorded — in fact the recovery of architectural fragments overwhelmed the 1993 excavation. The result was that some data input forms lacked full information, for the trench supervisors were so overwhelmed by the amounts of fallen fragments that they were distracted from the excavation process.

Forms were filled out with a description of the object including its material, composition and function, as well as its provenance, a rough sketch and often a photograph. Metal tags were affixed to each of the elements that might be used in reconstruction, and those objects too small to be tagged were coated with clear nail enamel and marked with their P/ST (Petra Southern Temple) numbers with an indelible pen.

To the west of the site we created a lapidary marked with grid squares that corresponded to the Site Grid. All the large, undecorated architectural fragments were stored in their respective grid designations.

When we returned to the site in 1994, we found that the aluminum tags had been removed by Bedouin children, and much of the identifying information had been lost. Additionally, the nail enamel had begun to peel away, and the numbers had been compromised. It was then decided to mark every fragment with an indelible marker. Large fragments that were exposed to the elements were marked in at least two places so that hopefully one number would remain.

Full-time recording in 1993 was undertaken by Meredith Chesson and Peter Lund, who coordinated the assignment of area sequence numbers to the finds. In successive seasons, each of the trench supervisors undertook the recording of the architectural fragments in their trenches. When a fragment was located outside a trench, it was assigned a grid number.

It was hoped that each fragment would also be surveyed, and we did survey a significant number of fragments. With time, the excavation was enlarged to include Trenches 1-4 and SP 4,

**Architectural Fragments Petra Great Temple**

Material |limestone          Phasing |II

AF2312

PST #          Sequence #   Grid          Area          Trench        Locus #                                D    M    Y
|C5/055          |2294          |C5-C6          |T (W)          |22          |7          ☐ Surface          Date |25  |VII  19|95

                                                                                                              Jul 25, 1995
Height        Diameter    Length        Width          Thickness
|              |              |44          |43          |27          ☐ No Dimensions          Excavator  |LAB

Composition              Composition 2            Feature                                Function                    Color
○ carved                 ○ bossed                 ○ ashlar          ○ sculpture          ◉ abacus                    ☐ red
◉ carved & incised       ○ drafted                ○ boss            ○ unknown            ○ arch                      ☐ black
○ dressed                ○ bossed & drafted       ◉ capital         ○ Other…             ○ column decoration         ☐ green
○ dressed diagonally     ○ painted                ○ column drum                          ○ door jamb                 ☐ blue
○ incised                ○ mason's mark           ○ column base                          ○ stylobate                 ☐ yellow
○ molded                 ○ unknown                ○ floor                                ○ wall                      ☐ gold leaf
○ unknown                ○ Other…                 ○ cornice                              ○ wall decoration           ☐ orange
○ Other…                                          ○ pediment/entablature                 ○ unknown
                                                                                         ○ Other…

Motif                    Motif 2                  Motif 3                  Comments
|volute                  |volute                  |                         |Double volute and abacus.

Sort by
[ Material ] [ Composition ] [ Phasing ]     [ Find Mode ] [ Find All ]     [ TBD ]                     [ Main Menu ]

*Figure 6.18.  Architectural Fragment Input Form.*

*Figure 6.19.  Architectural Fragment Reports Generated.*

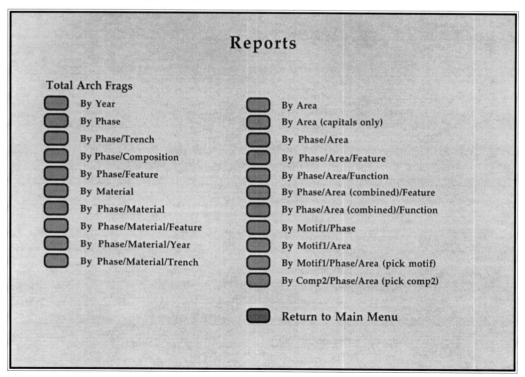

**Reports**

**Total Arch Frags**

By Year                                          By Area

By Phase                                         By Area (capitals only)

By Phase/Trench                                  By Phase/Area

By Phase/Composition                             By Phase/Area/Feature

By Phase/Feature                                 By Phase/Area/Function

By Material                                      By Phase/Area (combined)/Feature

By Phase/Material                                By Phase/Area (combined)/Function

By Phase/Material/Feature                         By Motif1/Phase

By Phase/Material/Year                            By Motif1/Area

By Phase/Material/Trench                          By Motif1/Phase/Area (pick motif)

                                                 By Comp2/Phase/Area (pick comp2)

                                    **Return to Main Menu**

the Subterranean Canalization System. The trench supervisors, with Meredith Chesson and Martha S. Joukowsky, undertook the continued recording of architectural elements. The overburden was so intense that as soon as we could, architectural fragments were removed by hand to the lapidary to the west of the site, and in many cases although fragments were identified as to their composition and function, many were not measured.

At the close of the first excavation season, column drums and ashlars were placed in their respective lapidary grid areas, and the larger sculpted fragments were covered with clean sand and metal sheeting in hopes they would be protected from the elements and would be out of sight. All the small carved pieces were marked and reburied in crates under one of the roofed sondages. They were, therefore, returned to their microenvironment, were out of sight and were protected from the elements.

Because the database construct designed in 1994 had become dysfunctional, a new database was completed in December 1997 to record architectural fragments. The Architectural Fragments Database was based on the "short" version of the Architectural Fragments Field Form (Figure 6.17) developed in 1994 from the cumbersome initial form designed in 1993. In 1997, Donna J. D'Agostino created the FileMaker Pro form, and Martha S. Joukowsky went through the 1993-1997 site notebooks to record the information for 5000+ architectural fragments. This database is a fairly straightforward reproduction of the paper form that we use in the field. Figure 6.18 shows the FileMaker Pro input form. The database includes the ability to report on architectural fragments by material, function, location found and measurements. Figure 6.19 shows the reports generated, all of which are available on the CD-ROM.

## Problems with the Architectural Fragments Database

Excavators were inconsistent about recording whether or not an item was a fragment, but we assumed, unless there was an annotation to that effect in the comment field, that the majority of the entries are fragments. There exists a standard way to record "tentativeness" about a categorization. We have included an "other" or "unknown" as a standard item in multivalue fields.

## Architectural Fragments: Results

Architectural fragments fallen from the Great Temple site have been found in large numbers. A total of 5078 architectural elements or fragments have been identified.[5] (Combining the Grosso Modo plaster fragments (8091), the total number of fragments is 13,169.)[6] The significance of these finds, however, takes on an added interest, because they throw the Temple's architectural importance into relief. A general outline of the architectural decorative elements is proposed in Chapter 5 by Erika L. Schluntz. Without a duplication of effort, the fragments cataloged and discussed here, by type and frequency of occurrence, utilize the computer database. Those interested in architectural specifics can access this database on the CD-ROM.

The types of architectural elements include ashlars, architectural elements such as arch elements and door jambs. As the largest single class, capital fragments contain a large and diversified body of decorative elements. These elements, we believe, constitute an accurate index of the sculptural priorities and canon that are representative of the Great Temple, and this, in turn, helps us in placing the precinct into the chronology of Petra. All the decorated fragments have been retained for study, and since many of them can be correlated to dateable structures in Petra, their chronological value for Petra is critical.

In the charts are graphs showing the distribution of architectural fragments classified by year (Figure 6.20) and by material (Figure 6.21); the distribution by phase is given in Figure 6.22, the distribution by area Figure 6.23 and by phase and area Figure 6.24. Of the total fragments classified, it will be noted that 32%, or 1647 fragments, are of sandstone; 63%, or 3189 fragments, are of limestone, and 3.5%, or 180 fragments, are of stucco or plaster. Three fragments were of basalt, which were probably not architectural fragments at all but served for domestic purposes.

Architectural fragments by area show that 53%, or 2672 fragments, were found in the confines of the Great Temple itself. Twenty-five percent, or 1258 fragments, were recovered from the Upper Temenos, and 1144 fragments, or 22%, were found in the Lower Temenos. A combined fragment area count shows that 78%

| Year | Total | Percent |
|------|-------|---------|
| 1993 | 697 | 13.7% |
| 1994 | 1,409 | 27.7% |
| 1995 | 1,235 | 24.3% |
| 1996 | 905 | 17.8% |
| 1997 | 832 | 16.4% |
| | 5,078 | 100.0% |

**Architectural Fragments by Year**

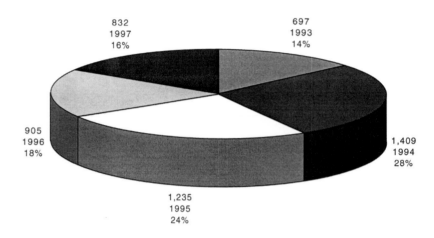

*Figure 6.20. Architectural Fragments by Year.*

*Figure 6.21. Architectural Fragments by Material.*

| Total Architectural Fragments by Material | |
|------|------|
| **Material** | **Total** |
| basalt | 3 |
| limestone | 3,135 |
| limestone/mortar | 11 |
| limestone/stucco | 43 |
| marble | 49 |
| other | 2 |
| sandstone | 1,553 |
| sandstone/mortar | 62 |
| sandstone/stucco | 32 |
| stucco (plaster) | 180 |
| unknown | 8 |
| *Total Arch Frags:* | ***5,078*** |

| Phase | Total | Percent |
|---|---|---|
| I | 9 | 0.2% |
| II | 219 | 4.3% |
| III | 36 | 0.7% |
| IV | 158 | 3.1% |
| V | 713 | 14.0% |
| VI | 3,943 | 77.6% |
| | 5,078 | 100.0% |

**Architectural Fragments by Phase**

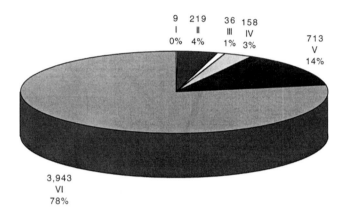

*Figure 6.22. Architectural Fragments by Phase.*

*Figure 6.23. Architectural Fragments by Area.*

| Area | Total | Percent |
|---|---|---|
| Lapidary | 3 | 0.1% |
| Lower Temenos | 1,144 | 22.5% |
| Temenos | 2,666 | 52.5% |
| Upper Temenos | 1,265 | 24.9% |
| | 5,078 | 100.0% |

**Architectural Fragments by Area**

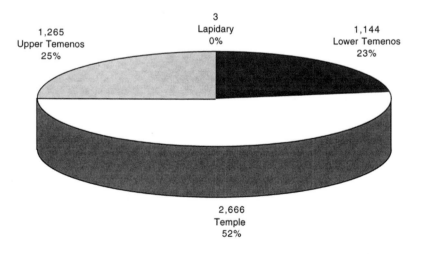

| Phase | Area | Total Frags |
|---|---|---|
| **I** | | |
| | LAP | 2 |
| | T | 7 |
| | | 9 |
| **II** | | |
| | LT | 48 |
| | T | 161 |
| | UT | 10 |
| | | 219 |
| **III** | | |
| | LT | 36 |
| | | 36 |
| **IV** | | |
| | LT | 76 |
| | T | 56 |
| | UT | 26 |
| | | 158 |
| **V** | | |
| | LT | 16 |
| | T | 690 |
| | UT | 7 |
| | | 713 |
| **VI** | | |
| | LAP | 1 |
| | LT | 968 |
| | T | 1,752 |
| | UT | 1,222 |
| | | 3,943 |
| **Total Arch Frags:** | | **5,078** |

*Figure 6.24. Architectural Fragments by Phase and Area.*

were from the Upper Temenos and the Temple areas, and 22% were recovered from the Lower Temenos.

**Ashlar Blocks:** Of the total collection of 5078 architectural fragments, 1237, or 24%, were ashlar blocks, and of these, 128, or 10%, of the ashlars were arch fragments, while the 72 door jambs recognized accounted for 6%. Some 66 ashlars were found with a marginal draft, and from the Temple Rear, 27 were identified with channels 0.06-0.08 m in depth cut into two sides. These channeled ashlars must have served for the theater seating, for they are like the blocks that are still *in situ*. These ashlar fragments were found where they had fallen along side other architectural elements. The circumstances of this fallen debris suggests that an earthquake caused the final collapse of the Temple.

Sandstone was the favored material for ashlars, representing the material for 81% of the

blocks, as opposed to 18% that were carved from limestone. Forty-one of the ashlars bore mason's marks, all of which were recorded. These are not presented in detail in this study; however, Figure 6.27 gives an illustration of several mason's marks.

**Column Drums:** Column drum fragments or complete drums numbered 526, or 10%, of the total collection. Almost all of the drums were of sandstone, 448 or 85%, and a few, 75 or 14% were of limestone. Seventy-four drums were found in the Lower Temenos; their diameters average 0.78 m, and they averaged 0.46 m in height.

The Great Temple Porch and Pronaos drums averaged 0.40-0.42 m in height, but the heights of these drums seem to decrease the higher the drum was positioned on the column. The fall of the Nadine and Pia Porch Columns was measured, and because the Nadine column had the greatest number of drums, 29 drums had fallen *in situ*, it was estimated that the height of the column shaft (without the capital or the base) originally stood about 12.4 m in height. These drums measured between 1.50-1.53 m in diameter. We know that the Pronaos columns were coated with a red stucco, for some of it remains on the lower column shaft. We are less sure about the color of the Great Temple Porch columns.

The Temple is decorated with eight columns on its east and west sides and six columns in the rear. The columns lying behind the East and West Antae (Pierre and Patricia, respectively) are two-part engaged columns (Loa and Paul Columns), and the columns in the rear are four- to five-part, heart-shaped columns (Leigh-Ann and Suleiman Columns). Excluding these engaged and heart-shaped columns, there were originally six free-standing columns that flanked the Temple sides and four in the rear. These 16 columns are better preserved in the rear of the Temple, where the unexcavated soil provides them with support and the Temple Inter-Columnar walls are in a better state of preservation. As the area is as yet incompletely excavated, we are not sure what the condition of these columns will be, but we anticipate finding many of these columns with their bases and

*Figure 6.25. Capital egg and dart motif.*

much of their shafts *in situ*. The west column drums that have been knocked away from their shafts fell to the east, into the Temple. Judging from the remains of the upper drums of these western columns (Lee, David and Peter Columns), which toppled into the

'Adyton' area, those drums that have been registered range from 1.08-1.10 m in diameter and from 0.32-0.65 m in height. These measurements correspond with those drums of the Temple East, which were found slumped further east.

**Column Bases:** The column bases of the Great Temple are well-articulated Attic bases that were sculpted in either a limestone or a white, fine-grained sandstone. The *in situ* Nadine and Pia Porch Column bases are what we have used as a guide for determining the height of the Porch and Pronaos. The Nadine base measures 0.63 m in height; however, the Pia Column base is smaller, measuring 0.60 m in height. These bases were manufactured in two parts, as two vertical halves. A rectangular, flat sandstone slab was used to support their bases. They are characterized by a torus (or large convex molding) at the bottom, the concave molding above the torus, known as the cavetto, and another torus above, above which is a finished top molding. Plaster was found as a bonding agent for the joins. Based on our excavations up to this point, we have found that the Great Temple side and rear columns are still *in situ*, and as they are excavated, we will have a better grasp of their architectural statement.

*Figure 6.26. Plaster fragment showing dentilation.*

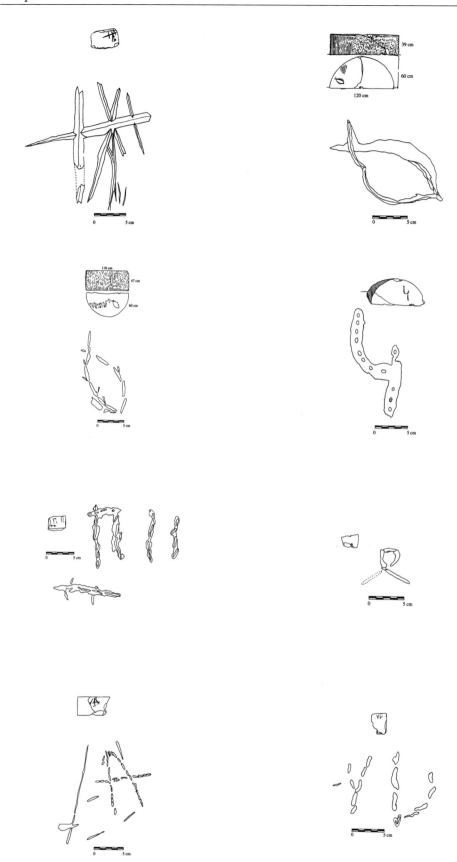

*Figure 6.27. Several examples of mason's marks.*

*Figure 6.28. Lower order of an acanthus-decorated capital.*

Column base elements numbered only 20, which is not surprising considering that the columns of the Lower Temenos colonnades were baseless, i.e., the columns rested directly on the stylobates of the colonnade. Those twin columns in the entry to the West and East Exedrae still rest on their bases.

**Architectural moldings:** Cornice fragments numbered 295, and of these, 202, or 68%, were manufactured from limestone; 60 were of sandstone, and 31 were fashioned from stucco. Egg and dart fragments numbered 61, and only two fragments were identified with an egg and tongue motif. The pattern of alternating short and long beads, otherwise known as bead and reel design (usually placed on the astragal below the egg and dart motif), decorated only five fragments, and these were fashioned both out of sandstone and limestone. As far as pediment and entablature fragments are concerned, only 32 pieces were registered, and they are found in all media — sandstone, limestone and stucco. Unfortunately, they do not offer a clear idea of the Temple's overall façade design.

**Capitals and Decorated Pieces:** Fifty percent of the Great Temple collection was represented by capital fragments. Registered were 2562 fragments as capitals or decorative capital elements. Of these, 2460, or 95%, were limestone; 67, or 2.6%, were of stucco, and 33, or 1%, were of sandstone. Twenty percent, or 514, of these were found in the Upper Temenos, and 543, or 21%, were found in the Lower Temenos. The majority, or 1505 (59%), were recovered from the Great Temple itself. It is not clear if we have found the capital elements of either the Porch or Pronaos columns; however, in style we assume that their capitals are similar in composition to the eight capitals that decorated the sides of the building and those in the Temple Rear.

The decorative program of the capitals flanking the Great Temple has been defined. These capitals are comprised of a two-part lower order of bushy acanthus leaves, which measure approximately 1.43 m in width and 0.58 m in height (Figures 6.28 and 6.32). The upper order is comprised of a four-part capital that measures as much as 0.89 m in height or as little as 0.78 m in height (Figure 6.33). Together, these elements measure 1.47 m in height.

*Figure 6.29. Detail of crossed-vine and blossom decoration.*

*Figure 6.30. Volute vegetal decoration.*

*Figure 6.31. Drawing of volute decoration showing drill holes. Drawing by Jean Blackburn.*

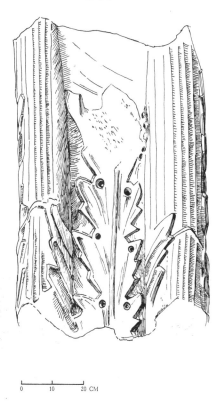

TOP VIEW

PLASTER

SIDE VIEW

BOTTOM VIEW

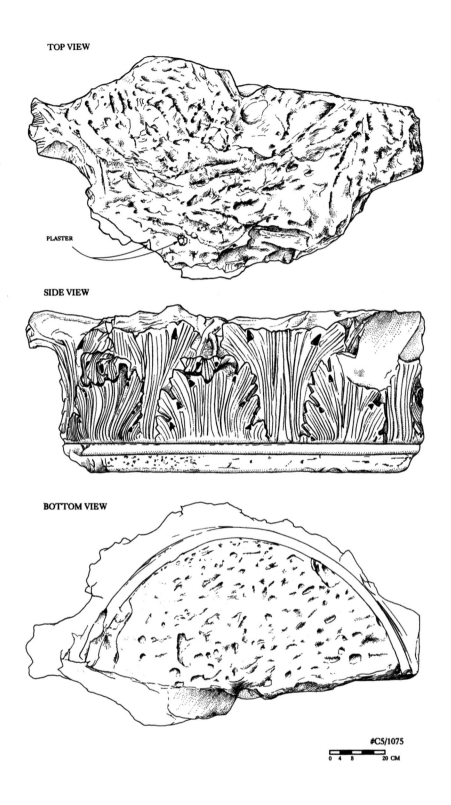

#C5/1075

0  4  8          20 CM

*Figure 6.32. Column capital, lower order, half drum. Drawing by Jean Blackburn.*

TOP VIEW

SIDE VIEW

BOTTOM VIEW

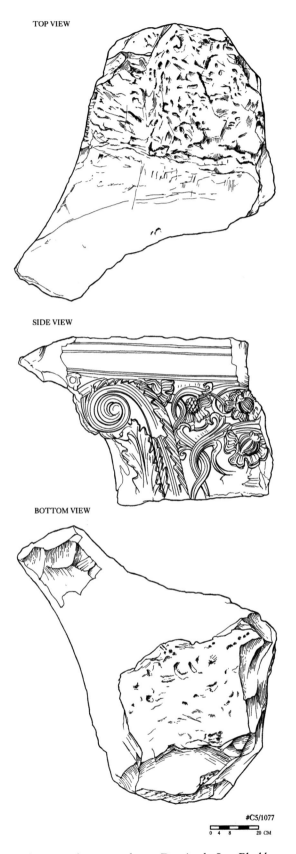

#C5/1077

0  4  8                    20 CM

*Figure 6.33. Column capital, upper order, quarter drum. Drawing by Jean Blackburn.*

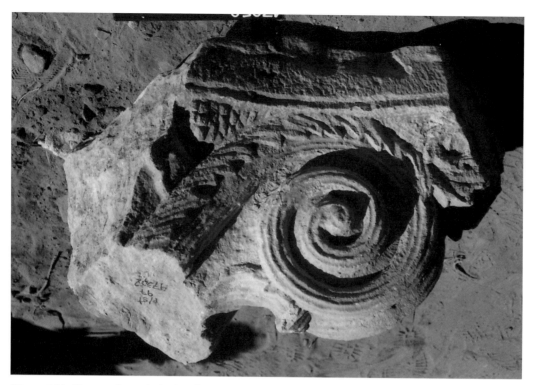

*Figure 6.34. Upper order, capital volute fragment.*

These capitals range around 0.69 m in width and are 0.56 m in thickness. The decoration is comprised of an intricate, deeply carved array of vines and plant stalks with hibiscus petals that frame different fruits — pine cones and

*Figure 6.35. Vine and poppy-pomegranate motif.*

pomegranates or poppies springing forth from their centers (Figures 6.29 and 6.35). These capitals resemble those of the lower order of the Al-Khazna (McKenzie 1990, Type 1 Floral Capital McKenzie 1990, f Plates 42 c, 43 a and b), and it can be reasoned they were manufactured by the same sculptural school at the same time as the Al-Khazna.

Twenty-one percent, or 1058 fragments, were identified with acanthus leaf decoration, accounting for 1044, or 98%, of the capital fragments. In the Great Temple, 696 acanthus fragments, or 66%, were recovered, and 183, or 17%, were found in the Upper Temenos. Only 179 acanthus fragments were recovered from the Lower Temenos, accounting for 17% of the assemblage. Thus, the Temple and the Upper Temenos combined represent 83% of the collection.

Fluted cauliculi represent 123, or 4.8%, of the Temple capital fragments; there were 150 volutes and an additional 12 corner volutes, together representing 162 pieces, or 6.3%, of the capital fragments. More minor in representation are hibiscus petals, numbering 67, or 2.6% of embellishments, but there were an additional 102 floral fragments that may have included hibiscus petals as well. Only 10 fragments were classified as spirals on the face of the capital (helices), but identified were 28 fragments of the convex molding around the base of the capital (the astragal) and 117 flat elements forming the top of a capital (abacus fragments). Other decorated fragments were vines representing 219, or 2.6%, of the capital fragments. Many of these were crossed vines. Sixty poppy-pomegranate fragments were recognized, representing 2.3% of the decorative motifs (Figure 6.35). Pine cones numbered 103, or 4%, of the capital fragments (Figure 6.36). Additionally, there were 42 boss fragments — that projection of the abacus that at the Great Temple, like the Al-Khazna, is decorated with a center pine cone (Figure 6.36).

The design of architectural decoration suggests that the vast majority of the elements cataloged in the database were originally part of the Great Temple architecture during the prime periods of the Temple's life. One of the few pieces that is puzzling is the sandstone Tyche head (Basile 1997), which may derive from the Great Temple (Figures 6.79 and 6.80) or from some other nearby structure. It may have been dumped on the site during one of the earthquakes that occurred at Petra, and she probably suffered damage to her face at that time.

**Elephant-headed capitals:** Also registered were a total of 106 elephant-headed fragments. Thus, only 4% of the capital fragments were decorated with either elephant heads or elephant parts. The majority, 105, were manufactured from limestone, and one was registered as being carved out of sandstone. Some of these were covered with a thin film of plaster. More prone to breakage, 73 are elephant-trunk fragments, which account for 69% of the elephant remains. Heads or partial heads numbered 15, or 14% of the elephants (three of these artifacts had heads with the ear); there were six separate pieces recognized as ears, six as skin fragments and eight separate eye fragments. As 100 fragments were recovered from the Lower Temenos, representing 94%, four fragments from the Temple and two fragments from the Upper Temenos, it is reasoned that the Lower Temenos colonnades must have been the area these zoomorphic capitals decorated.

**Masks:** Seven mask fragments were found in 1994 in the West Walkway of the Great Temple. They are all carved out of limestone, and three are carved out of a yellow limestone. Two (94-S-1 and 94-S-3) were the two halves of the same mask of a female head. Illustrated in the Chapter 5 discussion on architectural sculpture,

*Figure 6.36. Pine cone boss.*

these masks must have fallen from the Great Temple façade.

**Pilasters:** Although seven pilaster blocks were registered in the database, six were of human figures found near the Stairs of the Propylaeum on the Colonnaded Street in front of the precinct. Although we have included them in our database, these cannot be securely identified with the Temple. But one carved, limestone pilaster (a vertical, rectangular-shaped support block) of a partial human figure was found in Trench 18A in the Lower Temenos in 1997. Measuring 0.24 m in height, 0.86 m in length and 0.52 m in width, this relief represents a torso with drapery over its left arm and the right arm partially destroyed. There is a strap between the breasts. It is illustrated in Chapter 5.

**Painted stucco:** Some 120 fragments of either capitals or wall decoration were found painted. Of these, 24% were painted red; 17.5% were black-painted; 12% were green; 28% were blue; 16% were yellow, and of the remainder, three fragments were found with gold leaf, and one fragment was painted orange.

## Conclusion

The Architectural Fragment Database has provided us with a beginning to address the scholarly problems to be solved. Work to date has focused on the ordering of this collection. Simple patterns of cataloging and inventory have evolved that have identified the basic nature and attributes of the architectural data units. Now we have to question this data and inter-relate it to other factors of the site to amplify both its meaning and the meaning of the site as a whole.

We now turn to the Lamp and the Catalog corpus presented by Deirdre G. Barrett, followed by the Coin Database. Sara G. Karz will then present the Glass Database.

## The Catalog Database

The Catalog Database was originally created with an eye towards producing reports for the Jordanian Department of Antiquities; however, due to the usefulness of being able to generate reports of our most interesting finds, we expanded the database to handle recording of all catalog information pertaining to coins, pottery, glass, bone and architectural fragments, such as elephant heads and parts.

This database contains a series of "core" fields that are common to all cataloged items and a series of ancillary fields that are specific to the cataloging of coins. The database has input systems for general catalog items and for coins. Likewise, there are separate reporting layouts for general catalog items and coins. We have added a "culture" field to the general catalog input system and a "Munsell" field for the pottery input layout as well. We have now graduated to putting the catalog directly onto the computer and have eliminated the paper form altogether.

---

## Endnotes

[1] Although the osteological and materials have been scrupulously excavated, counted, recorded and retained for analysis, none has been performed on them to date. David S. Reese has offered to study our shell remains. The results of these studies will be presented in the Final Report.

[2] Notes from Geoffrey Bilder's observations are also drawn upon for this section.

[3] Another option was to return to our 1994 Newton experiment. A few of these would allow any number of excavators to enter data directly into the computer and thus bypass the lengthy and inefficient transcription process.

[4] For example, the tasks for the 1995 season were the following:

1) Update the existing FileMaker Pro input systems based on comments and suggestions made after 1994 experiences;

2) Develop a system in FoxPro for analyzing and reporting the data that was entered in FileMaker Pro;

3) Develop a system for transferring data from FileMaker Pro to FoxPro;

4) Migrate existing 1993 data from Fourth Dimension to FoxPro;

5) Migrate architectural fragment data from Microsoft Word to FoxPro.

In addition to the above consolidation and refining, we also developed a new database to assist us in publishing our catalog data. This database was designed with site report publishing as the immediate goal; however, with modifications, it evolved into a complete catalog database.

[5] Approximately 58 fragments from Trenches 40 and 47 excavated in 1997 inside the Great Temple have not been included in this database, because the site records were incomplete.

[6] Since at this writing the two databases have not been combined, we will confine our comments to the Architectural Fragment Database.

# THE LAMPS

Deirdre G. Barrett

## Introduction

The total number of lamp fragments discovered and cataloged from the Great Temple, Petra, amount to 342. Of these only seven are complete or almost complete lamps. We have identified two fragments as being of Hellenistic origin, 84 as Nabataean, 60 as Roman, 127 as Byzantine and two as Islamic, leaving 67 fragments unidentified. It would seem from this evidence and interpretation that the Great Temple saw its longest occupation from the first century BCE until the end of the fourth century CE, with possible intervening periods of abandonment after sporadic earthquake activity (e.g., the earthquake of 363 CE).

The destruction of the Temple, caused by the collapse of monumental architecture across the site, has rendered stratigraphic contextualization almost impossible. Indeed, very few artifacts *in situ* can be given absolute dates, due to the chaotic tumble of rock and masonry that has covered the area for over fourteen centuries. In some cases we have been able to ascertain a date for an area, where lamp fragments or coins have been found in a sealed context; however, these finds have been rare, demanding a more holistic overview of artifact patterning.

One method of sourcing the origination of clays used in lamp production is instrumental neutron activation analysis (NAA). As this is an extremely expensive and time-consuming procedure, only 12 lamp fragments were tested by Leigh-Ann Bedal, and the reader will find the results of such testing in Chapter 7. These results proved to be most rewarding, as they were able to dispel preconceived notions concerning some local lamps.

The lamps are classified into six cultural groups: Hellenistic, Nabataean, Roman, Byzantine and Islamic, with the last group representing the unidentified, or unknown, category. Due to the large corpus of fragments, only a representative group is described in this publication, and the reader will find the complete inventory in the companion CD-ROM.

## Discussion

### Hellenistic Lamps

The scanty evidence of lamps from this period (two identified fragments), renders any hypothesis a *canard*; therefore, I will not attempt to suggest an explanation for their presence within the Temple vicinity. As excavation continues within the site, further Hellenistic lamp fragments may be uncovered, providing us with a more substantial corpus that deserves mention.

### Nabataean Lamps

Joseph Patrich designates two Nabataean original styles that epitomize the local "avoidance of imitation of the surrounding Hellenistic-Roman culture" (Patrich 1990:130). These are the ω and 'volute' lamps. Patrich's perception of the ω in the lamp decoration, though, is subjective in that the design could also be read as a rosette, echoing the small clusters on the volute lamp. Other lamps bear this ω cipher, however, which lends credence to Patrich's designation (Rosenthal and Sivan 1978:131).[1]

The volute lamp, with its sunburst of ridges topped with small rosettes, would seem to demonstrate the Nabataean knack for adaptation. This marriage of classical (the volute) and baroque layering of decoration is uniquely Nabataean, a pattern that is replicated in that remarkable piece of rock-hewn architecture, the Al-Khazna.

Both these lamps are non-figurative, conforming to the tenets of the Nabataean Semitic faith prohibiting idolatry. Patrich observes that Nabataean non-figurative art reflects the most original expression of Nabataean creativity, citing the stelae representations of their gods, funerary architecture (the design of tomb façades), painted pottery, clay oil lamps, numismatics and jewelry (Patrich 1990:49).

Examples of these exquisitely molded Nabataean lamps have been found throughout the Great Temple precinct, 94-P-26 (Figure 6.37) being a particularly fine upper rim fragment of the volute lamp. The presence of these lamps attests to the Temple construction predating the Roman occupation of 106 CE, and may confirm our earlier premise that the Temple was part of Aretas IV's grand design at the end of the first century BCE, during the Augustan *Pax Romana*.

(Figure 6.38) was identified as an import from Parthia and "is not found in Nabataean contexts earlier than the first century AD" (Schmid personal communication). This last-mentioned lamp has double axes on its rim.[2]

## Roman Lamps

Unlike the Nabataeans, the Romans had no religious constraints regarding figurative expression. Indeed, they often decorated the whole upper concave surface of their lamps, which was known as the discus, and this provided a *tabula rasa* for the religious and mythological scenes that were *au courant* during the first century CE. As Donald Bailey has noted (1972:22), representations of aspects of daily life, the circus and theater, animals, inanimate objects and floral designs appeared on this clay backdrop, and these lamps are acknowledged to be the finest mold-made lamps ever produced in this period.

Appearing first in Italy during late Republican times, they continued to dominate the home market during the early Imperial period at the end of the first century BCE and then began to be exported throughout the Roman Empire from the late first century BCE to the first century CE. It did not take long before

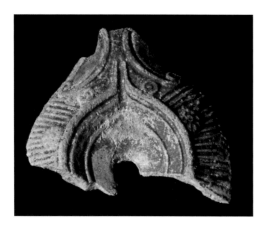

*Figure 6.37. 94-P-26, volute lamp.*

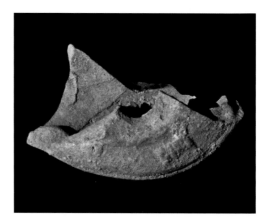

*Figure 6.38. 95-L-81, double axes.*

The NAA evidence is slender, as only four supposed Nabataean lamps were sent for analysis. Of these, two were found to be local (95-L-79 and 95-L-82), and they bear the sunray and a stamped design around their rims. However, a fragment from a volute lamp (95-L-38), whose origin unfortunately cannot be predicted accurately without further analysis, has been placed in the Odd/Anomalous Group. The remaining lamp (95-L-81)

they were copied by provincial workshops, despite an imperial policy that sought to protect such exports from plagiarism. Economic and political machinations throughout the Empire encouraged the imported lamps to be used as a patrix to produce a mold, and by the second century CE, the export trade in Italian-made lamps had disappeared.

Four samples from Roman lamps were sent to the MURR Reactor for an NAA report. Of these, two have been designated non-local (95-L-26 and 95-L-61) and one local (95-L-6). 95-L-33 has been assigned to the Odd Group, as its constituent elements differ sufficiently from the Local Group to exclude it from local manufacture. Lamps 95-L-81 (non-local) and 95-L-82 (local) have been reassigned as Roman lamps, examples of an import from Parthia and a Nabataean copy that could only be detected through chemical analysis.

Two lamps from the Great Temple that are notable for their discus decoration are 94-P-37 (Figure 6.39) and 95-L-179 (Figure 6.40). Both have figurative designs, 94-P-37 showing an erotic scene and 95-L-179 a mythological vignette of Eros in shackles. The same designs have been described by Khairy from lamps

*Figure 6.39. 94–P-37, erotic scene.*

discovered at Al-Katute in 1981 (Khairy 1990:87). He has dated his examples to 18-40 CE. The Al-Katute erotic lamp differs in material from the Great Temple fragment; Khairy describes its composition as light redware with a pink gritty slip, whereas 94-P-37 is of light yellow ware.

The erotic scene has been found in many sites at Petra (Horsfield and Conway 1942:196 Pl. XIV.424a and b, Hammond 1973:37, Nos. 149-152, Zayadine 1982:169 fig. 15: 392) and also throughout the Empire. The British Museum also has an excellent example (Registration No. 1971:4-26.3, Boardman et al. 1986:202).

Eros clothed and wearing leg shackles, accompanied by a basket and wielding a pickax, has been described by Rosenthal and Sivan (1978:34, No. 124) as possibly Nabataean

in origin, although the fabric of buff clay and black slip are not typically Nabataean. This lamp is a good candidate for NAA to assist in determining its source. A date of the first century CE has been ascribed by both Horsfield, and Rosenthal and Sivan. Because we have substantial documentation on both lamps, we can infer that they were popular in Petra during the first century CE, although the erotic lamp appears to have had a more widespread distribution than 'Eros in shackles.'[3]

The cheerful eroticism depicted on the discus of 94-P-37 was a favorite theme in Imperial Rome and was not confined to relief-decorated ceramics, appearing in domestic wall-painting and shop signs, for example, and thereby reaching out to the furthest ends of the Empire through trade and artistic expression. That the Nabataeans in Petra possessed and copied erotica on their lamps is certainly indicative of their exposure to such an ideology and is also proof of an imperial influence.[4]

Not all the Roman lamps found within the Temple were decorated on the discus; the majority were plain except for concentric circles used as a border on the rim of the lamp. These lamps do have a mixed heritage, as we have seen from the NAA results, evidence that the local economy was no different than our own in replicating popular material culture to its own advantage and profit.

*Figure 6.40. 95–P-179, Eros in shackles.*

## Byzantine Lamps

The Byzantine lamps found to date within the Great Temple constitute the largest culture represented, and at first glance one might assume that that was the longest residential period for the Temple. However, one must take into consideration that the Theatron area has not yet been completely excavated, which may well yield a large number of Nabataean artifacts, including lamps. In addition, the West Exedra, which has provided many of the Byzantine lamp fragments, may have been the site of a fifth-century Christian chapel. This tentative hypothesis has been made, because it is apsidal in shape, lending itself to the style of early classical Christian architecture. In addition, several items of value have been found there, e.g., an amethyst tessera, gold jewelry and a bronze drain cover. Oscar Broneer has stated that church rituals at that time required the use of many lamps to serve an ideo-technic function. "The lamps from the fourth and fifth centuries are more numerous than from any other period either before or after. This is due to the large role which the lamps played in the church service of the early Christians" (Broneer 1930:27).

The Byzantine lamp is unique in its "slipper" shape with a radial pattern on the rim and crosses, volutes and palm branches on the nozzle, which is an integral part of the body. The handle is usually a vestigial knob or pellet, and the lamps are unslipped (Rosenthal and Sivan 1978:112). Barag and Hershkovitz (1994:101) note in their Masada IV report that most Byzantine lamps from Palestine and Transjordan are notoriously difficult to date precisely within the fifth to early seventh century CE. Rosenthal and Sivan, though, cite a cache of these lamps found in a tomb at 'Ayn Yabrud, which also contained a gold coin of Constantine, thus providing a date in the second half of the fourth century CE. They also state that the practice of depicting the cross in any form whatsoever began in the middle of the fourth century (1978:112).

Khairy compares Byzantine lamps from other sites with those from Petra and concludes that the latter are more delicate and smaller in size with slightly concave sides between the nozzle and the filling hole. He describes another anomalous feature placed above some of the ring bases that is peculiar to Petra (Khairy 1990:20). This feature resembles three fingers, which could be a potter's mark, or it could represent the "thrice blessed" in Christianity. Examples of this mark appear on many of the Byzantine lamps found in the Great Temple (94-P-14, 94-P-34, 94-P-46, 95-L-91, 95-L-104). Christian symbols also appear on 95-L-126, 95-L-130 and 95-L-132 (Figures 6.41-6.45).

All four of the Byzantine lamps sent for NAA were designated as being local. These were 95-L-18, 95-L-39, 95-L-88 and 95-L-92. It would appear that by the late fourth century CE, local potters were responsible for the manufacture of these lamps.

When these lamps were created by the potters in Petra, were they aware of the supposed period of calm that we, looking back at the past, label their present? Their designs were dictated by a new foreign elite, one that was motivated by the creed of Nicaea. By a decree in 380 CE, only those who believed in the Trinity of the Father, Son and Holy Ghost were considered Catholic Christians; all others, "the mad and insane" people who adhered to "the infamy of heretic doctrine," had no right to call their meeting places churches and were subject to severe punishment (Codex Theodosianus, XVI, 1, 2 in Vasiliev 1952:80). Only followers of the Nicene symbol were allowed the right to assemble in the churches throughout the Byzantine Empire. Small wonder that Khairy's "thrice blessed" motif appears on so many Byzantine lamps in Petra.[5]

A period of calm and a drop in trade may appear to have been the way of the world in Petra in the late fourth century CE; however, the narrative portrayed on its lamps reveals another fingerprint of yet another empire striving to take control of the minds of its people.

## Islamic Lamps

With only two fragments to examine, any effect that the coming of Islam may have had upon the material culture of the Great Temple will be very difficult to decipher. By the law of superposition, later deposits should be found on or near the surface, and it is therefore unlikely that we will find further evidence of that particular empire as we delve deeper into the confines of the Temple. However, a succession of earthquakes throughout the last two millennia has deposited artifacts amid stratigraphy that is disturbed, and although contextually irrelevant, this material culture can still be important.

The presence of two identified fragments (96-L-47 and 96-L-50) may indicate that the Islamic Empire touched Petra at some time during the seventh century CE, when the Ummayad dynasty was centered in Damascus

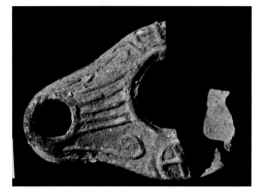

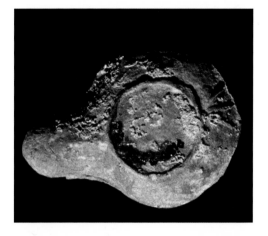

*Figures 6.41 and 6.42. Lamps with "three fingers."*

and before the city was abandoned to endure devastation by recurrent earthquakes and the later onslaught of the Crusaders and the construction of their castles.

## Conclusion

I believe some subversive undercurrents can be detected at work in the style and decoration of the material culture at Petra. Our site, the Great Temple, as an integral part of the city has experienced these cultural shifts and nuances of foreign ideology, influences that may be observed in the decoration and style of its lamps. Symbols of political power, religious domination, erotica and sexual restraint have been placed on this item of everyday use. An item in fact that has multiple functions and, therefore, multiple opportunities to "re-mind" its audience and operators, both consciously and unconsciously, of the prevailing ideology endorsed by the latest empire in power — a subtle message that its recipients often take for

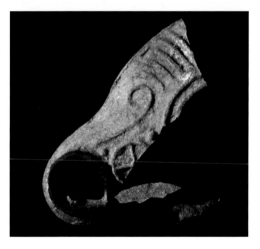

*Figure 6.43. 97–L–72. Figure 6.44. 95–L–132. Figure 6.45. 95–L–126.*

granted, so insidious is its appearance in the material culture. Power and persuasion do not have to be enveloped in chain mail to be effective; terracotta is cheaper and more appealing. It is ironic, however, that although its material will last for an eternity, the interpretation of its message may be lost after a few decades, as fingerprints of new empires make themselves manifest on the fabric of the lamp. (All following measurements are in centimeters and grams unless otherwise noted.)

## Nabataean

### 94-P-26 volute lamp

Object: Lamp fragment. Munsell: 5YR 8/4 pink, salmon-colored clay with black slip. Condition: Very good. Area UT, Trench SP 4, Locus 5. Length: 5.1, Width: 5.5, Diameter: 5.5, Thickness: 0.5, Filling Hole Diameter: 0.75. Description: Exquisite upper lamp segment with sunray rim edging and rosette decoration with double volutes on nozzle and concentric ridges around small convex filling hole.

### 95-L-85 ω lamp

Object: Lamp fragment. Munsell: 7.5YR 7/3, pink. Condition: Good. Area LT, Trench 20, Locus 13. Length: 5, Width: 3, Diameter: 6, Thickness: 0.3, Filling Hole Diameter: 2.0. Description: Double petal design on concave discus, herringbone border on shoulder rim. Soot-stained spout.

*Figure 6.46. 94–P-26.*     *Figure 6.47. 95–L-85.*

### 97-L-66 ovolo decorated rim, complete lamp

Object: Lamp. Munsell: 2.5YR 7/6, light red, pinkish clay with red slip. Condition: Good. Area UT, Trench 41, Locus 20. Diameter: 6.98, Height: 3.84. Description: Above spout is a tongue. Ovolo-decorated rim separated from plain depressed discus by two ridges. Double base ring marking. Perforated, ridged handle (Rosenthal and Sivan 1978:98 #399).

*Figures 6.48 and 6.49. 97–L-66.*

# Roman

### 94-P-37  erotic lamp

Object: Lamp fragment. Munsell: 7.5YR 8/3, pink. Condition: Very good. Area UT, Trench SP 4, Locus 5. Length: 5.7, Width: 4.9, Diameter: 7.7, Thickness: 0.3, Filling Hole Diameter: 0.75. Description: Large discus with flat base, traces of red and black paint with erotic design. Parallel: British Museum specimen, showing male/female coupling, dated to first half of third century CE, whose length is given as 10.8.

### 95-L-179  Eros in shackles

Object: Lamp fragment. Munsell: 7.5YR 6/2, pinkish gray, buff clay with black slip. Condition: Good. Area T, Trench 19, Locus 8. Length: 3.5, Width: 2.75, Thickness: 0.4, Filling Hole Diameter: 0.5. Description: Fragment of discus with Eros, clothed and wearing leg shackles (working with a pickax and basket in complete image, see Rosenthal and Sivan 1978:34, #124). Horsfield (1942) points out unusualness of subject, punished child Eros. Possibly Nabataean, although the fabric is not typically Nabataean. Similar lamp found on Al-Katute site (Khairy 1990).

*Figure 6.50.  94–P-37.*            *Figure 6.51.  95–P-179.*

### 97-L-73  small discus fragment/relief of horse/satyr

Object: Lamp fragment. Munsell: 2.5YR 6/8, red. Condition: Fair. Area T, Trench 34, Locus 14. Length: 3.48, Thickness: 0.32. Description: Small discus fragment with relief of horse or satyr.

### 95-L-81 Parthian/double axes

Object: Lamp fragment. Munsell: 7.5YR 6/3, light brown, buff clay with red slip. Condition: Fair. Area LT, Trench 16, Locus 8. Length: 6.5, Width: 3, Diameter: 6, Thickness: 0.4, Filling Hole Diameter: 1.0. Description: Syro-Palestinian (Antioch-on-the-Orontes), round lamp with double axes on shoulder. Second half first century CE; see Rosenthal and Sivan *QEDEM* 81978:85.

*Figure 6.52.  97–L-73.*            *Figure 6.53.  95–L-81.*

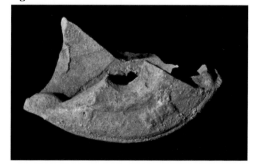

# Byzantine

## 97-L-57  nearly complete slipper lamp minus spout

Object: Lamp fragment. Munsell: 2.5YR 6/6, light red. Condition: Fair. Area T, Trench 47, Locus 13. Length: 5.42, Diameter: 5.16, Thickness: 0.4, Height: 2.5, Filling Hole Diameter: 1.86. Description: Byzantine lamp, complete except for the spout. Radials to the filling hole, some hardly visible. Perhaps the lamp was taken from a worn mold. Vestigial knob handle, ring base with a ridge from the ring to the shoulder.

*Figures 6.54 and 6.55.  97-L-57.*

## 97-L-72  spout

Object: Lamp fragment. Munsell: 2.5YR 5/8, red. Condition: Fair. Area T, Trench 34, Locus 12. Length: 4.77, Width: 4.36, Thickness: 0.23. Description: Partial Byzantine lamp with upper and lower sections of the spout. The lamp has radial ridging to the filling hole and partial volutes from the spout to the filling hole. The spout is also soot-stained.

## 95-L-126  cross

Object: Lamp fragment. Munsell: 5YR 6/2, reddish gray, redware with gray encrustations. Condition: Very good. Area LT, Trench 16, Locus 13. Length: 6.5, Width: 5, Diameter: 5, Thickness: 0.3, Height: 2.5, Filling Hole Diameter: 2. Description: Half lamp, upper and lower sections, spout end. Almond-shaped, very deep molding. Scrolls on nozzle and Christian symbols on shoulders, crosses in circles. Ring base with seams edging soot-stained spout. Fourth/fifth century CE.

## 95-L-132  cross

Object: Lamp fragment. Munsell: 10YR 7/2, light gray, redware with gray slip. Condition: Good. Area LT, Trench 16, Locus 13. Length: 7.25, Width: 5.25, Diameter: 5.5, Thickness: 0.3. Description: Religious symbol on front, cross inside circle. Deeply molded, scrolls on neck, partial ring base. Spout soot-stained. Fourth/fifth century CE.

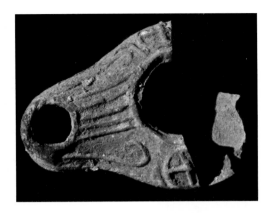
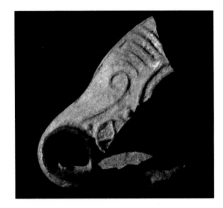

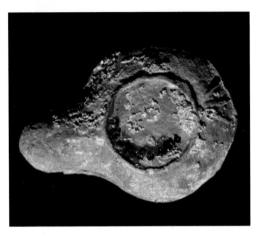

*Figure 6.56. 97–L–72. Figure 6.57. 95–L–126.*
*Figure 6.58. 95–L–132.*

## 95-L-130 three fingers/lamp base

Object: Lamp fragment. Munsell: 10YR 6/2, light brownish gray, gray slip on redware. Condition: Good. Area LT, Trench 16, Locus 13. Length: 7, Width: 5.25, Diameter: 5, Thickness: 0.2, Height: 2.5, Filling Hole Diameter: 2.2. Description: Deeply molded decoration. Knobs either side of neck, potter's mark — arrowhead on bowl of ring base. Some soot staining on spout rim. Fourth/fifth century CE.

## (Late Byzantine) Islamic

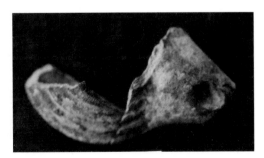
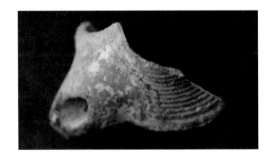

*Figure 6.59. 96–L–47, inkwell lamp.*      *Figure 6.60. 96–L–50, inkwell lamp.*

## 96-L-47  inkwell lamp

Object: Lamp fragment. Munsell: 7.5YR 7/4, pink. Condition: Fair. Area T, Trench 24, Locus 4. Length: 7.89, Thickness: 0.28. Description: Body of inkwell lamp with ridges (Rosenthal and Sivan). Mesopotamian influence fifth to seventh century CE. Also soot-stained spout that fits the body.

## 96-L-50  inkwell lamp

Object: Lamp fragment. Munsell: 2.5YR 6/6, light red. Condition: Good. Area T, Trench 34, Locus 7. Width: 5.15, Diameter: 6.26, Thickness: 0.34, Height: 3.05. Description: Upper fragment with spout and partial base of inkwell lamp. Wheel-made with soot-stained spout.

---

## Endnotes

[1] One hesitates to label this Greek letter rhetorically as metonymy without suggesting its alter ego. If the design is indeed composed of linked ωs, what significance might these letters convey to its past audience? Could the lamp, so embellished, have been used in a funerary rite conferring a finality upon the corpse? This assumption, I believe, is a suspect presentist approach, as it is documented that in antiquity only a few steps separated the house from the tomb. Death was not considered a separation and an ending, as it is in our contemporary Western society (Demosthenes, Cicero in Fustel de Coulanges 1864:32). If death was not an ending, perhaps the ω represented the ending of the year or the ending of an initiate's preparation before being presented to the Temple deity, both functions serving the socio- and ideo-technic properties suggested by Lewis Binford (1962: 217-226).

Ian Hodder warns us "to be wary about reading material culture evidence directly"; he suggests that material culture may have been made to seem as if change had occurred and produced as part of a narrative "which explained new forms of power as having been imposed by foreign 'élites' — tales of stranger-rulers" (1995:165). How interesting if the ω was part of a narrative, the result of telling stories about and to ourselves. Could the ω represent the ending of a reign? Aretas IV ruled the Nabataean kingdom from 9/8 BCE to 40 CE. Lamps may well have been produced to commemorate such an event.

If this is indeed the Greek letter ω, it must have percolated into the "grammar" of the Nabataean potter from the Hellenistic world. Why did he not use a Nabataean character in its stead if, as Patrich has argued, conscious avoidance was a primary motive in design? Nabataean script has been used in graffiti throughout the length and breadth of the kingdom, a constant conscious and unconscious reminder of their nativist vocabulary. Indeed Nabataean inscriptions have been found on the lamp bases, perhaps an indication of ritual use of the lamp (Khairy 1984:115-119).

[2] A Hodderian metonymy representing a powerful leader (Hodder 1995:165) is a narrative that begs interpretation. In 49 CE, the Roman legatus of Syria had attempted to place a pretender on the Parthian throne. The *coup d'état* was unsuccessful, but some propaganda may have been in place to tell the story to the people. Tacitus, a first-century-CE Roman storyteller of some distinction, writes, "Letters were written to the tetrarchs and kings, to *praefecti* and *procuratores* and to whatever *praetores* were governing the neighboring provinces instructing them to obey Corbulo's orders (the legatus)" (Tacitus in Millar 1993:67). Millar remarks that "in this period any conception which we can gain of the structure of the Empire in the Near East is still heavily dependent on the accidents of what subjects or areas are touched on by the available narratives" (ibid. 68). Perhaps the double axes are part of that narrative, depicting the concept of a ruler who never actually ruled but would *seem* to have ruled — a tale of a stranger-ruler backed by foreign elites.

[3] Michel Foucault, in *Beyond Structuralism and Hermeneutics* (1982), comments:

> The Greeks and Romans did not have any *ars erotica*...they had a *techne tou biou* (art of life) in which the economy of pleasure played a very large role. In this "art of life" the notion of exercising a perfect mastery over oneself soon became a main issue. And the Christian hermeneutics of the self constituted a new elaboration of this *techne*. It's quite clear from Socrates to Seneca or Pliny, for instance, that they didn't worry about the afterlife, what happened after death, or whether God exists or not...the problem was: which techne do I have to use in order to live as well as I ought to live? And I think that one of the main evolutions in ancient culture has been that this *techne tou biou* became more and more a *techne* of the self. A Greek citizen of the fifth and fourth century (BCE) would have felt that his *techne* for life was to take care of the city, of his companions. But for Seneca, for instance, the problem is to take care of himself. The idea of the *bios* as a material for an aesthetic piece of art is something which fascinates me. ...art has become something which is related only to objects and not to individuals or to life...But couldn't everyone's life become a work of art? Why should the lamp or the house be an art object, but not our life? (Foucault in Rabinow 1984:348-350)

If we accept Foucault's interpretation of the place of life in art during antiquity, we may be able to trace the passage of this philosophy through the Empire by the presence of erotica in the material culture. The lamp was a most mobile vehicle for the ideology of pleasuring oneself, serving both socio- and ideo-technic functions.

[4] How can we interpret Eros clothed and in shackles? Horsfield (1942:123, No. 49 and Pl. XI) has commented on the unusual theme of the punished child Eros. Was Eros's condition a reaction to the indulgence of sexual pleasure? Love in chains represents constraint of the emotional self, and it may be of some consequence that this design is peculiar to Petra. Perhaps the ideology of pleasure met a pocket of resistance in the desert kingdom, and the local potter was the agency used to express such dissatisfaction.

[5] Uniformity in religion, compulsory allegiance to the Trinity — conformity in fact — dictated the conscious and unconscious decoration of the "slipper" lamp. Its crosses, and perhaps the three fingers, conveyed an ideology that has since been named as a major cause for the demise of the Roman Empire. These symbols were metonymies of enormous power, rhetorical devices that told stories of good over evil, legitimating social strategies by claiming them to be universal (Hodder 1995:166).

# Bibliography

Bailey, D.

    1972    *Greek and Roman Pottery Lamps*. Oxford: The British Museum.

Barag, D. and M. Hershkovitz.

    1994    *Masada IV, The Yigael Yadin Excavations 1963-1965, Final Reports*. Jerusalem: Israel Exploration Society, The Hebrew University of Jerusalem.

Binford, L.

    1962    "Archaeology as Anthropology," *American Antiquity* 28, 2.

Boardman, J., J. Griffin and O. Murray.

    1986    *The Roman World*. Oxford.

Broneer, O.

1930    *Corinth, Results of Excavations Conducted by the American School of Classical Studies at Athens, Terracotta Lamps.* Vol. IV, Part II. Cambridge, MA: Harvard University Press.

Foucault, M.

1982    "On the Genealogy of Ethics: An Overview of Work in Progress." In *Michel Foucault: Beyond Structuralism and Hermeneutics*, by H.L. Dreyfus and P. Rabinow. 2nd ed. University of Chicago.

Fustel de Coulanges.

n.d.    *The Ancient City.* 1864. Reprint. Johns Hopkins University Press, 1980.

Hammond, P.C.

1973    "The Nabataeans — Their History, Culture and Archaeology." In *Studies in Mediterranean Archaeology.* Vol. 37. Gothenburg, Sweden.

Hodder, I.

1995    *Interpreting Archaeology.* London: Routledge.

Horsfield G. and A. Conway.

1942    "Sela-Petra, the Rock of Edom and Nabatene, IV, The Finds," *QDAP* 9.

Khairy, N.I.

1984    "Neither 'TLT' nor 'ALT' but 'RAYT'," *PEQ* 116.

———.

1990    *The 1981 Petra Excavations.* Vol. I. Abh. des Deutschen Palästinavereins, Wiesbaden.

Millar, F.

1993    *The Roman Near East 31 BC - AD 337.* Cambridge, MA: Harvard University Press.

Patrich, J.

1990    *The Formation of Nabataean Art.* Jerusalem: The Hebrew University.

Rabinow, P. (ed.)

1984    *The Foucault Reader.* New York: Pantheon Books.

Rosenthal, R. and R. Sivan.

1978    *Ancient Lamps in the Schloessinger Collection, Qedem 8.* The Hebrew University.

Vasiliev, A.A.

1973    *History of the Byzantine Empire 324-1453 AD.* Vol. I. Madison: University of Wisconsin.

Zayadine, F.

1982    "Recent Excavations and Restorations of the Department of Antiquities (1979-81)," *ADAJ* 26.

# OTHER SMALL FINDS

Deirdre G. Barrett

## Introduction

Included in the small finds catalog are objects of stone (159), bone (24), metal (29), pottery (37), terracotta figurines (10) and shell (3). The glass is cataloged at the end of this chapter. Our estimated chronology for the Great Temple has been confirmed by the dating of these objects. Because stratigraphy is problematic due to earthquake destruction, sealed contexts and extant structures (e.g., columns *in situ*) have been most useful in determining the period to which the artifact belongs. It would seem from the artifactual evidence, as with the lamps and coins, that the principal occupation period of the Great Temple first occurred during the latter part of the first century BCE, extending up to the latter part of the fourth century CE, with some intervening periods of abandonment probably due to earthquake devastation.

## Stone

We have a large corpus of limestone architectural fragments, providing details of capital, cornice and frieze decoration, which can be found in the Architectural Fragment Database. The overwhelming bounty of elephant heads, sometimes separated from their relative trunks, ears, mouths and eyes, is indicative of the crowning glory of many of the capitals, whose supporting columns surrounded the Lower Temenos. A small selection has been included in this chapter, these are 96-S-9, 97-S-9, 97-S-20 and 97-S-18. The remainder can be found in the CD-ROM. In all, 71 elephant fragments have been cataloged, and 106 were recorded.

In addition to elephants, we have discovered another excellent example of an animal carving in limestone. Found close to the Stairs of the Propylaeum was a diminutive lion's head (97-S-33) (Figures 6.67-6.69), with carefully executed features and a curling mane.

Despite the domination of elephants, they were not the only decorative element surmounting the capitals. Many vegetal/floral embellishments have been discovered amongst the rubble, lying often at the foot of column bases. These exquisitely carved flowers and fruits include the ambiguous pomegranates/ poppies, vine tendrils and pine cones. The latter have been cataloged as superlative examples of Nabataean stone carving (97-S-26 and 97-S-27) (Figures 6.70-6.72).

One intriguing aspect of Nabataean art lingers in the traces of paint found on the decorative architectural elements, in colors of white, cobalt blue, rust red, yellow ochre, moss green and black: even gold leaf has been found tucked within the inner coils of a volute. Other surfaces bearing traces of paint can be found on stucco fragments, some of which are included in the stone catalog. Plaster was used in the Temple to cover the columns, and its talent for plasticity has even been employed in the repair of statuary. For example, a life-size, flesh-color painted plaster nose (96-S-24) (Figure 6.73) was found in a tumble of plaster fragments, its parent face lost to us over the centuries of destruction and neglect.

Fragmented limestone face masks (94-S-1, 94-S-2, 94-S-3, 94-S-5, 94-S-8, 94-S-9) (Figures 6.74-6.78) have been found, but none fit our plaster nose. These exquisitely carved masks may be of deities worshipped by the Nabataeans. Although their Semitic religion forbade anthropomorphic reproduction, there are many examples of figurative art within Petra, the Al-Khazna being one such edifice that bears imitations of the human form. These betray a Hellenistic influence as do our masks with their flowing hair and mustaches. Perhaps our most impressive example of a deity is the limestone head of Tyche (95-S-14) (Figures 6.79 and 6.80), another victim of the powerful earthquake activity that probably felled all the Temple statuary. This city-goddess is well-documented in *ADAJ* 1997, XLI, by Joseph J. Basile, so we will let her virtues be extolled elsewhere.

Other remains of human statuary have been found that are not as monumental as the Tyche head, most notable of which is a hand with wrist (95-S-45) (Figures 6.81 and 6.82). Carved from marble, the small scale may be an indication of the local scarcity of this stone, which was a precious commodity imported in precut blocks and readied for the statuary and imperial inscriptions that abounded in the former Roman provinces. We have found an interesting selection of marble inscriptions within the Temple, three of which (96-S-32, 96-S-34 and 96-S-38) (Figure 6.83) have presented us with a Latin declaration that is examined in Chapter 8. We have two more inscriptions, one bearing a few Roman letters (93-S-1) and another cut with Greek characters (97-S-1) (Figures 6.84 and 6.85).

One inscribed limestone object of some interest is a loom weight that has the letters O H O carved on one side (96-S-13) (Figures 6.86 and 6.87). These letters have been found on Nabataean coins, the O signifying Sela, or Petra, and the H signifying Aretas, King of the Nabataeans (Christian Augé personal communication, July, 1998). We have no other parallels as yet that might suggest the meaning of these marks.

Before closing this section, we should mention the discovery of two tesserae cut from semiprecious stone, one of amethyst (95-S-4) and the other of malachite (95-S-7), among many others cut from limestone. They were found in the vicinity of the West Exedra, perhaps remnants of a fourth/fifth-century-CE mosaic, having a parallel in the Petra Church mosaics just across the wadi. An abundance of Byzantine lamps, some adorned with crosses (95-L-126 and 95-L-132), was also found nearby, suggesting that the West Exedra may have been reused for Christian religious practices during the fourth/fifth centuries CE.

## Selected catalog entries from the above text
(All measurements are in centimeters and grams unless otherwise noted.)

### 96-S-9  elephant head

Material: Limestone. Condition: Good. Culture: Nabataean. Area LT, Trench 18, Locus 17. Description: Elephant head, minus ears and trunk. Length: 23.5, Width: 19.0 (length measured from rear of head to beginning of trunk).

### 97-S-9  elephant trunk

Material: Limestone. Condition: Good. Culture: Nabataean. Area LT, Trench 42, Locus 14. Description: Upper trunk with tusk aperture. Length: 9.81, Thickness: 5.14.

### 97-S-18  elephant trunk

Material: Limestone. Condition: Good. Culture: Nabataean. Area LT, Trench 42, Locus 3. Description: Curved snout end of trunk. Snout is forked and ends are blunted. Length: 25.0, Thickness: 5.07 (measured at widest section).

### 97-S-20  elephant trunk

Material: Limestone. Condition: Good, broken in two. Culture: Nabataean. Area LT, Trench 42, Locus 16. Description: Middle section of trunk with ridging, small attachment underneath. Length: 9.95, Thickness: 4.77.

*Figure 6.61. 96-S-9, elephant head.*

*Figure 6.62. Drawing of 96-S-9 by Jean Blackburn.*

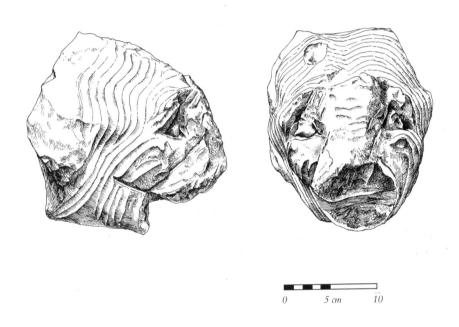

*Figure 6.63. 97-S-9, elephant trunk.*

*Figure 6.64. 97-S-20, elephant trunk.*

289

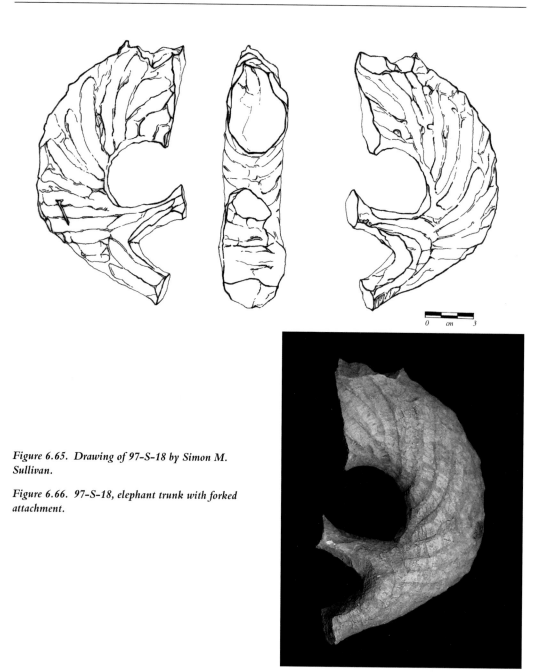

*Figure 6.65. Drawing of 97-S-18 by Simon M. Sullivan.*

*Figure 6.66. 97-S-18, elephant trunk with forked attachment.*

## 97-S-33 lion's head

Material: Limestone. Munsell: 10YR 7/3, very pale brown. Condition: Fair. Culture: Possibly Nabataean. Area P, Trench SP 53, Locus 1. Description: Partial head of lion. Both eyes, upper part of the nose, the left cheek and left-hand side of the mane present. There is some red/brown paint on the underside of the left cheek. Length: 12.38, Width: 6.61, Thickness: 4.87.

## 97-S-26 vegetal decoration

Material: Limestone. Munsell: 10YR 8/3, very pale brown. Condition: Good. Culture: Nabataean. Area T, Trench 47, Locus 6. Description: Small pine cone boss, surrounded by carved ribbed leaves. Length: 15.77, Width: 16.06, Thickness: 8.42.

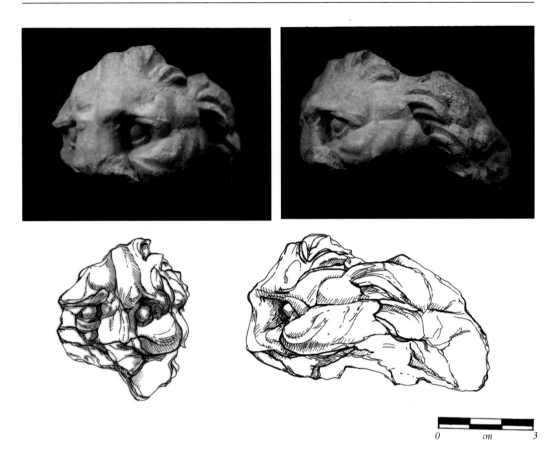

*Figures 6.67 and 6.68. 97-S-33, lion's head fragment.*

*Figure 6.69. Drawing of 97-S-33 by Simon M. Sullivan.*

*Figure 6.70. 97-S-26, vegetal decoration, pine cone boss.*

*Figure 6.71. Drawing of 97-S-26 by Simon M. Sullivan.*

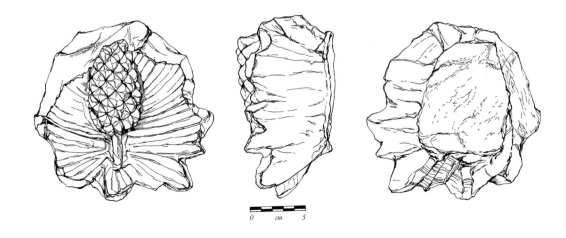

## 97-S-27  vegetal decoration

Material: Limestone. Munsell: 10YR 8/3, very pale brown. Condition: Good. Culture: Nabataean. Area T, Trench 47, Locus 6. Description: Pine cone boss (larger than 97-S-26). This pine cone has a stalk and is surrounded by ridged leaves. Length: 26.75, Width: 16.20, Thickness: 10.10.

*Figure 6.72. 97-S-27, vegetal decoration, pine cone boss.*

## 96-S-24  plaster nose

Material: Plaster. Munsell: 7.5YR 7/6, reddish yellow. Condition: Good. Area T, Trench 29, Locus 6. Description: Plaster nose, perhaps a reconstruction of a lost limestone feature. Length: 4.54, Width: 2.97. This object was discovered amongst a pile of retrieved plaster in the rockfall deposited in the trench.

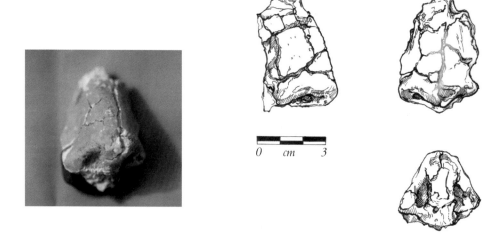

*Figure 6.73. 96-S-24, plaster nose. Drawing by Simon M. Sullivan.*

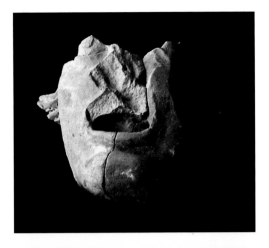

*Figure 6.74. 94–S–1, face mask.*
*Figure 6.75. 94–S–5, face mask. Photograph by David L. Brill.*

*Figure 6.76. 94–S–2, face mask. Photograph by David L. Brill.*

## 94-S-1 face mask *(see also Chapter 5 for further discussion of the masks)*

Material: Limestone. Condition: Good. Area T, Trench SP 2, Locus 6. Description: Head fragment of yellow limestone with open mouth and most of open eye, beginning of hair. Length: 12.0, Width: 8.5, Thickness: 5.0. Associated artifact: 94-S-3.

## 94-S-2 face mask

Material: Limestone. Good condition. Area T, Trench SP 2, Locus 6. Description: Larger than life-size limestone head fragment facing right, showing laurel leaf diadem, hair, nearly all of the eye and the beginning of a beard. Length 27.0, Width 8.5, Thickness 7.3. The width and thickness were measured at the eyebrow. This is probably part of a frieze. There is a pit in the eyebrow and a small crack in the beard line. The carving is well-defined.

## 94-S-3 face mask

Material: Limestone. Condition: Good. Area T, Trench SP 2, Locus 6. Description: Head fragment of yellow limestone, facing left with open mouth, lower chin and part of cheek. Length: 11.0, Width: 4.0, Thickness: 8.0. Associated artifact: 94-S-1.

*Figure 6.77. 94–S–8, face mask. Photograph by David L. Brill.*

*Figure 6.78. 94–S–3, face mask. Photograph by David L. Brill.*

*Figures 6.79a and 6.79b. 95–S–14, Head of Tyche. Photograph by David L. Brill.*

### 94-S-5  face mask

Material: Limestone. Condition: Good. Area T, Trench 8, Locus 1. Description: Head fragment of yellow limestone with garland around forehead and an elaborate arrangement of hair on top of head and at side of face. Well-executed. Length: 19.5, Width: 9.0, Thickness: 14.5.

### 94-S-8  face mask

Material: Limestone. Condition: Good. Area T, Trench SP 2, Locus 1. Description: Head/facial fragment of yellow limestone, with open mouth, lower chin and part of cheek facing to the right. Length: 20.1, Width: 14.2, Thickness: 10.8. Cheek and chin chipped during excavation. Part of eye and nose fragmented. Probably part of a frieze.

### 94-S-9  face mask

Material: Limestone. Condition: Good. Area T, Trench SP 2, Locus 1. Description: Head/facial fragment of yellow limestone, with eye and side curl well-defined, only corner of open mouth extant on the left side. Missing are the hair on top of head, nose and most of mouth. Length: 19.6, Width: 14.2, Thickness: 10.3.

### 95-S-14  Head of Tyche

Material: Sandstone. Munsell: 7.5YR 7/6, reddish yellow. Condition: Quite worn. Area LT, surface find. Description: Head of Tyche — facial features and turretted crown partially eroded. Hair set in waves. Nose missing. A counterpart to Isis in the east, serving as the city-goddess. Length: 38.3, Width: 31.5.

*Figure 6.80. Drawing of 95-S-14 by Jean Blackburn.*

## 95-S-45  hand with wrist

Material: Marble. Condition: Fair. Area T, Trench 23, Locus 7. Description: Wrist and part of hand, square opening in center of wrist for attachment to arm. Length: 11.5, Width: 14.5.

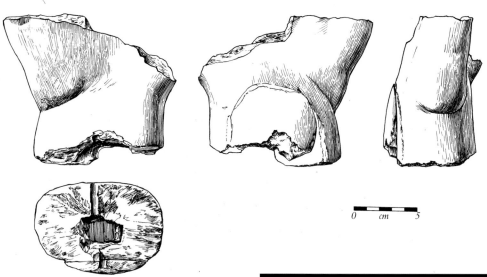

*Figure 6.81. Drawing of 95-S-45 by Jean Blackburn.*
*Figure 6.82. 95-S-45, hand with wrist.*

## 93-S-1  inscription

Material: Marble. Condition: Fair. Culture: Roman. Area UT, Trench 1, Locus 4. Description: Small fragment of marble with inscription. The upper line contains the lower portion of a rounded numeral or the letter O, with a flourish belonging to the letter or numeral to its right. The line below contains the upper portion of the numeral I with a small upper portion of the numeral II. Length: 9.34, Width: 8.31, Thickness: 2.27.

## 96-S-32  inscription *(see also Chapter 8 for further analysis of the inscriptions)*

Material: Marble. Condition: Fair. Culture: Roman. Area T, Trench 22, Locus 16. Description: Two fragments of marble, one bearing the letters RIB on the top line and perhaps EIV on the second line. The second fragment forms the lower half of V. First fragment: Length: 16.11, Width: 9.46, Thickness: 2.31; second fragment: Height: 5.36 (of V), Thickness: 2.25. Associated artifacts: 96-S-34, 96-S-38, 96-S-39.

## 96-S-34  inscription

Material: Marble. Condition: Good. Culture: Roman. Area T, Trench 22, Locus 16. Description: Second marble fragment, matches 96-S-32. Also possibly the letters VS period M. Length: 20.5, Width: 9.33, Thickness: 2.53. Associated artifacts: 96-S-32.

*Figure 6.83. 96-S-32, 96-S-34 and 96-S-38, marble inscription.*

## 96-S-38 inscription

Material: Marble. Condition: Good. Culture: Roman. Area T, Trench 22, Locus 16. Description: Third marble fragment, matches 96-S-32, 96-S-34 and 96-S-39. Includes punctuation mark, P and O. Length: 9.59, Width: 8.15, Thickness: 2.19. Associated artifacts: 96-S-32, 96-S-34, 96-S-39.

## 97-S-1 inscription

Material: Marble. Condition: Good. Culture: Unknown. Area LT, Trench 42, Locus 19. Description: Fragment with lettering (N, M, X) and beneath these three letters two perpendicular cuts, perhaps one being an I. Length: 12.34, Width: 9.06, Thickness: 3.59 (measured at widest points).

*Figure 6.84. 97-S-1, inscription.*

*Figure 6.85. Drawing of 97-S-1 by Simon M. Sullivan.*

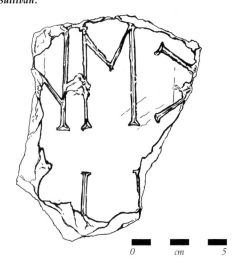

0  cm  5

## 96-S-13 loom weight with inscription

Material: Limestone. Munsell: 7.5YR 7/2, pinkish gray. Condition: Good. Culture: Unknown. Area LT, Trench 31, Locus 3. Description: Possible loom weight. Triangular shape with etched lines in a four-line crisscross pattern on the flat surface. On two sides there are four ridged lines, and on the third there is an inscription which may be in Greek (OHO). The other flat side has been damaged and therefore is no longer legible. There is a perforation measuring 0.8 cm through the weight. Found within a wall. Length: 4.33, Thickness: 2.31.

*Figures 6.86 and 6.87. 96-S-13, loom weight.*

## 95-S-4 amethyst tessera

Material: Amethyst. Condition: Good. Culture: Unknown. Area LT, Trench 16, Locus 3. Description: Mosaic component. Length: 1.0, Width: 1.0, Thickness: 1.0.

## 95-S-7 malachite tessera

Material: Malachite. Condition: Satisfactory. Culture: Unknown. Area LT, Trench 14, Locus 6. Description: If this is a tessera, it is not a cube but triangular in shape. Length: 2.0, Width: 1.5.

## Pottery

Forty-seven items of pottery, including 10 terracotta figurine fragments, have been cataloged. We have identified 14 objects of Nabataean origin, including five unguentaria, four bowls, three plates, one jug and one cup. The unguentaria are all damaged, most with their necks broken. The bowls are decorated with rouletting, stamping and incising, and the plates have vegetal/geometric designs painted in black or brown paint on the interior surface. One plate, for example, (97-P-9) (Figure 6.88) is from the second Nabataean style and is decorated with vegetal, dots and double cones designs that can be dated to 18-40 CE (Khairy 1990:40). Many thousands of small painted sherds have also been recovered from the Temple site, exhibiting the fine "eggshell"

quality of Nabataean pottery, which is dependent on well-levigated clay and even-firing in the kiln.

Two inscribed ceramic objects include a Rhodian jar handle complete with stamp (97-P-3), which is described in Chapter 8, and a small vessel base (95-P-14) (Figure 6.89) with an inscription yet to be deciphered. A ceramic fragment that is provisionally classified as North African Red Slip Ware (97-P-8) is stamped with concentric circles and interwoven with a leaf-like/feather motif. John W. Hayes (1997:62) comments, "Stamped patterns, at first floral but increasingly figurative, were introduced on both wares (*Terra Sigillata africana* C and D) around AD 325 and lasted until the fifth- and sixth-century."

A ceramic plaque (97-P-7) (Figures 6.90 and 6.91) has been found that may illustrate the impact of Ptolemaic religious influence on Petra. It is decorated with a relief of Harpocrates (the Roman/Greek name for the Egyptian deity Horus), son of Isis, sucking his thumb, subscribing to the Isisian belief-system that Philip C. Hammond (1990) has suggested pervaded the Temple of the Winged Lions — a close neighbor of the Great Temple.

Two finds with a later date are a small ribbed Byzantine bowl (96-P-3) and a green tin-glazed Islamic handle (96-P-1) (Figures 6.92 and 6.93).

## Selected catalog entries from the above text

(All measurements are in centimeters and grams unless otherwise noted.)

### 97-P-9  Nabataean plate

Material: Ceramic. Munsell: 10R 6/8, light red. Condition: Fair. Culture: Nabataean. Area LT, Trench 46, Locus 17. Description: Partially reconstructed Nabataean plate with conical base and a small vertical lip. The design is organized into a triangular subdivision (Schmitt-Korte 1968:29/3l, Figs. 15/17). The design is vegetal in form with dots and double cones. It typically demonstrates the "*horror vacuii*" of the second Nabataean style. Diameter: 18.3, Thickness: 0.17.

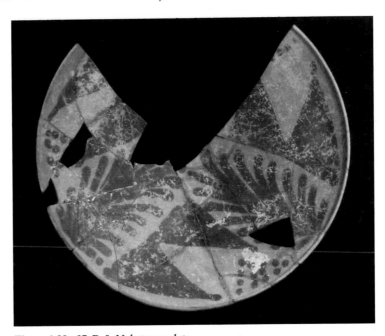

*Figure 6.88. 97-P-9, Nabataean plate.*

### 97-P-3  Rhodian jar handle

Material: Ceramic. Munsell: 5YR 6/6, reddish yellow. Condition: Fair. Culture: Rhodian. Area T, Trench 48, Locus 1. Description: Rhodian jar handle with stamped impression. Length: 8.17, Thickness: 3.63.

### 95-P-14  vessel base with inscription

Material: Ceramic. Munsell: 10R 5/8, red. Condition: Evidence of lime leaching. Culture: Unknown. Area T, Trench 19, Locus 9. Description: Ring base fragment, incised inscription above base. Length: 4.1, Width: 4.6, Diameter: 6.0.

Figure 6.89. 95-P-14, vessel base with inscription. Drawing by Simon M. Sullivan.

## 97-P-7  plaque of Harpocrates, son of Isis

Material: Ceramic. Munsell: 2.5YR 6/6, red. Condition: Fair. Culture: Unknown. Area T, Trench 47, Locus 13. Description: Small ceramic plaque with decorated border, with incised horizontal lines and circles. The relief in the center is of a male figure standing on a decorated plinth. The figure has its right arm raised and possibly a finger inserted in the mouth. Length: 8.40, Width: 4.33, Thickness: 1.08. (Thickness determined at the border. Thickness determined within the border is 0.72.) Note: Many fingerprints on back of plaque.

Figure 6.90. 97-P-7, plaque of Harpocrates.

Figure 6.91. Drawing of 97-P-7 by Simon M. Sullivan.

## 96-P-3 Byzantine bowl

Material: Ceramic. Munsell: 10YR 4/1, dark gray. Condition: Very good. Culture: Byzantine. Area T, Trench 24, Locus 1. Description: Small ribbed bowl with string-cut base. Gray slip over red clay. Height: 6.15, Thickness: 0.46.

## 96-P-1 Islamic glazed handle

Material: Ceramic. Munsell: 5Y 7/6, yellow. Condition: Two pieces reattached. Culture: Islamic. Area LT, Trench 18, Locus 3. Description: Handle, green tin-glaze. Length: 9.51, Width: 2.92, Thickness: 2.55.

*Figure 6.92. 96–P-3, Byzantine bowl.*

*Figure 6.93. 96–P-1, Islamic glazed handle.*

## Figurines

Terracotta figurines were made in molds and frequently followed Hellenistic patterns, which were often of goddesses associated with local cults. Many have been found in and around Nabataean sites, and particularly near temples and sanctuaries (Hammond 1973:84), suggesting that they may have been votive offerings or even served as "ushabti" figures (Higgins 1967:1). Their manufacture declined from the fourth century CE, possibly because of the increasing influence of Christianity (Jenkins 1978).

The figurine fragments discovered at the Temple site, 10 in all, are predominantly human in form, apart from 95-P-2, 97-P-1 and 97-P-12 (Figures 6.94-6.97), the latter being a fragment of an ibex horn. The human forms are broken, which begs the question whether this breakage was deliberate (Khairy 1981:23).

Attempting to date these figurines is difficult due to the lack of stratigraphic integrity; however, if we look at the assemblage found with each figurine (i.e., within the same locus), some sense of historic period may be deduced.

## 95-P-2 zoomorphic figurine fragment

Munsell: 5YR 9/6. Condition: Good, some salt encrustation. Area LT, Trench 14, Locus 14. Length: 6.2, Width: 2.6, Diameter: 1.8 (width measured at head, diameter measured at body). Description: Orange ware, zoomorphic figure. Body and head damaged. Associated artifacts: One lamp fragment that may be of Islamic origin (95-L-34) and one bronze coin (95-C-14) dated to the reign of Constantine I or II (335-361 CE) were found within this locus.

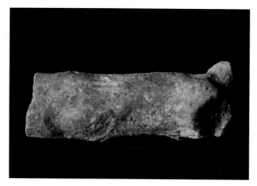

*Figure 6.94. 95-P-3, drapery fragment.*

*Figure 6.95. 95-P-6, figurine or baby feeder.*

## 95-P-3 drapery fragment from a human figure

Munsell: 5YR 7/6. Condition: Satisfactory. Area LT, Trench 20, Locus 4. Length: 5.5, Width: 3. Description: Fragment of drapery from a human figure. Found in association with this fragment were three lamp fragments (95-L-30, 95-L-38, 95-L-45) of unknown culture and 95-L-38, which is classified as a Nabataean volute lamp. (Neutron activation tests, however, show its clay is foreign to Petra; therefore, it must have been imported.) A Roman lamp (95-L-45), a bone spoon (95-B-1) whose origin/culture is unidentified and a Nabataean elephant trunk fragment (95-S-38) were also found in this locus. This assemblage does not demonstrate a dominant culture but suggests a late-first/early-second-century-CE dating, with the presence of Nabataean, Roman and imported material.

## 95-P-4 upper torso of human figure with drapery

Munsell: 10R 6/8. Condition: Good. Area LT, Trench 20, Locus 1. Length: 5.1, Width: 4.8. Description: Fragment of upper torso of a human figure, toga drapery and one arm holding a round object. Found in association with this fragment were five lamp fragments (95-L-26, 95-L-61, 95-L-20, 95-L-21, 95-L-22). Two of these lamp fragments (95-L-22 and 95-L-61) have been classified as Roman lamps, and neutron activation tests show their clays are foreign to Petra and that they originate possibly from Parthia with a dating of first/second century CE. The remaining three lamp fragments (95-L-20, 95-L-21, 95-L-22) are classified as Byzantine and are approximately dated to the late fourth century CE.

Included in this assemblage are four Nabataean elephant trunk fragments (95-S-12, 95-S-17, 95-S-18, 95-S-27) and one elephant head (95-S-28). The seemingly broad dating of the assemblage in this locus demonstrates the chaos caused by the earthquake tumble, a cataclysmic destruction of the Temple that strewed the Lower Temenos with elephant capital decorations, forcefully churning up the underlying strata. This earlier debris is now found covering artifacts of a later date, which were deposited by human agency, so confounding the law of superposition.

## 95-P-5 possible arm of figurine

Munsell: 5YR 6/6, reddish yellow. Condition: Fair. Area T, Trench 26, Locus 12. Length: 4.26, Thickness: 1.25. Description: Possible arm of a figurine. No other artifacts were found within this locus.

## 95-P-6 head of figurine or fragment of a baby feeder

Munsell: 10R 6/6. Condition: Ears broken away. Area LT, Trench 16, Locus 9. Length: 4.5, Width: 3.5. Description: Head of figurine (or possibly fragment of a baby feeder). Found in association with one Nabataean lamp fragment (95-L-97a), two Byzantine lamp fragments (95-L-88 and 95-L-99) and a Nabataean elephant trunk fragment (95-S-35). Four bronze coins, all dated to the late fourth century CE, were found in this locus (95-C-27, 95-C-29, 95-C-30, 95-C-31). This assemblage is mixed in culture; therefore, we cannot attribute a period, except an inclusive one of first century to fifth century CE. Possibly earthquake debris has contaminated the locus.

## 95-P-8 possible human figurine fragment, crudely modeled

Munsell: 10R 6/8. Condition: Good. Area LT, Trench 20, Locus 21. Description: Possibly human figure, arms and legs missing, crudely modeled. Found in association with this fragment were 17 Nabataean lamp fragments (95-L-110 through 125 and 95-L-145). Also found were a Nabataean unguentarium (95-P-7), a carved bone object (95-B-3) and an ivory eye socket (95-B-5), perhaps belonging to an elephant head. One bronze coin (95-C-40) was found in this locus, which has been dated to the reign of Septimius Severus (193-211 CE) or the reign of Caracalla (211-212 CE). Despite the dating of this coin, the overwhelming Nabataean assemblage indicates that the figurine is probably of Nabataean origin.

*Figure 6.96. 95-P-8, possible human figurine. Drawing by Simon M. Sullivan.*

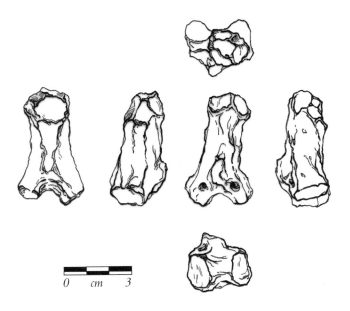

## 95-P-12 possible human figurine fragment with bead necklace

Munsell: 2.5YR 7/4. Condition: Good. Area T, Trench SP 30, Locus 12. Length: 3.4, Width: 1.7. Description: Possibly a fragment of a bust with bead necklace (or belt). This artifact stands alone, as no other items were found in this locus.

## 95-P-13  arms and upper torso of female figure

Munsell: 5YR 7/6. Condition: Some lime leaching. Area T, Trench 19, Locus 9. Length: 2.9, Width: 3.3. Description: Arms and bust of a female figure. Also found within this locus was a terracotta ring base fragment with an inscription that has yet to be deciphered.

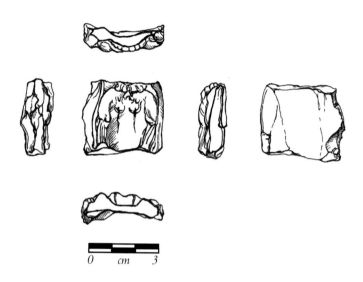

0     cm     3

*Figure 6.97.  95-P-13, female figure.  Drawing by Simon M. Sullivan.*

## 97-P-1  possible two front legs of animal figure

Condition: Fair. Area UT, Trench 44, Locus 7. Length: 2.25, Thickness: 1.78. Description: Perhaps the two front legs of an animal figure or part of an ornamental jug handle. Found in association with a spindle whorl (97-S-4) and four Roman lamp fragments dated to the latter two-thirds of the first century CE (97-L-14, 97-L-15, 97-L-30a, 97-L-30b).

## 97-P-12  fragment of ibex horn

Munsell: 2.5YR 6/6, red. Condition: Fair. Area T, Trench 48, Locus: 1. Length: 3.85, Thickness: 1.32. Description: Fragment of an ibex horn with notches and a small doughnut-shaped appendage, which could be an eye. Similar parallels come from the Christian basilica at 'Ayn Hanniye (Baramki 1934:113-117, Pl. XL.1), dated to the fifth to sixth centuries CE, and other churches such as Khirbat Asida, Khirbat al-Mefgir and Umm Sayhun (Zayadine 1982:389, Pl. CXXXVII 96) probably from the fifth century CE.

Also found within this locus were three Byzantine lamp fragments (97-L-39, 97-L-61, 97-L-62), three Nabataean lamp fragments (97-L-63, 97-L-64, 97-L-69) and a Rhodian jar handle with inscription (97-P-3). Two bronze coins (97-C-33 and 97-C-34) have been provisionally designated possibly Roman/Nabataean. The varied cultural mix suggests earthquake debris, particularly as this was the first locus opened in the trench.

## Metal

Twenty-nine metal objects were cataloged, with a total of 1151 metal objects recorded but not cataloged. Many were difficult to identify, as they were often too corroded or too fragmented. There were three bronze rings (96-M-1, 96-M-13, 95-M-4) (Figure 6.98), a possible bronze bracelet (95-M-3), a possible locket (94-M-3), a silver pendant (96-M-12), a lead pendant (95-M-6), three supposed bronze fastenings (96-M-16, 95-M-5, 97-M-1), three bronze/iron hooks (96-M-5, 96-M-9, 96-M-11) and six iron nails (96-M-3, 96-M-4, 96-M-7, 96-M-8, 96-M-10, 94-M-1), which were cataloged as examples (100 were recorded but not cataloged) (Figure 6.99).

Apart from the above objects, there were single finds as follows: one bead (95-M-7), one possible bronze earring (96-M-9), one bronze tag (93-M-1) (Figure 6.100), one bronze flask neck (96-M-14) (Figure 6.101), one iron arrowhead (94-M-2), one possible iron ax head (93-M-2), one bronze leaf-shaped fragment that could represent human hair (96-M-6) (Figures 6.102 and 6.103) and one bronze leaf with petal (96-M-15).

Most remarkable were two bronze handles (97-M-2 and 97-M-3) (Figures 6.104-6.108) that were found in a drain in the western Lower Temenos in Trench 42, Locus 24. These handles have a floral motif with a twelve-petalled flower and leafy stem. One might suggest that they belonged at one time to a jar or urn and were lost when the parent vessel broke. No parallel has yet been located. Their location in a drain makes them difficult to date, although two items were found in association with them. One was an incomplete Nabataean carinated bowl (97-P-2), and the other item was an incomplete Roman jar with a loop handle (97-P-4).

## Selected catalog entries from the above text

(All measurements are in centimeters and grams unless otherwise noted.)

### 95-M-4 bronze ring

Object: Finger ring. Condition: Heavily corroded. Area T, Trench 23, Locus 7. Diameter: 1.9. Description: Simple wire ring, seemingly twisted into a knot.

### 96-M-1 bronze ring

Object: Metal ring. Condition: Covered with verdigris. Area T, Trench 17, Locus 26. Diameter: 3.17, Thickness: 0.53. Description: Bronze ring, perhaps used for curtain or jewelry.

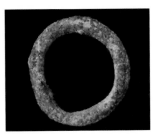

*Figure 6.98. 96-M-1, bronze ring.*

### 96-M-13 bronze ring

Object: Signet ring. Condition: Corroded. Area LT, Trench 31, Locus 51. Width: 2.32, Thickness: 0.25. Description: Copper/bronze ring with engraving that resembles an asterisk with brackets on either side.

## 94-M-3  locket

Object: Possible locket. Condition: Corroded. Area T, Trench 9, Locus 45. Length: 2.25, Width: 1.4. Description:  Bell-shaped ornament, perforated at the top. Possibly a locket or jewelry.

## 95-M-3  bronze bracelet

Object: Wire fragment. Condition: Corroded, broken in two. Area LT, Trench 20, Locus 13. Length: 12.4. Description:  Bent knob or twist at one end, possibly a bracelet.

## 95-M-6  lead pendant

Object: Amulet or pendant. Condition: Corroded. Area T, Trench 15, Locus 105. Length: 1.5, Width: 1.3, Thickness: 0.15. Description:  Oval on one side, a cross or possibly a man making an offering. On the other side the design is illegible, contains remains of a loop at top.

## 95-M-7  bead

Object: Bead (half). Condition: Fair. Area T, Trench 19, Locus 8. Length: 0.67, Width: 0.37, Thickness: 0.37. Description:  Half of a bead, black in color, found with two lamp fragments, one base (95-L-178) and the other a small discus fragment of a Nabataean lamp (95-L-179). The bead has been broken lengthwise.

## 96-M-12  silver pendant

Object: Pendant. Condition: Corroded. Area T, Trench 22, Locus 8. Length: 1.82, Thickness: 0.13. Description:  Small piriform pendant in silver.

## 96-M-5  hook

Object: Metal hook. Condition: Good. Area T, Trench 22, Locus 8. Length: 1.24, Thickness: 0.22. Description:  Small bronze/copper hook with eye and extra piece of wire.

## 96-M-9  hook

Object: Hooks and assorted metal wire strips. Condition: Good. Area T, Trench 22, Locus 8. Length: 2.25, Width: 1.31, Thickness: 0.36. Description: Possible bronze earring.

## 96-M-11  hook

Object: Hook/eye. Condition: Corroded. Area T, Trench 22, Locus 8. Length: 4.03, Thickness: 0.29. Description:  Small iron hook. Head corroded to post.

## 96-M-3  iron nail

Object: Nail. Condition: Covered in rust. Area T, Trench 29, Locus 7. Length: 8.51, Thickness: 1.31. Description:  Large iron nail with head and projection, perhaps a stone cemented to nail by rust.

## 96-M-7  iron nail

Object: Nail. Condition: Corroded. Area T, Trench 29, Locus 10. Length: 7.71, Thickness: 1.04. Description: Heavily corroded, large iron nail with head, which appears to have been made by bending over the top of the nail, possibly to hang a lamp.

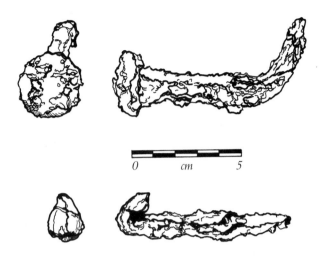

*Figure 6.99.  96-M-3 and 96-M-7, iron nails.  Drawings by Simon M. Sullivan.*

## 93-M-1  bronze tag

Object: Metal tag. Condition: Fair. Area UT, Trench 2, Locus 7. Length: 5.18, Width: 2.4, Thickness: 0.9. Description:  Small bronze "tag" with pinched ends. Function unknown.

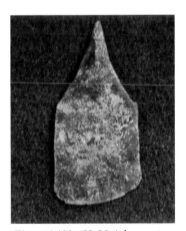

*Figure 6.100.  93-M-1, bronze tag.*

## 93-M-2  iron ax head

Object: Unknown metal. Condition: Poor. Area UT, Trench 3, Locus 10. Length: 4.98, Width: 3.41, Thickness: 1.16. Description:  Triangular-shaped metal with rough finish.  Could be from a metal clamp or ax head.

## 94-M-2  iron arrowhead

Object: Arrowhead. Condition: Corroded. Area LT, Trench 5, Locus 46. Length: 6.8, Width: 0.7, Thickness: 0.9. Description:  Fragment of an iron arrowhead tapered to a point, tip missing, elongated tang.

## 96-M-14  bronze flask neck

Object: Metal neck of flask. Condition: Fair. Area T, Trench 22, Locus 16. Length: 1.61, Thickness: 1.1. Description: Small bronze shoulder and neck of bottle or flask. Covered in verdigris.

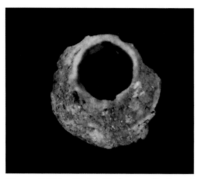

*Figure 6.101.  96-M-14, bronze flask neck.*

## 96-M-6  bronze leaf-shaped fragment

Object: Metal decorative piece. Condition: Good. Area T, Trench 23, Locus 12. Length: 5.16, Width: 2.46, Thickness: 0.14. Description:  Small leaf-shape piece. Could be hair, e.g., beard.

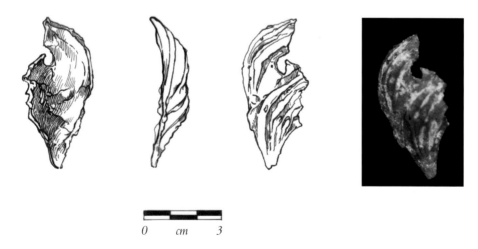

*0     cm     3*

*Figures 6.102 and 6.103.  96-M-6, bronze leaf-shaped fragment. Drawing by Simon M. Sullivan.*

## 96-M-15  bronze leaf with petal

Object: Metal decorative piece. Condition: Good. Area T, Trench 22, Locus 6. Length: 4.77, Thickness: 0.19. Description:  Small leaf-shaped piece with striations.

## 97-M-2 bronze handle

Object: Handle. Condition: Very good. Area LT, Trench 42, Locus 24. Length: 5.5, Width: 4.0. Description: Bronze handle, vegetal decoration. Attachment in the form of a curved leaf, backed by a scroll. A twelve-petalled flower provides the actual handle.

*Figures 6.104 and 6.105. 97-M-2, bronze handle, after cleaning. Photograph by Paul C. Zimmerman.*

## 97-M-3 bronze handle

Object: Handle. Condition: Very good. Area LT, Trench 42, Locus 24. Length: 6.7, Width: 1.64. Description: Bronze handle (the companion to 97-M-2). Leaf attachment backed by a scroll and twelve-petalled flower.

 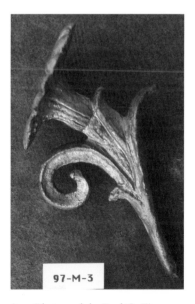

*Figures 6.106 and 6.107. 97-M-3, bronze handle, after cleaning. Photograph by Paul C. Zimmerman.*

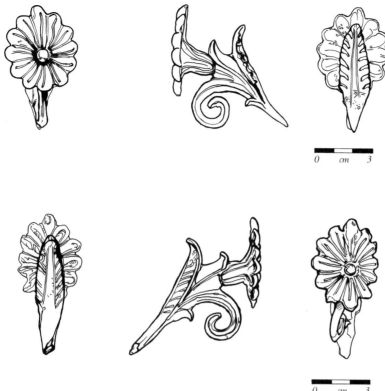

*Figure 6.108. Drawings of 97–M–2 and 97–M–3 by Simon M. Sullivan.*

## Bone

Although a total of 24 bone objects were cataloged, 7341 bone fragments were recovered on the site, and these have been recorded. Of the cataloged bone objects, we have two needles (96-B-3 and 96-B-5) (Figure 6.111), one cosmetic spatula found in the Temple (96-B-4) (Figure 6.110), one small *fleur-de-lis* decorative piece also found in the Temple (96-B-2) (Figure 6.109), one spindle whorl (96-B-1), eight pins (96-B-6, 94-B-1, 95-B-7, 95-B-11, 95-B-12, 97-B-1, 97-B-2, 97-B-4) (Figures 6.112-6.119), two spoon fragments (95-B-1 and 95-B-10), one peg (95-B-2) (Figure 6.120) two small unidentified carved pieces (95-B-3 and 97-B-3), one bone eye fragment, possibly belonging to an elephant head found in Trench 16 in the Lower Temenos (95-B-4), one elliptical eye socket that may have had a similar function to 95-B-3 (95-B-5), one ring fragment also found in the Lower Temenos in Trench 20 (95-B-6) and one inlay fragment with dots and grooves on one side found in the Temple in Trench 23 (95-B-9).

## Selected catalog items from the above text
(All measurements are in centimeters and grams unless otherwise noted.)

## 96-B-1 spindle whorl

Object: Spindle whorl. Munsell: 10YR 8/3. Condition: Fair. Area LT, Trench 18, Locus 3. Diameter: 3.05, Thickness: 0.68, Perforated Hole Diameter: 0.45.

## 96-B-2 *fleur-de-lis* decoration

Object: Decorative motif. Munsell: 10YR 8/2, very pale brown. Condition: Good. Area T, Trench 29, Locus 14. Length: 4.19, Thickness: 0.45. Description: Small decorative piece. *Fleur-de-lis* design with volute.

*Figure 6.109. 96–B–2,* **fleur-de-lis** *decoration.*

## 96-B-4 cosmetic spatula

Object: Possible cosmetic spatula. Munsell: 7.5YR 8/4, pink. Condition: Fragments glued together. Area T, Trench 22, Locus 16. Length: 6.48, Thickness: 0.14. Description: Small spatula with circular protrusion at one end.

*Figure 6.110. 96–B–4, cosmetic spatula.*

## 96-B-3 needle

Object: Bone needle. Munsell: 10YR 8/4. Condition: Very good. Area T, Trench 22, Locus 16. Length: 10.45, Thickness: 0.35. Description: Bone needle with eye (0.16 cm wide).

## 96-B-5 needle

Object: Needle. Condition: Fair. Area T, Trench 22, Locus 16. Length: 6.1, Thickness: 0.29. Description: Two fragments of bone needle

## 94-B-1 pin

Object: Bone pin. Condition: Fair. Area T, Trench 10, Locus 14. Length: 6.2; Diameter: 0.6, Thickness: 0.5. Description: Bone pin, stem, well-finished.

*Figure 6.111. 96–B–3, needle.*

*Figure 6.112. 94–B–1, pin.*

## 95-B-7 pin

Object: Pin. Condition: Good, complete. Area LT, Trench 16, Locus 13. Length: 10.3, Diameter: 0.4. Description: Shank tapered to point and polished, grooved below head. Head, conical and grooved.

## 95-B-11 pin

Object: Pin. Condition: Good, complete. Area T, Trench 23, Locus 7. Length: 5.3, Width: 0.35.
Description: Triple grooves below head, pointed, quadrilateral head, polished.

*Figure 6.113. 95-B-7, pin.* 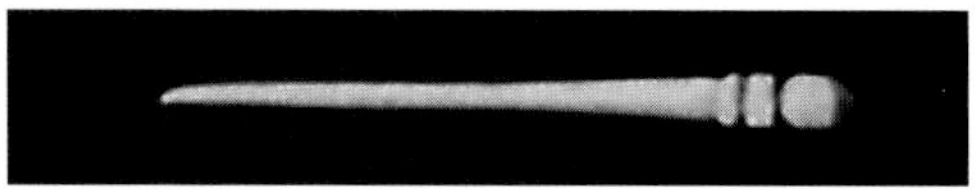      *Figure 6.114. 95-B-11, pin.*

## 95-B-12 pin

Object: Pin fragment. Condition: Good. Area LT, Trench 5, Locus 22. Length: 4.4, Width: 0.6.
Description: Rectangular, intricately carved and perforated head of pin, tapered to a small knob on top, polished.

## 96-B-6 pin

Object: Pin. Condition: Broken. Area T, Trench 34, Locus 10. Length: 2.75, Thickness: 0.44.
Description: Head of broken bone pin. End of pin has an encircling ridge with a dimple at end.

## 97-B-1 pin

Object: Pin/distaff. Condition: Fair. Area T, Trench 27, Locus 5. Length: 2.5, Thickness: 0.58.
Description: Broken pin with head separated from body by a ridge.

## 97-B-2 pin

Object: Pin/distaff. Condition: Fair. Area T, Trench 47, Locus 6. Length: 3.11, Thickness: 0.59.
Description: Head of a pin or distaff, with a rounded, etched head that has a dimple on the top. There is some small carving/marking on the side that resembles a spider or a flower without a center.

*Figure 6.115. 95-B-12, pin.*
*Figure 6.116. 96-B-2, pin.*

*Figure 6.117. 97-B-1, pin.*
*Figure 6.118. 97-B-6, pin.*

## 97-B-4 pin

Object: Pin. Condition: Good. Area T, Trench 34, Locus 14. Length: 4.3, Width: 1.82, Thickness: 0.26. Description: Small bone pin. The top has an ovoid opening and wings. The pin tapers to a point.

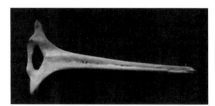

*Figure 6.119. 97-B-4, pin.*

### 95-B-1  spoon

Object: Spoon. Condition: Broken into two fragments. Area LT, Trench 20, Locus 4. Length: 6.4, Width: 2.1, Thickness: 0.2. Description: Bowl of oval spoon only, stub of handle behind one end of the bowl.

### 95-B-10  spoon

Object: Spoon fragment. Condition: Good except cracked. Area T, Trench SP 23. Length: 6.5, Width: 3.4. Description: Bowl only, handle missing. Oval.

### 95-B-2  peg

Object: Peg. Condition: Top end broken off. Area LT, Trench 20, Locus 22. Length: 2.6, Width: 0.6. Description: Tapered to point, two ridges carved below missing top end.

*Figure 6.120.  95-B-2, peg.*

### 95-B-3  carving

Object: Unidentified. Condition: Fair. Area LT, Trench 20, Locus 21. Length: 4.9, Width: 1.9. Description: Carved, image unidentifiable.

### 97-B-3  carving

Object: Unknown. Condition: Fair. Area UT, Trench 41, Locus 21. Length: 5.94, Width: 1.28, Thickness: 0.51. Description: Triangular-shaped, flat bone fragment with curved cutout on one side. The cutout is etched with a ridge.

### 95-B-4  eye fragment

Object: Unidentified fragment. Condition: Good. Area LT, Trench 16, Locus 13. Diameter: 2.4. Description: Half circle, white, polished, possibly from an elephant head.

### 95-B-5  eye fragment

Object: Eye socket. Condition: Good, stained from soil. Area LT, Trench 20, Locus 21. Length: 3.2, Width: 1.9, Thickness: 1.4. Description: Elliptical eye socket from an elephant head or statue.

### 95-B-6  ring

Object: Unidentified fragment. Condition: Discolored by soil. Area LT, Trench 16, Locus 23. Diameter: 3.2, Thickness: 0.6. Description: Half of a ring, slight ridges around side. Rough underside may indicate breakage.

## 95-B-9 inlay

Object: Unidentified ornamental fragment. Condition: Broken at both ends. Area T, Trench 23, Locus 7. Length: 3.3, Thickness: 0.8. Description: Carved design of dots and grooves on one side, random slashes on other side, tapered from center to thin end. Possibly a fragment of inlay or of a handle.

### Shell

Only three marine items have been cataloged, although 501 shells and shell fragments have been recorded and saved. Of these, the most notable was a complete brain coral found on the floor of the West 'Adyton' room (96-H-1) (Figure 6.121) and a fragment of a spotted shell found in the same context (96-H-2). One can only guess at the function of these two unusual finds, so far from their original seabed(s). If they were intended for ritual use, why were they left behind when the Temple was abandoned? The question of intentional and planned abandonment versus catastrophic abandonment is then brought to mind. Were the occupants of the Temple forced to flee at a moment's notice, or did they have time to collect themselves and their belongings in an orderly fashion before departure? No human remains have yet been found to present a 'Pompeii premise' for the excavators, and yet both the neighboring, contemporaneous sites of the Temple of the Winged Lions and Al-Katute have skeletal evidence that indicates a cataclysmic disaster. The brain coral and the spotted shell were found buried beneath an enormous tumble of architectural fragments, providing clues perhaps to the elusive past human behavior that once took place in the Great Temple nearly 2000 years ago.

### Selected catalog items from the above text

(All measurements are in centimeters and grams unless otherwise noted.)

## 96-H-1 brain coral

Object: Brain coral. Condition: Good. Area T, Trench 22, Locus 16. Description: Complete brain coral found at bottom of Trench 22, in context with 96-H-2. Possibly a ritual object.

*Figure 6.121. 96-H-2, brain coral.*

## 96-H-2 spotted shell

Object: Shell fragment. Condition: Broken. Area T, Trench 22, Locus 16. Length: 3, Thickness: 0.19. Description: Edge fragment of spotted shell, found in context with 96-H-1, brain coral. Possible ritual use.

# Bibliography

Baramki, D.C.

    1934     "An Early Christian Basilica at 'Ein Hanniya," *QDAP* 3.

Hammond, P.C.

    1973     "The Nabataeans — Their History, Culture and Archaeology." In *Studies in Mediterranean Archaeology*. Vol. 37. Gothenburg, Sweden.

————.

    1990     "The Goddess of the Temple of the Winged Lions at Petra (Jordan)." In Symposium organized at Petra in September, 1985. Amman.

Hayes, J.W.

    1997     *Handbook of Mediterranean Roman Pottery*. University of Oklahoma.

Higgins, R.A.

    1967     *Greek Terracottas*. London.

Jenkins, F.

    1978     "Some Interesting Types of Clay Statuettes of the Roman Period Found in London." In Collectanea Londiniensia. *Studies in London Archaeology and History Presented to Ralph Merrifield*, ed. J. Bird et al. London. 148-162.

Khairy, N.I.

    1990     *The 1981 Petra Excavations*. Vol. I. Abh. des Deutschen Palästinavereins, Wiesbaden.

Schmitt-Korte, K.

    1968     *Beitrag zur Nabatäischen Keramik*. ArAnz, Heft 3.

Zayadine, F.

    1982     "Recent Excavations and Restorations of the Department of Antiquities (1979-81)," *ADAJ* 26.

# THE COINS

Deirdre G. Barrett

## Introduction

We have discovered 195 copper or bronze coins and one silver coin (94-C-36) at the site of the Great Temple during the five-year period between 1993-1997. The coins have been read by Christian Augé, Université de Paris I.

Thirty-two of the coins have been designated as Nabataean, ranging in date from the reign of Aretas IV (8 BCE-40 CE) through the end of the Nabataean king line with Rabbel II (70-106 CE). Of these coins, 10 were found in the Lower Temenos, and 16 were found in the Temple area.

Fifty-six of the coins have been identified as Roman/late Roman, ranging in dates from

98/117 CE and the reign of Trajan through the reign of Theodosios II in 408-450 CE. Of these, six coins were found in the Lower Temenos, and 15 were found in the area of the Temple.

Two of the coins have been designated Islamic (97-C-4 and 97-C-5). The remaining coins cannot be identified due to damage caused by corrosion.

The complete catalog of coins can be found on the CD-ROM, but we are listing our most representative examples of Nabataean and Roman coins in the text below. One Jewish coin is included, dated to the First Jewish Revolt (66-70 CE). (All measurements are in centimeters and grams unless otherwise noted.)

## Jewish Coin

### 94-C-32     66-70 CE

Area T, Trench 9, Locus 45. Condition: Fragile. Obverse legend: Inscription (Hebrew, beginning on right below): ש [ת ־ש]תנש ש (year three) amphora (with narrow neck, fluted belly, small handles, foot, conical lid). Dotted circle. Reverse legend: Inscription (Hebrew, beginning on left): ץ ת ש [ m] תx9日 (deliverance of Zion) vine branch with large leaf and tendril. Dotted circle. Diameter: 1.55, Thickness: 0.14, Weight: 1.30. Mintmark: Jerusalem. Date minted: 66-70 CE (probably 68/9, year 3). First Jewish Revolt. References: e.g., G.F. Hill, *A Catalogue of the Greek Coins in the British Museum*, Palestine (London, 1914), p. 274-275, Nos. 42-54, Pl. XXXX, 12 and 14 (rather common, especially for year 3).

## Nabataean Coins

### 97-C-8    First century BCE

Area LT, Trench 18A, Locus 1. Obverse legend: Head of king right, circular lineal border. Reverse legend: Two parallel cornucopiae and legend. Diameter: 1.29, Thickness: 0.16. Die axis: ~12 o'clock. City/Dynasty: Petra, Aretas IV (beginning of reign). References: Possibly Meshorer No. 62a, p. 48, Pl. 5, 5 BCE.

### 97-C-38    First century BCE

Area: East Propylaeum, surface find. Obverse legend: King's laureated head facing right. Reverse legend: Queen's veiled head facing right. May be an **פצ** (Nabataean letters for Aretas) on right. Perhaps Queen Huldu, first wife of Aretas, as the coin is possibly a very early Minute coin. Diameter: 1.00, Thickness: 0.18. Die Axis: 11 o'clock. References: Possibly Meshorer No. 48, p. 94, Pl. 4, 9/8 BCE.

### 94-C-3    75-102 CE

Area T, Trench SP 2, Locus 1. Condition: Good. Obverse legend: Jugate busts right. Reverse legend: Crossed cornucopiae. Legend (two lines) **רבאל/גמלת**. Diameter: 1.69, Thickness: 0.27, Weight: 3.37. Date minted: ~75-102 CE. Country: Nabataean kingdom. City/Dynasty: possibly Petra/Rabbel II-Gamilat. References: From the shape of letters (according to Meshorer's chronology) between 75/6-85 CE (cf. Meshorer No. 163, p. 110-111, Pl. 8).

## Roman Coins

### 97-C-33    68-69 CE

Area T, Trench 48, Locus 1. Obverse legend: Galba ~68/69 CE. Reverse legend: SC within wreath. No dot present. Diameter: 2.12, Thickness: 0.38.

96-C-60          Second century CE

Area T, Trench 22, Locus 16. Condition: Worn but clean, short flan. Obverse legend: Victory to left, holding a crown. Reverse legend: Letters to left, between illegible letters, possibly B to right. Diameter: 1.02, Thickness: 0.23, Weight: 1.05. References: Perhaps coin from Berytos (beginning of Imperial epoch, second century CE. cf. BMC Phoen. p. 57 Nos. 40 and 42, Pl. VIII, 6), but the letters do not correspond (Berytos = C-B).

97-C-25          Second century CE

Area T, Trench 35, Locus 3. Obverse legend: Circular legend in Greek. ΑΥΤ ΚΟΜΜΟδ, broken. On right ΑΝΤωΝΙΝΟS SEB/. Bust facing right, laureated, bearded. Commodus, Emperor. Reverse legend: Inscription in wreath in Greek. ΡΕΤΛΑ/ΜΕΤROPOLIS/. Diameter: 1.81, Thickness: 0.59. Die axis: 12-1 o'clock. Date minted: second century CE, Commodus 177-192 CE. Country: Petra. Roman Provincial (Syria).

94-C-31          211-217 CE

Area T, Trench 9, Locus 45. Condition: Corroded. Obverse legend: [AVTMAVP or]-ANTWNINOCCEB (or — NEINOC CEB?). Bust of Caracalla right, laureated, cuirassed, wearing paludamentum. Circle of dots. Perhaps round countermark under the chin. Reverse legend: Inscription: Left, [AΔPI]; in exergue, ΠΕΤΡΑ; right, MHT within tetrastyle temple (without pediment), Tyche seated left on rock wearing turreted crown and long chiton, holding trophy on left shoulder with extended right hand (empty or holding small object, stele or bust). Diameter: 2.35, Thickness: 0.3, Weight: 8.04. Mintmark: Petra. Date minted: 211-217 CE. Country: Provincia Arabia Petra/Caracalla (Aug. 211-217). References: cf. A. Spijkerman, *The Coins of the Decapolis and Provincia Arabia* (1978), p. 232-233, No. 46, Pl. 51 (smaller diameter).

### 95-C-53     212-217 CE

Area T, Trench 15, Locus 101. Condition: Corroded. Obverse legend: D.V.T.K-C?-IAN—HN, perhaps -IAN—INOC. Bust to right, laureated, bearded, nude, although more likely to be draped, seen from back. Under the chin, large triangular countermark. Hallmark cut under the ear. Reverse legend: Legend effaced on left, perhaps-M.U.B.A at right. Mars standing, cuirassed, legs apart, wearing small boots, small circular shield and spear, thymiateria very effaced. No visible border. Diameter: 2.8, Thickness: 0.3, Weight: 12.47. Die axis: 11 o'clock. References: May be Caracalla (Nos. 25-27) instead of Geta (No. 32). The legend on the obverse may be ANTWNE.

### 96-C-16     218-222 CE

Area LT, surface find. Condition: Worn. Obverse legend: IMPC—(effaced)—A.N.T.U— Bust to right, bearded, laureated, possibly draped. Reverse legend: At the top PETΛA, and in the exergue COLONI -, perhaps A at the right. Founder with raised arm, harnessed oxen with humps, spread out feet, horns seen from face. Diameter: 1.85, Thickness: 0.21, Weight: 3.81. Die axis: 5 o'clock. References: Petra, Elagabalus, Spijkermann No. 56.

### 96-C-26     218-222 CE

Area T, Trench 22, Locus 16. Condition: Good. Obverse legend: IMPCM.A.V. —ANTWN.I. ? N.O.C. (with first N=H). Bust to right, bearded, laureated, perhaps nude or cuirassed and draped. Border out of flan. Reverse legend: At top PETΛA, exergue COLONI-A (at right). Founder with raised arms, with harnessed oxen at right, two beasts with spread out feet, humps, two heads facing with long horns. Diameter: 2.01, Thickness: 0.40, Weight: 5.42. Die axis: 6 o'clock. References: Foundation of Petra as a colony 218-222 CE.

**96-C-39**     218-222 CE

Area T, Trench 22, Locus 16. Condition: Good. Obverse legend: Continuous legend IMPCMAVPANTWNI (with w = W). Bust to right, bearded, diademed, cuirassed and draped, seen from back. Reverse legend: At the top PETΛA, at the bottom C.O.LONI (A not visible from the right). The founder has raised arm and harnessed team to right, feet apart, humps, two heads seen face forward with long horns. Diameter: 2, Thickness: 0.36, Weight: 6.67. Die axis: 7 o'clock. References: Petra, Elagabalus, Spijkerman No. 56.

**97-C-3**     253-268 CE

Area T, Trench 40, Locus 14. Condition: Fair. Obverse legend: Circular legend. Bust right, draped, Gallienus. Reverse legend: Circular legend BA.PU. Trophy with two prisoners. Diameter: 2.2, Thickness: 0.14. Die axis: ~12 o'clock. Dots: 0.19 and 0.2. Date minted: 253-268 CE. City/Dynasty: Late Roman. References: Compare with 97-C-13.

**97-C-13**     253-268 CE

Area LT, Trench 42, Locus 6. Condition: Good. Obverse legend: Circular legend, bust right, radiated. Reverse legend: Legend and type, standing figure. Diameter: 2.03, Thickness: 0.18. Die axis: 12 o'clock. Date minted: Late third-early fourth century CE. City/Dynasty: Roman. References: Compare with 97-C-3.

**94-C-24**     305-306 CE

Area T, Trench 10, Locus 10. Condition: Corroded. Obverse legend: DN[CONSTAN-] TIVS NOB C. Bust right, bareheaded, paludamentum. Dots. Reverse legend: FEL TEMP-REPARATIO Virtus or Emperor, spearing fallen horseman (type 3). Exergue SMHA. Diameter: 1.6, Thickness: 0.14, AE 3, Weight: 1.80. Mintmark: SMHA (Heraclea Thracica). Date minted: 351-354 CE. Country: Eastern Roman Empire. City/Dynasty: Constantius Gallus Caesar. References: *Late Roman Bronze Coinage II*, No. 1901.

**95-C-44**      312-324 CE

Area T, Trench 15, Locus 101. Condition: Corroded. Obverse legend: I.M.P.C.CONSTANTINVSPFAVG. Bust to right, diademed or laureated, cuirassed, draped. Reverse legend: IOVI CONSER-VATORIAVGG, exergue ALE. Jupiter standing, nude, head to left (chlamyde or short mantle hanging from arm left), star or point above the head, holding Victory, at foot an eagle holds crown. At left K, at right crown Q/A/X. Diameter: 1.9, Thickness: 0.2, Weight: 3.12. Die axis: 7 o'clock. References: Dated to Constantine, Alexandria, beginning of reign, between 312 and 324 CE.

**95-C-14**      335-337 CE

Area LT, Trench 14, Locus 14. Obverse legend: Legend extant — CONSTANTINVS — bust of Constantine at right, laureated, cuirassed, draped. Reverse legend: Legend effaced by concretion. —INV—T. Exergue SMANTH ? Type totally effaced. Diameter: 1.9, Thickness: 0.2, Weight: 2.84. Die axis: 11 o'clock. References: AE of Constantine I or Constantine II, probably 335-337 CE.

**95-C-4**      351-361 CE

Area LT, surface find. Condition: Very worn. Obverse legend: Legend out of flan to left, effaced on right. Bust to right, diademed, possibly cuirassed. Reverse legend: (SPES R)EI-PVBLIC(E) Virtus holding globe and spear. Line of exergue. Diameter: 1.2, Thickness: 0.1, Weight: 1.33. Mintmark: Julian. References: Small AE 3, period 355-361 CE (Constantine II, Julian).

**97-C-19**      351-361 CE

Area T, Trench 47, Locus 4. Obverse legend: TIVSAVG right of circular legend. Reverse legend: FEL TEMP REPARATIO, legend off flan. Virtus spearing the fallen horseman, who raises his hand. Exergue: -AN. Diameter: 1.98, Thickness: 0.24. Date minted: ~351-361 CE, Constantius II. Probably AE 3.

97-C-21    351-361 CE

Area T, Trench 47, Locus 4.  Obverse legend: DN CONSTAN -?  Bust right with diadem, cuirassed, paludamentum (draped).  Reverse legend: FEL TEMP-REPARATIO AN- left field letter-δ.  Virtus with fallen horseman.  Diameter: 1.58, Thickness: 0.30.  Date minted: Constantius II possibly 354-361 CE, AE 3 small.

94-C-13    364-367 CE

Area T, Trench 9, Locus 13.  Condition: Stable.  Obverse legend: Inscription: DN VALEN-SPFAVG.  Bust right, diademed (pearls), cuirassed, paludamentum.  Reverse legend: Inscription: GLORIA RO-MANORVM Type: Emperor or soldier, right holding labarum (decorated with a dot) and dragging captive.  Exergue: TESr.  Diameter: 1.6, Thickness: 0.14, Weight: 1.54.  Mintmark: Thessalonica, third officina.  Date minted: 364-367 CE.  Country: Roman Empire.  City/Dynasty: Thessalonica mint/Valens (Aug. 364-378 CE).  References: Late Roman AE 3, Thessalonica, Valens Gloria Romanorum (8) type, period 364-367 CE cf. *Late Roman Bronze Coinage II*, No. 1705.

96-C-27    364-375 CE

Area T, Trench 22, Locus 16.  Condition: Corroded.  Obverse legend: Circular legend, letters partly off the flan.  Perhaps —N—TINI-A.N.V.S.P.F.(—I ?).  Bust to right, diademed (pearled), cuirassed and draped.  Reverse legend: Probably GLORIA RO-MANO.R.U.M. (8).  Emperor holding labarum and captive.  Exergue off flan, border off flan.  Diameter: 1.53, Thickness: 0.25, Weight: 1.96.  Die axis: 12 o'clock.  References: AE 3, 364-375 CE, period Valentinian I (or Valens or Gratien ca. 367 CE).  Mint: (Antioch: LRBC 2653, for Valentinian I).

97-C-16    383-395 CE

Area LT, Trench 49, Locus 1.  Condition: Good, no oxidation.  Obverse legend: Circular legend, bust right, diademed, draped, cuirassed.  Reverse legend: SALVS REIPVBLICAE, cross left.  Exergue: ANA.  Victory holding trophy, dragging captive left.  Diameter: 1.27; Thickness: 0.12.  Date minted: Late fourth century CE (probably 383-395 CE).  AE 4.  Mintmark: Antioch.

### 95-C-11    383-395 CE

Area LT, Trench 16, Locus 5. Condition: Corroded. Obverse legend: Legend effaced, covered by concretion, with the exception of the letters DNE — Bust to right, diademed, cuirassed. Reverse legend: SALVS REI-PVBLICAE. Exergue: ANTr. Victory holding trophy and captive. Diameter: 1.2, Thickness: 0.1, Weight: 0.85. References: AE 4, Antioch, period 383-395 CE, Valentinian II (392 CE), Theodosios I, Arcadius or Honoris.

### 95-C-18    383-395 CE

Area LT, Trench 16, Locus 6. Condition: Corroded. Obverse legend: D.N.A.R.C.A.D.I.V.S.P.F.A.V.G. (:) Small bust to right, diademed, draped, cuirassed. Reverse legend: (SALVS REI-PV)BLICAE, exergue out of flan. Victory and captive. Diameter: 1.2, Thickness: 0.1, Weight: 0.78. References: AE 4, period 383-395 CE — perhaps Arcadius, Honoris, Theodosios I or Valentinian II.

# THE ROMAN AND BYZANTINE GLASS

## Sara G. Karz

## Glass History

Glass, a homogenous material with noncrystalline molecular structure, was invented in the eastern Mediterranean before 3000 BCE (Whitehouse 1988:5, Newton and Davidson 1989:19). Silica in the form of quartz sand is the most basic glass ingredient. Soda and lime, the other two basic ingredients in ancient glass, lower the melting point of silica from 1700°C to about 1100°C (Frank 1982:8-9, Fleming 1997:10).

Early methods of glass vessel production included core-forming, grinding, cold-cutting, and casting (Harden 1987:2). By 1500 BCE the Egyptians and the Mesopotamians were making core-formed vessels of molten glass wound around a mud and dung core (Auth 1976:15). For grinding and cold-cutting, solidified glass was cut on a wheel with metal instruments or hand-cut with tools. In casting, molten glass was forced into a mold to pro-duce the desired shape (Whitehouse 1993:53). Faience, a kind of glass paste made with ground sand and an alkali binder that has been fired, was a common method of glass bead production (Auth 1976:15). All of these methods were time-consuming, however, and glassware became an item of luxury and status. Core-forming, for example, required a new core for each vessel, because cores cannot be reused.

In the mid-first century BCE in Syro-Palestine there was a revolution in glass production. It was at this time that glass blowing was intro-duced (Whitehouse 1988:5). Glass blowing, the inflation of a bubble of air inside molten glass on the end of a blow pipe, allowed vessels to be produced quickly. With a blow pipe it

was possible to create as many as 100 simple vessels in an hour (Saldern 1968:6). Glass became cheaper and was used by people of all economic classes, even rivaling ceramics as common ware.

Mold-blowing, the blowing of molten glass into an open mold, entered wide usage at approximately the same time as did free-blowing. Mold-blowing allowed for an almost assembly-line-like production of the same vessel shape and design without variation. There is some debate over which method appeared first, but it is enough to say that mold-blowing and free-blowing were related inventions, and with the invention of one, the invention of the other must have occurred shortly thereafter (Harden 1987:151).

The Romans took advantage of this ability to reproduce the same design over and over again. By the first century CE, mold-blown vessels were so prolific in all workshops of the Roman Empire that they were popular with people of all classes (Harden 1987:152). At the height of the Roman Empire, all of the major glassmaking centers in the world were within the borders of the Empire. All glass vessels were basically Roman in character (with minor regional variations) regardless of point of origin, be it Cologne or Tyre (Newton and Davidson 1989:24). During the early cen-turies of the Empire, with the achievement of transparent glass color, there was a preference for color transparency over opacity (Corning 1957:47).

With the collapse of the western empire in the late fifth century CE, there was a decline in the quality of glass production. The eastern empire also experienced decline, although on a lesser scale (Whitehouse 1988:8). In the east, Byzantine-period glass is often characterized by ornate designs and decoration and inferior quality, such as seed bubbles incorporated in the fabric of the glass (Newton and Davidson 1989:31).

The glass assemblage of the Great Temple reflects both Roman and Byzantine influence. Blown and mold-blown glass accounts for almost 60% of the glass by weight. Of the Roman glass, over 40% is colorless, while over 40% of the Byzantine glass is light green, testifying to a change in character of the Petra glass between these two periods.

Lastly, it is important to point out that glass manufacture occurs in two stages. First is the actual creation of glass from raw materials: quartz sand, soda and lime. After these constituent materials have been melted and mixed, the glass can be formed into vessels, the second stage of production. These two stages, glass production and glass vessel manufacture, can and often do occur in different places. Thus, it is possible for glass to be created in one location and then moved to another location before it is made into a vessel or other final form. Brill considers this a notable distinction "because it is considerably more difficult to fuse a batch of raw materials into a glass melt than it is to fashion gathers of that glass melt into objects" (1967:95).

## Glass at the Great Temple

I have examined the glass from the first five seasons at the Petra Great Temple and have found it to be almost entirely Romano-Byzantine in origin. By comparing the Petra corpus with other contemporary sites in the eastern Roman Empire, I will demonstrate that the fall of the western Roman Empire, and this division between the Roman and Byzantine periods, has revealed itself in the east through changes in glass color resulting from the change in the use of manganese as a glass decolorant.

Glass, although not immune to age or burial, holds up remarkably well in archaeological contexts such as at Petra. Glass is particularly suitable for studies of trade because of its long-term durability. Other trade goods, such as textiles and foodstuffs, disappear from the archaeological record after a much shorter time (Meyer 1992:11). Over the course of the

Roman Empire, glass went from being a rare, labor-intensive, luxury item to a ware so common that it even began to rival ceramics in its popularity. Glass also moved around the Empire in the form of transport vessels, traded not because of the desirability of the vessel but because of the material the vessel contained.

In this contribution I will be using glass as an agent for discussing the repercussions of the fall of the western Roman Empire in the eastern Mediterranean. The date most commonly accepted for the fall of the west, 476 CE, is at best a compromise. The Empire deteriorated gradually, as did the trade networks which it supported. While there is no evidence at Petra for a sudden, punctuated change as a result of Odoacer's conquest of Rome, there is evidence of gradual change in the glass record. This gradual change represents the transition from the Roman to Byzantine periods in the eastern Roman Empire.

## Methodology

Glass from the previous four seasons at Petra Great Temple was requested on loan from the Jordanian Department of Antiquities to be cataloged, along with any glass discovered during the 1997 season.[1] Glass was discovered throughout the site with larger concentrations in a few areas, specifically in Trenches 5 and 16, to be discussed later. The catalog format is based on a pre-existing FileMaker Pro format for cataloging *all* artifacts. I made several glass-specific modifications based on glass catalog formats of *I Vetri Romani* and the Corning Museum of Glass. Modifications include recording the opacity, surface condition, glass color, method of production of the vessel and culture period. Each entry also includes a description of the object, the weight and number of fragments as well as measurements of dimension. This catalog format (Catalog A) was used to record all diagnostic pieces of glass, including such fragments as handles, rims, bases, spouts and all fragments with decoration or clear evidence of manufacture, such as applied threads or blobs, etch marks, evidence of molding and blow marks. Objects recorded in this catalog were given catalog identification codes (Catalog Number) according to the scheme *year-material code-object number*, as applied to all artifacts recovered at the Great Temple. Thus, the first glass object recovered

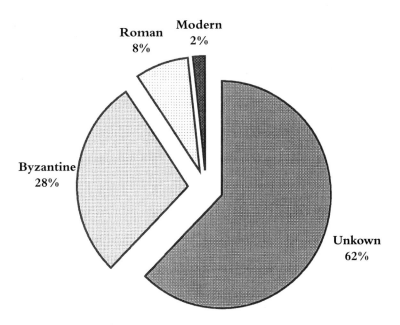

*Figure 6.122. Glass Culture by Weight (in grams).*

in the 1994 season received the Catalog Number 94-G-1, where G is the material code for glass.

Fragments considered non-diagnostic were recorded on an abbreviated catalog form (Catalog B) noting only opacity, glass color, number and weight of fragments and any associated artifacts. Culture period is not taken into account in Catalog B, because the small nature of the fragments made such identification impossible. All figures and tables that refer to an identified culture period (Roman, Byzantine, Modern, Unknown) take into account only the glass recorded in Catalog A. All figures and tables that refer to glass color take into account Catalogs A and B, the entire glass corpus. Both catalog formats include the fragment's original location, represented by sequence number, area, trench, locus and year of excavation.

All glass from the 1993 to 1997 excavation seasons, numbering 1988 fragments and weighing 3734.6 g, in addition to another 66 fragments that were unweighed, was recorded in these two catalogs. Catalog A consists of 897 fragments, weighing 2264.0 g, plus an additional 19 unweighed fragments. Catalog B consists of 1091 fragments, weighing 1470.8 g, and 47 unweighed fragments.

The figures referred to in this report are based on overall glass weight and disregard all unweighed glass. Since no complete vessels

were found and it is impossible to say with any certainty how many vessels the fragments originally represented, it was important to identify another criterion with which to quantify the glass. All of the glass was weighed and the number of fragments recorded. Basing all calculations on glass weight is more reliable than the number of fragments, because weight remains relatively constant over time, while the number of fragments is subject to change as breakage occurs.[2] The weathering process, however, resulting in iridescent flakes and heavy pitting, is also responsible for some (perhaps negligible) loss of mass of the glass fragments over time.

FileMaker Pro is well-suited to this project. I wanted to retain the overall format and feel of the previous site cataloging system so that the glass catalog would be compatible with the rest of the artifacts of the Great Temple. Performing searches on the catalogs or sorting data by a particular category is straightforward. The Excel spreadsheet program, however, is better adapted for making calculations and allowed me to see the breakdown of the catalog according to various categories, such as color, culture and location. These figures enhance the nature of the collection, especially with regard to color and location, in turn leading to more directed questions about the nature of the Great Temple glass assemblage.

One of the difficulties in describing glass is in the identification of color. Perception of color varies between individuals and with differences in lighting. In an attempt to mitigate these problems, I am the sole glass cataloger and identified color by morning sunlight as a light source. The translucent nature of glass, coupled with its varying stages of disintegration, however, make this process problematic. The color notations are kept at a minimum in order to avoid a catalog that consists of as many colors of glass as there are fragments. Thus, the resultant catalogs (Catalogs A and B) are divided into seven major categories by color: amber, blue (encompassing light blue, blue-green, cobalt blue and turquoise), dark green, green, light green, olive green and colorless. There is a small percentage of the glass that falls into none of these categories, such as red and orange or variegated colors. A larger percentage (almost 39%) of the glass has deteriorated to the point where color is not distinguishable and is recorded as "unknown."[3]

As can be seen in Figure 6.122, another problem area is the identification of culture period. The stratigraphy of the Great Temple did not allow for accurate stratigraphic dating. Unfortunately, there is no widely applicable test for the dating of glass.[4] All culture identification of glass from the Great Temple is based on stylistic attributes. As a result of the nature of the sample, much of it in small, deteriorating fragments, such dating is difficult and often impossible.[5]

## Manganese in Glass

Quartz sand, the largest constituent material in glass, is not entirely free of impurities and can contain up to 3% iron, giving glass a green or blue tint (Harden 1936:7). In order to make a truly colorless glass, it is necessary to add a decolorant to the glass batch, or mixture of raw materials (Whitehouse 1993:11), such as manganese or antimony. The Romans placed a high value on colorless glass and its resemblance to rock crystal, or colorless quartz. Eventually, the prestige of man-made colorless glass began to rival the natural crystal that it imitated (Stern 1997:195).

Manganese is one of the most common decolorants used to neutralize iron impurities present in sand and can be introduced to the batch either as pyrolusite ($MnO_2$)[6] or as rhodochrosite ($MnCO_3$)[7] (Newton and Davidson 1989:58). Too much manganese,

however, can color the glass purple. There are two methods of adding decolorant. The manganese can be added directly to the batch, or purple glass (made with intentionally large amounts of manganese) can be crushed into *cullet* and then added to the batch.

## Research Question

The total glass from the Petra Great Temple falls into two predominant categories based on color: light green and colorless. The percentage of each color based on *total* glass weight (taking into account both Catalogs A and B) is 30% and 22%, respectively, while 31% is unknown, 13% is olive green and 4% is other (Figure 6.123). Of the glass identified as Roman (taking into account only Catalog A), colorless glass is the most prevalent at 43%, while olive green glass accounts for 27%, and light green glass accounts for only 15% of the total glass identified by color. Ten percent of the Roman glass falls into the category of "other," encompassing blue, amber and green, and 6% of the glass is of unknown color (Figure 6.124). During the Byzantine period, the order of the three most prevalent colors of Roman glass is reversed. Forty-four percent of the glass is light green; 16% is olive green, and 13% is colorless. Twenty-three percent of the Byzantine glass is unknown, and 4% is "other" (Figure 6.125). It is clear that there has been a shift from colorless to light green glass at the Petra Great Temple between the Roman and Byzantine periods.

I intend to explore the reasons for this change in "colorless" glass from the predominantly untinted Roman glass to the light-green tinted Byzantine glass through discussion of contemporaneous sites in the Roman Near East and discussion of trade disruption around the time of the fall of the western Roman Empire in 476 CE as a potential explanation for the change in the use of manganese in its capacity as a glass decolorant.

At present, there is no known glass manufacture or vessel production at Petra. I undertook a surface survey in 1997, which although inconclusive, may have been a glass-producing facility. This site will be explored further in future excavation seasons.

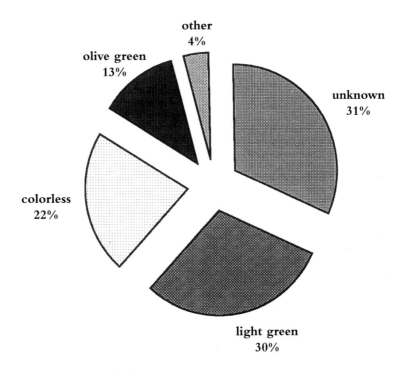

*Figure 6.123. Glass Color by Weight (in grams).*

## Comparative Sites

Several contemporary sites in the eastern Mediterranean illustrate the same trends in glass color as at the Great Temple. The uniformity of these trends suggests that the change in glass color at the Great Temple (from colorless to light green) was not, in fact, an isolated event. The following sites, Quseir

al-Qadim, Jalame, Beth She'arim and Jarash (Figure 6.126), share contemporaneity and a general location in the eastern Roman Empire with the Temple. Furthermore, these sites all possess glass from the Roman and/or Byzantine periods.

Quseir al-Qadim was a Roman port city on the western coast of the Red Sea, today in Egypt. The city was occupied for two distinct

*Figure 6.124. Roman Glass Color by Weight (in grams).*

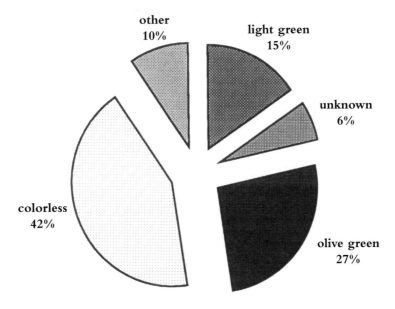

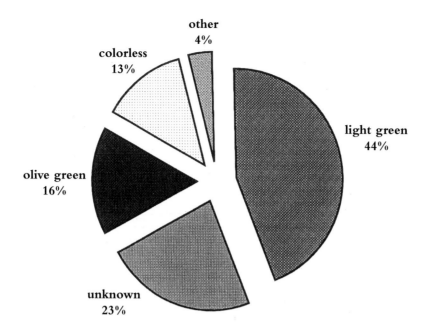

*Figure 6.125. Byzantine Glass Color by Weight (in grams).*

periods: from the first to second centuries CE and again from the thirteenth to fourteenth centuries CE, during the Mamluk period (Meyer 1992:1). During the Roman period the port was a trade center to the east with Arabia, East Africa and India (Meyer 1992:2). An almost total lack of both food and water resources meant that all supplies for Quseir al-Qadim had to be brought in from the Nile Valley and that the city's existence was, out of necessity, totally dedicated to trade (Meyer 1992:2). Interestingly, trade in the Red Sea region may have improved after the Roman annexation of Petra reduced the competition (Meyer 1992:5).

There is no evidence of glass production at the site, perhaps because of inadequate fuel supplies, although raw glass itself may have been exported to India (Meyer 1992:41). The vessels that came to Quseir al-Qadim, likely from Egypt and the Mediterranean, were then exported to the east to countries around the Indian Ocean (Meyer 1992:11). Table wares make up the bulk of the glass corpus, with the addition of some heavier, glass transport vessels as well as luxury wares.

At Quseir al-Qadim, colorless glass is well-represented in this Roman corpus, especially among the luxury wares. Much of the purple glass had been colorless originally, because of manganese additives, but changed to purple over time (Meyer 1992:16). It is evident that

manganese was a common ingredient in the Roman glass up through the second century CE.

Jalame, in modern-day Israel about 10 km southeast of Haifa, was a center of glass production during the late Roman period. The site was occupied, although not continuously, from the late first century BCE to the early fifth century CE (Weinberg 1988:2-3, 4). Jalame was a fairly wealthy villa by the mid- to late fourth century CE, to judge by the presence of both wine and olive presses in the area (Weinberg 1988:10-11). Jalame would have been caught in the midst of the greatest destruction during the Jewish Revolt against Gallus Caesar in 351 CE, although there is no evidence that the villa suffered at this time. The neighboring community of Beth She'arim, to be discussed later, was demolished during the revolt (Weinberg 1988:16).

The glass factory was operational during the fourth century CE for a very limited time — only about three decades sometime after 350 CE (Weinberg 1988:16, 19). The identification of the glass factory, created specifically for this purpose, is undisputed due to the large amounts of raw glass, cullet and vessel fragments found in and around the site (Weinberg 1988:24). There is no evidence for the production of raw glass, however, necessitating the importation of glass and cullet (Weinberg

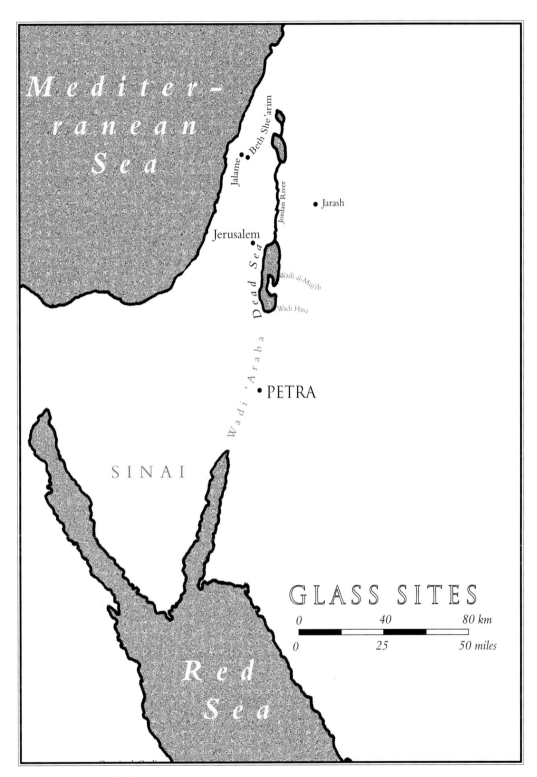

*Figure 6.126. Map of Glass Sites.*

1988:25). The Jalame factory mostly produced blown and mold-blown household vessels of average quality (Weinberg 1988:24, 39, 79).

The prevalent glass colors at Jalame are colorless, purple and various shades of green (Weinberg 1988:38). The natural color of Jalame glass, without colorants or decolorants, is described by Weinberg as a pale greenish-blue (1988:269). Chemical analysis has revealed the use of manganese as a decolorant in Jalame glass, demonstrating the presence and at least minimal availability of manganese in the area at this time (Weinberg 1988: 269).

Not far from Jalame is Beth She'arim, a late Roman-early Byzantine site southeast of Haifa. After the burial in Beth She'arim of Rabbi Judah Ha-Nassî, an influential Jewish leader in the early third century CE, the city became a burial center, and the rabbi's cemetery became sacred ground. Local industry became directed toward this activity, with the employment of undertakers, quarrymen, architects, builders, stonecutters and sculptors (Avigad 1976:2). In the mid-fourth century CE, Beth She'arim was destroyed and burned, possibly associated with the Jewish Revolt against Gallus Caesar in 351 CE, and although the city was not abandoned entirely, it never recovered (Avigad 1976:3).

Several hundred fragments and 19 complete vessels were recovered from a series of catacombs at Beth She'arim. There is no evidence that these vessels were produced here, although they are almost certainly local, and some may even have come from nearby Jalame. Most of the vessels were free-blown, and only a minority were the result of mold-blowing. Most of the glass was light green or light bluish-green (Barag 1976:198). Barag further states that "only a few vessels are made of colorless glass with a greenish tinge" (1976:198). Whether or not this implies the use of manganese (or another decolorant) is unclear.

The most unusual and perhaps most telling glass find at Beth She'arim was the discovery of a nine-ton block of purple glass, measuring 3.40 m long, 1.95 m wide and approximately 0.50 m thick. The slab was discovered in a filled-in cistern next to some of the catacombs on the site. The block was made *in situ* from raw materials after the cistern was no longer in use; this date is not precisely known. The chemical composition of the block was

consistent with Roman glass, with a high manganese content. The batch was imperfectly mixed, for the fusing of the raw materials remained incomplete, and the slab showed bands of higher and lower intensity purple and one band of green (Brill 1967:89). Dating of the cistern and other factors suggests a manufacture date somewhere between the fourth and early seventh centuries CE (Brill 1967:94-95).

The intended use for this slab is unknown, although there are two hypotheses. It is possible that the block was meant to be crushed into cullet and then distributed for use as a decolorant. Why the production of one large block instead of many smaller blocks of purple glass would be attempted is unknown. The other possibility is that the slab may have been commissioned for some other use besides remelting; it may have even served as an architectural component (Brill 1967:95). Regardless of its original purpose, the slab was ultimately flawed and unfit for use.

Last is Jarash, the well-preserved remains of a Roman city 48 km north of modern-day Amman, most famous today for its surviving monumental buildings. Colonnaded streets, temples to Artemis and Zeus, a forum and theaters were all constructed in the first and second centuries CE. Hadrian's Arch, built in honor of the emperor's visit in 129 CE, was also a product of this era of prosperity. The legalization of Christianity prompted a second wave of construction, most notably of churches, at the beginning of the Byzantine period (Meyer 1987:176). Jarash was a member of the Decapolis, a league of 10 commercial cities dating from the first century BCE. The city declined during the Byzantine period and declined further after an earthquake in the mid-eighth century CE (Meyer 1987:176).

Much of the Jarash glass was found in the North Theater, a building constructed in two phases the first phase in the mid-second century CE with additions in 230 CE (Meyer 1987:176). The glass, dating between 630-670 CE, was not found in its primary context, although it is likely that it was thrown down from residences uphill (Meyer 1987:176, 178, 180). There was no evidence that any glass was produced at Jarash. (Other known glass centers, such as Jalame, discussed previously, may have provided glass to Jarash, Meyer 1987:181.) The glass vessel forms at Jarash vary widely, and although table wares were common (Meyer 1987:219), the color of the Jarash Byzantine glass is fairly standardized. Almost all of the Byzantine-period glass is green, blue-green or light blue (Meyer 1987:188). The light blue glass is possibly the result of an unavailability of decolorant. That colorless glass is not prevalent at Jarash during the Byzantine period further supports this lack of decolorant.

All of these sites overlap in time with the Petra Great Temple. Quseir al-Qadim has the earliest glass corpus and has the largest amount of colorless glass. Jalame and Beth She'arim, true contemporaries, demonstrate that manganese was still in use as both a colorant and decolorant, even though the incidence of "tinted colorless" glass is higher. Jarash, with the latest glass corpus, shows a lack of true colorless glass. The Great Temple, therefore, seems to bridge the transition from the Roman to Byzantine periods, for it incorporates characteristics of both of these trends.

## Catalog Discussion

Most of the glass at the Petra Great Temple is identifiable as Romano-Byzantine in origin, although making the distinction between these two periods is much more difficult, especially when considering the fragmentary nature of the glass corpus. Although a few forms, such as the head vases, are distinctly Roman, most of the vessel forms were in widespread use during both periods. Byzantine vessels tend to be thicker-walled renditions of Roman forms, although they are not as thick-walled as the heavy glass transport vessels. Heavy, thick-walled Byzantine bases are a common find and perhaps most aptly characterize the decline in ability of glass production during this period.

The glass corpus itself, being the primary source, can also help address future questions. As several important and intriguing fragments fell outside the scope of this investigation, it is my hope that this Petra corpus will be of assistance in future research. Of particular note are the two head vases (94-G-4, 95-G-135), Roman mold-blown vessels that may be products of the same mold (Figures 6.127-6.130). The Petra vases appear to have come from two-part molds, with seams running along the sides of the face. Since neither vase has been preserved in the round, it is not possible to conclusively determine whether they were Janus heads, two-faced, although it is a distinct possibility.

Three counters, or game pieces, were found during the fifth season (97-G-71, 97-G-82, 97-G-83), made by simply dropping molten glass on a flat surface (Figure 6.131). Such game pieces are a common find throughout the Roman Empire in a wide range of colors (Meyer 1992:40). The three Petra examples are of indeterminate color.

Perhaps the most exciting glass find of 1997 was a millefiore flower tile (97-G-101) that was initially mistaken for a bone fragment until it was cleaned (Figures 6.132 and 6.133). Very similar millefiore tiles are represented in the Evan Gorga collection, most notable in panels from the villa of Lucius Verrus near Rome (Saguì, Bacchelli and Pasqualucci 1995:222). The Petra tile shows a flower with six white petals against a green background, inside a yellow border. The center of the flower appears to be blue and shows some signs of iridescence.

## Discussion

The movement of manganese, either in mineral or cullet form, is a potentially informative medium for examining the change in trade patterns between the Roman and Byzantine periods. Manganese appears to have been a very use-specific material, that is, it was primarily valued for its use as a glass decolorant. Any manganese identified within trade networks is likely to have been for this purpose.

Even though an in-depth chemical analysis of the Petra glass, and thus the identification of manganese source(s), was not feasible at this time, I hope that by comparing the trade practices of the western and eastern empire, both pre- and post-fall of Rome, and through discussion of Colin Renfrew's *modes of exchange* (as presented in the essay, "Trade as Action at a Distance") it may be possible to at least narrow down the geographic locations that were the manganese source(s).

Renfrew discusses 10 models of exchange and their spatial implications, in a rough order of increasing complexity.[8] Renfrew's models depend on nodes of exchange, while maritime commerce involves transportation that occurs

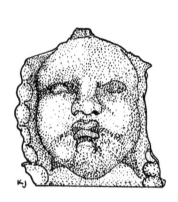

*Figure 6.127. 94-G-4, head vase. Photograph by Sara G. Karz.*

*Figure 6.128. Drawing of 94-G-4 by Karen Jacobson.*

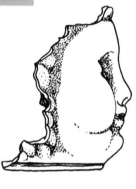

0    cm    2

*Figure 6.129. 95-G-135, head vase. Photograph by Sara G. Karz.*

*Figure 6.130. Drawing of 95-G-135 by Simon M. Sullivan.*

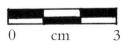

0    cm    3

*Figure 6.131. 97-G-83, game piece. Photograph by Sara G. Karz.*

between these nodes. If ports of trade are treated as nodes, however, his models may still be applicable to Roman maritime trade.

The nodes that I will refer to in the following are those of central place redistribution and down-the-line trading. In central place redistribution, "A takes his produce to p and renders it to P (no doubt receiving something in exchange, then or subsequently). B takes his produce to p and receives from P some of A's produce" (Renfrew 1975:43). Down-the-line trading is simply the reduplication of reciprocity trading, "so that the commodity travels across successive territories...through successive exchanges" (Renfrew 1975:41, 43).

Roman overseas trade was a very organized affair. Routes, alternative routes, destinations and cargoes were planned well in advance. Skippers did not find themselves moving from port to port in search of a market for their goods (Parker 1992:21). Such agendas were in part the result of "continuous urban needs for imported foodstuffs [that] created established patterns of voyaging" (Duncan-Jones 1990:32). Roman maritime trade was pursued on a large scale. "The freighters that carried government cargoes were commonly 340 tons burden, and those of the crack grain fleet ran to 1,200 tons; seventeen centuries were to pass before merchant fleets of such tonnage again sailed the seas" (Casson 1991:191). The multiple economic roles assumed by those involved in sea trade included the shipper (*navicularius*), the captain (*magister*) and the merchant (*mercator*, *negotiator*), roles that further illustrate the organization of the Roman period (Love 1991:156). There is even evidence to support the active involvement of senators engaging in sea trade for profit (Love 1991:157).

Roman colorless glass at the Petra Great Temple, and at the comparative sites previously

0    cm    2

*Figure 6.132. 97-G-101, millefiore tile. Photograph by Sara G. Karz.*

*Figure 6.133. Drawing of 97-G-101 by Simon M. Sullivan.*

discussed, may owe its presence to the existence of this rigorously controlled trading environment that allowed manganese to travel from a source in the west to the east. I suggest that Renfrew's model of *central place redistribution* is most applicable here in its reflection of the organization associated with Roman trade.

Byzantine-period trading was much smaller-scale and more opportunistic in nature than previously in the Roman period. Smaller ships replaced their larger counterparts as the state-financed fleets faded from prominence, and there was a "diminution in the frequency and size of long-distance navigation" (Lopez 1959:71). Many of the individual economic roles of the Roman period were often played by one person serving as owner, captain and merchant (McCann and Freed 1994:51). The master of the Yassi Ada, a wreck from the seventh century CE, was possibly an example of this conflation of roles and played the role of trader as well (Parker 1992:21). Trade gradually became provincial and local instead of international (Walbank 1969:51). However, trading opportunities did not deteriorate in the eastern empire as much as in the western empire, in part due to the Christian pilgrim industry that attracted tourists to religious sites (Evans 1996:239).

Despite the continuation of more efficient trade networks in the eastern empire, there was still a noticeable shift away from the colorless glass of the Roman period, toward glass with a light green tint. I suggest that Renfrew's model of *down-the-line* trading is applicable here. If manganese came from the west, in order for it to reach the more-advanced networks of the east, it would have had to first go through the now haphazard networks of the western empire, passing from one port to another only if thought profitable by merchant-traders. Manganese, probably never a lucrative cargo because of its limited usage, would have been traded less and less.

What minerals or geologic formations did the Roman and Byzantine glass makers exploit for manganese? What were the geographic locations of these sources, utilized in antiquity? Manganese is a widely occurring secondary deposit in "crystalline rocks whence, like iron, it is dissolved out and it re-deposited as the oxide, hydroxide or carbonate" (Sully 1955:3). The Romans knew about pyrolusite, widespread in occurrence and the most common manganese ore (Klein and Hurlbut 1985:306). Rhodochrosite is common in "hydrothermal vein deposits and in unmetamorphosed and metamorphosed sedimentary manganese deposits" (Roy 1981:56) and would also have been available.

Desert varnish, "a black-to-brown coating of iron, manganese, and clay, commonly [formed] on exposed rock and artifact surfaces that are embedded in desert pavements" (Waters 1992:207), is not a likely manganese source. The varnish consists of only a thin layer that would not have been worth the effort necessary for removal.[9] Had desert varnish been the primary source of manganese in glass decoloration, I firmly believe that colorless glass would have been a luxury item, available only to the upper classes rather than the popularly available item that is evident in the archaeological record.

Manganese is wide in its geographic occurrence. The geographic locations where manganese was recovered in antiquity are not widely known today. In Europe, manganese, specifically pyrolusite, is found in Moravia, Bohemia, Romania, Spain and in the Caucasus (Heichelheim, Yeo and Ward 1984:351, 355, Merriman 1958:264, Davies 1935:48). In the eastern Mediterranean, within the reach of Petra, manganese occurs in the Sinai Peninsula

and in the Aqaba region (Garland and Bannister 1927:32, Groves 1938:65). Manganese ore, specifically pyrolusite, has been even identified in the nearby Wadi Dana (Bender 1974:154, 156).

The aforementioned locations, however, are geographic locales where we know that manganese exists *today*. It is not known with a great degree of certainty which, if any, of these sources were exploited in antiquity. A heap of manganese ore, found near a possible furnace at a Romano-British site near Cardiff, has been tentatively identified as Spanish in origin, with connections to glass industry (Davies 1935:48, 98). An association between this manganese and glass manufacture is tenuous at best, but this is one of the only connections that has been made between a manganese source and its use as a glass colorant or decolorant.

If the decolored glass in the eastern Roman Empire was in fact decolorized with manganese retrieved locally, there are two possible explanations for its discontinued use. The first possibility is that even though manganese was available in the east and decolorized glass was still desirable, glass manufacturers were no longer able to utilize this tool due to a decline in their ability. The second explanation, an aesthetic one, is that there was no longer a demand for truly colorless glass because of a change in taste. Even though the materials for decolorization were still readily available, they were no longer used.

If the manganese is considered to be a product of the western Roman Empire, it becomes clear why the eastern Empire, despite its own surviving trade networks, no longer produced high-quality colorless glass. The manganese was not moving efficiently or predictably from its origin in the west and thus rarely reached the ports in the east. Manganese that did reach eastern ports probably arrived as the result of a greater dependence on free-lance and opportunistic trading.

Of these three possibilities, the first is the most easily dismissed. Moorey (1994:203) describes glass manufacture as the combination of the correct proportions of the three basic glass ingredients (silica, soda and lime) with the desirable colorants, decolorants and/or opacifiers and then heating the mixture in a furnace at the correct temperature. It is difficult to believe that there was a deterioration in knowledge so great that glass makers no longer knew when to add a decolorant. An alternative explanation for this scenario is that the knowledge necessary to extract the manganese from its geologic setting was no longer available.

The aesthetic explanation deserves further consideration because of the manganese and, more specifically, pyrolusite deposits in the vicinity of Petra. However, it is difficult to ignore that the Byzantine glass is of inferior quality than the Roman in both quality of material and skill of execution. The fact that non-decolorized glass requires less work and fewer steps to produce seems to suggest that glass was no longer colorized not because it was desirable, but because it was a simpler, less-complex feat to accomplish. Whether or not this coloration eventually evolved into a desirable feature is unknown.

The socio-economic explanation is intriguing because of what it may be able to tell us about the state of trade and trade networks throughout the Roman Empire after the fall of Rome. A serious problem with this explanation is that the geographical sources of manganese used in glass manufacture remain unknown. Furthermore, the existence of manganese in such close proximity to Petra means that it was possible that the manganese did not come from the west at all.

## Summary

When the glass from the Petra Great Temple is sorted by culture, as based on stylistic attributes, a difference in glass color between the Roman and Byzantine periods becomes obvious. Forty-three percent by weight of the Roman glass is colorless, while an almost equal percentage, 44%, of the Byzantine glass is light green. Only 15% of the Roman glass is light green, while only 13% of the Byzantine glass is colorless.

This sudden reversal of the relative amounts of these two glass colors between the Roman and the Byzantine periods strongly suggests that there was a change in the production and/or distribution of glass at this time in the Roman Empire. I say "Roman Empire" because all glass produced during this time was essentially Roman in character.

Manganese, useful as a glass decolorant, can be incorporated into a glass batch either as the minerals pyrolusite or rhodochrosite. The Greek name, pyrolusite, is even suggestive of the mineral's usage as a decolorant. Manganese, regardless of mineralogic form, is still used for this purpose.

Glass from contemporary sites in the eastern Roman Empire, like the Great Temple, also demonstrates a decreasing amount of truly colorless glass through time. In all cases, manganese is the primary decolorant responsible for colorless glass. The earliest comparative site in this investigation, Quseir al-Qadim, has the greatest proportion of colorless glass, while the latest site, Jarash, has the least colorless glass.

There is no question that glass vessels were produced in the east, at sites such as Jalame, although there is more debate surrounding the question of where the glass was manufactured from raw materials. There is also the still unanswered question of exactly where the manganese originated.

While it was clearly the absence of manganese or some other decolorant that was physically responsible for the change in glass from colorless to light green, there are two possible explanations for the reason for this change: aesthetic and socio-economic. Did glass color change between the Roman and Byzantine periods because there was a change in local preference for light green glass over colorless or because the materials necessary to produce colorless glass were no longer widely available to the eastern Roman Empire?

Since the glass of the Roman Empire demonstrates relatively little variation from one end of the Empire to the other, and regional differences did not become marked until after the fall of Rome, an aesthetic explanation becomes possible. Byzantine-period glass in the eastern Roman Empire may have been light green because the local populations preferred it to colorless glass, but it was not until after the fall of Rome, and Rome's subsequent declining influence, that these local preferences could be exhibited. If manganese sources that were utilized during the Roman period are identified in the eastern Mediterranean, for example, the aesthetic explanation becomes more plausible. It implies that during the transition between Roman and Byzantine periods there was

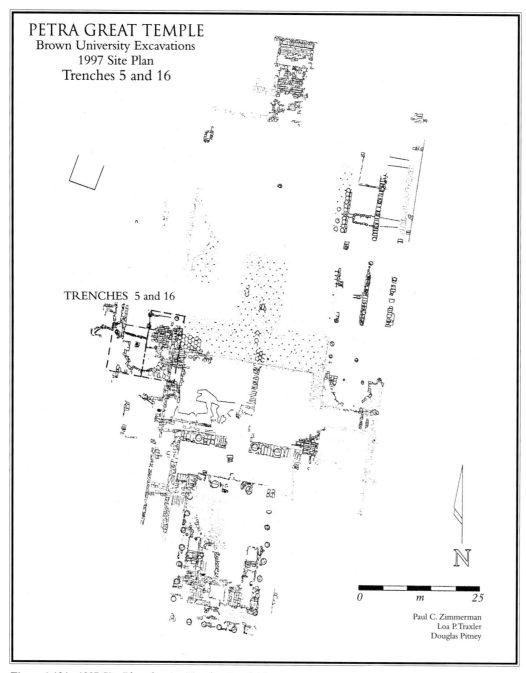

**PETRA GREAT TEMPLE**
Brown University Excavations
1997 Site Plan
Trenches 5 and 16

TRENCHES 5 and 16

N

0          m          25

Paul C. Zimmerman
Loa P. Traxler
Douglas Pitney

*Figure 6.134. 1997 Site Plan showing Trenches 5 and 16.*

access to glass decolorant in the east after all, and therefore manganese was not left out of glass batches because of unavailability in the east but for some other (perhaps aesthetic) reason.

The socio-economic explanation, however, favors the idea that the change in glass color was a response to the collapse of Roman trade and transport systems. Byzantine-period glass is generally of poorer quality than its predecessor, as exemplified by seeds, or air bubbles, included in the glass fabric. Light green glass was easier to produce than colorless glass, because it did not require the addition of a separate decoloring ingredient to the glass batch. Both of these changes, a decrease in glass quality and a change in color by removing a step from the production process, are steps in the same direction — away from the more-skilled work associated with Roman-period glass. If manganese could no longer efficiently reach the eastern Roman Empire, then colorless glass would become less prevalent in the area over time as existing supplies were depleted. By attempting to identify the source of Roman glass decolorants and the trade networks that would have distributed these decolorants, it may be possible to test this hypothesis.

With the fall of the western Roman Empire came a change in how trade was conducted. Roman-period trade was conducted on a larger-scale than during the Byzantine period. Byzantine trade, especially in the west, is best characterized as more provincial in nature. The decline in the east was less severe, although glass color was nonetheless affected, as demonstrated by the glass at Petra and contemporary sites. It is possible that the Roman Empire depended on a western source of manganese that became less accessible after the fall of Rome and thus affected its distribution throughout the Mediterranean.

## Conclusion

Between the Roman and the Byzantine periods the definition of colorless glass changed. For the Romans, colorless glass was originally an imitation of rock crystal and was almost entirely lacking in color. During the Byzantine period, however, "colorless" glass meant merely that no intentional colorants were added to the glass batch. Iron impurities in sand would be considered an unintentional colorant. Colorless Byzantine glass did not entail the absence of color, but rather the absence of intentional color.

Byzantine-period glass has a reputation for being heavily colored, although this strong coloration was not clear in the glass from the Great Temple. Perhaps this preference was because colorants other than manganese were much more readily available and because a strong color was preferable to a weakly tinted colorless glass.

This change in glass after the fall of the western Roman Empire, from colorless to faintly colored, may have been adopted as a desirable characteristic for glass during the Byzantine period, although it is possible that it was not initially desirable. Byzantine glass was inferior to Roman glass in both the quality of the glass and the quality of execution of the form. That the most common glass color in the Byzantine period, light green, required fewer steps to produce (no chemical additives necessary), agrees with a trend of decreasing ability and substandard materials. That the Petra Great Temple is only one of several

contemporary sites exhibiting this color change suggests that they were all dependent on another source, or sources, for glass decolorants.

While it is not possible to make any identification of the geographic origin of the manganese decolorant except in the broadest possible manner, it is hoped that further investigation of trade networks in the Mediterranean during this time of transition between the Roman and Byzantine periods may lead to a more specific location and add to our understanding of how overseas trade changed in the late fifth century CE.

Stratigraphy at the Great Temple is often convoluted, making dating a difficult proposition. It may someday be possible to use these known color differences to aid in dating when large amounts of glass, or hoards, are present. Two such examples at the Great Temple are the adjacent Trenches 16 and 5 (Figure 6.134). Trench 16, with over 600 fragments, is 25% light green by weight and 21% colorless. Nine percent of Trench 16 was identified as olive green, 2% as other and 43% as unknown. Trench 5, with over 400 fragments, is 37% light green and only 12% colorless. Thirty-three percent of Trench 5 is olive green; 1% is other, and 17% is unknown. These percentages suggest that the glass from Trench 16, with its almost equal amounts of light green and colorless glass is earlier than Trench 5. The glass from Trench 5, with three times as much light green glass as colorless, possibly represents a later deposit, perhaps during the Byzantine period. It may be argued that these hoards were in fact intentional dumps with the intention of sorting by color for future remelting, thus accounting for a color preference. However, this cannot be the case for either of these hoards because of the significant amounts of other glass colors present. Nine percent of Trench 16 and 33% of Trench 5, for example, consist of olive green glass.

It is hoped that these ideas regarding gradual change in glass color will be applicable to further exploration of the Petra Great Temple and will serve as an impetus for further research into the mineral sources exploited in antiquity.

# Endnotes

[1] One objective I had hoped to achieve was to have some of the glass chemically analyzed to learn its chemical content and, thus, (potentially) its point of origin. However, after consultation with Jutta Page, Associate Curator of European Glass at the Corning Museum of Glass, I learned that such testing is prohibitively expensive, especially for use on a "fishing expedition" as this effort would have been.

[2] Personal communication from Richard A. Gould, March 1998.

[3] Initially, I divided the light green glass into two categories: "light green" and "green tint." The former was meant to be indicative of intentional coloring of the glass by chemical additives, while the latter indicates glass that is unintentionally light in color because of natural impurities in the sand. This distinction, however, proved to be both too arbitrary and too difficult to identify, so instead I recorded all such fragments as light green.

[4] Radiocarbon dating is not effective for dating glass because of its minimal carbon content (Frank 1982:65).

[5] I depended heavily on the photographs, dates and descriptions in exhibition catalogs and excavation reports to form the basis for cultural affiliation. Harden's 1987 *Glass of the Caesars*, Stern and Schlick-Nolte's 1994 *Early Glass of the Ancient World* and Whitehouse's 1988 *Glass of the Roman Empire* were particularly helpful in this respect.

[6] Pyrolusite, the common name for manganese dioxite, is a term derived from the Greek words for *fire* and *to wash*, in direct reference to its use as a glass decolorant (Klein and Hurlbut 1985:306).

[7] Rhodochrosite, or manganese carbonate, is most commonly found in the silver mines of Saxony and Romania, possible exploitative territory for the Romans. Its mineral name, also derived from the Greek, means *rose* and *color*, in reference to the mineral's pink color (Klein and Hurlbut 1985:333-334).

[8] The first and simplest model is that of *direct access*, where access to a given resource is not hindered and no exchange transaction actually occurs (Renfrew 1975:41). Renfrew's tenth model is *port-of-trade*, such that trade between two groups occurs in a neutral, central location where emissaries of both groups exchange goods (1975:43).

[9] Personal communication, G. Rapp, August 1998.

# Bibliography

Auth, S.H.

    1976    *Ancient Glass from the Newark Museum*. Newark: Newark Museum.

Avigad, N. (ed.)

    1976    *Beth She'arim: Report on the Excavations During 1953-1958*. Vol. III. New Brunswick, NJ: Rutgers University Press.

Barag, D.

    1976    "Glass Vessels." In *Beth She'arim: Report on the Excavations During 1953-1958*, ed. N. Avigad. Vol. III. New Brunswick, NJ: Rutgers University Press. 198-209.

Bender, F.

    1974    *Geology of Jordan*, trans. M.K. Khdeir. Berlin: Gebrüder Borntraeger.

Brill, R.H.

    1967    "A Great Glass Slab from Ancient Galilee," *Archaeology* 20.2:88-95.

Casson, L.

    1991    *The Ancient Mariners: Seafarers and Sea Fighters of the Mediterranean in Ancient Times*. Princeton, NJ: Princeton University Press.

Corning Museum of Glass.

    1957    *Glass from the Ancient World*. Corning, NY.

Davies, O.

    1935    *Roman Mines in Europe*. Oxford: Clarendon Press.

Duncan-Jones, R.

    1990    *Structure and Scale in the Roman Economy*. Cambridge: Cambridge University Press.

Evans, J.A.S.

    1996    *The Age of Justinian*. London and New York: Routledge.

Fleming, S.J.

    1997    *Roman Glass: Reflections of Everyday Life*. Philadelphia: University of Pennsylvania Museum of Archaeology and Anthropology.

Frank, S.

    1982    *Glass and Archaeology*. New York: Academic Press Inc. (London) Ltd.

Garland, H. and C.O. Bannister.

    1927    *Ancient Egyptian Metallurgy*. London: Charles Griffin and Company, Ltd.

Groves, A.W.

    1938    *Manganese*. London: Imperial Institute.

Harden, D.B.

    1936    *Roman Glass from Karanis*. Ann Arbor: University of Michigan Press.

————.

    1987    *Glass of the Caesars*. Milan: Olivetti.

Heichelheim, F.M., C.A. Yeo and A.M. Ward.

    1984    *A History of the Roman People*. Englewood Cliffs, NJ: Prentice-Hall, Inc.

Klein, C. and C.S. Hurlbut, Jr.

    1985    *Manual of Mineralogy*. New York: John Wiley.

Lopez, R.S.

    1959    "The Role of Trade in the Economic Readjustment of Byzantium in the Seventh Century," *Dumbarton Oaks Papers* 13:69-85.

Love, J.R.

    1991    *Antiquity and Capitalism: Max Weber and the Sociological Foundations of Roman Civilization.* London: Routledge.

McCann, A.M. and J. Freed.

    1994    *Deep Water Archaeology: A Late-Roman Ship from Carthage and Ancient Trade Route Near Skerki Bank off Northwest Sicily,* ed. J.H. Humphrey. JRA, supplementary series no. 13. Ann Arbor, MI.

Merriman, A.D.

    1958    *A Dictionary of Metallurgy.* London: MacDonald and Evans, Ltd.

Meyer, C.

    1987    "Glass from the North Theater Byzantine Church, and Soundings at Jerash, Jordan, 1982-1983," *BASOR Supplement* 25:175-222.

—————.

    1992    *Glass from Quseir al-Qadim.* Chicago: Oriental Institute of the University of Chicago.

Moorey, P.R.S.

    1994    *Ancient Mesopotamian Materials and Industries: The Archaeological Evidence.* Oxford: Clarendon Press.

Newton, R. and S. Davidson.

    1989    *Conservation of Glass.* Boston: Butterworths.

Parker, A.J.

    1992    *Ancient Shipwrecks of the Mediterranean and the Roman Provinces. BARIS.* 580.

Renfrew, C.

    1975    "Trade as Action at Distance." In *Ancient Civilization and Trade,* ed. J. Sabloff and C.C. Lamberg-Karlovsky. Albuquerque: University of New Mexico Press. 3-59.

Roy, S.

    1981    *Manganese Deposits.* New York: Academic Press.

Saguì, L., B. Bacchelli and R. Pasqualucci.

    1995    "Un Patrimoine Unique au Monde: Les Verres de la Collection Gorga," *Annales du 13e Congrès de l'Association Internationale pour l'Histoire du Verre* 13:213-224.

Simona, S.B.

    1991    *I Vetri Romani: Provenienti dalle terre dell'attuale Cantone Ticino.* Vol. II. Locarno: Tutti I Diritti Riservati.

Stern, E.M. and B. Schlick–Nolte.

    1994    *Early Glass of the Ancient World*. Germany: Verlag Gerd Hatje.

Stern, E.M.

    1997    "Glass and Rock Crystal: A Multifaceted Relationship," *JRA* 10:192–206.

Sully, A.H.

    1955    *Manganese*. New York: Academic Press, Inc. Publishers.

Saldern, A. von.

    1968    *Ancient Glass in the Museum of Fine Arts, Boston*. Meriden, CT: The Meriden Gravure Co.

Walbank, F.W.

    1969    *The Awful Revolution*. Canada: University of Toronto Press.

Waters, M.R.

    1992    *Principles of Geoarchaeology: A North American Perspective*. Tucson: The University of Arizona Press.

Weinberg, G.D.

    1988    *Excavations at Jalame: Site of a Glass Factory in Late Roman Palestine*. Columbia: University of Missouri Press.

Whitehouse, D.

    1988    *Glass of the Roman Empire*. Corning, NY: The Corning Museum of Glass.

————.

    1992    *Glass: A Pocket Dictionary of Terms Commonly Used to Describe Glass and Glassmaking*. Corning, NY: The Corning Museum of Glass.

# CHAPTER SEVEN

# NEUTRON ACTIVATION ANALYSIS of POTTERY

Leigh-Ann Bedal

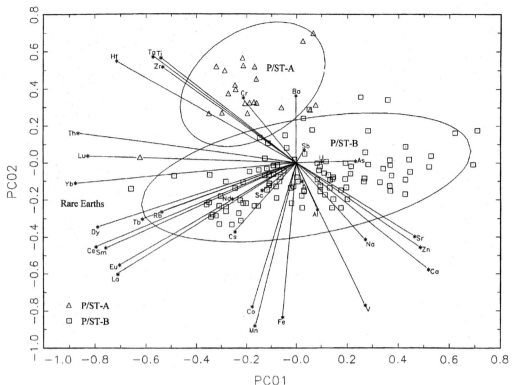

*Figure 7.1. RQ-mode plot of principal components 1 and 2 of the P/ST data set. Ellipses represent 95% confidence limits for membership in a pottery group. Radiating lines represent enrichment of samples by the material indicated at the asterisks; samples that are plotted nearer to the asterisk are relatively enriched in this material compared to samples that are plotted further away.*

*Figure 7.2. Plot of principal components 2 and 3 derived from PCA of 'Amr's Group XV (1987) showing its separation into two groups, XVa and XVb. Ellipses represent 95% confidence limits for membership in a pottery group.*

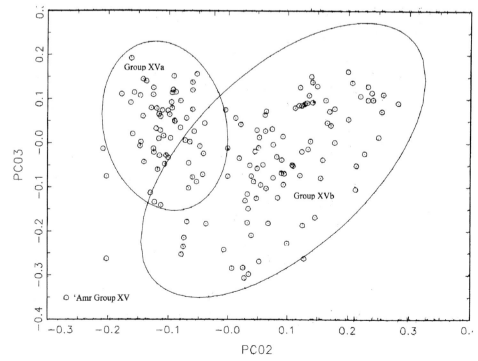

# NEUTRON ACTIVATION ANALYSIS of POTTERY

## Leigh-Ann Bedal

*(for clarity, Figures 7.9-7.15 are located at the end of the chapter)*

In addition to qualitative analysis of Nabataean wares based on form, fabric and decoration to determine chronology,[1] quantitative analysis using neutron activation (NAA) has focused on identifying clay composition and place of manufacture. 'Amr (1987) compared the composition of Nabataean ceramics from Petra and other Nabataean sites with that of contemporary pottery and clay artifacts identified as locally produced at those sites as well as with clay samples obtained from the potters' workshops at 'Avdat and Zurrabah and clay sources in the vicinity of Petra ('Ayn at-Tina, Asem, Mu'allaq, Tawilan, Wadi Musa). Non-contemporary samples of pottery from Umm al-Biyara, the pre-Nabataean Edomite settlement at Petra, and pottery and clay samples from a modern potters' workshops were included for chronological and regional comparisons. Gunneweg, et al. (1991) analyzed Nabataean fine wares, wasters and clays from 'Avdat/Oboda and other sites in the Negev as well as some clays, wasters and bricks from Petra, in order to draw some conclusions regarding the place of manufacture of Nabataean fine wares found at Negev sites. The overall conclusion of these two studies was that Nabataean painted and unpainted fine wares were manufactured in and around the site of Petra and exported to other settlements within the Nabataean kingdom ('Amr 1987:198, Gunneweg, et al. 1991:342). The major discrepancy between these two studies, however, is that the former study, which had samples originating mostly from the vicinity of Petra, identified a single composition ('Amr Group XV) for Nabataean wares, whereas the latter study, which had samples originating mostly from the Negev, identified two compositional groups (Gunneweg NAB-I and NAB-II) for the same wares.

While the overall conclusion of these two NAA studies regarding place of manufacture may be accurate, it is difficult to resolve the discrepancy between them regarding the number of compositional groups for Nabataean wares due to the fact that the reactors used by the studies — the University of London Reactor Centre and Hebrew University, respectively — provide measurements for a limited number of elements, only 12 of which are common to both studies (Ce, Co, Cr, Cs, Eu, Fe, La, Lu, Na, Sc, Sm, Th). The purpose of conducting additional NAA analyses was to obtain a more complete chemical "fingerprint" for Petra ceramics by using the facilities of the Missouri University Research Reactor (MURR), which is capable of reliably determining the concentration for a total of 32 elements commonly found in pottery. In addition, powerful computer programs for multivariate statistical analysis developed at MURR can be applied to the new measurements as well as the results from past NAA studies to conduct a more accurate cluster analysis.

## Sampling

Pottery samples were collected during the 1994 and 1995 excavation seasons at Petra's Great Temple (P/ST). Although pottery was found within the fill of the Temple proper during the 1994 excavation season, little was found in reliable stratigraphic context. Therefore, most of the samples were taken from the Lapidary West, a sounding 44 m west of the Temple in the area used as a lapidary by the archaeological expedition. Two meters below the surface, under several layers of topsoil, is the top of a wall constructed of well-dressed ashlar blocks with the diagonal chisel marks characteristic of Nabataean masonry. A well-stratified deposit, dense with pottery sherds, extends up against the south face of this wall and overlies its top. It is from this deposit that most of the sampled pottery originated.

A typological and chronological analysis of the Lapidary West pottery was conducted in October 1994 by Stephan G. Schmid.[2] The pottery consists of Nabataean painted and unpainted fine ware, ridged jars made of sand-tempered red and gray fabric, several domestic vessels of greenish clay, including two examples of strainer jars, and a few examples of terra sigillata (TS). From the architectural and stratigraphic evidence, Schmid identified four main phases, with the third phase divided into four subphases:

**Phase I:** the construction of the wall (Locus 11) with a *terminus post quem* at the late first century BCE.

**Phase II:** the repair of the wall (Locus 14), which cannot be securely dated.

**Phase IIIa:** the fill abutting the lower half of the southern face of the wall (Loci 13, 15 and 16) assigned to the early first century CE, with pottery dated between 50 BCE and 20 CE.

**Phase IIIb:** the fill abutting the upper half of the southern face of the wall (Loci 8, 9 and 12) assigned to the late first century CE.

**Phase IIIc:** the fill abutting the upper course of the north face of the wall (Locus 10) assigned generally to the first century CE.

**Phase IIId:** the fill immediately overlying the top of the wall (Loci 4-7) dated to the early second century CE, with pottery dated between 75 CE and the early second century CE.

**Phase IV:** surface strata (Loci 1-3) dated to the second and third centuries CE.

Samples were taken from a representative selection of 120 sherds from Phase IIIa and IIIb in the Lapidary West. In addition, a few samples were taken from other parts of the Temple for comparison; this included a few examples of complete vessels (Figures 7.3-7.6), a kernos ring (Figures 7.7 and 7.8) and 12 lamps of Nabataean, Roman and Byzantine forms (95-L-6, 95-L-18, 95-L-26, 95-L-33, 95-L-38, 95-L-39, 95-L-61, 95-L-79, 95-L-81, 95-L-82, 95-L-88, 95-L-92 in Deirdre G. Barrett's article in Chapter 6).

The initial sampling procedure was conducted on site with proper precautions to prevent contamination. All of the pottery selected for analysis was individually numbered, recorded and drawn before sampling was undertaken. An area of the sherd was selected and its surface cleaned using a battery-operated drill and grinding bit. The cleaned section was then carefully snipped off using an end-cutter and placed into a small plastic bag with the field number and a description written on it. The extreme thinness of Nabataean fine ware and the relatively small size of the sherds made it difficult to attain the ideal sample size of 400 mg without destroying the entire sherd. Since it is useful to retain a representative portion of each sampled sherd for reference after the NAA results are obtained, the goal of a minimal sample weight of 200 mg was set.[3] A total of 149 samples were taken and hand-carried back to MURR for compositional analysis using NAA.

## NAA and Statistical Analysis

As mentioned above, the reactor at MURR is capable of reliably determining the concentration for a total of 32 elements

*Figure 7.3. 94-P-3, cup fragment of light red ware, carinated just above ring base. Uneven interior and exterior red 2.5YR 5/8 slip.*

*Figure 7.4. 94-P-4, cup fragment with interior and exterior red 2.5YR 5/8 slip and fugitive white 2.5YR 7/4 slip on exterior rim.*

*Figure 7.5. 94-P-5, bowl fragment of light red ware, with interior and exterior red 2.5YR 5/8 slip and fugitive white 2.5YR 7/4 slip on exterior rim.*

*Figure 7.6. 94-P-11, juglet of piriform shape with carination just above ring base, two rings in base center, long flared neck ending in an everted rim, lightly ribbed body of light red wash; one-grooved handle extends from the shoulder to just below the rim.*

*Figures 7.7 and 7.8. 94-P-13, fragment of a hollow, circular tube with the lower part of a cup standing upright on the tube, which is perforated at the base with two more perforations in the tube.*

*Figure 7.3*

*Figure 7.4*

*Figure 7.5*

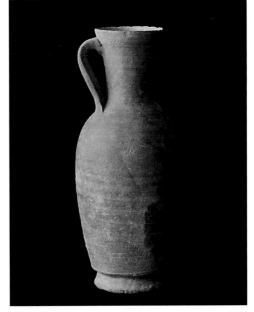

*Figure 7.6*

*Figure 7.7*

*Figure 7.8*

commonly found in pottery. These include 10 major and minor elements (Na, Al, K, Ca, Ti, Mn, Fe, Sr, Ba, Zr), 13 trace elements (Sc, V, Cr, Co, As, Rb, Sb, Cs, Hf, Th, Ta, U, Z) and nine rare earth elements (La, Lu, Nd, Sm, Yb, Ce, Eu, Tb, Dy). Once the results are obtained from the detector, the elemental concentrations for each sample are organized in a computer database for statistical analysis using a version of the Gauss program especially designed for the purposes of NAA by Hector Neff at MURR.[4] Using principal-components analysis, or PCA (Bishop and Neff 1989, Baxter 1993), RQ-mode principal-components analysis (Neff 1994) and standard Mahalanobis distance probabilities, the measurements for 32 elements for the entire sample group are calculated and clusters of samples with similar compositions are identified. These clusters represent groups of artifacts all of which were made of the same clay and therefore, in theory, originate from the same source and manufacture center. Along this line, the samples that fall into different clusters have different compositions and, therefore, must be made of a different clay from a different source (Glascock 1992, Neff 1992, 1994).

## Results

The NAA results for 149 samples of pottery from the Great Temple (P/ST) show two major composition groups, P/ST-A and P/ST-B; a third composition group, P/ST-C, is represented by three samples, and several "Outliers" are generally attributed to imported wares. The results are compared with the previous NAA studies of pottery from Petra and other Nabataean sites in addition to the NAA study of pottery from Tell Anafa, Israel, conducted at MURR (Elam, et al. 1989; Slane, et al. 1994), which includes comparable TS wares (i.e., Eastern Sigillata A). The three compositional groups, P/ST-A, P/ST-B and P/ST-C, are found to have matches in one or both of the other two studies. The following is a description of each Great Temple (P/ST) group and comparisons from other studies.

### P/ST-A and PST-B

Of the 149 samples analyzed, 23 formed a compositional group (P/ST-A), which is made up of 20 examples of Nabataean painted and unpainted fine wares (Figure 7.15, Nos. 1-13), two jars (Figure 7.15, Nos. 14 and 17), three cooking pots (Figure 7.15, Nos. 15, 16 and 18) and one Roman lamp (Barrett 95-L-6). In contrast, over 70% of the analyzed P/ST ceramics (109 out of 149) form a single compositional group (P/ST-B). Most of the samples that fall into this group are Nabataean painted and unpainted fine ware cups and bowls (Figure 7.13), everted bowls (Figure 7.14, Nos. 1-7), jars and jugs (Figure 7.14, Nos. 8-24), cooking pots (Figure 7.15) and six lamps — one Nabataean (Barrett 95-L-79), one Roman (Barrett 95-L-82) and four early Byzantine (Barrett 95-L-18, 95-L-39, 95-L-88 and 95-L-92) [For the individual measurements for samples in P/ST-A and P/ST-B, see Bedal Tables A and B on the accompanying CD-ROM.]

The results of NAA and multivariate statistical analysis show that P/ST-A and P/ST-B are very similar compositionally, as can be seen when comparing the means and standard deviations for the elements measured (Figure 7.9). However, the two groups are distinguished from each other based on differences in their concentrations of several major elements (Ba, Ca, Fe, Mn, Sr, Ti, Zr) and trace elements (Co, Cr, Hf, V, Zn). The RQ-mode principal-components diagram in Figure 7.1 illustrates how PST-A and PST-B cluster in relation to each other due to differences in these elements. This diagram also serves to illustrate how much of the compositional difference within P/ST-B is attributed to variation in the measurement of rare earth elements.

The identification of two compositional groups among Nabataean wares was originally made through the analysis of 105 samples of Nabataean painted fine wares (NABPF) from Petra, 'Avdat/Oboda and other sites in the region (Gunneweg, et al. 1991). In this study, both compositional groups (NAB-I and NAB-II) were shown to match with clays and wasters from the vicinity of Petra, indicating that NABPF was exported from Petra to western Nabataean sites. The compositions of these two groups correspond with P/ST-A and PST-B, respectively, as illustrated by a list of the means and standard deviations of 17 elements measured in both NAA studies (Figure 7.10). Since the results of two separate studies are in agreement — that Nabataean pottery was produced in the vicinity of Petra using two different clays with chemically distinct compositions — it is necessary to address the discrepancy with the earlier NAA study by 'Amr, which identified only one chemical composition (Group XV) for 211 samples, including NABPF, red ware, cooking pots, figurines, lamps and samples from the kiln at Zurrabah, a pottery production site located just outside of Petra (Zayadine 1981:350-51, 1982:380-93; Homes-Fredericq and Franken 1986:185-89), which are determined to be locally produced ('Amr 1987:198).[5] Subjecting the published NAA measurements for Group XV to the same multivariate analytical techniques used on the P/ST samples helps to solve this discrepancy.

Using Mahalanobis distance probabilities, both P/ST-A and P/ST-B can be matched compositionally with Group XV, which has a large standard deviation. After applying the same multivariate analyses to the measurements for Group XV ('Amr 1987:Tables 4.15 a, b and c) as were applied to the P/ST assemblage, 'Amr's Group XV was shown to consist of two separate compositional groups, which will be referred to hereafter as XVa and XVb; their separation is best illustrated in a plot of principal-components 2 and 3 (Figure 7.2) derived from PCA of 'Amr's Group XV pottery. The compositions of these two groups (XVa and XVb) are shown to correspond with P/ST-A/NAB-I and PST-B/NAB-II, respectively, as illustrated by a list of the means and standard deviations of elements common to the three studies (Figure 7.10). One reason the separation between Groups XVa and XVb was not identified in the original study is that measurements were obtained for only three elements (Co, Cr, Fe) of the 11 elements already shown to be key in the separation of the two Petra clays. It took a combination of multivariate statistical analysis and principal-components analysis to tease out this distinction.[6]

The results from three NAA studies of Nabataean pottery are in agreement that pottery production in and around Petra, including the production of NABPF, made use of two different clays with chemically distinct compositions. In addition to the chemical separation of Nabataean ware, the current study was able to investigate the claim of "a visual prescription for distinguishing vessels belonging to one [compositional] group from those of another" (Gunneweg, et al. 1991:326).

This claim was made based on the fact that the pottery with the chemical composition NAB-I could be dated on the basis of typology (form and painted decoration) to the earliest phases of the production of Nabataean fine wares (first century BCE-early first century CE), whereas the pottery with the chemical composition NAB-II was dated typologically to later phases of production (first century-early second century CE) (Gunneweg, et al. 1991:Figures 8 and 9, Table 6). Could the same correspondence between composition, typology and chronology be observed when comparing P/ST-A/Group XVa with P/ST-B/Group XVb?

Verification for a typological and chronological correspondence with compositional groups is found in the NABPF analyzed by 'Amr. Although both XVa and XVb contain examples of the full range of pottery types that make up the entire Group XV, one notable difference is that all of the NABPF of the "Type 1" category (defined as the earliest chronological phase) ('Amr 1987:18, Pl. 1) fall into the sub-Group XVa. By contrast, all of the painted ware of "Type 2," "Type 3a" and "Type 3b" categories (ibid.:18f, Pls. 2-5), which are attributed to the succeeding classical and later Nabataean phases ('Amr 1987:18-19), fall into the sub-Group XVb (see 'Amr 1987:Table B.2 for the individual compositions of the analyzed painted ware).[7]

A look at the forms and painted designs associated with the compositional groups from this study, P/ST-A (Figure 7.12, Nos.1-18) and P/ST-B (Figures 7.13-7.15), which represent local Petra production, shows that there is some correspondence between chemical composition and typology. The forms and painted designs of the nine NABPF samples with the chemical composition P/ST-A (947L13/15.88, 947L13/15.92, 947L13/15.93, 947L13/15.94, 947L13/15.95, 947L13/15.96, 947L9.109, 947L9.115 and 947L9.118) are consistent with those of NAB-I (specifically Decoration Motifs 7, 8 and 9 and Basic Forms 2 and 3; see Gunneweg, et al. 1991:Figure 8). Each has a feather or wreath motif that is lightly drawn, leaving much of the background visible and uncongested. Those with diagnostic forms are bowls with simple inturned rims (Figure 7.12, Nos. 1, 5, 6, 8, 10), with one example of a carinated bowl (Figure 7.15, No. 13), which is similar to NAB-I Form Type 3 except that its rim is flared rather than inturned.

Of the 20 NABPF samples with the chemical composition P/ST-B, the forms and painted designs of 17 (947L13/15.89, 947L13/15.91 (Figure 7.13, No. 30), 947L12.99, 947L12.100, 947L9.101, 947L9.102, 947L9.103, 947L9.104, 947L9.105 (Figure 7.13, No. 14), 947L9.107 (Figure 7.13, No. 18), 947L9.110 (Figure 7.13, No. 17), 947L9.111 (Figure 7.13, No. 13), 947L9.112 (Figure 7.13, No. 19), 947L9.113 (Figure 7.13, No. 12), 947L9.114 (Figure 7.13, No. 15), 947L9.116 (Figure 7.13, No. 11) and 947L9.119) are consistent with those of NAB-II (specifically Decorative Motifs 5-8 and Basic Form 1; see Gunneweg, et al. 1991:Figure 9). Their painted decorations include feathers or wreaths, dotted chevrons and background fillers of dots and fine lines, all generally rendered in a bold manner relative to the P/ST-A/NAB-I examples. Those with diagnostic forms are bowls with carinated rims, several unpainted examples of which also have the P/ST-B composition (Figure 7.13, Nos. 20, 27, 35). Although no painted examples of the NAB-II Basic Form 3 (shallow bowl with upright rim above carination) were included as part of the P/ST assemblage, several unpainted examples of this form were analyzed and determined to have the chemical composition P/ST-B (Figure 7.13, Nos. 28, 32-34, 36-42). Interestingly, however, two of the P/ST-B NABPF samples are consistent with NAB-I, based on design (the use of a light feather motif on 947L13/15.90) and form (shallow bowl with simple inturned rim, 947L9.106) (Figure 7.13, No. 16). There are also several examples of unpainted hemispherical bowls and unpainted carinated bowls with vertical sections above the carination, which are consistent with the NAB-I Basic Forms 1 and 4 (Gunneweg, et al. 1991:Figure 1) but have the P/ST-B chemical composition.

The results of the comparison of the NAA results for the P/ST assemblage with those of previous studies is the confirmation of the claim that two different clays were utilized for the production of pottery in and around Petra (Gunneweg, et al. 1991). The transition in the use of clay sources, from clay with the chemical "fingerprint" of P/ST-A (NAB-I and 'Amr Group XVa) to clay with the chemical "fingerprint" P/ST-B (NAB-II and 'Amr Group XVb) occurred sometime during the first half of the first century CE (between 9 BCE and 40 CE) and coincided with a typological transition illustrated most clearly by a change in the form and painted decoration of NABPF. The analysis of lamps dating to the early Byzantine period shows that the P/ST-B clay continued to be utilized for the production of ceramics as late as the fourth century CE.

## P/ST-C

Three examples of terra sigillata (TS) make up the composition group P/ST-C, including a distinctive krater form (Figure 7.15, No. 19). While this is statistically too small of a number to reliably determine a composition group, Figure 7.11 illustrates how the elemental concentrations from these three samples are nearly identical with those of 'Amr's Group V (1987:Table 4.15 a-c), which consists of 38 samples of TS (composed of Eastern Sigillata A and Eastern Sigillata C) as well as a group of 25 samples of Eastern Sigillata A (ESA) from excavations at Tell Anafa (Elam, et al. 1989). The three P/ST-C samples, therefore, can be assumed to belong to this larger compositional group. According to the Tell Anafa analysis, ESA has a Syrian provenance, although the identification of the specific production center has not yet been accomplished. The P/ST analysis indicates, though, that some of the TS excavated from Petra had the same Syrian provenance as the TS at Tell Anafa. [For the individual measurements for samples in P/ST-C, see Bedal Table C on the accompanying CD-ROM.]

## Outliers

In addition to the 132 P/ST samples of locally produced pottery and the three imported TS samples, there are 14 samples of the analyzed P/ST assemblage that could not be matched compositionally to the previous groups nor do they form a group themselves. In a preliminary attempt to identify their provenance based on chemical composition, the NAA results for each of the outlying samples was run against a database containing the NAA data on over 5000 samples in the MASCA expansion on the Brookhaven Laboratory database. Based on mean Euclidean distance (MED) calculations, with matches determined by an MED of less than 0.08, five of the 14 P/ST Outliers were matched to Brookhaven samples, providing a general indication as to their provenance. Three Roman lamps (Barrett 95-L-26, 95-L-61, 95-L-81) were matched compositionally with Brookhaven samples from sites in coastal Palestine. One sample of a TS body sherd (9SP4L5.130, not illustrated) and a distinctive knob base (Figure 7.15, No. 25) matched samples from Cyprus. [For a list of the Brookhaven samples whose compositions match closely with these six P/ST samples, see Bedal Table E on the accompanying CD-ROM.] All other P/ST Outliers, including two jars (Figure 7.15, Nos. 21 and 23), an amphora base (Figure 7.15, No. 27), a TS bowl (Figure 7.15, No. 20), a Roman lamp (Barrett 95-L-33) and a Nabataean lamp (Barrett 95-L-38), remain unprovenanced; the Nabataean lamp's status as an Outlier may indicate its production at another site within the Nabataean kingdom, although sampling error cannot be ruled out. Also unprovenanced are samples from strainer-spouted and strainer-necked jars (Figures 7.12, Nos. 24 and 26) made of a distinctive light greenish-brown ware. Their chemical "fingerprint" differs from the rest of the analyzed samples included in this study, particularly in the elements Fe, Ba, Sc, Cr, Co and Cs. Stephan G. Schmid suggests that they may be imports from the Parthian area, based on ware and form.[8] However, when run against the Brookhaven database, these two samples were shown to be compositionally distinct from everything, including those samples from the general Parthian region. Further comparative work must be done to determine the provenance of the P/ST Outliers. [For the individual measurements for Outliers, see Bedal Table D on the accompanying CD-ROM.]

## Conclusion

By using the facilities and statistical programs of MURR, a chemical "fingerprint" comprised of the measurements for 32 elements was obtained for pottery excavated at Petra, making it possible to compare the P/ST results to the results of other relevant NAA studies, with an overlap in a significant number of common elements measured. The most important result of this study is the verification of a change in clay source for locally produced ceramics at Petra sometime in the early first century CE, as originally presented by Gunneweg, et al. (1991), by matching P/ST-A and P/ST-B with NAB-I and NAB-II, respectively. The application of multivariate statistical methods to 'Amr's NAA results allowed the separation of her local Group XV into two compositions with the same chronological and typological associations, thus solving the discrepancy between the two earlier studies. Further work is needed to determine the provenance for several of the P/ST imported wares (Outliers).

*Figure 7.9. Mean and standard deviation for compositional Groups P/ST-A (n=23) and P/ST-B (n=109).*

| Major and Minor elements (as %) | | | Trace elements (as ppm) | | | Rare Earth elements (as ppm) | | |
|---|---|---|---|---|---|---|---|---|
| | P/ST-A | P/ST-B | | P/ST-A | P/ST-B | | P/ST-A | P/ST-B |
| Na | 1.98 ± 1.25 | 2.62 ± 1.23 | Sc | 20.9 ± 1.1 | 20.5 ± 1.1 | La | 25.2 ± 1.0 | 26.6 ± 1.1 |
| Al | 10.14 ± 1.07 | 10.17 ± 1.48 | V | 96 ± 1 | 124 ± 1 | Lu | 0.45 ± 1.0 | 0.41 ± 1.13 |
| K | 2.3 ± 1.1 | 2.4 ± 1.1 | Cr | 141 ± 1 | 122 ± 1 | Nd | 25 ± 1 | 27 ± 1 |
| Ca | 1.4 ± .1 | 3.7 ± .1 | Co | 16.9 ± 1.1 | 20.2 ± 1.1 | Sm | 5.6 ± 1.1 | 5.9 ± 1.1 |
| Ti | .75 ± .01 | .56 ± .01 | As | 7.9 ± 1.9 | 8.1 ± 1.4 | Yb | 3.0 ± 1.1 | 2.9 ± 1.1 |
| Mn | .019 ± .001 | .044 ± .001 | Rb | 74 ± 1 | 72 ± 1 | Ce | 57.2 ± 1.0 | 58.6 ± 1.1 |
| Fe | 4.49 ± .01 | 5.10 ± 1.07 | Sb | .469 ± 1.137 | .426 ± 1.583 | Eu | 1.3 ± 1.1 | 1.4 ± 1.1 |
| Sr | .010 ± .001 | .017 ± .001 | Cs | 4.1 ± 1.1 | 4.2 ± 1.1 | Tb | 0.75 ± 1.31 | 0.80 ± 1.18 |
| Ba | .157 ± .001 | .118 ± .001 | Hf | 8.2 ± 1.1 | 5.7 ± 1.2 | Dy | 4.5 ± 1.1 | 4.7 ± 1.1 |
| Zr | .018 ± .001 | .013 ± .001 | Th | 8.6 ± 1.0 | 7.8 ± 1.1 | | | |
| | | | Ta | 1.2 ± 1.1 | 0.9 ± 1.1 | | | |
| | | | U | 2.8 ± 1.2 | 2.8 ± 1.2 | | | |
| | | | Zn | 62 ± 2 | 83 ± 1 | | | |

*Figure 7.10. Comparison of compositional Groups P/ST-A and P/ST-B and their corresponding NAB-I and NAB-II from Gunneweg, et al. (1991) and XVa and XVb from 'Amr (1987), based on mean and standard deviation. ★*

|  | P/ST-A | NAB-I | XVa | P/ST-B | NAB-II | XVb |
|---|---|---|---|---|---|---|
| Na** | 1.98 ± 1.25 | .23 ± .08 | 1.82 ± .53 | 2.62 ± 1.23 | 0.22 ± .6 | 2.35 ± .75 |
| K | 2.3 ± 1.1 | xxx | 2.3 ± 1.1 | 2.4 ± 1.1 | xxx | 2.4 ± 1.1 |
| Ca | 1.4 ± .1 | 1.4 ± 0.6 | xxx | 3.7 ± 0.1 | 5.6 ± 1.8 | xxx |
| Ti | .75 ± .01 | .75 ± .07 | xxx | .56 ± .01 | .54 ± .05 | xxx |
| Fe | 4.49 ± .01 | 4.54 ± .28 | 4.32 ± 1.10 | 5.10 ± 1.07 | 5.36 ± .51 | 5.05 ± 1.10 |
| Sc | 20.9 ± 1.1 | 23.8 ± 1.4 | 21.6 ± 1.1 | 20.5 ± 1.1 | 22.8 ± 1.4 |  |
| Cr | 141 ± 1 | 154 ± 4 | 139 ± 1 | 122 ± 1 | 134 ± 11 | 119 ± 1 |
| Co | 16.9 ± 1.1 | 17.9 ± 1.8 | 17.4 ± 1.1 | 20.2 ± 1.1 | 21.7 ± 2.0 | 21.1 ± 1.1 |
| Rb | 74 ± 1 | xxx | 86 ± 1 | 72 ± 1 | xxx | 82 ± 1 |
| Cs | 4.1 ± 1.1 | 4.5 ± .3 | 3.3 ± 1.1 | 4.2 ± 1.1 | 4.8 ± 5.0 | 3.4 ± 1.1 |
| Hf | 8.2 ± 1.1 | 8.3 ± .7 | xxx | 5.7 ± 1.2 | 5.0 ± .8 | xxx |
| Th | 8.6 ± 1.0 | 9.4 ± 1.2 | 9.6 ± 1.1 | 7.8 ± 1.1 | 8.0 ± .6 | 8.6 ± 1.1 |
| Ta | 1.2 ± 1.1 | 1.2 ± .1 |  | .9 ± 1.1 | .8 ± .1 |  |
| La | 25.2 ± 1.0 | 26.7 ± 2.1 | 27.0 ± 1.1 | 26.6 ± 1.1 | 26.2 ± 2.2 | 28.4 ± 1.1 |
| Lu | .45 ± 1.07 | .48 ± .03 | .43 ± 1.09 | .41 ± 1.13 | .40 ± .05 | .40 ± 1.15 |
| Sm | 5.6 ± 1.1 | 5.3 ± .3 | 5.4 ± 1.1 | 5.9 ± 1.1 | 5.3 ± .5 | 5.8 ± 1.1 |
| Yb | 3.0 ± 1.1 | 3.1 ± .2 | xxx | 2.9 ± 1.1 | 2.7 ± .1 | xxx |
| Ce | 57.2 ± 1.0 | 59.6 ± 4.3 | 65.3 ± 1.2 | 58.6 ± 1.1 | 58.6 ± 4.8 | 68.9 ± 1.2 |
| Eu | 1.3 ± 1.1 | 1.3 ± .1 | 1.5 ± 1.1 | 1.4 ± 1.1 | 1.3 ± .1 | 1.4 ± 1.2 |

\* Formal calibrations between the results of the three study groups was not done since the numbers were similar.

\*\* The difference in the measurements for Na between the P/ST and NAB groups is most likely a result of contamination during deposition rather than from differences in clay composition.

*Figure 7.11. Comparison of compositional Group P/ST-C and the corresponding TS samples from other studies.*

|  | P/ST-C samples | | | ESA (Slane et. al.) | Group V ('Amr) |
|---|---|---|---|---|---|
|  | 947L9.10 | 947L9.45 | 947L13/15.83 | | |
| Na | 11.21 | 7.78 | 2.51 | 7.80 ± .70 | xxx |
| K | 1.1 | 1.5 | 2.1 | xxx | 1.9 ± 0.3 |
| Ca | 12.1 | 11.9 | 8.5 | 10.4 ± 1.1 | xxx |
| Ti | 0.38 | 0.32 | 0.73 | .44 ± .05 | xxx |
| Fe | 5.48 | 5.19 | 5.72 | 5.56 ± .18 | 5.56 ± .34 |
| Sc | 20.9 | 18.1 | 25.0 | 20.9 ± .7 | 22.2 ± 1.5 |
| Cr | 459 | 332 | 319 | 357 ± 40 | 327 ± 37 |
| Co | 33.3 | 26.7 | 30.7 | 32.6 ± 1.6 | 34.0 ± 3.0 |
| Cs | 5.1 | 4.1 | 5.3 | 5.2 ± .4 | 4.34 ± .57 |
| Hf | 3.2 | 2.7 | 3.1 | 31 ± .1 | xxx |
| Th | 6.8 | 5.7 | 6.4 | 6.8 ± 0.2 | 7.8 ± 0.6 |
| Ta | 0.8 | 0.7 | 0.8 | 0.8 ± .1 | xxx |
| La | 21.0 | 18.6 | 21.3 | 23.9 ± 0.7 | 22.7 ± 1.3 |
| Lu | 0.31 | 0.28 | 0.34 | 0.36 ± 4.1 | 0.31 ± .02 |
| Sm | 4.2 | 3.5 | 4.3 | 4.1 ± .1 | 4.2 ± 0.3 |
| Yb | 2.2 | 2.0 | 1.9 | 2.4 ± .1 | xxx |
| Ce | 42.8 | 35.9 | 39.7 | 41.6 ± 1.3 | 53.9 ± 6.2 |
| Eu | 1.1 | 0.9 | 1.0 | 1.1 ± .1 | xxx |

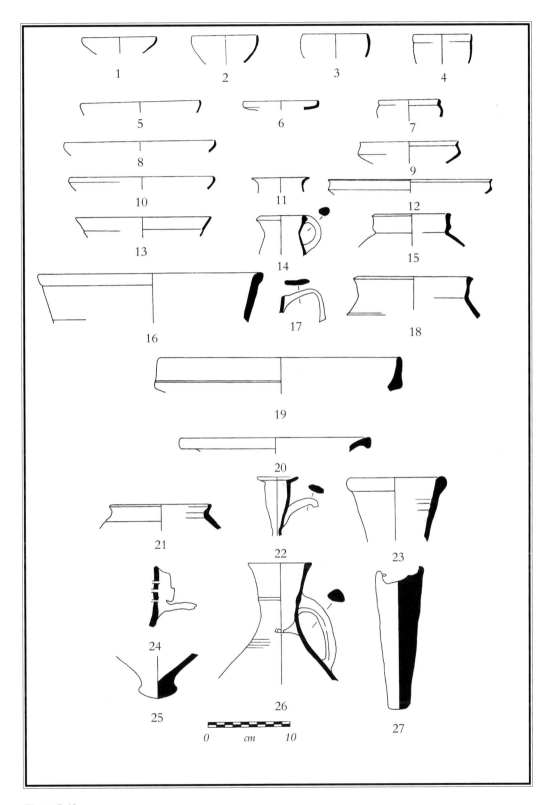

*Figure 7.12*

Drawings and descriptions by Martha S. Joukowsky.
All cores are even unless otherwise expressed.
Ceramics are all from the Trench 7, 1994, Lapidary West excavations unless otherwise indicated.

*Figure 7.12. Nabataean pottery forms with composition P/ST-A (Nos. 1-18), terra sigillata with composition P/ST-C (No. 19), Outliers (Nos. 20-27).*

| No. | Catalog no. | Description | MURR no. |
|---|---|---|---|
| | **P/ST-A:** | | |
| 1 | 947L13/15.94 | Bowl of light red 2.5YR7/8 ware with interior reddish brown 2.5YR5/4 painted feather design. | LAB094 |
| 2 | 947L8.61 | Small bowl/cup of light red 2.5YR7/6 ware with a light red 2.5YR7/6 slip over the exterior rim and the interior. | LAB061 |
| 3 | 947L13/15.84 | Bowl of light red 2.5YR7/8 ware with an exterior pinkish white 7.5YR8/2 slip. | LAB084 |
| 4 | 947L13/15.85 | Bowl/cup of light red 2.5YR7/8 ware with an exterior flaky 2.5YR6/6 slip. | LAB085 |
| 5 | 947L13/15.93 | Bowl of light red ware 2.5YR7/8 with interior light red 2.5YR6/6 painted feather design and the exterior rim slipped in pinkish white 7.5YR8/2. | LAB093 |
| 6 | 947L9.115 | Decorated bowl of light red 2.5YR7/8 ware, red 10R5/6 interior paint, pinkish white 5YR8/2 slip on exterior, interior feather design. | LAB115 |
| 7 | 947L9.42 | Small bowl of cooking pot reddish yellow 5YR6/8 ware, black core. | LAB042 |
| 8 | 947L13/15.92 | Bowl of reddish yellow 5YR6/8 ware with interior light red 2.5YR6/6 paint with a V on the rim and feather designs. | LAB092 |
| 9 | 947L9.41 | Everted bowl of reddish yellow ware 5YR7/8, with exterior rim pinkish white 5YR8/2 slip-paint. | LAB041 |
| 10 | 947L9.118 | Decorated bowl of light red 2.5YR7/8 ware, red 10R5/6 interior painted feather design, exterior banded rim in reddish gray 10R6/1. | LAB118 |
| 11 | 947L9.58 | Jug of light red 2.5YR7/6 ware with interior-exterior self-same slip. | LAB058 |
| 12 | 947L9.44 | Bowl of light red 2.5YR6/8 ware and self-same slip. | LAB044 |
| 13 | 947L9.109 | Decorated bowl with carinated body, of light red 2.5YR7/8 ware with red 10R5/6 interior painted feather design. | LAB109 |
| 14 | 947L13/15.81 | Jug of light red 2.5YR7/6 ware with an exterior pinkish white 7.5YR8/2 slip. | LAB081 |
| 15 | 947L13/15.80 | Jar of light red 2.5YR6/6 ware, exterior and over top of rim reddish brown 2.5YR5/3 slip. | LAB080 |
| 16 | 947L9.23 | Work pot/jar of reddish brown ware 5YR5/4, with traces of secondary burning on the exterior and interior. | LAB023 |
| 17 | 947L9.36 | Triple strand jar handle of reddish yellow 5YR6/8 with a pink slip 5YR7/3. | LAB036 |
| 18 | 947L12.67 | Cooking pot of light red 10R6/6 ware, exterior blackened by secondary firing, ribbing present on shoulders. | LAB067 |
| | 947L13/15.88 | Body sherd (located just above the base) of light red ware 2.5YR7/8 with a red-painted 2.5YR5/6 clustered needle design with dots on the interior (P/ST-A, not illustrated). | LAB088 |
| | 947L13/15.95 | Two joining body sherds of light red 2.5YR7.8 ware with interior red 10R5/6 feather designs (P/ST-A, not illustrated). | LAB095 |
| | 947L13/15.96 | Body sherd of light red 2.5YR7/8 ware with interior light red 2.5YR6/6 painted feather design (P/ST-A, not illustrated). | LAB096 |
| Figure 7.5 | 94-P-5 | Jar; see caption, p. 348. | LAB134 |
| Barrett | 95-L-6 | Roman lamp fragment; upper part with short and slightly arched spout; smoke-stained, decorated with raised ridges; pink ware 5YR 7/4 (dated 1st century CE). | LAB137 |
| | **P/ST-C:** | | |
| 19 | 947L9.10 | Krater of pink 7.5YR8/3 ware, exterior-interior fugitive, flaky self-same slip re-covered with a red 2.5YR4/8 slip. | LAB010 |

*Figure 7.12 (continued)*

| | | | |
|---|---|---|---|
| | 947L9.45 | Body sherd of *terra sigillata* light red 2.5YR7/6 ware, interior-exterior red 10R5/8 slip. Slip is worn away on the interior (P/ST-C, not illustrated). | LAB045 |
| | 947L13/15.83 | Body sherd of *terra sigillata* reddish yellow 7.5YR8/6 ware with exterior red 2.5YR4/8 slip (P/ST-C, not illustrated). | LAB083 |

**Outliers:**

| | | | |
|---|---|---|---|
| 20 | 9411L6.129 | Large bowl of *terra sigillata* light red 2.5YR7/8 ware with an interior-exterior light red 10R6/8 slip. | LAB129 |
| 21 | 947L9.20 | Small jar with pronounced neck ridge of reddish yellow ware 5YR7/6 with an interior-exterior pink 7.5YR8/3 slip. | LAB020 |
| 22 | 947L13/15.79 | Jug of light red 10YR6/8 ware with exterior and over interior rim light red 10R6/6 slip-wash. | LAB079 |
| 23 | 947L9.24 | Coarse ware jar of light red ware 2.5R6/8 with a flaky very pale brown 10YR8/3 slip over the top of the interior rim and exterior. | LAB024 |
| 24 | 947L9.14 | Sieve spout of a jug of very pale brown ware 10YR8/3 with a self-same slip. | LAB014 |
| 25 | 947L9.34 | Knob base of reddish yellow 5YR6/6 ware with exterior self-same slip (import from Cyprus). | LAB034 |
| 26 | 947L12.69 | Jug with sieve neck of pinkish white 7.5YR8/2 ware with exterior-interior self-same slip. | LAB069 |
| 27 | 947L9.60 | Amphora base of yellowish red 5YR5/8 ware. | LAB060 |
| | 94SP4L5.130 | Base sherd of *terra sigillata* light red 10R6/6 ware with an interior-exterior red 10R5/6 slip (from Lower Channel of the Canalization System) (unprovenienced, not illustrated). | LAB130 |
| Barrett | 95-L-38 | Nabataean lamp shoulder fragment; sunray design with superimposed rosettes and small filling hole; pink ware 5YR 8/3 (1st century CE). | LAB141 |
| Barrett | 95-L-81 | Roman lamp fragment; round with double axes on shoulder; buff ware 7.5YR 6/3 with red slip; (late 1st century CE; import from coastal Palestine). | LAB145 |
| Barrett | 95-L-26 | Roman lamp rim fragment; ridges around a large discus; pink ware 7.5YR 7/4 (1st-2nd centuries CE; import from coastal Palestine). | LAB139 |
| Barrett | 95-L-61 | Roman lamp fragment; deep plain discus and central filling hole surrounded by three grooves; tongue on neck; buff clay 10YR 7/4 with black slip (1st-2nd centuries CE; import from coastal Palestine). | LAB143 |
| Barrett | 95-L-33 | Roman lamp fragment; upper shoulder showing three border ridges around large discus; pinkish white ware 7.5YR 8/2 (compare with 'Amr 1987:pl. 32). | LAB140 |

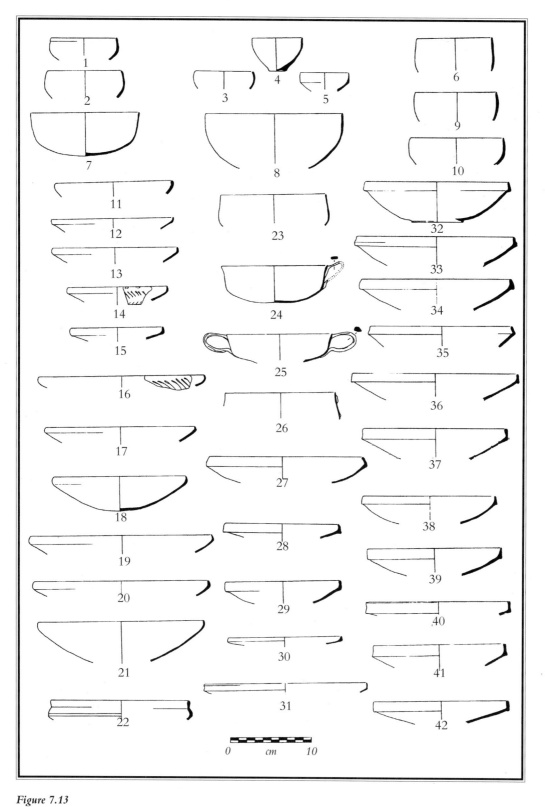

*Figure 7.13*

*Figure 7.13. P/ST cups and bowls with composition P/ST-B.*

| No. | Catalog no. | Description | MURR no. |
|---|---|---|---|
| 1 | 947L9.50 | Bowl of light red 2.5YR5/6 ware with a self-same slip. | LAB050 |
| 2 | 947L9.49 | Bowl of light red 2.5YR6/6 ware with the exterior rim pink 7.5YR8/3 slip. | LAB049 |
| 3 | 94SP4L5.124 | Bowl/cup of light red 2.5YR6/6 ware (from Lower Channel of the Canalization System). | LAB124 |
| 4 | 947L9.8 | Small bowl/cup of light red 2.5YR6/6 ware, partial pinkish white slip-wash 7.5YR8/2 over exterior rim and upper body. | LAB008 |
| 5 | 94SP4L5.126 | Bowl/cup of light red 2.5YR6/8 ware with a self-same slip (from Lower Channel of the Canalization System). | LAB126 |
| 6 | 947L9.39 | Small bowl of light red 2.5YR 6/8 ware with a streaky pale red wash/slip exterior and over the interior rim. | LAB039 |
| 7 | 947L9.9 | Bowl of light red 2.5YR5/3 ware. White wash over exterior spiral incised base. | LAB009 |
| 8 | 947L9.12 | Bowl of red 2.5YR5/8 ware with pinkish white 7.5YR8/2 slip on the exterior rim. | LAB012 |
| 9 | 947L12.66 | Fine ware bowl of light red 10R6/8 ware with interior-exterior self-same slip. | LAB066 |
| 10 | 94SP4L5.125 | Bowl of light red 2.5YR6/8 ware, heavily encrusted with silt (from Lower Channel of the Canalization System). | LAB125 |
| 11 | 947L9.116 | Decorated bowl of light red 2.5YR7/8 ware, red 10R5/6 interior paint, pinkish white 5YR8/2 slip on exterior rim all but worn away, feather design with blobs painted over the feather design. | LAB116 |
| 12 | 947L9.113 | Decorated bowl of light red 2.5YR7/8 ware, red 10R5/6 interior paint, exterior rim slipped in a light red 10R6/6, interior dots and fruit motif. | LAB113 |
| 13 | 947L9.111 | Decorated bowl of pale red 10R6/8 ware with exterior rim slipped in a very pale brown 10YR8/2. Rim motif of red 10R5/6 interior painted chevrons around dots. | LAB111 |
| 14 | 947L9.105 | Decorated bowl of pale red 10R6/8 ware with interior pale red 10R6/4 painted feather design. | LAB105 |
| 15 | 947L9.114 | Decorated bowl of light red 2.5YR7/8 ware, red 10R5/6 interior painted feather design, pinkish white slip on exterior rim all but worn away. | LAB114 |
| 16 | 947L9.106 | Decorated bowl of pale red 10R6/8 ware with interior feather design in pale red 10R6/4 paint. | LAB106 |
| 17 | 947L9.110 | Decorated bowl of pale red 10R6/8 ware with exterior rim slipped in very pale brown 10YR8/2 and red 10R5/6 interior painted feather design with heavily dotted background. | LAB110 |
| 18 | 947L9.107 | Decorated bowl of light red 2.5YR7/8 ware with paint of varying colors: light red 2.5YR6/6 and red 2.5YR5/6. Exterior rim covered in pinkish white 5YR8/2, black core. | LAB107 |
| 19 | 947L9.112 | Decorated bowl of light red 2.5YR7/8 ware with exterior rim slipped in a light reddish brown 10YR 8/2 with a light reddish brown band inside the rim. Red 10R5/6 interior painted feather designs. | LAB112 |
| 20 | 947L9.117 | Decorated bowl of light red 2.5YR7/8 ware, red 10R5/6 interior painted feather design ending in blobs. | LAB117 |
| 21 | 947L9.108 | Decorated bowl of light red 2.5YR7/8 ware with exterior rim of flaky pinkish white 7/5YR8/2 slip that has been all but worn away; interior red 10R5/6 painted feather design, dots and 'pollywogs.' | LAB108 |
| 22 | 947L9.43 | Bowl of light red 2.5YR6/8 ware with an exterior pinkish gray 7.5YR7/2 slip. | LAB043 |
| 23 | 947L12.65 | Bowl of light red 2.5YR6/8 ware, with a light red 10R6/8 slip. over the interior and partial exterior black core. | LAB065 |
| 24 | 947L8.131 | Two-handled cup of red 2.5YR5/8 ware. Fugitive pinkish white 7.5YR8/2 wash over exterior. Base string-cut before smoothing. (947L8, Locus 8, sequence 7036). | LAB131 |
| 25 | 947L9.13 | Two-handled cup/bowl of light red 2.5YR6/8. | LAB013 |

**Figure 7.13** *(continued)*

| | | | |
|---|---|---|---|
| 26 | 947L9.40 | Bowl or cup with handle vestige of reddish yellow 5YR6/6 ware. | LAB040 |
| 27 | 947L9.11 | Bowl of cooking fabric of dark reddish gray 2.5YRN4/ ware with blackened interior, even black core. | LAB011 |
| 28 | 947L9.97 | Bowl of light red 10R6/8 ware, exterior pinkish white 5YR8/2 and smudged; exterior core darker than interior. | LAB097 |
| 29 | 947L9.6 | Bowl of light red 10R6/8 ware with white 5YR8/1 slip over exterior rim and fugitive gray wash at base, black core. | LAB006 |
| 30 | 947L13/15.91 | Bowl of light red 2.5YR6/8 ware with interior light red 2.5YR6/6 painted feather designs. | LAB091 |
| 31 | 947L8.73 | Bowl of light red 2.5YR7/8 ware with a flaky pinkish white 7.5YR8/2 slip over the exterior rim. | LAB073 |
| 32 | 947L9.1 | Inverted bowl of gray 7.5YR5/1 ware. Very pale brown 10YR8/3 slip-wash on exterior rim. | LAB001 |
| 33 | 947L12.76 | Bowl of light red 2.5YR6/6 with pinkish white 5YR8/2 slip on the exterior rim. | LAB076 |
| 34 | 947L9.7 | Bowl of light red 2.5YR6/8 ware with pinkish white 7.5YR8/2 slip over exterior rim. | LAB007 |
| 35 | 947L8.74 | Bowl of light red 2.5YR6/8 ware with exterior rim pinkish white 5YR8/2 slip and black core. | LAB074 |
| 36 | 947L9.4 | Bowl of light red 10R6/6 ware with pinkish white 5YR8/2 slip over exterior rim. | LAB004 |
| 37 | 947L9.3 | Bowl of light red 2.5YR6/8 ware. Light red 5YR8/1 slip over exterior rim, black core. | LAB003 |
| 38 | 947L9.2 | Bowl of light red 10R6/8 ware. Pale red 2.5YR7/2 fugitive slip over exterior rim. | LAB002 |
| 39 | 947L9.5 | Bowl of light red ware 2.5YR6/8, smudged to a light reddish gray 2.5YR7/1, wheel marks on the exterior, light red slip on exterior rim, black core. | LAB005 |
| 40 | 947L13/15.78 | Bowl of light red 2.5YR6/8 ware with an interior-exterior pink 5YR8/3 slip. | LAB078 |
| 41 | 947L12.71 | Bowl of light red 2.5YR6/6 ware with a very pale brown 10YR8/3 slip on the exterior rim. | LAB071 |
| 42 | 947L12.77 | Bowl of light red 2.5YR6/8 ware, discolored due to secondary firing to a 2.5YR5/4 reddish brown color. | LAB077 |
| | 947L9.38 | Body sherd of light red 2.5YR6/8 ware with an exterior very pale brown 10YR8/2 slip (P/ST-B, not illustrated). | LAB038 |
| | 947L9.101 | Body sherd of light red 10R6/8 ware, interior red 10R5/4 painted design with dots, needle clusters and dotted chevrons (P/ST-B, not illustrated). | LAB101 |
| | 947L9.119 | Decorated body sherd of light red 2.5YR7/8 ware, red 10R5/6 interior painted design with bold and fine lines (P/ST-B, not illustrated). | LAB119 |
| | 947L9.102 | Decorated body sherd of light red 10R6/8 ware, interior pale red 10R6/4 painted feathers, dots and dotted chevrons (P/ST-B, not illustrated). | LAB102 |
| | 947L9.104 | Decorated body sherd of light red 10R6/8 ware with pale red 10R6/3 painted feathers and dots, black core (P/ST-B, not illustrated). | LAB104 |
| | 947L9.103 | Decorated body sherd of light red 10R6/8 ware with interior pale red 10R6/4 paint of the feather design, black core (P/ST-B, not illustrated). | LAB103 |
| | 947L12.98 | Body sherd of light red 10R6/8 ware with interior light red paint 10R6/6 (P/ST-B, not illustrated). | LAB098 |
| | 947L13/15.90 | Bowl body sherd of light red 2.5YR7/8 ware with interior light red 2.5YR6/6 painted feather design (P/ST-B, not illustrated). | LAB090 |
| | 947L12.100 | Body sherd of light red 10R6/8 ware with interior pale red 10R 6/4 painted rows of dots (P/ST-B, not illustrated). | LAB100 |
| | 947L12.99 | Body sherd of pale red 10R6/8 ware with interior light red 10R6/6 painted dots (P/ST-B, not illustrated). | LAB099 |
| | 947L13/15.89 | Body sherd of light red 2.5YR7/6 ware with interior light reddish brown 2.5YR6/4 to light red 2.5YR6/6 small and large dot design (P/ST-B, not illustrated). | LAB89 |
| Figure 7.3 | 94-P-3 | Bowl; see caption, p. 348. | LAB132 |
| Figure 7.4 | 94-P-4 | Bowl; see caption, p. 348. | LAB133 |

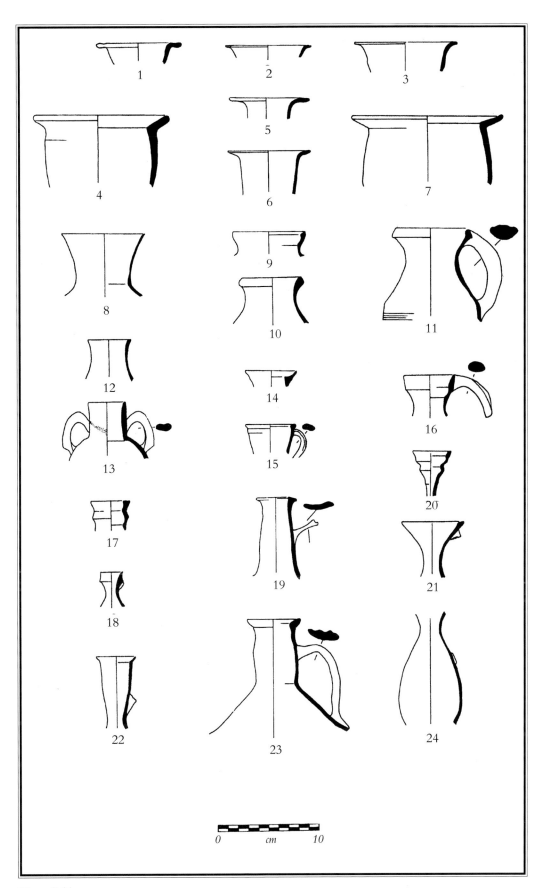

*Figure 7.14*

*Figure 7.14. P/ST everted bowls, jars and jugs with composition P/ST-B.*

| No. | Catalog no. | Description | MURR no. |
|-----|-------------|-------------|----------|
| 1 | 94SP4L5.122 | Everted rim of light red 2.5YR7/6 ware with ridged neck. Self-same slip (from Lower Channel of the Canalization System). | LAB122 |
| 2 | 94SP4L4.121 | Everted rim of light red 10R6/8 ware with self-same slip, gray core. Ridges on top of the rim (from Lower Channel of the Canalization System). | LAB121 |
| 3 | 947L9.56 | Everted bowl of light red 2.5YR6/8 ware with interior-exterior self-same slip, black core. | LAB056 |
| 4 | 947L8.62 | Everted bowl of coarse light red 10R6/8 ware. Exterior mottled pinkish white 5YR8/2 discolored slip. | LAB062 |
| 5 | 947L9.57 | Everted rim of light red 2.5YR6/6 ware with a self-same slip on the interior and exterior. | LAB057 |
| 6 | 947L9.55 | Everted rim of light reddish brown 2.5YR6/3 ware, with a see-through wash-slip 2.5YR6/3 on the exterior and over the interior rim. | LAB055 |
| 7 | 947L9.59 | Everted bowl of light red 2.5YR6/8 ware. Rim and exterior slipped in pinkish white 7.5YR8/2. | LAB059 |
| 8 | 947L9.22 | Jug or tankard of light red ware 2.5YR6/6 with an exterior glossy self-same slip, uneven core. | LAB022 |
| 9 | 94SP4L5.123 | Juglet rim  f light red 2.5YR6/8 with an exterior pinkish white 7.5YR8/2 slip, exterior smudged, black core (from Lower Channel of the Canalization System). | LAB123 |
| 10 | 947L13/15.72 | Jar rim of reddish yellow 5YR7/6 ware with a very pale brown 10YR8/4 slip on the exterior and over the interior rim. | LAB072 |
| 11 | 947L9.31 | Cooking jug of pinkish gray 7.5YR7/2 ware and black core. | LAB031 |
| 12 | 947L9.53 | Jug rim of reddish yellow 5YR6/6 ware with interior-exterior light red 2.5YR7/6 slip. | LAB053 |
| 13 | 947L9.52 | Pilgrim bottle of light red 2.5YR6/8 ware with a flaky, very pale brown 10YR8/2 slip on the exterior. The handles are affixed sloppily. | LAB052 |
| 14 | 947L9.37 | Small jug of light red 2.5YR6/8 ware with a self-same slip. | LAB037 |
| 15 | 947L9.18 | Jug of light red 2.5YR6/8 ware with self-same slip. | LAB018 |
| 16 | 947L9.16 | Jug of light red 2.5YR6/8 ware with interior-exterior pinkish white 5YR8/2 slip. | LAB016 |
| 17 | 947L12.86 | Jug of light red 2.5YR6/8 ware with a very pale brown 10YR8/2 slip. | LAB086 |
| 18 | 947L9.17 | Small jug of pinkish gray 5YR6/2 ware with interior and exterior self-same slip. Fragmented handle attachment. | LAB017 |
| 19 | 947L9.54 | Jug of light red 2.5YR6/8 ware with exterior and over interior rim pink 5YR8/3 slip. The potter's fingerprints remain on the handle attachment. | LAB054 |
| 20 | 947L8.64 | Jug rim of light red 2.5YR6/8 ware. Exterior and over the top of the interior pale red 2.5YR7/2 slip, black core. | LAB064 |
| 21 | 947L8.63 | Jug rim with fragmented handle of light red 2.5YR6/8 ware with self-same slip on the exterior and over the interior rim. | LAB063 |
| 22 | 947L12.87 | Decanter/jug of light red 2.5YR6/8 ware with a pinkish white 5YR8/2 slip on the exterior and over the top of the rim. | LAB087 |
| 23 | 947L9.21 | Jug of red ware 10R5/8 with an interior-exterior of reddish yellow 7.5YR8/6. | LAB021 |
| 24 | 94SP4L5.120 | Juglet of light red 10R6/8 ware, exterior washed away light red 10R6/6 pitted surface. Fragmented handle. This is Catalog number 94-P-27 (from Lower Channel of the Canalization System). | LAB120 |
| Figure 7.6 | 94-P-11 | Jar; see caption, p. 348. | LAB135 |
| | 947L9.35 | Triple strand jar handle light pink ware 2.5YR6/8 with pinkish white 5YR8/2 slip (P/ST-B, not illustrated). | LAB035 |
| | 947L8.75 | Five strand-ribbed handle of light red 2.5YR6/8 ware (P/ST-B, not illustrated). | LAB075 |

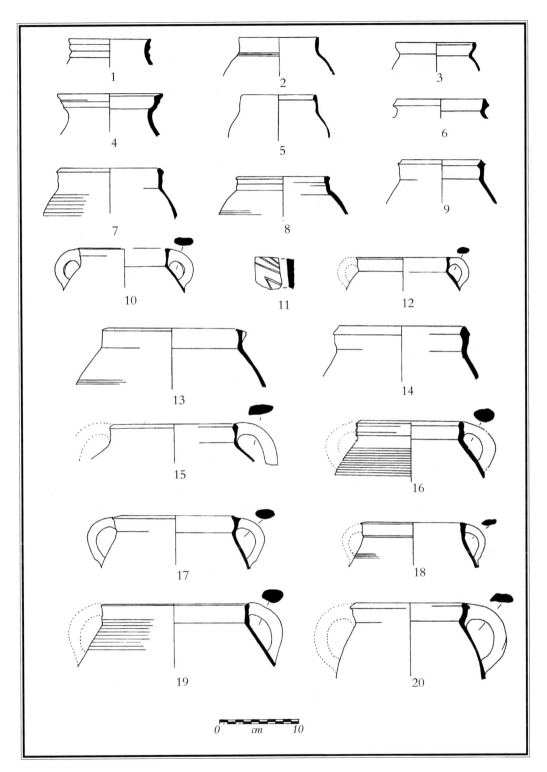

**Figure 7.15**

*Figure 7.15. P/ST cooking pots, lamps and a kernos ring with composition P/ST-B.*

| No. | Catalog no. | Description | MURR no. |
|-----|-------------|-------------|----------|
| 1 | 947L9.26 | Jar/jug of light red ware 2.5YR6/8, exterior discolored self-same slip. | LAB026 |
| 2 | 947L9.19 | Jar of light red ware 2.5YR6/8 with exterior pinkish gray 7.5YR6/2 slip. | LAB019 |
| 3 | 94SP4L5.127 | Small jar of light red 2.5YR6/6 ware with an exterior very pale brown slip 10YR8/2, uneven core (from Lower Channel of the Canalization System). | LAB127 |
| 4 | 947L9.48 | Cooking pot of weak red 2.5YR5/3 ware with an exterior flaky pinkish white 7.5YR5/2 slip and three exterior ridges. | LAB048 |
| 5 | 947L9.15 | Jug or cooking pot light red 2.5YR6/8 ware; discolored from secondary burning. | LAB015 |
| 6 | 947L9.51 | Jar rim of light red 2.5YR6/8 ware, interior-exterior self-same slip. | LAB051 |
| 7 | 947L9.27 | Cooking pot of light brown 2.5YR6/8 ware with exterior pinkish white 7.5YR8/2 slip, exterior ribbed, black core. | LAB027 |
| 8 | 947L9.46 | Jar of coarse light red 2.5YR6/8 ware, with an exterior white 5YR8/1 flaky slip, ribbed exterior, uneven core. | LAB046 |
| 9 | 947L9.25 | Jar of red 10R5/8 ware with a very pale brown 10YR8/2 slip on the exterior. | LAB025 |
| 10 | 947L9.47 | Cooking pot or jug of light red 2.5YR6/8 ware with an exterior pale red 2.5YR7/2 flaky slip, black core. | LAB047 |
| 11 | 9411L6.128 | Body sherd with excisions of light reddish brown 2.5YR7/3 ware with a black core (Trench 11). | LAB128 |
| 12 | 947L9.11 | Cooking pot fabric of weak red ware 2.5YR5/2, over exterior rim weak red 2.5YR5/2 slip. | LAB011 |
| 13 | 947L12.70 | Cooking pot of light red 10R6/6 ware with a flaky very pale brown 10YR6/2 exterior slip. | LAB070 |
| 14 | 947L9.32 | Cooking pot of reddish yellow 5YR6/8 ware, black core. | LAB032 |
| 15 | 947L13/15.82 | Cooking pot of pinkish gray 7.5YR6/2 ware with a self-same slip, even gray core. | LAB082 |
| 16 | 947L9.33 | Cooking pot of 5YR7/6 ware, black core. | LAB033 |
| 17 | 947L12.68 | Cooking pot or jug/jar of light red 10R6/8 ware with exterior pinkish white 5YR8/2 slip, uneven core. | LAB068 |
| 18 | 947L9.29 | Cooking pot of reddish yellow 5YR7/6 ware with large limestone inclusions. | LAB029 |
| 19 | 947L9.30 | Cooking pot of reddish yellow ware 5YR7/6, black core. | LAB030 |
| 20 | 947L9.28 | Cooking pot of light red ware 2.5YR6/8 with an exterior slip of very pale brown 10YR8/2, uneven core. | LAB028 |
| Figure 7.7 | 94-P-13 | Kernos ring; see caption, p. 348. | LAB136 |
| Barrett | 95-L-79 | Nabataean lamp fragment; shoulder with sunray design and possible rosette decoration; light reddish-brown ware 5YR 6/4 (1st century CE). | LAB144 |
| Barrett | 95-L-82 | Roman lamp fragment; shoulder rim and soot-stained spout with stamped tongue/horseshoe design; pink ware 7.5YR 7/3. | LAB146 |
| Barrett | 95-L-18 | Byzantine lamp spout; upper and lower segments with radiating lines and volute, raised ridges around the filling hole; soot-stained; dark grayish brown ware 10YR 3/2 (Broneer Type XXVIII 4th century CE). | LAB138 |
| Barrett | 95-L-39 | Byzantine lamp spout; upper and lower segments with ridges radiating from spout and one ridge bordering filling hole; soot-stained (4th century CE). | LAB142 |
| Barrett | 95-L-88 | Byzantine lamp fragment; shoulder with ridges radiating from filling hole, an encircling ridge, and a vestigial handle; light brown ware 7.5YR 6/2 (4th century CE). | LAB147 |
| Barrett | 95-L-92 | Byzantine lamp; small upper shoulder with vestigial knob handle and radiating ridges from filling hole; light brown ware 10YR 7/3 (4th century CE). | LAB148 |

# Endnotes

[1] G.M. Crowfoot 1936; P.C. Hammond 1959, 1962, 1964; P.J. Parr 1970; K. Schmitt-Korte 1971, 1974, 1979; A. Negev 1972, 1974, 1986; A. Negev and R. Sivan 1977; J.-M. Dentzer 1985.

[2] A copy of Stephan G. Schmid's report is on file with Martha S. Joukowsky.

[3] The original sample weighing 400 mg is ultimately divided into two samples of 200 mg each. One is sealed is a polyethylene vial and used for measuring the short-lived elements, while the other 200 mg is sealed in a quartz tube and used to measure the long-lived elements. When only the minimal 200 mg are obtained, the sample can be irradiated twice, first for short-lived elements and then for long-lived elements.

[4] My appreciation to Hector Neff and Michael Glascock, with whom I spent four months as an intern at MURR learning the process of NAA and application of multivariate analysis.

[5] 'Amr attributes all of her Group XV to local Petra production (1987:198), but she also notes that the Group XV composition is similar to that of Palestinian limestone hill clays and that it is difficult to determine the difference between the clays of the Petra area and those of the Palestinian hill clays, since they are all from the same geological limestone formation. She states, "a Palestinian origin for some of the samples included in G XV cannot be ruled out" ('Amr 1987:192).

[6] The k-means (or optimization) method of cluster analysis was used in this study, in which the number of groups is predetermined by the operator ('Amr 1987:131).

[7] For a thorough description of the differences between Types 1, 2 and 3 and their correspondence to chronological phases, see K. 'Amr 1987:17-19, P.J. Parr 1970:369-72, K. Schmitt-Korte 1971: 53f, A. Negev and R. Sivan 1977.

[8] See endnote 2.

# Bibliography

'Amr, K.

    1987    *The Pottery from Petra. A Neutron Activation Analysis Study. BARIS.* Oxford. 324.

Baxter, M.J.

    1993    "Principal Component Analysis in Archaeometry," *Archaeologia e calcolatoria.*

Bishop, R.L. and H. Neff.

    1989    "Multivariate Analysis of Compositional Data in Archaeology." In *Archaeological Chemistry IV*, ed. R.O. Allen. Washington DC: Am. Chem. Soc. Advances in Chemistry. Ser. 220. 576-586.

Cogswell, J., H. Neff and M.D. Glascock.

    1995    "Archaeometric Research Using Neutron-Activation Analysis at the Missouri University Research Reactor," *MAS Quarterly* 12-19.

Crowfoot, G.M.

    1936    "The Nabataean Ware of Sbaita," *Palestine Exploration Fund, Quarterly Statement*: 14-27.

Dentzer, J.-M.

1985    "Ceramique et Environnement Naturel: La ceramique Nabateene de Bosra." In *SHAJ II,* ed. A. Hadidi. Amman: Department of Antiquities. 149-153.

Elam, J.M., M.D. Glascock and K.W. Slane.

1989    "A Re-examination of the Provenance of Eastern Sigillata A," *Proceedings of the International Symposium on Archaeometry 1988.* Toronto.

Glascock, M.D.

1992    "Characterization of Archaeological Ceramics at MURR by Neutron Activation Analysis and Multivariate Statistics." In *Chemical Characterization of Ceramic Pastes in Archaeology,* ed. H. Neff. Madison, WI: Prehistory Press.

Glueck, N.

1940    *The Other Side of the Jordan.* New Haven: ASOR.

Gunneweg, J., I. Perlman and F. Asaro.

1991    "The Origin, Classification and Chronology of Nabataean Fine Ware." In *Jahrbuch des Romisch-Germanischen Zentralmuseums Mainz.* 35:315-345.

Gunneweg, J., I. Perlman and J. Yellin.

1983    *The Provenience, Typology and Chronology of Eastern Sigillata. Qedem 17.* Jerusalem: Hebrew University.

Hammond, P.C.

1959    "Pattern Families in Nabataean Painted Ware," *AJA* 63:371-382.

————.

1962    "A Classification of Nabataean Fine Ware," *AJA* 66:169-79.

————.

1964    "The Physical Nature of Nabataean Fine Ware," *AJA* 68:259-268.

Homes-Fredericq, D. and H.J. Franken.

1986    *Pottery and Potters – Past and Present.* Tubingen: Attempo Verlag.

Iliffe, J.H.

1935    "Nabataean Pottery from Negeb," *QDAP* 3:132-35.

Khairy, N.I.

1975    "A Typological Study of the Unpainted Pottery from the Petra Excavations," Ph.D. Dissertation, University of London.

————.

1985    "Fine Nabataean Ware with Impressed and Rouletted Decorations." In *SHAJ I,* ed. A. Hadidi. Amman: Department of Antiquities. 275-283.

Neff, H.

1994    "RQ-mode Principal Components Analysis of Ceramic Compositional Data," *Archaeometry* 36:115-30.

Neff, H. (ed.)

 1992 *Chemical Characterization of Ceramic Pastes in Archaeology*. Madison, WI: Prehistory Press.

Negev, A.

 1972 "Nabataean Sigillata," *RB* 79:381–398.

———.

 1974 *The Nabataean Potters' Workshop at Oboda*. Bonn: Habelt.

———.

 1986 *The Late Hellenistic and Early Roman Pottery of Nabataean Oboda, Final Report. Qedem 22*. Jerusalem.

Negev, A. and R. Sivan.

 1977 "The Pottery of the Nabataean Necropolis at Mampsis," *Rei Cretaria Romanae Fautorum Acta* 17/18:109–131.

Parr, P.J.

 1970 "A Sequence of Pottery from Petra." In *Near Eastern Archaeology in the Twentieth-Century: Essays in Honor of Nelson Glueck*, ed. J.A. Sanders. New York. 348–381.

Schmitt-Korte, K.

 1971 "A Contribution to the Study of Nabataean Pottery," *ADAJ* 16:47-60.

———.

 1974 "Die Bemalte Nabataeische Keramik: Verbreitung, Typologie und Chronologie." In *Petra und das Koenigreich der Nabataeer*. 2nd ed. Munich. 70-93.

———.

 1979 *Nabataean Pottery, Typology and Chronology*. Riadh Symposium 2. Frankfurt.

Slane, K.W., J.M. Elam, M.D. Glascock and H. Neff.

 1994 "Compositional Analysis of Eastern Sigillata A and Related Wares from Tel Anafa (Israel)," *Journal of Archaeological Science* 21:51-64.

Zayadine, F.

 1981 "Recent Excavations and Restorations of the Department of Antiquities," *AJA* 25: 341-55.

 1982 "Recent Excavations at Petra (1979-1981)," *AJA* 26:365-93.

# CHAPTER EIGHT

# INSCRIPTIONS

## AN IMPERIAL INSCRIPTION

## INSCRIBED FINDS

Stephen V. Tracy

*Figures 8.1 and 8.2. The assembled fragments of the Imperial inscription. Drawing by Jean Blackburn.*

# AN IMPERIAL INSCRIPTION[1]

## Stephen V. Tracy

Four joining pieces of white marble and one non-joining (96-S-32, 96-S-34, 96-S-38, 96-S-39) (Figures 8.1 and 8.2) were found in the West 'Adyton' of the Petra Great Temple (Area T, Trench 22) on July 30-31 and August 2, 1996. Figure 8.3 shows the West 'Adyton' during the course of excavation. There were abundant traces of dark red paint in the letters of the inscription when found. The back is preserved flat and very smooth, indeed finely finished. The thickness of the four joined pieces is not uniform but is thinner at the top (0.018 m) than at the bottom (0.025 m). Their dimensions are 0.19 m in height and 0.26 m in width. The letters measure 0.047-0.05 m in height for Lines 1 and 2 and 0.04 m for Line 3. The inscription reads:

M[AX•]TRIB•PO[T]

FINIVM

VS•M

I
•

ca. a. 112-114 CE p.?

The non-joining piece likewise increases in thickness from 0.018 m at the top to 0.0199 m at its bottom. The lines of breakage follow the central strokes of an M. The thickness situates this small piece in the first line. The M in all likelihood belongs to the title [Pont(ifex)] M[ax(imus)] or, if the inscription is Trajanic, to the epithet [Ger]m(anicus). The fragments were found in fill above the floor of the West 'Adyton'; the room was cleared to floor level (Figure 8.3), and no further fragments came to light.

Erika L. Schluntz, one of the student excavators, has called my attention to another non-joining fragment of this inscription (93-S-1) (Figures 8.4 and 8.5) found on the last day of the 1993 excavation season. Though battered, it is of white marble and

exhibits the same calligraphic lettering as the foregoing text; it preserves the back (smooth) and was found on the stairway leading into the Temple (Trench 1) on August 18, 1993. This fragment too tapers in thickness, from 0.022 m at the bottom to 0.0192 m at the top. It measures 0.092 m in height and 0.085 m in width. The inscription reads:

ON

IV̇

To the right of the O appears a lozenge-shaped serif — the lower left part of N. The sharply curving serif to the right of I is probably part of a V. The thickness reveals that this fragment preserves part of the first two lines of the text. The ON may be from the word [P]on[t(ifex)].

It is to be greatly regretted that so little of this important text survives. It is not possible to determine, for example, the original lengths of the lines nor to know how many lines are lost above and below. Line 1 preserves unmistakably part of the titulature of the emperor, i.e., *trib(unicia) po[t(estate)]*. If in fact this text dates to 112 to 114 CE, there are a number of inscriptions that reveal the style of nomenclature and titles Trajan used during these years. This gives an idea of what is missing from this part of the present text. The emperor was styled during the year 112 CE, as we may see from *ILS* 292-293: *imp(erator) Caesar divi Nervae f(ilius) Nerva Traianus Aug(ustus) Germ(anicus) Dac(icus) pont(ifex) max(imus) trib(unicia) pot(estate) XVI imp(erator) VI co(n)s(ul) VI p(ater) p(atriae).*

By the year 114 CE, *ILS* 295-296 reveals that this had become *imp(erator) Caesar divi Nervae f(ilius) Nerva Traianus Optimus Aug(ustus) Germ(anicus) Dac(icus) pont(ifex) max(imus) trib(unicia) pot(estate) XVIII imp(erator) VII co(n)s(ul) VI p(ater) p(atriae).*

*Figure 8.3. The West 'Adyton' from above, looking south.*

The genitive plural *finium* (if correct) in the second line is intriguing.[2] This text apparently dealt in some way with territorial borders. Boundaries naturally were a frequent matter of concern, which ultimately rested with the emperor. During the year 116/7 CE, for example, C. Avidius Nigrinus, Trajan's legate, settled a complex of disputes between Delphi and its neighbors (*FD* III.4 290-295). See also the very informative letter of the proconsul Q. Gellius Sentius Augurinus concerning the boundary dispute between Lamia and Hypata in Thessaly, which reads in part: *cum optimus maximusque princeps Traianus Hadrianus Aug(ustus) scripserit mihi uti adhibitis mensoribus de controversiis finium inter Lamienses et Hypataeos cognita causa terminarem...placet initium finium esse ab eo loco...*(*ILS* 5947a).[3] It is highly doubtful, however, that the present text deals with a boundary dispute; we should rather think of some such phrase of the emperor as the preserver (*conservator*) or founder (*auctor*) of the territory. See the dedicatory inscription to Trajan from early in the year 115 CE on the north gate at Jarash (Gerasa/Jerash) that refers to him as σ[ω]τήρ and, if it has been restored correctly, [κ]τί[στης] (*Gerasa* 401 No. 56/57, Line 5). Finally, if we are here dealing with a dedication to the emperor, one should probably interpret the letters in Line 3 as part of a proper name.

That the language of the inscription is Latin is, in the first place, notable. Apart from a few private gravestones left by Roman soldiers, Latin was the language of the Roman administration. We see it in Arabia particularly on milestones and on military texts. The present text then *prima facie* is likely to be an official document emanating ultimately from Rome.

The discovery of an inscription on white marble at this site is unusual. The known inscriptions are mostly rock-cut or are inscribed on local stone. White marble is used for architectural decoration, mostly in the form of small inlays but occasionally in bigger slabs for wall veneer and steps.[4] Such stone is not local but had to be imported, probably from somewhere in the Aegean. The large size of the letters and the excellent quality of the writing too are most striking. There are very few inscriptions thus far known from Petra that can serve as comparanda.[5] There is a series of seven votive altars dedicated about the year 206 CE by the legate of Arabia, Q. Aiacius Modestus (*IGLJord* IV Nos. 1-7). There is the inscription on the imposing tomb of T. Aninius Sextius Florentinus, who served as governor of the province in the year 127 CE (*Prov. Arabia* I 382 No. 763=*IGLJord* IV No. 51).[6] There is also the dedication to Trajan of the year 114 CE from the area of the Market (*IGLJord* IV No. 37)[7] and two very fragmentary ones to emperors of the late second or third centuries CE from the excavations at the temple of Qasr al-Bint (*IGLJord* IV Nos. 24-25). These last three inscriptions are in Greek; the first is on fine sandstone blocks, and the other two are on marble.

All of these inscriptions have thin, rather tall, lightly inscribed letters with strokes that curve slightly. C.M. Bennett and D.L. Kennedy (*Levant* 10, 1978, 163-165=*IGLJord* IV No. 52) published a sandstone funerary plaque of C. Antonius Valens that dates to the first half of the second century CE. The shapes of the letters on this plaque,[8] particularly the way the right slanting strokes of M and N extend above the strokes that meet them, are the most similar to the present text. The similarities, however, stop at the level of shape. The letters of the new inscription are very large, 0.04-0.05 m in height, while those of the Valens marker are 0.13-0.19 m. The calligraphic quality of these deeply incised, shaded letters contrasts sharply with the rather tall, lightly

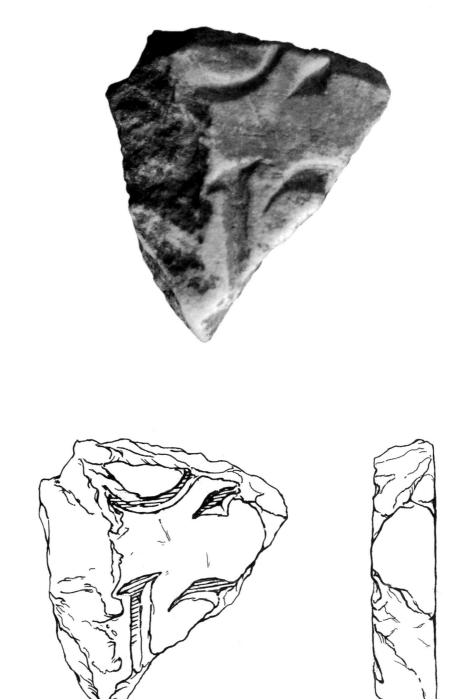

**Figures 8.4 and 8.5.** *Non-joining fragment of the Imperial inscription, recovered in 1993. Drawing by Simon M. Sullivan.*

inscribed letters of the funerary plaque. The fineness of the lettering of our monument can be most truly appreciated by considering the lettering of the dedicatory inscription in Greek to Trajan from the agora at Petra. Fortunately, reasonably good photographs of this text have been published as Plate IX.2 in *ADAJ* 4/5, as Plate 6 figure 25 in Spijkerman and in *IGLJord* IV Plates XXII-XXIII. The lettering is tall and thin, almost cursive in quality. It has a wispy fineness that differs entirely from the handsome calligraphy of the new text. In sum, the lettering of our inscription has no close parallel from Petra. There have also been found at Bostra and Jarash (Gerasa/Jerash) to the north a large number of inscriptions (*IGLS* XIII.1; *Gerasa*). None of the letter-shapes have much of a similarity to the lettering of the present text; indeed, study of the plates of those volumes will quickly convince one of the unusual quality of the lettering of our text from Petra.

Outside of Arabia, we may usefully compare with it a Latin inscription which Arabia's legion, the Third Cyrenaica, had inscribed in honor of Trajan on a triumphal arch at Dura-Europos in the year 115 CE. The lettering of this text is plain, unshaded capitals that are not deeply incised (see Plates XIII and XIV in *Excavations Dura-Europus* 4). In Lebanon, Baalbek has produced a number of Latin inscriptions (*IGLS* VI pp. 45-164); Nos. 2749-2750 on pages 77-78, dedications of the Folni, have letter shapes that are somewhat similar to the new text.

The closest parallels to the present lettering, however, are to be found in Rome, where for the capitol and the surrounding area we have the invaluable *Album of Dated Latin Inscriptions* (*ADLI*) of Joyce and Arthur Gordon. The style to which it belongs can be characterized as follows. E and F are perhaps its most characteristic letters. Instead of block capitals, *à la* the printed capitals at the opening of the previous sentence, the horizontals curve upward and taper to points as though under the influence of brush strokes. Such shapes begin to occur during the reign of Augustus (*ADLI* I No. 28)[9] and especially characterize the small lettering of the records of the Arval brethren — *ADLI* I Nos. 57, 58 (*CIL* 6.32340), 69 (*CIL* 6.32342) and 127 (*CIL* 6.2051), ranging in date from 20 to 69 CE.

The style was already employed for larger letters by the year 45 CE (*ADLI* I No. 91; see also No. 128 of the year 70 CE) and became quite common during the first half of the second century CE — *ADLI* II Nos. 169 (*CIL* 6.2075), 177 (*CIL* 6.2080), 184 (*CIL* 6.30901), 194 (*CIL* 6.8991) and 213 (*CIL* 6.10235), with dates of 105, 120, 128, ca. 130 and 149 CE, respectively. Of these inscriptions, Nos. 128 of the year 70 CE, 184 of 128 CE and 213 of 149 CE are rather close to the present lettering. The shapes of F, M, N and V, in particular, are very similar. The style is quite clearly one that emanates from the capitol and is characteristic of official documents.

The fineness of the lettering, their monument-al size and the unusual use of white marble, not to mention the inclusion of the emperor's name and full titulature, all suggest that we have before us the debris from an imposing as well as important official document. The lettering, based on parallels from Rome and its environs, suggests a date anytime from the first century to middle of the second century CE. It is, of course, normally quite improper to date the inscriptions of one locale based on the styles from another. Styles of lettering were, for the most part, strictly local. In this case, however, there are almost no local inscriptions that are comparable. None shows a similar degree of shading; indeed, few have any shading to speak of. Moreover, there seems good reason to think that the present text reproduces a chancery style emanating from Rome.

The inscription naturally will not predate Trajan's annexation of Arabia in 106 CE.[10] It could be related to Hadrian's visit to the area during the year 130 CE, when Petra took on the epithet *Hadriane*. It seems unlikely that it can be as late as the time of Septimius Severus and his transformation of the boundaries of Arabia.[11] While it is hazardous to speculate based on so little evidence, I am inclined to think, if fortune is kind enough to give us more fragments of this inscription, that it will prove to be Trajanic. I would not be surprised in fact if it turns out to be the inscription celebrating the conferral on Petra of the status of Metropolis or a text memorializing the completion of the *Via Nova Traiana*.[12] In any case, it will date somewhere around the years 112 to 114 CE.

# Endnotes

[1] The excavation has been carried out under the auspices of Brown University. I thank the director, Martha S. Joukowsky, and the Jordanian authorities for granting me the opportunity to publish the present text. The photographs were taken by Artemis A. W. Joukowsky, and the drawings were done by Jean Blackburn and Simon M. Sullivan. A travel grant from the College of Humanities of the Ohio State University allowed me to spend a week in June of 1998 at Petra studying these fragments in the storeroom of the new Petra Museum. I am also indebted to the members of the Brown University excavation for their wonderful on-site hospitality.

[2] The neuter noun *confinium* as an alternative reading appears unlikely, for part of the right side of N ought to be visible to the left of F. That space is blank; see Figures 8.2 and 8.3.

[3] This text has also been published as *CIL* 3.586 and 12306; in addition, it is printed in *IG* IX.2 p. 20. Other such disputes known to us include several in Thessaly, one under Tiberius (*IG* IX.2 261) and two under Trajan (*Ath.Mitt.* 52, 1927, 90-91 No. 6 and *AE* 1923 161-162 No. 386y), one in Macedonia in the middle of the second century CE (Hatzopoulos 1996:65 No. 3) and one in Lycia at the time of Caracalla (*TAM* V 859).

[4] I am indebted to a letter from Peter J. Parr for this information.

[5] For the inscriptions of Petra, see now *IGLJord* IV Nos. 1-93.

[6] On the date of Florentinus' governorship, see Glen W. Bowersock 1983:86 and No. 34. There are no legible photographs or facsimiles of this text known to me.

[7] Glen W. Bowersock first published this text in *JRS* 72, 1982, 198 and also in his *Roman Arabia* 84-85 No. 28. I am grateful to Glen W. Bowersock for pointing out to me that he was misled about the inscription coming from the arch at the west end of the Colonnaded Street. He printed a correction in *Journal of Roman Archaeology* 4, 1991, 336-344 No. 7. For an improved text of this inscription, see the present author's forthcoming study entitled "The Dedicatory Inscription to Trajan at Petra."

[8] See Pl. XXVb in *Levant* 10, 1978.

[9] The so-called *laudatio Turiae* (*CIL* 6.37053) of ca. 5 BCE.

[10] See Freeman (1996) for a discussion of the complex nature of this.

[11] On Septimius Severus' activities in Syria and Arabia at the end of the second century CE and beginning of the third, Glen W. Bowersock 1983:110-122.

[12] The text of the inscription to Trajan from the agora published in 1982 (see endnote 7 above for references) revealed that the city had that status by the year 114 CE.

[13] The project was completed under the governorship of C. Claudius Severus. See PIR2 C 1023 for the milestones with his name. Interestingly, given the language of the present text, these milestones speak of the road which Trajan, *redacta in formam provinciae Arabia, a finibus Syriae usque ad mare rubrum aperuit et stravit.*

I am most indebted to Glen W. Bowersock, C. Habicht and J. Bodel for reading this paper and offering many helpful suggestions.

# INSCRIBED FINDS

Stephen V. Tracy

## Amphora Handle

A Rhodian stamped amphora handle (97-P-3) (Figure 8.6) was found in the summer of 1997 (see Chapter 6 for find information). The text of the stamp is as follows:

ἐπὶ Καλ̣[λι]–

ξείνου

῾Υ[ακινθίου]

There are 19 occurrences of this eponym in the collection of the amphora project in the Athenian Agora, including one (unpublished) from Alexandria that appears to be identical to the present stamp. It dates late in Period V to early in Period VI.[1] V. Grace has established that Period V extends from approximately 146–108 BCE, and Period VI extends from 108–88 BCE.[2] The present handle belongs, then, toward the end of the second century BCE.

## Greek Inscription

The summer of 1997 also produced one very fragmentary Greek inscription (97-S-1) (Figures 8.7 and 8.8) (see Chapter 6 for find information). It preserves one complete letter and parts of three or four others.

Π̣

ΚωΝ

*s.* II–III *p.*

The date is based on the letter shapes. Above ω appear the lower halves of two vertical strokes; the left one occurs just along the line of fracture. These strokes could be part of π, or they could be parts of two separate letters, such as ΝΙ, ΝΤ, ωΙ or Ι Ι. It is impossible, based on such exiguous remains, to suggest any probable restorations.

*Figure 8.6. Inscribed amphora handle.*

*Figures 8.7 and 8.8. Fragment of a Greek inscription. Drawing by Simon M. Sullivan.*

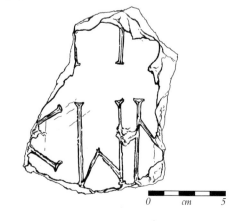

# Endnotes

[1] I am greatly indebted to Carolyn Koehler and to Maria Petropoulakou of the Athenian Amphora project for this information.

[2] V. Grace, "The Middle Stoa by Amphora Stamps," *Hesperia* 54 (1985) 42.

# Abbreviations and Bibliography

*ADAJ* 4/5.

    1960      *Annual of the Department of Antiquities of Jordan* 4/5.

*AE* 1923 161–162.

    Arvanitopoulos, A. S. θεσσαλικαὶ ἐπιγραφαί. Ἀρχαιολογικὴ Ἐφημερις 1923:123–162.

*Ath.Mitt.* 52: 90–91.

    1927      Stählin, F. Inschriften aus Thessalien. *Mitteilungen des Deutschen Archäologischen Instituts, Athenische Abteilung.*

Bennett, C.M. and D.L. Kennedy.

    1978      A New Roman Military Inscription from Petra. *Levant* 10:163–165.

Bowersock, G.W.

    1982      Review of A. Spijkerman, "The Coins of the Decapolis and Provincia Arabia," in *Journal of Roman Studies* 72:197–198.

————.

    1983      *Roman Arabia.* Cambridge, Massachusetts:Harvard University Press.

————.

    1991      The Babatha Papyri, Masada, and Rome. *Journal of Roman Archaeology* 4:336–344.

*CIL.*

    *Corpus Inscriptionum Latinarum.* Berlin:de Gruyter.

*Excavations Dura-Europus 4.*

    1933      Bauer, P.V. C.; Bellinger, A. R. and Rostovtzeff, M. I. *The Excavations at Dura Europus, Preliminary Report of the Fourth Season of Work, October 1930-March 1931.* New Haven:Yale University Press.

*FD III.4.*

    1970      Plassart, A. *Fouilles de Delphes III Epigraphie, fascicule IV.* Paris:de Boccard.

Freeman, P.

    1996    The annexation of Arabia and imperial Grand Strategy. *The Roman Army in the East. Journal of Roman Archaeology* Supplementary series 18:91–118.

*Gerasa.*

    1938    Welles, C. B. *Gerasa, City of the Decapolis: The Inscriptions.* New Haven: American Schools of Oriental Research.

Gordon, J.S. and A.E. Gordon.

    1958    *Album of Dated Latin Inscriptions* I. Berkeley: University of California Press.

———.

    1964    *Album of Dated Latin Inscriptions* II. Berkeley: University of California Press.

Hatzopoulos, M.B.

    1996    *Macedonian Institutions under the Kings.* Meletemata 22. Athens/Paris: de Boccard.

*IG IX.2.*

    1908    Kern, O. *Inscriptiones Graecae: Inscriptiones Thessaliae.* Berlin: G. Reimer.

*IGLJord IV.*

    1993    Sartre, M. *Inscriptions grecques et latines de la Syrie XXI, inscriptions de la Jordanie* IV. Paris: Libraire orientaliste P. Geuthner.

*IGLS VI.*

    1967    Rey-Coquais, J.-P. *Inscriptions grecques et latines de la Syrie: Baalbek et Beqa.* Paris: Libraire orientaliste P. Geuthner.

*IGLS XIII.1.*

    1982    Sartre, M. *Inscriptions grecques et latines de la Syrie: Bostra.* Paris: Libraire orientaliste P. Geuthner.

*ILS.*

    1892-1916  Dessau, H. *Inscriptiones Latinae Selectae.* Berlin: Weidmann.

*PIR².*

    1933-1987  Groag, E.; Stein, A. and Petersen, L. *Prosopographia Imperii Romani* ed. 2. Berlin/Leipzig: de Gruyter.

*Prov. Arabia I.*

    1904    Brünnow, R.E., and Domaszewski, A. von *Die Provincia Arabia* I. Strassburg: Verlag von Karl J. Trübner.

Spijkerman, A.

    1978    *The Coins of the Decapolis and Provincia Arabia.* Jerusalem: Franciscan Printing Press.

*TAM V.*

    1981, 1989  Herrmann, P. *Tituli Asiae Minoris V: Tituli Lydiae.* Vienna: Austrian Academy of Sciences.

# INDEX

Mediterranean Sea 150, 152, 153, 154, 325, 326, 329, 330, 336, 337

Mesha 44

Mesha Stele *See* Moab: Moabite Stone

Mesolithic 15, 44

Mesopotamia(ns) 325

Microsoft Excel 245, 258, 327

Microsoft Word 142, 274

Midia 16

Miller, Cynthia xliv

MiniCAD 51, 109, 181, 185

Missouri University Research Reactor (MURR) 347, 348, 350, 353, 365

Mitten, Barbara xliv

Moab 3, 4, 17, 23, 43, 44, 146
    Moabite Stone 17, 44
    Moabites 17, 35

Modestus, Q. Aiacius 372

Mohammad 28

Monastery *See* Ad-Dayr

Moses 4, 16, 17, 29, 33, 44

Mount Hor *See* Jabal Harun

Mu'allaq 347

Murray, Margaret 40

Murshed, Mohammad 40

Musil, Alois 40

Muslim Conquest 28

Myers, J. Wilson and Eleanor E. xliv, 51, 64, 141, 143

Myros Hormos 4

# N

Nabaitaeans (Nabayot) 44

Nabataea(ns) 2, 4, 13, 15, 17, 19, 21, 22, 24, 25, 26, 27, 33, 37, 41, 45, 49, 50, 125, 128, 136, 139, 140, 145, 154, 171, 179, 231, 234, 277, 353
    architecture 14, 61, 147
    army 22
    art 225, 287
    building techniques 14, 157
    coins *See* coins
    culture 50, 156
    customs 19
    deities 26
        Al-'Uzza 9, 35, 36, 46
        Allat 36
        Dushara (Dusares) 4, 8, 9, 11, 24, 33, 35–36
        Illaalge 35, 36
        Manawat 35, 36
        Sai' Al-Qaum 35, 36
    engineering systems 5, 15, 153, 156, 223
    geography 3
    lamps *See* lamps
    languages 26, 33–35, 284
    Nabataean Tomb Inscriptions 33
    pottery *See* pottery
    religion 35–37, 125, 276, 287
    rulers 22–26, 41, 125, 222, 234
        Aretas I 22, 23, 45
        Aretas II 23, 38
        Aretas III Philhellenos 6, 21, 22, 23–24

Aretas IV Lover of His People 6, 11, 22, 23, 24–25, 40, 43, 45, 108, 139, 156, 276, 284, 317, 318
        Gamilat 25, 318
        Hagru 25
        Huldu 24, 318
        Malichus I 21, 23, 24, 136
        Malichus II 23, 25, 45, 139
        Obodas I 22, 23, 27, 33
        Obodas II 23, 24, 136
        Obodas III 23, 24, 44
        Rabbel I 23
        Rabbel II 23, 25, 26, 139, 317, 318
        Shuqailat I (Shaqilat I) 24, 45
        Shuqailat II 25, 45
    small finds *See* catalog
    trade 15, 18, 20, 21, 22, 26, 171
    water supply and conservation 81, 156, 171, 176 *See also* Petra: water supply and conservation

Nabt 33

Nahal Hever 27, 145, 146

Najjar, Elizabeth A. xliii

Nalle, Peter xliv, 144, 176

Natufian 15

Nazzal's Camp *See* Burckhardt Archaeological Center, J.L.

Near East 3, 18, 20, 21, 30, 198, 284, 328

Neff, Hector 350, 365

Negev 3, 20, 23, 25, 28, 29, 40, 43, 347

Neolithic 15, 33, 44

Nero 45

Nerva 45

Nessana 3

neutron activation analysis (NAA) xlii, xlvi, 78, 93, 114, 275, 276, 277, 278, 347

Nicaea, creed of 278

Nigrinus, C. Avidius 372

Nimri, Kathy xliii

Nimrud 38

Nitzana *See* Nessana

# O

Oboda 3, 23, 347, 350 *See also* 'Avdat

Odoacer 326

Orientalism 14

Orontes River 20, 281

Otho 45

Ottoman period 30, 31, 32

Oultre-Jourdain *See* Transjordan

# P

Page, Jutta 340

PageMaker 6.0 xlvi

Palaeolithic 15, 154

Palestina Salutaris/Tertia 27

Palestine 18, 20, 21, 28, 40, 44, 221, 223, 278, 353
    Palestrina 206, 207

Palma, A. Cornelius 26

Palmyra 26, 28, 36

palynological analysis 167–168

Roman(s) xli, 3, 4, 14, 20, 21, 22, 25, 26–27, 28, 35, 49, 125, 128, 139, 140, 145, 153, 154, 156, 157, 195, 198, 221, 222, 231, 325, 326, 328, 329, 333, 335, 336, 337, 339, 340

    Rome 14, 21, 23, 24, 26, 27, 42, 45, 139, 234, 277, 326, 333, 337, 339, 372, 374

        Ara Pacis Augustae 234

    small finds *See* catalog

    Trajanic period 43

    western 326, 328, 336, 339

Roman Road 175

Royce, Charles M. xliv

Ruheibeh *See* Rehovot-in-the-Negev

Russell, Kenneth W. 41

# S

Saba 4, 26, 43

Sabra 154, 171

Sahr 148

Salah-ed-Din (Saladin) 30

Samaria 45

San'a 43

Saudi Arabia 3, 4, 25, 38, 41, 42, 44, 147

Savingac, R. 40

Sbeita 3

Scaurus, Marcus Aemilius 23

Schluntz, Erika L. xliii, xliv, xlv, 55, 93, 108, 109, 128, 131, 133, 144, 145, 207, 261, 371

Schmid, Stephan G. xlvi, 61, 143, 145, 203, 207, 239, 240, 348, 353, 365

Seetzen, Ulrich J. 38

Sela (Selah) 17, 44, 45, 288 *See also* Jokteel

Seleucid Empire 20

    coins *See* coins

    sculptural decoration 14

    Seleucids 13, 20, 21, 26, 27

    Seleucus (Seleucia) 20, 148

Seleucus I 20

Seleucus IV Philopater 20

Severus, C. Claudius 375

Severus, Septimius 303, 374, 375

Shaer, May xliii, 63

Shara (Sharra) Mountains 4

Sheba *See* Saba

Sheba, Queen of 43

Shivta *See* Sbeita

Si' 148

Sinai 3, 38, 41, 336

Siq al-Barid 41

Sisson, Lawrence 58

Slaughter, Michael F. xlv

Smart, David xlv, 108, 145

Smolenski, John 142

Sobata *See* Sbeita

Solomon 17, 43

Stephens, J.L. 155

Stone Age 15

Strabo 18, 19, 20, 44, 155, 222

Streets of Façades 8

stucco *See* architectural fragments; catalog; Great Temple: architectural sculpture

Stucky, Rolf A. xlvi, 41, 60, 147

Suez 21

Sullivan, Simon M. xliv, xlv, xlvi, 14, 133, 145, 290, 291, 292, 297, 300, 303, 304, 307, 308, 310, 334, 335, 373, 375, 376

Sur 148

Susa 45

Syllaeus, minister-general 24

Sylvester, Monica L. 239

Syria 3, 4, 13, 18, 20, 21, 23, 24, 26, 41, 42, 45, 50, 162, 221, 284, 319, 352, 375

    deities

        Atargatis 36, 148

    Syrians 26, 35

Syro-Palestine 281, 325

# T

Tacitus 284

Tall (Tel) al-Kheleifih 42

Tawilan 17, 347

Taylor, Jane xlv, 80

Teixidor, Javier xli

Tell Anafa 350, 352

Tell, Safwan xlii, 66, 71

Temple *See* Great Temple

Temple of the Winged Lions 9, 11, 13, 14, 27, 36, 37, 38, 40, 147, 192, 198, 206, 229, 299, 314

Terracina 206, 207

Theodosios I 324

Theodosios II 317

Theodosios, Saint (Koinobiarches) 28

Thessalonica 323

Thessaly 372, 375

Third Winter Palace 222

3D Studio MAX 133

Tiberias, Lake 42, 151

Tiberius 45, 375

Tigranes 24

Tigris River 20, 148

Tillack, Susan B. 227

Titus 45

tombs 6, 8, 11, 25, 27, 35, 40, 41, 43, 139, 151, 152, 153, 154, 156, 276

    At-Turkmaniyya 35

    cliff-sculpted 11

    Corinthian 9, 11, 214

    Obelisk 6

    Palace 9, 11

    Royal 8

    shaft 11

    stylistic groups 11

    T. Aninius Sextius Florentinus 13, 45, 372

    Urn 8, 28, 214

Topcon 51

Trachontis 45

Tracy, Stephen V. xli, xlvi, 106

Trajan 15, 26, 27, 45, 139, 156, 206, 317, 371, 372, 374, 375

Trajan, Forum of 206

Transjordan 18, 20, 28, 31, 35, 40, 153, 278

Traxler, Loa P. xlii, 52, 183, 185, 207